ENCYCLOPEDIA OF EDUCATION

SECOND EDITION

EDITORIAL BOARD

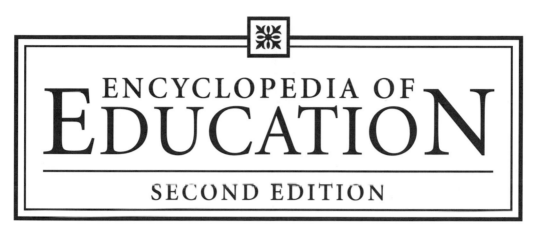

ENCYCLOPEDIA OF EDUCATION

SECOND EDITION

James W. Guthrie, Editor in Chief

VOLUME

4

IEA–Lowenfeld

**MACMILLAN
REFERENCE
USA**™

THOMSON
™
GALE

New York • Detroit • San Diego • San Francisco • Cleveland • New Haven, Conn. • Waterville, Maine • London • Munich

Encyclopedia of Education, Second Edition

James W. Guthrie, Editor in Chief

For permission to use material from this product, submit your request via Web at http://www.gale-edit.com/permissions, or you may download our Permissions Request form and submit your request by fax or mail to:

Permissions Department
The Gale Group, Inc.
27500 Drake Road
Farmington Hills, MI 48331-3535
Permissions Hotline: 248-699-8006 or
800-877-4253 ext. 8006
Fax: 248-699-8074 or 800-762-4058

While every effort has been made to ensure the reliability of the information presented in this publication, The Gale Group, Inc. does not guarantee the accuracy of the data contained herein. The Gale Group, Inc. accepts no payment for listing; and inclusion in the publication of any organization, agency, institution, publication, service, or individual does not imply endorsement of the editors or publisher. Errors brought to the attention of the publisher and verified to the satisfaction of the publisher will be corrected in future editions.

LIBRARY OF CONGRESS CATALOGING-IN-PUBLICATION DATA

Encyclopedia of education / edited by James W. Guthrie.—2nd ed.
   p. cm.
Includes bibliographical references and index.
   ISBN 0-02-865594-X (hardcover : set : alk. paper)
   1. Education—Encyclopedias. I. Guthrie, James W.
   LB15 .E47 2003
   370'.3—dc21
                                       2002008205

ISBNs
Volume 1: 0-02-865595-8
Volume 2: 0-02-865596-6
Volume 3: 0-02-865597-4
Volume 4: 0-02-865598-2
Volume 5: 0-02-865599-0
Volume 6: 0-02-865600-8
Volume 7: 0-02-865601-6
Volume 8: 0-02-865602-4

Printed in the United States of America
10 9 8 7 6 5 4 3 2 1

I

IEA

See: INTERNATIONAL ASSESSMENTS, *subentry on* INTERNATIONAL ASSOCIATION FOR EDUCATIONAL ASSESSMENT.

IMMIGRANT EDUCATION

UNITED STATES
Charles L. Glenn
INTERNATIONAL
Charles L. Glenn

UNITED STATES

The United States is often called a "nation of immigrants"; more accurately the nation always comprised both newcomers and those who worry about the impact of the newcomers on the existing society. The relationship between newcomers and established families has always been in some sense filled with tensions, uncertainties, and even bitter conflicts. It has also been characterized by varied efforts at accommodation and adaptation, often but not always on the part of the newcomers alone.

Immigration to the United States

Between 1820 and 1996, 63 million immigrants arrived in the United States. Germans were cumulatively the largest group, with 7.1 million, followed by Mexicans, with 5.5 million (60 percent of the Mexican immigrants over the 176-year period had arrived in the last 15 years). Other groups of immigrants, in order, were from Italy (5.4 million), the United Kingdom (5.2 million), Ireland (4.8 million), Canada (4.4 million, however, many Irish immigrants came via Canada), and Russia (which used to include much of Poland and the Baltic states—3.8 million).

Immigrants who arrived before the 1840s were for the most part similar to the native population, if not superior in education and ambition; they were rarely considered a problem by the native-born population. With the arrival of large numbers of Irish and German Catholics in the two decades before the Civil War, however, immigrants began to be seen as a threat to American society. The number of immigrants tripled between the 1830s and the 1840s, and the country received as many immigrants in the 1850s as in the two previous decades combined. Between 1845 and 1854 immigration increased the American population by 17.6 percent, a much higher rate than in the latter half of the twentieth century.

After many decades of essentially unrestricted admission, the United States imposed restrictions in 1882 excluding criminals, prostitutes, and the physically and mentally ill. "Nine years later the category of excluded undesirables was extended to take in as well believers in anarchism and in polygamy. These minimal controls reflected no disposition to check the total volume of immigration" (Handlin, p. 287).

Late in the nineteenth century and early in the twentieth century immigrants from southern and eastern Europe, widely considered to come from "inferior stock," were restricted, though much needed by an expanding economy. In the wave of xenophobia that swept over the United States during World War I, a literacy requirement was imposed in 1917. The phase of qualitative restrictions ended with the National Origins Act of 1924, which placed strict quantitative restrictions on the number of immigrants allowed from various nations, explicitly designed to limit immigration from countries that were considered less desirable sources of future citizens.

Puerto Ricans, as United States citizens, enjoyed an unrestricted right to migrate in search of better economic conditions. With the introduction of air service between San Juan and New York City after World War II, the United States experienced what was surely the world's first mass migration by air, with almost 136,250 Puerto Ricans coming to the U.S. mainland in 1947 alone.

The Immigration and Naturalization Act Amendments of 1965 repealed the quotas favoring northwestern Europe (such as those established by the National Origins Act of 1924) but set a limit of 20,000 immigrants per year from each nation of the Eastern Hemisphere and for the first time placed restrictions on immigration from the Western Hemisphere. The Immigration Reform and Control Act of 1986 and subsequent laws have continued to tinker with the terms for the admission of immigrants and refugees.

Reactions to Immigrants

The American colonists' own adaptation to the new circumstances of their life, especially in the mid-Atlantic colonies, involved a largely unproblematic mixing of people who had had much less contact in their home countries of early modern Europe. By the time of the American Revolution, the French immigrant turned American farmer St. John de Crève-coeur would write that the nations of Europe had been combined to create: "the American, this new man . . . leaving behind all his ancient prejudices and manners . . . he must therefore entertain new ideas and form new opinions" (pp. 49–50).

The prominent physician and signer of the Declaration of Independence Benjamin Rush published an essay in 1786 that called for the establishment of public schools in Pennsylvania. A remarkable feature of his proposal was its recommendation that children "be taught to read and write the English and German languages," and attendance districts be so arranged that "children of the same religious sect and nation may be educated as much as possible together" (pp. 5, 7).

In fact, until the 1830s most schooling in Pennsylvania (and in the states to its south) was provided by church initiatives, usually on a denominational

and thus ethnic basis. Quaker, Anglican, and Presbyterian schools, schools of German Lutheran and Reformed congregations, and a whole range of other variations provided what schooling was available. State authorities sought to meet their obligation to provide for the schooling of those whose parents could not afford to pay tuition by providing what would now be called *vouchers,* enabling them to go to existing nonpublic schools and academies, including church schools.

In Pennsylvania, what would become a widespread anxiety about the effects on American society of immigration was anticipated (like so much else) by Benjamin Franklin. In 1752 he asked "Why should Pennsylvania, founded by the English, become a colony of Aliens, who will shortly be so numerous as to Germanize us rather than our Anglifying them, and will never adopt our language or customs?" On the eve of the American Revolution, Franklin returned to this theme, noting "the vast unpeopled [sic] Territories of North America," and warning that "Germans are now pouring into it, to take possession of it, and fill it with their Posterity" (pp. 374, 709–710).

Similarly, Thomas Jefferson warned in 1787 that immigrants would "bring with them the principles of the governments they leave, imbibed in their early youth; or, if able to throw them off, it will be in exchange for an unbridled licentiousness . . . . These principles, with their language, they will transmit to their children" (p. 211).

It was only in the 1830s, though, that concern about the cultural and religious differences of immigrants began to be a basis for educational policy. In 1836 Calvin Stowe of Ohio warned that "unless we educate our immigrants, they will be our ruin . . . . The intellectual and religious training of our foreign population has become essential to our own safety" (p. 993). This was a primary motivation for the extension of the "common school" system of publicly controlled education, and for opposition to public funding for Catholic schools.

When Catholic immigrants (first Germans, then other groups) began to organize their own schools, as did some Protestant and Jewish immigrants, it was perceived by many as an expression of refusal to accept the requirements of life in American society. Their children "will be shut up," warned a prominent Protestant minister in 1853, "in schools that do not teach them what, as Americans, they most of all need to know . . . . They will be instructed mainly into the foreign prejudices and superstitions of their fathers." If, instead, the children of immigrants could be gathered into the common public school, "we may be gradually melted into one homogeneous people" (Bushnell, pp. 209–303).

In fact, religious schools do not seem to have retarded what came to be called *Americanization*; to the contrary, they have provided a safe setting for millions of immigrant children to learn American ways without turning their backs on their families. In a study of Mexican-American children in San Antonio, Philip Lampe found that those who attended Catholic schools "were more likely to have non-Hispanic friends, were more willing to date and marry outside their own ethnic group, were more willing to identify with the WASP value system, showed significantly less prejudice against other ethnic groups, and were more willing to perform their civic duties" than their public school counterparts (Walch, p. 202).

As anxiety about Catholicism began to fade, other cultural differences came to be the primary concern. The immigrants arriving from southern and eastern Europe in the late nineteenth and early twentieth centuries seemed to many commentators to be of an inferior stock. As John R. Commons, a leading social scientist of the Progressive era wrote in 1907, "If in America our boasted freedom from the evils of social classes fails to be vindicated in the future, the reasons will be found in the immigration of races and classes incompetent to share in our democratic opportunities." After all, he pointed out, "race differences are established in the very blood and physical constitution. They are most difficult to eradicate, and they yield only to the slow processes of the centuries. Races may change their religions, their forms of government, their modes of industry, and their languages, but underneath all these changes they may continue the physical, mental, and moral capacities and incapacities which determine the real character of their religion, government, industry, and literature" (pp. 12, 7).

More optimistic observers insisted upon the capacity of the public school to transform the children of immigrants into "real Americans," and it was this impulse which led to several decades of emphasis upon Americanization through schools and other agencies of popular education like settlement houses and civic associations. Ellwood Cubberley, the enormously influential Stanford University professor, ar-

gued in 1909 that the highest mission of public education was "to assimilate and amalgamate those people as part of our American race, and to implant in their children, so far as can be done, the Anglo-Saxon conception of righteousness, law and order, and popular government, and to awaken in them a reverence for our democratic institutions and for those things in our national life which we as a people hold to be of abiding worth" (Cremin, p. 68).

Although the "intelligence tests" conducted by the U.S. Army during World War I seemed to confirm the intellectual inferiority of Slavic, Jewish, and southern European immigrants, the findings reflected a generational phenomenon. Although immigrants in the early decades of the twentieth century had low levels of education compared to their native-born contemporaries, there was a "massive educational jump among the new Europeans in the cohort born between 1925 and 1935 in the concentration in professional jobs . . . . The analogous change for native whites of native parentage was much smaller" (Sollors, pp. 206, 329).

Immigrants and Language

The desire to preserve German language and culture had been one of the motivations behind the organization of Catholic and Lutheran parochial schools in the nineteenth century, and Polish, Bohemian, and other immigrant groups made efforts in the same direction. Public schools in some cities responded to this competition by offering classes designed to maintain and develop the languages that pupils spoke at home. In 1877 the superintendent of schools in San Francisco argued that public schools should begin offering French and German. Public schools in Chicago began offering German in confidence that "the number of private schools now to be found in every nook and cranny of the city will decrease, and the children of all nationalities will be assembled in the public schools, and thereby be radically Americanized" (Peterson, pp. 54–55). By the late 1880s, eight states had statutes authorizing bilingual instruction in public schools.

Such measures on the part of public authorities should not be construed as reflecting acceptance of bilingualism as a long-term educational goal; the mounting concern about how immigrants seemed to be building separate communities led by 1911 seventeen states to require that English be the sole language of instruction at the elementary level in public schools. The anti-German sentiment of World War

I led twenty-one states to add such a requirement for private schools as well—a requirement that the U.S. Supreme Court struck down in *Meyer v. State of Nebraska* in 1923.

The supposed failure of immigrants and their children to learn English is the basis for much concern about immigration and about bilingual education in the early twenty-first century. In fact, there is no reason to believe that current immigrants, any more than those in the past, will seek or be able to persuade their children to remain linguistically separate. Two leading supporters of bilingual education concede that "the United States is, at the societal level, staunchly monolingual. Legislating monolingualism as a requirement for citizenship could hardly have been more successful in creating a monolingual society than have been the unofficial economic and social forces at work." Among immigrant minority groups, "only the old folks, the very young, and the recent arrivals, in general, speak these other languages; the school children and young adults have often switched to 'dominance' in English" (Snow and Hakuta, p. 385). The continuing use of Spanish in California has not slowed the rate of shift to English as the primary language for individuals of Hispanic descent; while "in most areas of the United States approximately 70 percent of the native born currently are adopting English as their usual language," the rate is 85 percent in California (Veltman, p. 66).

It is sometimes suggested that the heavy concentrations of Hispanics constitutes an exception to the usual pattern of language shift, but this seems to reflect mostly the language use of newcomers. A 1973 study by Alejandro Portes and Ruben G. Rumbaut in Los Angeles found that, among third-generation Mexican-American women, 4 percent spoke only Spanish at home, and 84 percent only English. The transition to English among men was even more rapid.

Because of this pattern of language loss, some argue that the public schools have an obligation to help maintain minority languages and cultures. It would be more accurate to say that, while this policy option certainly could be justified on educational grounds, it is not a legal requirement. In no case have the courts found a legal right to public support in maintaining a group's identity or language as a remedy of past discrimination.

Even if language maintenance were to be accepted as an educational goal, there is little reason to believe that even full-time bilingual classes would have the effect of maintaining the active use of minority languages, unless these languages were strongly supported outside the school.

Immigrant parents are especially likely to question language-maintenance efforts in schools if they believe there is any chance this will limit their children's acquisition of the majority language that they themselves cannot teach their children well. Mexican-American parents surveyed by the Educational Testing Service in 1987 supported bilingual education and said it was important that their children speak Spanish well, but rejected instruction in Spanish nearly four to one if it would take away from learning English. In a 1998 survey, the foundation Public Agenda posed the question: "With students who are new immigrants, which is more important for the public schools to do? Teach them English as quickly as possible, even if this means they fall behind in other subjects, or teach them other subjects in their native language, even if this means it takes them longer to learn English?" Foreign-born parents favored "English as quickly as possible" by 75 percent to 21 percent, while Hispanic parents supported that option by 66 percent to 30 percent.

Educating the Children of Immigrants

No special arrangements were made for immigrant pupils through most of the nineteenth century, apart from being in a public school classroom, with what was then a strong emphasis upon basic skills and upon patriotism and civic morality. In some cases, indeed, they were not allowed to attend school with native children. Children of Chinese immigrants were segregated by law in a number of states. The California legislature enacted a requirement during its 1859–1860 session that "Negroes, Mongolians, and Indians, shall not be admitted into the public schools." The legislature, however, did allow local school boards to establish separate schools for such children; this segregation was reaffirmed in the school code adopted ten years later.

Such discrimination was not confined to California. The U.S. Supreme Court ruled in *Gong Lum v. Rice* (1927) that school officials in Mississippi could exclude a Chinese-American child from the local "white" school. Martha Lum had "the right to attend and enjoy the privileges of a common school education in a colored school" or her father could send her to a private school at his own expense.

Although persons of Mexican descent were considered "white" under state laws requiring school segregation of blacks, they were often segregated by local practices. Local practices included drawing school attendance lines to correspond with residential segregation—and the segregation already existing within schools—and assigning all Mexican-American children automatically to the lowest instructional track, according to Guadalupe Salinas's 1971 study. As a result of such practices, "in 1931, 85 per cent of California schools surveyed by the state government reported segregating Mexican students either in separate classrooms or in separate schools . . . . By 1930, 90 per cent of the schools in Texas were racially segregated" (Donato, Menchaca, and Valencia, p. 35).

Separation was not always permanent, or motivated by distaste for the immigrant. Special reception classes to teach essential language skills in an otherwise unmodified school program were considered an especially progressive measure in the period of heaviest immigration to the United States in the early twentieth century. So-called steamer classes were provided in many cities for children newly arrived "off the boat" from Europe. In Massachusetts alone, twenty-six cities and towns reported providing such classes in 1914. The Boston school superintendent asserted that "there is general agreement in the practice of progressive communities in grouping older immigrant children in special classes for intensive work in English, in order that they may acquire the common tongue as a tool for work through which they can be advanced rapidly to classes of children of their own age" (Thompson, p. 118).

Special language support did not become a right until the Supreme Court's 1974 decision in *Lau v. Nichols*. This decision stated that San Francisco was violating the Civil Rights Act of 1964 by failing to provide programs that met the needs of several thousand pupils of Chinese ancestry who did not speak English. The implication of the decision was that no violation would have been found if all of the pupils in question had participated in supplemental English instruction (ESL), as did about a thousand others. The court left the method of meeting this obligation to the discretion of school districts. "Teaching English to the students of Chinese ancestry who do not speak the [English] language is one choice. Giving instructions to this group in Chinese is another. There may be others." The court took care to point out that it would not be appropriate to sepa-

rate minority children more than was required by their educational needs, citing an earlier federal government regulation specifying that any ability grouping or tracking system employed by the school system to deal with the special language skill needs of national origin, minority children must be designed to meet such language skill needs as soon as possible and must not operate as an educational dead-end or permanent track.

In retrospect, however, it seems almost inevitable that such a targeted program would develop a momentum of its own and that those educators who made it their specialty would discover an ever-increasing need for what only they could provide, and ever new reasons not to integrate language minority children into the mainstream. The "Lau remedies" issued in draft form subsequently by the federal government, influenced by bilingual education advocates, leaned heavily toward requiring use of the home language for instruction in a separate program, so-called transitional bilingual education. School administrators had every reason to believe that they were not only permitted but required to educate language minority pupils separately, at least for whatever period of time was required to bring them up to speed in English. The argument, by some linguists and minority language advocates, that the best way to learn English was through a number of years (five to seven years is the figure most commonly used) of a bilingual program provided a strong rationale for extending this period of separation.

Much conflicting research exists on the issue of whether children should first be instructed through their home language if that is not the language of their continuing education. Fortunately, a very complete review of more than thirty years of studies was carried out on behalf of the National Research Council. "It is clear," the experts note,

> that many children first learn to read in a second language without serious negative consequences. These include children in early-immersion, two-way, and English as a second language (ESL)-based programs in North America, as well as those in formerly colonial countries that have maintained the official language [of the colonizer] as the medium of instruction, immigrant children in Israel, children whose parents opt for elite international schools, and many others . . . . The high literacy achievement of Spanish-speaking children in English-

medium Success for All schools . . . that feature carefully-designed direct literacy instruction suggests that even children from low-literacy homes can learn to read in a second language if the risk associated with poor instruction is eliminated. (August and Hakuta, p. 60)

Later in the report, indeed, Diane August and Kenji Hukuta conclude candidly that "we do not yet know whether there will be long-term advantages or disadvantages to initial literacy instruction in the primary language versus English, given a very high-quality program of known effectiveness in both cases" (p. 177). This would seem to argue for allowing the individual school to adopt whatever method produces satisfactory results.

Bilingual education was developed initially not as a remedial program but as an enrichment of the education of middle-class children, responding to demands of a relatively high-status refugee group that included many teachers, the Cubans who fled to Miami from the Castro regime in the early 1960s. According to James Crawford, this group, expecting to return to Cuba, was strongly motivated to maintain Spanish. The Dade County school system launched the first experiment in bilingual education at the Coral Way School. This was an unabashed Spanish-maintenance program for Cuban children and at the same time a Spanish immersion program for Anglo children. The goal was fluency in both languages for both groups.

Transitional bilingual education (TBE) programs have a different goal: they provide support in the home language while the pupil becomes proficient in English. TBE has been provided by hundreds of local school systems as a result of the requirements of state laws (the first was enacted in Massachusetts in 1971) or as a means of complying with the requirements of the 1974 *Lau v. Nichols* case. While federal law leaves it up to local education officials to determine how to overcome language barriers, a strong encouragement has been given to bilingual programs by federal funding that supports "educational programs using bilingual education practices, techniques and methods."

Pupils are assigned to TBE programs on the basis of an assessment that they are unable to perform ordinary classwork in English and speak another language at home. Pupils stay in these separate classes typically for three years, though many remain longer and advocates argue that five to seven years would be preferable. "Late-exit" bilingual programs, with an explicit intention of maintaining and developing the home language while English is learned, are less common.

A 1980 survey found that local school districts in thirty-eight of the fifty states provided TBE for Spanish-speaking youngsters, in twenty states they did so for Vietnamese children, in twelve for Korean youngsters, in ten for French-speaking children, and in nine for speakers of Greek. Half the states had laws that mandated or permitted bilingual instruction as needed—or were in the process of enacting such legislation—and the other half did not seem to have significant enrollments of affected students. The 1980s were probably the high-water mark of this approach to educating the children of immigrants.

California adopted a mandate of bilingual and "bicultural" education in 1976, requiring school districts with more than fifty pupils of limited proficiency in English to develop and implement district master plans. This law was not reenacted in 1987, but most large school systems continued to implement bilingual programs until the referendum (Proposition 227) organized by Ron Unz. In June 1998 California voters decisively mandated that the children of immigrants be given one year of "structured immersion" in English before mainstreaming into regular classes, unless a sufficient number of parents petitioned for a bilingual class.

Voters in Arizona followed the California example and, as of 2001, similar efforts are under way in Colorado and Massachusetts. Even liberal newspapers like the *New York Times* have begun to criticize bilingual programs, which face new demands for accountability and results. The alternative offered is no longer "sink-or-swim," but carefully designed programs that focus (like those in other countries with large numbers of immigrants) on developing an initial proficiency in English so that the pupil can as soon as possible be placed with classmates for whom that is the first language and with whom he will communicate naturally and so become more and more proficient.

It should be noted that proficiency in a language other than that of the school is by no means of itself a barrier to success in school, and may indeed be associated (whether as cause or effect) with academic achievement, provided that the pupil is also proficient in the school language. A study conducted by the Educational Testing Service in conjunction with the National Assessment of Educational Progress concluded that "whether or not one comes from a home where a second language [that is, other than English] is frequently spoken is not the critical issue, but rather the central question is whether or not one is competent in English" (Baratz-Snowden et al., p. iii).

In the early twenty-first century American education seems to be entering a period in which a variety of approaches to the education of immigrant children will be employed, based upon local judgments about what will work best and what parents want; a new emphasis on accountability for results will prevent schools from sliding back into the old complacency about whether immigrant students learn or not.

See also: BILINGUALISM, SECOND LANGUAGE LEARNING, AND ENGLISH AS A SECOND LANGUAGE; BILINGUAL EDUCATION; CURRICULUM, SCHOOL; ELEMENTARY EDUCATION LANGUAGE MINORITY STUDENTS; RACE, ETHNICITY, AND CULTURE; SECONDARY EDUCATION.

BIBLIOGRAPHY

AUGUST, DIANE, and HAKUTA, KENJI, eds. 1997. *Improving Schooling for Language Minority Children: A Research Agenda.* Washington, DC: National Academy Press.

BARATZ-SNOWDEN, JOAN; ROCK, DAVID; POLLACK, JUDITH.; and WILDER, GITA. 1988. *The Educational Progress of Language Minority Students: Findings from the NAEP 1985–1986 Special Study.* Princeton, NJ: Educational Testing Service.

BUSHNELL, HORACE. 1880. *Life and Letters,* ed. Mary A. Bushnell Cheney. New York: Harper.

CASTELLANOS, DIEGO, with LEGGIO, PAMELA. 1983. *The Best of Two Worlds: Bilingual/Bicultural Education in the U.S.* Trenton: New Jersey State Department of Education.

COMMONS, JOHN R. 1920. *Races and Immigrants in America* (1907). New York: Macmillan.

CRAWFORD, JAMES. 1992. *Hold Your Tongue: Bilingualism and the Politics of English Only.* Reading, MA: Addison-Wesley.

CREMIN, LAWRENCE A. 1961. *The Transformation of the School: Progressivism in American Education, 1876–1957.* New York: Random House.

DONATO, RUBEN; MENCHACA, MARTHA; and VALENCIA, RICHARD R. 1991. "Segregation, Desegregation, and Integration of Chicano Students: Problems and Prospects." In *Chicano School Failure and Success: Research and Policy Agendas for the 1990s,* ed. Richard Valencia. London: Falmer.

FRANKLIN, BENJAMIN. 1987. *Writings,* ed. J. A. Leo Lemay. New York: The Library of America.

GLENN, CHARLES L. 1988. *The Myth of the Common School.* Amherst: University of Massachusetts Press.

GLENN, CHARLES L. 1997. "What Does the National Research Council Study Tell Us about Educating Language Minority Children?" *READ Perspectives* 4(2):66–95.

GLENN, CHARLES L., with DE JONG, ESTER J. 1996. *Educating Immigrant Children: Schools and Language Minorities in Twelve Nations.* New York: Garland.

HANDLIN, OSCAR. 1951. *The Uprooted: The Epic Story of the Great Migrations that Made the American People.* Boston: Little, Brown.

JEFFERSON, THOMAS. 1984. "Notes on the State of Virginia." In *Writings,* ed. Merrill D. Peterson. New York: The Library of America.

LIEBERSON, STANLEY. 1980. *A Piece of the Pie: Blacks and White Immigrants since 1880.* Berkeley: University of California Press.

PETERSON, PAUL. 1985. *The Politics of School Reform: 1870–1940.* Chicago: University of Chicago Press.

PORTES, ALEJANDRO, and RUMBAUT, RUBEN G. 1990. *Immigrant America.* Berkeley: University of California Press.

ROSS, WILLIAM G. 1994. *Forging New Freedoms: Nativism, Education, and the Constitution, 1917–1927.* Lincoln: University of Nebraska Press.

RUSH, BENJAMIN. 1965. "Plan for the Establishment of Public Schools." In *Essays on Education in the Early Republic,* ed. Frederick Rudolf. Cambridge, MA: Harvard University Press.

SNOW, CATHERINE E., and HAKUTA, KENJI. 1992. "The Costs of Monolingualism." In *Language Loyalties,* ed. James Crawford. Chicago: University of Chicago Press.

SOLLORS, WERNER. 1986. *Beyond Ethnicity.* New York: Oxford University Press.

ST. JOHN DE CRÈVECOEUR, J. HECTOR. 1981. *Letters from an American Farmer; and Sketches of Eigh-*

teenth-Century America. New York: Penguin Books.

STOWE, CALVIN. 1974. "Calvin Stone on the Americanization of the Immigrant." In Education in the United States: A Documentary History, Vol. 2, ed. Sol Cohen. New York: Random House.

THOMPSON, FRANK V. 1971. Schooling of the Immigrant (1920). Montclair, NJ: Patterson Smith.

VELTMAN, CALVIN. 1988. The Future of the Spanish Language in the United States. New York and Washington, DC: Hispanic Policy Development Project.

WALCH, TIMOTHY. 1996. Parish School. New York: Crossroad.

CHARLES L. GLENN

INTERNATIONAL

The social and cultural effects of immigration have been in the forefront of policy debate a number of times in U.S. history (and in that of Canada and of Australia) but it is a largely unfamiliar and thus all the more difficult question in Europe. As the late Willem Fase noted, "Western Europe quickly moves in the direction of immigration countries such as the United States, Canada and Australia" but there is "crossnational variation in social and educational provisions for ethnic minority groups" (p. 7). The focus here will be upon the members of the European Union and Canada, Australia, and New Zealand.

Ethnicity and its consequences are among the most difficult and potentially destabilizing political issues in most of the Western democracies, as well as in the former Soviet Union and Yugoslavia and the developing nations. In recent years, commentators in Germany, France, Australia, and elsewhere have ranked immigration as the leading "hot button" topic in political discourse. The education of the children of immigrants is a challenge that professionals in the United States have faced for many years, but it is a relatively recent concern in Europe.

Certain countries, such as Australia, Canada, the United States, and South Africa, have long welcomed immigrants, though often with restrictions based upon origin, race, or skills. Migrant workers have been moving, and often settling, within Europe for centuries. Since World War II, Western Europe has absorbed millions of "guest workers," immigrants from former colonies who became permanent residents and brought their families; and more recently, millions of migrants from Eastern Europe. Even countries like Italy, Spain, Portugal, and Greece that were long exporters of their citizens to other countries now find themselves seeking to integrate hundreds of thousands of immigrants from North Africa, Eastern Europe, and elsewhere. Most European cities now have areas inhabited mostly by immigrant families.

Exceptional groups aside, the educational outcomes of immigrant children are generally inferior to those of native children. This has led to high rates of grade-retention and to frequent failure of students to obtain qualifications for technical or university education. Immigrant children are also often concentrated in schools that, in some cases, enroll no native pupils at all. Policy responses have included "reception classes" for pupils who are not proficient in the language of the school, supplemental programs to support home language and culture, and the designation of special zones or schools that receive additional funding to permit a more favorable pupil–teacher ratio and other supports. In a few cases that have not been widely copied, authorities have provided bilingual education or made efforts to desegregate schools.

Reception Classes

Typically, children of immigrant parents who are older than primary school age when they arrive are placed in reception classes for a year, where they are given an intensive program in the language of the school as well as orientation to life in the host society. In France, for example, it is assumed that young immigrant children should be treated like and integrated with French children of the same age; should learn numbers, colors, and reading in French; and should receive supplemental help only as individually needed, just as a child from a French-speaking home would. Special reception programs are regarded as an essential transitional measure only for pupils who start French schools at ages when their classmates would already be well advanced in their studies.

Some classes have a teacher who speaks the language of most of the children, as well as a native teacher. The role of the former is to assist with explanations and not to instruct in academic subjects through the home language; the goal is to prepare pupils as quickly as possible for participation in a regular class.

Supplemental Home Language and Culture Programs

In the countries under consideration some arrangement has been made to enable immigrant children to continue to develop their home language and to gain some knowledge of the culture of the country from which their parents came. Some of these programs are funded by the governments of the sending countries or by ethnic organizations, but many are supported by the educational system of the host society. Typically, pupils attend these classes on a voluntary basis for several hours per week, so arranged as not to conflict with regular academic instruction.

Supplemental language programs should not be confused with "bilingual education" (BE) as it is practiced in the United States. The intent is not, as in BE, to develop initial literacy in the home language or to teach the academic subjects through that language, but rather to enable immigrant children to retain some link with the homeland and the culture of their families.

Extra Resources for Immigrant Pupils

A number of efforts have been made to increase the effectiveness of the schooling provided to children from immigrant families by devoting additional resources to their schools. France has a system of "priority educational zones" (ZEPs) that receive additional support and attention.

Bilingual Education

Although instruction provided in two languages is common in some areas with linguistically mixed native populations, such as Catalonia in Spain, Friesland in the Netherlands, Schleswig-Holstein in Germany, and Wales, bilingual education has seldom been provided for the children of immigrants. The exceptions include some programs for Finnish immigrants in Sweden and experimental classes in other countries. The results have not been sufficiently positive to encourage widescale adoption of this approach.

School Desegregation

Only a few scattered attempts have been made in Western Europe to ensure that ethnic minority children are not concentrated in certain schools. It has frequently been pointed out that the growing tendency toward segregation of the children of immigrants has a negative effect upon their opportunities to learn the language of the school and reduces the motivation of foreign pupils and their parents to take seriously schooling in which no native pupils participate.

One German community that made a determined and comprehensive effort to promote ethnic integration is Krefeld in North Rhine/Westphalia. While the "Krefeld Model" was most notable for its stress upon pedagogical integration, it also included an element of deliberate assignment of pupils to create the preconditions for successful integration. Similar efforts have been made in Gouda and Amsterdam in the Netherlands, and in a number of cities of Flanders in Belgium.

See also: BILINGUALISM, SECOND LANGUAGE LEARNING, AND ENGLISH AS A SECOND LANGUAGE; BILINGUAL EDUCATION; LANGUAGE MINORITY STUDENTS; WESTERN EUROPE.

BIBLIOGRAPHY

BOOS-NÜNNING, URSULA. 1981. *Schulmodelle für ethnische Minderheiten: Drei Bundesländer im vergleich* (School models for ethnic minorities: Three German states compared). Essen/Landau, Germany: ALFA.

BOULOT, SERGE, and BOYZON-FRADET, DANIELLE. 1991. "De qui parle-t-on?" (Who are we talking about?) *Hommes et Migrations* 1146 (September):4–8.

BULLIVANT, BRIAN. 1981. *The Pluralist Dilemna in Education.* Sydney, Australia: George Allen and Ulwin.

DICKOPP, KARL-HEINZ. 1982. *Erziehung ausländischer Kinder als pädagogische Herausforderung: Das Krefelder Modell* (The education of foreign children as a pedagogical challenge: The Krefeld model). Dusseldorf, Germany: Schwann.

EDWARDS, JOHN, ed. 1984. *Linguistic Minorities, Policies and Pluralism.* London: Acadamic Press.

FASE, WILLEM. 1994. *Ethnic Divisions in Western European Education.* Munster, Germany: Waxmann.

GLENN, CHARLES L., with DE JONG, ESTER J. 1996. *Educating Immigrant Children: Schools and Language Minorities in Twelve Nations.* New York: Garland.

NIEKE, WOLFGANG; BUDDE, HILDEGARDE; and HENSCHEID, RENATE. 1983. *Struktuelle*

Benachteiligung ausländischer Jugendlicher: Die Marginalisierung der zweiten Generation (Structural disadvantaging of foreign youth: The marginalization of the second generation). Essen/Landau, Germany: ALFA.

PAULSTON, CHRISTINA BRATT. 1982. *Swedish Research and Debate about Bilingualism.* Stockholm: National Swedish Board of Education.

VERLOT, MARC. 1999. "Allochtonen in het onderwijs: Een politiek-anthropologisch onderzoek naar het integratie- en onderwijsbeleid in de Vlaamse Gemeenschap en de Franse Gemeenschap van België (1988–1998)." (Foreigners in the educational system: A political-anthropological investigation into integration and educational policy in the Flemish and French communities of Belgium, 1988–1998). Ph.D. diss., University of Ghent.

CHARLES L. GLENN

IMMUNIZATION AND CHILDREN'S PHYSICAL HEALTH

With the exception of safe water, no other public health intervention has had a greater impact in reducing deaths related to infectious disease than vaccinations. Smallpox was eradicated in 1977; wild-type poliomyelitis was eliminated from the Western hemisphere in 1991. Among children under five, measles and invasive *Haemophilus influenzae* type b (Hib) have both been reduced to record low numbers. Deaths associated with smallpox, diphtheria, pertussis, tetanus, paralytic poliomyelitis, measles, mumps, rubella, congenital rubella syndrome, and Hib decreased an average of nearly 100 percent during the twentieth century.

Though the United States is reaching record low levels of vaccine-preventable disease, continued immunization is important. Pathogenic viruses and bacteria still circulate in the United States, and with continuing globalization, the threat of disease spread increases. Immunization protects the general population from disease; individuals who are immunized have inherent protection from disease while those who are not immunized are protected by the limited likelihood that they will be exposed to another unimmunized and infected individual. Furthermore, immunization protects a population from disease; vaccinated individuals acquire immunologic protection from pathogens for themselves. As a consequence, immunized individuals are protected secondary to a decreased incidence of disease. This phenomenon of *herd immunity,* however, will not be achieved unless 80 percent to 95 percent of the population is immunized.

Childhood Immunizations

A detailed childhood immunization schedule is released yearly by the National Immunization Program (NIP), the American Academy of Pediatrics (AAP), and the American Academy of Family Physicians (AAFP). This schedule informs parents and health care providers which vaccines children need to receive and when they should receive them. An updated schedule can be found at the website of the Centers for Disease Control and Prevention.

State governments are responsible for passing and enforcing school immunization laws. Currently all fifty states have immunization requirements for children entering school. The vaccinations required may be different for different states. Additionally, states may also differ in the number and types of philosophical or religious exemptions they allow for children entering school. Vaccination decreases the risk of infection and outbreaks in schools by reducing the number of unprotected people who may be infected that are capable of transmitting the disease within their schools and communities.

Immunizations are available either free of charge or for a reduced cost at local health departments for children whose parents cannot afford to take their children to private physicians for immunization. Furthermore, on August 10, 1993, the Omnibus Budget Reconciliation Act (OBRA) created the Vaccines for Children Program (VFC) program as Section 1928 of the Social Security Act in order to increase access to immunizations. The program began on October 1, 1994; it provides vaccinations at no cost to VFC-eligible children seeing either public or private providers.

Vaccine-Preventable Diseases

The following eleven vaccine-preventable diseases are addressed through standard vaccination programs. A number of these diseases are covered by mandatory school immunization laws.

Diphtheria is a respiratory disease caused by a virus that is spread by coughing and sneezing. Symptoms include sore throat and low-grade fever. Left untreated, diptheria can lead to airway obstruction, coma, and death. Vaccines that contain the diptheria toxoid include the DTP, DtaP, DT, and Td vaccines.

Tetanus (lockjaw) is a disease of the nervous system that is caused by bacteria that enters the body through a break in the skin. Early symptoms include lockjaw, stiffness in the neck and abdomen, and difficulty in swallowing. Later onset symptoms include fever, elevated blood pressure, and severe muscle spasms. Death occurs in one third of all cases, especially among the elderly. Tetanus toxoid is also contained in the DTP, DT, DtaP, and Td vaccines.

Pertussis (whooping cough) is a highly contagious bacterial respiratory disease spread through coughing and sneezing. Symptoms include severe fits of coughing that may interfere with eating, drinking, and breathing. Pertussis may cause pneumonia, encephalitis, and infant death. The pertussis vaccine is contained within the DTP and DtaP vaccines.

Haemophilus influenzae type b is a bacterial infection that predominantly affects infants. It is spread by coughing and sneezing. Symptoms include skin and throat infections, meningitis, pneumonia, sepsis, and arthritis and may be severe for children under the age of one. Risk of disease is reduced after the age of five. A Hib vaccine can prevent the disease.

Hepatitis A is caused by the Hepatitis A virus and is spread most commonly through the fecal-oral route when the stool of an infected person is put into another person's mouth. It can also be transmitted by ingesting food or water that contain the virus. The disease affects the liver. Symptoms are unlikely, but if present they may include yellow skin or eyes, fatigue, stomach ache, loss of appetite, and nausea. This disease is prevented using the Hepatitis A vaccine.

Hepatitis B is caused by the Hepatitis B virus and is spread through sexual contact or through contact with the blood of an infected person. As with the initial clinical presentation of Hepatitis A, infection with Hepatitis B may follow an indolent course and manifest no symptoms. The likelihood of developing Hepatitis B increases with age. If present, symptoms are similar to Hepatitis A. The Hepatitis B vaccine prevents the disease.

Mumps is caused by a virus and is spread through coughing and sneezing. It is a disease that affects the lymph nodes. Symptoms include fever, headache, muscle ache and swelling of the lymph nodes close to the jaw. Infection with the mumps virus may also lead to meningitis, inflammation of the testicles or ovaries, inflammation of the pancreas and permanent deafness.

Measles is a highly contagious respiratory disease caused by a virus that is transmitted through coughing or sneezing. Symptoms include rash; high fever; cough; runny nose; and red, watery eyes lasting about a week. The measles may cause diarrhea, ear infections, pneumonia, encephalitis, seizures, and death. The measles vaccine is contained within the MMR, MR and measles vaccines.

Rubella (German measles) is a viral respiratory disease spread through coughing and sneezing. Symptoms may include a mild rash and fever for two to three days in children and young adults. Complications are severe for pregnant women, whose children frequently have congenital birth defects. The rubella vaccine is contained within the MMR, MR, and rubella vaccines.

Polio is a viral disease of the lymphatic and nervous systems. Transmission occurs through contact with an infected person. Symptoms include fever, sore throat, nausea, headaches, stomach aches, and stiffness in the neck, back and legs. OPV and IPV are the vaccines in current use.

Varicella (chickenpox) is a highly contagious disease caused by bacteria and is spread by coughing or sneezing. Symptoms are a skin rash of blister-like lesions on the face, scalp, or trunk. The varicella vaccine prevents this disease.

Immunization Safety

Before vaccines are approved by the Food and Drug Administration, they undergo rigorous scientific testing to ensure that they are safe and effective. However, differences in each individual's response to an antigenic vaccine challenge account for the rare occurrences ranging from vaccine failure to anaphylaxis. The National Childhood Vaccine Injury Act (NCVIA) of 1986 created the National Vaccine Program Office within the Department of Health and Human Services. It requires that all providers who administer vaccines provide a Vaccine Information Statement that explains the disease and the risks and benefits of vaccination to the vaccine recipient, parent, or legal guardian. The NCVIA also created the Vaccine Adverse Event Reporting System, a mandatory reporting system for health care providers. The National Vaccine Injury Compensation Program was also created under the NCVIA as a no-fault system for compensating people injured by vaccination.

See also: HEALTH EDUCATION; HEALTH SERVICES, *subentry on* SCHOOL.

BIBLIOGRAPHY

PLOTKIN, STANLEY A., and ORENSTEIN, WALTER A. 1999. *Vaccines,* 3rd edition. Philadelphia: W. B. Saunders Co.

INTERNET RESOURCES

CENTERS FOR DISEASE CONTROL AND PREVENTION. 2002. "Immunization Laws." <www.cdc.gov/od/nvpo/law.htm>.

CENTERS FOR DISEASE CONTROL AND PREVENTION. 2002. "Parent's Guide to Childhood Immunizations." <www.cdc.gov/nip/publications/Parents-Guide>.

CENTERS FOR DISEASE CONTROL AND PREVENTION. 2002. "Recommended Childhood Immunization Schedule." <www.cdc.gov/nip/recs/child-schedule.htm>.

ANGELA HUANG

IMPACT AID, PUBLIC LAWS 815 AND 874

Public Laws 81-815 and 81-874 were approved by the U.S. Congress in 1950 to assist local school districts with the construction and cost of public educational activities impacted by federal defense efforts. The so-called impact laws were an extension of a 1941 federal emergency measure, the Lanham Act. The precedence of the Lanham Act, the rising educational burden placed on local school districts near military bases, and the advent of the Korean War (1950–1953) contributed to the subsequent passage of the impact laws. A House Committee on Education and Labor studied the strain on local districts and concluded that unless federal assistance were provided, "more than 1.8 million children in these federally impacted areas would not receive normal school services" (National Association of Federally Impacted Schools, p. 9).

To ameliorate the loss of local taxes from personnel residing on federal lands, the authorizing committees of both the House and the Senate passed legislation (H.R. 7940 and S. 2317) to provide federal aid for the construction and maintenance of new schools in defense areas. On July 13, 1950, Public Law 81-874 was initially authorized for four years. Public Law 81-815 was passed on August 22, 1950 for an initial two-year authorization. The passage of the impact laws in 1950 and subsequent reauthorization during the 1950s represented a significant exception to the contentious federal school politics of the 1940s and early 1950s. Numerous federal aid-to-education bills had failed because of racial and religious dissent. Until the passage of the Elementary and Secondary Education Act in 1965, impact laws were the only form of federal general aid for K–12 education. Furthermore, school districts receiving impact aid funds were generally free from federal governmental interference. For example, until the 1964 Civil Rights Bill enabled the U.S. Office of Education to withhold federal money from districts maintaining racial segregation, impact aid schools were not pressured to desegregate.

Children attending schools in impacted areas or federally connected children were (1) children who lived on federal property and whose parents worked on federal property; (2) children who either lived on federal property or whose parents worked on federal property; and (3) children whose parents came into the district as a result of federal contracts with private firms. A minimum of 3 percent or 400 federally connected children had to be in average daily attendance in a given district to qualify for impact aid.

The Elementary and Secondary Education Act (ESEA) of 1965 and subsequent amendments altered the original criteria for impact laws to assist not only areas affected by military personnel but also those with high poverty rates and other hardships such as rapid growth. Under Title I, Public Law 81-874 created a new three-year program of basic federal grants to the states. Funds would be allotted to districts where at least 100 school-age children, or 3 percent of the total number of school-age children were from families with low annual incomes. Under Title VI of the 1966 ESEA amendments the stipulation that three percent of children in a district must be federally connected to receive impact aid was altered to substitute a minimum of 400 children even if three percent were not federally connected. Public Law 81-815 also was broadened under the 1966 ESEA amendments to allow districts with rapid enrollment to qualify for aid.

Native American children living on federally owned lands also were eligible for funds under Public Law 81-874 and Public Law 81-815. However, it was not until passage of Title IV of the 1972 Amendments, the Indian Education Act, that Native Americans were explicitly included. In that year Public Law 81-874 was amended to financially assist local educational agencies for the education of Indian children.

Impact Aid funds flow primarily through basic support payments on behalf of federally connected children. Additional payments are made for federally connected children with disabilities, for heavily impacted districts, for federal property removed from local tax rolls after 1938, and for construction and renovation of school facilities. The bulk of the appropriation goes directly to student compensation. For fiscal year 1999, the Department of Education found that close to 97 percent of the $864 million allocation was for federally connected children, whereas little more than 3 percent was targeted for school districts that lost significant local assessed value due to the acquisition of property by the federal government since 1938.

Program Analysis

Researchers from RAND's National Defense Research Institute analyzed the Impact Aid Program, with an emphasis on its effect on the children of military personnel. Their findings are documented in a 2001 publication by Richard Buddin, Brian P. Gill, and Ron Zimmer. The authors drew the following conclusions.

- The complex Impact Aid formula results in large payment disparities for the same type of students.

- Differences in how school districts are defined makes the link between them and reimbursements inherently flawed.

- Educational opportunities of military and civilian children appear roughly comparable.

- Concern over the extra cost of military children may be misplaced.

- Military children have a much higher migration rate than do civilian children.

Future Directions

The U.S. Department of Education continually proposes changes for funding via appropriations language and annual budget requests to best serve the needs of all federally connected children, and to improve the targeting of districts experiencing the greatest impact from federal activities. To improve the timely processing of Impact Aid payments, the department is increasing its use of technology and endeavoring to establish improved review procedures. According to the department's biennial report for the fiscal year 1995–1996, however, the program objectives have remained substantially the same: to support local school districts impacted by children who reside on military bases, Indian lands, federal properties, or in federally subsidized housing; or to a lesser extent, for children who have parents in the uniformed services or who are employed on eligible federal properties, but do not also reside there.

See also: FEDERAL EDUCATIONAL ACTIVITIES; FEDERAL SCHOOLS AND COLLEGES.

BIBLIOGRAPHY

BUDDIN, RICHARD; GILL, BRIAN P.; and ZIMMER, RON. 2001. *Impact Aid and the Education of Military Children.* Santa Monica, CA: RAND.

CONGRESSIONAL QUARTERLY SERVICE. 1967. *Federal Role in Education,* 2nd edition. Washington, DC: Congressional Quarterly.

LAPATI, AMERICO D. 1975. *Education and the Federal Government: A Historical Record.* New York: Mason-Charter.

NATIONAL ASSOCIATION OF FEDERALLY IMPACTED SCHOOLS. 1996. *Impact Aid Handbook.* Washington, DC: The National Association of Federally Impacted Schools.

RAVITCH, DIANE. 1983. *The Troubled Crusade: American Education 1945–1980.* New York: Basic Books.

TIEDT, SIDNEY, W. 1966. *The Role of the Federal Government in Education.* New York: Oxford University Press.

U.S. DEPARTMENT OF EDUCATION. 2000. *OESE Impact Aid: What Is Impact Aid?* Washington, DC: U.S. Department of Education.

U.S. DEPARTMENT OF EDUCATION: OFFICE OF THE UNDER SECRETARY. 1996. *Biennial Evaluation Report, Fiscal Years 1995–1996.* Washington, DC: U.S. Department of Education.

CAROLYN D. HERRINGTON
VICTORIA-MARÍA MACDONALD

INCLUSION
See: SPECIAL EDUCATION.

INDEPENDENT SCHOOLS
See: PRIVATE SCHOOLING.

INDEPENDENT STUDY

Independent study programs are found at nearly every level of education in the United States, from elementary school through graduate school. Although the concept of independent study was not new, a spectacular increase in interest in the subject occurred in elementary and secondary schools in the 1960s. In the early twenty-first century, many courses delivered within a traditional format are expected to have some component of independent study and to build independent learning skills. The major elements of independent study are the following:

- Individualized teaching and learning takes place through the student's activity.
- A tutorial relationship exists.
- Learning is made convenient for the student.
- The learner takes responsibility for progress.

Independent study programs are sometimes criticized because they release students from group-learning situations. Students themselves, while they may select or volunteer for independent study experiences, are frequently unprepared because they lack experience with any other way to learn except in a classroom. However, some research has shown that computer-based learning is as effective as traditional instruction. Students were able to organize their own learning effectively, were generally positive about using this form of instruction, and scored similarly on examinations.

Purposes and Goals of Independent Study

Successful independent study programs provide preparation for students and guidance along the way:

- Students are taught knowledge and skills that cannot easily be communicated in classrooms.
- As evaluated by exams, independent students learn at least as well as students in classes.
- Independent study provides useful practice in the process of learning.

- Independent study is viable when an educational institution is inaccessible to the learner.
- Independent study meets the convenience needs of many learners.
- Independent study develops self-motivation, concentration, and discipline.
- The learner is taught to identify a problem, gather data, and take responsibility for conclusions.
- The learner does all the work and cannot slide by on the anonymity of group activity.

Independent Study and Extensiveness in Grades K–12

The amount of time that students devote to independent study could be much greater than is the case in most schools. Although often identified as a tool for meeting the needs of gifted students, independent study should be available for all. Each year, teachers demand more group attention on the part of students, leaving less time for independent study even though the students' capacity for independent study grows. Of course, students differ in their degree of self-direction, creativity, and performance, but all can profit from a greater amount of independence. In the past independent study has too often been viewed as being synonymous with learning by doing or with special term projects. Independent study needs to be viewed as an integral part of the total process of learning in all fields. Each curricular area needs sequenced materials that enable students to learn independently effectively. The materials first should describe the required outcomes in terms that each student can understand. Concepts and skills should be defined in behavioral terms. For example, if students are asked to research an issue through independent study, the exact parameters of their project, depth and breadth, the types and numbers of sources, the form conclusions should take, and the formats that may be used to present the results should be clearly spelled out, so that each student will know precisely what the school expects. Each segment in the learning sequence should provide a variety of learning activities that may be used to arrive at specified outcomes. Pretests and self-tests that enable monitoring of learning and suggestions of some ways to study in greater depth should be included. Motivation is enhanced by self-selection of learning strategies that work well for individual students and by the immediate reinforcement of self-testing. Provocative questions or activities to stimulate the learner's creativity such as those described by Phil Schlemmer (1999) for students in grade six and above can be used in concert with a traditional curriculum. Students no longer fail; they simply make less progress in the learning sequence. Each student's special projects should be recorded as part of an educational portfolio (now required by some states for graduation).

The University of Missouri-Columbia High School (MU High School), part of the University of Missouri Center for Distance and Independent Study, has an accredited diploma program for students of varying ages interested in alternatives to traditional high school. These include students who are home schooled, rural students wishing for additional college preparation, gifted students who need coursework above their current grade level, and students who need to make up courses. More than 150 different courses can be applied toward credit to a high school transcript. John Marlowe (2000) recommends that educators offering independent study to high school students analyze individual needs, match needs to options, use a paper trail to manage each program, enlist teacher support, guarantee academic rigor, and include some component that allows for students to socialize. Programs to teach independent and strategic learning skills to this age student also exist. In summary, students at the high school level use independent study to do the following:

- Earn university credit before they begin college.

- Earn extra credits to finish high school early.

- Supplement schedules with courses not offered at their schools.

- Enrich their high school experiences.

- Make up credits to graduate on time.

- Earn a high school diploma.

Similar programs also exist at the elementary and middle school level. The University of Missouri's Distance and Independent Study Center also offers a program for elementary and middle school students in grades three through eight that covers curriculum in language arts, mathematics, science, and social studies. All the courses were written by licensed teachers and are equivalent to a semester of work. Coursework can be completed through the mail, online, or by fax.

Trends, Issues, and Controversies

The movement toward independent study at the elementary and middle school level has been fueled by an increase in the number of students who are home schooled. Although developed primarily for this consumer group, such courses are being offered to schools as supplements to the regular curriculum and as a way to meet the needs of diverse learners. Schools may opt for these programs for use in enrichment programs, especially for students in accelerated programs or those identified as gifted, for remediation, for use with students with identified learning problems, or in place of summer school programs. Programs to teach independent and strategic learning skills also exist for grades K–12.

There are several reasons for this trend. First, independent study programs have been successful in meeting the needs of students who lack other educational opportunities. Second, increasing pressure on adults to continue learning to upgrade skills for their current job or to prepare themselves for new careers has created a concomitant expectation that students will learn how to do this in grades K–12. Third, educational technology has gained increasing acceptance as an ally of the teacher and student in accomplishing tasks that would be more difficult and expensive in conventional formats. Fourth, improved understanding of the nature of the individual process of learning has yielded greater emphasis on teaching the student to learn and solve problems independently and with less emphasis on information transfer.

At the beginning of the twenty-first century, the infusion of technology (particularly the Internet and video-conferencing) has made independent learning and distance education a focus for all schools. Carefully conducted research and a rigorous evaluation of the effectiveness of independent study programs, especially those that rely heavily on technology over a long period of time, are needed. Such evaluation should analyze not only differences in achievement, as measured by existing standardized tests, but also changes in student attitudes and the quality of their experience. The changes that independent study and distance education bring in the learning and teaching environment must also be a focus of study.

See also: Alternative Schooling; Curriculum, School; Elementary Education, *subentries on* Current Trends, History of; Gifted and Talented Education; Home Schooling; Secondary

EDUCATION, *subentries on* CURRENT TRENDS, HISTORY OF.

BIBLIOGRAPHY

DEWHURST, DAVID; MACLEOD, HAMISH A.; and NORRIS, TRACY A. 2000. "Independent Student Learning Aided by Computers: An Acceptable Alternative to Lectures?" *Computers and Education* 35(3):223–241.

KIEWRA, KENNETH, and DUBOIS, NELSON F. 1998. *Learning to Learn: Making the Transition from Student to Lifelong Learner.* Boston: Allyn and Bacon.

MARLOW, JOHN. 2000. "Learning Alone." *The American School Board Journal* 87(12):56–62.

MEDINA, KATHLEEN; PIGG, MATTHEW; DELAR, GAIL; and GOROSPE, GIL. 2001. "Teaching Generation.com." *Phi Delta Kappan* 82(8):616–619.

SCHLEMMER, PHIL, and SCHLEMMER, DORI. 1999. *Challenging Projects for Creative Minds: Twenty Self-Directed Enrichment Projects that Develop and Showcase Student Ability: For Grades Six and Up.* Minneapolis, MN: Free Spirit Press.

SCHUNK, DALE H., and ZIMMERMAN, BARRY J. 1998. *Self-Regulated Learning: From Teaching to Self-Reflective Practice.* New York: Guildford Press.

WASSERRNAN, SELMA. 2001. "Curriculum Enrichment with Computer Software." *Phi Delta Kappan* 82(8):592–597.

WEINSTEIN, CLAIRE E., and HUME, LAURA M. 1998. *Study Strategies for Lifelong Learning.* Washington, DC: American Psychological Association.

ZIMMERMAN, BARRY J.; BONNER, SEBASTIAN; and KOVACH, ROBERT. 1996. *Developing Self Regulated Learners: Beyond Achievement to Self-Efficacy.* Washington, DC: American Psychological Association.

INTERNET RESOURCES

UNIVERSITY OF MISSOURI'S CENTER FOR DISTANCE AND INDEPENDENT STUDY. 2002. "Elementary/Middle School." <http://cdis.missouri.edu/elementary>.

UNIVERSITY OF MISSOURI'S CENTER FOR DISTANCE AND INDEPENDENT STUDY. 2002. "MU High School." <http://cdis.missouri.edu/MUHigh School/Hshome.htm>.

MARY ANN RAFOTH

INDIVIDUAL DIFFERENCES

ABILITIES AND APTITUDES

Abilities are cognitive or mental characteristics that affect one's potential to learn or to perform. Aptitudes are sometimes treated as interchangeable with abilities, particularly when they focus on prediction of performance in other settings or on other occasions. Cognitive abilities have been conceived very broadly (e.g., intelligence) and also in terms of specialized abilities such as verbal, spatial, memory, reasoning, problem solving, and psychomotor ability. Some authors have defined aptitudes more broadly than abilities, to include any number of individual-differences factors—affective, cognitive, and personality characteristics—that influence one's readiness or likelihood of learning or performing successfully.

During the twentieth century, there have been significant changes in conceptions of ability, moving from atheoretical models that have their basis in measurement and psychophysics to ones that are based largely on cognitive theories of human performance. Social issues continue to influence conceptions of ability and practices of ability testing. The scientific measurement of abilities has been viewed as either enabling or stifling social progress, and such controversy continues in the twenty-first century.

History

Ability testing in education began in 1905 in Paris when Alfred Binet along with his assistant Théodore Simon developed the Binet-Simon scale to solve the practical problem of reliably differentiating between educable, educable with special help, and uneducable children. Prior to the development of the scale, such classifications were made subjectively and inconsistently; thus the scale was considered a significant practical achievement. The scale consisted of thirty tests, such as "naming objects in pictures," "defining common words by function," and "retaining a memory of a picture." In historical treatments, Binet and Simon's approach is sometimes referred to as a task-sampling approach, in that the tests are essentially samples of typical educational events.

The task-sampling approach may be contrasted with another tradition in ability testing, a basic elements approach. This tradition began with Francis Galton's development of a battery of basic sensory-motor, reaction time, and memory tests. Galton believed that a general mental ability with biological underpinnings underlay performance on these tests, but to his disappointment, he found no relationship with educational or occupational levels. Charles Spearman developed a statistical method known as factor analysis, which demonstrated that Galton's hypothesis of a general ability was supported after all. Later, researchers such as Louis Thurstone and J.P. Guilford refined Spearman's notion, by adding various kinds of tests to the more basic batteries, and identifying "group factors" such as spatial and verbal ability in addition to general ability (Spearman's "g") to account for patterns of performance.

Developing conceptions of ability and aptitude have proceeded in tandem with practical applications, particularly in military, educational, and employment settings. In the military, the development of the "Army Alpha and Beta" intelligence tests during World War I, which helped efficiently sort 1.7 million World War I conscripts into job classifications (training, frontline, officer, and so forth) has been cited by Frederick McGuire as one of psychology's most influential contributions to American society. The Army Alpha, used essentially as a measure of general cognitive ability, consisted of eight subtests (oral directions, arithmetic problems, practical judgment, antonyms, disarranged sentences, number series, analogies, and information), most of which are still being used in test batteries today. During World War II and through the 1950s the number of abilities measured was expanded to include such constructs as verbal and quantitative ability, technical knowledge, and psychomotor abilities, the latter being particularly important for pilot and navigator selection. In the early twenty-first century the U.S. military services use a multidimensional test battery, the Armed Services Vocational Aptitude Battery (ASVAB), for both selecting applicants and assigning them to training and occupational specialties.

Following the success of the Army Alpha, there was general optimism about the role ability assessment could play in "social engineering," such as providing opportunities for higher education to students based on merit rather than on birthright. An example was the Scholastic Aptitude Test (now known as the SAT) during the period between World War I and World War II. The SAT was designed, in the words of the American educator James Bryant Conant, to "reorder the 'haves and have-nots' in every generation to give flux to our social order." The composition of the SAT has fluctuated minimally over the years, consistently yielding "verbal" and "mathematical" scores, relying on tasks that are arguably work samples of academic tasks (e.g., reading comprehension) to those that are more abstract from such tasks (e.g., verbal analogies).

A third major application of abilities and aptitudes is in employment testing. The General Aptitude Test Battery (GATB) was developed around the time of World War II, by a commission of industrial psychologists and measurement experts for the U.S. Department of Labor. The test measures general ability, verbal aptitude, numerical aptitude, psychomotor ability (motor coordination, finger dexterity, and manual dexterity), and general perceptual ability (spatial aptitude, form perception, and clerical perception). The GATB was designed to predict job performance. More than seven hundred validity studies have demonstrated that it does so, and consequently the test is widely used as an employment screen. A meta-analysis of these studies conducted by John Hunter and Ronda Hunter has shown that general cognitive ability is the primary determinant of job success, but that psychomotor ability is important for relatively low complexity jobs.

Modern Views

The major aptitude batteries—the ASVAB, GATB, and SAT, in the military, industrial, and educational sectors, respectively—were developed in the post–World War I period, and although still in use in the early twenty-first century, have not fundamentally changed over the years in what they measure or how they measure it. But advances in the knowledge of how people think, learn, and solve problems, since the 1970s, has triggered a reevaluation of what abilities are and how they ought to be measured.

Information processing. The information-processing view likens the individual to an information-processing system, suggesting that the parameters governing the performance of an information-processing system, such as speed and memory capacity, might be the abilities that govern human learning and performance. Since the 1960s, numerous studies have examined the relationship between mental speed and learning and performance. The conclusion has been that increased sophistication in the procedures for measurement are responsible for a slightly more favorable view than Galton had of the importance of mental speed in everyday life. Still, the work has primarily been of theoretical interest, and there have been few suggestions that mental speed is an important ability to begin routinely including it in large-scale aptitude batteries. In fact, to the contrary, the military services are in the process of removing their "speed" composite from the ASVAB because it has proven not to be a valid predictor of training success or job performance. Similarly, ETS routinely considers speed to be an irrelevant factor for most of its measures.

There has been considerable support, though, for the notion that another aspect of information processing, working-memory capacity, is central to human performance. Several studies have shown that working-memory capacity (as measured by tasks such as mental arithmetic) is indistinguishable from Spearman's "g" and therefore is the primary ability governing learning and performance. Ian Deary has suggested that Spearman's "g" is simply being relabeled to have a more contemporary-sounding title. But information-processing explanations of abilities have several advantages. One is that they allow for the construction of ability measures based not simply on previous measures, but on the understanding of how people learn, think, and solve problems. A second is that an information-processing scheme has potential use in task analysis. For example, as Susan Embretson has demonstrated, the requirements of a task can be characterized in information-processing terms, enabling the a priori prediction of item difficulty. A third advantage is that information-processing based concepts connect with wider areas of inquiry such as cognitive and brain sciences, and therefore allow for the uniting of what Lee Cronbach referred to as the two disciplines of scientific psychology, the correlational and the experimental.

Knowledge and expertise. A second perspective based on new conceptions in cognitive science might be called the knowledge and expertise view. In this view, characteristics such as working-memory capacity and information-processing speed are not viewed as fixed characteristics of an individual, but as dependent upon knowledge and skill that is developed over long periods of time. So, for example, expert chess players have the ability to recall actual chess positions with impressive accuracy and to a much greater extent than novice players. However, when chess pieces are arranged in random fashion, the two groups have equal recall. Similarly, many studies have demonstrated that processing speed is a direct function of repeated practice. These studies have demonstrated that efficient information processes are, in large part, the residue of well-organized knowledge structures that are developed over years of active engagement and practice within a domain. Further, well-developed knowledge structures in a domain make one a much more effective learner of other concepts in that domain, since there is an established knowledge organization within which to embed and connect new information.

This emphasis on domain specific expertise has profound implications for considering ability testing and ability development. The implication of the expertise approach is to assess and then facilitate the development of knowledge structures and processing skills that will support performance and learning within a domain, without significant attention paid to broad, domain-independent skills. Clearly, the debate over how much of ability is specific to or independent of particular domains continues, and has profound implications for the selection, education, and training of individuals.

Hierarchical model. A third new development might be called the hierarchical model of ability differences. This work continues the factor analytic tradition began by Spearman, and further refined by Thurstone and Guilford. The key idea behind the hierarchical model is that what had been thought to be rival hypotheses concerning the number and organization of human abilities can be now seen as compatible. Even into the 1980s one had to take a position on whether the evidence was more favorable towards the Spearman view of one general ability (along with number test-specific abilities); with Thurstone's view of eight to eleven primary mental abilities; or Guilford's 120 or 160 ability models. The hierarchical model, as developed by Jan-Eric Gustafsson and John Carroll, shows the fruitfulness of considering abilities as varying in their generality from fairly specific abilities (e.g., memory span, associative memory, and free recall memory), to broader ones (e.g., general memory and learning), to the most broad (general intelligence). In fact, this example is taken from Carroll's "Three-stratum structure of cognitive abilities," which posits sixty-seven or so "Stratum I" abilities, eight "Stratum II" abilities, and one "Stratum III" ability. Gustafsson's scheme is similar in spirit, but he did not consider nearly as many datasets as Carroll did, and so consequently his proposal may be seen as a subset of Carroll's.

Multiple intelligences. A final new development might be called the "multiple intelligences" view. There are actually two quite distinct notions that might be considered in this category, the "triarchic theory" of Robert Sternberg and the "multiple intelligences" theory of Howard Gardner. Sternberg's idea is that the field, the testing industry, and the application sectors themselves (education, industry, and the military) are preoccupied with one notion of abilities, which he playfully refers to as the "g-ocentric view." He also calls this analytic intelligence, and suggests that while important, success in school and in life is perhaps equally if not more importantly determined by other intelligences, namely creativity and practical intelligence. Although this work has not yet resulted in any widescale applications, preliminary work, particularly in the area of practical intelligence appears promising.

Gardner has proposed a different scheme, called "multiple intelligence theory," which identifies eight abilities—linguistic, logical-mathematical, musical, spatial, bodily-kinesthetic, interpersonal, intrapersonal, and naturalist intelligences. This scheme is quite popular in educational circles, perhaps attributable to its elevation of abilities other than the usual linguistic and logical-mathematical abilities, encouraging the recognition of some students for talents normally overlooked. However, the scheme is often dismissed in scientific circles because by eschewing measurement, it fails to allow for its validity to be tested. As Nathan Brody has pointed out, multiple-intelligence theory is at odds with the rest of the field in its rejection of a general cognitive ability, and with its choice of the particular eight abilities—neither empirical nor theoretical justifications for these features of the theory have been produced.

Controversies

Discussions and investigations of aptitudes, abilities, and individual differences have been fraught with controversy throughout their history. Certainly one of the most contentious issues is that of the heritability of abilities. Comparisons of monozygotic and dizygotic twins, twins reared apart versus together, adoption studies, and various other behavioral genetics studies, suggest that abilities are somewhat heritable, although the issue of by what amount remains unsettled. There is ample evidence for notably high consistency in test scores over time. A study reported by Ian Deary showed that Scottish eleven-year-olds performed remarkably similarly on an identical test of mental ability administered sixty-six years later, when they were seventy-seven years old.

Some of the reason for the intense interest in heritability seems to be inappropriately due to a misconception that to the degree that abilities are inherited, there is not much one can do to improve one's abilities. Heritability, however, is not synonymous with immutability, as can be proven with a simple thought experiment. Height is highly heritable, but has steadily increased over the twentieth century due to improvements in environmental factors such as nutrition. Similarly, as documented by James Flynn, intelligence scores have been shown to have risen quite dramatically in the second half of the twentieth century in numerous parts of the world. Early childhood intervention programs, such as Head Start, have met with mixed success, but others, such as the Carolina Abecedarian project, have shown strong and persistent gains in cognitive skills, academic test scores, and language use in follow-up studies through the age of fifteen.

Another area of some controversy in the abilities and aptitudes literature concerns the role of other factors such as metacognition, attitudes, motivation, and concepts such as emotional intelligence, in performance in school and the workplace. Concepts such as test anxiety have for a long time been cited as a threat to the validity of an estimate of a student's ability. Claude Steele has suggested that additional attitudinal factors, "disidentification" and "stereotype threat," may impair the performance of minority students in certain contexts. Motivation has long been considered an important factor in governing learning and performance success and related concepts such as goal setting, self-efficacy, and optimism are being investigated for their role in learning. Emotional intelligence refers to a wide variety of factors that may mediate the relationship between abilities and performance, or may serve as abilities and aptitudes in their own right.

A third controversy centers on the extent to which ability can even be considered as an individual phenomenon. In the situated cognition view, abilities can only be considered as they are manifest and develop within social situations. The interaction of the person with the social environment is what defines ability —it is not a construct that can be defined independent of such interaction. Much of the support for this work comes from examining very sophisticated cognitive strategies that develop without the benefit of any formal academic training or ability to demonstrate the strategies in traditional academic ways.

Further Directions

The predominant use of individual differences in abilities and aptitudes in education has been in assigning students to special remedial programs, selecting them for admission into schools (e.g., colleges), or identifying them for receiving awards such as scholarships or fellowships. Although this use will undoubtedly continue, it is likely that an increasing emphasis will be put on new uses, opening the door to additional opportunities, in the form of diagnosis, tailored educational programs, and self-assessments to facilitate more efficacious career choices. It is likely that the noncognitive ability and aptitude variables, including interests, personality, motivation, and the like, will prove particularly important for the new uses role.

Another trend in ability and aptitude testing in education is an increased emphasis on the assessment of achievements rather than the more basic abilities. Some of this is due to what some have characterized as the pernicious effects of test coaching, and is certainly consistent with cognitive conceptions of expertise. The idea is that as long as there are high-stakes ability tests, there will be a coaching industry designed to help students improve their chances of succeeding on those tests. To the extent that the tests directly reflect the achievements that are supposed to be learned in school, coaching then becomes a positive force, a productive adjunct to the school curriculum, reinforcing lessons learned in school. Another reason for this trend is that test users and the public in general have increasingly demanded tests that look more like the learning or performance activities that the tests are designed to predict. There seems to be less patience with arguments based exclusively on predictive validity statistics. One sees this in military and industry testing as well as educational testing.

A third trend in abilities and aptitude assessment is what is sometimes called "embedded assessment" or the insertion of abilities tests within the context of instruction itself. This trend fits with the general trend toward the increased use of achievement testing, but for the specific purpose of tailoring instruction to a particular individual, based on that individual's changing knowledge and understanding of a particular topic area. Richard Snow and Valerie Shute have suggested both "macroadaptive" and "microadaptive" responding on the part of a computerized ("intelligent") tutoring system. Microadaptive instruction refers to the specific reactions a tutor makes in response to its continually updated understanding of what a student knows and is learning; macroadaptive instruction refers to more global approaches to delivering coaching and feedback the tutor makes based on more general assessments of a student's abilities.

Finally, a possible future trend is increasing attention paid to what might be called "mediators" for their role in affecting abilities and aptitudes. These include factors such as nutrition, psychopharmacology, fatigue, and circadian rhythms. Nutritional explanations have begun to appear more frequently in discussions of changes in abilities, and the role of nutrition, vitamins, and glucose has been investigated but as of yet, little is known. Similarly, there have been some investigations of "smart drugs," such as caffeine, ginseng, and ginko biloba, as well as other psychopharmacological agents, particularly cholinergic enhancers. Finally, much has been learned over the past decade about the role of circadian rhythms in affecting hormonal production and concommittant behavioral effects such as fatigue and alertness over the course of the day. There has been some work suggesting that "morningness" and "eveningness" may be characteristic dispositions that mediate both cognitive abilities and personality factors.

See also: ASSESSMENT; INTELLIGENCE; TESTING.

BIBLIOGRAPHY

ATKINSON, RICHARD C. 2001. "Tests and Access to American Universities." The 2001 Robert H. Atwell Distinguished Lecture Delivered at the 83rd

Annual Meeting of the American Council on Education, Washington, DC.

BENTON, DAVID; GRIFFITHS, REBECCA; and HALLER, JURG. 1997. "Thiamine Supplementation Mood and Cognitive Functioning." *Psychopharmacology* 129(1):66–71.

BINET, ALFRED, and SIMON, THÉODORE. 1916. *The Development of Intelligence in Children (The Binet-Simon Scale),* trans. Elizabeth S. Kite. Baltimore: Williams and Wilkins.

BRODY, NATHAN. 1992. *Intelligence,* 2nd edition. San Diego, CA: Academic.

CAMPBELL, FRANCIS A., and RAMEY, CRAIG T. 1994. "Effects of Early Intervention on Intellectual and Academic Development: A Follow-Up Study of Children from Low-Income Families." *Child Development* 65:684–698.

CARROLL, JOHN B. 1993. *Human Cognitive Abilities.* New York: Cambridge University Press.

COULL, JENNIFER T., and SAHAKIAN, BARBARA J. 2000. "Psychopharmacology of Memory." In *Memory Disorders in Psychiatric Practice,* ed. German E Berrios and John R Hodges. New York: Cambridge University Press.

CRONBACH, LEE J. 1957. "The Two Disciplines of Scientific Psychology." *American Psychologist* 12:671–684.

DEARY, IAN J. 2000. *Looking Down on Human Intelligence: From Psychometrics to the Brain.* Oxford: Oxford University Press.

DEARY, IAN J., et al. 2000. "The Stability of Individual Differences in Mental Ability from Childhood to Old Age: Follow-Up of the 1932 Scottish Mental Survey." *Intelligence* 28:49–55.

EMBRETSON, SUSAN E. 1995. "The Role of Working Memory Capacity and General Control Processes in Intelligence." *Intelligence* 20:169–190.

FLYNN, JAMES R. 1987. "Searching for Justice: The Discover of IQ Gains over Time." *American Psychologist* 54:5–20.

FUREY, MAURA; PIETRINI, PIETRO; and HAXBY, JAMES V. 2000. "Cholinergic Enhancement and Increased Selectivity of Perceptual Processing during Working Memory." *Science* 290 (5500):2315–2319.

GALTON, FRANCIS. 1973. *Inquiries into Human Faculty and Its Development* (1883). New York: AMS Press.

GUILFORD, JOY P. 1967. *The Nature of Human Intelligence.* New York: McGraw-Hill.

GUSTAFSSON, JAN ERIC. 1984. "A Unifying Model for the Structure of Intellectual Abilities." *Intelligence* 8:179–203.

HUNTER, JOHN E. 1994. "The General Aptitude Test Battery." In *Encyclopedia of Human Intelligence,* ed. Robert J. Sternberg. New York: Macmillan.

HUNTER, JOHN E., and HUNTER, RONDA F. 1984. "Validity and Utility of Alternate Predictors of Job Performance." *Psychological Bulletin* 96:72–98.

JENSEN, ARTHUR R. 1998. *The g Factor: The Science Of Mental Ability.* Westport, CT: Praeger.

KYLLONEN, PATRICK C. 2001. "'g': Knowledge, Speed, Strategies, or Working-Memory Capacity? A Systems Perspective." In *The General Factor of Intelligence: How General Is It?* ed. Robert J. Sternberg and Elena L. Grigorenko. Mahwah, NJ: Erlbaum.

KYLLONEN, PATRICK C., and CHRISTAL, RAYMOND E. 1990. "Reasoning Ability Is (Little More Than) Working-Memory Capacity?!" *Intelligence* 14(4):389–433.

LEHMAN, NICHOLAS. 1999. *The Big Test: The Secret American Meritocracy.* New York: Farrar, Strauss and Giroux.

LAVE, JEAN, and WENGER, ELLEN. 1991. *Situated Learning: Legitimate Peripheral Participation.* Cambridge, Eng.: Cambridge University Press.

LOHMAN, DAVID F. 2000. "Complex Information Processing and Intelligence." In *Handbook of Intelligence,* ed. Robert J. Sternberg. New York: Cambridge University Press.

LYNN, RICHARD. 1987. "Nutrition and Intelligence." In *Biological Approaches to the Study of Intelligence,* ed. Phillip. A. Vernon. Norwood, NJ: Ablex.

MAYER, JACK D., CARUSO, DAVID R., and SALOVEY, PETER. 2000. "Selecting a Measure of Emotional Intelligence: The Case for Ability Scales." In *The Handbook of Emotional Intelligence: Theory, Development, Assessment, and Application at Home, School, and in the Workplace,* ed. Reuven Bar-On. San Francisco: Jossey-Bass.

McGUIRE, FREDERICK L. 1994. "Army Alpha and Beta Tests of Intelligence." In *Encyclopedia of Human Intelligence,* ed. Robert J. Sternberg. New York: Macmillan.

MOTOWIDLO, STEPHAN J.; DUNNETTE, MARVIN D.; and CARTER, GARY W. 1990. "An Alternative

Selection Procedure: The Low-Fidelity Simulation." *Journal of Applied Psychology* 75:640–647.

PENTLAND, ALEX. 1998. "Wearable Intelligence." *Scientific American.* 9(4):90–95.

ROBERTS, RICHARD R., and KYLLONEN, PATRICK C. 1999. "Morningness–Eveningness and Intelligence: Early to Bed, Early to Rise Will Likely Make You Anything but Wise!" *Personality and Individual Differences* 27(6):1123–1133.

SCHOLEY, ANDREW. 2001. "Fuel for Thought." *Psychologist* 14(4):196–201.

SHUTE, VALERIE J. 1992. "Aptitude-Treatment Interactions and Cognitive Skill Diagnosis." In *Cognitive Approaches to Automated Instruction,* ed. J. Wesley Regian and Valerie J. Shute. Hillsdale, NJ: Erlbaum.

SNOW, RICHARD E. 1992. "Aptitude Theory: Yesterday, Today, and Tomorrow." *Educational Psychologist* 27:5–32.

SPEARMAN, CHARLES. 1904. "General Intelligence Objectively Determined and Measured." *American Journal of Psychology* 15:201–293.

SPIELBERGER, CHARLES D., and VAGG, PETER R. 1995. *Test Anxiety: Theory, Assessment, and Treatment.* Philadelphia: Taylor and Francis.

STEELE, CLAUDE M. 1997. "A Threat in the Air: How Stereotypes Shape Intellectual Identity and Performance." *American Psychologist* 52(6):613–629.

STERNBERG, ROBERT J. 1997. *Successful Intelligence.* New York: Plume.

STERNBERG, ROBERT J., et al. 2000. *Practical Intelligence in Everyday Life.* New York: Cambridge University Press.

THURSTONE, LOUIS L. 1938. *Primary Mental Abilities.* Chicago: University of Chicago Press.

VAN DONGEN, HANS P. A., and DINGES, DAVID F. 1999. "Circadian Rhythms in Fatigue, Alertness and Performance." In *Principles and Practice of Sleep Medicine,* 3rd edition, ed. Meir H. Kryger, Thomas Roth, and William C. Dement. Orlando, FL: Saunders.

PATRICK C. KYLLONEN
DREW H. GITOMER

AFFECTIVE AND CONATIVE PROCESSES

People react emotionally to their own and others' performances, often in characteristic ways. Getting a grade of "B" in a course can produce devastation in an anxious student who expected an "A." Psychologists believe that the student's temperament interacts with expectations for the course grade to produce a negative emotional response.

Characteristic emotional reactions and certain qualities of temperament are examples of psychological processes that are affective. Affective processes include all feelings and responses, positive or negative, related to emotion-laden behavior, knowledge, or beliefs. Affect can alter perceptions of situations as well as outcomes of cognitive effort; it can also fuel, block, or terminate cognition and behavior.

Affective processes intertwine with aspects of motivation and volition. In educational situations, students' motivational beliefs and judgments of their own capabilities influence their intentions and plans. Thus students who see themselves as "not good at math" will prefer other subjects and struggle in math class. Conation, an ancient psychological concept whose dictionary definition refers to purposive striving, covers the range of motivational and volitional processes that human beings display. Motivational processes underlie the decision to pursue a goal; they are the wishes and desires that lead to intentions, in turn dictated by interest and experience. Volitional processes come into play after goals and intentions are formed; these processes reflect steps to implement goals, and ways of managing resources. Modern psychology has come to see motivation and volition as category labels for distinct conative processes.

In 1980 Ernest Hilgard wrote that the main agenda for modern scientific psychology ought to be to understand the processes underlying three central human functions—cognition (perception, memory, and the processing of information), affection, and conation. Indeed, since the beginning of the twentieth century, psychology in education has been peppered with programs of research on the qualities and characteristics of people that fit into one of these three functional categories. Intelligence, for example, is cognitive, impulsivity is affective, and self-concept is conative. Within conation, some well-studied processes influence commitments and are therefore considered motivational. One example is self-efficacy, a kind of personal capability belief. Other research examines processes that people use to protect commitments already formed—for example, self-monitoring and self-rewards. When these processes occur once a commitment is made, they are volitional.

As early as the mid-twentieth century, theories began to identify the range of variables within and between categories that could be measured validly and reliably in persons. But despite much progress up to and past Hilgard's writing in 1980, more effort is needed to explain how the triad of human functions works together at the process level. Moreover, this research agenda is virtually unknown to those outside psychology, and laypeople are frequently unaware of how psychologists use these terms.

For some purposes, affective and conative processes have proven to be so interconnected that it makes little sense even to psychologists to separate them. One group of researchers, the Stanford Aptitude Seminar, invented the hybrid term, *affcon,* to reflect this viewpoint. Given the complicated sociocultural context in which schooling takes place today, it is hard to dismiss the importance for educators, parents, and counselors of understanding how changes in affect can influence conation and vice versa: Both play central roles in the willingness to work and quality of effort invested by students in academics.

Three examples serve to illustrate how the interplay between academic-intellectual processes and affcon processes affects objectives of educational practitioners, decision makers, and students. The examples reflect current issues as well as persistent problems.

Cognitive Engagement

A school classroom is a social context offering many opportunities for students to be distracted from their work. At the same time, the organization of a classroom demands behavioral self-control. This paradoxical combination of opportunities and demands suggests the need for creative curricular experiences that engage students fully in classroom work, making them want to succeed. The concept of cognitive engagement is a prominent goal of classroom teaching, at virtually all levels of education.

Part of what new paradigms for instruction are about is providing teachers with a repertoire of strategies for promoting cognitive engagement. Modern education reform emphasizes success as its own reward, but encourages teachers to use other incentives to move students along. Activities and experiences grounded in students' own interests,

and assignments that require meaningful discussion of topics and material, help to promote cognitive engagement. Also supported by empirical research are inquiry teaching methods that make thinking explicit, and uncover hidden assumptions in content ranging from narratives to persuasive arguments. Research on teaching conducted between 1970 and the early twenty-first century makes it clear that students tune out in tired models of conventional teaching, where students listen and teachers talk.

Knowledge about which reforms and strategies work in different situations has been informed by evaluations of educational programs. Frequently, these demonstrate the insufficiency of seeking direct impact on learning outcomes such as achievement scores. Rather, achievement improves as a result of tapping into the affcon responses of students as they engage in and with schoolwork.

Student Responsibility

A student who takes responsibility for learning is self-regulated and self-motivated, intentionally directing energy toward learning tasks. Self-starters have long reaped academic rewards. Research conducted between 1980 and the early twenty-first century has uncovered the attitudes, skills, and behavior that characterize self-regulated learners, and emphasized the important role played by self-regulation skills in schooling outcomes. Researchers have also designed programs to help weaker students acquire self-regulation knowledge and skills. Counselors and teachers can use such programs to teach students responsibility. Likewise, parents can model self-regulation and strategies for doing homework.

Self-regulation and personal responsibility involve affcon processes. Careful self-management is necessary when follow-through is in jeopardy; for example, when a student experiences boredom or perceives that a task will be difficult to perform. The effortful processes that mark volition come forward then, with the sense to "buckle down." Not all academic situations demand volitional control, however. In some activities in the curriculum, learning can seem to occur with no effort, almost automatically. When a person is in the affective state that Mihalyi Csikszentmihalyi called "flow," there is no need to drain volitional reserves.

Astute teachers and parents will listen and watch closely for evidence of emotional stress in school children, and encourage the highly motivated to enjoy their time between work and play. Negative physiological as well as emotional changes can result from too much pressure on children in school. Although the ability to monitor and control emotions increases developmentally, some variation remains even among adults.

Adaptive Teaching

An increasingly diverse population of students leads teachers to differentiate curriculum and instruction. Some common differentiation strategies have proven ineffective from an academic standpoint; for example, teaching to the bottom third of the class. There are also well-documented negative social consequences to other differentiation strategies, most notably the common practices of tracking and retention in grades. To accommodate individual differences in students, a teacher must do only good.

Some types of cooperative work groups, formed to reflect the heterogeneity of students within classes, produce positive affcon outcomes: Students give and receive help from peers; they learn how to organize and manage due dates; the whole group incurs rewards when individuals contribute best efforts. But even effective grouping arrangements work best in short bursts of time; motivation and affect are buoyed by flexibility. In forming cooperative groups teachers should take into account students' affect and self-regulatory styles as well as their status characteristics and levels of achievement. The importance of considering the affcon profile of students has historically been left out of adaptive teaching discussions and decisions.

Another important point to make about adaptive teaching is that good teachers have always addressed students according to attitudinal and work styles. For any given task, what a student presents in the way of interest and attitude, as well as prior knowledge, often dictates a particular explanation, example, or suggestion for improvement. Different explanations, examples, and suggestions will reach students with other interests or markedly opposite styles of behavior. Moreover, teaching adaptively means shifting with the student's own development. Hence, the teacher's dictum of "If you can't reach them one way, then try another" comes into play. Adaptive teaching not only requires a teacher to circumvent observed student weaknesses, but also to capitalize on strengths. When a student is removed from conventional instruction for compensatory purposes, there ought to be simultaneous efforts to develop an aptitude for conventional instruction directly. It is, after all, to the regular classroom that many special program students eventually will return.

Despite the growing body of research on affective and conative processes in education, many programs remain disjointed, even when constructs overlap considerably. There are important theoretical issues still contested, including the need for distinctions between concepts as interrelated as motivation and volition, and the precise nature of the connections in Hilgard's trilogy of mental functions. Some highly regarded theorists, such as Richard Snow and Julius Kuhl, offer sophisticated and situated (context-dependent) models, models that suggest the need for new language as well as new methods of practical assessment and clinical treatment. As the twenty-first century continues, work will advance in these directions, ultimately producing entirely different ways of thinking about affect and conation in education.

See also: AFFECT AND EMOTIONAL DEVELOPMENT; INSTRUCTIONAL STRATEGIES.

BIBLIOGRAPHY

BERLINER, DAVID C., and CALFEE, ROBERT C., eds. 1996. *Handbook of Educational Psychology.* New York: Macmillan.

COHEN, ELIZABETH. 2001. "Equity in Schools and Classrooms." In *Education across a Century: The Centennial Volume,* ed. Lyn Corno. Chicago: National Society for the Study of Education.

CORNO, LYN. 1993. "The Best-Laid Plans: Modern Conceptions of Volition and Educational Research." *Educational Researcher* 22(2):14–22.

CORNO, LYN. 2000. "Looking At Homework Differently." *Elementary School Journal* 100:529–548.

CSIKSZENTMIHALYI, MIHALYI. 1975. *Beyond Boredom and Anxiety.* San Francisco: Jossey-Bass.

GOLEMAN, DANIEL. 1997. *Emotional Intelligence.* New York: Bantam.

HIDI, SUZANNE; RENNINGER, K. ANN; and KRAPP, ANDREAS. 1992. "The Present State of Interest Research." In *The Role of Interest in Learning and Development,* ed. Suzanne Hidi, K. Ann Renninger, and Andreas Krapp. Hillsdale, NJ: Erlbaum.

HILGARD, ERNEST R. 1980. "The Trilogy of Mind: Cognition, Affection, and Conation." *Journal of The History of Behavioral Sciences* 16:107–117.

KUHL, JULIUS. 2000. "The Volitional Basis of Personality Systems Interaction Theory: Applications." In *Learning and Treatment Contexts. International Journal of Educational Research* 33:665–703.

OAKES, JEANNE. 1985. *Keeping Track: How Schools Structure Inequality.* New Haven, CT: Yale University Press.

PINTRICH, PAUL R., and SCHUNK, DALE H. 1996. *Motivation in Education: Theory, Research, and Applications.* Englewood Cliffs, NJ: Prentice Hall.

RANDI, JUDI, and CORNO, LYN. 1997. "Teachers as Innovators." In *International Handbook of Teachers and Teaching,* Vol. 2, ed. Bruce J. Biddle, Thomas L. Good, and Ivor F. Goodson. Dordrecht, the Netherlands: Kluwer.

REIGELUTH, CHARLES M., ed. 1999. *Instructional-Design Theories and Models: A New Paradigm of Instructional Theory,* Vol. 2. Mahwah, NJ: Erlbaum.

STANFORD APTITUDE SEMINAR. 2001. *Remaking the Concept of Aptitude: Extending the Legacy Of Richard E. Snow.* Mahwah, NJ: Erlbaum.

WEBB, NOREEN M., and PALINCSAR, ANNMARIE S. 1996. "Group Processes in the Classroom." In *Handbook of Educational Psychology,* ed. David C. Berliner and Robert C. Calfee. New York: Macmillan.

ZIMMERMAN, BARRY J. 1990. "Self-Regulated Learning and Academic Achievement: An Overview." *Educational Psychologist* 25:3–17.

LYN CORNO

ETHNICITY

As the student population in the United States continues to become more ethnically diverse, the central challenge facing education is how to provide schooling experiences that maximize the participation and academic success of all students. The representation of ethnic minority students rose from 22 percent in 1972 to 38 percent in 2000, and is expected to increase dramatically through the year 2020, when more than two-thirds of the total public-school student population will be African American, Asian American, Hispanic, or Native American. Meanwhile, comparison studies continue to show a consistent gap in school achievement for various ethnic school populations.

Derived from the Greek term *ethnos,* meaning *people,* ethnicity refers to a sense of membership in and identification with a distinct group in which members perceive themselves, and are perceived by outside observers, to be bound together by a common origin, history, and culture. Cultural features that define an ethnic group include shared expectations for behavior, such as family roles, health practices, and work and recreational activities; shared values, such as religion, politics, and concepts of achievement, beauty, time and space; and shared symbols, such as language, art, music, and modes of dress. Although broad ethnic categories such as African American, Asian American, Hispanic, Native American, and white are used conventionally in the United States, there are, in fact, important national, linguistic, religious, tribal, regional, and generational differences within each of these broad categories.

Empirical Approaches: Cross-Cultural and Cultural Process

In the social sciences, two main approaches, distinct in their assumptions, foci, and methodologies, are used to investigate the role of ethnicity and culture in education: a *cross-cultural* approach and a *cultural-process* approach. In a cross-cultural approach, ethnicity and culture are viewed as separate from human behaviors. Cross-cultural researchers focus on the influence that ethnicity and culture have on human behavior. Alternatively, the cultural-process approach treats ethnicity and culture as interdependent with social processes; in other words, ethnicity and culture influence human interactions, and, at the same time, are constructed within those interactions.

Cross-cultural researchers tend to view ethnicity as relatively stable and fixed, while cultural-process researchers tend to view ethnicity as more dynamic with its content and boundaries continually under revision and redefinition. Cross-cultural researchers usually employ quantitative methodologies, such as survey questionnaires and experiments, with a focus on the attributes of individuals. Cultural-process researchers almost exclusively utilize qualitative methodologies, such as observations and interviews, with a focus on actions and interactions in context. For example, in studying parent involvement, a researcher using a cross-cultural approach might conduct a survey on a large sample of families from different ethnic groups to assess group differences in the amount of time parents spend on a variety of activities related to their child's schooling. A researcher using a cultural-process approach might interview parents from several ethnic groups on what it means to be involved with their child's school, while also engaging in an observational study of the interactions between students and parents, in order to detail the processes through which the parents engage with their children in their schoolwork. Ultimately, the combination of both a cross-cultural approach and a cultural-process approach is beneficial for a more in-depth understanding of the role of ethnicity and culture in education.

The Achievement Gap

The results of numerous cross-cultural studies indicate that many ethnic minority students are not faring well in U.S. schools. Ethnic group differences are found in school grades, standardized achievement tests, course enrollment, grade retention rates, high school graduation, and level of educational attainment. The achievement gap appears in the early school years, increases during the elementary school years, and persists through the secondary school years. While achievement gaps narrowed between 1971 and 1999, the average scores of African-American and Hispanic students have remained significantly below those of non-Hispanic white students.

Rates of grade retention tend to be higher for African-American and Hispanic students (particularly males), when compared to other groups. High school dropout rates tend to be highest for Hispanic students, followed by African-American students. African-American males tend to be disproportionately represented in special education classes. With the exception of Asian Americans, ethnic minority students are not adequately represented within programs for gifted and talented education (GATE).

In general, Asian-American students fare well academically, displaying high levels of performance on standard achievement indicators. With respect to the educational attainment level of students, high school graduation rates since 1971 have greatly increased overall for ethnic minority youth, however the rates in 2000 were lower for Hispanic and African-American students than for Asian-American

and white students. Asian-American students, in general, show higher college graduation rates, as well as higher graduate degree attainment, than white students. It may be noted that for some of the cross-cultural studies, comparisons were not made across all of the major ethnic groups due to the relatively small sample sizes of Native American students and, in some cases, Asian-American students.

A number of issues require consideration in light of these general findings of ethnic group differences in school achievement. First, many studies do not account for socioeconomic differences, such as family income, parental employment and education, when examining ethnic groups. Given that the average socioeconomic status (SES) differs substantially among ethnic groups, the failure to disentangle ethnicity and SES can lead to erroneous interpretations. SES is a significant predictor of academic success, and ethnic minority families are disproportionately represented in the lower SES bracket. Moreover, schools with the highest proportion of low-income students are more likely to have fewer qualified teachers, have substantially fewer resources (computers, enrichment materials), and be located in a neighborhood with fewer informal educational resources (such as museums and libraries). Economic pressures at home, compounded by poor neighborhoods and poor schools, makes the separation of socioeconomic factors from ethnic cultural factors even more difficult. Thus, it is imperative for future studies to examine comparability as well as account for the disparities among ethnic groups with respect to SES levels.

Many educators and policymakers often perceive technology as a promising tool for leveling inequities in educational achievement. However, studies show that children who come from lower-income families (which are disproportionately ethnic minority families) have fewer computers in the home. The provision of updated educational technology within schools is uneven at best, and this, combined with unequal access within the home, limits such computer-based activities as homework completion, research, word processing of reports, and presentations.

Second, while many comparative studies typically focus on the major ethnic groups as broad groups, it is important to acknowledge that individual differences within each ethnic group are substantial. Such categorization may give the illusion of overall cultural similarity and obscure substantial national, tribal, or other subgroup differences. For example, the broad category of Asian Americans is comprised of diverse national backgrounds, including Cambodian, Chinese, Filipino, Korean, Japanese, Vietnamese, Thai, Khmer, and Asian Indian. Additionally, much variation within an ethnic group is likely to exist with respect to variables such as gender, social class, generation/immigrant status, and level of assimilation.

Studies that examine differences within an ethnic group are useful for a variety of reasons. First, within-group studies may serve to weaken the uniform, and often stereotyped, views associated with particular ethnic groups. Second, studies of within-group differences in which the subgroups differ on various demographic variables would be helpful in understanding the role that variables such as generation/immigration status, level of assimilation, language, and socioeconomic status may play. Third, within-group studies may provide a further understanding of the cultural processes underlying achievement-related outcomes.

Theoretical Models Explaining the Achievement Gap

Researchers have attempted to explain the consistent achievement gap among ethnic groups from a number of different perspectives. The explanations offered may be grouped into three theoretical models. The first, a *cultural deprivation,* or *deficit,* model, explains the poor performance of ethnic minority students as the result of an impoverished and restricted home life. The underlying theory is that "culturally deprived" or "socially disadvantaged" students do not achieve because they lack a cognitively stimulating environment. Research may identify, for example, a lack of parental support, a low value placed on education, a language-poor environment, or even low intellectual capacity. The use of whites as the norm against which other ethnic minority groups are compared may perpetuate a deficit model in which ethnic minority groups are perceived as second-rate to the majority group.

The second theoretical model, the *cultural difference* model, points to differences in values, expectations, languages, and communication patterns between teachers and students—or between schools and families—as a source of difficulty for ethnic minority students. The underlying theory is that the social organization, learning formats and expectations, communication patterns, and sociolinguistic environment of schools are incongruent with the cultural patterns of different ethnic groups, and therefore limit the opportunities for student success. For some researchers in this area, the important differences exist at the level of interpersonal communication, where teachers and students are unable to fully understand each other. Important communicative differences may be identified at many levels, including formal language (e.g., English versus Spanish), conventions for interacting (e.g. distance between speakers, acceptable physical contact, and turn-taking rules), preferences for rhetorical style (e.g., the use of emotion in persuasion), and storytelling patterns.

A number of studies have also suggested that differences between social worlds, such as home and school, can be difficult for ethnic minority students to negotiate. For example, where U. S. public schooling tends to encourage independence, with competition and rewards for individual achievement, some ethnic groups may tend to encourage interdependence among members, with rewards for collaborative effort. Socialization practices also vary across ethnic groups, so that, for example, the parenting styles acceptable within one ethnic group may vary significantly from the parenting styles valued by schools and educators. Likewise, expectations for the role of parents in education may differ across ethnic groups, so that while some teachers expect active parent involvement at school, parents' conceptions of involvement may be altogether different. Additionally, some parenting practices may focus on social and observational learning and apprenticeship examples, and thus favor visual rather than auditory information processing. Insofar as early learning experiences may vary systematically by ethnic group, ethnicity can have important consequences for learning in (and out) of school.

Some researchers argue that the cultural difference model presumes ethnic differences to be inherently problematic when, in fact, it is the perception of differences and how people act on such perceived differences that is an important source of difficulty for minority students. These researchers typically utilize a cultural-process approach and focus on social interactions. Barriers to school success are identified by examining how students, teachers, and parents understand patterns of language use and socialization. In any case, the cultural difference model has made important contributions to understanding the relationship between ethnicity and school achievement by pointing out that children from different ethnic groups may vary in culturally patterned ways, some of which are relevant for educators.

A third theoretical model, which can be termed *sociosystemic,* moves outside the classroom in an effort to identify the social, economic, and political forces that contribute to the achievement gap. Researchers have come to recognize how differences in perceived economic opportunity affect the level of school engagement for ethnic minority students. For example, when students' families, peers, and community members hold beliefs that economic and social opportunities are limited, regardless of school achievement, students are far less likely to engage in meaningful ways with formal educational activities. Such beliefs may lead to a youth's active resistance to school or a "disidentification" with schooling overall (i.e., when students are apathetic or disaffected toward schooling). Some studies have identified patterns of differences within ethnic minority groups, where school achievement varies according to the conditions of one's minority status. Specifically, members of *voluntary* minority groups, including those who immigrated for improved economic opportunity, often do better in school than members of *involuntary* minority groups, such as those who were colonized or whose residency was forced (e.g., through slavery). Research utilizing a sociosystemic model has also identified schools as the places where societal pressure to assimilate is most keenly perceived—and often resisted. Many researchers and practitioners, for example, have noted that student peer groups link school achievement to the acceptance or rejection of various identities.

Each of the theoretical models on the achievement gap—cultural deficit, cultural difference, and sociosystemic—corresponds with specific policies (federal, state, regional, district, school), curricula, and teaching practices seeking to narrow the gap. Within the cultural deficit model, educators are encouraged to intervene as early as possible in children's development. Many federal and state programs, such as Head Start, focus on the compensation of deficits. From the cultural difference model, schools and teachers are encouraged to make better use of the knowledge and practices of diverse cultures and to form home–school connections. The various forms of multicultural education also derive from a basic cultural difference model, as do some bilingual education programs. Also included in this model are recent efforts to develop theories and practices of *culturally-relevant pedagogy,* an approach to teaching that modifies both curriculum and communication to reflect the diverse cultural practices of students. The cultural difference model appears to decrease the pressure on children to conform to mainstream culture standards, yet increase the pressure on teachers and schools to transform their practices to better reflect the diversity that is present around them.

For those with a sociosystemic perspective, repairing the achievement gap demands a commitment to an ongoing examination of the social and political systems, along with direct action to counter systemic bias. Few formal policies or programs with this model exist, although *critical theory* and *critical pedagogy* are actively promoted within this perspective. Critical theory seeks to make systemic injustice visible and critical pedagogy encourages teachers and students to understand and contend with stereotyping, racism, sexism, and other forms of prejudice.

Because of the tremendous variation within any ethnic group, it would be inappropriate to make generalizations about the needs and abilities of any individual student based solely on his or her membership in a given ethnic group. That said, there is no doubt that variation does exist along several lines, and educators should be aware of this. Perhaps most important of all, members of the teaching and learning community should be reflective of their own perceptions and actions with respect to all learners. It must be recognized that just as schools themselves vary, so do the students within them. Schools are the spaces where a great deal of a youth's development occurs, and on multiple levels, including academic achievement, identity, and social competence. In the end, ethnicity and culture must become part of the face of education in order to reflect and better serve our youth as they encounter an increasingly diverse world.

See also: LITERACY AND CULTURE; MULTICULTURAL EDUCATION; POVERTY AND EDUCATION; RACE, ETHNICITY, AND CULTURE.

BIBLIOGRAPHY

BANKS, JAMES A. 1999. *An Introduction to Multicultural Education.* Needham Heights, MA: Allyn and Bacon.

BARTH, FREDERICK. 1969. *Ethnic Groups and Boundaries.* Boston: Little, Brown.

BENNETT, CHRISTINE. 1997. "Teaching Students as They Would Be Taught: The Importance of Cultural Perspective." In *Culture, Style, and the Educative Process,* ed. Barbara J. Shade. Springfield, IL: Charles C. Thomas.

ERICKSON, FREDERICK. 1987. "Transformation and School Success: The Politics and Culture of Educational Achievement." *Anthropology and Education Quarterly* 18(4):335–356.

FAN, XITAO. 2001. "Parental Involvement and Students' Academic Achievement: A Growth Modeling Analysis." *Journal of Experimental Education* 70(1):27.

GREENFIELD, PATRICIA M. 1997. "Culture as Process: Empirical Methods for Cultural Psychology." In *Handbook of Cross-Cultural Psychology,* Vol. 1, ed. John W. Berry, Ype H. Poortinga, and Janek Pandey. Needham Heights, MA: Allyn and Bacon.

MCDERMOTT, RAYMOND P. 1997. "Achieving School Failure, 1972–1997." In *Education and Cultural Process: Anthropological Approaches,* 3rd edition, ed. George D. Spindler. Prospect Heights, IL: Waveland Press.

MEECE, JUDITH L., and KURT-COSTES, BETH. 2001. "The Schooling of Ethnic Minority Children and Youth." *Educational Psychologist* 36(1):1–7.

NATIONAL CENTER FOR EDUCATION STATISTICS. 2000. *National Assessment of Educational Progress (NAEP), 1999 Long-Term Trend Assessment.* Washington, DC: U.S. Department of Education, Office of Educational Research and Improvement.

NATIONAL CENTER FOR EDUCATION STATISTICS. 2001a. *The Condition of Education.* Washington, DC: U.S. Department of Education, Office of Educational Research and Improvement.

NATIONAL CENTER FOR EDUCATION STATISTICS. 2001b. *Dropout Rates in the United States: 2000.* Washington, DC: U.S. Department of Education, Office of Educational Research and Improvement.

OGBU, JOHN, and SIMONS, HERBERT. 1998. "Voluntary and Involuntary Minorities: A Cultural-Ecological Theory of School Performance With Some Implications For Education." *Anthropology and Education Quarterly* 29(2):155–188.

OKAGAKI, LYNN. 2001. "Triarchic Model of Minority Children's School Achievement" *Educational Psychologist* 36(1):9–20.

PHELAN, PATRICIA; DAVIDSON, ANN L.; and YU, HAN C. 1991. "Students' Multiple Worlds: Navigating the Borders of Family, Peer, and School Cultures." *Anthropology and Education Quarterly* 22:224–250.

SHIELDS, MARGIE K., and BEHRMAN, RICHARD E. 2000. "Children and Computer Technology: Analysis and Recommendations." *The Future of Children* 10(2):4–30.

STEELE, CLAUDE. 1992. "Race and the Schooling of African-American Americans." *Atlantic Monthly* 269(4):68–78.

HSIU-ZU HO
JASON DUQUE RALEY
ANGELA D. WHIPPLE

GENDER EQUITY AND SCHOOLING

The 1992 publication of the landmark report *How Schools Shortchange Girls,* by the American Association of University Women (AAUW) Educational Foundation, brought gender equity to the forefront of educational reform. Since then, the focus of discussions about quality education for all students has shifted from *equality* to *equity.* In the context of gender, equitable education appropriately addresses the needs of both girls and boys rather than assuming that those needs are identical. Thus, equity in education provides equal opportunities for reaching a shared standard of excellence. Simply defined, gender equity in education is the absence of gender differences in educational outcomes.

Researchers struggling to identify the origins of gender differences have examined a range of theories, including biological, psychoanalytic, social learning, and cognitive developmental approaches to gender differences. While there has been ongoing debate about the role of biology as a source of cognitive differences, educators agree that changes in educational outcomes must focus on the psychosocial aspects of behavior. Regardless of the specific causes of gender gaps, schools have a mission to ensure that all students can fully participate in and experience educational success. While acknowledging that individual differences within each gender are substantial, this analysis will focus on girls and boys as aggregate groups in an examination of similarities and differences in schooling experiences and outcomes. These differences will be reviewed in relation to mathematics, science, humanities, technology, and extracurricular activities, including differences in both attitudes and outcomes. Except where noted, the information presented here is based on data from public schools in the United States, for kindergarten through twelfth grade. Statistical findings reported are based primarily upon results from a number of large-scaled studies and reports, such as those of the American Association of University Women, the U.S. Department of Education, and the National Center for Education Statistics.

Gender Equity Pertains to Boys and Girls

Because much of the literature regarding gender in education has focused on areas where girls are underserved, some have argued that gender equity appeared to pertain to girls only. Near the turn of the new millennium, however, a few authors brought attention to the education gender gap for boys, showing that the national phenomenon of male underachievement has been nearly invisible in the gender-equity literature. Gender equity is not "for girls only," and improvement for one gender should not imply a disadvantage for the other.

Early Behavioral Outcomes

Girls and boys appear to have similar types and amounts of opportunities to help them prepare for elementary school. For example, equal numbers of girls and boys are enrolled in center-based preschool programs and receive equivalent amounts of literacy activities at home. Preschool girls perform higher on tests of small motor skills than boys, and they show fewer signs of developmental difficulties in areas such as physical activity, attention, and speech. Boys in the early grades are more likely to be identified as learning disabled, to be tracked into remedial and special education classes, to be diagnosed with attention-deficit disorder, to be involved with crimes and violence on school property, to repeat a grade, and to be suspended from school. Subsequently, boys are more likely to drop out of school altogether. Girls, on average, receive higher grades than boys in all subjects beginning in the early grades—a trend that continues throughout middle and secondary school.

Classroom Environment

Aspects of the classroom environment have been found to foster and/or reinforce gender biases. Often unintentionally, many teachers exhibit gender biases when interacting with students. For example, teachers generally give more attention to boys than to girls. Ironically, this is partly caused by the fact that girls tend to be better behaved in the classroom and more attentive to assigned tasks. Teachers' attention is often consumed by boisterous or aggressive behaviors more typical of boys. Teachers also tend to give less feedback (positive or negative) to female students. Without such feedback, girls may be deprived of valuable opportunities to evaluate their own behaviors and ideas and to learn to cope with constructive criticism. Boys, on the other hand, when reinforced for their boisterous behaviors, may fail to learn self-control, listening skills, and respect for others.

Classroom materials may also serve to reinforce gender biases in the schools. Although editors of textbooks and other instructional materials have made greater efforts to include women since 1992, female characters continue to play a smaller role than male characters in classroom materials. Moreover, when female characters are represented, they are often shown in stereotypical roles that reinforce gender biases.

Attitudes

Among the core academic subjects, some are considered typically "male," and others "female." In spite of increased female enrollment in mathematics and science courses, ideas persist that these subjects are for boys, while the humanities and social sciences are for girls. Students often act on these stereotypes in class activities by self-selecting into groups and roles according to gender norms. In science classes, for example, boys often dominate laboratory equipment, controlling hands-on experiments while girls observe and take notes. Similarly, when boys and girls work together on computers, boys tend to sit where they can more easily view the monitor and take control of the mouse. Also, computer usage is typically dominated by boys during after-school activities.

Differences remain in boys' and girls' attitudes toward academic subjects. On average, girls report liking mathematics and science less than boys, and having less confidence in their ability to succeed at these subjects. Girls also rate themselves lower in computer abilities than boys, and are far more likely to suffer from *math anxiety* or *tech anxiety*. They tend to perceive these subjects as being less useful in their lives, which may diminish their achievement motivation in these areas. Hence, fewer girls plan to choose careers in mathematics, science, or technology. Additionally, whereas boys tend to believe their success in academics is the result of ability, girls tend to attribute academic successes and failures to luck and other external factors. This attribution of success to factors other than effort may lead some girls to feel "helpless," particularly in subjects they perceive as male domains.

Mathematics and Science

Encouragingly, the gender gap in mathematics and science course enrollment is closing. At least as many girls as boys are now enrolling in algebra, geometry, precalculus, calculus, trigonometry, and statistics/probability courses. Moreover, girls receive higher grades than boys, on average, in math classes (as in all academic subjects). Nevertheless, girls consistently lag behind boys in scores on standardized mathematics assessments, including the mathematics sections of the Preliminary SAT (PSAT), the SAT, the National Assessment of Educational Progress (NAEP), and mathematics Advanced Placement (AP) exams. Such "high-stakes" exams are critical factors in determining college admission and scholarship awards, and lower scores can therefore limit career opportunities.

Gender differences found in science are similar to those in mathematics. In high school, girls are more likely than boys to take biology and chemistry, while about equal numbers of girls and boys enroll in engineering and geology. Physics, however, continues to be a male-dominated subject. Girls also take fewer AP science exams than boys, and they receive proportionately fewer top grades.

Humanities

Humanities, an area in which female students typically excel, receives little attention in the research about gender in education. With the shrinking of gender gaps in math and science, however, the humanities are quickly becoming an area in which the most substantial gender differences can be found. More girls than boys enroll in English, sociology, psychology, foreign languages, and fine arts. Particularly notable because of its role in standardized testing is the subject of English. Girls consistently outnumber boys in English classes, and significantly outperform them in most reading and writing assessments, with the notable exception of the AP English exam.

Technology

Many educators, administrators, and policymakers advocate technology as a tool for empowering other-

wise disadvantaged groups, thus leveling inequities in educational achievement. Nevertheless, a number of disturbing gender inequities have already been observed in educational technology use. For example, female enrollment in computer science courses lags significantly behind that of males. Moreover, only a small percentage of the students taking the AP exam in computer science (17% in 1995 and 1996) is female. Many more men than women are computer educators, and women remain greatly underrepresented in computer technology careers. Such disparities are of particular concern because technology skills are increasingly crucial for high-skill, well-paying jobs.

Several hypotheses have been suggested to explain the gender gaps in technology. Social and parental expectations, along with teacher biases, are commonly suggested reasons. Differential access to computers is also thought to play a significant role in creating gender disparities. It is often reported that parents are more likely to buy computers for boys than girls. Moreover, even when given equal access, boys use computers at home more frequently than girls. Additionally, computer software may appeal more to boys than to girls. Computer-related toys and games, designed mostly by males, are marketed primarily to boys and are typically found in the "boys' aisles" in toy stores. Games, which play a significant role in computer use, are dominated by images of competition, sports, and violence, which typically appeal more to males. These games, along with other technology-based materials, may help to perpetuate gender stereotypes.

Extracurricular School Activities

Girls and boys tend to participate in different types of extracurricular activities, representing traditional areas of gender dominance. Females, for example, are more likely than males to participate in performing arts, belong to academic clubs, work on the school newspaper or yearbook, or participate in the student council or government. Females are also more active than males in community service. Males, on the other hand, are more likely than females to play on athletic teams. While girls' rates of participation in team sports have increased since 1972, equity has not been achieved.

The differences in boys' and girls' choices of extracurricular activities may have important consequences. For example, sports participation has been linked to higher academic achievement as well as greater leadership capacity, better overall health, higher self-esteem, and more positive attitudes toward school. On the other hand, participation in non-sports-based extracurricular activities has also been found to build self-esteem, leadership, and social skills; to improve general health; and is associated with higher mathematics and reading test scores.

Individual Differences

It is important to acknowledge that the gender differences described above are based on average group scores. Girls (and boys) are not a uniform group and their needs are certainly not singular. In fact, large differences exist within each gender across different racial, ethnic, and socioeconomic groups. For example, African-American girls, despite the existence of both racial and gender discrimination, have a higher self-esteem, healthier body image, and greater social assertiveness than their white female counterparts. These girls also perform better on many academic indicators than their black male counterparts. Similarly, Latino girls score higher than Latino boys in mathematics by the eighth grade, and in science by the twelfth grade—contradicting patterns for girls on the whole. However, Latino females also have the highest dropout rate of all groups of girls, with one in five leaving school by the age of seventeen.

Race, ethnicity, and socioeconomic status (SES) appear to play a larger role than gender in determining enrollment in remedial and special education classes; and participation rates are lower in all extracurricular activities for low-SES students. Furthermore, students in ethnically diverse and low socioeconomic schools have less access to technology. Finally, regional differences may also contribute to gaps in educational outcomes. Girls in rural southern regions of the country consistently perform below girls from rural and nonrural areas in other regions. Greater understanding of gender, racial, ethnic, regional, and socioeconomic class differences and needs can only improve U.S. schooling. Building on all students' cultures, interests, and ways of knowing can make schooling experiences meaningful to their lives and useful for addressing social problems. At its core, educational equity seeks to enrich classrooms, expand choices, and widen opportunities for reaching a shared standard of excellence for all students.

See also: DEVELOPMENTAL THEORY, *subentry on* COGNITIVE AND INFORMATION PROCESSING; GEN-DER ISSUES, INTERNATIONAL; MORAL DEVELOPMENT; MOTIVATION, *subentry on* INSTRUCTION; SINGLE-SEX INSTITUTIONS; TITLE IX.

BIBLIOGRAPHY

AMERICAN ASSOCIATION OF UNIVERSITY WOMEN. 1992. "How Schools Shortchange Girls: The AAUW Report, A Study of the Major Findings on Girls and Education." Washington, DC: American Association of University Women Educational Foundation.

AMERICAN ASSOCIATION OF UNIVERSITY WOMEN. 1998. "Gender Gaps: Where Schools Still Fail Our Children." Washington, DC: American Association of University Women Educational Foundation.

BAE, YUPIN; CHOY, SUSAN; GEDDES, CLAIRE; SABLE, JENNIFER; and SNYDER, THOMAS. 2000. "Educational Equity for Girls and Women." NCES publication 2000-030. Washington, DC: National Center for Education Statistics.

FOX, LYNN H., and SOLLER, JANET F. 2001. "Psychosocial Dimensions of Gender Differences in Mathematics." In *Changing the Faces of Mathematics: Perspectives on Gender,* ed. Walter G. Secada, Joanne R. Becker, and Gloria F. Gilmer. Reston, VA: National Council of Teachers of Mathematics.

GREENFIELD, TERESA A. 1996. "Gender and Grade Level Differences in Science Interest and Participation." *Science Education* 81:259–276.

HARRELL, WILLIAM, JR. 1998. "Gender and Equity Issues Affecting Educational Computer Use." *Equity and Excellence in Education* 31(3):46–53.

NATIONAL CENTER FOR EDUCATION STATISTICS. 2000. *National Assessment of Educational Progress (NAEP), 1999 Long-Term Trend Assessment.* Washington, DC: U.S. Department of Education, Office of Educational Research and Improvement.

ORENSTEIN, PEGGY. 1994. *Schoolgirls: Young Women, Self-Esteem, and the Confidence Gap.* New York: Bantam Doubleday.

POLLACK, WILLIAM. 1998. *Real Boys: Rescuing Our Sons From the Myths of Boyhood.* New York: Random House.

SADKER, MYRA, and SADKER, DAVID. 1994. *Failing at Fairness: How America's Schools Cheat Girls.* New York: Scribner's.

Sommers, Christina H. 2000. *The War against Boys: How Misguided Feminism Is Harming Our Young Men.* New York: Simon and Schuster.

Valentine, Elizabeth. 1998. "Gender Differences in Learning and Achievement in Mathematics, Science and Technology Strategies for Equity: A Literature Review." ERIC Document Reproduction Service ED446915.

Hsiu-Zu Ho
Heather A. Tomlinson
Angela D. Whipple

INDIVIDUALIZED INSTRUCTION

The improvement of instruction has been a goal of educators as far back as the teachings of the Greek philosopher Socrates. Although there are a wide variety of approaches, in most cases instruction can be characterized by the following tasks: setting objectives, teaching content based on these objectives, and evaluating performance. This formula is indeed the most common; however, there have been many advocates of alternative approaches. Among the alternative approaches there is a focus on a more individualized approach to instruction, where the traits of the individual learner are given more consideration. Each approach to individualizing instruction is different, but they all seek to manipulate the three following fundamental variables:

- **Pace:** the amount of time given to a student to learn the content
- **Method:** the way that the instruction is structured and managed
- **Content:** the material to be learned

Pace

There are two basic extremes when the pace of instruction is considered. The first is when someone other than student, usually a teacher or instructor, controls the amount of time spent learning the material. In this case specific due dates are defined before instruction begins. This is currently the predominant model in most educational systems. The opposite extreme would be if the learner had exclusive control over the pace of instruction, without a time limit. Between these two extremes are situations where control of the pace of instruction is shared or negotiated, not necessarily equally, by the teacher and learner.

Method

As theories of learning and instruction develop and mature, more and more consideration is given to the way in which learning occurs. In an attempt to account for the way that students learn, instructors may apply a combination of theories and principles in preparing instruction. This can influence whether instruction is designed for one homogenous group, or is flexible, in anticipation of individual differences among learners. In the majority of cases, instruction is designed for the average learner, and is customized ad-hoc by the teacher or instructor as needed once instruction begins. This type of instruction, although it does give some consideration to individual differences among learners during instruction, does not fall into the typically accepted definition of individualized instruction. For instruction to be considered individualized, the instruction is usually designed to account for specific learner characteristics. This could include alternative instructional methods for students with different backgrounds and learning styles.

To help clarify this point, the instructional method used can be considered in terms of extremes. In the first extreme, one instructional method is used for everyone. Terms like *inclusion* and *mainstreaming* have been used to describe this first case. In the second extreme, a specific instructional method is used for each individual. Between these extremes lie situations where students are arranged into groups according to the their characteristics. These groups can vary in size, and the instructional method is tailored to each group.

Content

Perhaps the least frequently modified component is the actual learning content. However, it is possible to vary the content taught to different learners or groups of learners. Both "tracking" and "enrichment" are examples of customizing instructional content. A renewed movement toward learner-centered principles in education has given this component more consideration in the 1990s. It has become possible to find examples of instructional settings in which students define their own content, and pursue learning based on their own interests. In most cases, however, this opportunity is limited to high-achieving students. In terms of extremes, content can be uniform for everyone, or unique to each individual. Between these extremes lie cases where the content can be varied, but only within a predefined range. The range of activities available to the learner is an indicator of how individualized the content is in an instructional setting.

Examples of Individualized Instruction

There are many examples of instructional approaches that have modified some or all of these three components. In all of these examples, the goal was to improve the instructional experience for the individual learner. Some of the most historically notable approaches are discussed below. Within each example both the benefits and criticisms of each approach are discussed.

Personalized System of Instruction. Introduced in 1964 by Fred Keller, the Personalized System of Instruction, or the Keller Plan, is perhaps one of the first comprehensive systems of individualized instruction. Keller based his system on ten accepted educational principles (McGaw, p. 4):

1. Active responding
2. Positive conditions and consequences
3. Specification of objectives
4. Organization of material
5. Mastery before advancement
6. Evaluation/objectives congruence
7. Frequent evaluation
8. Immediate feedback
9. Self-pacing
10. Personalization

None of these ten principles should be considered unique, as they all can be easily found in other more traditional educational settings. Rather, it is the components of the Keller plan—based on these ten principles—that makes the Keller Plan somewhat different: self-pacing; unit mastery; student tutors; optional motivational lectures; and learning from written material. It is the first component, self-pacing, that is the most obvious attempt at individualizing the instruction. From the second component, unit mastery, it can be seen that the content does not vary, as the unit content is fixed. To illustrate the static nature of the content, Mike Naumes describes the basic design of a course using Keller's personalized system of instruction:

> breaking the material of the course into several units. . . . dividing the material into units one to two weeks long. . . . [and] as each unit of material is covered, specific

learning objectives are given to the students. These state exactly what a student must know to pass a unit quiz. (p. 2)

The last three components indicate that the method of instruction does vary slightly from individual to individual. Although all students learn from written material and student tutors, the motivational lectures are optional. Making these lectures optional does constitute some flexibility in terms of instructional method, albeit extremely limited. Fundamentally, it is the self-pacing that more or less stands alone as the individualized component of this instructional system.

Proponents of the Keller Plan cite many benefits, including better retention and increased motivation for further learning. At the same time, there are others with criticisms of the Keller Plan such as the following: limited instructional methods, high dropout rates, and decreased human interaction. The debate over the effectiveness of Keller's Personalized System of Instruction, with its advantages and disadvantages, raises fundamental questions about the nature of self-contained, self-paced learning. There are indeed opportunities for designing instruction that lend themselves to the Personalized System of Instruction approach. This would apply especially to cases where enrollment is high, course material is standardized and stable, and faculty resources are scarce. On the other hand, when there is not a shortage of faculty, or the class size is not large, the course would be better taught with more conventional methods, yet still based on sound educational principles. Where the line is drawn on the continuum between these two extremes is a matter of opinion, and should be based on the context in which the instruction is to take place. It would be inappropriate to claim that one of the extremes is completely right, and the other wrong, given the vast number of studies and evaluations that support either side.

Audio-Tutorial. Audio-Tutorial is a method of individualized instruction developed by Samuel N. Postlethwait in 1961 at Purdue University. His goal was to find an improved method of teaching botany to a larger number of college students and to effectively assist the students who possessed only limited backgrounds in the subject. The development of an Audio-Tutorial program requires a significant amount of planning and time by the instructor. Although there is some room for modification for each specific program, the general principles remain the same. Students have access to a taped presentation of a specifically designed program that directs their activities one at a time. The basic principles of Audio-Tutorial are "(1) repetition; (2) concentration; (3) association; (4) unit steps; (5) use of the communication vehicle appropriate to the objective; (6) use of multiplicity of approaches; and (7) use of an integrated experience approach" (Couch, p. 6).

The major benefits of Audio-Tutorial are that "students can adopt the study pace to their ability to assimilate the information. Exposure to difficult subjects is repeated as often as necessary for any particular student" (Postlethwait, Novak, and Murray, p. 5). In addition to taking more time if they wish, students can also accelerate the pace of their learning. Other benefits are that students feel more responsible for their learning, and more students can be accommodated in less laboratory space and with less staff.

Some of the major criticisms that are common to Audio-Tutorial courses were illustrated by Robert K. Snortland upon evaluating a course in graphics design. The primary criticism concerns the claim of responsibility. It seems that some students respond to the responsibility placed upon them, while others do not. There was a problem with the initial dropout rate, which seemed to be explained by the lack of willingness of some students to take on the amount of responsibility that was required in order to complete the course. Snortland advised that "since many freshmen students are not ready for additional self-discipline required of them in the A-T format, the choice of either a structured approach or an individualized approach should always remain open" (p. 8). Many other criticisms of Audio-Tutorial courses are concerned with teacher control. The instructor dictates all of the material including the learning and feedback procedures. The criticism is that this is a severe form of teacher control over the student.

Like the Keller Plan, Audio-Tutorial allows the individual student to determine his or her own pace, and the content is fixed. Unlike the Keller Plan, however, there are more instructional delivery methods available when designing the course. Yet the locus of control remains with the instructor in the Audio-Tutorial as well.

Computer-Assisted Instruction (CAI). Most proponents of individualized instruction saw the computer as a way to further improve the design and delivery of individualized instruction—now in an electronic environment. With the advent of the computer came the potential to deliver individualized instruction in a more powerful way. This potential was anticipated long before the proliferation of the home computer. John E. Coulson wrote in 1970: "A modern computer has characteristics that closely parallel those needed in any educational system that wishes to provide highly individualized instruction" (p. 4). He also noted the specific benefits that the computer could offer (p. 5):

1. "It has a very large memory capacity that can be used to store instructional content material or . . . to generate such material."
2. "The computer can perform complex analyses of student responses."
3. "The computer can make decisions based on the assessments of student performance, matching resources to individual student needs."

Although there were many anticipated benefits to using the computer to deliver instruction, in practice, CAI has been heavily criticized for its hidden side-effects. These are nicely articulated by Henry F. Olds:

Learning is in control of some unknown source that determines almost all aspects of the interactive process. To learn one must suspend all normal forms of interaction and engage only in those called for by the program. Learning is an isolated activity to be carried on primarily in a one-to-one interaction with the computer. Normal inter-human dialogue is to be suspended while learning with the computer. Learning involves understanding (psyching out) how the program expects one to behave and adapting one's behavior accordingly. One must suspend idiosyncratic behavior. Learning (even in highly sophisticated, branching programs) is a linear, step-by-step process. In learning from the computer, one must suspend creative insights, intuitions, cognitive leaps, and other nonlinear mental phenomena. (p. 9)

Olds even offered some solutions to these problems, indicating that "time on-line needs to be mixed with plenty of opportunities for human interaction" and that computer should allow people to "jump around within the program structure" (p. 9).

CAI became the forerunner in individualized instruction during the 1980s and early 1990s, as the home computer became more powerful and less expensive. The changes that the computer environment helped to make were predominantly a change in the delivery mechanism of individualized instruction, rather than a fundamental change in purpose or method. In a sense, the computer, especially the home computer, offered a convenience that other delivery mechanisms lacked. This convenience was accelerated with the proliferation of the Internet in late 1990s. Starting as an extension of computer-based instruction, online education became increasingly popular and eventually began to supplant CAI as the predominant form of individualized instruction.

Distance education. A surge in the number of nontraditional students attending college in the 1990s, combined with the technological potential of the Internet, has caused a renewed effort to deliver instruction in a nontraditional fashion. Accessibility and convenience—not research—are the primary driving forces in this movement toward instruction in the form on online education. When reviewing more than 200 articles on online instruction over the 1990s, James DiPerna and Robert Volpe found that only one article directly addressed the impact of the technology on learning. Partnerships between businesses and institutions of higher learning have arisen to address the increased need for continuing education.

Whether it is more effective or less effective than traditional education seems less a concern. In many cases, the audience addressed is nontraditional, and they have limited access to traditional education. Additionally, many students who could otherwise attend brick-and-mortar institutions are choosing online education for the convenience. In other words, what was established initially due to necessity has now expanded as students choose this route because of its convenience. The rate of expansion of online education has accelerated to a point where the general feeling among institutions of higher learning is of willing participation. In terms of pace, method, and content, there is a large variety of competing approaches to distance education, and no dominant model has emerged. Like previous iterations of individualized instruction, it is usually the pace of instruction that most often varies. The content is still fixed in most cases, as is the method (predominantly via the Internet).

Final Issues

Individualized instruction comes in many forms, all of which seek to improve instruction in some way. As can be seen in the examples above, alternative instructional approaches most often vary the pace and method of instruction, but not the content itself. The content is usually consistent with traditional instruction, although it may be segmented differently.

Other benefits are also significant, but not as consistent among approaches. Each approach has its own set of prescriptions, and each has been heavily criticized—yet that is to be expected. Even now, individualized instruction in its various forms is still a relatively recent innovation, and will remain under scrutiny until several criticisms are accounted for.

Perhaps the most profound criticism comes in the article "Individualization: The Hidden Agenda," by Ronald T. Hyman. He was concerned with the latent functions of individualization generally. In the push for individualization, the most common approach is to divide the subject matter up into segments and teach it at a self-taught level, but Hyman warns that "Segmented Junk Is Still Junk" (p. 414). There is no concern for what really is the problem, and that is the subject matter itself. He claims that individualized instruction typically does not alter the subject matter based on the needs of the student. Without doing this, there is a compromise of individualized instruction.

In summary, individualized instruction has the potential to improve instruction by varying the pace of instruction, the instructional method, and the content. Most approaches allow for self-pacing, yet variation in method and content is rare, and when it does occur, is usually very limited. As of the early twenty-first century, there are no indications that this trend will change in the immediate future, although as the research base in this area increases, major improvements are certain to come.

See also: INSTRUCTIONAL STRATEGIES; TECHNOLOGY IN EDUCATION, *subentry on* CURRENT TRENDS.

BIBLIOGRAPHY

COUCH, RICHARD W. 1983. "Individualized Instruction: A Review of Audio-Tutorial Instruction, Guided Design, the Personalized System of Instruction, and Individualized Lectures Classes." Paper written for partial fulfillment of doctor of philosophy degree, University of Kansas. ERIC Document ED252178.

DiPerna, James C., and Volpe, Robert J. 2000. *Evaluating Web-Based Instruction in Psychology.* Poster presented at the Annual Meeting of the American Psychological Association, Washington, DC.

Hyman, Ronald T. 1973. "Individualization: The Hidden Agenda." *Elementary School Journal* 73:412–423.

Keller, Fred S. 1968. "Good-Bye Teacher . . . ." *Journal of Applied Behavior Analysis* 1:78–89.

Keller, Fred S. 1982. *Pedagogue's Progress.* Lawrence, KS: T.R.I.

McGaw, Dickinson. 1975. "Personalized Systems of Instruction." Paper prepared for the annual meeting of the American Political Science Association, San Francisco.

Naumes, Mike. 1977. "The Keller Plan: A Method for Putting the Responsibility of Learning Upon the Student." *Perspectives* 1977:1–7.

Olds, Henry F. 1985. "The Microcomputer and the Hidden Curriculum." *Computers in Schools* 2(1):3–14.

Postlethwait, Samuel N.; Novak, Joseph D.; and Murray, Hallard Thomas. 1972. *The Audio-Tutorial Approach to Learning.* Minneapolis, MN: Burgess.

Snortland, Robert K. 1982. "An Individualized Teaching Approach: Audio-Tutorial." College Teaching Monograph. ERIC Document ED22 6656. Bismarck: University of North Dakota.

Anthony K. Betrus

INDIVIDUAL WITH DISABILITIES EDUCATION ACT (IDEA)

See: People with Disabilities, Federal Programs to Assist.

INDUSTRIAL ARTS EDUCATION

See: Technology Education.

INFANT SCHOOLS IN ENGLAND

Infant schools in England provide publicly funded education for children age five to seven and represent the first level of compulsory education in England. Infant schools and junior schools are often housed together in primary schools. Together, they furnish education to children until they reach eleven years of age. As of 1998 there were 18,230 primary schools in England providing full-time education for almost 4 million children. Twelve percent of these schools were infant schools, providing children with two years of education only. All infant schools educate children age five to seven, but the traditional infant school approach to education has influenced educational programs for younger and older children.

Children enter infant schools shortly after their fifth birthday, and it is here that they learn to manipulate numbers, read, and write. Traditional infant schools offer an informal education using child-centered techniques. They encourage hands-on manipulation, group and individual learning, and learning through play. Infant schools have been characterized as progressive, child-centered, open and exploratory; they educate children in a way that recognizes their development from a holistic perspective.

Classes are typically vertically grouped to accommodate children age five through seven. Class size may be as large as forty children. Infant schools use an open classroom approach where children move freely from indoor to outdoor environments. The teachers' role is one of facilitation; he or she (usually she) works individually with students or with small groups of students and provides students the opportunity to choose from a range of options appropriate to their developmental level. Infant schools utilize an integrated day, where children pursue various interests or themes without rigid time periods.

Infant schools have a rich conceptual heritage. Their approach draws on the ideas of Friedrich Froebel, who emphasized the importance of play and object in learning; Maria Montessori, who emphasized self-correcting play and an individualized pace in learning; John Dewey, who characterized the community of the school and emphasized integration among subject areas; and Jean Piaget, who supported a developmentally-sensitive approach to learning and advocated hands-on exploration of materials.

Most infant schools encourage children's choice. For example, children typically choose where to sit and whether they would like to work individually or with peers. Infant schools permit freedom of movement and conversation, encouraging children's natural curiosity and exploratory tendencies.

Infant school teachers are trained to understand the interrelation between social, emotional, and intellectual development, and accommodate children's individual variability within these developmental domains. Infant school teachers are expected to acknowledge the immaturity, innocence, and lack of self-control of young children, employing oblique, indirect strategies toward discipline. Teachers are expected to demonstrate pleasantness, affection, and level-headedness toward misbehaving children. For example, when a child misbehaves, it is more typical for a teacher to chide, "Someone's being silly" rather than scold, "Don't do that!"

A History of Infant Schools

Robert Owen established the first infant school in 1816 in Scotland. His goal was to shield children from the effects of poverty. This school was designed to provide children with a pleasant school environment where they could think about practical problems and experience little punishment. Teachers encouraged children to help each other, dance, sing, and play outside.

In nineteenth-century England, many mothers worked outside of the home. Forty-five percent of children under the age of five were enrolled in school. Consistent with Owen's objectives, infant schools aimed to protect children and promote a better society. In 1870 the official age for school entrance was set at five, but infant schools accepted poor children of two to seven years, space permitting. During this period, the government imposed standards for children to attain so that children would be prepared to enter school (first standard) at age six. When these standards were relaxed at the end of the nineteenth century, infant schools began a new period of development that strengthened their child-centered ideology.

An early step in this direction was an 1893 government circular encouraging educators to consider all facets of children's development in creating educational programs. By the 1920s and 1930s the infant schools adopted a child-centered approach. The *Report of the Hadow Committee* in 1933, written by the Consultative Committee of the Board of Education on the Primary School, stated explicitly that primary schools should provide discovery learning and child-centered practice.

The Education Act of 1944 required that primary education be available to all children age five through eleven. The act was vague on what this entailed, mandating "[education] suitable to the requirements of junior pupils." Because this definition was imprecise, curriculum decisions were ceded to the schools. Infant schools offered a wide variety of curricula, structures, and functions. This same act created a selective system of secondary education. As a result, one of the implicit goals for primary education was to begin the process of streaming or tracking, a goal that was discredited gradually over subsequent decades.

In 1967 the Central Advisory Council for Education issued "Children and Their Primary Schools," known as the Plowden Report. This report was based on observations in infant schools. It described the state of primary education in Britain, and endorsed those schools subscribing to "informal, child-centered education." As a result of this report, teachers were given increased freedom to teach children as they saw fit, with less emphasis on strict schedules and specific curricula.

The Plowden Report also assessed the effectiveness of the child-centered infant schools. It asserted that children in traditional, formal classes performed slightly better on conventional tests than children in child-centered, open classrooms. These differences were greatest for arithmetic, smallest for reading, and disappeared in later school years. Some proponents of the child-centered infant schools dismissed these findings on the basis that traditional, formal schools spend time teaching children how to take conventional tests. Despite these results, the Plowden Report advocated the child-centered approach.

The Education Reform Act of 1988 produced a radical restructuring of British education. This included infant schools. England was experiencing uncertainty about its status in the world, and these new laws represented an attempt by the government to control the content and the balance of the curriculum. The Education Reform Act of 1988 required that children be offered "a balanced and broadly based curriculum which promotes the spiritual, moral, cultural, mental and physical development of pupils at the school and of society; and prepares such pupils for the opportunities, responsibilities, and experiences of adult life."

The Education Reform Act ushered in a new national curriculum and a matching set of assessment procedures. Primary schools, including infant schools, were required to teach a core curriculum of mathematics, English, science, history, geography, technology, music, art, and physical education, requiring approximately 70 percent of the instructional time. Specific provisions were created for children with special educational needs.

The act also mandated testing. Children's achievement was to be measured based on a combination of teachers' assessment and Standardized Assessment Tasks (SAT). The SATs were integrated into the normal classroom routines; children were to experience them as normal classroom tasks that they might do individually or with other children, but would reflect their academic progress. Children had to attain specific English, mathematics, and science competencies by age seven.

The Education Reform Act supported parents' rights to choose their children's schools and encouraged competition among schools. By imposing free market models on educators, the government hoped to provide more cost-effective and efficient schools.

Several studies have examined the implications of the Education Reform Act on educational practice and effectiveness. The PACE (Primary Assessment Curriculum and Experience) study found less use of an integrated day, more use of whole class teaching, and a new emphasis on assessment compared to the traditional infant school model. According to the PRINDEP (Primary Needs Independent Evaluation Project) study, teachers found the national curriculum burdensome, but reported few changes in their balance between individual, group, and whole class pedagogy. Teachers in the PRINDEP study reported increased professionalism in the climate at their school following the act. Finally, the new ORACLE (Observational Research and Classroom Learning Evaluation) study compared basic skills in 1976 with basic skills in 1996, cross-sectionally, and showed declines in mathematics, language, and reading skills between these time periods.

Influences of the Infant Schools on Education in Other Countries

France, Switzerland, Belgium, the Netherlands, and other European countries adopted infant schools in the early to mid-1800s. Their goal was to buffer children from poverty-related stressors. Infant schools on the Continent were similar to those in England, providing children with a child-centered educational environment.

Infant schools of England were again influential throughout Europe during the 1960s and 1970s. Existing programs adopted aspects of the English child-centered approach. For example, the Netherlands fully subsidized infant schools and included them as part of their public school system in 1965. In the 1970s the German Federal Republic's Council on Education opened *Eingangsstufe,* a transitional class in primary schools for five-year-old children that resembled infant schools in England.

Several infant schools were established in the United States in the 1820s in response to Owen's writings, but these disappeared within ten years. The infant school movement had a larger influence on preschool and primary education in the United States during the 1960s and 1970s. At this time, U.S. preschool programs were viewed as "preparatory programs for rigid kindergarten classrooms" (Featherstone 1967, p. 19). To U.S. observers, the infant schools in England offered a demonstration that a child-centered, informal education for young children could exist within in the public schools. As Lillian Weber wrote in 1971, "By observing somewhat analogous situations in the industrial cities of England, I sought relevant answers to the problems of present preschool expansion in the United States and to the needs of children in our deteriorated areas of our cities" (p. 7).

Thus, as Head Start and Follow-Through programs developed, they incorporated practices from the English infant schools. British heads and teachers ran workshops on "informal education." They trained American teachers to recognize individual and uneven patterns of development, reorganize classrooms to enable teachers to interact with small groups and individuals, and establish opportunities for children to manipulate and discover materials independently. There was a proliferation of books designed specifically for early childhood teachers wanting to provide an informal education to their students. These books were rooted in the infant school philosophy, and explained the role of the school, teachers, and families; appropriate curricula; approaches to discipline; the physical organization of schools; and the construction of materials, such as easels and aquariums, to promote children's curiosity.

Also during the 1970s, infant schools influenced practice in U.S. elementary schools. Open schools, which grew from infant school principles, emphasized the holistic development of the child and children's interests as the basis for school learning. Schools implementing this approach offered decentralized learning, freedom of movement from one space to another, unstructured periods of study, and individualized and group-oriented student activities. This approach faced implementation problems in the U.S., which included improper training of teachers and unsupportive administrators and families.

Summary

Infant schools offer a child-centered, informal approach to education that has been recognized as being sensitive to the development of young children. Educational reforms late in the twentieth century have demanded higher levels of competency from young children and have affected the direction and practices of infant schools in England. English infant schools have had a lasting impact on educational policy and practice in many countries.

See also: EARLY CHILDHOOD EDUCATION, *subentries on* OVERVIEW, PREPARATION OF TEACHERS; EARLY CHILDHOOD EDUCATION IN AN INTERNATIONAL CONTEXT.

BIBLIOGRAPHY

ALEXANDER, ROBIN. 1995. *Versions of Primary Education.* London: Routledge.

FEATHERSTONE, JOSEPH. 1967. "Schools for Children." *New Republic* (August 19):17–21.

FEATHERSTONE, JOSEPH. 1971. *An Introduction.* New York: Citation.

GALTON, MAURICE, et al. 1999. *Inside the Primary Classroom: Twenty Years On.* London: Routledge.

GRUGEON, DAVID, and GRUGEON, ELIZABETH. 1971. *An Infant School.* New York: Citation.

HADOW, WILLIAM HENRY. 1933. *Report of Consultative Committee on Infant and Nursery Schools.* Ministry of Education. London: H.M. Stationery Office.

POLLARD, ANDREW. 1990. *An Introduction to Primary Education.* London: Cassell.

POLLARD, ANDREW, et al. 1994. *Changing English Primary Schools?* London: Cassell.

RATHBONE, CHARLES. 1971. *Open Education: The Informal Classroom.* New York: Citation.

TAYLOR, JOY. 1976. *The Foundations of Maths in the Infant School.* London: Allen and Unwin.

TIZARD, BARBARA, et al. 1988. *Young Children at School in the Inner City.* London: Erlbaum.

WEBER, LILLIAN. 1971. *The English Infant School and Informal Education.* Englewood Cliffs, NJ: Prentice-Hall.

WHITBREAD, NANETTE. 1972. *The Evolution of the Nursery-Infant School.* London: Routledge and Kegan Paul.

YARDLEY, ALICE. 1976. *The Organisation of the Infant School.* London: Evans.

SARA E. RIMM-KAUFMAN

INSTITUTE OF INTERNATIONAL EDUCATION

The Institute of International Education (IIE) is a world leader in the international exchange of people and ideas. Its mission is to foster international understanding by opening minds to the world. It does this by assisting college and university students to study abroad; advising institutions of higher education on ways to internationalize their student body, faculty, and curriculum; fostering sustainable development through training programs in energy, the environment, enterprise management, and leadership development; and partnering with corporations, foundations, and governments in developing people's ability to think and work on a global basis.

Program

Sponsors of IIE's more than 250 programs include government departments and agencies in industrialized and developing countries, the World Bank, major philanthropic foundations, public corporations, and individuals. Nearly 4,000 men and women from the United States and 14,000 people from 175 countries study, conduct research, receive practical training, or provide technical assistance through these programs each year. IIE has administered the Fulbright Program on behalf of the U.S. Department of State since its inception in 1946, and, since 1948, has also conducted the annual *Open Doors* census on international student mobility to and from the United States.

IIE's programs are managed by professional staff with expertise in fields such as higher education and scholarship administration, energy and the environment, business and public administration, human rights, economic development, and the arts. The institute's program staff serve in four departments:

- **Exchange Programs and Regional Services.** This department manages the U.S. and Foreign Fulbright Student Programs and the International Visitor Program, both funded by the U.S. Department of State, as well as other privately funded academic and professional exchange programs. With 140 staff in New York, Washington D.C., Chicago, Denver, Houston, and San Francisco, this department conducts extensive outreach to local communities throughout the United States.

- **Center for Global Development (CGD).** The CGD administers capacity-building programs serving participants from developing countries. CGD professional exchange programs have allowed participants to gain industry expertise and learn leadership and technical skills in national energy and environmental program implementation, health care, and civil society development. With a staff of more than 100 people in sixteen countries, CGD is IIE's primary mechanism for initiating multisector development assistance contracts worldwide.

- **Educational and Corporate Services.** This department administers scholarship programs and leadership development and skills training programs for midcareer professionals. Educational Services staff also conduct policy and statistical research on international academic mobility and provide educational advising and testing services in the institute's international offices. The department has 100 staff members in nine offices around the world.

- **Council for the International Exchange of Scholars (CIES).** CIES was founded in 1947 to administer the Fulbright Scholar Program and has grown to house other international scholarly exchange initiatives. In 1997 CIES became a department of IIE, based in Washington D.C. More than 1,600 U.S. academics and international scholars are served by CIES programs annually. The day-to-day work of the department is carried out by more than forty-five program officers and staff.

Organizational Structure

IIE has a staff of more than 475 professionals and relies on the services of more than 6,000 volunteers who serve on regional advisory boards, scholarship screening and selection panels, and program committees. In addition to its headquarters in New York City, IIE has offices in Chicago, Denver, Houston, San Francisco, and Washington, D.C. International offices are located in Bangladesh, Brazil, China, Egypt, Hong Kong, Hungary, India, Indonesia, Kazakhstan, Mexico, Philippines, Russia, South Africa, Thailand, Ukraine, and Vietnam.

Staff members in U.S. offices administer IIE-related programs, mobilize community support for international exchange, provide information and counseling to individuals and institutions, and maintain contact with grantees and the institutions they attend.

Personnel in the international offices assist students and scholars wishing to study or conduct research in the United States; administer U.S. admissions tests for international applicants; report on educational systems, institutions, and developments; cooperate with other private and government agencies abroad to facilitate international exchange; and provide technical assistance and training in selected development fields. The institute is governed by an international board of trustees composed of corporate executives, diplomats, college and university presidents, and artistic and civic leaders.

IIE disburses more than $150 million annually on programs and services. Most funds provide direct support to sponsored students and professionals. These funds also materially assist the universities and research and training institutions at which IIE grantees study and work.

History and Development

Until the twentieth century there were no programs for study abroad in American higher education. The U.S. Bureau of Education began collecting data on foreign students in 1904, and published a guidebook in 1915. The YMCA formed a Committee on Friendly Relations Among Foreign Students in 1911, and three bilateral exchange programs came into existence during this time: the Rhodes Trust, the American-Scandinavian Foundation, and the China Foundation for the Promotion of Education and Culture. IIE was established in 1919 as the first independent, nonprofit organization dedicated to promoting all aspects of educational exchange on a global basis. The founders were Elihu Root, the Nobel Prize–winning secretary of state; Nicholas Murray Butler, then president of Columbia University and subsequently a recipient of the Nobel Peace Prize; and Dr. Stephen Duggan, a professor at the City College of New York. These men were deeply committed internationalists in an age when this was not popular. They believed that academic travel abroad would promote mutual understanding and closer cultural relations between Americans and leaders of other countries. Dr. Duggan became the first director, and the institute's first programs were supported by grants from the Carnegie Endowment for International Peace.

The institute lobbied for the creation of non-immigrant student visas in 1921 and designed a new application to assist American consular officials to process visa requests. Its first student exchange was negotiated in 1922 with five American and five Czechoslovakian students. In 1925 the institute created a junior year abroad program for American undergraduates. In 1933 it established the Emergency Committee in Aid of Displaced German Scholars, under the institute's then assistant director, Edward R. Murrow. Its activities saved more than 300 European scholars from the Holocaust. In 1941, the U.S. State Department called upon IIE to administer the country's first nationally sponsored educational exchange scholarships with Latin America under the Buenos Aires Cultural Convention Program. Additional work for the U.S. government necessitated the institute's opening an office in Washington, D.C., in 1943. In 1948, the State Department appointed the institute to screen, place, and supervise student exchange under the Fulbright program.

As African nations emerged from colonial rule in the 1950s, IIE created new U.S. scholarship opportunities for African students. In 1952 the Educational Associates program was established by the institute, providing services for U.S. colleges and universities. In the late 1970s IIE designed and implemented the U.S. government's Hubert H. Humphrey Fellowship program for midcareer professionals from developing nations, as well as creating the South African Education Program to help prepare black South Africans for leadership in a post-apartheid future. The institute also assumed responsibility for a portion of the U.S. government's International Visitor Program and began to run the ITT Corporation's International Fellowship Program, which for seventeen years was an exemplary model of corporate involvement in international educational exchange. In the 1980's, the institute began managing short-term, hands-on professional development projects and internships for sponsors such as USAID, expanding its service for scientific and technical development, and establishing a division to undertake energy training programs. IIE has created innovative programs in journalism and human rights, and opened new offices in Jakarta, Zimbabwe, Sri Lanka, and Cairo.

Taking advantage of improving relations with Communist governments, IIE developed the U.S.-USSR Student Exchange Program in cooperation with the Soviet State Committee for Public Education and extended its educational advising services in the People's Republic of China.

In the 1990s IIE initiated programs for leaders, managers, professors, and students in formerly Communist countries to enable them to learn about market economics and democratic institutions. It also developed collaborative programs with Japan and Southeast Asian nations to deepen mutual understanding and address issues of common concern. In response to the Balkan conflicts and the Asian currency crisis, IIE designed and implemented Balkan-Help and Asia-Help emergency assistance funds to enable students from these regions to stay in the United States to complete their degrees.

In 2000 the Ford Foundation turned to the institute to help administer the single largest program in the foundation's history—The International Fellowships Program. This program recruits candidates that lack systematic access to higher education from social groups and communities around the world. These individuals are provided with full scholarships for graduate education in the hope that they will become leaders in their respective fields, furthering social justice and economic development in their own countries.

The institute also helped to develop, and now administers, the Benjamin A. Gilman International Scholarship Program on behalf of the State Department. This program provides awards for undergraduate study abroad for U.S. students who are receiving federal need-based financial aid under Pell Grants, Federal Work-Study, Stafford Loans, Perkins Loans, and Supplemental Educational Opportunity Grants.

BIBLIOGRAPHY

ALTBACH, PHILIP G., and PETERSON, PATTI MC-GILL., eds. 1999. *Higher Education in the Twenty-First Century: Global Challenge and National Response.* New York: Institute of International Education.

CHANDLER, ALICE. 1999. *Paying the Bill for International Education: Programs, Partners, and Possibilities at the Millennium.* Washington, DC: NAFSA: Association of International Educators.

DAVIS, TODD M. 2000. *Open Doors: Report on International Educational Exchange.* New York: Institute of International Education.

HALPERN, STEPHEN MARK. 1969. *The Institute of International Education: A History.* New York: Columbia University Press.

HARVEY, THOMAS. 2001. *Opening Minds to the World: 2000 Annual Report.* New York: Institute of International Education.

INSTITUTE OF INTERNATIONAL EDUCATION. 1997. *Towards Transnational Competence-Rethinking International Education: A U.S.-Japan Case Study.* New York: Institute of International Education.

TAYLOR, MARY LOUISE. 1994. *Investing in People Linking Nations: The First Seventy-Five Years of the Institute of International Education.* New York: Institute of International Education.

INTERNET RESOURCE

INSTITUTE OF INTERNATIONAL EDUCATION. 2002. <www.iie.org>.

ALLAN E. GOODMAN

INSTITUTIONAL ADVANCEMENT IN HIGHER EDUCATION

With the rapid increase in the costs associated with higher education, there has been an ever-increasing pressure placed upon colleges and universities to raise funds for institutional support. Fund-raising drives in excess of $1 billion are commonplace among top tier institutions in the early twenty-first century. The responsibility for identifying individuals capable of making gifts to the institution falls under the umbrella of institutional advancement.

Offices of institutional advancement are typically responsible for all of the institution's relationships with individuals external to the institution. This discussion of institutional advancement in higher education includes two sections. First, it presents a brief history of institutional advancement. In the second section, the four functional areas of institutional advancement are discussed (public relations, publications, alumni relations, and development).

Historical Background

The philanthropic support of educational institutions is not a new concept. Some of the earliest examples of educational philanthropy include Greek philanthropist Cimon's support of the Academy of Socrates and Plato and Alexander the Great's assistance in opening Aristotle's Lyceum through his financial support.

The history of educational philanthropy in the United States can be traced back to medieval universities in twelfth-century Europe. In these institutions, founders were forced to approach potential donors for money and resources for college operations. Wealthy individuals established endowments to support the universities of Paris, Oxford, and Cambridge. The idea of the chief faculty member raising funds for the institution was transferred to the early colonial American colleges.

The first president of Harvard College, Henry Dunster, counted generating resources as part of his duties. While the first solicitation for Harvard College in 1641 is cited as the beginning of fund-raising in this country, Kathleen Kelly commented in 1998 that the extent of the solicitation efforts tends to be overstated and presents a misleading portrayal of early educational institutions as heavily dependent on financial donations. Others also dismiss the notion that fund-raising began in the 1600s given that most early colleges were supported by government funds and taxes. Systematic fund-raising traces its roots to the twentieth century; early efforts were limited and involved only a few wealthy benefactors.

In 1821 Williams College established the first alumni association and in 1823 Brown University established the first alumni fund. Not until 1897 did the first public university, the University of Michigan, establish an alumni association. This difference in organizational behavior between public and private institutions is repeated throughout fund-raising history, although only minor differences exist today.

One of the first great institutional fundraisers was William Lawrence, an Episcopal bishop, who raised more than $2 million for Harvard in 1904–1905 as president of the alumni association and who led a drive at Wellesley College that brought in nearly $2 million. From 1905 to 1915 Charles Sumner Ward and Lyman L. Pierce conducted the first "capital campaign" for the YMCA that raised about $60 million in capital funds.

However, in 1936 fewer than fifty percent of colleges and universities had alumni funds in place and. According to Kelly "apart from a few exceptions related to annual giving . . . the first full-time staff fundraisers did not appear on the scene until the late 1940's" (p. 149). Private, rather than public institutions employed the first fundraisers, "with only 25 percent of all institutions reporting a centralized development function as recently as 1970" (Brittingham and Pezzulo, p. 82). The majority of those were private institutions. In 1912, twenty-three men who were responsible for organizing former students of their universities founded the Association of Alumni Secretaries (AAS). While some of those involved had responsibilities for raising funds, the majority were engaged in the organization of alumni to support their universities in ways other than financial. By 1938 only one fifth of those surveyed by the American Alumni Council (the new name adopted by the AAS) were engaged in fund-raising activities.

In the spring of 1958 the American Public Relations Association (ACPRA) and the American Alumni Council (AAC) met at the Greenbrier Hotel in White Springs, Virginia. The purpose of the meeting was to discuss the need for administrative coordination of the functions of public relations, alumni relations, and fund-raising. In 1974 the AAC and ACPRA merged to form the Council for the Advancement and Support of Education (CASE). This organization brought together the organizational functions of public relations, publications, fund-raising, and alumni relations under the umbrella of institutional advancement.

Areas of Institutional Advancement

Public relations. The first functional area within institutional advancement is public relations. Through this department, an institution crafts messages for its various publics. Frequently the director of public relations serves as the institution's chief spokesperson. The public relations arm of institutional advancement also cultivates and manages the university's re-

lationships with members of the media, which may consist of being available to members of the media when they have questions about the institution or its activities or contacting the media to get placement of stories. Many public relations offices facilitate media relationships by maintaining a list of faculty members who are experts on specific subject areas and having them available for media interviews when comments are needed for news stories.

In some public relations offices, there is an individual or a team that is responsible for planning special events for the institution. These may include commencement events or other large-scale special occasions that will increase the public visibility of the institution.

Publications. The second functional area within institutional advancement is publications. Publications offices are responsible for all print materials used by the institution. Within publications offices are graphic designers, proofreaders, and photographers.

Typically, an institution's publications office is responsible for the design and production of the alumni magazine. This is frequently the largest and most visible of the publications produced by an institution. Depending upon the size of a college or university, individual colleges, schools, or departments may have their own magazines or newsletters. The design and maintenance of the college or university web pages also falls to members of the publications staff.

Publications departments are also responsible for the consistency of an institution's print image and the proper use of university symbols. This is frequently accomplished by requiring internal production of all print pieces or by subjecting anything that has been designed outside of the publications office to scrutiny by a member of the publications staff. This review, coupled with the office having the ability to stop the printing of a publication that does not conform to university standards, allows for a tight maintenance of the institution's graphic identity.

Alumni relations. The alumni relations office is primarily responsible for maintaining ties between graduates of a higher education institution and their alma maters. This is typically accomplished through events held for alumni either at the university or college or by scheduling programs away from campus. For example, a college or university alumni office may be responsible for organizing homecoming festivities for alumni at the institution.

The activities of the alumni office are frequently directed by an alumni board. At some colleges and universities, the board has hiring and firing authority over the director of alumni relations. The board helps to direct the activities of the association and to shape the programming for alumni. Two different types of alumni associations exist in higher education. The first is a dues-based organization that requires graduates to join the association by paying yearly dues (or perhaps by making a certain level of gift to the annual fund). The other type is an alumni association to which all alumni become members automatically without any required contribution or dues payment.

The office of alumni relations is also responsible for maintaining a chapter or club system for the institution. These clubs or chapters are separate organizations located in cities in which there are large concentrations of alumni. Frequently these organizations have their own officers and may have responsibility for their own finances.

Alumni offices also design programs targeted to specific alumni affinity groups, for example, a program designed for graduates of an institution who were members of a fraternity or sorority. These programs help maintain the bond created by the extra-curricular activities alumni participated in while they were students on campus.

Development. The development office frequently contains the largest number of positions within an institutional advancement division. The office's organization may be centralized, decentralized, or a hybrid of these two. Organization is often dependent upon the size of the institution. In a centralized environment, all individuals responsible for fund-raising are housed in one physical location and report either directly or indirectly to the same person. This type of organization is better suited to smaller colleges and universities. In a decentralized environment, development officers are spread out among the various academic units of the institution. The fund-raisers in these schools and colleges report to the deans of their respective areas. This organization is often found in larger institutions. The hybrid model mixes the centralized and decentralized, with development officers physically located in a college or school, yet reporting to both a dean and a chief development officer.

Within a development office, there are a number of distinct areas of operation, each of which are discussed in detail.

Annual fund. The primary responsibility of the annual fund of a college or university is to ask graduates of the institution for small gifts that are given yearly. Annual fund gifts can range from one dollar to ten thousand dollars or more. These gifts are solicited primarily through the mail or by telephone. Occasionally, high-end annual fund gifts are solicited in person. Annual fund gifts can be either restricted (to be used only for a specific purpose) or unrestricted (to be used however the institution deems appropriate).

The annual fund is one of the most important components of a mature development program. Not only does it provide annual operating dollars for the institution's budget, it also helps to identify individuals who are interested in making gifts to the institution and who may want to make larger gifts in the future.

The annual fund office may also help to organize a senior class gift program through which graduating seniors make a pledge (either for a single year or over a number of years) to donate for a specific project identified by the graduating class. Many annual funds are also responsible for a parents fund, through which parents of current and former students are asked for gifts.

Annual fund offices are also the coordinators of matching gift solicitations. Some companies have standing agreements with their employees that the company will match any gifts made to a charitable organization. Annual fund officers craft specific solicitations to their graduates who are employees of those companies, asking them for gifts and reminding them that their donation comes with additional funds for the institution.

Major gifts. Major gifts are larger than annual gifts. They frequently are composed of a pledge, on which payments are spread over a number of years. Because of the large amounts of money involved in major gift solicitations, individuals who have long-standing relationships with the potential donors usually solicit them.

Major gift prospects are identified in many ways. They may be annual fund donors who have a history of providing support to the institution. Other individuals are identified because they have a level of wealth that would allow them to make a major gift to the institution and they have an interest in an area which the institution is seeking support.

Once major gift prospects have been identified, they are assigned either to a development officer or to an individual who is engaged in major gifts fundraising. At most institutions the president has a list of individuals with whom close relationships must be developed or already exist. Other individuals who are involved in the major gift process include deans, some department chairs, and select faculty members and administrators.

These individuals bring their prospects closer to the institution by involving them in programs, inviting them to serve on advisory committees or on boards of trustees. Throughout this process, the prospect's interests emerge. Once the development officer has an idea of what sort of gift the prospect might make, a team is assembled of individuals who are closest to the prospect and who are best suited to ask the prospect to consider the donation. The actual solicitation is usually done face-to-face. Actually getting a definitive "yes" to a major gift solicitation may take a considerable amount of negotiation. The prospective donor may want to change how the gift would be used, the amount of the gift, or other specifics related to the request.

Capital campaigns. Capital campaigns are intensive efforts to raise a significant amount of money for an institution over a limited period of time in order to increase the institution's capital assets, either physical (through the erection of buildings, etc.) or financial (by increasing the institution's endowment). Many institutions also conduct comprehensive campaigns that raise operating funds in addition to capital funds.

Campaigns generally progress in four phases: the planning phase, the silent phase, the public phase, and the accounting phase. In the planning phase, the institution determines what dollar amount could realistically be raised over the period of the campaign. Additionally, the organization ascertains what volunteers will be recruited to help with the campaign, how many staff members will be needed to meet the goal, and how many individuals will be identified as campaign prospects. Colleges and universities may employ outside counsel to assist with this phase of the campaign.

In the silent phase, individuals who have been cultivated are solicited for campaign gifts. The institution's prospects who have been cultivated the most and have the capacity to make the largest gifts are usually solicited first. While active requests are being made during this phase, only individuals who are very close to the institution would be aware that a

campaign is in progress. Most institutions attempt to raise between one-half to two-thirds of the dollar total in this phase of the campaign. Doing so reduces the risk that the institution will not make the campaign goal in the next phase.

In the public phase of a campaign, the institution lets all of its constituencies know that a campaign is in progress, what the dollar goal for the campaign is, the total amount of money raised to date, and the date selected for the end of the campaign. This is usually done in conjunction with a special event for those who have been involved in the campaign and those who will be asked to be major contributors. Additionally, press conferences may be held for the media and if building projects are involved, official groundbreaking ceremonies may be conducted. During the public phase, individuals who have been cultivated through the silent phase are solicited. Finally, in the closing months of the campaign, a large-scale mailing is frequently conducted so that individuals who cannot contribute at a major gift level have the opportunity to participate and feel included.

The final phase of a campaign is the accounting phase. During this phase staff members who were brought on board specifically for the campaign may be let go, the institution tries to collect unfulfilled pledges, and the plans are made for either restarting the campaign cycle or returning to noncampaign operations.

Planned giving. Planned giving is the term given to any gift which involves a transfer of assets other than cash. These gifts are planned because they frequently have tax consequences or involve other structuring. The most familiar of all planned gifts is the bequest, where an individual leaves either a portion or all of their estates to a higher education institution after their death. Also quite common is the transfer of stock or real estate to the institution. However, many other vehicles exist for potential donors to make planned gifts, including those that create a lifetime income for the donor or a beneficiary.

Planned giving officers are often attorneys familiar with tax and estate law. While other development officers may have the ability to discuss planned giving options with prospects, many institutions have planned giving officers on staff to deal with the details of a structured gift.

Prospect research. Within the development department, identification of individuals who have the ability to make major gifts to the institution falls to the prospect research department. Once these prospects have been identified, prospect research, through the use of print and electronic resources, develops dossiers on each individual. These profiles include information on the prospect's family background, interests, previous giving history for the institution and other institutions, a rating indicating for how much the prospect should be solicited, and a cultivation and solicitation strategy based upon the office's research.

Advancement records. The advancement records area is responsible for all gifts and pledges that come into the university. Specifically, advancement records documents donations and pledges electronically for each donor in the university's alumni and donor record system. Address information is kept on each alumnus or alumna, parent, and friend of the institution. Additionally, information that is frequently attached to each address record can include previous gifts and pledges, interests, names of family members, year of graduation and degree type (if a graduate), and other biographical information.

Donor records also generates receipts for those making gifts and may also generate acknowledgement letters letting donors know that their gifts were received and that the college or university appreciates the gift.

Advancement records also sees that daily receipts are deposited into the university accounts and that restricted gifts are posted to the correct funds. At the end of each month this office also generates income statements breaking down gift totals in many categories, and may provide year-to-date totals along with comparisons to previous years.

Corporate and foundation relations. Depending upon the size of the development operation, there may be a department of corporate and foundation relations or an individual who has the same responsibility. Because of the intense writing required for submitting a foundation proposal, individuals in corporate and foundation relations spend much of their time writing grant proposals. In smaller offices, the responsibility for developing relationships with foundations and corporations falls to individual development officers.

Stewardship. Once an individual, foundation, or corporation makes a gift to an institution, the responsibility of maintaining the relationship falls to the stewardship office (in addition to those involved in the solicitation). Being good stewards of a gift includes providing donors with annual reports detailing how their gifts were used and which individuals benefited from the generosity. Additionally, the stewardship office maintains the record of the things to which pledges are designated and to whom the end of the year reports should be sent. The institution also has a responsibility to the donor that it will be a good steward of the donated funds and that they will be used according to the donor's wishes. Finally, the process of thanking a donor is critical to the development process because individuals who have made gifts in the past are the best prospects for the future.

See also: BOARD OF TRUSTEES, COLLEGE AND UNIVERSITY; PRESIDENCY, COLLEGE AND UNIVERSITY; STRATEGIC AND LONG-RANGE PLANNING IN HIGHER EDUCATION.

BIBLIOGRAPHY

ASSOCIATION OF ALUMNI SECRETARIES. 1913. *Report of the First Conference of the Association of Alumni Secretaries.* Ann Arbor, MI: Association Office of the Secretary.

BRITTINGHAM, BARBARA E., and PEZZULLO, THOMAS R. 1990. *The Campus Green: Fund Raising in Higher Education.* Washington, DC: George Washington University School of Education and Human Development.

CARTER, LINDY KEANE. 1988. "Diamond Jubilee: Advancement's Founding Field Looks Back on 75 Eventful Years." *CASE Currents* (February):17–20.

COUNCIL FOR ADVANCEMENT AND SUPPORT OF EDUCATION (CASE). 1994. *CASE Campaign Standards: Management and Reporting Standards for Educational Fund-Raising Campaigns.* Washington, DC: Council for Advancement and Support of Education.

COWLEY, WILLIAM H. 1980. *Presidents, Professors, and Trustees.* San Francisco: Jossey-Bass.

CURTI, MERLE, and NASH, RODERICK. 1965. *Philanthropy in the Shaping of American Higher Education.* New Brunswick, NJ: Rutgers University Press.

CUTLIP, SCOTT M. 1990. *Fund Raising in the United States: Its Role in America's Philanthropy.* New Brunswick, NJ: Rutgers University Press.

FISHER, JAMES L. 1989. "A History of Philanthropy." In *The President and Fund Raising,* ed. James L.

Fisher and Gary H. Quehl. New York: American Council on Education and Macmillan.

HALL, PETER DOBKIN. 1992. *Inventing the Nonprofit Sector and Other Essays on Philanthropy, Voluntarism, and Nonprofit Organizations.* Baltimore, MD: Johns Hopkins University Press.

KELLY, KATHLEEN S. 1998. *Effective Fund-Raising Management.* Mahwah, NJ: Erlbaum.

MARTS, ARNAUD C. 1953. *Philanthropy's Role in Civilization.* New York: Harper and Brothers.

MILLER, M. T. 1991. *The College President's Role in Fund Raising.* ERIC Document No. No. ED 337 099. Washington, DC: ERIC Document Reproduction Service.

PRAY, FRANCIS C., ed. 1981. *Handbook for Educational Fund Raising: A Guide to Successful Principles and Practices for Colleges, Universities and Schools.* San Francisco: Jossey-Bass.

SCHACHNER, NATHAN. 1962. *The Medieval Universities.* New York: A. S. Barnes.

TIMOTHY C. CABONI

INSTITUTIONAL RESEARCH IN HIGHER EDUCATION

Institutional research is research activity carried out in colleges and universities to collect and analyze data concerning students, faculty, staff, and other educational facilities. The primary purpose of institutional research is to promote institutional effectiveness. It does this by providing information for institutional planning, policy formation, and decision-making within the college or university.

Largely as a result of the significant role institutional research plays in keeping track of the performance of the institution, higher educational institutions have created a special office, called the Office of Institutional Research. This office usually is placed in the higher hierarchy of the administrative units of the institution.

The size of the Office of Institutional Research depends upon the educational programs and services of the institution. The Office of Institutional Research for a larger higher educational institution usually reports to the provost. In a smaller institution, the Office of Institutional Research reports to the vice-president for academic affairs. No matter the size or the organizational structure, all institutional research offices exist to provide information for institutional planning, policy formation and implementation, and decision-making.

Tasks Performed

The primary role of the Office of Institutional Research in the institutional setup is to collect, analyze, and interpret institutional data on students, faculty, educational programs, and administrative and support services so as to provide accurate information to support planning and decision making activities within the educational institution.

It is the responsibility of the Office of Institutional Research to compile data on course enrollments every semester or quarter. The course enrollment data shows the distribution and major of students enrolled in each department and course. With this knowledge, the institution is in a better position to discontinue a program that is not attracting students. It also allows the administration to allocate more funds to programs that are attractive to students. This helps the institution to utilize its resources for efficient organization and management.

The Office of Institutional Research gathers and maintains data on student retention in terms of gender, race, age, geographic location, and test scores, and shares this information with the student admission office. Student retention is the ability of an educational institution to recruit and retain a student until the student graduates from that institution. A higher retention rate is a reflection of the effectiveness of the programs the institution offers students. Any higher educational institution with a higher retention rate takes delight in displaying this information in a brochure to showcase the effectiveness of their educational programs to prospective students and the general public. Therefore, at the end of every term, the Office of Institutional Research looks into the student population and provides the admissions office data that it needs for its recruitment and retention efforts.

Apart from recruitment and retention records, the Office of Institutional Research keeps track of degrees granted by every department of the institution. In particular, it identifies students who graduate with certificate, associate, bachelor, master, or doctoral degrees. This information is often compiled in terms of discipline or area of study, gender, race, age, or number of years the student studied to complete the program. Information on graduation records is essential because it reflects the number of students who are able to successfully complete their studies in the institution. It also makes the administration aware of educational programs or fields of study that are or are not attracting and maintaining students through graduation.

Of primary importance to the work of the Office of Institutional Research is enrollment management. Often the Office of Institutional Research collaborates with the Student Affairs Office to engage in enrollment and retention management activities to find out how best to retain students in their programs. As a result of such collaborative activities, many colleges and universities have established special programs such as scholarships or grants to attract students who are under-represented in their institutions.

The Office of Institutional Research maintains a plethora of data relating to the financial status of the institution. It shares this information with the Finance Office, which in turn uses this data to conveniently determine and allocate funds for such institutional programs as faculty development, instructional materials, research, work-study students, and faculty and staff salary.

The Office of Institutional Research at the end of every term or year also examines and evaluates the performance of its program faculty. It examines such variables as faculty publications, research, and general contributions to the academic community. Through student evaluations of faculty at the end of every semester or quarter, the Office of Institutional Research is able to document the performance of its program faculty. Students evaluate faculty on such items as grading procedures, knowledge of content, pace of instruction, and respect for student views in the learning process. Assessment of program faculty is done essentially for the purposes of faculty development, retention, recruitment, and promotion.

Institutional research offices produce what is called a "fact book" about the institution. The fact book presents, at a glance, general information and data concerning academic programs, students, degrees conferred, faculty and staff, finances, institutional facilities such as library holdings, and research activities by the institution. The fact book serves as a window to the institution. It provides a summary of the achievements, programs, progress, and facilities of the institution. The Office of Institutional Re-

search takes great pains to prepare it because it gives the public a taste of what awaits students who decide to enroll in that institution.

By the nature of its work, the Office of Institutional Research provides vital data for internal and external surveys and reports. It compiles data for institutional self-study and accreditation by external agencies. Institutional self-study is an attempt that every institution makes to evaluate the effectiveness of its programs and activities. It reveals strengths and weaknesses in the institution. It is done with the aim of making sure the institution is working to accomplish its educational mission. Accreditation is also of significant importance to all colleges and universities because it is an indication that the academic programs of the institution conform to federal or state established standards. Accreditation acts as a benchmark for institutional effectiveness and gives the institution a higher academic ranking.

Institutional research offices also serve as contact points for reports and surveys requested from governmental and nongovernmental agencies such as the United States Department of Education. These agencies may require this data to compile reports on issues such as affirmative action and college guidebooks.

The smooth functioning of educational institutions, like any other organization, depends upon the ability of the institution to identify problems and find appropriate solutions for them. Without this ability, no organization can function effectively. The Office of Institutional Research conducts research into specific problems facing the institution. The research may be focused on such areas as student attrition or retention rate, faculty turnover, or student diversity. It shares the research findings with other departments in the institution. Many of the research activities may be carried out annually or otherwise as needed. The Office of Institutional Research carries out such research with the sole purpose of finding solutions to challenges the institution might encounter in the future. At other times, the research may be conducted with the aim of finding a solution to an existing problem or adding a new program to the curriculum of the institution.

Facilities in educational institutions have the potential effect of attracting students to that institution. Therefore, the Office of Institutional Research compiles data on educational facilities in the institution for organizational purposes. The data on facilities indicates the number of classrooms, teaching laboratories, meeting or conference rooms, offices, libraries, media and technology, space utilization, housing, and vehicles. In addition to compiling the data, the Office of Institutional Research presents an annual report on facility utilization in the institution.

As in all organizations, educational institutions need common guidelines and procedures for implementing policies. The Office of Institutional Research defines common data sets used by the college or university to establish policies for administrative procedures. It is the responsibility of this office to define a part-time student or a part-time faculty member, as well as the concepts of doctoral degree, bachelor's degree, master's degree, a commuter, credit hour, contact hour, credit, or grade point average. The common data set is essential to the smooth administration of the institution because it helps the institution to develop rules, regulations, and policies to guide staff, student, and faculty conduct in the service of the institution.

See also: Colleges and Universities, Organizational Structure of; Presidency, College and University.

BIBLIOGRAPHY

Delaney, Anne Marie. 1996. "The Role of Institutional Research in Higher Education: Enabling Researchers to Meet New Challenges." Paper presented at the 36th annual forum of the Association for Institutional Research, Albuquerque, NM, May 5–8, 1996. ERIC Document Reproduction Service, ED 397752.

Hanson, Gary R., and Denzine, Gypsy M. 2000. "Student Affairs Research: The Work We Do." In *Collaboration Between Student Affairs and Institutional Researchers to Improve Institutional Effectiveness,* ed. James W. Pickering. San Francisco: Jossey-Bass.

Harrington, Charles F., and Chen, Hong Yu. 1995. "The Characteristics, Roles, and Functions of Institutional Research Professionals in the Southern Association for Institutional Research." Paper presented at the 35th annual forum of the Association for Institutional Research, Boston, May 28–31, 1995. ERIC Document Reproduction Service, ED 386136.

Harrington, Charles; Knight, William; and Christie, Ray. 1994. "An Examination of the Institutional Research Functions and Structures in Georgia Higher Education." Paper presented at the 34th annual forum of the Association for Institutional Research, May 29–June 1, 1994. ERIC Document Reproduction Service, ED 372722.

Middaugh, Michael F.; Trusheim, Dale W.; and Bauer, Karen W. 1994. *Strategies for the Practice of Institutional Research: Concepts, Resources, and Applications.* Tallahassee, FL: Association for Institutional Research.

Owens, Robert G. 2001. *Organizational Behavior in Education.* Boston: Allyn and Bacon.

Saupe, Joe L. 1990. *The Functions of Institutional Research,* 2nd edition. Tallahassee, FL: Association for Institutional Research.

Seybert, Jeffery A. 1991. "The Role of Institutional Research in College Management." *School Organization* 11(2):231–239.

Volkwein, J. Fredericks. 1999. "The Four Faces of Institutional Research." In *What Is Institutional Research All About: A Critical and Comprehensive Assessment of the Profession,* ed. J. Fredericks Volkwein. San Francisco: Jossey-Bass.

Zikopoulos, Marianthi, and Hourigan, Christopher. 2001. *The Role of Institutional Research Office in the Institutional Accreditation Self-Study Process.* ERIC Document Reproduction Service, ED 453286.

Kwabena Dei Ofori-Attah

INSTRUCTIONAL DESIGN

OVERVIEW

Instructional-design theory provides guidance on how to help people learn (or develop) in different situations and under different conditions. This guidance includes what to teach and how to teach it. To do this, instructional-design theory must take into account both methods and situations. Just as a carpenter uses different tools for different situations, so do instructional design theories offer instructional designers and teachers different tools for facilitating learning in different situations.

Elements of Instructional-Design Theory

Elements of instructional-design theory include instructional outcomes, conditions, methods, and values. Instructional values are an individual's or group's philosophy or beliefs about instruction. Instructional design theories ought to inform possible users (teachers and instructional designers) of the values about learning and instruction with which the theory was constructed, for they are the values that users and students must hold in order for the theory to work well.

Instructional outcomes include both results that are intentional and those that are incidental. Outcomes include the instruction's effectiveness, efficiency, and appeal. Instructional outcomes should not be confused with learning outcomes. Instructional outcomes focus on the degree of success in attaining the desired learning outcomes (the effectiveness of instruction) but also include the efficiency and appeal of the instruction.

Instructional conditions are factors beyond the influence of the instructional designer that impact upon the effects of the methods of instruction. Conditions may include the nature of what is being learned (the content), the learner, the learning environment, and the instructional development constraints (e.g., time and money). Instructional-design theory, in attempting to provide guidance for people to help others learn, ought to state explicitly the conditions under which different methods should and should not be used.

Instructional methods are the "how to" for facilitating human learning. They are the elements of guidelines that inform designers and teachers what to do to help students learn. They can be very general, such as "provide opportunities for practice," or they can be broken down into much more detailed specifications, such as (for learning concept classifi-

cation) presenting previously unencountered examples and nonexamples of the concept in random order and asking the learner to identify those that are examples of the concept.

Instructional methods are situational rather than universal. This means that there are values, desired instructional outcomes, and instructional conditions (collectively referred to as instructional situations) in any context that influence whether or not a given instructional method should be used. Hence, instructional-design theory should specify the values, outcomes, and conditions for which each method should be used. Also, instructional methods are probabilistic rather than deterministic. That is, their use can only increase the probability that the desired outcomes will be attained.

Differences

Instructional design theories differ most importantly by the methods they offer. But the methods differ because of differences in the outcomes, values, and conditions for which they are intended.

For example, regarding instructional outcomes, some theories may focus more on effectiveness of the instruction, while others may focus more on appeal or efficiency. Also, regarding learning outcomes, different instructional theories can promote very different kinds of learning: from memorization to deep understandings or higher-order thinking and self-regulatory skills; from cognitive goals to such affective goals as emotional and social development.

Instructional values may differ, and they lead one to select different goals and different methods to attain those goals. Traditional instruction systems design (ISD), "a systematic approach to the planning and development of a means to meet instructional needs and goals" (Briggs, p. xxi), specifies that goals should be selected based on an assessment of learners' needs. However, in 1999 Charles Reigeluth proposed that users also consider teachers' and learners' values about goals. Furthermore, designers have tried to rely on experimental research to determine which methods are best for any given situation. Reigeluth countered that users also consider teachers' and learners' values about methods. If a teacher does not value learner-centered methods, then forcing the teacher to use them is not likely to ensure success.

Instructional conditions may also differ across instructional design theories. First, the nature of what is to be learned (the content) may differ. For example, some theories, such as those of David Perkins and Chris Unger, focus on deep understandings, which are taught differently than skills. Second, the nature of the learner may differ, including prior knowledge, skills, understandings, motivation to learn, and learning strategies. Third, the nature of the learning environment may differ. And finally, different instructional design theories may be intended for different constraints on instructional development (time and money). In essence, different instructional theories use different methods to attain different outcomes under different conditions and based on different values.

Major Trends

Two major trends in the field of instructional-design theory are apparent: the increasing predominance of an information-age paradigm of theories and the broadening of the kinds of learning and human development addressed by instructional theorists.

Information-age paradigm. Scholars, such as Bernie Trilling and Paul Hood, are increasingly drawing attention to the need for an attainment-based, "learning-focused paradigm" of instruction to meet learners' new educational needs in the information age, compared to the time-based, "sorting-focused paradigm" of the industrial age. Reigeluth (1999) distinguishes between the industrial and information ages with certain "key markers" (see Table 1).

In the early twenty-first century there is a growing recognition that the current system of education is beginning to fail society, not in its ability to attain traditional goals, but in its ability to provide what is increasingly needed in the emerging information society. There has begun a societal transition in which the complexity of human activity systems is growing dramatically, and learning has become the "indispensable investment" according to the National Commission on Excellence in Education 1983 report, *A Nation at Risk*. This has important implications for both what should be taught and how it should be taught.

Broadening the scope of instructional theory. Much of the work that has been done in relation to and with instructional-design theory has been focused on teaching and learning procedural tasks, which are performed by following sets of defined mental or physical steps that were predominant in the industrial age. However, educational and corpo-

rate settings increasingly require people to solve problems in ill-structured and complex domains—problems for which there is not a clear solution or just one way of doing things. These "heuristic" tasks entail the use of causal models and "rules of thumb," along with other kinds of typically tacit knowledge that require different methods of instruction. This heuristic knowledge because of its nature often takes years for experts to develop through trial and error, if at all. Therefore, it would be valuable for schools and corporations to be able to teach it well.

Several new methods and tools are designed to assist learners with real-world problem solving, including just-in-time instruction and electronic performance support systems (EPSSs). However, they do not provide the appropriate amount or types of support for learning this usually tacit heuristic knowledge. Only toward the close of the twentieth century have instructional deign theorists seriously attempted to address this complex type of learning. Promising work has been done in the area of problem-based learning by such theorists as John D. Bransford and colleagues, David Jonassen, Laurie Nelson, and Roger Schank.

Other current areas of promising instructional-design theory include collaborative learning, self-regulated learning, and such affective areas as emotional development and social development.

Peter Senge highlighted the importance of the "learning organization," which he defined as "an organization that is continually expanding its capacity to create its future" (p.14) through the use of five disciplines: systems thinking, personal mastery, mental models, building shared vision, and team learning. A challenge for instructional design theorists is to develop comprehensive theories that foster such organizational learning.

The preceding offers only a sampling of areas in which instructional-design theory is currently being developed. Due to the nature of human learning, there exist many more domains of instructional guidance that require greater study.

Controversial Issues

Three controversial or problematic issues are discussed below: (1) Should instructional design theories be "theoretically pure" or eclectic? (2) Are traditional research methods appropriate for advancing instructional design theories, or is a different paradigm of research needed? (3) Should instructional-design theories be strictly "local" in scope, or should they generalize across settings?

Eclecticism versus purism. Some scholars, such as Anne K. Bednar and colleagues, argue that an instructional-design theory should be "theoretically pure" in that it should follow a set of assumptions from a single theoretical perspective, such as constructivism or behaviorism. Others, such as Peggy Ertmer and Timothy Newby, believe that such is true for descriptive theories, but that design theories, with their goal orientation, should draw on all useful methods for accomplishing the stated goals. For example, a behaviorist perspective would offer the method of drill and practice to help learners remember important information, whereas a cognitive perspective would offer the use of mnemonics to relate the new information to meaningful information. Perhaps there are some situations where good mnemonics cannot be developed, in which case drill and practice would be suggested by a design theory. Is it unwise for a teacher to draw on both kinds of methods because they hail from different theoretical perspectives? This issue is particularly important because it greatly influences the nature of an instructional theory.

Traditional versus new research methods. Many scholars advocate experimental and/or descriptive case studies or other kinds of descriptive research to advance our knowledge about design theories. Other theorists, such as James Greeno and colleagues, advocate new forms of research, such as "design experiments" and "formative research" (Reigeluth and Frick). "Design experiments" is the term Greeno, Allan Collins, and Lauren Resnick have come to use to refer to educators collaborating to analyze and design changes in institutional practice. "Formative research" is a form of research developed by Charles Reigeluth and Theodore Frick that is meant to help improve instructional-design theory. In an analysis of this issue, Glenn Snelbecker argued in 1974 that descriptive theories in the field are evaluated by how truthfully they describe why learning occurs, whereas instructional theories are evaluated by how useful their methods are for attaining their stated goals. Given this very different orientation toward usefulness rather than truthfulness, Reigeluth (1999) has proposed that the major concern in research on design theory should be "preferability" (whether or not a given method is more useful than the alternatives), rather than "validity" (whether or not the description is truthful). He has also suggested that the

TABLE 1

Key markers of the industrial and information ages that affect education

Industrial age	Information age
Standardization	Customization
Bureaucratic organization	Team-based organization
Centralized organization	Autonomy with accountability
Adversarial relationships	Cooperative relationships
Autocratic decision-making	Shared decision-making
Compliance	Initiative
Conformity	Diversity
One-way communications	Networking
Compartmentalization	Holism
Parts-oriented	Process-oriented
Planned obsolescence	Total quality
CEO or boss as "king"	Customer as "king"

SOURCE: Reigeluth, Charles M. 1999. "What Is Instructional-Design Theory and How Is It Changing?" In *Instructional-Design Theories and Models, Vol. II: A New Paradigm of Instructional Theory*, ed. Charles M. Reigeluth. Mahwah, NJ: Erlbaum. Page 17. Reprinted with permission.

focus for research on a design theory should be to improve it rather than to prove it, because most of our methods of instruction are not nearly as successful as we need them to be. There is also clearly a role for descriptive research on instructional design theories, however. It is occasionally helpful to compare one method with another for a given situation, and descriptions of what a highly effective teacher or computer program does can be helpful for improving an instructional theory.

Although most researchers recognize that different research methods are useful for different purposes, perhaps there has not been enough emphasis on research to improve the preferability of instructional-design theories.

Generalizable versus local knowledge. Some scholars argue that instructional design theories should be "local" in scope because every situation is unique and methods that work well in one situation may not work well in another. Others believe that the purpose of an instructional-design theory is to generalize across situations—that if it loses this quality, it has little usefulness. Given that the standard for a design theory is usefulness rather than truthfulness, the issue may boil down to whether a highly local theory is more useful than a highly generalizable theory, or even whether a design theory that is intermediate between local and general may be the most useful.

There is another consideration that may enlighten this issue. Design theories are made up of not only methods, but also situations (values, desired outcomes, and conditions) that serve as a basis for deciding when to use each method. If a design theory offers different methods for different situations, the theory is at once both local and generalizable. It recognizes the unique needs of each situation but also offers methods for a wide range of situations. In this manner perhaps the profession can transcend "either–or" thinking and be both local and global.

Further Directions

Instructional-design theory bridges the gap between descriptive theory and practice and offers powerful guidance for practitioners. It has the potential to spur tremendous improvements in practice, but it currently constitutes a minor percentage of scholarly efforts devoted to education. Partnering of researchers and practitioners to develop and improve more powerful instructional-design theories can provide valuable insights and improvements for more useful design theory to facilitate human learning and development.

See also: COOPERATIVE AND COLLABORATIVE LEARNING; INSTRUCTIONAL DESIGN, *subentries on* ANCHORED INSTRUCTION, DIRECT INSTRUCTION, LEARNING THROUGH DESIGN, PROBLEM-BASED LEARNING.

BIBLIOGRAPHY

BEDNAR, ANNE K.; CUNNINGHAM, DONALD; DUFFY, THOMAS. M.; and PERRY, J. DAVID. 1991. "Theory into Practice: How Do We Link?" In *Instructional Technology: Past, Present, and Future,* ed. Garry J. Anglin. Englewood, CO: Libraries Unlimited.

BIELACZYC, KATERINE, and COLLINS, ALLAN. 1999. "Learning Communities in Classrooms: A Reconceptualization of Educational Practice." In *Instructional-Design Theories and Models,* ed. Charles M. Reigeluth. Mahwah, NJ: Erlbaum.

BRIGGS, LESLIE, ed. 1977. *Instructional Design: Principles and Applications.* Englewood Cliffs, New Jersey: Educational Technology.

CORNO, LYN, and RANDI, JUDI. 1999. "A Design Theory for Classroom Instruction in Self-Regulated Learning?" In *Instructional-Design Theories and Models,* ed. Charles M. Reigeluth. Mahwah, NJ: Erlbaum.

ERTMER, PEGGY A., and NEWBY, TIMOTHY J. 1993. "Behaviorism, Cognitivism, Constructivism: Comparing Critical Features from an Instructional Design Perspective." *Performance Improvement Quarterly* 6(4):50–72.

GREENO, JAMES G.; COLLINS, ALLAN; and RESNICK, LAUREN B. 1996. "Cognition and Learning." In *Handbook of Educational Psychology,* ed. David C. Berliner and Robert C. Calfee. New York: Macmillan.

KEMP, JERROLD E.; MORRISON, GARY R.; and ROSS, STEVEN M. 1998. *Designing Effective Instruction,* 2nd edition. Upper Saddle River, NJ: Merrill.

LEWIS, CATHERINE; WATSON, MARILYN; and SCHAPS, ERIC. 1999. "Recapturing Education's Full Mission: Educating for Social, Ethical, and Intellectual Development." In *Instructional-Design Theories and Models,* ed. Charles M. Reigeluth. Mahwah, NJ: Erlbaum.

MERRILL, M. DAVID. 1999. "Instructional Transaction Theory: Instructional Design Based on Knowledge Objects." In *Instructional-Design Theories and Models,* ed. Charles M. Reigeluth. Mahwah, NJ: Erlbaum.

NATIONAL COMMISSION ON EXCELLENCE IN EDUCATION. 1983. *A Nation at Risk: The Imperative for Educational Reform.* Washington, DC: U.S. Government Printing Office.

NELSON, LAURIE M. 1999. "Collaborative Problem Solving." In *Instructional-Design Theories and Models,* ed. Charles M. Reigeluth. Mahwah, NJ: Erlbaum.

REIGELUTH, CHARLES M. 1999. "What Is Instructional-Design Theory and How Is It Changing?" In *Instructional-Design Theories and Models,* Vol. II: *A New Paradigm of Instructional Theory,* ed. Charles M. Reigeluth. Mahwah, NJ: Erlbaum.

REIGELUTH, CHARLES M., and GARFINKLE, ROBERT J. 1994. *Systemic Change in Education.* Englewood Cliffs, NJ: Educational Technology Publications.

SENGE, PETER M. 1990. *The Fifth Discipline: The Art and Practice of the Learning Organization.* New York: Doubleday.

SNELBECKER, GLENN E. 1974. *Learning Theory, Instructional Theory, and Psychoeducational Design.* New York: McGraw-Hill.

STONE-McCOWN, KAREN, and McCORMICK, ANN H. 1999. "Self-Science: Emotional Intelligence for Children." In *Instructional-Design Theories and Models,* ed. Charles M. Reigeluth. Mahwah, NJ: Erlbaum.

TRILLING, BERNIE, and HOOD, PAUL. 1999. "Learning, Technology, and Education Reform in the Knowledge Age or 'We're Wired, Webbed, and Windowed, Now What?'" *Educational Technology* 39(3):5–18.

DANIEL F. OSWALD
CHARLES M. REIGELUTH

ANCHORED INSTRUCTION

Anchored instruction (AI) is an example of an approach to curriculum and instruction that provides opportunities for students to learn important content while attempting to understand and solve authentic problems that arise within particular disciplines. Other related approaches are case-based learning, which is used in law and business education, and problem-based learning, sometimes used in medical education. Another way of organizing instruction around problem solving is through project-based learning.

The Problem of Inert Knowledge

In 1929 the English philosopher Alfred Whitehead identified a major problem in schools, namely the problem of *inert knowledge.* Inert knowledge is knowledge than can be recalled when people are explicitly prompted to remember it, but is not spontaneously used to solve problems even though it is relevant. A major goal of AI is to create learning environments that overcome the inert knowledge problem.

Research suggests that the degree to which knowledge remains inert is strongly affected by the way the information was learned initially. One factor contributing to the problem of inert knowledge is that traditional instruction too often consists of learning isolated facts and procedures. As a consequence, students do not learn when or how to use what they have learned. The knowledge is not organized in memory with information on the conditions under which to apply it. In AI students are provided with opportunities to solve realistic problems—called anchors—that help them learn when and how to apply knowledge.

The Role of Prior Knowledge in Learning

Research indicates that learning is affected by the knowledge that people bring to the learning situation. Sometimes people's prior knowledge of a situation enables them to understand with little effort the meaning and significance of new information. More typically, especially in the case of young learners, prior knowledge of the situation is limited and the learner is unable to make sense of new information and has difficulty discriminating important from less important aspects of the information. When learners lack sufficient prior knowledge, information is treated as facts to be memorized. Anchored instruction was developed to compensate for learners' lack of experience and knowledge. Anchors consist of multimedia (e.g., video or audio with pictures) scenarios that are designed to improve learners' understanding of the problems to be solved.

Experience Being an Expert

Another major goal of AI is to help people learn the kinds of problems that experts in various areas encounter and to experience how experts identify, represent, and solve problems. The problems that experts encounter are more complex and open ended than the problems that students are asked to solve in school. Experts also assume greater autonomy than students in solving problems, including learning new skills and knowledge on an as-needed basis to solve problems. Anchors are designed to afford these kinds of experiences.

An Example of AI: *The Adventures of Jasper Woodbury*

Some of the original work on AI was conducted in the domain of middle school mathematics by the Cognition and Technology Group at Vanderbilt. These efforts culminated in a series called *The Adventures of Jasper Woodbury. Jasper* consists of twelve anchors (on videodisc or CD-ROM) that are designed for students in grades five and up. To promote transfer of learning, multiple related anchors are available to provide extra practice on core concepts and problem schemas. Three anchors relate to each of the following topics: statistics and business planning, trip planning, geometry, and algebra. Each anchor contains a short (about fifteen minutes) story on video, which ends in a complex challenge. The adventures are like good detective novels, where all the data necessary to solve the adventure (plus additional solution-irrelevant data) are embedded in the story.

In *The Big Splash,* one of the anchors related to statistics and business planning, the main character is a junior high school student named Chris. Chris's school is having a Fun Fair to raise money to buy a new camera for the school TV station. Chris wants to set up a dunking booth at the fair. Students would buy tickets for the opportunity to try to dunk their teachers in a pool of water. Chris needs to develop a business plan to get his dunking booth project approved by the school and to obtain a loan from the school principal. The plan must include an estimate of revenue and expenses for the dunking booth and must meet constraints set by the principal with respect to the maximum amount of the loan and the requisite profit. The video story shows Chris collecting information for his business plan.

Design principles. *Jasper* anchors were designed according to a set of principles. Each is video based. Research indicates that video helps students, especially poor readers, comprehend problems better. Video is also motivating to students. Anchor problems are presented in story form, instead of expository form. Stories are used because they are easy to remember.

Anchors are not simply traditional word problems on video—they are more representative of problems that an expert might solve. They are complex; more than one solution is possible and many steps (and hours) are required to solve them. Traditional story problems explicitly present the problem to be solved (there is usually only a single problem) and the relevant data. Anchors use a generative format. Each story ends with a challenge and students must generate the problems to be solved. For example, in *The Big Splash* many different business plans can be generated, based on the information presented. There are several options for filling the dunking booth with water and each option differs in terms of cost, risk, and the amount of time required. The challenge also involves some important statistical concepts. Chris conducts a survey to collect information on whether students at his school would be interested in dunking a teacher and how much they would pay to do so. Data from the survey can be used to extrapolate an estimate of revenue for the whole school.

All of the data needed to solve each challenge is contained in the story; students revisit the videos on an as-needed basis to look for and record data. Some of the *Jasper* anchors also contain ideas for how to solve parts of the challenge. These are called embed-ded teaching scenes. The embedded teaching scenes provide students with models for how to approach particular problems that may not be familiar to them.

Perspective on Pedagogy

Anchored instruction is consistent with a class of instructional theories known as constructivist theories. Constructivism rejects the idea that students learn by passively "soaking up" knowledge that is transmitted to them by teachers or others. Instead they assume students learn more if the teacher engages them in activities, such as defining problems, clarifying misunderstandings, generating solutions, and so forth, instead of lecturing or "telling" students how to solve problems.

Because of their complexity, anchors are effective for use in cooperative learning groups. Depending on the skill level of the class, teachers may structure the small-group work in different ways. If the class is quite skilled, the teacher may simply ask students to solve the challenge posed at the end of the video. For other classes, the teacher may ask groups to work and report on some part of the challenge or may focus the task even more by asking groups to brainstorm and report on ideas for how to solve a part of the challenge. An important aspect of AI pedagogy relates to how teachers mediate group problem solving. Because a goal of AI is for students to be as intellectually autonomous as possible in solving the anchors, it is important for teachers to interact with student in ways that do not usurp this autonomy.

Research on Anchored Instruction

One of the largest studies on AI involved a field implementation of four anchors from *The Adventures of Jasper Woodbury.* These anchors were used over the course of a school year by teachers in seventeen classes in seven states in the southeastern United States. In the majority of the classes, the *Jasper* instruction took the place of the students' regular mathematics instruction. Ten comparison classes that were matched on key demographic variables, including socioeconomic status, location, gender, minority representation, and mathematical achievement, were included in research. All students were administered a series of tests at the beginning and end of the school year. One test examined students' word-problem-solving skills. In spite of the fact that *Jasper* students had not received additional practice on written word problems, they performed significantly better than comparison students at the end of the school year. In this way, *Jasper* students were able to transfer the skills they had acquired in the context of solving *Jasper* problems to written word problems.

Students were also administered a series of tests designed to assess their abilities to define and formulate problems. They were given complex story problems in written form and were asked to identify goals that would need to be addressed to solve these problems. They were also shown mathematical formulations and were asked to identify the goal that each formula would satisfy. These aspects of problem solving are unique to the *Jasper* anchors and are not part of traditional problem-solving instruction. As expected, *Jasper* students performed better than comparison students on the posttest.

Finally, self-report measures of students' attitudes were collected. *Jasper* students showed more positive change relative to comparison students in five areas: they showed a reduction in mathematics anxiety, an increase in their beliefs about their ability to perform successfully in mathematics, greater interest in mathematics, greater interest in solving complex problems, and they thought mathematics was more useful in solving problems from everyday life.

The goal of anchored instruction is to help students learn information such that it can be remembered later on and flexibly applied to solve problems. Relevant research suggests that pedagogical approaches such as anchored instruction can enhance students' complex problem solving skills and positive attitudes towards learning.

See also: INSTRUCTIONAL DESIGN, *subentries on* CASE-BASED REASONING, LEARNING THROUGH DESIGN, PROBLEM-BASED LEARNING.

BIBLIOGRAPHY

BARRON, BRIGID J. S.; SCHWARTZ, DANIEL L.; VYE, NANCY J.; MOORE, ALLISON; PETROSINO, ANTHONY; ZECH, LINDA; BRANSFORD, JOHN D.; and COGNITION AND TECHNOLOGY GROUP AT VANDERBILT. 1998. "Doing with Understanding: Lessons from Research on Problem- and Project-Based Learning." *The Journal of the Learning Sciences* 7:271–311.

BARROWS, HOWARD S. 1985. *How to Design a Problem-Based Curriculum for the Preclinical Years.* New York: Springer.

BEREITER, CARL. 1984. "Implications of Postmodernism for Science, or Science as Progressive Discourse." *Educational Technology* 29:3–12.

BRANSFORD, JOHN D.; BROWN, ANN L.; and COCKING, RODNEY R. 2000. *How People Learn: Brain, Mind, Experience, and School.* Washington, DC: National Academy Press.

BRANSFORD, JOHN. D.; FRANKS, JEFFERY J.; VYE, NANCY J.; and SHERWOOD, ROBERT D. 1989. "New Approaches to Instruction: Because Wisdom Can't Be Told." In *Similarity and Analogical Reasoning,* ed. Stella Vosniadou and Andrew Ortony. New York: Cambridge University Press.

COGNITION AND TECHNOLOGY GROUP AT VANDERBILT. 1990. "Anchored Instruction and Its Relationship to Situated Cognition." *Educational Researcher* 19:2–10.

COGNITION AND TECHNOLOGY GROUP AT VANDERBILT. 1992. "The Jasper Experiment: An Exploration of Issues in Learning and Instructional Design." *Education Technology Research and Development* 40:65–80.

COGNITION AND TECHNOLOGY GROUP AT VANDERBILT. 1997. *The Jasper Project: Lessons in Curriculum, Instruction, Assessment, and Professional Development.* Mahwah, NJ: Erlbaum.

DEWEY, JOHN. 1933. *How We Think, A Restatement of the Relation of Reflective Thinking to the Educative Process.* Boston: Heath.

GICK, MARY L., and HOLYOAK, KEITH J. 1983. "Schema Induction and Analogical Transfer." *Cognitive Psychology* 15:1–38.

PAIVIO, ALLAN. 1971. *Imagery and Verbal Processes.* New York: Holt, Rinehart and Winston.

SHARP, DIANA L.; BRANSFORD, JOHN D.; GOLDMAN, SUSAN R.; RISKO, VICTORIA J.; KINZER, CHARLES K.; and VYE, NANCY J. 1995. "Dynamic Visual Support for Story Comprehension and Mental Model Building by Young, At-Risk Children." *Educational Technology Research and Development* 24:417–435.

VYGOTSKY, LEV S. 1978. *Mind in Society: The Development of the Higher Psychological Processes.* Cambridge, MA: Harvard University Press.

WHITEHEAD, ALFRED N. 1929. *The Aims of Education.* New York: Macmillan.

WILLIAMS, SUSAN M. 1992. "Putting Case-Based Instruction into Context: Examples from Legal and Medical Education." *The Journal of the Learning Sciences* 2:367–427.

NANCY J. VYE

CASE-BASED REASONING

Case-based reasoning (CBR) is a kind of analogical reasoning that focuses on reasoning based on previous experience. A previous experience can play several roles, such as:

- suggesting a solution to a new problem or a way of interpreting a situation,
- warning of a problem that will arise, or
- allowing the potential effects of a proposed solution to be predicted.

These are the types of inference necessary for addressing the kinds of ill-defined or complex problems that occur every day in the workplace, at school, and at home. One might, for example, create a new recipe by adapting one made previously. To understand why someone's boss reacted a certain way, one might remember a situation when his own boss reacted similarly. People might persuade themselves that a strategic plan will work based on the similarities between their company's situation and that of another company that is progressing in a similar way.

Cognitive Foundations

Case-based reasoning views analogical reasoning as the centerpiece of the ability to function as human beings. It posits that the most natural and powerful learning strategies are the automatic ones that situate learning in real-world experience. Previous experience and knowledge are naturally brought to bear in interpreting new situations, trying to explain when things are not as expected (based on the predictions made by previous experiences and knowledge), drawing conclusions based on explanations and on similarities between situations, and anticipating when some new thing just learned might be applicable. To do these things automatically there must be some internal processes and representations that allow a new experience to call up similar ones from memory.

Key to such reasoning is a memory that can access the right experiences (cases) at the times they are needed (the indexing problem). Case-based reasoning identifies two sets of procedures that allow such recognition to happen. First, at insertion (encoding) time, while engaging in an experience, a reasoner interprets the situation and identifies at least some of the lessons it can teach and when those lessons might most productively be applied. The case is labeled according to its applicability conditions, that is, the circumstances in which it ought to be retrieved. The most discriminating labels on a case will be derived by a reasoner who has taken the time and effort, and who has the background knowledge, to carefully analyze a case's potential applicability. Second, at retrieval time, while engaging in a new situation, a reasoner uses his or her current goals and understanding of the new situation as a probe into memory, looking for cases that are usefully similar to the new one. The extent to which a reasoner is willing or able to interpret the new situation determines the quality of the probe into memory. An uninterpreted situation is likely to yield poorer access to the contents of memory than is one that is more embellished. The more creative a reasoner is at interpreting a situation, the more likely he or she is to find relevant knowledge and experience to use in reasoning about it.

Learning, in the CBR paradigm, means extending one's knowledge by interpreting new experiences and incorporating them into memory, by reinterpreting and reindexing old experiences to make them more usable and accessible, and by abstracting out generalizations over a set of experiences. Interpreting an experience means creating an explanation that connects one's goals and actions with resulting outcomes. Such learning depends heavily on the reasoner's ability to create such explanations, suggesting that the ability and need to explain are key to promoting learning.

Case-based reasoning thus gives failure a central role in promoting learning because failure promotes a need to explain. When the reasoner's expectations fail, he or she is alerted that his or her knowledge or reasoning is deficient. When such failures happen in the context of attempting to achieve a personally meaningful goal, the reasoner wants to explain so that he or she can be more successful. Crucial to recognizing and interpreting failure is useful feedback from the world. A reasoner who is connected to the world will be able to evaluate his or her solutions with respect to what results from them, allowing indexing that discriminates usability of old cases and allowing good judgments later about reuse.

Because one's first explanations might not be complete or accurate, iterative refinement is central to CBR. Explanations (and thus, knowledge) are revised and refined over time. People explain and index any experience the best they can at the time, and later on, when a similar situation comes up, remember and try to apply what was learned from the past experience. The ability to accurately explain develops over time through noticing similarities and differences across diverse situations, suggesting that a variety of experiences with a concept or skill—personal ones and vicarious ones—are necessary to learn it to its full complexity.

Implications for Promoting Learning

Case-based reasoning suggests five important facilitators for learning effectively from experience:

1. having the kinds of experiences that afford learning what needs to be learned;

2. interpreting those experiences so as to recognize what can be learned from them, to draw connections between their parts so as to transform them into useful cases, and to extract lessons that might be applied elsewhere;

3. anticipating the usefulness of those extracted lessons so as to be able to develop indexes for these cases that will allow their applicability to be recognized in the future;

4. applying what one is learning and experiencing failure of one's conceptions to work as expected, explaining those failures, and trying again (iteration); and

5. learning to use cases effectively to reason.

Case-based reasoning suggests that the easiest kinds of experiences to learn from are those that afford concrete, authentic, and timely feedback, so that learners have the opportunity to confront their conceptions and identify what they still need to learn. It also suggests that learners be given the opportunity to iteratively move toward increasingly better development of the skills and concepts they are learning so as to experience them in a range of situations and under a variety of conditions, and that, with each iteration, they have a chance to explain things that did not go exactly as expected and identify what else they need to learn. According to CBR,

the iterative cycle of applying what is known, interpreting feedback, explaining results, and revising memory explains how expertise is developed and how an expert uses personal experiences and those of others to reason and learn.

Designing Instruction

Case-based reasoning makes two kinds of suggestions about designing instruction. First it suggests ways of orchestrating and sequencing classroom activities, including the roles teachers and peers can play in that orchestration and ways of integrating hands-on activities, software tools, and reflection. Second it suggests several kinds of software tools for scaffolding and enhancing reasoning and for promoting productive kinds of reflection.

Design of learning environments. Case-based reasoning suggests a style of education in which students learn by engaging in problem solving and other activities that motivate the need to learn and that give students a chance to apply what is being learned in ways that afford real feedback. In such an environment students might engage in solving a series of real-world problems (e.g., managing erosion, planning for a tunnel, designing locker organizers) requiring identification of issues that need resolution and knowledge that needs to be learned to address those issues; exploration or investigation or experimentation to learn the needed knowledge; application of that knowledge to solve the problem; and generation and assessment of a solution. Thinking about the problem they are trying to solve should help learners identify what they need to learn; they should have opportunities to learn those things; and they should get to apply what they are learning over and over again, with help along the way aimed at allowing them to successfully solve the problem and successfully learn the targeted knowledge and skills. Two approaches to the design of full learning environments have come from CBR. Roger C. Schank's group at Northwestern University's Institute for the Learning Sciences proposed the notion of a goal-based scenario as a fully automated learning environment. Janet L. Kolodner's group at Georgia Institute of Technology proposes the notion of their trademarked Learning by Design, a way of orchestrating a classroom for combined learning of content and important skills.

Goal-based scenarios (GBS). A goal-based scenario is a learning environment that places students in a situation where they have to achieve some interesting goal that requires them to learn targeted knowledge and skills. In Advise the President, for example, students play the role of advisers to the president in dealing with a hostage situation in a foreign land, in the process learning about several hostage-taking events, which have happened in history, and also learning some foreign policy. In Sickle-Cell Counselor students advise couples about their risk of having children with sickle-cell anemia, in the process learning about genetics in the context of sickle-cell disease. Using Broadcast News students put together a news story, in the process learning both history and writing skills. Students learn about history or genetics or writing because they need to learn those things to successfully achieve the challenge set for them. The trick is to design challenges that both engage the students and focus them on whatever content and skills they should be learning.

The student engaged in a goal-based scenario is provided with a case library of videos of experts telling their stories, strategies, and perspectives, which might help them with their task. When they reach an impasse in achieving their goal, they ask a question of the case library, and an appropriate video is retrieved and shown. Sometimes a story will suggest a topic they should learn more about or a skill they need to learn; other times it will tell how that expert dealt with some difficult issue the student is addressing. Based on suggestions made by the case library students move forward with their task—choosing a policy to recommend to the president, choosing a blood test, making recommendations to couples about whether or not they should have children, or deciding how to refer to a leader. The software takes on an additional role to clearly inform students when they have failed at their task. The case library can be consulted again, this time to help with explaining and recovering from a failure.

Learning by Design. Learning by Design is a project-based inquiry approach to middle school science, which uses design challenges as compelling contexts for learning science concepts and skills. Design challenges provide opportunities for engaging in and learning complex cognitive, social, practical, and communication skills. For example students design miniature vehicles and their propulsion systems to learn about forces, motion, and Newton's laws; and ways of managing the erosion near a basketball court to learn about erosion and accretion, erosion management, and the relationship between people and the environment.

Learning by Design's curriculum units are centered on the design and construction of working devices or models that illustrate physical phenomena. Learning by Design's focus on design challenges comes from CBR's suggestion that learning requires impasses and expectation failures. Designing, building, and testing working devices provides the kinds of failure experiences and feedback that promote good learning as well as opportunities for trying again to achieve the challenge based on what's been newly learned.

Case-based learning purports that learning from experience requires reflecting on one's experiences in ways that will allow learners to derive well-articulated cases from their experiences and insert them well into their own memories. Learning by Design includes integration of classroom "rituals" that promote such reflection. "Poster sessions" provide a venue for reporting on and discussing investigative results and procedures. "Pin-up sessions" give small groups the opportunity to share their plans with the whole class and hear other students' ideas. "Gallery walks" provide a venue for presenting one's designs in progress to the rest of the class and explaining why one's device behaves the way it does. Each provides opportunities for students to publicly present the way they engaged in important science skills, to see how others have engaged in those skills, and to discuss the ins and outs of the skills being practiced. Preparing for presentations requires doing the kinds of reflection on their activities that CBR suggests will lead to lasting learning.

Successfully engaging in design and investigative activities and in reflecting on those activities in ways that lead to productive learning requires help, and in Learning by Design, that help is distributed among the teacher, peers, cases, software, and paper-and-pencil tools. Cases that are read as part of the investigation or during design planning help students identify what they need to learn more about and give them ideas for their designs. Paper-and-pencil design diary pages help them keep track of decisions they make and data they collect while designing and testing so that they will be able to remember and reconstruct their experiences. SMILE's (Supportive Multi-User Interactive Learning Environment) Design Discussions help students plan investigative activities, summarize investigative experiences, justify design decisions, and explain design experiences, and its Lessons Learned helps them reflect back on a full design experience (several weeks long) and articulate what they've learned. The tools act as resources to help students create cases for others to use, help students keep track of what they have been doing, and help students reflect on their experiences and turn them into cases in their own memories. Learning by Design's classroom rituals get students and teachers involved in sharing and discussing experiences, providing advice, and abstracting across the experiences of different groups in a class.

Design of instructional tools. Case-based reasoning suggests three types of software tools for promoting learning: (1) case libraries as a resource; (2) supports for reflection; and (3) realistic simulation and modeling environments.

Case libraries as a resource. The most common place where CBR has influenced learning tools is in the creation of case libraries. A case library offers the opportunity for students to learn from others' experiences. Case libraries as a resource can offer a variety of different kinds of information of value to learners:

- Advice in the form of stories

- Vicarious experience using a concept or skill

- The lay of the domain and guidance on what to focus on

- Strategies and procedures

- How to use cases

Archie–2, for example, provides cases for architecture students to use while designing. Its cases describe public buildings, focusing on libraries and courthouses. As students work on designing buildings they consult Archie periodically for advice. Another program, STABLE, is designed to help students learn the skills involved in doing object-oriented design and programming. It uses a web-based (hypermedia) collection of cases made from previous students' work. Many goal-based scenarios include case libraries at their cores.

The context in which case libraries are used is critical to their effectiveness. For cases to be a useful resource to students, the students must be engaged in an activity where their impasses might be answered by cases in the case library. If students are facing challenges that arise naturally in problem solving (e.g., "How do I model a situation like this?" or "What's a good starting point for this kind of problem?"), then a case library of relevant situations and problems can help them address those impasses.

Building case libraries can be as valuable educationally as using case libraries, sometimes even more valuable. One of the findings in using Archie–2 was that the graduate students who were *building* the case library seemed to be learning as much or more than the students who were *using* the case library in their design work. The activity of building a case library is frequently motivating for students because it is creating a public artifact whose purpose is to help future students. Cognitively the need to explain to others in a way that will allow them to understand requires reflecting on a situation, sorting out its complexities, making connections between its parts, and organizing what one has to say into coherent and memorable chunks.

Support for reflection. Case-based reasoning purports that the most productive reflection for deep and lasting learning includes connecting one's goals, plans, actions, and their outcomes to tell the fully interpreted story of an experience, and then extracting the lessons learned and making predictions about the circumstances when those lessons might be applicable in the future. Several software tools have been designed to help learners engage in such reflection, each asking learners to be authors of cases describing their experiences. Jennifer Turns's Reflective Learner helps undergraduate engineering students write "learning essays" about their design experiences. Its prompting asks students to (a) identify and describe a problem that they had encountered when undertaking the current phase of their design project; (b) describe their solution to the problem; (c) say what they had learned from the experience; and (d) anticipate the kinds of situations where a similar solution might be useful. Amnon Shabo's Javacap and its successor, Kolodner's and Kris Nagel's Storyboard Author, provide structuring and prompts to help middle school students summarize their project-based science experiences, extract from them what they have learned, and write them up as stories for publication in a permanently accessible case library for use by other students. The networked computer creates motivation for the students' reflection; students enhance their own learning as they write summaries, which can act as guides and supports to future students. Nagel and Kolodner's Design Discussions, mentioned earlier, provides prompting to help students write up the results of experiments they've done, ideas about achieving project challenges or solving problems they are working on, or what happened when they constructed and tested a design idea.

Realistic modeling and simulation. Case-based reasoning's model of learning puts emphasis on experiencing failure as a motivation for deep learning. Case-based reasoning thus suggests that learners should have opportunities to try out their conceptions, failing softly when their predictions fail, and getting timely and interpretable feedback that they can use to identify and explain their misconceptions. Thus, the ability to try out and see the results of one's conceptions is fundamental to any learning environment based on CBR's model. Sometimes one can construct artifacts and try them out. For example, in Learning by Design, students design, construct, and test miniature vehicles to learn about combining forces. But often processes have time scales, size, cost, or safety constraints that make authentic feedback impractical. In those situations, CBR suggests making available to students realistic modeling and simulation environments.

Evidence of Learning

There has not been a great deal of evaluation and assessment of case-based tools and learning environments, but indicators are positive. Teachers and trainers who use CBR-informed materials come back energized. Teachers feel that they are able to reach more of their students with this methodology. Both students at the top and those at the bottom seem to be drawn in more by these activities than they are in a normal aim-toward-the-middle classroom. Concepts and skills are being learned, teachers think, in ways that will encourage students to remember and reuse them. Students surprise the teachers with ideas they come up with and the connections they are able to draw.

Evaluation and assessment in Learning by Design classrooms shows that indeed students are learning, often better than students in a traditional classroom. Results indicate that students who participate in Learning by Design learn the science content as well as or better than students in more traditional science classes. More important, results show that Learning by Design students learn targeted science skills and communication, collaboration, project, and learning practices such that they can apply them in novel situations. Indeed, Learning by Design students in typical-achievement classes perform these skills and practices as well as or better than honors students who have not been exposed to Learning by

Design, while Learning by Design honors students perform the targeted skills and practices almost like experts.

See also: INSTRUCTIONAL DESIGN, *subentries on* ANCHORED INSTRUCTION, LEARNING THROUGH DESIGN, PROBLEM-BASED LEARNING.

BIBLIOGRAPHY

BAREISS, RAY, and BECKWITH, RICHARD. 1993. "Advise the President: A Hypermedia System for Teaching Contemporary American History." Paper presented at the annual meeting of the American Educational Research Association, Atlanta, GA.

BELL, BENJAMIN; BAREISS, RAY; and BECKWITH, RICHARD. 1994. "Sickle Cell Counselor: A Prototype Goal-Based Scenario for Instruction in a Museum Environment." *Journal of the Learning Sciences* 3:347–386.

DOMESHEK, ERIC A., and KOLODNER, JANET L. 1993. "Using the Points of Large Cases." *Artificial Intelligence for Engineering Design, Analysis and Manufacturing (AIEDAM)* 7(2):87–96.

FERGUSON, WILLIAM; BAREISS, RAY; BIRNBAUM, LARRY; and OSGOOD, RICHARD. 1992. "ASK Systems: An Approach to the Realization of Story-Based Teachers." *Journal of the Learning Sciences* 2(1):95–134.

GUZDIAL, MARK, and KEHOE, COLLEEN. 1998. "Apprenticeship-Based Learning Environments: A Principled Approach to Providing Software-Realized Scaffolding through Hypermedia." *Journal of Interactive Learning Research* 9:289–336.

HAMMOND, KRISTIAN J. 1989. *Case-Based Planning.* New York: Academic Press.

HMELO, CINDY E.; HOLTON, DOUGLAS L.; and KOLODNER, JANET L. 2000. "Designing to Learn About Complex Systems." *Journal of the Learning Sciences* 9(3):247–298.

HOLYOAK, KEITH J. 1984. "Analogical Thinking and Human Intelligence." In *Advances in the Psychology of Human Intelligence,* Vol. 2, ed. R. J. Sternberg. Hillsdale, NJ: Erlbaum.

KASS, ALEX, and GURALNICK, D. 1991. "Environments for Incidental Learning: Taking Road Trips Instead of Memorizing State Capitals." In *Proceedings of the International Conference on the*

Learning Sciences (ICLS) 1991. Evanston, IL: American Association for Computers in Education.

KOLODNER, JANET L. 1993. *Case-Based Reasoning.* San Mateo, CA: Kaufmann.

KOLODNER, JANET L. 1997. "Educational Implications of Analogy: A View from Case-Based Reasoning." *American Psychologist* 52:57–66.

KOLODNER, JANET L.; CRISMOND, DAVID; GRAY, JACKIE; HOLBROOK, JENNIFER; and PUNTAMBEKAR, SADHANA. 1998. "Learning by Design from Theory to Practice." In *Proceedings of the International Conference on the Learning Sciences (ICLS) 1998.* Charlottesville, VA: American Association for Computers in Education (AACE).

KOLODNER, JANET L., and GUZDIAL, MARK. 1999. "Theory and Practice of Case-Based Learning Aids." In *Theoretical Foundations of Learning Environments,* ed. Daniel H. Jonassen and Susan M. Land. Mahwah, NJ: Erlbaum.

KOLODNER, JANET L.; HMELO, CINDY E.; and NARAYANAN, N. HARI. 1996. "Problem-Based Learning Meets Case-Based Reasoning." In *Proceedings of the International Conference on the Learning Sciences (ICLS) 1996,* ed. Daniel C. Edelson and Eric A. Domeshek. Charlottesville, VA: American Association for Computers in Education (AACE).

KOLODNER, JANET L., and NAGEL, KRIS. 1999. "The Design Discussion Area: A Collaborative Learning Tool in Support of Learning from Problem-Solving and Design Activities." In *Proceedings of Computer Support for Collaborative Learning (CSCL) 1999.* Palo Alto, CA: Stanford University.

KOLODNER, JANET L., and SIMPSON, ROBERT L. 1989. "The MEDIATOR: Analysis of an Early Case-Based Reasoner." *Cognitive Science* 13:507–549.

NAGEL, KRIS, and KOLODNER, JANET L. 1999. "SMILE: Supportive Multi-User Interactive Learning Environment. Poster Summary." In *Proceedings of Computer Support for Collaborative Learning (CSCL) 1999.* Palo Alto, CA: Stanford University.

PUNTAMBEKAR, SADHANA, and KOLODNER, JANET L. 1998. "The Design Diary: A Tool to Support Students in Learning Science by Design." In *Proceedings of the International Conference of the Learning Sciences (ICLS) 1998.* Charlottesville,

VA: American Association for Computers in Education (AACE).

REDMOND, MICHAEL. 1992. "Learning by Observing and Understanding Expert Problem Solving." Ph.D. diss., College of Computing, Georgia Institute of Technology.

RIESBECK, CHRISTOPHER K., and SCHANK, ROGER C. 1989. *Inside Case-Based Reasoning.* Mahwah, NJ: Erlbaum.

SCHANK, ROGER C. 1982. *Dynamic Memory.* New York: Cambridge University Press.

SCHANK, ROGER C. 1999. *Dynamic Memory Revisited.* New York: Cambridge University Press.

SCHANK, ROGER C., and CLEARY, CHIP. 1994. *Engines for Education.* Mahwah, NJ: Erlbaum.

SCHANK, ROGER C.; FANO, ANDREW; BELL, BENJAMIN; and JONA, MENACHIM. 1994. "The Design of Goal-Based Scenarios." *Journal of the Learning Sciences* 3:305–346.

SHABO, AMNON; NAGEL, KRIS; GUZDIAL, MARK; and KOLODNER, JANET. 1997. "JavaCAP: A Collaborative Case Authoring Program on the WWW." In *Proceedings of Computer Support for Collaborative Learning (CSCL) 1997.* Toronto: University of Toronto/OISE.

TURNS, JENNIFER A.; NEWSTETTER, WENDY; ALLEN, JANET K.; and MISTREE, FARROKH. June 1997. "The Reflective Learner: Supporting the Writing of Learning Essays That Support the Learning of Engineering Design through Experience." In *Proceedings of the 1997 American Society of Engineering Educators' Conference.* Milwaukee, WI: American Society of Engineering Education.

ZIMRING, CRAIG M.; DO, ELLEN; DOMESHEK, ERIC.; and KOLODNER, JANET L. 1995. "Supporting Case-Study Use in Design Education: A Computational Case-Based Design Aid for Architecture." In *Computing in Engineering: Proceedings of the Second Congress,* ed. Jafar P. Mohsen. New York: American Society of Civil Engineers.

JANET L. KOLODNER

DIRECT INSTRUCTION

Instruction is an illusive term that is often used indiscriminately to describe any presentation of information. In this discussion instruction is limited to those situations that, in addition to providing relevant information, include the following characteristics: (1) a particular educational goal has been specified; (2) the information has been organized to facilitate the acquisition of the desired knowledge or skill; (3) appropriate practice with feedback has been provided; and (4) guidance is available to assist learners to acquire the desired knowledge or skill.

Learning is also a term that is often equated with instruction. Learning occurs in all situations, whether or not there was a deliberate attempt to promote acquisition of a particular goal. Instruction is limited to those situations where there is a deliberate attempt to promote learning of specified knowledge or skill.

Direct instruction is a subset of instructional situations in which there is some instructor or instructional agent that is not only providing information but also monitoring the instructional activities of the student and providing guidance and feedback as appropriate. Ruth Clark describes four instructional architectures: receptive, directive, guided discovery, and exploratory. *Receptive instruction* is typified by a lecture where information is provided, but there is no attempt to ensure learning by providing practice or guidance. *Directive instruction,* often called tutorial instruction, involves presenting segments of information followed by appropriate practice with feedback and guidance. This is the type of instruction that is the subject of this entry. *Guided discovery* provides students with problems to solve and engages them in microworlds or simulations of the real world where they can explore a variety of approaches. The amount of guidance provided varies widely in this type of instruction. Highly guided situations are very similar to direct instruction, whereas those with little or no guidance depend more on student discovery of the knowledge or skill being promoted. *Exploratory architectures* are typically unstructured. Learners are provided some problem to solve and given a rich library of resource material. Students must structure their own learning as they investigate various resources and attempt to solve the problem.

Types of Instructional Models

There are a wide variety of instructional models and theories available to guide the design of directive instructional products. Charles M. Reigeluth includes summaries of more than twenty such models. Robert Tennyson et al. and Sanne Dijkstra et al. include summaries of a number of international models of instruction. David Jonassen includes a number of articles summarizing research related to direct instruction. Perhaps the most widely used model for direct instruction is the 1985 work of Robert Gagné, elaborated and extended by David Merrill in 1994. A newer model of some importance is the 4C/ID model of J. J. G. van Merriënboer.

The author has examined the above and other sources to identify instructional principles prescribed by this body of theory and research to which all of these authors would agree. These instructional design models represent a wide range of philosophical orientation and each emphasizes different aspects of the instructional situation. Some of these models apply more directly to architectures other than direct instruction but have implications for direct instruction nevertheless.

Many of these instructional models suggest that the most effective learning situations are those that are problem-based and involve students in four distinct phases of learning: (1) activation of prior experience; (2) demonstration of skills; (3) application of skills; and (4) integration of these skills into real-world activities.

Principles for Direct Instruction

The various instructional theorists and researchers all seem to agree on the following underlying principles for direct instruction:

1. Learning is promoted when learners are engaged in solving real-world problems.
   a. Learning is promoted when learners are shown the task that they will be able to do or the problem they will be able to solve as a result of completing a module or course.
   b. Learning is promoted when learners are engaged at the problem or task level, not just the operation or action level.
   c. Learning is promoted when learners solve a progression of problems that are explicitly compared to one another.
2. Learning is promoted when relevant previous experience is activated.
   a. Learning is promoted when learners are directed to recall, relate, describe, or apply knowledge or skill from relevant past experience that can be used as a foundation for the new knowledge or skill.
   b. Learning is promoted when learners are provided relevant experience that can be used as a foundation for the new knowledge or skill.

c. Learning is promoted when learners are provided or encouraged to recall a structure than can be used to organize the new knowledge.

3. Learning is promoted when the instruction demonstrates what is to be learned rather than merely telling information about what is to be learned.

a. Learning is promoted when the demonstration is consistent with the learning goal: examples and nonexamples for concepts, demonstrations for procedures, visualizations for processes, and modeling for behavior.

b. Learning is promoted when learners are provided appropriate learner guidance including some of the following: learners are directed to relevant information, multiple representations are used for the demonstrations, and multiple demonstrations are explicitly compared.

c. Learning is promoted when media plays a relevant instructional role.

4. Learning is promoted when learners are required to apply their new knowledge or skill to solve problems.

a. Learning is promoted when the application (practice) and the posttest are consistent with the stated or implied objectives: *information-about practice* is to recall or recognize information; *parts-of practice* is to locate, name, and/or describe each part; *kinds-of practice* is to identify new examples of each kind; *how-to practice* is to do the procedure; and *what-happens practice* is to predict a consequence of a process given conditions, or find faulted conditions given an unexpected consequence.

b. Learning is promoted when learners are guided in their problem solving by appropriate feedback and coaching, including error detection and correction, and when this coaching is gradually withdrawn.

c. Learning is promoted when learners are required to solve a sequence of varied problems.

5. Learning is promoted when learners are encouraged to integrate (transfer) the new knowledge or skill into their everyday life.

a. Learning is promoted when learners are given an opportunity to publicly demonstrate their new knowledge or skill.

b. Learning is promoted when learners can reflect on, discuss, and defend their new knowledge or skill.

c. Learning is promoted when learners can create, invent, and explore new and personal ways to use their new knowledge or skills.

See also: INSTRUCTIONAL DESIGN, *subentry on* OVERVIEW.

BIBLIOGRAPHY

ANDRE, THOMAS. 1997. "Selected Microinstructional Methods to Facilitate Knowledge Construction: Implications for Instructional Design." In *Instructional Design: International Perspective: Theory, Research, and Models*, Vol. 1, ed. Robert D. Tennyson, Franz Schott, Norbert Seel, and Sanne Dijkstra. Mahwah, NJ: Erlbaum.

CLARK, RUTH. 1998. *Building Expertise: Cognitive Methods for Training and Performance Development.* Washington, DC: International Society for Performance Improvement.

DIJKSTRA, SANNE; SEEL, NORBERT; SCHOTT, FRANZ; and TENNYSON, ROBERT D. 1997. *Instructional Design International Perspective,* Vol. 2: *Solving Instructional Design Problems.* Mahwah, NJ: Erlbaum.

GAGNÉ, ROBERT M. 1985. *The Conditions of Learning and Theory of Instruction,* 4th edition. New York: Holt, Rinehart and Winston.

JONASSEN, DAVID H. 1996. *Handbook of Research for Educational Communications and Technology.* New York: Macmillan.

MCCARTHY, BERNICE. 1996. *About Learning.* Barrington, IL: Excell.

MERRILL, M. DAVID. 1994. *Instructional Design Theory.* Englewood Cliffs, NJ: Educational Technology.

REIGELUTH, CHARLES M. 1999. *Instructional Design Theories and Models: A New Paradigm of Instructional Theory,* Vol. 2. Mahwah, NJ: Erlbaum.

SCHWARTZ, DANIEL; LIN, XIAODONG; BROPHY, SEAN; and BRANSFORD, JOHN D. 1999. "Toward the Development of Flexibly Adaptive Instructional Designs." In *Instructional Design Theories and Models: A New Paradigm of Instructional Theory,* Vol. 2. Mahwah, NJ: Erlbaum.

Tennyson, Robert D.; Schott, Franz; Seel, Norbert; and Dijkstra, Sanne. 1997. *Instructional Design: International Perspective*, Vol. 1: *Theory, Research, and Models.* Mahwah, NJ: Erlbaum.

van Merriënboer, Jeroen J. G. 1997. *Training Complex Cognitive Skills.* Englewood Cliffs, NJ: Educational Technology.

M. David Merrill

LEARNING COMMUNITIES

At the end of the twentieth century in America there has developed a *learning-communities* approach to education. In a learning community the goal is to advance the collective knowledge and, in that way, to support the growth of individual knowledge. The defining quality of a learning community is the presence of a culture of learning in which everyone is involved in a collective effort of understanding.

There are four characteristics that such a culture must have: (1) diversity of expertise among its members, who are valued for their contributions and given support to develop; (2) a shared objective of continually advancing the collective knowledge and skills; (3) an emphasis on learning how to learn; and (4) mechanisms for sharing what is learned. It is not necessary that each member assimilate everything that the community knows, but each should know who within the community has relevant expertise to address any problem. This marks a departure from the traditional view of schooling, with its emphasis on individual knowledge and performance and the expectation that students will acquire the same body of knowledge at the same time. Classrooms organized as learning communities differ from most classrooms along a number of dimensions.

Learning Activities

Because the goals focus on fostering a culture of learning, the activities of learning communities must provide a means for (1) both individual development and collaborative construction of knowledge, (2) sharing knowledge and skills among members of the community, and (3) making learning processes visible and articulated. The learning activities described in a learning-communities approach and those found in most classrooms may share some similarities. For instance, methods such as cooperative learning can be used to support a learning community's goals, but they can equally well support more traditional learning aimed at inculcating particular knowledge among students.

Teacher Roles and Power Relationships

In a learning-communities approach the teacher takes on roles of organizing and facilitating student-directed activities, whereas in most classrooms the teacher tends to direct the activities. The power relationships shift as students become responsible for their own learning and the learning of others. Students also develop ways to assess their own progress and work with others to assess the community's progress. In contrast, in most classrooms the teacher is the authority, determining what is studied and assessing the quality of students' work.

Identity

As members of a learning community take on different roles and pursue individual interests toward common goals, students develop individual expertise and identities. In contrast, in most classrooms students work on the same things and are all expected to reach a base level of understanding. Students tend to form their identity through being measured or by measuring themselves against this base level. In a learning-communities approach there is also the notion of a community identity. By working toward common goals and developing a collective awareness of the expertise available among the members of the community, a sense of "who we are" develops.

Resources

Both a learning-communities approach and many traditional classrooms use resources outside of the classroom, including disciplinary experts, telementors, the Internet, and so forth. However, in learning communities both the content learned and the processes of learning from the outside resources are shared more among members of the community and become part of the collective understanding. A further distinction between learning communities and most classrooms is that in learning communities, both the members themselves and the collective knowledge and skills of the communities are viewed as important resources.

Discourse

In the learning-communities approach, the language for describing ideas and practices in the community emerges through interaction with different knowledge sources and through co-construction and negotiation among the members of the community. Also, learning communities develop a common language for more than just content knowledge and skills. The community develops ways to articulate learning processes, plans, goals, assumptions, and so forth. In contrast, in most classrooms the teacher and texts tend to promulgate the formal language to be learned.

Knowledge

In learning communities the development of both diverse individual expertise and collective knowledge is emphasized. In order for students to develop expertise, they must develop an in-depth understanding about the topics that they investigate. There is also a circular growth of knowledge, wherein discussion within the community about what individuals have learned leads individuals to seek further knowledge, which they then share with the community. In most classrooms the goals tend toward covering all the topics in the curriculum (breadth over depth) and teaching everyone the same thing.

Products

In a learning-communities approach, members work together to produce artifacts or performances that can be used by the community to further their understanding. There is sustained inquiry and development of products over months. In contrast, most classrooms tend toward individual or small group assignments with little sharing or collective products. Usually work is produced in short periods of time.

A key idea in the learning-communities approach is to advance the collective knowledge of the community, and in that way to help individual students learn. This is directly opposed to the approaches found in most schools, where learning is viewed as an individual pursuit and the goal is to transmit the textbook's and teacher's knowledge to students. The culture of schools often discourages sharing of knowledge by inhibiting students talking, working on problems or projects together, and sharing or discussing their ideas. Testing and grading are administered individually. When taking tests, students are prevented from relying on other resources, such as students, books, or computers. The whole approach is aimed at ensuring that students have all the knowledge in their heads that is included in the curriculum. Thus the learning-community approach is a radical departure from the theory of learning and knowledge underlying traditional schooling.

See also: COMPUTER-SUPPORTED COLLABORATIVE LEARNING; COOPERATIVE AND COLLABORATIVE LEARNING; PEER RELATIONS AND LEARNING.

BIBLIOGRAPHY

BIELACZYC, KATERINE, and COLLINS, ALLAN. 1999. "Learning Communities in Classrooms: A Reconceptualization of Educational Practice." In *Instructional Design Theories and Models: A New Paradigm of Instructional Theory,* ed. Charles M. Reigeluth. Mahwah, NJ: Erlbaum.

BROWN, ANN, and CAMPIONE, JOSEPH. 1996. "Psychological Theory and the Design of Innovative Learning Environments: On Procedures, Principles, and Systems." In *Innovations in Learning: New Environments for Education,* ed. Leona Schauble and Robert Glaser. Mahwah, NJ: Erlbaum.

SCARDAMALIA, MARLENE, and BEREITER, CARL. 1994. "Computer Support for Knowledge-Building Communities." *Journal of the Learning Sciences* 3:265–283.

KATERINE BIELACZYC

LEARNING THROUGH DESIGN

Design principles, perspectives, and processes in K–12 classroom practice became a topic of educational research during the final decade of the twentieth century. Research was preceded by design-based practices in the classrooms of many K–12 teachers, who engaged students in a variety of design projects and activities, such as proposing environmental strategies, creating plans for future communities, building bridges, designing machines, creating art and theater, and planning for community events. Classroom design projects thrived among teachers, who appreciated their value, but received little notice from researchers of learning. Design activities were the legacy of John Dewey and other progressive influences on schools and teachers, with roots in "experiential education," "learning by doing," and "project work." This entry is concerned exclusively with the nascent research field exploring the cognitive, metacognitive, and social contributions of design-based approaches to learning.

Research Background and Interests

The research community's interest in design-based approaches to curriculum overlap with several movements in education during the last two decades of the twentieth century. During the 1980s an education policy atmosphere developed that called for connecting what was taught and learned in school with the emerging demands of the work world. At the same time, cognitive and social research on learning evolved in new directions. Finally, research and development efforts with educational technologies emerged, bringing new concerns, tools, and methods to classroom research. In each of these arenas there was interest in problem solving, multidisciplinary approaches to content learning, social aspects of the learning process, applications of school content to the real world, and development of new tools. Because design embodies these qualities, it became a focus of research.

Policy. At the policy level, standards documents supported the importance of design-based learning experiences. The national science content standards included a strand titled "Science and Technology Standards," which called for students to engage actively in design work, from stating problems to designing solutions and evaluating them. The standards "emphasize abilities associated with the process of design and the fundamental understandings about the enterprise of science and its various linkages with technology" (National Research Council, p. 106). The *Standards for Technological Literacy* included design activities, stating that design is "as fundamental to technology as inquiry is to science and reading is to language arts" (International Technology Education Association, p. 90). Although not pointing directly to design, other standards documents from the National Council of Teachers of Mathematics supported problem solving, modeling, and connecting schoolwork to real applications. The trend to include design was international as well. In a 1996 multinational examination of science, mathematics, and technology curricula in thirteen countries, Paul Black and J. Myron Atkin identified movement toward design-oriented curricula that coincided with the desire of educators to have relevant, applied contexts as well as contexts for students to develop their practical knowledge and understandings. Although the policy call was clear, there was little account of existing school practices and no evidence of their effectiveness.

Design-based curricula. The most comprehensive examination of design-based learning in the United States, a 1997 report by Meredith Davis and colleagues under the umbrella of the National Endowment for the Arts, attempted to find and study design-based curricula to show what teachers and students do in design and the promise it holds for educational reform. The study used an "exploratory, hypothesis-generating approach" because design practices in classrooms were not widespread. Scores of design approaches were discovered and examined. The study's contribution was in providing descriptions of design practice in classrooms and identifying effective models and outcomes for using design. The study emphasized the ways design opens learning opportunities across curriculum subjects for teachers and learners and connects them to the world and a future beyond school.

Designing for Results

Changes took place in what was of interest to study as well as in the ways social and cognitive researchers approached and conducted research. Concerns about the learning goals of schools and their connections to students' futures as citizens and workers interested cognitive and social-learning researchers. Prior research results indicated that, under the right conditions, children were capable of complicated understandings and skills, and more researchers became interested in identifying and understanding learning in practice. This brought researchers out of laboratories and into the rough and tumble of classroom life. Researchers began to connect with teachers and reformers, expanding the goals, methods, and reach of their research. New models of research became established, such as the "design experiment" and "interactive research and design," both less aimed at researching design-based learning and more focused on researchers designing, implementing, studying, and tweaking classroom activities until they achieved sought-after results. Some researchers partnered with teachers to conduct classroom-based cognitive research and to develop tools and curriculum based on research findings that specifically incorporated design.

Middle-School Mathematics through Application Project (MMAP). Research and development of educational technologies became an additional and significant intersection point. Technology and design have a symbiotic relationship. Once technology tools for problem solving were in the hands of teachers and students, design-based activities became a possibility for widespread use. The Middle-School Mathematics through Application Project (MMAP) developed and researched an approach to middle school mathematics that integrated technology as a tool for mathematics learning in the context of design-based projects. Students were introduced to mathematics as they needed it, to solve pre-specified and constrained design problems, such as building a research station in Antarctica or recommending environmental population-control policies. Design contexts were treated as resources for mathematical interaction and explanation, and they led to increasing student engagement with mathematics topics. Design contexts made real-world connections of mathematics obvious to students and gave them situational resources for developing mathematical concepts. Design contexts provided opportunities for problem definition, problem solving, and performance-based assessments.

Jasper Project. The Jasper Project incorporated design-based approaches to upper-elementary mathematics learning with technology. The Jasper series focused on mathematical problem finding and solving, reasoning, communications, and making connections to other content areas for elementary students. The Jasper Project encouraged collaborative activity on extended problems over time, while offering deep understanding of mathematical concepts. Both MMAP and the Jasper Project emphasized the emergent aspects of problem solving and the utilization of various mathematical concepts and skills along the way to solving real-world problems. They both emphasized the roles technologies could play in supporting complex, design-based work in the mathematics curriculum and the supports needed for teacher professional development and assessment.

Yasmin Kafai and Mitchell Resnick bring together research from both school and informal technology, using settings to demonstrate how design activities with games, textile patterns, and robots empower children and connect them to important mathematics and science ideas. They examined subject-matter learning and provided compelling cases for how design processes provide meaningful and productive learning settings.

Learning by Design. Research independent of technology has concentrated on connections between design contexts and content learning, especially in mathematics and science. The Learning by Design project employed design approaches in science learning. The researchers based their work on prior results to create environments for learning science concepts and their applicability through a curriculum focused on "design and build challenges." They studied how, in the context of design work, students gained a conceptual understanding of complex systems and practices and created and field tested pedagogical rituals and processes for making design projects effective.

Modeling. With a concentration in both mathematics and science, work by Richard Lehrer and Leona Schauble investigated students' understanding of modeling, which is central to design work. They studied four schools where teachers were moving away from emphasizing facts and procedures to approaches focusing on constructing, evaluating, and reviewing models. They chronicled the development of models across the K–5 years and outlined key features in teacher professional development. In other analyses, they examined the development of mathematical inscription devices for representing and communicating about data in experiments and designs.

Geometry. Several studies of geometry understanding explored design contexts. In a 1998 study on understanding space, Lehrer, Cathy Jacobson, and colleagues examined how the geometric ideas of transformation and symmetry were developed through a quilt-design activity. They found that quilt design provided students with opportunities to explore ideas of symmetry and transformation and that informal knowledge of drawing and aesthetics played a mutual role in mathematical argumentation and notation. James Middleton and Robert Corbett examined the contexts of engineering and architecture to see if realistic situations helped students develop notions of physical structure that they could in turn connect to their understanding of geometry. Students made toothpick models of geometric solids, tested their strengths, then created suspension bridges and tested their stability. Results were mixed, with conceptions of geometric contributions to stability present but applied naively in designs.

Features of Design-Based Learning under Study by Researchers

A closer look at the features of design ideas and practices reveals what has made them appealing to teachers and researchers and indicates areas for future research. As a collaborative process, design requires discussion and clarification of goals, problems, sub-problems, and actions. Researchers of learning have interests in problem exploration, the development of organizational skills and logic, and the ways they connect to, or enhance, learning of content and concepts.

Once problems and solution constraints are understood, design-based brainstorming encourages participation because it requires students to offer ideas and suggestions for solving problems in the context of a low-pressure forum. This engages students as stakeholders at the start of a complex set of activities. Brainstorming reinforces equity principles by providing for cultural knowledge to be relevant, brought to the table, and consequential for engagement and participation.

Success and inclusion are encouraged because multiple solutions to design problems are sought and appreciated. Variation is an expected outcome of the design experience. Variation in response to problems requires that students keep track of their decisions and provide rationales for them.

The features mentioned, including problem definition, brainstorming, open access to varied solution paths, and collaborative work, provide support for specific discourse processes in the classroom. Discussion, making and testing conjectures, rationales, argumentation, and explanation are necessary. Students must talk about possibilities, resources, and constraints. The more students discuss the problems they are trying to solve, the more they suggest and assess the viability of specific solutions while trafficking in the vocabulary and discourse practices of the discipline, then the more they are learning.

Design work and its tools require students to interact with multiple media and representations of information and data, and these are an increasing focus of research. Students may have to create constraint lists, flowcharts, data tables, graphs, and drawings as they use numbers and number sense, measurement, and both natural language and symbolic formulas while working from problem definition to solution. Researchers recognize the ability and ease with which technologies and media can put multiple representations of problems and processes on the student's desktop.

Research on design-based approaches creates opportunities for studying performance-based assessment practices. Iterative review processes are part of design work, leaving teachers and students with more opportunities for performance-based and peer-based assessment. Elaborating and agreeing on goals, evaluating processes, giving and receiving feedback, and prioritizing and making revisions are practices in design and worthwhile assessment practices as well.

In design, students' work with extended real-world problems connects them to practical professions, such as art, architecture, and engineering. Links are created between the real world and models, between simulations and solution processes, giving students access to practical knowledge and general processes of problem solving.

Finally, design-based learning has examined teacher practices. Evidence from MMAP suggests that the design process has the effect of decentering instruction from the teacher, and provides students with more explanation opportunities, more agency, and a more balanced position of power in relation to their work progress.

Barriers to widespread design-based approaches are also evident. Design-based learning is considered difficult to adopt and implement and remains only a specialized classroom practice. Design-based projects and activities are disruptively different from traditional approaches and perspectives. They impact on "business as usual" in the classroom in terms of management, planning, pedagogy, and content focus, disrupting classroom routines and requiring new kinds of work and attention. They are complex and take extended periods of time, making it necessary to reorganize classroom activity structures.

Design projects place new demands on teachers and students. Teachers need professional development to learn how to structure and manage design-based activities and many of the design-focused research projects also depend on teacher learning and preparation. Design work supports new levels of participation from students as well. Students often make strong connections to their design projects, taking extra time and often working at home. This is a positive effect, with implications for supporting partnerships between school, home, and community, but one that needs to be negotiated.

With collaborative work, emergent, complex problems, and real-world distractions, design projects are difficult to grade. Researchers are working to find ways to articulate standards, assessments, and complex learning environments, such as design projects.

Summary

Design-based approaches to learning have a long-standing place in the K–12 classroom, yet research attention to the role and effects of design-based learning experiences is in its infancy. Recent movements in educational reform, changes in the conduct of social and cognitive research on learning, and the growth of research and development in educational technologies have contributed to design-based learning becoming a topic of interest and inquiry. Current research reports findings from work in the social and cognitive sciences on problem solving, discourse and learning, teaching and learning processes, culture and learning processes, and classroom assessment.

See also: INSTRUCTIONAL DESIGN, *subentries on* ANCHORED INSTRUCTION, CASE-BASED REASONING, PROBLEM-BASED LEARNING.

BIBLIOGRAPHY

BARRON, BRIGID J. 2000. "Achieving Coordination in Collaborative Problem-Solving Groups." *Journal of the Learning Sciences* 9:403–436.

BARRON, BRIGID J.; SCHWARTZ, DANIEL L.; VYE, NANCY J.; MOORE, A.; PETROSINO, ANTHONY; ZECH, LINDA; BRANSFORD, JOHN D.; and COGNITION AND TECHNOLOGY GROUP AT VANDERBILT. 1998. "Doing with Understanding: Lessons from Research on Problem- and Project-Based Learning." *Journal of the Learning Sciences* 7:271–312.

BERG, RICK, and GOLDMAN, SHELLEY. 1996. "Why Design Activities Involve Middle Schoolers in Learning Mathematics." Paper presented at the American Educational Research Association Meeting, New York.

BLACK, PAUL, and ATKIN, J. MYRON, eds. 1996. *Changing the Subject: Innovations in Science, Mathematics and Technology Education.* New York: Routledge.

BOTTRILL, PAULINE. 1995. *Designing and Learning in the Elementary School.* Reston, VA: International Technology Education Association.

BUSHEY, BEVERLY. 1997. "Student Reflection in Emergent Mathematical Activity." Ph.D. diss., Stanford University.

COGNITION AND TECHNOLOGY GROUP AT VANDERBILT. 1997. *The Jasper Project: Lessons in Curriculum, Instruction, Assessment, and Professional Development.* Mahwah, NJ: Erlbaum.

COLE, KAREN; COFFEY, JANET; and GOLDMAN, SHELLEY. 1999. "Using Assessments to Improve Equity in Mathematics Education." *Educational Leadership* 56(6):56–58.

COLLINS, ALLAN. 1990. *Toward a Design Science of Education.* New York: Bank Street College of Education.

DAVIS, MEREDITH. 1998. "Making a Case for Design-Based Learning." *Arts Education Policy Review* 100(2):7–14.

DAVIS, MEREDITH; HAWLEY, PETER; McMULLAN, BERNARD; and SPILKA, GERTRUDE. 1997. *Design as a Catalyst for Learning.* Alexandria, VA: Association for Supervision and Curriculum Design.

DEWEY, JOHN. 1900. *Education and Society.* Chicago: University of Chicago.

GOLDMAN, SHELLEY, and GREENO, JAMES G. 1998. "Thinking Practices: Images of Thinking and Learning in Education." In *Thinking Practices in Mathematics and Science Education,* ed. James G. Greeno and Shelley Goldman. Hillsdale, NJ: Erlbaum.

GOLDMAN, SHELLEY; KNUDSEN, JENNIFER; and LATVALA, MICHELLE. 1998. "Engaging Middle Schoolers in and through Real-World Mathematics." In *Mathematics in the Middle,* ed. Larry Leutzinger. Reston, VA: National Council of Teachers of Mathematics.

GOLDMAN, SHELLEY, and MOSCHKOVICH, JUDIT. 1998. "Technology Environments for Middle School: Embedding Mathematical Activity in Design Projects." In *Proceedings of the ICLS 98: International Conference of the Learning Sciences,* ed. Amy Bruckman et al. Atlanta: Georgia Tech University.

GREENO, JAMES G.; McDERMOTT, RAY; COLE, KAREN; ENGLE, RANDI A.; GOLDMAN, SHELLEY; KNUDSEN, JENNIFER; LAUMAN, BEATRICE; and LINDE, CHARLOTTE. 1999. "Research, Reform, and Aims in Education: Modes of Action in Search of Each Other." In *Issues in Education Research: Problems and Possibilities,* ed. Ellen Lagemann and Lee Shulman. San Francisco: Jossey-Bass.

GREENO, JAMES G., and MIDDLE-SCHOOL MATHEMATICS THROUGH APPLICATIONS PROJECT GROUP. 1997. "Theories and Practices of Thinking and Learning to Think." *American Journal of Education* 106:85–126.

HMELO, CINDY; HOLTON, DOUG; and KOLODNER, JANET. 2000. "Designing to Learn about Complex Systems." *The Journal of the Learning Sciences* 9:247–298.

INTERNATIONAL TECHNOLOGY EDUCATION ASSOCIATION. 2000. *Standards for Technological Literacy: Content for the Study of Technology.* Reston, VA: International Technology Education Association.

KAFAI, YASMIN, and RESNICK, MITCHEL, eds. 2000. *Constructionism in Practice: Designing, Thinking, and Learning in a Digital World.* Mahwah, NJ: Erlbaum.

KATZ, LILLIAN G., and CHARD, SILVIA C. 2000. *Engaging Children's Minds: The Project Approach.* Stamford, CT: Ablex.

KOLODNER, JANET; GRAY, JACQUELYN T.; and BURKS FASSE, BARBARA. 2000. *Promoting Transfer through Case-Based Reasoning: Rituals and Practices in Learning by Design Classrooms.* Atlanta, GA: Georgia Institute of Technology.

LEHRER, RICHARD, and CHAZAN, DANIEL, eds. 1998. *Designing Learning Environments for Developing Understanding of Geometry and Space.* Mahwah, NJ: Erlbaum.

LEHRER, RICHARD; JACOBSON, CATHY; THOYRE, GREG; KEMENY, VERA; STROM, DOLORES; HORVATH, JEFFREY; GANCE, STEPHEN; and KOEHLER, MATTHEW. 1998. "Developing Understanding of Geometry and Space in the Primary Grades." In *Designing Learning Environments for Developing Understanding of Geometry and Space,* ed. Richard Lehrer and Daniel Chazan. Mahwah, NJ: Erlbaum.

LEHRER, RICHARD, and SCHAUBLE, LEONA. 2000. "Modeling in Mathematics and Science." In *Advances in Instructional Psychology: Educational Design and Cognitive Science,* Vol. 5, ed. Robert Glaser. Mahwah, NJ: Erlbaum.

LEHRER, RICAHRD; SCHAUBLE, LEONA; CARPENTER, S.; and PENNER, D. 2000. "The Interrelated Development of Inscriptions and Conceptual Understanding." In *Symbolizing and Communicating in Mathematics Classrooms: Perspectives in Discourse, Tools, and Instructional Design,* ed. Paul Cobb, Eerna Yackel, and Kay McClain. Mahwah, NJ: Erlbaum.

LEHRER, RICHARD; SCHAUBLE, LEONA.; and PETROSINO, ANTHONY. 2001. "Reconsidering the Role of Experimentation in Science Education." In *Designing for Science: Implications from Everyday, Classroom, and Professional Settings,* ed. Kevin Crowley, Christian Schunn, and Takeshi Okada. Mahwah, NJ: Erlbaum.

LICHENSTEIN, GARY; WEISSGLASS, JULIAN; and ERCIKAN-ALPER, KADRIYE. 1998. *Final Evaluation Report: Middle School Mathematics through Applications Project: MMAP II.* Denver, CO: Quality Education Designs.

MIDDLETON, JAMES A., and CORBETT, ROBERT. 1998. "Sixth-Grade Students' Conceptions of Stability in Engineering Contexts." In *Designing Learning Environments for Developing Understanding of Geometry and Space,* ed. Richard Lehrer and Daniel Chazan. Mahwah, NJ: Erlbaum.

NATIONAL COUNCIL OF TEACHERS OF MATHEMATICS. 1989. *Curriculum and Evaluation Standards for School Mathematics.* Reston, VA: National Council of Teachers of Mathematics.

NATIONAL COUNCIL OF TEACHERS OF MATHEMATICS. 2000. *Principles and Standards for School Mathematics.* Reston, VA: National Council of Teachers of Mathematics.

NATIONAL RESEARCH COUNCIL. 1996. *National Science Education Standards.* Washington, DC: National Academy Press.

OWEN-JACKSON, GWYNETH. 2000. *Learning to Teach Design and Technology in the Secondary School: A Companion to School Experience.* New York: Routledge Falmer.

PERKINS, DAVID. 1997. *Design as Knowledge.* Hillsdale, NJ: Erlbaum.

STEVENS, REED. 2000. "Who Counts What as Math? Emergent and Assigned Mathematics Problems in a Project-Based Classroom." In *Multiple Perspectives on Mathematics Teaching and Learning,* ed. Jo Boaler. Westport, CT: Ablex.

TODD, RONALD. 1999. "Design and Technology Yields a New Paradigm for Elementary Schooling." *Journal of Technology Studies* 25(2):26–33.

WATT, DANIEL L. 1998. "Mapping the Classroom Using a CAD Program: Geometry as Applied Mathematics." In *Designing Learning Environments for Understanding of Geometry and Space,* ed. Ricahrd Lehrer and Daniel Chazan. Mahwah, NJ: Erlbaum.

WOLF, DENNIE PALMER, and BARON, JOAN BOYKOFF. 1996. *Performance-Based Assessment: Challenges and Possibilities.* Chicago: University of Chicago Press.

SHELLEY GOLDMAN

PEDAGOGICAL AGENTS AND TUTORS

The creation of pedagogical agents is a fairly new enterprise that has emerged from previous work done in autonomous agents, intelligent tutoring systems, and educational theory. *Pedagogical agents* are autonomous agents that occupy computer learning environments and facilitate learning by interacting with students or other agents. Although intelligent tutoring systems have been around since the 1970s, pedagogical agents did not appear until the late 1980s. Pedagogical agents have been designed to produce a range of behaviors that include the ability to reason about multiple agents in simulated environments; act as a peer, colearner, or competitor; generate multiple, pedagogically appropriate strategies; and assist instructors and students in virtual worlds.

Animated Pedagogical Agents

A new breed of pedagogical agents has begun to appear in learning environments and on websites: *animated* pedagogical agents. The advent of animated pedagogical agents is the result of recent advancements in multimedia interfaces, text-to-speech software, and agent-generation technologies. Some of the more high-profile systems are described below.

- ALI is an automated laboratory instructor that monitors and guides undergraduates as they solve problems while interacting with chemistry simulations.
- ADELE (Agent for Distance Learning–Light Edition) helps students work through problem-solving exercises for courses that are delivered over the Internet. ADELE-based courses have been developed for continuing medical education and geriatric dentistry.
- AutoTutor simulates the dialogue moves of human tutors while participating in conversations with students. AutoTutor is currently designed to help college students learn about topics in computer literacy and conceptual physics.
- Cosmo exploits deictic behaviors to offer problem-solving advice to students learning about network routing mechanisms in the Internet Advisor learning environment.

- Herman the Bug inhabits the Design-A-Plant learning environment and helps children learn about botanical anatomy and physiology.
- PPP Persona provides online help instructions while helping users navigate through web-based materials.
- STEVE (Soar Training Expert for Virtual Environments) interacts with learners in an immersive virtual environment and has been used in naval training tasks such as operating engines on U.S. Navy surface ships.
- Vincent helps workers in shoemaking factories learn about production-line control time.

These agents exhibit lifelike behaviors and have the potential to bolster student-learning outcomes by exploiting both the auditory and visual channels of the learner. In general, animated pedagogical agents are lifelike personas, which execute behaviors that involve emotive responses, interactive communication, and effective pedagogy.

Emotive responses. Clark Elliott, Jeff Rickel, and James Lester argue in their 1999 article that animated agents displaying appropriate emotions provide a number of educational benefits to learners. First, agents that appear to care about students' progress may convince students to care about their own progress. Second, agents that are sensitive to learners' emotions (e.g., boredom or frustration) can provide feedback that prevents students from losing interest. Third, agents that convey enthusiasm for the subject matter are more likely to evoke the same enthusiasm in learners. Finally, agents that have rich and interesting personalities make learning more enjoyable for the learner.

Agents can display appropriate emotions through facial expressions, gestures, locomotion, and intonation variations. For example, Cosmo uses a recorded human voice and full-body emotive behaviors to express a wide range of pedagogically appropriate emotions. When a student experiences success in the Internet Advisor learning environment, Cosmo may applaud, point to relevant information on the screen, and provide positive feedback (e.g., "You chose the fastest subnet. Also, it has low traffic. Fabulous!"). Another system, AutoTutor, synchronizes facial expressions and intonation variations to provide feedback that reflects the quality of students' natural language contributions. If a student provides a good answer to a question, AutoTutor may respond simultaneously with an enthusiastic

"Okay!" a fast head nod, and a smile. However, if the student's answer is only partially correct, AutoTutor may respond with a less enthusiastic "Okay," a slower head nod, and no smile.

Interactive communication. Most educational websites and software packages are designed to be mere information delivery devices that occasionally employ unsophisticated reward systems as metrics of student understanding. Pedagogical agents, however, facilitate interaction in learning environments and force students to be active participants in the learning process. Agents and learners can collaboratively perform tasks, solve problems, and construct explanations. STEVE, the agent that teaches procedural knowledge involved in operating engines on navy ships, demonstrates for learners how to perform tasks and solve problems. A learner may choose to intervene and finish the demonstration. When this happens, STEVE monitors the learner's actions and a mixed-initiative demonstration occurs. Specifically, learners can take the initiative by asking questions or performing actions, or STEVE can mediate the interaction by providing hints, asking questions, giving feedback, or demonstrating a task. Learning sessions with ADELE are interactive in that ADELE interrupts students when "she" detects student errors and suggests alternative actions to be performed instead (e.g., "Before ordering a chest X ray, it would be helpful to listen to the condition of the lungs."). Students who reach impasses during problem solving may receive hints and ask "why" questions while interacting with ADELE and STEVE. In other systems, such as AutoTutor, the agent and student have a conversation with each other. Throughout the conversation, AutoTutor simulates human-tutor-dialogue moves (e.g., hints, prompts, assertions, and corrections), which allow the agent and student to jointly construct answers and explanations to deep-reasoning problems.

Effective pedagogy. In order to be considered value-added entities of learning environments, pedagogical agents must be effective teachers and, therefore, adaptive and dynamic in their teaching strategies. They must be able to adjust their teaching to fit a particular problem state or learning scenario, and they must be capable of adjusting their pedagogy to accommodate students' knowledge and ability levels. Pedagogical agents should be able to ask and answer questions, provide hints and explanations, monitor students' understanding, provide appropriate feedback, and keep track of what has been covered in the learning session. All of the pedagogical agents mentioned above are, to some extent, capable of each of these functions. Of course the litmus test for any pedagogical agent is whether it produces positive student-learning outcomes.

Learning Outcomes

It has been well documented that users prefer learning environments with animated agents over those that do not have agents. Specifically, participants assigned to learning conditions with animated agents (even ones that are not particularly expressive) perceive their learning experiences to be considerably more positive than participants assigned to learning conditions that do not include animated agents. This recurring finding is known as the *persona effect*. The persona effect is somewhat enigmatic in that it generally is not related to student outcome or performance measures. That is, most researchers who report evidence of the persona effect also report no differences between agent and no-agent conditions for retention and learning measures.

Several recent empirical studies, however, indicate that pedagogical agents do promote learning on both retention and transfer tasks. Robert Atkinson reported that students who received explanations from an animated agent about how to solve proportion word problems outperformed other learning conditions on both near and far transfer problems. In a study conducted by Roxana Moreno et al., college students and seventh graders attempted to learn about how to design plants that could survive in a number of different environments. One group of students interacted with a pedagogical agent, Herman the Bug, while another group of students received identical graphics and textual explanations but no pedagogical agent. The results indicated that students in the pedagogical agent condition outperformed students in the no-agent condition on transfer tests but not on retention tests. In another study, Natalie Person et al. (2001) reported that the effect size for AutoTutor was .6 compared to the other learning conditions; human tutoring studies typically report effect sizes around .5 compared to other learning controls. Given the results of these learning-outcome studies and the fact that learners perceive their interactions with agents quite favorably, the future for pedagogical agents looks quite promising.

See also: COOPERATIVE AND COLLABORATIVE LEARNING; PEER RELATIONS AND LEARNING; TECHNOLOGY IN EDUCATION, *subentry on* TRENDS.

BIBLIOGRAPHY

ANDRÉ, ELISABETH; RIST, THOMAS; and MÜLLER, JOCHEN. 1998. "Integrating Reactive and Scripted Behaviors in a Life-Like Presentation Agent." In *Proceedings of the Second International Conference on Autonomous Agents.* Minneapolis-St. Paul, MN: ACM Press.

BAYLOR, AMY L. 2001. "Investigating Multiple Pedagogical Perspectives through MIMIC (Multiple Intelligent Mentors Instructing Collaboratively)." In *Artificial Intelligence in Education: AI-ED in the Wired and Wireless Future,* ed. Johanna D. Moore, Carol L. Redfield, and W. Lewis Johnson. Amsterdam: IOS Press.

CARBONELL, JAMIE R. 1970. "AI in CAI: An Artificial Intelligence Approach to Computer-Assisted Instruction." *IEEE Transactions on Man-Machine Systems* 11:190–202.

CASSELL, JUSTINE; PELACHAUD, CATHERINE, BADLER, NORMAN; STEEDMAN, MARK; ACHORN, BRETT; BECKET, TRIPP; DOUVILLE, BRETT; PREVOST, SCOTT; and STONE, MATTHEW. 1994. "Animated Conversation: Rule-Based Generation of Facial Expression, Gesture and Spoken Intonation for Multiple Conversational Agents." *Computational Graphics* 28:413–420.

CHAN, TAK-WEIL. 1996. "Learning Companion Systems, Social Learning Systems, and the Global Social Learning Club." *Journal of Artificial Intelligence in Education* 7:125–159.

CHAN, TAK-WEIL, and BASKIN, ARTHUR B. 1990. "Learning Companion Systems." In *Intelligent Tutoring Systems: At the Crossroads of Artificial Intelligence in Education,* ed. Claude Frasson and Gilles Gauthier.

DILLENBOURG, PIERRE; JERMANN, PATRICK; SCHNEIDER, DANIEL; TRAUM, DAVID; and BUIU, CATALIN. 1997. "The Design of MOO Agents: Implications from an Empirical CSCW Study." In *Proceedings of Eighth World Conference on Artificial Intelligence in Education,* ed. Ben du Boulay and Riichiro Mizoguchi. Amsterdam: IOS Press.

D'SOUZA, AARON; RICKEL, JEFF; HERREROS, BRUNO; and JOHNSON, W. LEWIS. 2001. "An Automated Lab Instructor for Simulated Science Experiments." In *Artificial Intelligence in Education: AI-ED in the Wired and Wireless Future,* ed. Johanna D. Moore, Carol L. Redfield, and W. Lewis Johnson. Amsterdam: IOS Press.

ELLIOTT, CLARK; RICKEL, JEFF; and LESTER, JAMES CARL. 1999. "Lifelike Pedagogical Agents and Affective Computing: An Exploratory Synthesis." In *Artificial Intelligence Today,* ed. Michael Wooldridge and Manuela Veloso. Berlin: Springer-Verlag.

FRASSON, CLAUDE; MANGELLE, THIERRY; and AIMEUR, ESMA. 1997. "Using Pedagogical Agents in a Multi-Strategic Intelligent Tutoring System." In *Proceedings of the AI-Ed '97 Workshop on Pedagogical Agents.* Amsterdam: IOS Press.

FRASSON, CLAUDE; MANGELLE, THIERRY; AIMEUR, ESMA; and GOUARDERES, GUY. 1996. "An Actor-Based Architecture for Intelligent Tutoring Systems." In *Proceedings of the Third International Conference on Intelligent Tutoring Systems, LNCS.* Berlin: Springer-Verlag.

GRAESSER, ARTHUR C.; HU, XIANGEN; SUSARLA, SURESH; HARTER, DEREK; PERSON, NATALIE K.; LOUWERSE, MAX; OLDE, BRENT; and TUTORING RESEARCH GROUP. 2001. "AutoTutor: An Intelligent Tutor and Conversational Tutoring Scaffold." In *Artificial Intelligence in Education: AI-ED in the Wired and Wireless Future,* ed. Johanna D. Moore, Carol L. Redfield, and W. Lewis Johnson. Amsterdam: IOS Press.

GRAESSER, ARTHUR C.; PERSON, NATALIE K.; HARTER, DEREK; and TUTORING RESEARCH GROUP. 2000. "Tactics in Tutoring in AutoTutor." In *ITS 2000 Proceedings of the Workshop on Modeling Human Teaching Tactics and Strategies.* Montreal, Canada: Springer-Verlag.

JOHNSON, W. LEWIS, and RICKEL, JEFF. 1998. "STEVE: An Animated Pedagogical Agent for Procedural Training in Virtual Environments." *SIGART Bulletin* 8:16–21.

JOHNSON, W. LEWIS; RICKEL, JEFF; and LESTER, JAMES C. 2000. "Animated Pedagogical Agents: Face-to-Face Interaction in Interactive Learning Environments." *International Journal of Artificial Intelligence in Education* 11:47–78.

LESTER, JAMES C.; CONVERSE, SHAROLYN A.; KAHLER, SUSAN E.; BARLOW, S. TODD; STONE, BRIAN A.; and BHOGAL, RAVINDER S. 1997. "The Persona Effect: Affective Impact of Animated Pedagogical Agents." In *Proceedings of CHI 1997.* Atlanta, GA: ACM Press.

LESTER, JAMES C.; VOERMAN, JENNIFER L.; TOWNS, STUART G.; and CALLAWAY, CHARLES B. 1999.

"Deictic Believability: Coordinating Gesture, Locomotion, and Speech in Life-Like Pedagogical Agents." *Applied Artificial Intelligence* 13:383–414.

LOYALL, A. BRYAN, and BATES, JOSEPH. 1997. "Personality-Rich Believable Agents That Use Language." In *Proceedings of the First International Conference on Autonomous Agents.* Marina del Rey, CA: ACM.

MARSELLA, STACY C., and JOHNSON, W. LEWIS. 1997. "An Instructor's Assistant for Team-Teaching in Dynamic Multi-Agent Virtual Worlds." In *Proceedings of the Fourth International Conference on Intelligent Tutoring Systems, LNCS.* Berlin: Springer-Verlag.

MORENO, ROXANA; MAYER, RICHARD E.; SPIRES, HILLER A.; and LESTER, JAMES C. 2001. "The Case for Social Agency in Computer-Based Teaching: Do Students Learn More Deeply When They Interact with Animated Pedagogical Agents?" *Cognition and Instruction* 19:177–213.

PAIVA, ANA, and MACHADO, ISABEL. 1998. "Vincent, an Autonomous Pedagogical Agent for on-the-Job Training." In *Intelligent Tutoring Systems,* ed. Valerie Shute. Berlin: Springer-Verlag.

PERSON, NATALIE K.; CRAIG, SCOTTY; PRICE, PENELOPE; HU, XIANGEN; GHOLSON, BARRY; GRAESSER, ARTHUR C.; and TUTORING RESEARCH GROUP. 2000. "Incorporating Human-Like Conversational Behaviors into AutoTutor." In *Agents 2000 Proceedings of the Workshop on Achieving Human-like Behavior in the Interactive Animated Agents.* Barcelona, Spain.

PERSON, NATALIE K.; GRAESSER, ARTHUR C.; KREUZ, ROGER J.; POMEROY, VICTORIA; and TUTORING RESEARCH GROUP. 2001. "Simulating Human Tutor Dialog Moves in AutoTutor." *International Journal of Artificial Intelligence in Education* 12:23–29.

PERSON, NATALIE K.; KLETTKE, BIANCA; LINK, KRISTEN; KREUZ, ROGER J.; and TUTORING RESEARCH GROUP. 1999. "The Integration of Affective Responses into AutoTutor." In *Proceedings of the International Workshop on Affect in Interactions.* Siena, Italy: Springer-Verlag.

RICKEL, JEFF, and JOHNSON, W. LEWIS. 1999. "Animated Agents for Procedural Training in Virtual Reality: Perception, Cognition, and Motor Control." *Applied Artificial Intelligence* 13:343–382.

SHAW, ERIN; GANESHAN, RAJARAM; JOHNSON, W. LEWIS; and MILLAR, DOUGLAS. 1999. "Building a Case for Agent-Assisted Learning As a Catalyst for Curriculum Reform in Medical Education." In *Proceedings of the International Conference on Artificial Intelligence in Education.* Berlin: Springer-Verlag.

SHAW, ERIN; JOHNSON, W. LEWIS; and GANESHAN, RAJARAM. 1999. "Pedagogical Agents on the Web." In *Proceedings of the Third International Conference on Autonomous Agents.* New York: ACM Press.

SLEEMAN, DEREK, and BROWN, JOHN, eds. 1982. "Intelligent Tutoring Systems." New York: Academic Press.

TOWNS, STUART G.; CALLAWAY, CHARLES B.; VOERMAN, JENNIFER L.; and LESTER, JAMES C. 1998. "Coherent Gesture, Locomotion, and Speech in Life-Like Pedagogical Agents." *IUI '98: International Conference on Intelligent User Interfaces.* New York: ACM Press.

WENGER, ETIENNE. 1987. *Artificial Intelligence and Tutoring Systems: Computational and Cognitive Approaches to the Communication of Knowledge.* Los Altos, CA: Morgan Kaufmann.

NATALIE K. PERSON
ARTHUR C. GRAESSER

PROBLEM-BASED LEARNING

Problem-based learning (PBL) is one of a class of instructional methods that situates learning in complex contexts. In PBL, students learn through guided experience in solving complex, open-ended problems, such as medical diagnosis or designing a playground. Developed by Howard Barrows for use in medical schools, it has expanded to other settings such as teacher education and K–12 instruction.

Problem-based learning was designed with five goals: to help students (1) construct flexible knowledge; (2) develop effective problem-solving skills; (3) develop self-directed learning skills; (4) become effective collaborators; and (5) become motivated to learn.

With its emphasis on learning through problem solving and on making key aspects of expertise visible, PBL exemplifies the cognitive apprenticeship model. In this model, knowledge is constructed by learners working on real-world problems. One key characteristic that distinguishes PBL from other cognitive apprenticeship approaches is its potential for covering an entire integrated curriculum through a well-chosen set of problems. Concepts and thinking skills are used in a variety of problems. This redundancy affords learners the opportunity to construct a deep understanding by revisiting concepts from many perspectives and by experiencing a variety of situations in which skills are applied.

The Problem-Based Learning Tutorial Process

A PBL tutorial session begins by presenting a group, typically 5 to 7 students, with a small amount of information about a complex problem. From the outset, students question the facilitator to obtain additional problem information; they may also gather facts by doing experiments or other research. At several points, students pause to reflect on the data they have collected so far and generate questions about that data and ideas about solutions. Students identify concepts they need to learn more about to solve the problem (i.e., learning issues). After considering the case with their existing knowledge, students divide up and independently research the learning issues they identified. They then regroup to share what they learned, and reconsider their ideas. When completing the task, they reflect on the problem to consider the lessons learned, as well as how they performed as self-directed learners and collaborative problem solvers.

While working, students use white boards to help guide their problem solving. The white board is divided into four columns to help them record where they have been and where they are going. The columns help remind the learners of the problem-solving process. The white board serves as a focus for group deliberations. Figure 1 shows an example of white board entries made by engineering students working on a chemical release problem. The *Facts* column holds information that the students obtained from the problem statement. The *Ideas* column serves to keep track of their evolving hypotheses about solutions, such as reducing the storage of hazardous chemicals. The students place their questions for further study into the *Learning Issues* column. They use the *Action Plan* column to keep track of plans for resolving the problem or obtaining additional information.

The Role of the Problem

Cognitive research and experience with PBL suggest that to foster learning, good problems have several

FIGURE 1

The problem-based learning tutorial process

Examples of white-board entries used by engineering students solving a chemical release problem.

Facts	Ideas	Learning Issues	Action Plan
Hazardous chemical	Minimize onsite storage	What are the safety standards for cyanide storage?	Call FPA to find out standards
Near population center	Provide safety training		
	Improve early warning systems	What technology is available to safely store hazardous chemicals?	

SOURCE: Courtesy of author.

characteristics. Problems need to be complex and open ended; they must be realistic and connect with the students' experiences. Good problems require multidisciplinary solutions and provide feedback that allows students to evaluate the effectiveness of their knowledge, reasoning, and learning strategies. Problems should promote conjecture and discussion and should motivate the students' need to go out and learn. As students generate and defend their ideas, they publicly articulate their current understanding, thus enhancing knowledge construction and setting the stage for future learning.

Each problem requires a final product or performance that allows the students to demonstrate their understanding. For example, PBL has been used to help middle school students learn life science by designing artificial lungs. They conducted experiments and used a variety of other resources to learn about breathing. Their final products were models of their designs.

The Role of the Facilitator

The term *facilitator* refers to someone trained to facilitate student learning through PBL. In PBL facilitators are expert learners, able to model good learning and thinking strategies, rather than being content experts. The facilitator is responsible for moving students through the various stages of PBL and for monitoring the group process—ensuring that all students are involved and encouraging them to externalize their own thinking and to comment on each other's thinking. The facilitator plays an important role in modeling the thinking skills needed when self-assessing reasoning and understanding. For example, the facilitator encourages students to explain and justify their thinking as they propose solutions to problems. Their questions help model the use of hypothetical-deductive reasoning as they encourage students to tie inquiry to their hypotheses. Facilitators progressively fade their scaffolding as students become more experienced with PBL, until their questioning role is largely adopted by the students. However, they continue to actively monitor the group, making moment-to-moment decisions about how to facilitate the PBL process.

Collaborative Learning in Problem-Based Learning

Collaborative problem-solving groups are a key feature of PBL. Its small group structure helps distribute the work among the members of the group, taking advantage of individual strengths by allowing the whole group to tackle problems that would normally be too difficult for any student alone. Students often become experts in particular topics. Small group discussions and debate enhance higher-order thinking and promote shared knowledge construction.

Reflection in Problem-Based Learning

Reflection on the relation between doing and learning is needed to help the learners understand that the tasks they are doing are in the service of the questions they have asked and that these questions arise from the learning goals they have set. Thus, each task is not an end in itself but a means to achieve a self-defined learning goal.

One potential danger of PBL is that knowledge may become bound to the problem in which it is learned. Learners need to understand what principles are at play in a given task and further understand how those principles might apply to new problems. To avoid this difficulty, learners must use concepts and thinking skills in multiple problems and to reflect on their learning. Reflection is important in helping students (1) relate their new knowledge to prior understanding; (2) mindfully abstract knowledge; and (3) understand how the strategies might be applied in new situations. Problem-based learning incorporates reflection throughout the tutorial process and when completing a problem. As students make inferences that tie the general concepts and skills to the specifics of the problem that they are working on, they construct more coherent understanding. The facilitator-guided reflection helps students prepare to take what Gavriel Salomon and David Perkins, in their 1989 study, call the "high road" to transfer as they consider how their new knowledge might be useful in the future and the effectiveness of their learning and problem-solving strategies.

Empirical Support for Problem-Based Learning

Research results are converging to show that some of these goals have been successfully met. Students in problem-based curricula are more likely to use their knowledge during problem solving and to transfer higher-order thinking skills to new situations. Cindy Hmelo has studied PBL in medical students and found that when asked to provide an explanation for a patient problem, the students in problem-based curricula were more accurate in their diagnoses, more likely to apply scientific concepts, and constructed better quality explanations than students in traditional curricula. This study provides evidence that PBL students transfer their knowledge and strategies to new problems. Shelagh Gallagher and William Stepien have studied the effects of PBL on gifted high school students. In one study, they examined the effect of a PBL intervention on content knowledge in social studies and found that students in PBL learned as much content as students in traditional instruction. In another study Gallagher, Stepien, and Hilary Rosenthal, comparing students taking a PBL science and society elective with students taking other classes, found that PBL students became better at problem-finding than comparison students. Most studies of PBL have been conducted either in medical schools or in other highly selected populations such as gifted high school students, but Hmelo, Douglas Holton, and Janet Kolodner conducted a 2000 preliminary study with middle school students learning life science. The students in the PBL intervention learned more than a comparison class, but because the students were not actually able to get feedback by implementing their solution, they did not achieve as deep an understanding as the investigators had expected.

Conclusion

Problem-based learning was designed to help students become flexible thinkers. Although the research on PBL is promising, the effects of PBL need to be examined more widely. The challenge ahead lies in understanding how the potential of PBL can be harnessed in diverse settings. Understanding the nature of the tutorial process, including the role of the problem and facilitator, collaboration among peers, and the importance of student reflection is necessary to successfully implement PBL and to prepare students to think in the world beyond school.

See also: INSTRUCTIONAL DESIGN, *subentries on* ANCHORED INSTRUCTION, CASE-BASED LEARNING, LEARNING THROUGH DESIGN.

BIBLIOGRAPHY

BARROWS, HOWARD S. 1985. *How to Design a Problem-Based Curriculum for the Preclinical Years.* New York: Springer

BLUMENFELD, PHYLLIS C.; MARX, RONALD W.; SOLOWAY, ELLIOT; and KRAJCIK, JOSEPH S. 1996. "Learning with Peers: From Small Group Cooperation to Collaborative Communities." *Educational Researcher* 25(8):37–40.

CHI, MICHELINE T. H.; BASSOK, MIRIAM; LEWIS, MATTHEW W.; REIMANN, PETER; and GLASER, ROBERT. 1989. "Self-Explanations: How Students Study and Use Examples in Learning to Solve Problems." *Cognitive Science* 13:145–182.

COLLINS, ALLAN; BROWN, JOHN SEELY; and NEWMAN, SUSAN E. 1989. "Cognitive Apprenticeship: Teaching the Crafts of Reading, Writing, and Mathematics." In *Knowing, Learning, and Instruction: Essays in Honor of Robert Glaser,* ed. Lauren B. Resnick. Hillsdale, NJ: Erlbaum.

GALLAGHER, SHELAGH A., and STEPIEN, WILLIAM J. 1996. "Content Acquisition in Problem-Based Learning: Depth Versus Breadth in American Studies." *Journal for the Education of the Gifted* 19:257–275.

GALLAGHER, SHELAGH A.; STEPIEN, WILLIAM J.; and ROSENTHAL, HILARY. 1992. "The Effects of Problem-Based Learning on Problem Solving." *Gifted Child Quarterly* 36:195–200.

HMELO, CINDY E. 1998. "Cognitive Consequences of PBL for the Early Development of Medical Expertise." *Teaching and Learning in Medicine* 10:92–100.

HMELO, CINDY E. 1998. "Problem-Based Learning: Effects on the Early Acquisition of Cognitive Skill in Medicine." *Journal of the Learning Sciences* 7:173–208.

HMELO, CINDY E.; HOLTON, DOUGLAS; and KOLODNER, JANET L. 2000. "Designing to Learn About Complex Systems." *Journal of the Learning Sciences* 9:247–298.

HMELO, CINDY E., and LIN, XIAODONG. 2000. "Becoming Self-Directed Learners: Strategy Development in Problem-Based Learning." In *Problem-Based Learning: A Research Perspective on Learning Interactions,* ed. Dorothy H. Evensen and Cindy E. Hmelo. Mahwah, NJ: Erlbaum.

KOLODNER, JANET L.; HMELO, CINDY E.; and NARAYANAN, N. HARI. 1996. "Problem-Based Learning Meets Case-Based Reasoning." In *Proceedings of the Second International Conference of the Learning Sciences,* ed. Daniel C. Edelson and Eric A. Domeshek. Charlottesville, VA: Association for the Advancement of Computing Education.

KOSCHMANN, TIMOTHY D.; MYERS, ANN C.; FELTOVICH, PAUL J.; and BARROWS, HOWARD S. 1994. "Using Technology to Assist in Realizing Effective Learning and Instruction: A Principled Approach to the Use of Computers in Collaborative Learning." *Journal of the Learning Sciences* 3:225–262.

SALOMON, GAVRIEL, and PERKINS, DAVID N. 1989. "Rocky Roads to Transfer: Rethinking Mechanisms of a Neglected Phenomenon." *Educational Psychologist* 24:113–142.

TORP, LINDA, and SAGE, SARA. 1998. *Problems As Possibilities: Problem-Based Learning for K–12 Education.* Alexandria, VA: Association for Supervision and Curriculum Development.

WILLIAMS, SUSAN M.; BRANSFORD, JOHN D.; VYE, NANCY J.; GOLDMAN, SUSAN R.; and CARLSON, KRISTEN. 1993. "Positive and Negative Effects of Specific Knowledge on Mathematical Problem Solving." Paper presented at the American Educational Research Association annual meeting, Atlanta, Georgia.

CINDY E. HMELO-SILVER

INSTRUCTIONAL DESIGN AND COMPUTER-ASSISTED INSTRUCTION

See: TECHNOLOGY IN EDUCATION, *subentry on* CURRENT TRENDS.

INSTRUCTIONAL OBJECTIVES

Most people would agree that the goal of education is learning. Most would also agree that education is likely to be more effective if educators are clear about what it is that they want the learners to learn. Finally, most would agree that if teachers have a clear idea about what learners are expected to learn, they can more easily and more accurately determine how well students have learned.

Enter instructional objectives. Because instructional objectives specify exactly what is supposed to be learned, they are helpful to the teacher as well as the learner throughout the learning process and are invaluable in the evaluation process.

Instructional objectives (also known as *behavioral objectives* or *learning objectives*) are basically statements which clearly describe an anticipated learning outcome. When objectives were first coming into their own in education, they almost always began with the phrase: "Upon completion of this lesson, the student should be able to . . . ." This phrase focused on the outcome of learning rather than on the learning process. In fact, one of the criteria for a well-written objective is that it describe the outcome of learning, that is, what the learners can do after learning has occurred that they might not have been able to do before the teaching and learning process began.

Characteristics of a Well-Written Objective

A well-written objective should meet the following criteria: (1) describe a learning outcome, (2) be student oriented, (3) be observable (or describe an observable product).

A well-written objective should describe a learning outcome (e.g., to correctly spell the spelling words on page seventeen). It should not describe a learning activity (e.g., to practice the words on page seventeen by writing each one ten times). Learning activities are important in planning and guiding instruction but they are not to be confused with instructional objectives.

A student-oriented objective focuses on the learner, not on the teacher. It describes what the learner will be expected to be able to do. It should not describe a teacher activity (e.g., to go over the words on page seventeen with the students, explaining their meaning and telling them how the words are pronounced). It may be helpful to both the teacher and the student to know what the teacher is going to do but teacher activities are also not to be confused with instructional objectives.

If an instructional objective is not observable (or does not describe an observable product), it leads to unclear expectations and it will be difficult to determine whether or not it had been reached. The key to writing observable objectives is to use verbs that are observable and lead to a well defined product of the action implied by that verb. Verbs such as "to know," "to understand," "to enjoy," "to appreciate," "to realize," and "to value" are vague and not observable. Verbs such as "to identify," "to list," "to select," "to compute," "to predict," and "to analyze" are explicit and describe observable actions or actions that lead to observable products.

There are many skills that cannot be directly observed. The thinking processes of a student as she tries to solve a math problem cannot be easily observed. However, one can look at the answers she comes up with and determine if they are correct. It is also possible to look at the steps a student takes to arrive at an answer if they are written down (thus displaying his thinking process). There are many end products that also can be observed (e.g., an oil painting, a prose paragraph, a 3-dimensional map, or an outline.)

Characteristics of a Useful Objective

To be useful for instruction, an objective must not only be well written but it also must meet the following criteria: (1) be sequentially appropriate; (2) be attainable within a reasonable amount of time; (3) be developmentally appropriate.

For an objective to be sequentially appropriate it must occur in an appropriate place in the instructional sequence. All prerequisite objectives must already have been attained. Nothing thwarts the learning process more than having learners trying to accomplish an objective before they have learned the necessary prerequisites. This is why continuous assessment of student progress is so important.

A useful objective is attainable within a reasonable time. If an instructional objective takes students an inordinately long time to accomplish, it is either sequentially inappropriate or it is too broad, relying on the accomplishment of several outcomes or skills rather than a single outcome or skill. An objective should set expectations for a single learning outcome and not a cluster of them.

Developmentally appropriate objectives set expectations for students that are well within their level of intellectual, social, language, or moral development. Teachers, parents, and others who are working with preschool or elementary school children should be especially aware of the developmental stages of the children they are working with. No author or researcher has more clearly defined the stages of intellectual development than Jean Piaget. Familiarity with his work as well as with the work of other child development specialists (e.g., Lev Vygotsky's language development, Lawrence Kohlberg's moral development and Erik Erikson's social development) should produce better instructional objectives.

Kinds of Instructional Objectives

Instructional objectives are often classified according to the kind or level of learning that is required in order to reach them. There are numerous taxonomies of instructional objectives; the most common taxonomy was developed by Benjamin Bloom and his colleagues. The first level of the taxonomy divides objectives into three categories: cognitive, affective, and psychomotor. Simply put, cognitive objectives focus on the mind; affective objectives focus on emotions or affect; and psychomotor objectives focus on the body.

Cognitive objectives call for outcomes of mental activity such as memorizing, reading, problem solving, analyzing, synthesizing, and drawing conclusions. Bloom and others further categorize cognitive objectives into various levels from the simplest cognitive tasks to the most complex cognitive task. These categories can be helpful when trying to order objectives so they are sequentially appropriate. This helps to insure that prerequisite outcomes are accomplished first.

Affective objectives focus on emotions. Whenever a person seeks to learn to react in an appropriate way emotionally, there is some thinking going on. What distinguishes affective objectives from cognitive objectives is the fact that the goal of affective objectives is some kind of affective behavior or the product of an affect (e.g., an attitude). The goal of cognitive objectives, on the other hand, is some kind of cognitive response or the product of a cognitive response (e.g., a problem solved).

Psychomotor objectives focus on the body and the goal of these objectives is the control or manipulation of the muscular skeletal system or some part of it (e.g., dancing, writing, tumbling, passing a ball, and drawing). All skills requiring fine or gross motor coordination fall into the psychomotor category. To learn a motor skill requires some cognition. However, the ultimate goal is not the cognitive aspects of the skill such as memorizing the steps to take. The ultimate goal is the control of muscles or muscle groups.

The Role of Objectives in Teaching and Testing

Objectives can be helpful in instructional planning, during the teaching/learning process, and when assessing student progress. Instructional objectives are often either ignored (by both teachers and students) or are, at best, occasionally referred to. However, it can be argued that instructional objectives should guide the teaching and learning process from beginning to end.

Most lesson plan forms include a place for the objectives of the lesson to be recorded. However, to write an objective down and then to plan the lesson around the topic of the lesson rather than around the learning outcomes to be reached is missing the point. There is good evidence in the human learning literature that different kinds of outcomes are learned differently. Robert Gagné was one of the first researchers to articulate this; it follows from his research that instructional planning must take into account the kind of learning the students will be engaged in as they seek to reach an objective. Effective teachers learn to categorize their instructional objectives and then develop the teaching and learning activities that will help students do the kind of thinking required for that kind of learning.

It's time to evaluate. How does an educator know what to measure? Look at the objectives. How does a teacher know what kind of information gathering tools to use (test, rubric, portfolio)? Study the objectives. Any test item, any rating scale or checklist, any technique devised to collect information about student progress must seek to measure the instructional objectives as directly and as simply as possible. Instructional objectives are an extremely valuable teaching tool that guide both teachers and students through the teaching and learning process.

See also: ASSESSMENT, *subentry on* PERFORMANCE ASSESSMENT; INSTRUCTIONAL DESIGN, *subentry on* OVERVIEW; STANDARDS FOR STUDENT LEARNING.

BIBLIOGRAPHY

ANDERSON, LORIN W., KRATHWOHL, DAVID R., and BLOOM, BENJAMIN SAMUEL, eds. 2000. *Taxonomy for Learning, Teaching, and Assessing: A Revision of Bloom's Taxonomy of Educational Objectives.* White Plains, NY: Longman.

COOPER, JAMES M., ed. 1999. *Classroom Teaching Skills,* 6th edition. Boston, MA: Houghton Mifflin Company.

DICK, WALTER; CAREY, LOU; and CAREY, JAMES O. 2001. *The Systematic Design of Instruction,* 5th edition. Boston, MA: Addison Wesley.

DUCHASTEL, P. 1977. "Functions of Instructional Objectives: Organization and Direction." ERIC Clearing House No: SP010829. Paper presented at the American Educational Research Association, New York, April 4–8.

ERIKSON, ERIK H. 1968. *Identity: Youth and Crisis.* New York: Norton.

GAGNÉ, ROBERT MILLS. 1985. *The Conditions of Learning,* 4th edition. New York: Holt, Rinehart and Winston.

KOHLBERG, LAWRENCE. 1969. "Stage and Sequence: The Cognitive-Developmental Approach to Socialization." In *Handbook of Socialization Theory and Research,* ed. David A. Goslin. Chicago: Rand McNally.

MAGER, ROBERT FRANK. 1997. *Preparing Instructional Objectives: A Critical Tool in the Development of Effective Instruction.* Atlanta, GA: Center for Effective Performance Press.

PIAGET, JEAN. 1958. *The Growth of Logical Thinking from Childhood to Adolescence,* trans. Anne Parsons and Stanley Milgram. New York: Basic Books.

STUART, J., and BURNS, R.W. 1984. "The Thinking Process: A Proposed Instructional Objectives Classification Scheme." *Technology* 24 7:21–26.

VYGOTSKY, LEV. 1962. *Thought and Language.* Cambridge, MA: MIT Press.

TERRY D. TENBRINK

INSTRUCTIONAL STRATEGIES

Since the inception of formal, classroom-based instruction, a fundamental aspect of teaching has been the way teachers arrange the classroom environment so students can interact and learn. The instructional strategies teachers use help shape learning environments and represent professional conceptions of learning and of the learner. Some strategies consider students empty vessels to be filled under the firm direction of the teacher; other strategies regard them as active participants learning through inquiry and problem solving—still others tell children they are social organisms learning through dialogue and interaction with others.

History

The instructional strategies used in the early twenty-first century began in antiquity. In ancient Greece, Socrates illustrated a questioning strategy intended to facilitate the learner's independent discovery of important truths. An instructional strategy similar to direct instruction was reported by Samuel Griswold Goodwich's account of teaching in a rural Connecticut school during the early eighteenth century.

> The children were called up one by one to Aunt Delight, who sat on a low chair and required each, as a preliminary, "to make his manners," which consisted of a small, student nod. She then placed the spelling book before the pupils and with a penknife pointed, one by one, to the letters of the alphabet saying, "What's that?" (Edward and Richey, p. 172).

As education extended beyond society's elite, educators became interested in instructional strategies that would accommodate large numbers of students in efficient ways. One example, the Lancaster Method, popular in the early nineteenth century, consisted of gathering as many as a hundred students in one large room, sorting them into groups of similar abilities, and having monitors (teacher aides) guide pupil recitations from scripted lesson plans. Nineteenth-century instructional strategies were teacher centered, intended mainly to transmit basic information clearly. In the early part of the twentieth century, however, this emphasis started to shift. John Dewey and his disciples of Progressive education left a legacy of student-centered instructional methods aimed at helping students acquire higher-level thinking and problem-solving skills. Of particular importance was the project method that provided the intellectual heritage for such contemporary methods as cooperative learning, problem-based instruction and other approaches emphasizing active student learning and group interaction.

The early work of the Progressives, fueled later by new theories and research about learning by such eminent theorists as European psychologists Lev Vygotsky and Jean Piaget and Americans Jerome Bruner and Albert Bandura extended thinking in the profession about instructional strategies in the post-*Sputnik* reforms of the 1950s and 1960s. Cognitive psychology and constructivist perspectives produced instructional strategies such as discovery learning and inquiry teaching that were at the center of the curriculum reforms of that era, and the cooperative learning and problem-based strategies popular today became more widely known and used.

In the late 1960s Bruce Joyce began describing the various approaches to teaching that had been developed over the years. He developed a classification system to analyze each approach according to its theoretical basis, the learner outcomes it was designed to accomplish, and the teacher and student behaviors required to make the approach work. Joyce used the term *model* rather than *teaching strategy* to refer to a particular approach to instruction. In his initial work (Joyce and Weil, 1972) more than twenty models were identified. Joyce's conceptualization of the field was a significant contribution and has influenced greatly how educators have thought about instructional strategies worldwide.

Nature and Categories of Instructional Strategies

In the early twenty-first century there are many instructional strategies. Similarly, there are tactics used by teachers to support particular strategies. The following provides a framework for thinking about instructional strategies, and then provides descriptions of seven strategies used frequently by teachers.

Instructional organizers, strategies, and tactics. A number of educators over the years, such as Barrie Bennett and Carol Rolheiser, have developed conceptual frameworks for thinking about instructional strategies. The frameworks most often include instructional organizers, instructional strategies, and tactics. Instructional organizers are at one end of a complexity continuum, and provide the "big ideas" that allow us to think about instructional practices. Examples of instructional organizers would be Howard Gardner's multiple intelligences or Benjamin Bloom's taxonomy for organizing instructional objectives. On the other end of the continuum are what

are often labeled *instructional tactics.* These are specific, and for the most part, simple actions taken by teachers within the confines of particular teaching strategies. Asking questions, checking for student understanding, providing examples or visual representations, or examining both sides of an argument are examples of instructional tactics. Many tactics have grown out of the practices of experienced teachers. In the middle of the continuum are instructional strategies that involve a series of steps, are supported by theory and research, and have been designed to produce certain types of student learning. Examples of instructional strategies would include direct instruction, cooperative learning, and the others described later in this article.

Finally, some teaching strategies are tightly tied to the content of particular lessons. *Pedagogical content knowledge* is a term coined by Lee Shulman in 1987 to describe the relationship between content and strategy and to illustrate how what is being taught influences the way it is taught. For example, an English teacher teaching a Shakespearian tragedy would use different strategies than the biology teacher who is trying to help students understand photosynthesis. Similarly, a fourth-grade teacher would use different methods to teach reading, fractions, or the concept of scarcity.

Learning environments and instructional strategies. Classrooms are places where teachers and students interact within a highly interdependent environment. At particular times, some types of learning environments have been deemed more appropriate than others. For example, prior to the mid-twentieth century in the United States, environments that kept students quiet and in their seats were the preferred environment compared to later times when more open and active environments were in vogue. Both formal and informal learning emanates from the particular environments that teachers create, and these are highly influenced by the strategies being used. For instance, lecturing creates a tightly structured learning environment where students are expected to listen, observe, and take notes. On the other hand, if the teacher divides students into cooperative learning groups, an environment is created where students are actively engaged and in charge of their own interactions.

Instructional strategies and learner outcomes. Learning is defined as a process where experience (instruction) causes a change in an individual's knowledge or behavior; different learning theories propound different perspectives about what is important and how learning occurs. Behavioral learning theories generally view the outcome of learning as change in behavior and emphasize the effects of the external environment. Cognitive and constructivist learning theories, on the other hand, view learning as change in cognition and focus mainly on internal mental activity. Instructional strategies used by teachers stem from particular learning theories and in turn produce certain kinds of outcomes. For most of the twentieth century, arguments persisted about which learning theories and which instructional strategies were the most accurate and most effective in affecting student learning. Debates among educators and the general public have surrounded lecture versus discussion; direct instruction versus discovery learning; and phonics versus whole language. These debates led nowhere mainly because the selection of effective instructional strategies can not always be precisely pinpointed, and mainly depends on what the teacher is trying to accomplish.

Contemporary conceptions of instructional strategies acknowledge that the goals of schooling are complex and multifaceted, and that teachers need many approaches to meet varied learner outcomes for diverse populations of students. A single method is no longer adequate. Effective teachers select varied instructional strategies that accomplish varied learner outcomes that are both behavioral and cognitive. To illustrate this point consider strategies teachers might use to teach the Bill of Rights to a group of eighth-grade students. The teacher might begin with a lecture describing each of the ten articles and the reasons they were included as the first ten amendments to the Constitution. Students might then be asked to match each amendment with its purpose. Use of the lecture and direct instruction methods facilitates the transmission of fairly large amounts of information to students in an efficient manner and helps them retain it in memory. However, it does not encourage students to think very deeply or critically about the Bill of Rights, or consider its significance to contemporary life. Nor would listening to a teacher promote the development of social discourse skills. Instead, the teacher might use more interactive strategies such as concept teaching and cooperative learning. If, however, teachers use more interactive methods, they have less time to explain the Bill of Rights. Particular strategies, then, have been designed to achieve particular learner outcomes, but no single strategy can

address them all. Appropriate use of particular strategies depends upon the type of learning outcomes the teacher wants to achieve.

Taxonomies for Categorizing Instructional Methods

Several taxonomies have been developed that categorize instructional strategies based on the strategy's theoretical underpinnings and on the type of learner outcomes that result from using the strategy. Joyce's taxonomy divided instructional models into four major families: information processing, behavioral, personal, and social. Behavioral strategies are designed to help students acquire basic information and skills. Information processing strategies help the learner process and use information and data. Social strategies help develop a sense of community and facilitate the learning of social skills. Personal methods emphasize the development of personal growth and awareness.

Others have made distinctions among strategies based on achieving learning outcomes most closely associated with behavioral theory as compared to those outcomes that stem from information processing, cognitive, and constructivist theories of learning. Still others have found the student-centered and teacher-centered categorization scheme useful for thinking about the relationship between student learning and instructional strategies. The seven strategies are categorized according to the degree of student versus teacher centeredness and the theoretical basis for the strategy (see Table 1).

Frequently Used Instructional Strategies

The rationale and theoretical background for each strategy is described in the table, along with the learner outcomes the strategy in intended to produce and the syntax and learning environment required to make the strategy effective. Syntax refers to the steps or phases through which a lesson progresses. Learning environment refers to the classroom context and required teacher and student behaviors. Each strategy described has been subjected to substantial research and evaluation and has been deemed highly effective. Positive effects, however, are sizeable only if the strategy is implemented faithfully.

Direct instruction. Direct instruction is a method for imparting basic knowledge or developing skills in a goal-directed, teacher-controlled environment. The teacher identifies clearly defined learning outcomes, transmits new information or demonstrates a skill, and provides guided practice. Direct instruction is designed to maximize academic learning time through a highly structured environment in which students are "on task" and experience high degrees of success.

Direct instruction has its roots in behaviorism. Behavioral theorists emphasize breaking behaviors and skills into component tasks and mastering each subcomponent. They emphasize the importance of modeling desired behavior and using feedback and reinforcement to guide students toward desired goals. The clearest empirical support for direct instruction came from the teacher effectiveness research of the 1970s and 1980s. By studying the relationship between teaching behaviors and student achievement in classrooms, researchers concluded that direct instruction produced greater time-on-task and higher student achievement, particularly for the acquisition of basic information and skills.

Direct instruction can be used effectively to promote acquisition of knowledge that is well structured and that can be taught in a step-by-step fashion, such as parts of speech, the multiplication tables, or the capitals of the fifty states. It is also effective in teaching how to perform simple and complex skills such as how to subtract, read a map, or swing a golf club. Although direct instruction is widely used, it is not appropriate for teaching concepts and generalizations, higher-level thinking, inquiry, problem solving, group processes, or independent learning.

In general, a direct instruction lesson proceeds through five phases. Teachers begin the lesson with an orientation phase. The teacher clarifies the goals of the lesson, explains why the lesson is important, ties the lesson to previous lessons and students' prior knowledge, and motivates students. This establishes the students' mental set and prepares them for the lesson. This initial phase is followed by phase 2, presentation or demonstration. The teacher demonstrates the skill or presents new information. If a skill is being taught, each step must be identified and demonstrated accurately. If new information is being taught, the information must be well organized and logically presented. Effective teachers give multiple examples, provide accurate demonstrations, restate the information often, and use visual models or illustrations.

The third phase is guided practice. The teacher structures the initial practice by walking the students

TABLE 1

Categorizing instructional methods		
Learning theory	Mainly teacher-directed	Mainly student-centered
Behavioral/social learning theories	Direct instruction	Simulation
Information processing	Lecture with advance organizers	Concept teaching
Cognitive/ constructivist theories	Discussion	Cooperative learning Problem-based instruction

SOURCE: Courtesy of author.

through, step-by-step, and giving feedback on correct and incorrect responses. When students understand, the teacher moves to guided practice in which students work independently while the teacher monitors student work and gives individual feedback. Guided practice is most effective in short increments repeated over time. At the end of guided practice, phase 4 checks for understanding and provides feedback, informally or formally, verbally or in writing. The most common tactic in this phase of the lesson is teacher questioning, but assessing independent work, giving a quiz, or observing a live or taped performance may also be appropriate. Feedback must be given as soon as possible after practice and be specific and focused on behavior.

The final phase of a direct instruction lesson is extended practice. Extended practice reinforces the knowledge or skill. It can be accomplished through seatwork or homework, but should only be given when students are at or near mastery and timely feedback can be given. Extended practice over time increases retention, transfer, and automaticity.

The learning environment in a direct instruction lesson is highly structured by the teacher. Students are expected to be careful listeners and keen observers.

Simulation. Simulation involves students playing roles in simulated situations in order to learn skills and concepts transferable to "real life." Students make decisions and learn from successes and failures. Simulations enable the learning of complex concepts or mastery of dangerous tasks in more simple and safe environments. Simulations include hands-on games such as Monopoly (real estate), social-political-economic role-playing or problem solving (model United Nations or feeding a family of four on $100 a week), software games ("Where in the World Is Carmen Sandiego?" for geography) and experiments (chemical changes), and simulators (driving a car or landing a plane). Although some simulations are done individually (such as driving), others occur in groups.

Simulation is grounded in a branch of behavioral psychology called cybernetics, which holds the perspective that learning occurs in an environment in which the learner receives immediate feedback, experiences the consequences of behavior, and continually self-corrects until mastery occurs. When learning to land a plane in a flight simulator, for example, the "pilot" receives feedback on the speed, height, and angle of descent, and corrects (or under- or over-corrects) until the plane "lands" or "crashes." With continued practice, corrective behaviors become automatic until the "pilot" lands the plane safely each time.

Simulations are effective for teaching complex skills or concepts. Simulations can be used to practice skills such as driving, to teach concepts such as how political, social, and economic systems work, or to discern scientific principles through simulated experiments. Additional outcomes include problem solving, decision making, cause-effect relationships, cooperation or competition, and independent learning. Simulations are not effective for teaching large amounts of fact-based information.

Simulation has four phases. The teacher begins the lesson by explaining the purposes of the simulation and providing an overview of how it will proceed. This is followed by phase 2, where students are trained in the rules, procedures and goals of the simulation and provided time for abbreviated practice.

During phase 3, the simulation itself, the teacher serves as a coach, giving feedback, clarifying misconceptions, and maintaining the rules. The teacher does not tell students what to do or provide direct assistance. The debriefing aspect of the simulation, phase 4, allows time to describe and analyze experiences, make comparisons to real world situations, and relate the experience to the subject they are studying. The teacher's role is critical at this final phase in helping students make sense of the simulated experience and tie it to course content.

The teacher structures and facilitates the learning environment fairly tightly; however, students are active in determining their own experiences during the simulation. Students work individually or cooperatively in a nonthreatening atmosphere in which feedback comes from the simulation or from peers. The teacher helps students apply their learning to real world situations.

Presentation using advance organizers. Presentation (or lecture) is among the most commonly used strategies for knowledge acquisition and retention. But presentation is more than teachers talking. An effective presentation requires a highly structured environment in which the teacher is an active presenter and students are active listeners and thinkers. Teachers use advance organizers—powerful concepts to which subordinate ideas and facts can be linked—to provide structure and then involve students in processing the new information.

The presentation strategy is grounded in information processing theory, which describes how learning occurs and how the mind organizes knowledge. The brain utilizes short-term memory for complex thought processes and long-term memory for information storage. Stored information is organized according to hierarchically ordered concepts and categories called cognitive structures. New information must be processed actively in short-term memory and tied to students' existing cognitive structures in long-term memory. Just as the mind has cognitive structures, every discipline has an organizational structure. Presentations should be organized around key ideas and structures and these structures should be made explicit to students.

Presentation enables teachers to organize and convey large amounts of information efficiently. It is an appropriate strategy for instructing students about the key ideas in a subject, for acquisition and retention of factual information linked to these ideas, and for comparing similarities and differences among ideas. Presentation is less appropriate for higher-level thinking, problem solving, and inquiry, although it may be used prior to such activities to ensure that students have the necessary foundational information.

There are four phases in a presentation lesson. The teacher begins the presentation by explaining the goals, sequence, and expectations of the lesson, and by helping students retrieve appropriate prior knowledge. In phase 2 the advance organizer is presented. Advance organizers are "scaffolds" that help learners link new information to what they already know. Advance organizers may be expository, comparative (relationships), or sequential (steps), and work best when accompanied by graphic or visual representations.

Phase 3 is the presentation itself. As new learning material is presented, the teacher pays particular attention to order and clarity, and provides concrete examples and illustrations that help students make required connections to what they already know.

In the final phase of a presentation, the teacher checks for student understanding and helps them integrate what they have learned. The teacher asks questions to encourage precise and critical thinking. Effective questions might involve asking for summaries, definitions, examples, comparisons, descriptions, analysis, or connections to the advance organizer. It is in this final phase that students integrate the new knowledge into their prior knowledge, build more complex cognitive structures, and develop understanding of complex relationships.

The teacher carefully structures the learning environment during a presentation so students can hear and see the presentation, uses procedures to ensure a smooth and effective pace, and addresses off-task behaviors immediately.

Concept teaching. Concept teaching helps students learn concepts and develop higher level thinking skills. Concepts (such as round and integer in mathematics, scarcity and freedom in social studies, energy and motion in science, and comedy and tragedy in literature) serve as the foundation for knowledge, increase complex conceptual understanding, and facilitate social communication. There are several different approaches to concept teaching. The approach described here is called concept attainmenta and is an inductive process in which students construct, refine, and apply concepts through teacher-directed activities using examples and nonexamples and in which students learn to classify, recognize members of a class, identify critical and noncritical attributes, and define and label particular concepts.

Cognitive theorists such as Jean Piaget and Jerome Bruner and information processing psychologists such as Robert Gagne emphasized that thinking is organized around conceptual structures. Children begin learning concepts very early through interaction with concrete objects. Conceptual structures continue to develop with increasing complexity and abstraction throughout life. Concept formation requires students to build categories (an island is land

surrounded by water; a noun is a name for a person, place or thing). Concept attainment requires students to figure out the attributes of a category (e.g., a triangle has three sides and three angles; an adjective describes a noun). Young children can categorize using one rule or attribute (a bird has feathers), but students gradually develop the ability to use multiple rules or attributes (birds have feathers, lay eggs, have feet, and are warm-blooded) and to distinguish noncritical attributes (some birds fly, but not all birds). Examples and nonexamples are used to help students construct new concepts (a diary is a primary source, but a novel is not).

The primary purpose of concept teaching is to learn new concepts. It is also effective for teaching higher-level thinking, including inductive reasoning, hypothesis formation, logical reasoning, concept building strategies, and taking multiple perspectives (Is a slave's concept of slavery different from a master's concept?). Although not designed to convey large amounts of information, students must process information as they formulate new concepts.

Concept teaching has four phases. In phase 1 the teacher explains the purposes of the lesson, describes why concepts are important, and gets students ready to learn. The second phase consists of presentation of examples and nonexamples of the concept. The teacher gives examples and nonexamples, and the students strive to discover the concept and its attributes through inductive reasoning.

After the concept has been discovered, the teacher gives more examples and nonexamples, then asks students to provide examples and nonexamples. The purpose of this tactic is to test student understanding of the concept and its attributes. A concept lesson concludes with the teacher asking students to analyze their thinking patterns, strategies, and decisions in order to develop more effective thinking skills and to help students integrate the new concepts into existing knowledge.

The learning environment for concept teaching has a moderate degree of structure in that the teacher controls the first three phases of the lesson rather tightly. The fourth phase is more open and student interaction is encouraged. As students gain more experience with concept learning, they can assume increasing responsibility for how the lesson proceeds.

Discussion. Discussion is central to all aspects of teaching. Classroom discussion may serve as a strategy in itself or as part of another strategy. Teachers and students talking about academic content and students displaying their ideas and thinking processes to the teacher and to each other characterize discussions. Effective discussions go beyond question-and-answer recitations. The more involved students are in the discussion, the more effective the learning.

Theoretical support for classroom discussions stems from the study of language and patterns of discourse and from constructivist psychologists, such as Lev Vygotsky, who believed that most learning occurs through language-based social interactions.

Discussion is an appropriate strategy for improving student thinking; promoting engagement in academic content; and learning communication and thinking skills in a social environment. Discussion is particularly appropriate for topics that are subjective or controversial and that involve several points of view, such as the causes of World War I or funding of stem-cell research.

Classroom discussion proceeds through five phases. The teacher introduces the discussion by providing a clear purpose for the discussion and engaging students so they will become involved. This is followed by phase 2 where the teacher sets the ground rules, then poses a question, raises an issue, or presents a puzzling situation.

Phase 3 is the discussion itself. The teacher asks questions, uses wait-time, responds to students' ideas, and enforces the ground rules. The teacher keeps the discussion focused and encourages all students to participate. Using visual cues and posting a written record of main ideas keeps the discussion focused. Skillful, well-planned questioning is critical, and each discussion should include a mixture of factual and thought-provoking questions. Pairing students or putting them in small groups can increase their participation during a discussion.

The teacher provides closure in phase 4 by (1) summarizing; (2) asking students to summarize the content and meaning of the discussion; and (3) tying it back to the initial question or problem. Finally, the teacher debriefs the process of the discussion by having students examine their thinking processes and reflect on their participation.

The teacher focuses and moderates the discussion, but broad and active student participation characterizes the learning environment. The atmosphere is one of open communication in which students feel free to express their ideas and ask questions. Teaching students to have high regard for other's ideas and to use interpersonal communication skills improves cognitive and social learning.

Cooperative learning. In cooperative learning students work together in small groups on a common learning task, coordinate their efforts to complete the task, and depend on each other for the outcome. Cooperative learning groups are characterized by student teams (of 2–6) working to master academic goals. Teams are normally comprised of learners of mixed ability, ethnicity, and gender. Rewards systems (grades) are designed for the group as well as individuals.

Cooperative learning is rooted in two theoretical traditions. First, it is based on the progressivism of John Dewey, particularly his idea that the school should mirror the values of the society and that classrooms should be laboratories for learning democratic values and behaviors. Students are prepared for civic and social responsibilities by participating in democratic classrooms and small problem-solving groups. Cooperative learning also has roots in constructivist theory and the perspective that cognitive change takes place as students actively work on problems and discover their own solutions. Particularly important is Lev Vygotsky's theories that students learn through language-based interactions with more capable peers and adults.

Cooperative learning has three distinct goals: academic achievement, acceptance of diversity through interdependent work, and development of cooperative social skills.

There are numerous approaches to cooperative learning and each proceeds in slightly different ways. However, in general, a cooperative learning lesson has six phases. The teacher begins the lesson by presenting the goals of the lesson, motivating students, and connecting the forthcoming lesson to previous learning. Procedures, timelines, roles and rewards are described. Required group processes or social skills may also be taught at the beginning of a cooperative learning lesson.

In phase 2 the teacher facilitates the acquisition of the academic content that is the focus of the lesson. This may be done verbally, graphically, or with text. The teacher during phase 3 explains how the teams are formed and helps students make transitions into their groups. Phase 4 is teamwork. Students work together on cooperative tasks and the teacher assists students and groups, while reminding them of their interdependence.

The final phases of a cooperative learning lesson consists of phase 5 (assessment) and phase 6 (recognition). The teacher tests student knowledge or groups present their work. Individual students and groups are assessed on cooperation as well as academic achievement. The effort of individuals and groups are recognized through displays, newsletters, presentations, or other public forums.

The learning environment for cooperative learning differs markedly from the traditional individualistic classroom environment. Students assume active roles and take responsibility for their own learning. The social atmosphere is collaborative and respectful of differences. Students learn group processes and problem-solving skills and become increasingly independent in using them. Students construct their own learning through active engagement with materials, problems, and other students. The teacher forms the teams, structures the group work, provides materials, and determines the reward structure, but the students direct their own work and learning.

Problem-based instruction. In problem-based instruction students are presented with authentic, meaningful problems as a basis for inquiry and investigation. Sometimes called project-based instruction, inquiry learning, or authentic investigation, this strategy is designed to promote problem solving and higher-level thinking skills. All problem-based instruction strategies include more or less the following features: a driving question or problem, interdisciplinary focus, authentic investigation, production of artifacts or exhibits, and collaboration. This strategy is designed to involve students in the kinds of real-world thinking activities they will encounter outside of school from childhood through adulthood. Sample problems include the following:

- Why did the settlers at Jamestown die?

- How can we recycle in the school cafeteria?

- What causes clouds to form different shapes?

- How much peanut butter does our school need for a year and how much would it cost?

- Why did some civilizations thrive while others died out?

- What will happen if the world population doubles in five years?

Like cooperative learning, problem-based instruction has its roots in the progressivism of John Dewey and the constructivism of Jean Piaget, Lev Vygotsky, and Jerome Bruner. Dewey argued that learning should be relevant and engaging through the involvement of students in group projects of their own interest. Piaget theorized that learning occurs through active investigations of the environment in which students construct personally meaningful knowledge. Vygotsky stressed the importance of social, language-based learning. Bruner emphasized the importance of learners working with their own ideas and finding meaning through active involvement and personal discovery.

The primary goal of problem-based instruction is learning content through inquiry that can be applied in authentic situations. Students learn to think and behave like adult workers, scholars, and problem solvers and to regulate their own learning. They learn collaboration skills and research and inquiry strategies, and gain an understanding of knowledge as complex, multifaceted, and uncertain.

Problem-based instruction involves five phases similar to those in cooperative learning. A lesson may extend over several days or even weeks. Phase 1 is orientation to the problem. The teacher presents the problem or driving question, provides the parameters for student inquiry, and motivates students to engage in problem-solving activities. In phase 2 the teacher assists students in forming study groups and assists the groups in defining, planning, and organizing tasks and timelines, and by clarifying roles and responsibilities.

During the students' investigation, phase 3, the teacher encourages, questions, and assists students in data/information gathering, hypothesis formulation and testing, and the generation of explanations and solutions. Guiding and coaching is emphasized, not directing and telling.

Problem-based lessons are brought to conclusion through student presentation of products and exhibits, phase 4, and through reflection, phase 5. The teacher assists students in planning, preparing, and presenting products that share their work with others. These might include reports, videos, multimedia presentations, murals, plays, reenactments, models, diaries, or computer programs. After presentations, the teacher helps students reconstruct and analyze their thinking processes and integrate their learning.

Problem-based instruction is the most student centered of the strategies presented. Students work actively and independently on problems that interest them. This requires an environment that is open and safe for asking questions, forming hypotheses, and sharing ideas. The teacher's role is to pose problems, ask questions, facilitate investigation and dialogue, and provide support for learning.

See also: CURRICULUM, SCHOOL; DEVELOPMENTAL THEORY, *subentry on* VYGOTSKYAN THEORY; DEWEY, JOHN; ELEMENTARY EDUCATION, *subentry on* CURRENT TRENDS; PIAGET, JEAN; SECONDARY EDUCATION, *subentry on* CURRENT TRENDS.

BIBLIOGRAPHY

ARENDS, RICHARD I. 2001. *Learning to Teach,* 5th edition. New York: McGraw-Hill.

AUSUBEL, DAVID P. 1963. *The Psychology of Meaningful Verbal Learning.* New York: Grune and Stratton.

BANDURA, ALBERT. 1977. *Social Learning Theory.* Englewood Cliffs, NJ: Prentice Hall.

BENNETT, BARRIE, and ROLHEISER, CAROL. 2001. *Beyond Monet: The Artful Science of Instructional Integration.* Toronto: Bookation.

BRUNER, JEROME. 1960. *The Process of Education.* Cambridge, MA: Harvard University Press.

CAZDEN, COURTNEY B. 1988. *Classroom Discourse.* Portsmouth, NH: Heinemann.

CRUICKSHANK, DONALD, et al. 1999. *The Act of Teaching,* 2nd edition. New York: McGraw-Hill.

DEWEY, JOHN. 1916. *Democracy and Education.* New York: Macmillan.

EDWARDS, NEWTON, and RICHEY, HERMAN G. 1963. *The School in the American Social Order.* Boston: Houghton Mifflin.

GAGNE, ELLEN D.; YEKOVICK, CAROL W.; and YEROVICH, FRANK R. 1993. *The Cognitive Psychology of School Learning,* 2nd edition. New York: HarperCollins.

GAGNE, ROBERT M. 1985. *The Conditions of Learning and Theory of Instruction,* 4th edition. New York: Holt, Rinehart and Winston.

JOYCE, BRUCE, and WEIL, MARSHA. 2000. *Models of Teaching,* 6th edition. Boston: Allyn and Bacon.

PIAGET, JEAN. 1954. *The Construction of Reality in the Child.* New York: Basic Books.

PIAGET, JEAN. 1963. *Psychology of Intelligence.* Patterson, NJ: Littlefield Adams.

RICHARDSON, VIRGINIA, ed. 2001. *Handbook of Research on Teaching,* 4th edition. New York: Macmillan.

SCHMUCK, RICHARD A., and SCHMUCK, PATRICIA A. 1997. *Group Processes in the Classroom,* 7th edition. Dubuque, IA: Brown and Benchmark.

SLAVIN, ROBERT E. 1997. *Educational Psychology: Theory and Practice,* 6th edition. Boston: Allyn and Bacon.

SMITH, KARL, and SMITH, MARY. 1966. *Cybernetic Principles of Learning and Educational Design.* New York: Holt, Rinehart and Winston.

TENNYSON, ROBERT D., and COCCHIARELLA, MARTIN. 1986. "An Empirically Based Instructional Design Theory for Teaching Concepts." *Review of Educational Research* 56:40–71.

VYGOTSKY, LEV. 1962. *Thought and Language.* Cambridge, MA: MIT Press.

WITTROCK, MERLIN C., ed. 1986. *Handbook of Research on Teaching,* 3rd edition. New York: Macmillan.

RICHARD I. ARENDS
SHARON CASTLE

INTELLECTUAL PROPERTY RIGHTS

Intellectual property law, once thought of as an arcane and unpopular area of law, came to the forefront of legal disciplines in the 1990s, in large part due to the increased use of computers and the commercialization of the World Wide Web. Because of the widespread use of technology and computers to conduct research and teach, intellectual property law greatly impacts the educational enterprise in the early twenty-first century. The use of computer networks and the Web to create classrooms in cyberspace, communicate with students and faculty, write and publish scholarly material, and conduct research is considered the norm for many educational institutions. And each of these activities involves the use of copyrighted information. As a consequence educators and administrators need to have a basic understanding of copyright in order to avoid misusing copyrighted material.

Copyright Framework and Exclusive Rights

Intellectual property in the United States is a property right created by the law in intangible property. Specifically, *copyright* is a subset of *intellectual prop-*

erty, which protects creative works such as literature and art. Other types of intellectual property are patents, which protect inventions and processes, and trademarks, which protect names and logos.

Copyrights and patent rights originate from the Patent and Copyright Clause of the United States Constitution, which states "The Congress shall have power to . . . promote the progress of science and useful arts, by securing for limited times to authors and inventors the exclusive right to their respective writings and discoveries" (Art. 1, sec. 8, clause 8). The policy behind the copyright framework, embodied in this clause, is that economic incentive, in the form of monopoly rights in an author's work, is needed to generate new creative works in society and thus promote "the progress of science and useful arts."

The monopoly rights that authors possess are outlined in section 106 of the Copyright Act of 1976 (the Act). These rights include the right to make copies, create derivative works, and distribute, display, and perform works publicly. The copyright owner is entitled to exercise and authorize these rights, and prevent others from exercising these rights. Unless a use is exempted or considered fair, users must seek the permission of copyright owner and/or pay license fees to use a copyrighted work.

The digital environment implicates the exclusive rights of authors quite easily. For example, every time a person saves a work to a disk, the right to make copies is invoked. Scanning, digitizing, uploading, downloading, and file transfer all involve the right to make copies. A work is publicly displayed each time someone posts copyrighted information on a bulletin board, website, or online class. When a display or performance is done through a digital network transmission, temporary RAM copies are made in computers through which the material passes.

Copyright Protection and the Public Domain

In order to qualify for copyright protection, a work must meet the statutory requirements set out in section 102(s) of the Act. The work must be an original work of authorship fixed in a tangible medium of expression. Copyright protection exists from the moment of fixation in a tangible medium. The protection is automatic and notice is not required; however, registration carries certain benefits and is required to bring a lawsuit. Section 102 of the Copy-

right Act of 1976 includes eight categories of subject matter that fall under copyright protection: literary works; musical works; dramatic works; pantomimes and choreographic works; pictorial, graphic, and sculptural works; motion pictures and audiovisual works; sound recordings; and architectural works. Examples of copyrighted expression also include computer programming, animations, video footage, java applets, web pages, and photographs.

An important aspect of the copyright framework is that facts, ideas, and government works are not protected. Those items are generally considered within the public domain and freely available for use without permission or payment of license fees. The logic behind this is clear. If facts and ideas in particular were considered copyrighted information, then the process of innovation, research, and scholarship would be considerably slowed due to the increased time and monetary costs of getting permission and paying fees. Moreover, the possibility of great constraint of academic freedom would be quite high under those circumstances because those who exercised control over controversial facts or ideas might be hesitant to grant access to those materials. Facts, ideas, government information, and items with expired terms of copyright are also within the public domain. To determine whether a copyright term has expired, one should consult Chapter 3 of the Copyright Act. Another helpful resource is a chart developed by Laura N. Gasaway of the University of North Carolina School of Law that helps determine when works pass into the public domain. The chart can be found online at <www.unc.edu/~unclng/public-d.htm>.

Copyright Ownership

The exclusive rights in copyright are initially given to the owner of the copyrighted work. Although the author may transfer the copyright to someone else, any analysis of copyright ownership should begin with the principle that the author is the owner. Section 201 of the Act provides four types or categories for ownership: (1) author; (2) joint ownership; (3) collective works; and (4) works made for hire.

The primary exception to the *author is owner* approach is the *work-for-hire* category. When a work is made for hire, the employer, not an employee, is considered the owner/author of a work. Section 101 of the Act outlines two ways a work is made for hire: (1) the employee creates the work within the scope of his or her employment; or (2) the work meets the statutory criteria of being an independently contracted work made for hire.

The work-for-hire doctrine has always played a role in academic production. Many institutions have asserted ownership over research and other scholarly works by claiming the work is made for hire. However, an exception to this rule was developed in the common law for things such as syllabi, lectures, textbooks, and articles that professors write. There is no such explicit exception in the Copyright Act of 1976.

The factors to be considered in determining whether or not a person is an employee were outlined in the Supreme Court's decision in *Community for Creative Non-Violence (CCNV) v. Reid* (1989). The *CCNV* factors applied by the U.S. Court of Appeals for the Second Circuit in *Aymes v. Bonelli* include: the right of the hiring party to control the manner and means of creation; employee benefits provided by the hiring party; whether the hiring party has the right to assign more projects to the hired party; tax treatment of the hired party; and skill required to complete the project.

If a creator is not an employee, but is hired to create something, and both parties sign a written contract before the work begins that states the work is a work made for hire, and if the work fits into one of the statutory categories, it will be considered a work made for hire and the hiring party will own the work. The statutory categories are: contribution to a collective work; part of a movie or other audiovisual work; a translation; a supplementary work; a compilation; an instructional text; a test; answer material for a test; an atlas.

The controversy over the availability of the academic exception under the 1976 act has been exacerbated by the onset of digital distance education. Many educators claim that distance-education courses delivered online are nothing less than lecture notes, and that these items have historically been the property of faculty. Institutions counter that online courses are not developed in isolation, but that various persons help to develop them, and the institution therefore has an ownership interest in such courses. Because of the lack of clarity in this area, it is very important that colleges and universities develop copyright policies. University copyright policies can affect the application of copyright law by designating certain activities as being outside the scope of employment and/or incorporating the traditional academic exception.

Copyright Limitations and Exemptions

Although copyright owners have exclusive rights in their creations, these exclusive rights are limited by certain statutory exemptions and defenses. The most used and notable of these for the education community are: fair use, library copying, first sale, and the educational *performance and display* exemptions. The primary limitation in copyright on the exclusive rights of copyright owners is *fair use.* The fair use privilege allows for the reasonable use of a copyrighted work without permission or payment of license fees if the use is fair pursuant to statutory factors. Section 107 of the Act includes four factors that must be weighed to determine whether or not a use is fair: (1) the purpose and character of the use; (2) nature of the copyrighted work; (3) the amount and substantiality of the portion used; and (4) the effect of the use on the potential market for, or value of, the copyrighted work. All four factors are weighed or balanced, and no one factor ensures a finding of fair use. Fair use is critical to the teaching and research that takes place in educational institutions. If fair use did not exist, then the research process would be greatly frustrated, since many small and relatively inconsequential research uses copyrighted material that could be considered unlawful reproductions such as photocopying a page from a journal in order to write a research paper.

Exemptions that are directly applicable to the classroom and to distance education are located in Section 110 of the Copyright Act. The classroom exemption, 110(1), allows for the performance and display rights to be used in the course of "face to face" teaching at a nonprofit educational institution. The use must be within a "classroom or similar place devoted to instruction." The right to public display may occur whenever a picture, graphic, text, or chart is shown directly or by means of a projecting mechanism. A performance may occur when a work is recited or acted, or when an audiovisual work, such as a videotape, is played. Thus, in the course of teaching students in the classroom one can read text out loud, sing a song, or play a movie.

The types of activities permitted in the course of face-to-face instruction under the act, as of May 2002, may not be permitted in an online class, pursuant to the distance education exemption. The distance education exemption, 110(2), allows for the performance only of nondramatic literary or musical works or the display of a work if: (1) the use is part of "systematic instructional activities" of a nonprofit educational institution or governmental body; (2) the use is "directly related and of material assistance to the teaching content of the transmission;" and (3) the transmission must be "primarily" for "reception in classrooms or similar places normally devoted to instruction," or for persons whose disabilities or other special circumstances prevent their coming to classrooms.

The distance education provision was created in the 1970s and does not address the issues involved in transmitting content in the online classroom. This exemption does not provide for the use of audiovisual works such as educational videos, theatrical films, and film clips. The U.S. Copyright Office documented some of the limitations in 110(2) in a report given in 1999. The copyright owner and user communities have attempted to negotiate an amendment to Copyright Act, known as the Technology Education and Copyright Harmonization Act (TEACH Act). As of May 2002, the TEACH Act had yet to be adopted by Congress.

Infringement and Liability

Use of a copyrighted work without permission, unless it is covered under an exemption, infringes on the exclusive rights of the author outlined in Section 106 of the Copyright Act. Infringement can be direct, vicarious, or contributory. Direct infringement occurs when someone violates any of the exclusive rights of the copyright owner. Vicarious infringement occurs when one has the right to control the infringement of another or profits from infringement. This type of liability is based on the relationship with the direct infringer. Contributory infringement occurs when a person has knowledge of infringing activity and/or induces, causes, or contributes to infringing conduct. Educational institutions and faculty may be liable under all three types of liability.

Digital Millennium Copyright Act

Educational institutions that are heavily networked with high student and faculty use of computers need to become well versed in the liability limits in the Digital Millennium Copyright Act (DMCA), a 1998 amendment to the Copyright Act. Specifically, the DMCA limits liability for Internet Service Providers (ISPs) and provides safe harbors from liability for conduit activities, system caching, hyperlinks, directories, and location tools and stored material on an ISP system. There are specific requirements that

must be met in order to get statutory protection, however. Service providers qualifying for these limits in subsections (a)–(d) are shielded from damage awards. Section 512(j) limits the availability of injunctive relief.

The DMCA has a specific provision for nonattribution of infringing conduct by graduate students and faculty of nonprofit educational institutions. This provision, 512(e), applies to the conduct of graduate students and faculty involved in teaching and research if: (1) the activities do not involve online access to instructional materials that are required or recommended for a course taught at the institution within the preceding three-year period; (2) within that same three year period, the institution received two or fewer DMCA notifications that a particular faculty member or graduate student engaged in infringement and no actionable misrepresentations were made in connection with such notifications; and (3) the institution provides information on copyright compliance.

Anti-Circumvention

The DMCA also adds sections 1201–1205 to the Copyright Act, implementing the World Intellectual Property Organization treaty provisions prohibiting the circumvention of technological copyright protection measures and protecting the integrity of copyright management information. Section 1201 defines circumvention of technological measures and prohibits circumvention of technological measures that restrict access to a copyrighted work and trafficking in the means to circumvent protective measures restricting access to a copyrighted work. A technological measure that controls access is defined as one in which the authorized access to a copyrighted work requires either application of information (such as a password) or a process or treatment— with the authority of the copyright owner. Circumvention occurs whenever such technological measures are avoided, bypassed, deactivated, or impaired without the authority of the copyright owner.

Section 1201(d) exempts nonprofit libraries, archives, or educational institutions that circumvent technological measures controlling access to a protected work that is not reasonably available in another form. Such conduct must be for the sole purpose of making a good faith determination of whether to acquire that work. This exemption does not apply to acts that fall under section 1201(a)(2) or 1201(b)(1), which prohibit trafficking in a product or service that is intended to circumvent technological copyright protection measures.

There is also a narrowly limited reverse-engineering exception, found in section 1201(f), for circumvention of technological measures controlling access to a computer program. The exception exists for the sole purpose of identifying and analyzing those elements of a copyrighted work necessary to achieve interoperability with other independently created programs. *Interoperability* is defined as the ability of computer programs to exchange and share information. This section does not exempt acts of reverse engineering, but merely the circumvention of measures controlling access.

Computer Software

The issue of reverse engineering as copyright infringement was litigated before the Court of Appeals for the Ninth Circuit in *Sega Enterprises Ltd. v. Accolade* (1992). The court observed that "intermediate copying of computer object code may infringe the exclusive rights granted to the copyright owner in section 106 of the Copyright Act regardless of whether the end product of the copying also infringes those rights." The court held, however, that disassembly of copyrighted object code was a fair use, since it was a necessary step in the examination of unprotected ideas and functional concepts. The court recognized that there is no "settled standard" for identifying protected expression and unprotected ideas involved in determining copyright infringement of computer software.

See also: FACULTY AS ENTREPRENEURS; FACULTY CONSULTING; FACULTY PERFORMANCE OF RESEARCH AND SCHOLARSHIP; UNIVERSITY-INDUSTRIAL RESEARCH COLLABORATION.

BIBLIOGRAPHY

Abernathy v. Hutchinson, 3 L.J. 209, 214–215 (1825).

American Geophysical Union v. Texaco Inc., 37 F.2d 881 (2d Cir. 1994).

Amyes v. Bonelli, 980 F.2d 857, 862 (2d Cir. 1992).

Campbell v. Acuff-Rose Music, Inc., 114 S.Ct. 1164 (1994).

Community for Creative Non-Violence v. Reid, 490 U.S. 730 (1989).

Gershwin Pub'g Corp. v. Columbia Artists Management, 443 F.2d 1159 (2d Cir. 1971).

Harper & Row Publishers, Inc. v. Nation Enterp., 471 U.S. 539 (1985).

Hays v. Sony Corp. of Am., 847 F.2d 412 (7th Cir. 1998).

Sega Enterprises v. Accolade, Inc., 977 F.2d 1510, 1519 (9th Cir. 1992).

Universal City Studios, Inc., 464 U.S. 417 (1984).

Weinstein v. University of Illinois, 811 F.2d 1091 (1987).

INTERNET RESOURCES

AMERICAN LIBRARY ASSOCIATION WASHINGTON OFFICE. 2002. *Distance Education: Technology Education and Copyright Harmonization Act (The TEACH Act).* <www.ala.org/washoff/disted.html>.

CENTER FOR INTELLECTUAL PROPERTY AT UMUC. 2002. *(c)Primer.* <www.umuc.edu/distance/cip/index.html>.

COPYRIGHT MANAGEMENT CENTER AT INDIANA UNIVERSITY. 2001. *Fair Use Checklist.* <www.iupui.edu/~copyinfo/fuchecklist.html>.

CREWS, KENNETH D. 1999. *Summary of U.S. Copyright Office Report on Distance Education.* <www.iupui.edu/~copyinfo/distedsum.html>.

GASAWAY, LAURA N. 2002. "When Works Pass into the Public Domain." <www.unc.edu/~unclng/public-d.htm>.

UNITED STATES COPYRIGHT OFFICE. 1999a. *Copyright Office Study on Distance Education.* <www.loc.gov.copyright/docs/de_rprt.pdf>.

UNITED STATES COPYRIGHT OFFICE. 1999b. *Factsheet* <www.loc.gov/copyright/fls/fl102.pdf>.

UNITED STATES COPYRIGHT OFFICE. 2000. *Copyright Law of the United States.* Circular 92, April. <www.loc.gov.copyright/title17>.

UNITED STATES COPYRIGHT OFFICE. 2002. *Background and Testimony Related to the Copyright Office Study on Distance Education.* <www.loc.gov/copyright/disted>.

KIMBERLY M. BONNER

INTELLIGENCE

EMOTIONAL INTELLIGENCE

The term *emotional intelligence* was introduced in a 1990 article by Peter Salovey and John D. Mayer. They described emotional intelligence as a set of skills that involve the ability to monitor one's own and others' feelings and emotions, to discriminate among them, and to use this information to guide one's thinking and action. Salovey and Mayer introduced the term as a challenge to intelligence theorists to contemplate an expanded role for the emotional system in conceptual schemes of human abilities, and to investigators of emotion who had historically considered the arousal of affect as disorganizing of cognitive activity. In the spirit of Charles Darwin, who, in his 1872 book *The Expression of the Emotions in Man and Animals*, viewed the emotional system as necessary for survival and as providing an important signaling system within and across species, Salovey and Mayer emphasized the functionality of feelings and described a set of competencies that might underlie the adaptive use of affectively charged information.

Associated Concepts and Formal Definition

The idea of an emotional intelligence was anticipated, at least implicitly, by various theorists who argued that traditional notions of analytic intelligence are too narrow. Emotional intelligence adds an affective dimension to Robert Sternberg's 1985 work on practical intelligence, is consistent with theorizing by Nancy Cantor and John Kihlstrom (1987) about social intelligence, and is directly related to research on children's emotional competencies by Carolyn Saarni (1999) and others. Emotional intelligence is most similar to one of the multiple intelligences characterized by Howard Gardner in *Frames of Mind* (1983). Gardner delineated *intrapersonal intelligence* as awareness of one's feelings and the capacity to effect discriminations among these feelings, label them, enmesh them in symbolic codes, and draw upon them as a means of understanding and guiding one's behavior.

Mayer and Salovey described emotional intelligence more specifically in 1997 by outlining the competencies it encompasses. They organized these competencies along four branches: (1) the ability to perceive, appraise, and express emotion accurately; (2) the ability to access and generate feelings when they facilitate cognition; (3) the ability to understand affect-laden information and make use of emotional knowledge; and (4) the ability to regulate emotions to promote growth and well-being.

Individuals can be more or less skilled at attending to, appraising, and expressing their own emotional states. These emotional states can be harnessed adaptively and directed toward a range of cognitive tasks, including problem solving, creativity, and decision-making. Emotional intelligence also includes essential knowledge about the emotional system. The most fundamental competencies at this level concern the ability to label emotions with words and to recognize the relationships among exemplars of the affective lexicon. Finally, emotional intelligence includes the ability to regulate feelings in oneself and in other people. Individuals who are unable to manage their emotions are more likely to experience negative affect and remain in poor spirits.

Measures and Findings

There are two types of measures of emotional intelligence: self-report questionnaires and ability tests. Self-report measures essentially ask individuals whether or not they have various competencies and experiences consistent with being emotionally intelligent. Ability tests require individuals to demonstrate these competencies, and they rely on tasks and exercises rather than on self-assessment. Self-report and ability measures may yield different findings, because asking people about their intelligence is not the same as having them take an intelligence test.

Self-report measures include relatively short scales, such as Niccola Schutte and colleagues' (1998) scale, intended to assess Salovey and Mayer's original model of emotional intelligence, and the Trait Meta-Mood Scale (TMMS), designed to assess people's beliefs about their propensity to attend with clarity to their own mood states and to engage in mood repair. More comprehensive self-report inventories, such as the Bar-On Emotional Quotient Inventory (EQ-i) encompass a larger number of subscales that tap into personality and other traits related to emotional experience and self-reported, noncognitive competencies.

The advantage of self-report measures is that they provide a global self-evaluation of emotional competence. They draw upon a rich base of self-knowledge and reflect people's experiences across different settings and situations. However, these measures have important limitations: they measure perceived, rather than actual, abilities; and they are susceptible to mood and social desirability biases, as well as deliberate or involuntary self-enhancement. Moreover, self-report measures overlap substantially with personality, and it is unclear whether they contribute to the understanding of social and emotional functioning over and above what personality traits might explain.

To overcome such problems, Mayer, David Caruso, and Salovey (1999) developed an ability test of emotional intelligence. Their first test, called the Multidimensional Emotional Intelligence Scale (MEIS), paved the way for a more reliable, better normed, and more professionally produced test, the Mayer, Salovey, and Caruso Emotional Intelligence Test (MSCEIT). This test asks people to process emotional information and use it to solve various problems, and to rate the effectiveness of different strategies for dealing with emotionally arousing situations. It consists of eight tasks, including decoding facial expressions and visual displays of emotion, understanding blends of emotions and emotional dynamics, integrating emotional information with other thinking processes, and managing emotions for purposes of self-regulation and social interaction. The test can be scored using either expert or consensus norms, and Mayer and his colleagues demonstrated in 2001 that these scoring methods yield similar results.

Ability tests of emotional intelligence avoid the self-enhancement and other biases that plague self-report measures, and they are very different from personality inventories. These are substantial advantages. However, these tests also have limitations. To assess emotional regulation, the MSCEIT evaluates people's knowledge of appropriate strategies for handling various situations, rather than their actual skill in implementing these strategies. It is not known to what extent the abilities assessed by ability tests generalize across situations and social or cultural contexts. While they are intended to assess skills, relying on consensus scoring can make it difficult to distinguish enacted skills from adjustment or conformity, especially because emotionally intelligent behavior necessarily reflects attunement to social norms and expectations.

Evidence suggests that emotional intelligence, assessed through ability tests, represents a coherent and interrelated set of abilities, distinct from (but meaningfully related to) traditional measures of intelligence, and developing with age. Initial studies also suggest that ability measures of emotional intelligence are associated with a range of positive outcomes, including lower peer ratings of aggressiveness and higher teacher ratings of prosocial behavior among school children; less tobacco and alcohol consumption among teenagers; higher self-reported empathy, life satisfaction, and relationship quality among college students; and higher manager ratings of effectiveness among leaders of an insurance company's customer claims teams. Emotional intelligence also seems to explain the perceived quality of social relationships over and above what personality traits and traditional measures of intelligence might explain.

Stronger evidence that emotional skills are associated with social adaptation comes from studies with children, using very different measures. In a large number of studies, children's abilities to read emotions in faces, understand emotional vocabulary, and regulate their emotions have been associated with their social competence and adaptation, as rated by peers, parents, and teachers.

Emotional Intelligence in the Schools

During the 1980s and 1990s, the idea that the social problems of young people (e.g., dropping out of school, illicit drug use, teenage pregnancy) can be addressed through school-based prevention programs became popular among educational reformers. Earlier programs focused primarily on social problem-solving skills or conflict resolution strategies. After the 1995 publication of a best-selling trade book on the topic of emotional intelligence by science writer Daniel Goleman, the concept of emotional intelligence gained enormous popular appeal, and school-based programs of social and emotional learning multiplied. These programs usually deal with emotions explicitly, and they can help children to build a feelings vocabulary, recognize facial expressions of emotion, control impulsive behavior, and regulate feelings such as sorrow and anger.

There is evidence that programs of social and emotional learning that are well designed and well implemented can promote children's social and emotional adjustment. Programs such as Promoting Alternative Thinking Strategies (PATHS), the Seattle

Social Development Project, and Resolving Conflict Creatively have been evaluated through studies that track children's development over time. Benefits from these programs may include gains in children's social and emotional bonding to school, lowered dropout rates, a reduced incidence of aggressive or risky behaviors, and improvements in cognitive and emotional functioning. However, social and emotional learning programs usually address a very broad range of competencies, and it is not known to what extent the benefits observed in these studies can be attributed specifically to the training of emotional skills. Moreover, the success of these interventions depends on many factors, including the quality and motivation of the teachers, as well as their capacity to promote informal learning and generalization of skills.

Researchers associated with the Collaborative to Advance Social and Emotional Learning (CASEL) and others have drafted useful guidelines to help educators choose, adapt, and implement effective social and emotional learning programs. Important questions remain to be addressed, however. In dealing with others, people draw upon a very wide range of social and emotional skills, and it may be difficult to address all these competencies through formal or explicit instruction. It is not clear exactly what skills to emphasize, what are the best ways of teaching these skills, and to what extent they generalize across settings and situations.

Emotional skills may contribute to academic achievement in various ways. The ability to perceive and understand emotions may facilitate writing and artistic expression, as well as the interpretation of literature and works of art. Emotional regulation may help children to handle the anxiety of taking tests, or the frustrations associated with any pursuit requiring an investment of time and effort. It may also facilitate control of attention, sustained intellectual engagement, intrinsic motivation, and enjoyment of challenging academic activities.

See also: INTELLIGENCE, *subentry on* MYTHS, MYSTERIES, AND REALITIES.

BIBLIOGRAPHY

BAR-ON, REUVEN. 1997. *EQ-I: Bar-On Emotional Quotient Inventory.* Toronto: Multi-Health Systems.

CANTOR, NANCY, and KIHLSTROM, JOHN F. 1987. *Personality and Social Intelligence.* Englewood Cliffs, NJ: Prentice-Hall.

DARWIN, CHARLES. 1872. *The Expression of the Emotions in Man and Animals.* Chicago: University of Chicago Press.

GARDNER, HOWARD. 1983. *Frames of Mind: The Theory of Multiple Intelligences.* New York: Basic Books.

GOLEMAN, DANIEL. 1995. *Emotional Intelligence.* New York: Bantam.

MAYER, JOHN D.; CARUSO, DAVID R.; and SALOVEY, PETER. 1999. "Emotional Intelligence Meets Traditional Standards for an Intelligence." *Intelligence* 27:267–298.

MAYER, JOHN D., and SALOVEY, PETER. 1997. "What Is Emotional Intelligence?" In *Emotional Development and Emotional Intelligence,* ed. Peter Salovey and David Sluyter. New York: Basic Books.

MAYER, JOHN D.; SALOVEY, PETER; CARUSO, DAVID R.; and SITARENIOS, GILL. 2001. "Emotional Intelligence As a Standard Intelligence." *Emotion* 1:232–242.

SAARNI, CAROLYN. 1999. *The Development of Emotional Competence.* New York: Guilford Press.

SALOVEY, PETER, and MAYER, JOHN D. 1990. "Emotional Intelligence." *Imagination, Cognition, and Personality* 9:185–211.

SALOVEY, PETER; MAYER, JOHN D.; GOLDMAN, SUSAN L.; TURVEY, CAROLYN; and PALFAI, TIBOR P. 1995. "Emotional Attention, Clarity, and Repair: Exploring Emotional Intelligence Using the Trait Meta-Mood Scale." In *Emotion, Disclosure, and Health,* ed. James Pennebaker. Washington, DC: American Psychological Association.

SALOVEY, PETER, and SLUYTER, DAVID J., eds. 1997. *Emotional Development and Emotional Intelligence: Educational Implications.* New York: Basic Books.

SCHUTTE, NICOLLA S.; MALOUFF, JOHN M.; HALL, L. E.; HAGGERTY, D. J.; COOPER, JOAN T.; GOLDEN, C. J.; and DORNHEIM, L. 1998. "Development and Validation of a Measure of Emotional Intelligence." *Personality and Individual Differences* 25:167–177.

STERNBERG, ROBERT J. 1985. *Beyond IQ: A Triarchic Theory of Human Intelligence.* Cambridge, Eng.: Cambridge University Press.

PETER SALOVEY
PAULO N. LOPES

MEASUREMENT

Introductory treatments of the measurement of intelligence often begin with a discussion of three pioneers in the field: the French psychologist Alfred Binet (1857–1911), the English psychologist Charles Spearman (1863–1945), and the American psychologist Lewis Terman (1877–1956). Binet initiated the applied mental measurement movement when, in 1905, he introduced the first test of general mental ability. Spearman offered support for a psychologically cohesive dimension of general intellectual ability when, in 1904, he showed that a dominant dimension (called *g*) appears to run through heterogeneous collections of intellectual tasks. And Terman championed the application of intelligence testing in schools and in the military. Subsequently, Terman also illustrated how tracking intellectually talented youth longitudinally (i.e., via long-term studies) affords fundamental insights about human development in general.

Binet: The Testing of Mental Ability

Binet was not the first to attempt to measure mental ability. Operating under the maxim of the fourth century B.C.E. Greek philosopher Aristotle, that the mind is informed to the extent that one's sensory systems bring in clear and reliable information, the English scientist Francis Galton (1822–1911) and others had aimed to measure intellect through fundamental psychophysical procedures that indexed the strength of various sensory systems. In contrast, Binet examined complex behaviors, such as comprehension and reasoning, directly. In doing so, his methods could not compare to psychophysical assessments in terms of *reliability.* But Binet more than made up for this in the *validity* of his assessment procedure in predicting school performance. Binet's insight was to use an external criterion to validate his measuring tool. Thus, he pioneered the empirically keyed or external validation approach to scale construction. His external criterion was chronological age, and test items were grouped such that the typical member of each age group was able to achieve 50 percent correct answers on questions of varying complexity. With Binet's procedure, individual differences in scale scores, or mental age (MA), manifested wide variation around students of similar chronological age (CA). These components were synthesized by William Stern to create a ratio of mental development: MA/CA. This was later multiplied by 100 to form what became known as the intelligence quotient ("IQ"), namely IQ = MA/CA × 100.

Spearman: The Discovery of *g*

While Binet was creating the first valid test of general intellectual functioning, Spearman was conducting basic research that offered tangible support for the idea that a psychologically cohesive dimension of general intelligence (*g*) underlies performance on any set of items demanding mental effort. In a groundbreaking publication from 1904 called "'General Intelligence': Objectively Determined and Measured," Spearman showed that *g* appears to run through all heterogeneous collections of intellectual tasks and test items. Ostensibly, items aggregated to form such groupings were seen as a hodgepodge. Yet when such items are all positively correlated and they are summed, the signal received by each is successively amplified and the noise carried by each is successively attenuated. And the total score paints a clear picture of the attribute under analysis.

Spearman and William Brown formalized this property of aggregation in 1910. The Spearman-Brown Prophecy formula estimates the proportion of common or reliable variance running through a composite: $r_{tt} = kr_{xx} \div 1 + (k - 1)r_{xx}$ (where: r_{tt} = common or reliable variance, r_{xx} = average item intercorrelation, and k = number of items). This formula reveals how a collection of items with uniformly light (weak) positive intercorrelations (say, averaging $r_{xx} = .15$) can create a composite dominated by common variance. If fifty $r_{xx} = 15$ items were available, for example, their aggregation would generate an individual differences measure having 90 percent common variance (and 10 percent random error). Stated another way, aggregation amplifies signal and lessens noise. As Bert Green stated in his 1978 article "In Defense of Measurement," "given enough sow's ears you can indeed make a silk purse" (p. 666). A large number of weak positive correlations between test items is, in fact, the ideal when measuring broad psychological attributes.

Terman: The Application of IQ

Binet's approach to assessing mental ability was impressive because, unlike psychophysical assessments of sensory systems, his test forecasted teacher ratings and school performance. And Spearman's work identified the dominant dimension responsible for the validity of these forecasts. Subsequently, Terman cultivated the new enterprise of applied psychological testing. For example, he played a key role in America's military effort when he combined forces with the American psychologist Robert Yerkes (1876–1956) to facilitate personnel selection during World War I. The U.S. armed forces needed an efficient means to screen recruits, many of whom were illiterate. One of Terman's students, Arthur Otis, had devised a nonverbal test of general intelligence, and his work was heavily drawn on to build one of the two group intelligence tests used for the initial screening and the appropriate placement of recruits: the Army Alpha (for literates) and Beta (for illiterates). The role that mental measurements played in World War I and, subsequently, in World War II constitutes one of applied psychology's great success stories. Even today, an act of the U.S. Congress mandates a certain minimum score on tests of general mental ability, because training efficiency is compromised prohibitively at IQs less than or equal to 80 (the bottom 10% of those tested).

Following World War I, Terman was one of the first to draw a generalization between the utility of military intellectual assessments and problems in America's schools. In the early 1920s, Terman developed one of the most famous longitudinal studies in all of psychology, exclusively devoted to the intellectually gifted (the top 1%). Terman, a former teacher himself, was aware of the ability range found in homogeneous groupings based on chronological age and became an advocate of homogeneous grouping based on mental age. Drawing on solid empirical findings from his study of 1,528 intellectually precocious youth (a study that continued after his death in 1956 and into the twenty-first century), he proposed that, at the extremes (say, two standard deviations beyond either side of IQ's normative mean), the likelihood of encountering special student needs increases exponentially. Terman noted that structuring educational settings around chronological age often results in classes of students with markedly different rates of learning (because of markedly different mental ages). Optimal rates of curriculum presentation and complexity vary in gradation throughout the range of individual differences in general intelligence. With IQ centered on 100 and a standard deviation of 16, IQs extending from the bottom 1 percent to the top 1 percent in ability cover an IQ range of approximately 63 to 137. But because IQs are known to go beyond 200, this span covers less than half of the possible range. Leta Hollingworth's classic 1942 study, *Children above 180 IQ*, provided empirical support for the unique educational needs of this special population. These needs have been empirically supported in every decade since.

The Modern Hierarchical Structure of Mental Abilities

Modern versions of intelligence tests index essentially the same construct that was uncovered at the turn of the twentieth century in Spearman's 1904 work, "'General Intelligence': Objectively Determined and Measured"—albeit with much more efficiency and precision. For example, g is a statistical distillate that represents approximately half of what is common among the thirteen subtests comprising the Wechsler Adult Intelligence Scale. As noted by intelligence researcher Ian J. Deary in "Intelligence: A Very Short Introduction," the attribute g represents the research finding that "there is something shared by all the tests in terms of people's tendencies to do well, modestly, or poorly on all of them" (p. 10). In 2001 Deary's team published the longest temporal stability assessment of general intelligence to date (covering a span of sixty-six years, from age eleven to age seventy-seven); they observed a correlation of .62, which rose to over .70 when statistical artifacts were controlled.

John B. Carroll and other modern psychometricians have come to a consensus that mental abilities follow a hierarchical structure, with g at the top of the hierarchy and other broad groups of mental abilities offering psychological import beyond g. Specifically, mathematical, spatial-mechanical, and verbal reasoning abilities all have demonstrated incremental (value-added) validity beyond g in forecasting educational and vocational criteria. Although mathematical, spatial, and verbal reasoning abilities do not have the breadth or depth of external correlates that g does, the incremental validity they offer makes them especially important for educational and vocational planning.

Psychological and Social Correlates of *g*

Psychologists at poles of the applied educational–industrial spectrum, such as Richard Snow and John Campbell, respectively, have underscored the real-world significance of general intelligence by incorporating it in lawlike empirical generalizations, as in the following two passages:

> Given new evidence and reconsideration of old evidence, [*g*] can indeed be interpreted as "ability to learn" as long as it is clear that these terms refer to complex processes and skills and that a somewhat different mix of these constituents may be required in different learning tasks and settings. The old view that mental tests and learning tasks measure distinctly different abilities should be discarded. (Snow, p. 22)

> General mental ability is a substantively significant determinant of individual differences in job performance for any job that includes information-processing tasks. If the measure of performance reflects the information processing components of the job and any of several well-developed standardized measures used to assess general mental ability, then the relationship will be found unless the sample restricts the variances in performance or mental ability to near zero. The exact size of the relationship will be a function of the range of talent in the sample and the degree to which the job requires information processing and verbal cognitive skills. (Campbell, p. 56)

Modern research on general intelligence has sharpened validity generalizations aimed at forecasting educational outcomes, occupational training, and work performance. But empiricism also has escalated in domains at the periphery of general intelligence's network of external relationships, such as aggression, delinquency and crime, and income and poverty. For some benchmarks, general intellectual ability covaries .70–.80 with academic achievement measures, .40–.70 with military training assignments, .20–.60 with work performance (higher correlations reflect greater job complexity), .30–.40 with income, and around .20 with law-abidingness.

An excellent compilation of positive and negative correlates of *g* can be found in a 1987 work by Christopher Brand that documents a variety of weak correlations between general intelligence and diverse phenomena. For example, *g* is positively correlated with altruism, sense of humor, practical knowledge, responsiveness to psychotherapy, social skills, and supermarket shopping ability, and negatively correlated with impulsivity, accident-proneness, delinquency, smoking, racial prejudice, and obesity. This diverse family of correlates is especially thought-provoking because it reveals how individual differences in general intelligence "pull" with them cascades of direct and indirect effects.

Charles Murray's 1998 longitudinal analysis of educational and income differences between siblings is also illuminating. Murray studied biologically related siblings who shared the same home of rearing and socioeconomic class yet differed on average by 12 IQ points. He found that the differences in IQ predicted differences in educational achievement and income over the course of 15 years. His findings corroborate those of other studies that use a similar control for family environment, while not confounding socioeconomic status with biological relatedness.

Experts' definitions of general intelligence appear to fit with *g*'s nexus of empirical relationships. Most measurement experts agree that measures of general intelligence assess individual differences pertaining to "abstract thinking or reasoning," "the capacity to acquire knowledge," and "problem-solving ability." Naturally, individual differences in these attributes carry over to human behavior in facets of life outside of academic and vocational arenas. Abstract reasoning, problem solving, and rate of learning touch many aspects of life in general, especially in the computer-driven, information-dense society of the United States in the early twenty-first century.

Biological Correlates of *g*

General intelligence may be studied at different levels of analysis, and, as documented by Arthur Jensen in "The g Factor," modern measures of *g* have been linked to a variety of biological phenomena. By pooling studies of a variety of kinship correlates of *g* (e.g., identical and fraternal twins reared together and apart, and a variety of adoption designs), the heritability of general intelligence in industrialized nations has been estimated to be between 60 and 80 percent. These estimates reflect genetic factors responsible for individual differences between people, not overall level of g. In addition, research teams in molecular genetics, led by Robert Plomin, are working to uncover DNA markers associated with *g*.

Using magnetic resonance imaging technology, total brain volume covaries in the high .30s with *g* after removing the variance associated with body size. Glucose metabolism is related to problem-solving behavior, and the highly gifted appear to engage in more efficient problem-solving behavior that is less energy expensive. Also, highly intellectually gifted individuals show enhanced right hemispheric functioning, and electroencephdographic (EEG) phenomena have been linked to individual differences in *g*. Finally, some investigators have suggested that dendritic arborization (the amount of branching of dendrites in neurons) is correlated with *g*.

A Continuing Field of Debate

The above empiricism is widely accepted among experts in the measurement/individual differences field. Yet, it has been common for empiricism pertaining to general intelligence (and interpretative extrapolations emanating from it) to stimulate contentious debate. Indeed, psychologists can be found on all sides of the complex set of issues engendered by assessing individual differences in general intelligence. But this is not new, and it is likely to continue. Because psychological assessments are frequently used for allocating educational and vocational opportunities, and because different demographic groups differ in test score *and* criterion performance, social concerns have followed the practice of intellectual assessment since its beginning in the early 1900s. In the context of these social concerns, alternative conceptualizations of intelligence, such as Howard Gardner's theory of multiple intelligences, Daniel Goleman's theory of emotional intelligence, and Robert Sternberg's triarchic theory of intelligence have generally been positively received by the public. Yet, measures of these alternative formulations of intelligence have not demonstrated incremental validity beyond what is already gained by conventional measures of intelligence. That is, they have not yet demonstrated incremental validity beyond conventional psychometric tests in the prediction of important life outcomes such as educational achievement, occupational level, and job performance. This is not to say that there is no room for improvement in the prediction process. Innovative measures of mental abilities, however, need to be evaluated against existing measures before one can claim that they capture something new.

See also: ASSESSMENT TOOLS, *subentry on* PSYCHOMETRIC AND STATISTICAL; BINET, ALFRED; INTELLI-GENCE, *subentry on* MYTHS, MYSTERIES, AND REALITIES; TERMAN, LEWIS.

BIBLIOGRAPHY

BRAND, CHRISTOPHER. 1987. "The Importance of General Intelligence." In *Arthur Jensen: Consensus and Controversy,* ed. Sohan Magil and Celia Magil. New York: Falmer.

CAMPBELL, JOHN P. 1990. "The Role of Theory in Industrial and Organizational Psychology." In *Handbook of Industrial and Organizational Psychology,* 2nd edition, ed. Marvin D. Dunnette and Leaette M. Hough. Palo Alto, CA: Consulting Psychologists Press.

CARROLL, JOHN B. 1993. *Human Cognitive Abilities: A Survey of Factor-Analytic Studies.* Cambridge, Eng.: Cambridge University Press.

DEARY, IAN J. 2001. *Intelligence: A Very Short Introduction.* New York: Oxford University Press.

GOTTFREDSON, LINDA S., ed. 1997. "Intelligence and Social Policy" (special issue). *Intelligence* 24(1).

GREEN, BERT F. 1978. "In Defense of Measurement." *American Psychologist* 33:664–670.

HOLLINGWORTH, LETA S. 1942. *Children above 180 IQ.* New York: World Book.

JENSEN, ARTHUR R. 1998. *The g Factor: The Science of Mental Ability.* Westport, CT: Praeger.

MURRAY, CHARLES. 1998. *Income, Inequality, and IQ.* Washington, DC: American Enterprise Institute.

SNOW, RICHARD E. 1989. "Aptitude-Treatment Interaction as a Framework for Research on Individual Differences in Learning." In *Learning and Individual Differences: Advances in Theory and Research,* ed. Phillip. L. Ackerman, Robert J. Sternberg, and Robert G. Glasser. New York: Freeman.

SNYDERMAN, MARK, and ROTHMAN, STANLEY. 1987. "Survey of Expert Opinion on Intelligence and Aptitude Testing." *American Psychologist* 42:137–144.

SPEARMAN, CHARLES. 1904. "'General Intelligence': Objectively Determined and Measured." *American Journal of Psychology* 15:201–292.

TERMAN, LEWIS. 1925–1959. *Genetic Studies of Genius,* 4 vols. Stanford, CA: Stanford University Press.

THORNDIKE, ROBERT M., and LOHMAN, DAVID F. 1990. *A Century of Ability Testing.* Chicago: Riverside.

DAVID LUBINSKI
APRIL BLESKE-RECHEK

MULTIPLE INTELLIGENCES

The theory of multiple intelligences (MI) was developed by Howard Gardner, a professor of cognition and education at Harvard University. Introduced in his 1983 book, *Frames of Mind,* and refined in subsequent writings, the theory contends that human intelligence is not a single complex entity or a unified set of processes (the dominant view in the field of psychology). Instead, Gardner posits that there are several relatively autonomous intelligences, and that an individual's intellectual profile reflects a unique configuration of these intelligences.

Definition of Intelligence

In his 1999 formulation of MI theory, *Intelligence Reframed,* Gardner defines intelligence as "a biopsychological potential to process information that can be activated in a cultural setting to solve problems or create products that are of value in a culture." By considering intelligence a potential, Gardner asserts its emergent and responsive nature, thereby differentiating his theory from traditional ones in which human intelligence is fixed and innate. Whether a potential will be activated is dependent in large part on the values of the culture in which an individual grows up and the opportunities available in that culture, although Gardner also acknowledges the role of personal decisions made by individuals, their families, and others. These activating forces result in the development and expression of a range of abilities (or intelligences) from culture to culture and also from individual to individual.

Gardner's definition of intelligence is unique as well in that it considers the creation of products such as sculptures and computers to be as important an expression of intelligence as abstract problem solving. Traditional theories do not recognize created artifacts as a manifestation of intelligence, and therefore are limited in how they conceptualize and measure it.

Criteria for intelligences. Gardner does not believe that the precise number of intelligences is known, nor does he believe that they can be identified through statistical analyses of cognitive test results. He began by considering the range of adult end-states that are valued in diverse cultures around the world. To uncover the abilities that support these end-states, he examined a wide variety of empirical sources from different disciplines that had never been used together for the purpose of defining human intelligence. His examination yielded eight criteria for defining an intelligence:

- Two criteria derived from biology: (1) an intelligence should be isolable in cases of brain damage, and (2) there should be evidence for its plausibility and autonomy in evolutionary history.

- Two criteria derived from developmental psychology: (3) an intelligence has to have a distinct developmental history along with a definable set of expert end-state performances, and (4) it must exist within special populations such as idiot savants and prodigies.

- Two criteria derived from traditional psychology: (5) an intelligence needs to be supported by the results of skill training for its relatively independent operation, and (6) also by the results of psychometric studies for its low correlation to other intelligences.

- Two criteria derived from logical analysis: (7) an intelligence must have its own identifiable core operation or set of operations, and (8) it must be susceptible to encoding in a symbol system—such as language, numbers, graphics, or musical notations.

To be defined as an intelligence, an ability has to meet most, though not all, of the eight criteria.

Identified intelligences. As of 2001, Gardner has identified eight intelligences:

1. Linguistic intelligence, exemplified by writers and poets, describes the ability to perceive and generate spoken or written language.

2. Logical-mathematical intelligence, exemplified by mathematicians and computer programmers, involves the ability to appreciate and utilize numerical, abstract, and logical reasoning to solve problems.

3. Musical intelligence, exemplified by musicians and composers, entails the ability to create, communicate, and understand meanings made out of sound.

4. Spatial intelligence, exemplified by graphic

designers and architects, refers to the ability to perceive, modify, transform, and create visual or spatial images.

5. Bodily-kinesthetic intelligence, exemplified by dancers and athletes, deals with the ability to use all or part of one's body to solve problems or to fashion products.

6. Naturalistic intelligence, exemplified by archaeologists and botanists, concerns the ability to distinguish, classify, and use features of the environment.

7. Interpersonal intelligence, exemplified by leaders and teachers, describes the ability to recognize, appreciate, and contend with the feelings, beliefs, and intentions of other people.

8. Intrapersonal intelligence, apparent when individuals pursue a particular interest, choose a field of study or work, or portray their life through different media, involves the ability to understand oneself—including emotions, desires, strengths, and vulnerabilities—and to use such information effectively in regulating one's own life.

Gardner does not claim this roster of intelligences to be exhaustive; MI theory is based wholly on empirical evidence, and the roster can therefore be revised with new empirical findings. In the MI framework, all intelligences are equally valid and important, and though significantly independent of one another, they do not operate in isolation. Human activity normally reflects the integrated functioning of several intelligences. An effective teacher, for example, relies on linguistic and interpersonal intelligences, and possesses knowledge of particular subject areas as well.

Relationship to Other Theories

MI theory bears similarities to several other contemporary theories of intelligence, yet it remains distinct. Although it shares a pluralistic view of intelligence with Robert Sternberg's triarchic theory, MI theory organizes intelligences in terms of content areas, and no single cognitive function, such as perception or memory, cuts across all domains. The triarchic theory, in contrast, posits three intelligences differentiated by functional processes, and each intelligence operates consistently across domains.

Daniel Goleman's theory of emotional intelligence resonates with MI theory in that both acknowledge the social and affective aspects of intelligence. Whereas Goleman views intelligence from a moral and ethical perspective, however, Gardner regards all intelligences as value-free: He does not judge individuals as inferior or superior based on their configuration of intelligences, nor does he judge cultures as inferior or superior because they value one intelligence over another.

MI theory has been criticized on two grounds. First, some critics contend that psychometric research finds correlations, not autonomy, among abilities. Gardner has argued that these correlations are largely due to the use of psychometric instruments designed to measure only a given set of abilities. Second, critics have suggested that human intelligence is different from other human capabilities, such as musical talent. Gardner believes that such a narrow use of the word *intelligence* reflects a Western intellectual mind-set that does not recognize the diversity of roles that contribute to society.

Implications for Educational Practice

The primary intent for developing MI theory was to chart the evolution and topography of the human mind, not to prescribe educational practice. Nonetheless, MI theory has been discussed widely in the educational field and has been particularly influential in elementary education, where it has provided a useful framework for improving school-based practice in the areas of curricula, instruction, and assessment.

Curricula and instruction. From an MI perspective, curricula, particularly for young children, should encompass a broad range of subject areas that include (but go beyond) reading, writing, and arithmetic, because all intelligences are equally valuable. The visual arts, for example, are a serious domain in and of themselves, and not just as a means to improve reading scores. According to MI theory, the talented artist is just as intelligent as the excellent reader, and each has an important place in society. In *The Disciplined Mind,* Gardner cautions that an authentic MI-based approach goes beyond conveying factual knowledge about various domains: He stresses the importance of promoting in-depth exploration and real understanding of key concepts essential to a domain.

Because each child's biopsychological potential is different, providing a broad range of subject areas at a young age also increases the likelihood of discovering interests and abilities that can be nurtured and appreciated. Educators who work with at-risk children have been particularly drawn to this application of MI theory, because it offers an approach to intervention that focuses on strengths instead of deficits. By the same token, it extends the concept of the gifted child beyond those who excel in linguistic and logical pursuits to include children who achieve in a wide range of domains.

MI theory can be applied to the development of instructional techniques as well. A teacher can provide multiple entry points to the study of a particular topic by using different media, for example, and then encouraging students to express their understanding of the topic through diverse representational methods, such as pictures, writings, three-dimensional models, or dramatizations. Such instructional approaches make it possible for students to find at least one way of learning that is attuned to their predispositions, and they therefore increase motivation and engagement in the learning process. They also increase the likelihood that every student will attain at least some understanding of the topic at hand.

Assessment. When applied to student assessment, MI theory results in the exploration of a much wider range of abilities than is typical in the classroom, in a search for genuine problem-solving or product-fashioning skills. An MI-based assessment requires "intelligence-fair" instruments that assess each intellectual capacity through media appropriate to the domain, rather than through traditional linguistic or logical methods. Gardner also argues that for assessment to be meaningful to students and instructive for teachers, students should work on problems and projects that engage them and hold their interest; they should be informed of the purpose of the task— and the assessment criteria as well; and they should be encouraged to work individually, in pairs, or in a group. Thus, the unit of analysis extends beyond the individual to include both the material and social context.

MI-based assessments are not as easy to design and implement as standard pencil-and-paper tests, but they have the potential to elicit a student's full repertoire of skills and yield information that will be useful for subsequent teaching and learning. As part of Project Spectrum, Gardner and colleagues developed a set of assessment activities and observational guidelines covering eight domains, including many often ignored by traditional assessment instruments,

such as mechanical construction and social understanding. Project Spectrum's work also included linking children's assessments to curricular development and bridging their identified strengths to other areas of learning.

Evidence of the Value of the Theory

MI theory has been incorporated into the educational process in schools around the world. There is much anecdotal evidence that educators, parents, and students value the theory, but, as of 2001, little systematic research on the topic has been completed. The main study was conducted by Mindy Kornhaber and colleagues at Harvard University's Project Zero in the late 1990s. They studied forty-one elementary schools in the United States that had been applying MI theory to school-based practice for at least three years. Among the schools that reported improvement in standardized-test scores, student discipline, parent participation, or performance of students with learning differences, the majority linked the improvement to MI-based interventions. Kornhaber's study also illuminates the conditions under which MI theory is adopted by schools and integrated into the educational process.

The difficulty of research on MI theory in education is correlating changes specifically to the theory, since schools are complex institutions that make it difficult to isolate cause-and-effect relationships. Indeed, since MI theory is meaningful in the context of education only when combined with pedagogical approaches such as project-based learning or arts-integrated learning, it is not possible to study the precise contribution of the theory itself to educational change, only the effect of interventions that are based on it or incorporate it.

See also: ASSESSMENT, *subentries on* CLASSROOM ASSESSMENT, PERFORMANCE ASSESSMENT, PORTFOLIO ASSESSMENT.

BIBLIOGRAPHY

CHEN, JIE-QI; KRECHEVSKY, MARA; and VIENS, JULIE. 1998. *Building on Children's Strengths: The Experience of Project Spectrum.* New York: Teachers College Press.

GARDNER, HOWARD. 1993. *Frames of Mind: The Theory of Multiple Intelligences.* New York: Basic Books.

GARDNER, HOWARD. 1993. *Multiple Intelligences: The Theory in Practice.* New York: Basic Books.

GARDNER, HOWARD. 1999. *Intelligence Reframed: Multiple Intelligences for the 21st Century.* New York: Basic Books.

GARDNER, HOWARD. 2000. *The Disciplined Mind: Beyond Facts and Standardized Tests: The K–12 Education That Every Child Deserves.* New York: Penguin Books.

GOLEMAN, DANIEL. 1995. *Emotional Intelligence: Why It Can Matter More Than IQ.* New York: Bantam Books.

KORNHABER, MINDY L. 1999. "Multiple Intelligences Theory in Practice." In *Comprehensive School Reform: A Program Perspective,* ed. James H. Block, Susan T. Everson, and Thomas R. Guskey. Dubuque, IA: Kendall/Hunt.

STERNBERG, ROBERT J. 1988. *The Triarchic Mind: A New Theory of Human Intelligence.* New York: Viking.

JIE-QI CHEN

MYTHS, MYSTERIES, AND REALITIES

Intelligence and intelligence tests are often at the heart of controversy. Some arguments concern the ethical and moral implications of, for example, selective breeding of bright children. Other arguments deal with the statistical basis of various conclusions such as whether tests are biased, or how much of intelligence is genetically determined. What one hears less often is discussion of the construct of intelligence itself: What is intelligence? How does it grow? How and why do people differ intellectually? Questions like these, along with many others, which are central to any discussion of intelligence and intelligence testing, are less often raised, much less answered.

Historical Roots of Intelligence Tests

Intelligence testing began as a more or less scientific pursuit into the nature of differences in human intellect. However, it soon acquired practical significance as a tool for predicting school achievement and selecting individuals for various educational programs. Sir Francis Galton's work in the late 1800s formed the background for much of the research and theory pursued during the twentieth century on the assessment of individual differences in intelligence.

Galton believed that all intelligent behavior was related to innate sensory ability but his attempts to empirically validate that assumption were largely unsuccessful. In France, Alfred Binet and Victor Henri (1896) criticized the approach advocated by Galton in England and James McKeen Cattell in the United States and argued that appropriate intelligence testing must include assessment of more complex mental processes, such as memory, attention, imagery, and comprehension. In 1904, Binet and Théodore Simon were commissioned by the French Minister of Public Instruction to develop a procedure to select children unable to benefit from regular public school instruction for placement in special educational programs. In 1905 Binet and Simon published an objective, standardized intelligence test based on the concepts developed earlier by Binet and Henri. The 1905 test consisted of thirty subtests of mental ability, including tests of digit span, object and body part identification, sentence memory, and so forth. Many of these subtests, with minor modifications, are included in the Stanford-Binet intelligence test of the early twenty-first century.

In 1908 and again in 1911, Binet and Simon published revised versions of their intelligence test. The revised tests distinguished intellectual abilities according to age norms, thus introducing the concept of *mental age.* The subtests were organized according to the age level at which they could be successfully performed by most children of normal intelligence. As a result, children could be characterized and compared in terms of their intellectual or mental age. The Binet and Simon intelligence test was widely adopted in Europe and in the United States. Lewis Terman of Stanford University developed the more extensive Stanford-Binet test in 1916. This test has been used extensively in several updated versions throughout the United States.

A major change in intelligence testing involved the development of intelligence tests that could be simultaneously administered to large groups. Group tests similar to the original Binet and Simon intelligence test were developed in Britain and the United States. During World War I, group-administered intelligence tests (the Army Alpha and Army Beta tests) were used in the United States to assess the abilities of recruits who could then be selected for various duties based on their performance. In England, from the 1940s to the 1960s, intelligence tests were administered to all children near the age of eleven years to select students for different classes of vocational training.

An enormous number of "mental" tests are available in the early twenty-first century and are typically divided into those involving group versus individual administration. Whereas IQ (the intelligence quotient) was originally reported as the ratio of an individual's mental age to chronological age multiplied by 100 (100 x MA/CA), IQ has long been based upon normative score distributions for particular age groups. All individual and group tests currently yield such deviation IQs where 100 typically represents the 50th percentile and 68 percent of all scores fall between 85 and 115.

Factor Theories of Intelligence

What is intelligence and what do these tests actually assess? Very early in the psychological study of intelligence, Charles Spearman (1904) sought to empirically determine the similarities and differences between various mental tests and school performance measures. He found that many seemingly diverse mental tests were strongly correlated with each other. This led him to postulate a general factor of intelligence, g, that all mental tests measure in common while simultaneously varying in how much the general factor contributes to a given test's performance. On the basis of correlational studies, Spearman argued that intelligence is composed of a general factor that is found in all intellectual functioning plus specific factors associated with the performance of specific tasks. Spearman's theoretical orientation and methods of analysis served as the foundation of all subsequent factor analytic theories of intelligence. Spearman (1927) later developed a more complex factor theory introducing more general "group factors" made up of related specific factors. However, he adhered to his main tenet that a common ability underlies all intellectual behavior. For lack of a better definition, he referred to this as a mental energy or force.

The concept that intelligence is characterized by a general underlying ability plus certain task- or domain-specific abilities constitutes the basis of several major theories of intelligence, including those offered by Cyril L. Burt (1949), Philip E. Vernon (1961), and Arthur Jensen (1998). Quite distinct from theories of intelligence that emphasize g are those that emphasize specific abilities that can be combined to form more general abilities. Lloyd L. Thurstone (1924, 1938) developed factor analytic techniques that first separate out specific or primary factors. Thurstone argued that these primary factors represent discrete intellectual abilities, and he developed distinct tests to measure them. Among the most important of Thurstone's primary mental abilities are verbal comprehension, word fluency, numerical ability, spatial relations, memory, reasoning, and perceptual speed.

Raymond Cattell (1963, 1971) attempted a rapprochement of the theories of Spearman and Thurstone. In an attempt to produce a g factor, he combined Thurstone's primary factors to form secondary or higher-order factors. Cattell found two major types of higher order factors and three minor ones. The major factors were labeled gf and gc, for fluid and crystallized general intelligence. Cattell argued that the fluid intelligence factor represents an individual's basic biological capacity. Crystallized intelligence represents the types of abilities required for most school activities. Cattell labeled the minor general factors gv, gr, and gs for visual abilities, memory retrieval, and performance speed, respectively. Cattell's initial theory has been substantially extended by individuals such as John L. Horn (1979, 1985).

The most recent psychometric research supports a hierarchical model of intellect generally in accord with the outlines of the Cattell-Horn theory. At the top of the hierarchy is g and under g are broad group factors such as gf and gc. Below these broad group factors are more specific or narrow ability factors. The majority of intelligence tests focus on providing overall estimates of g (or gf and gc) since this maximizes the prediction of performance differences among people in other intellectual tasks and situations, including performance in school.

Alternative Theoretical Perspectives

The hierarchical model of human intelligence that has evolved from the psychometric or measurement approach is not the only influential perspective on human intellect. A second view of intelligence, that provided by developmental psychology, stems from the theory of intellectual development proposed by the Swiss psychologist Jean Piaget. This tradition is a rich source of information on the growth and development of intellect. A third view on intelligence, the information-processing or cognitive perspective, is an outgrowth of work in cognitive psychology since the 1970s. It provides elaborate descriptions and theories of the specific mental activities and representations that comprise intellectual functioning. The three perspectives are similar with regard to the general skills and activities that each associates with "being or becoming intelligent." For all three, reasoning and problem-solving skills are the principal components of intelligence. A second area of overlap among the three involves adaptability as an aspect of intelligence.

The differences and separate contributions of the three perspectives to an understanding of human intellect also stand out. The emphasis on individual differences within the psychometric tradition is certainly relevant to any complete understanding of intelligence. A theory of intelligence should take into account similarities and differences among individuals in their cognitive skills and performance capabilities. However, a theory of human intellect based solely on patterns of differences among individuals cannot capture all of intellectual functioning unless there is little that is general and similar in intellectual performance.

In contrast, the developmental tradition emphasizes similarities in intellectual growth and the importance of organism–environment interactions. By considering the nature of changes that occur in cognition and the mechanisms and conditions responsible, one can better understand human intellectual growth and its relationship to the environment. This requires, however, that one focus not just on commonalities in the general course of cognitive growth, but consider how individuals differ in the specifics of their intellectual growth. Such a developmental-differential emphasis seems necessary for a theory to have adequate breadth and to move the study of intelligence away from a static, normative view, where intelligence changes little over development, to a more dynamic view that encompasses developmental change in absolute levels of cognitive power.

Finally, the cognitive perspective helps to define the scope of a theory of intelligence by further emphasizing the dynamics of cognition, through its concentration on precise theories of the knowledge and processes that allow individuals to perform intellectual tasks. Psychometric and developmental theories typically give little heed to these processes, yet they are necessary for a theory of intelligence to make precise, testable predictions about intellectual performance.

No theory developed within any of the three perspectives addresses all of the important elements and issues mentioned above. This includes the more recent and rather broad theories such as Howard

Gardner's multiple intelligences theory (1983, 1999) and Robert J. Sternberg's triarchic theory (1985). Both theories represent an interesting blending of psychometric, developmental, and cognitive perspectives.

Uses and Abuses of Tests

Above it was noted that testing was developed in response to pragmatic concerns regarding educational selection and placement. The use of intelligence tests for educational selection and placement proliferated during the decades from the 1930s through 1960s as group tests for children became readily available. Since the early 1980s, however, general intelligence testing has declined in public educational institutions. One reason for diminished used of such tests is a trend away from homogeneous grouping of students and attendant educational tracking. A second reason is that achievement rather than aptitude testing has become increasingly popular. Not surprisingly, such tests tend to be better predictors of subsequent achievement than aptitude or intelligence tests. Even so, it is an established fact that measures of general intelligence obtained in childhood yield a moderate 0.50 correlation with school grades. They also correlate about 0.55 with the number of years of education that individuals complete.

Intelligence and aptitude tests continue to be used with great frequency in military, personnel-selection, and clinical settings. There are also two major uses of intelligence tests within educational settings. One of these is for the assessment of mental retardation and learning disabilities, a use of tests reminiscent of the original reason for development of the Binet and Simon scales in the early 1900s. The second major use is at the postsecondary level. College entrance is frequently based upon performance on measures such as the SAT, first adopted in the United States by the College Entrance Examination Board in 1937. Performance on the SAT, together with high school grades, is the basis for admission to many American colleges and universities. The ostensible basis for using SAT scores is that they moderately predict freshman grade point average—precisely what they were originally designed to do. However, considerable debate has arisen about the legitimacy and value of continued use of SAT scores for college admission decisions.

Throughout the history of the testing movement, dating back to the early 1900s and extending to the early twenty-first century, there has been controversy concerning the (mis)use of test results. One of the earliest such debates was between Lewis Terman, who helped develop the revised Stanford-Binet and other tests, and the journalist Walter Lippman. A frequent issue in debates about the uses and abuses of intelligence tests in society is that of bias. It is often argued that most standardized intelligence tests have differential validity for various racial, ethnic, and socioeconomic groups. Since the tests emphasize verbal skills and knowledge that are part of Western schooling, they are presumed to be unfair tests of the cognitive abilities of other groups. As a response to such arguments, attempts have been made to develop culture-fair or culture-free tests. The issue of bias in mental testing is beyond this brief review and Arthur R. Jensen (1980; 1981) can be consulted for highly detailed treatments of this topic. Evidence in the 1990s suggests that no simple form of bias in either the content or form of intelligence tests accounts for the mean score differences typically observed between racial and ethnic groups.

Factors Affecting Test Scores

Much of the research on intelligence has focused on specific factors affecting test scores. This includes research focused on environmental versus genetic contributions to IQ scores, related issues such as race differences in IQ, and overall population trends in IQ.

One of the most extensively studied and hotly debated topics in the study of intelligence is the contribution of heredity and environment to individual differences in test scores. Given a trait such as measured intelligence on which individuals vary, it is inevitable for people to ask what fraction is associated with differences in their genotypes (the so-called heritability of the trait) as well as what fraction is associated with differences in environmental experience. There is a long history of sentiment and speculation with regard to this issue. It has also proven difficult to answer this question in a scientifically credible way, in large measure due to the conceptual and statistical complexity of separating out the respective contributions of heredity and environment. Adding to the complexity is the need to obtain test score data from people who have varying kinship and genetic relationships, including identical and fraternal twins, siblings, and adoptive children with their biological and adoptive parents. Nonetheless, evidence has slowly been gathered that heritability is sizeable and that it varies across populations. For IQ, heritability is markedly lower for children, about 0.45, than for adults where it is about 0.75. This means that with age, differences in test scores increasingly reflect differences in the genotype and in individual life experience rather than differences in the families within which they were raised. The factors underlying this shift as well as the mechanism by which genes contribute to individual differences in IQ scores are largely unknown. The same can be said for understanding environmental contributions to those differences. A common misconception is that traits like IQ with high heritability mean that the results are immutable, that the environment has little or no impact, or that learning is not involved. This is wrong since heritable traits like vocabulary size are known to depend on learning and environmental factors.

Perhaps no topic is more controversial than that of race differences in IQ, especially since it is so often tied up with debates about genetics and environmental influences. It is an established fact that there are significant differences between racial and ethnic groups in their average scores on standardized tests of intelligence. In the United States, the typical difference between Caucasians and African Americans is 15 points or one standard deviation. A difference of this magnitude has been observed for quite a long period of time with little evidence that the difference has declined despite significant evidence that across the world IQ scores have risen substantially over the last fifty years. The latter phenomenon is known as the "Flynn Effect," and it, like so many other phenomena associated with test scores, begs for an adequate explanation.

There is a tendency to interpret racial and ethnic differences in mean IQ scores as being determined by genetic factors since, as noted above, IQ scores in general have a fairly high level of heritability and the level of heritability seems to be about the same in different racial and ethnic groups. There is, however, no logical basis on which to attribute the mean difference between racial groups to either genetic or environmental factors. As one group of researchers stated, "In short, no adequate explanation of the differential between the IQ means of Blacks and Whites is presently available" (Neisser et al., p. 97).

Age and Intelligence

Although most intelligence tests are targeted for school-age populations, there are instruments developed for younger age groups. Such tests emphasize the assessment of perceptual and motor abilities. Unfortunately, measures of infant and pre-school intelligence tend to correlate poorly with intelligence tests administered during the school years. However, there appears to be a high degree of stability in the IQ scores obtained in the early primary grades and IQ scores obtained at the high school level and beyond. Often this is misinterpreted as indicating that an individual's intelligence does not change as a function of schooling or other environmental factors. What such results actually indicate is that an individual's score relative to his or her age group remains fairly constant. In an absolute sense, an individual of age 16 can solve considerably more difficult items and problems than an individual of age 8. Comparing IQ scores obtained at different ages is akin to comparing apples and oranges since the composition of tests changes markedly over age levels.

Research has also studied changes in IQ following early adulthood. A frequent conclusion from research examining age groups ranging from 21 to 60 and beyond is that there is an age-related general decline in intellectual functioning. However, there are serious problems with many such studies since they involve cross-sectional rather than longitudinal contrasts. In those cases where longitudinal data are available, it is less obvious that intelligence declines with age. John L. Horn and Cattell (1967) presented data indicating a possible differential decline in crystallized and fluid intelligence measures. Crystallized intelligence measures focus on verbal skills and knowledge whereas fluid intelligence measures focus on reasoning and problem solving with visual and geometric stimuli. The latter also often place an emphasis on performance speed. Fluid intelligence measures tend to show substantial declines as a function of age, whereas crystallized intelligence measures often show little or no decline until after age 65. Research in the 1990s based on combinations of longitudinal and cross-sectional samples supports the conclusion that there are age-related declines in intelligence, which seem to vary with the type of skill measured, and that the declines are often substantial in the period from age 65 to 80.

Future Outlook

After more than 100 years of theory and research on the nature and measurement of intelligence there is much that researchers know but even more that they don't understand. Still lacking is any agreed upon definition of intelligence and many of the empirical findings regarding intelligence test scores remain a puzzle. In their summary paper "Intelligence: Knowns and Unknowns," Ulric Neisser and colleagues (1996) stated:

> In a field where so many issues are unresolved and so many questions unanswered, the confident tone that has characterized most of the debate on these topics is clearly out of place. The study of intelligence does not need politicized assertions and recriminations; it needs self restraint, reflection, and a great deal more research. The questions that remain are socially as well as scientifically important. There is no reason to think them unanswerable, but finding the answers will require a shared and sustained effort as well as the commitment of substantial scientific resources. (p. 97)

See also: GIFTED AND TALENTED, EDUCATION OF; INDIVIDUAL DIFFERENCES, *subentry on* ABILITIES AND APTITUDES.

BIBLIOGRAPHY

BINET, ALFRED, and HENRI, VICTOR. 1896. "La Psychologic Individuelle." *Année Psychologie* 2:411–465.

BLOCK, NED J., and DWORKIN, GERALD. 1976. *The IQ Controversy.* New York: Pantheon Books

BRODY, NATHAN. 1992. *Intelligence.* San Diego, CA: Academic Press.

BURT, CYRIL L. 1949. "The Structure of the Mind: A Review of the Results of Factor Analysis." *British Journal of Educational Psychology* 19:100–111, 176–199.

CARROLL, JOHN B. 1978. "On the Theory-Practice Interface in the Measurement of Intellectual Abilities." In *Impact of Research on Education,* ed. Patrick Suppes. Washington, DC: National Academy of Education.

CARROLL, JOHN B. 1993. *Human Cognitive Abilities: A Survey of Factor Analytic Studies.* Cambridge, Eng.: Cambridge University Press.

CATTELL, RAYMOND B. 1963. "Theory of Fluid and Crystallized Intelligence: A Critical Experiment." *Journal of Educational Psychology* 54:1–22.

CATTELL, RAYMOND B. 1971. *Abilities: Their Structure, Growth and Action.* Boston: Houghton Mifflin.

FLYNN, JOHN R. 1987. "Massive IQ Gains in 14 Nations: What IQ Tests Really Measure." *Psychological Bulletin* 101:171–191.

GARDNER, HOWARD. 1983. *Frames of Mind: The Theory of Multiple Intelligences.* New York: Basic Books.

GARDNER, HOWARD. 1999. *Intelligence Reframed: Multiple Intelligences for the 21st Century.* New York: Basic Books.

GOULD, STEPHEN, J. 1996. *The Mismeasure of Man.* New York: Norton.

GUSTAFSSON, JAN-ERIC. 1988. "Hierarchical Models of Individual Differences in Cognitive Abilities." In *Advances in the Psychology of Human Intelligence,* Vol. 4, ed. Robert J. Sternberg. Hillsdale, NJ: Erlbaum.

HERRNSTEIN, RICHARD, and MURRAY, CHARLES. 1994. *The Bell Curve: Intelligence and Class Structure in American Life.* New York: Free Press.

HORN, JOHN L. 1979. "The Rise and Fall of Human Abilities." *Journal of Research on Developmental Education* 12:59–78.

HORN, JOHN L. 1985. "Remodeling Old Models of Intelligence." In *Handbook of Intelligence: Theories, Measurements, and Applications,* ed. Benjamin B. Wolman. New York: Wiley.

HORN, JOHN L., and CATTELL, RAYMOND B. 1967. "Age Differences in Fluid and Crystallized Intelligence." *Acta Psychologica* 26:107–129.

JENSEN, ARTHUR R. 1980. *Bias in Mental Testing.* New York: Free Press.

JENSEN, ARTHUR R. 1981. *Straight Talk on Mental Tests.* New York: Free Press.

JENSEN, ARTHUR R. 1998. *The g Factor: The Science of Mental Ability.* Westport, CT: Praeger.

LEMANN, NICHOLAS. 1999. *The Big Test: The Secret History of the American Meritocracy.* New York: Farrar, Strauss, and Giroux.

NEISSER, ULRIC, et al. 1996. "Intelligence: Knowns and Unknowns." *American Psychologist* 51:77–101.

SPEARMAN, CHARLES. 1904. "General Intelligence, Objectively Determined and Measured." *American Journal of Psychology* 15:201–293.

SPEARMAN, CHARLES. 1927. *The Abilities of Man: Their Nature and Measurement.* New York: Macmillan.

STERNBERG, ROBERT J. 1985. *Beyond IQ: A Triarchic Theory of Human Intelligence.* New York: Cambridge University Press.

THURSTONE, LLOYD L. 1924. *The Nature of Intelligence.* London and New York: Harcourt Brace.

THURSTONE, LLOYD L. 1938. *Primary Mental Abilities.* Psychometric Monographs No. 1. Chicago: University of Chicago Press.

VERNON, PHILIP E. 1961. *The Structure of Human Abilities.* London: Methuen.

JAMES W. PELLEGRINO

TRIARCHIC THEORY OF INTELLIGENCE

The triarchic theory of intelligence is based on a broader definition of intelligence than is typically used. In this theory, intelligence is defined in terms of the ability to achieve success in life based on one's personal standards—and within one's sociocultural context. The ability to achieve success depends on the ability to capitalize on one's strengths and to correct or compensate for one's weaknesses. Success is attained through a balance of analytical, creative, and practical abilities— a balance that is achieved in order to adapt to, shape, and select environments.

Information-Processing Components Underlying Intelligence

According to Robert Sternberg's proposed theory of human intelligence, a common set of universal mental processes underlies all aspects of intelligence. Although the particular solutions to problems that are considered "intelligent" in one culture may be different from those considered intelligent in another, the mental processes needed to reach these solutions are the same.

Metacomponents, or executive processes, enable a person to plan what to do, monitor things as they are being done, and evaluate things after they are done. *Performance components* execute the instructions of the metacomponents. *Knowledge-acquisition components* are used to learn how to solve problems or simply to acquire knowledge in the first place. For example, a student may plan to write a paper (metacomponents), write the paper (performance components), and learn new things while writing (knowledge-acquisition components).

Three Aspects of Intelligence

According to the triarchic theory, intelligence has three aspects: analytical, creative, and practical.

Analytical intelligence. Analytical intelligence is involved when the components of intelligence are applied to analyze, evaluate, judge, or compare and contrast. It typically is involved in dealing with relatively familiar kinds of problems where the judgments to be made are of a fairly abstract nature.

In one study, an attempt was made to identify the information-processing components used to solve analogies such as: A is to B as C is to: D1, D2, D3, D4 (e.g., lawyer is to client as doctor is to [a] nurse, [b] medicine, [c] patient, [d] MD). There is an *encoding* component, which is used to figure out what each word (e.g., *lawyer*) means, while the *inference* component is used to figure out the relation between *lawyer* and *client.*

Research on the components of human intelligence has shown that although children generally become faster in information processing with age, not all components are executed more rapidly with age. The encoding component first shows a decrease in processing time with age, and then an increase. Apparently, older children realize that their best strategy is to spend more time in encoding the terms of a problem so that they later will be able to spend less time in making sense of these encodings. Similarly, better reasoners tend to spend relatively more time than do poorer reasoners in global, up-front metacomponential planning when they solve difficult reasoning problems. Poorer reasoners, on the other hand, tend to spend relatively more time in detailed planning as they proceed through a problem. Presumably, the better reasoners recognize that it is better to invest more time up front so as to be able to process a problem more efficiently later on.

Creative intelligence. In work with creative-intelligence problems, Robert Sternberg and Todd Lubart asked sixty-three people to create various kinds of products in the realms of writing, art, advertising, and science. For example, in writing, they would be asked to write very short stories, for which the investigators would give them a choice of titles, such as "Beyond the Edge" or "The Octopus's Sneakers." In art, the participants were asked to produce art compositions with titles such as "The Beginning of Time" or "Earth from an Insect's Point of View." Participants created two products in each domain.

Sternberg and Lubart found that creativity is relatively, although not wholly, domain-specific. In other words, people are frequently creative in some domains, but not in others. They also found that correlations with conventional ability tests were modest to moderate, demonstrating that tests of creative intelligence measure skills that are largely different from those measured by conventional intelligence tests.

Practical intelligence. Practical intelligence involves individuals applying their abilities to the kinds of problems that confront them in daily life, such as on the job or in the home. Much of the work of Sternberg and his colleagues on practical intelligence has centered on the concept of tacit knowledge. They have defined this construct as what one needs to know, which is often not even verbalized, in order to work effectively in an environment one has not been explicitly taught to work in—and that is often not even verbalized.

Sternberg and colleagues have measured tacit knowledge using work-related problems one might encounter in a variety of jobs. In a typical tacit-knowledge problem, people are asked to read a story about a problem someone faces, and to then rate, for each statement in a set of statements, how adequate a solution the statement represents. For example, in a measure of tacit knowledge of sales, one of the problems deals with sales of photocopy machines. A relatively inexpensive machine is not moving out of the showroom and has become overstocked. The examinee is asked to rate the quality of various solutions for moving the particular model out of the showroom.

Sternberg and his colleagues have found that practical intelligence, as embodied in tacit knowledge, increases with experience, but that it is how one profits, or learns, from experience, rather than experience *per se,* that results in increases in scores. Some people can work at a job for years and acquire relatively little tacit knowledge. Most importantly, although tests of tacit knowledge typically show no correlation with IQ tests, they predict job performance about as well as, and sometimes better than, IQ tests.

In a study in Usenge, Kenya, Sternberg and colleagues were interested in school-age children's ability to adapt to their indigenous environment. They devised a test of practical intelligence for adaptation to the environment that measured children's informal tacit knowledge of natural herbal medicines that the villagers used to fight various types of infections. The researchers found generally negative correlations between the test of practical intelligence and tests of academic intelligence and school achievement. In other words, people in this context often emphasize practical knowledge at the expense of academic skills in their children's development.

In another study, analytical, creative, and practical tests were used to predict mental and physical health among Russian adults. Mental health was measured by widely used paper-and-pencil tests of depression and anxiety, while physical health was measured by self-report. The best predictor of mental and physical health was the practical-intelligence measure, with analytical intelligence being the second-best measure and creative intelligence being the third.

Factor-Analytic Studies

Factor-analytic studies seek to identify the mental structures underlying intelligence. Four separate factor-analytic studies have supported the internal validity of the triarchic theory of intelligence. These studies analyzed aspects of individual differences in test performance in order to uncover the basic mental structures underlying test performance. In one study of 326 high school students from throughout the United States, Sternberg and his colleagues used the so-called Sternberg Triarchic Abilities Test (STAT) to investigate the validity of the triarchic theory. The test comprises twelve subtests measuring analytical, creative, and practical abilities. For each type of ability, there are three multiple-choice tests and one essay test. The multiple-choice tests involve verbal, quantitative, and figural content. Factor analysis on the data was supportive of the triarchic theory of human intelligence, as it was measured relatively separate and independent analytical, creative, and practical factors. The triarchic theory also was consistent with data obtained from 3,252 students in the United States, Finland, and Spain. The study revealed separate analytical, creative, and practical factors of intelligence.

Instructional Studies

In another set of studies, researchers explored the question of whether conventional education in school systematically discriminates against children with creative and practical strengths. Motivating this work was the belief that the systems in most schools strongly tend to favor children with strengths in memory and analytical abilities.

The Sternberg Triarchic Abilities Test was administered to 326 high-school students around the United States and in some other countries who were identified by their schools as gifted (by whatever standard the school used). Students were selected for a summer program in college-level psychology if they fell into one of five ability groupings: high analytical, high creative, high practical, high balanced (high in all three abilities), or low balanced (low in all three abilities). These students were then randomly divided into four instructional groups, emphasizing memory, analytical, creative, or practical instruction. For example, in the memory condition, they might be asked to describe the main tenets of a major theory of depression. In the analytical condition, they might be asked to compare and contrast two theories of depression. In the creative condition, they might be asked to formulate their own theory of depression. In the practical condition, they might be asked how they could use what they had learned about depression to help a friend who was depressed.

Students who were placed in instructional conditions that better matched their pattern of abilities outperformed students who were mismatched. In other words, when students are taught in a way that fits how they think, they do better in school. Children with creative and practical abilities, who are almost never taught or assessed in a way that matches their pattern of abilities, may be at a disadvantage in course after course, year after year.

A follow-up study examined learning of social studies and science by 225 third-graders in Raleigh, North Carolina, and 142 eighth-graders in Baltimore, Maryland, and Fresno, California. In this study, students were assigned to one of three instructional conditions. In the first condition, they were taught the course they would have learned had there been no intervention, which placed an emphasis on memory. In the second condition, students were taught in a way that emphasized critical (analytical) thinking, and in the third condition they were taught in a way that emphasized analytical, creative, and practical thinking. All students' performance was assessed for memory learning (through multiple-choice assessments) as well as for analytical, creative, and practical learning (through performance assessments).

Students in the triarchic-intelligence (analytical, creative, practical) condition outperformed the other students in terms of the performance assessments. Interestingly, children in the triarchic instructional condition outperformed the other children on the multiple-choice memory tests. In other words, to the extent that one's goal is just to maximize children's memory for information, teaching triarchically is still superior. This is because it enables children to capitalize on their strengths and to correct or to compensate for their weaknesses, allowing them to encode material in a variety of interesting ways.

In another study, involving 871 middle-school students and 432 high school students, researchers taught reading either triarchically or through the regular curriculum. At the middle-school level, reading was taught explicitly. At the high school level, reading was infused into instruction in mathematics, physical sciences, social sciences, English, history, foreign languages, and the arts. In all settings, students who were taught triarchically substantially outperformed students who were taught in standard ways.

Conclusion

The triarchic theory of intelligence provides a useful way of understanding human intelligence. It seems to capture important aspects of intelligence not captured by more conventional theories. It also differs from the theories of Howard Gardner, which emphasize eight independent multiple intelligences (such as linguistic and musical intelligence), and from the theory of emotional intelligence. The triarchic theory emphasizes processes of intelligence, rather than domains of intelligence, as in Gardner's theory. It also views emotions as distinct from intelligence. Eventually, a theory may be proposed that integrates the best elements of all existing theories.

See also: CREATIVITY; INTELLIGENCE, *subentry on* MYTHS, MYSTERIES, AND REALITIES.

BIBLIOGRAPHY

GARDNER, HOWARD. 1983. *Frames of Mind: The Theory of Multiple Intelligences.* New York: Basic Books.

GARDNER, HOWARD. 1999. *Intelligence Reframed: Multiple Intelligences for the 21st Century.* New York: Basic Books.

STERNBERG, ROBERT J. 1977. *Intelligence, Information Processing, and Analogical Reasoning: The Componential Analysis of Human Abilities.* Hillsdale, NJ: Erlbaum.

STERNBERG, ROBERT J. 1981. "Intelligence and Nonentrenchment." *Journal of Educational Psychology* 73:1–16.

STERNBERG, ROBERT J. 1993. *Sternberg Triarchic Abilities Test.* Unpublished test.

STERNBERG, ROBERT J. 1997. *Successful Intelligence.* New York: Plume.

STERNBERG, ROBERT J. 1999. "The Theory of Successful Intelligence." *Review of General Psychology* 3:292–316.

STERNBERG, ROBERT J.; FERRARI, MICHEL; CLINKENBEARD, PAMELA R.; and GRIGORENKO, ELENA L. 1996. "Identification, Instruction, and Assessment of Gifted Children: A Construct Validation of a Triarchic Model." *Gifted Child Quarterly* 40(3):129–137.

STERNBERG, ROBERT J.; FORSYTHE, GEORGE B.; HEDLUND, JENNIFER; HORVATH, JOE; SNOOK, SCOTT; WILLIAMS, WENDY M.; WAGNER, RICHARD K.; and GRIGORENKO, ELENA L. 2000. *Practical Intelligence in Everyday Life.* New York: Cambridge University Press.

STERNBERG, ROBERT J.; GRIGORENKO, ELENA L.; FERRARI, MICHEL; and CLINKENBEARD, PAMELA R. 1999. "A Triarchic Analysis of an Aptitude-Treatment Interaction." *European Journal of Psychological Assessment* 15(1):1–11.

STERNBERG, ROBERT J., and LUBART, TODD I. 1995. *Defying the Crowd: Cultivating Creativity in a Culture of Conformity.* New York: Free Press.

STERNBERG, ROBERT J., and RIFKIN, BATHSEVA. 1979. "The Development of Analogical Reasoning Processes." *Journal of Experimental Child Psychology* 27:195–232.

STERNBERG, ROBERT J.; TORFF, BRUCE; and GRIGORENKO, ELENA L. 1998. "Teaching Triarchically Improves School Achievement." *Journal of Educational Psychology* 90: 374–384.

ROBERT J. STERNBERG

INTERDISCIPLINARY COURSES AND MAJORS IN HIGHER EDUCATION

Interdisciplinary studies, broadly defined, is the process of answering a question, solving a problem, or addressing a problem that is so broad or complex that it cannot be addressed through a single discipline or field. In higher education in the United States, interdisciplinary studies are conducted through individual courses, including independent studies; in specific programs of study such as major or minor concentrations; as part of a student's general education requirements; through practica, internships, and other educational experiences that focus on the application of theory and knowledge to the workplace and society; and occasionally through honors programs. In a few cases entire colleges or universities are organized in interdisciplinary units that replace discipline- or field-based departments or divisions.

The goal of most interdisciplinary courses and programs is to integrate the contributions of different academic disciplines or fields of study so that topics, problems, and phenomena under study are better understood. (*Disciplines* have traditionally have been defined as specializations within the arts and sciences; the term *fields* is often used to distinguish disciplines from professional fields, such as business, education, law, and medicine, which draw their content and methods from a number of different disciplines.) However, some scholars such as Jean Francois Lyotard contest the usefulness of academic disciplines as ways of organizing and generating knowledge, and thus challenge the idea that disciplines are the basis for interdisciplinarity. These scholars consider interdisciplinarity to be a critique of the disciplines; in their view, the goal of interdisciplinarity is to subvert, rather than to utilize, the disciplines as they are currently organized.

Rationale for Interdisciplinary Courses and Programs

Arguments favoring interdisciplinary teaching emphasize the need to bring multiple disciplinary perspectives to bear on real-world issues. Proponents of interdisciplinarity argue that the disciplines arbitrarily fragment the world and allow their adherents to select only those dimensions of a problem that their discipline can adequately address, thus leaving important dimensions of the problem unaddressed.

The views offered by the disciplines are therefore considered partial; they provide a single lens or perspective from which to study and understand complex phenomena or issues. Advocates of interdisciplinarity argue that disciplinary approaches to education are therefore reductionist; they divide knowledge rather than generate comprehensive explanations of the world. Although many if not most proponents of interdisciplinarity believe that disciplines are necessary for the advancement of knowledge, they view overspecialization, in the form of increasing disciplinary isolationism, as impeding communication and understanding among disciplinary experts, their students, and the larger public that might be consumers or beneficiaries of their work.

Those who encourage interdisciplinary education seek holistic understandings of the social and natural worlds. Real-world problems, they argue, are not separated into disciplinary components; rather, they are complex, hard to define, challenging to solve, and often have more than one right answer. Such problems require that individuals know what kinds of information are needed and where to find that information. By requiring students to work on such problems, the argument proceeds, interdisciplinary education develops a number of intellectual skills. These include skills in problem solving, critical thinking, evaluation, synthesis, and integration. In addition, interdisciplinary courses are believed to develop the ability to see and employ multiple perspectives; to encourage tolerance and respect for the perspectives of others; to expand students' horizons or perspectives; to increase their willingness and capacity to question assumptions about the world and about themselves; to promote the ability to think in creative and innovative ways; and to create sensitivity to disciplinary and other biases. As a result, advocates argue, interdisciplinary study is excellent preparation for the role of citizen and worker in a pluralistic, technological, and democratic society.

Proponents such as James R. Davis, William H. Newell, and William J. Green also claim that interdisciplinary curricula are more engaging, capturing students' intellectual interests and encouraging them to make connections among the disparate realms of information provided by discrete disciplines. Even scholars, this argument continues, need to know about developments in other disciplines so that they may adapt or incorporate these into their own work as appropriate. Interdisciplinary training has therefore been recommended by Joseph Klockmans as a way to build bridges to overcome disciplinary isolation. Others argue that interdisciplinary courses can improve faculty morale by revitalizing instructors' interest in teaching introductory or survey courses that are not closely related to their areas of specialization. Similarly, supporters contend that interdisciplinary courses promote faculty development, offering instructors the opportunity to explore new areas of interest and collaborate with colleagues and thereby expand their repertoire of knowledge and skills.

Arguments, such as Thomas C. Benson's, opposing undergraduate interdisciplinary courses and programs typically focus on perceived detriments to student learning. Interdisciplinary study, opponents argue, cannot be effective unless students are first adequately schooled in at least one of the disciplines contributing to an interdisciplinary course or program. Without this foundation, students cannot marshal arguments, methods, or insights from the disciplines in an interdisciplinary course. Critics also assert that substantial commitment to interdisciplinary study as an undergraduate student, as is required in a minor or major program, may impede a student's development of disciplinary competencies. A third argument—that interdisciplinary courses are shallow and lacking in intellectual rigor—builds on the previous arguments. This criticism maintains that because students do not have the foundational knowledge of the involved disciplines that allows them to participate in demanding intellectual discussions in interdisciplinary courses, instructors emphasize what is entertaining and most accessible to the majority of students. Opponents also argue that interdisciplinary courses are costly because they often rely on team-teaching, independent studies, and low faculty-student ratios.

Interdisciplinary Study in U.S. Higher Education

The first interdisciplinary courses in U.S. colleges and universities were part of the general education, or core, requirements of the undergraduate curriculum. (General education is that component of the undergraduate curriculum intended to provide students with the knowledge, skills, and values required for life as a contributing member of society.) Although general education has a long history in higher education, interdisciplinary general education courses in the United States did not appear until the twentieth century when World War I prompted

U.S. colleges and universities to institute general education courses designed to strengthen Americans' sense of cultural and national identity and responsible citizenship. These comprehensive survey courses, which relied on a number of disciplines for their subject matter, attempted to sustain the content and values of Western civilization. The courses required instructors who could effectively synthesize knowledge and make it accessible to undergraduates and therefore highlighted the need for interdisciplinary approaches to education. Despite concerns about disciplinary fragmentation and academic overspecialization, only a few institutions offered more than a handful of interdisciplinary survey courses; the Experimental College at the University of Wisconsin, which lasted only from 1928 to 1932, is perhaps the most famous example of an institution committed to an extensive interdisciplinary general education.

During the 1930s and 1940s, war again influenced interdisciplinary curricula as institutions developed area studies programs designed to provide knowledge about foreign cultures and peoples involved in World War II. Although international education was spurred by private foundation support before the war, these efforts diversified during and after World War II as programs focused on more and more geographic areas. By 1988, there were more than 600 area studies programs on American campuses.

The social and cultural transformations of the 1960s and 1970s inspired additional interdisciplinary educational efforts. As the civil rights, women's liberation, and Vietnam War protests created demands for more personally and socially relevant, student-centered curricula, institutions responded by offering interdisciplinary courses and programs in a variety of areas. While a few institutions developed interdisciplinary organizational models, most institutions developed interdisciplinary courses and programs that supplemented the usual disciplinary offerings. By the 1970s, interdisciplinary minor and major programs in Black, Chicano, Environmental, Urban, and Women's Studies appeared on campuses across the United States. In the year 2000 Barrie Thorne reported there were more than 700 women's studies programs in U.S. institutions. According to a report published by the National Center for Education Statistics in 2001, in 1998 more than 6,200 associate and baccalaureate degrees were conferred in area, ethnic, and cultural studies. In addition more than 35,000 students earned associate's or baccalaureate degrees in multi/interdisciplinary studies.

During the 1980s concerns about general education heightened and curricular reform in this area was often motivated by a desire to create more meaningful and less fragmented educational experiences for college students. General education distribution requirements, typically filled by allowing students to choose from a variety of introductory courses in selected disciplines, were replaced by a core of interdisciplinary courses common to all students in an institution. Proponents believed the goals of general education would be better served if students engaged in a common conversation regarding cultural and societal issues rather than haphazardly choosing courses from approved lists with little concern for their connection to one another. Interdisciplinary general education requirements often include multicultural studies, environmental studies, Western Civilization, and the Great Books. In the final decades of the twentieth century, the number and type of interdisciplinary curricula greatly increased as programs in cultural studies, interdisciplinary science fields (e.g., neuroscience, molecular biology, and environmental sciences), human ecology, information technology, public policy, and legal and labor studies gained prominence in U.S. colleges and universities.

Interdisciplinary Courses

A distinction is often made between multidisciplinary and interdisciplinary courses, although the difference is more likely one of degree. In multidisciplinary courses, instructors present disciplinary perspectives, often one at a time, without special attention to integrating those perspectives or examining their assumptions. In contrast, instructors in interdisciplinary courses not only examine the underlying assumptions of the disciplines that contribute to the course, but also assist students in integrating the separate disciplinary contributions that have been brought to bear on a topic into an inclusive understanding.

Typically an interdisciplinary course is organized around a topic, broadly defined as an issue, theme, problem, region, era, institution, person, or idea. Different disciplinary (and potentially other) perspectives on the topic are incorporated into readings and assignments. Interdisciplinary courses take a variety of formats and espouse a number of purposes. First-year seminar courses can provide a com-

prehensive orientation to a field or fields of study, often by probing a single issue, problem, or question. Advanced seminars usually have an integrative purpose, serving as culminating or capstone courses in which students refine analytical and critical methodologies. Fieldwork, internship, service learning, and travel-study courses may also employ interdisciplinary approaches to assist students in connecting life experiences with classroom learning.

Individual instructors often plan and teach interdisciplinary courses, but teams of two or more faculty members from different disciplines or fields of study are also common. Collaboration among faculty teaching interdisciplinary courses can involve course planning, content integration, teaching, and assessment. All members of the faculty team may be involved in planning a course or a single individual can take primary responsibility for this role. Responsibility for instruction can also vary. In some team-taught courses, all members are present in the classroom for each session; they may all contribute to each class session or team members may take responsibility for specific components of the course. In other team-based courses, a core of faculty supplement their lectures and discussions by inviting guest lecturers to provide instruction in a specific area of interest. In a dispersed team model, large classes of students meet together for one class session per week in which all members of the faculty team are present. Subsequent weekly meetings take place in smaller sections taught by a single faculty member. No matter what delivery model is used, team members must make decisions about how student work will be assessed. Faculty may share this task, with each team member reading and commenting on all student work, or they may divide the task among them.

Coordinated studies and learning community models are a variation on the team-taught course. In these models, members of a faculty team coordinate two or more courses that focus on a prearranged theme or topic rather than teaching about that theme or topic in the context of a single course. Each coordinated course is designed to contribute to a wide-ranging understanding of the subject under study; in addition to coordinating content across these courses, instructors may also coordinate course activities and assignments to enhance the learning experience. The multiple-course format is intended to achieve the goal of depth of learning; a few institutions seek to further enhance depth by extending coordinated courses over an academic year rather than confining them to a single semester.

Instructors who teach interdisciplinary courses alone rather than in a team must present disciplinary information and perspectives that are not part of their area of specialization in order to teach an interdisciplinary topic. Most proponents of interdisciplinary courses and programs argue that faculty must have a broad background in the disciplines that are engaged in a particular interdisciplinary course before they can teach it without assistance from other disciplinary experts; faculty teaching an interdisciplinary course must be able to present their own, as well as different, disciplinary perspectives accurately and in depth. Until instructors develop the requisite base of knowledge and skills, proponents of this view believe that "solo" efforts should be discouraged. Faculty development in the form of seminars in which faculty teach one another their disciplines can provide the kind of faculty development needed to support interdisciplinary courses, but can be costly in terms of human and financial resources.

Many interdisciplinary courses are never taught in teams; individual faculty design and teach all the perspectives needed in the course. Faculty trained in interdisciplinary programs may have the necessary background for teaching such courses. Others develop expertise once asked to teach an interdisciplinary course. Interdisciplinary programs sometimes offer incentives to persuade and reward faculty who serve the program. These incentives can take the form of salary stipends, teaching or research assistants, travel money, or funding for the purchase of books or other materials. These incentives provide helpful resources for course preparation and also recognize the time and effort dedicated to the preparation and teaching of an interdisciplinary course.

Team-taught courses are frequently used for general education course sequences and in interdisciplinary programs in which the variety of disciplinary perspectives engaged are disparate, each requiring in depth knowledge of a specific set of methods or concepts, such as in environmental sciences, biochemistry, or urban planning. Individually taught interdisciplinary courses are particularly common in the humanities, women's studies, cultural studies, and ethnic studies, and often include a critique of disciplinary knowledge.

Interdisciplinary Programs

Interdisciplinary major and minor programs take a number of organizational forms, but three forms are prominent: (1) established programs with permanent staffs and program budgets; (2) interdepartmental committees, programs, or colleges with defined curricula but no faculty members appointed solely to the unit; and (3) individually designed majors or other programs that permit students to design, with faculty guidance, customized degree programs to meet their educational needs.

Typically, established programs have a full- or part-time director who provides administrative leadership and who also teaches in the program. Individual faculty in established programs may hold joint appointments with the interdisciplinary program and with one or more departments related to their area of expertise. They may also be appointed for a fixed term to serve an interdisciplinary program (for a portion or all of their time). The number of faculty associated with such programs can vary, but this mode provides stability to the interdisciplinary program because it guarantees at least a portion of a faculty member's time will be dedicated to program responsibilities at a given time.

In interdepartmental committees, programs, or colleges, the program director is either full- or part-time and is responsible for arranging courses to be taught by faculty from different departments. These faculty are not permanent members of the program but are rather borrowed temporarily from their home departments. Such budgetary arrangements leave interdisciplinary programs vulnerable in times of resource and financial stress. Advocates of interdisciplinarity note however that the closer the interdisciplinary program is tied to the mission of the institution, the less likely it is to suffer financially during difficult periods in an institution's history.

Interdisciplinary Colleges and Universities

Most institutions that adopt an interdisciplinary approach value team teaching, student and faculty involvement in curriculum development and in governance, and active participation by the students both in the classroom and in external research or work internships. Academic departments based on disciplinary affiliations are either nonexistent or more fluid than in other institutions. "Great Books" colleges, characteristically small institutions such as St. John's College of Maryland and of Santa Fe, are often labeled interdisciplinary because they explore the foundational ideas and questions that distinguish a civilization. The few Great Books colleges in the U.S. organize their curricula around reading and discussion of what they believe to be a set of classic texts of Western civilization. Proponents of this approach believe that students are best prepared for life when they interact and wrestle with the greatest minds of our civilization, and they opt for a nondisciplinary structure because "neither the world nor knowledge of it is arbitrarily divided up as universities are" (Hutchins, p. 59).

Other interdisciplinary institutions organize curricula around specific societal or environmental issues, and encourage individualized programs of study developed collaboratively by students and faculty. In 1965 the Wisconsin legislature chartered the University of Wisconsin-Green Bay to devise a future-oriented innovative curriculum. Influenced by the ecology movement of the time, Green Bay offered an interdisciplinary curriculum focused on the relationships between humans and their environment. The university organized its colleges around environmental themes rather than academic disciplines and divided its curriculum into nine problem-centered concentrations. Over time, however, Green Bay added disciplinary majors and interdisciplinary minors to its original structure. A smaller institution, the College of the Atlantic, established in Bar Harbor, Maine, in 1969 maintained its commitment to one primary issue. It offers individually tailored bachelor's and master's degrees in human ecology, a field that emphasizes the interrelationships between humans and their social and physical environments.

Other institutions, such as Evergreen State College in Olympia, Washington, offer a more extensive interdisciplinary curriculum. In 1967 Evergreen opened as a nontraditional liberal arts college. Its coordinated studies program allows students to participate in full-time interdisciplinary study through a combination of team-taught programs and student-designed areas of concentration. Hampshire College in Massachusetts also offers students the opportunity to create individualized programs of study built upon a core multidisciplinary curriculum. The number of colleges and universities offering exclusively interdisciplinary curricula is relatively small; the majority of higher education institutions in the United States either prescribe or offer interdisciplinary tracks within their general education offerings.

See also: ACADEMIC DISCIPLINES; CAPSTONE COURSES IN HIGHER EDUCATION; CURRICULUM, HIGHER EDUCATION; GENERAL EDUCATION IN HIGHER EDUCATION.

BIBLIOGRAPHY

AMERICAN ASSOCIATION OF COLLEGES. 1991. "Interdisciplinary Studies." In *Liberal Learning and the Arts and Sciences Major*, Vol.2: *Reports from the Fields*. Washington, DC: Association of American Colleges.

BENSON, THOMAS C. 1982. "Five Arguments Against Interdisciplinary Studies." *Issues in Integrative Studies* 1:38–48.

CHAMBERLIN, MARIAM, ed. 1988. *Women in Academe: Progress and Prospects.* New York: Russell Sage Foundation.

DAVIS, JAMES R. 1995. *Interdisciplinary Courses and Team Teaching: New Arrangements for Learning.* Phoenix, AZ: American Council on Education and Oryx Press.

HURSH, BARBARA; HAAS, PAUL; and MOORE, MICHAEL. 1983. "An Interdisciplinary Model to Implement General Education." *Journal of Higher Education* 54 (1):42–49.

HUTCHINS, ROBERT MAYNARD. 1976. *The Higher Learning in America.* New Haven, CT: Yale University Press.

KLEIN, JULIE THOMPSON. 1990. *Interdisciplinarity: History, Theory, and Practice.* Detroit, MI: Wayne State University Press.

KLEIN, JULIE THOMPSON. 1996. *Crossing Boundaries: Knowledge, Disciplinarities, and Interdisciplinarities.* Charlottesville: University Press of Virginia.

KLEIN, JULIE THOMPSON, and NEWELL, WILLIAM T. 1996. "Advancing Interdisciplinary Studies." In *Handbook of the Undergraduate Curriculum: A Comprehensive Guide to Purposes, Structures, Practices, and Change,* ed. Jerry G. Gaff and James L. Ratcliff. San Francisco: Jossey-Bass.

KOCKLEMANS, JOSEPH. 1979. "Why Interdisciplinarity?" In *Interdisciplinarity and Higher Education,* ed. Joseph Kocklemans. University Park: Pennsylvania State University Press.

LYOTARD, JEAN FRANCOIS. 1984. *The Postmodern Condition: A Report on Knowledge,* trans. Geoff Bennington and Brian Massume. Minneapolis: University of Minnesota Press.

NATIONAL CENTER FOR EDUCATION STATISTICS. 2001. *Degrees and Other Awards Conferred by*

Title IV Participating, Degree-granting Institutions: 1997–98. NCES 2001-177. Washington DC: U.S. Department of Education, Office of Educational Research and Improvement.

NEWELL, WILLIAM H. 1990. "Interdisciplinary Curriculum Development." *Issues in Integrative Studies* 8:69–86.

NEWELL, WILLIAM H. 1994. "Designing Interdisciplinary Courses." In *Interdisciplinary Studies Today.* New Directions for Teaching and Learning 58, ed. Julie T. Klein and William G. Doty. San Francisco: Jossey-Bass.

NEWELL, WILLIAM H., and GREEN, WILLIAM J. 1982. "Defining and Teaching Interdisciplinary Studies." *Improving College and University Teaching* 30(1):23–30.

THORNE, BARRIE. 2000. "A Telling Time for Women's Studies." *Signs* 24:1183–1187.

TOWNSEND, BARBARA K.; NEWELL, L. JACKSON; and WIESE, MICHAEL D. 1992. *Creating Distinctiveness: Lessons from Uncommon Colleges and Universities.* ASHE-ERIC Higher Education Report No. 6. Washington, DC: George Washington University, School of Education and Human Development.

LISA R. LATTUCA
LOIS J. VOIGT

INTEREST GROUPS

See: EDUCATIONAL INTEREST GROUPS.

INTERGOVERNMENTAL RELATIONS IN EDUCATION

Relationships between branches and levels of government are important in the administration and delivery of educational services in all countries. National ministries of education may wish to control all phases of education, but they inevitably must delegate significant aspects of the operation and delivery of educational services to lower levels of government. The more decentralized the governance system, and the more branches and levels of government there are, the more complex intergovernmental relationships may be. But, even in nations with highly centralized approaches to governance, the relationship between the central ministry of education and schools and colleges is important. Any government's policies are only as effective as their design and implementation permit, and effective implementation is heavily influenced by the character of the relationship that exists between branches and levels of government.

Governance Structures

Most nations have a unitary government, which means that the central government holds sovereign power over all lower levels of government. The lower levels of government are subordinate to the national government, which can overrule or even abolish them. By contrast, some nations have adopted federal governance systems, in which power is shared between the national government and state or regional units, which cannot be abolished. These federations with constitutions developed in nations, such as Australia, Canada, Germany, and the United States, where regional differences are important and where former colonies or semiautonomous states banded together out of common interest. In federal systems, education usually is the legal responsibility of the state governments rather than the national government. Still, even in federal systems, national interests in such matters as equality of opportunity and educational adequacy and excellence inevitably cause the national governments to play a role in education.

Whether control over a nation's government is democratic or autocratic, and whether a unitary or federal system is used, there can be significant variation in the degree to which the government is centralized or decentralized. By definition, one expects decentralization in federal systems, but this is not always the case. For example, until the mid-1980s Australia's states ran highly centralized statewide education systems in which all but the simplest decisions were made in the state ministries of education in the capitol cities. For the most part, Germany's states continue to run highly centralized education systems.

Beginning in the 1980s, a reform movement advocating decentralization and much greater decision-making at the school level (school-based management or "self-managing schools") began to spread across the world, especially the English-speaking world. School-based management sought to restructure the decision-making chain of command by shifting authority from highly centralized bureaucracies to the school site level. New Zealand adopted this approach completely, and some Australian states have moved in this direction. Britain presents a complex and interesting example of these trends. It has reduced the power of the local education authorities (roughly equivalent to American and Canadian school districts) and given schools much more decision-making authority, but the entire system operates under a powerful central government in London. In the United States, more than one-third of all school districts have implemented some version of school-based management, and at least five states—Colorado, Florida, Kentucky, North Carolina, and Texas—have legislated participatory decision-making at each school.

The high degree of decentralization in the structure of educational governance in the United States is unusual. The kind of local control that exists in the United States, through the delegation by states of substantial decision-making power to elected school boards of lay citizens in some 15,000 local school districts, is rare. Most nations have far more centralized arrangements. In European nations, such as France and Germany, civil servants operating within highly bureaucratized agencies or ministries of education tightly control the education system. In these settings, local citizens have little or no voice in decision-making for schools, and a highly professionalized (or at least bureaucratized) cadre of educators hold sway.

The stark contrast between, on the one hand, highly centralized and bureaucratized systems of governance and, on the other hand, decentralized systems that allow for local and lay participation in educational policy-making raises the question of how best to structure the governance of education. Here, it is common to see a tension between competing values. Efficiency, it can be argued, is best served by a centralized system that can better ensure consistent standards throughout a nation than a decentralized system. On the other hand, centralized systems are prone to develop bureaucratic rigidities that can ultimately impede efficiency, not to mention liberty and democracy. Debates about the proper governance of public services, in fact, often seem to revolve around the tension between the competing values of democracy and efficiency. Unfortunately, by themselves neither centralized nor decentralized approaches to government can guarantee either democracy or efficiency.

Standards, Accountability, and Capacity-Building

Many nations require students to pass national examinations in order to advance in school or exit from the school system. These high-stakes exams and the accompanying national curriculum provide a common standard for all students and schools and help establish a coherent educational system. In the United States, however, a debate continues over curriculum standards, testing, and accountability measures and over which level of government (local, state, or federal) should be responsible for these measures. The long tradition of local control over education impedes state and national efforts to impose standards and accountability systems. Further, high-stakes examinations conflict with American beliefs in freedom, individualism, and multiple opportunities for success. Inevitably, national goals, individual and minority rights, and regional differences conflict and contribute to tensions in intergovernmental relations.

Most U.S. states have established academic and curricular standards with testing and other accountability requirements, and many have experienced increasingly tense intergovernmental relations. The highly publicized takeover of the academically and fiscally distressed School District of Philadelphia by the Commonwealth of Pennsylvania in December 2001 illustrates how volatile intergovernmental conflicts can become when serious consequences are attached to school accountability measures. When higher levels of government intervene in or take over failing schools or school districts, the assumption is that the higher levels have the capacity to correct the problems. But, owing to underinvestment, state education departments sometimes lack the capacity to provide the technical assistance and professional development necessary to reinvigorate failing schools. Many schools lack the organizational capacity to respond effectively to the demands of higher academic standards, so staff professional development and capacity-building efforts are key activities in which higher levels of government need to assist them.

The Financing of Schools and Intergovernmental Relations

The costs of professional development efforts, not to mention the basic costs of operating and maintaining schools, lead to the important question of intergovernmental arrangements for the finance of education, including the relative share of the costs different levels of government should contribute.

Ideally, there are provisions, such as in Australia, to ensure that the same amount of government tax money is provided to finance a child's education regardless of where the child lives. But arrangements can be far less logical and equitable than that. The tradition of local control of education in the United States has produced a situation in which the funding of schools is heavily influenced by the wealth of individual communities. Even though American states try to equalize funding through contributions of state funds to augment local property tax revenue, many states still allow large disparities to exist between the levels of spending in local school districts that vary in wealth. Since the 1960s, this inequitable pattern has been challenged in numerous court cases, and reformers have succeeded in reducing the disparities in some states.

The funding of schools is likely to become even more complicated as governmental agencies are now having to determine who is responsible and at what level for the costs of educating students who no longer attend local schools but instead receive their education through "cyber schools" over the Internet. Cyber schools and other technological advances pose new challenges to intergovernmental relations and raise new politically charged questions. Policymakers must determine, for example, if cyber schools—in which students primarily stay home and access materials online with little direct contact with teachers—should be counted and financed as public education. Further, cyber schools raise new questions about school funding for which there have been no clear answers. Who should pay? What amount should come from local funds and what from state or national? Beyond fiscal questions, cyber schools also raise accountability and regulatory issues.

Intergovernmental Relations and School-Linked Social-Services Coordination

Children worldwide face a multitude of modern problems that include increased incidents of substance abuse, inadequate and unaffordable housing, racism, sexism, child abuse and family violence, sexual promiscuity and teen pregnancy, poverty, hunger, and limited or poor health care. These problems place children at risk and put schools at the epicenter of interconnected social problems. Yet the services needed to respond to these problems are typically fragmented across a variety of uncoordinated government agencies. Consequently, many Westernized

nations are increasingly adopting policies to have schools and external agencies collaborate to help meet students' nonacademic needs and provide more comprehensive support services for at-risk students and their families.

School-linked social-services efforts illustrate the complicated nature of intergovernmental relations in education. Although each school, social-service agency, or branch of the government seeks to assist those in need, jurisdictional and organizational problems can limit their ability to work together to find sustainable solutions that help those most at risk. Coordinated, school-linked services create new expectations and complexities and introduce new actors, thereby increasing organizational demands, ambiguities, and, potentially, loss of control. A fundamental challenge in intergovernmental collaborative efforts is to overcome the barriers created by the effects of competing institutional interests that emphasize protecting jobs, budgets, programs, facilities, and the agency's "turf" and clientele.

Organizational and professional differences among various government and nonprofit agencies, including schools, create barriers that include a lack of a common outlook and professional language, communication problems, licensure issues, and confidentiality issues. Also problematic are issues such as space and facilities management; funding issues and resource mingling; differing salary and personnel policies; new roles and relationships between educators and other agency personnel; leadership issues; deficits and differences in professional preparation programs and training; information sharing and retrieval; and control and legal issues. Research indicates that these are significant barriers that can impede intergovernmental/interagency collaboration.

See also: GOVERNMENT AND EDUCATION, THE CHANGING ROLE OF; SCHOOL-LINKED SERVICES; STATES AND EDUCATION; STATE DEPARTMENTS OF EDUCATION.

BIBLIOGRAPHY

CALDWELL, BRIAN J., and SPINKS, JIM M. 1988. *The Self-Managing School.* London: Taylor and Francis.

CROWSON, ROBERT L., and BOYD, WILLIAM L. 1993. "Coordinated Services for Children: Designing Arks for Storms and Seas Unknown." *American Journal of Education* 101(2):140–179.

DAVID, JANE. 1995/1996. "The Who, What, and Why of Site-Based Management." *Educational Leadership* 53:4–9.

DRYFOOS, JOY G. 1990. *Adolescents at Risk: Prevalence and Prevention.* New York: Oxford University Press.

DRYFOOS, JOY G. 1994. *Full-Service Schools: A Revolution in Health and Social Services for Children, Youth, and Families.* San Francisco: Jossey-Bass.

FOWLER, FRANCES. 2000. *Policy Studies for Educational Leaders.* Upper Saddle River, NJ: Merrill/Prentice-Hall.

KIRST, MICHAEL W. 1991. *Integrating Children's Services.* Menlo Park, CA: EdSource.

LEVY, JANET E., and COPPLE, CAROL. 1989. *Joining Forces: A Report from the First Year.* Alexandria, VA: National Association of State Boards of Education.

SMREKAR, CLAIRE E., and MAWHINNEY, HANNE B. 1999. "Integrated Services: Challenges in Linking Schools, Families, and Communities." In *Handbook of Research on Educational Administration,* ed. Joseph Murphy and Karen S. Louis. San Francisco: Jossey-Bass.

SMYLIE, MARK A.; CROWSON, ROBERT L.; CHOU, VICKI; and LEVIN, REBECCA A. 1996. "The Principal and Community-School Connections in Chicago's Radical Reform." In *Coordination among Schools, Families, and Communities: Prospects for Educational Reform,* ed. James G. Cibulka and William J. Kritek. Albany: State University of New York Press.

TROTTER, ANDREW. 2001. "Cyber Schools Carving Out Charter Niche." *Education Week* October 24.

TROTTER, ANDREW. 2001. "Federal Study Details Major Barrier to Internet Learning." *Education Week* January 10.

WILLIAM LOWE BOYD
BONNIE C. JOHNSON

INTERNATIONAL ASPECTS OF EDUCATION COMMERCE

The use of government financial resources to support public basic-education provision is well established and widely accepted across the globe. However, since 1990 there has been a noticeable shift in the traditional ways that provision of higher education and, to a lesser extent, secondary education is regulated. In different contexts there are new financing strategies being implemented in the public sector, with a view toward generating additional revenues from public assets, mobilizing additional resources from students and their families, encouraging donations from third-party contributions, and involving the private sector in the provision of essential services to educational institutions. Future demand for private provision of education services, especially at the higher levels of education, is predicted to grow even more in the first decade of the twenty-first century.

All governments are concerned about investment in human capital, and, despite significant improvements in education coverage in developing countries, there is still a large unmet demand for both access and quality education at all levels.

The private sector's role as a potential partner with the public sector in both the provision and financing of education is widely recognized in the early twenty-first century. There is substantial evidence to show that the private sector can: (1) ease the pressure on governments' financial constraints; (2) encourage and demonstrate efficiency, effectiveness and innovation; (3) promote social mobility and contribute to the growth of an emerging middle class; (4) expand educational diversity; and (5) increase access and quality across all education levels and societal groups.

Private Higher Education

In higher and continuing education, private-sector provision has become a practical way for economies to scale up their investment in human capital, especially in developing countries. More than 2.3 billion people, or 53 percent of the total population of the developing world, live in the poorest countries—those that have annual per capita incomes of less than $885. These countries have a small proportion (12 million students) of the global tertiary education market (90 million). Innovative action has been necessary in these lower-income countries to provide an acceptable standard of tertiary education in order to provide the education needed to generate economic growth. In these settings, low-income countries are providing positive legal frameworks where private, specialized two- or three-year tertiary education institutions (such as technical institutes or community colleges) can provide training for technicians and applied specialists.

Studies done between 1998 and 2000 show that the size of the private higher-education sector varied significantly across developing countries. Levels of private-sector ownership included:

- 100 percent of professional training market in Cote d'Ivoire
- 44 percent of skills training market in The Gambia
- 75 percent of tertiary colleges in India
- 1,274 private institutions, with 4 million students, in China
- 37 tertiary institutions in Ghana
- 60 percent of tertiary institutions in Brazil

A common characteristic of private higher-education provision is that tuition fees are the main source of revenue. Private institutions also serve both the rich and poor, which often includes *second chance* students who cannot gain admission to public universities. These institutions also exist in different forms, including franchises, school groups, sole proprietorships, for-profit companies, nonprofit institutions, and religious organizations. Some higher-education institutions may also offer a limited range of professional and practically oriented courses (e.g., accounting, management, English information technology), often using part-time staff (including trained professionals, practitioners, or professors from public institutions).

Student loan schemes are also emerging in places where positive regulatory conditions are in place for banks to provide for an individual student's access to credit. This is particularly the case at postsecondary levels, where private financial institutions can use students' increased expected earnings from their education as future collateral to provide individual credit.

Private Schools

Evidence shows that, in many cases, private schools can introduce and encourage better effectiveness in terms of education outcomes. A 2000 study by Arjun Bedi and Ashish Garg on the effectiveness of private versus public schooling in Indonesia showed a positive correlation between increased labor market earnings (as a proxy for more effective education) and private school attendance. Results from the Do-

minican Republic, the Philippines, Tanzania, and Thailand show evidence of better education results, at lower costs, for private schools—through better management practices, more efficient use of inputs, and the introduction of innovative cost-saving techniques. Likewise, two studies in India concluded that private initiatives provide better education at lower costs. The Fé y Alegria School network in Latin America is also known to provide more effective schooling than its public-sector counterparts; its per student costs are only 60 percent of those in the public sector; yet many of the schools achieve similar or better learning outcomes.

For-Profit and Nonprofit Institutions

Many countries regulate that private schools only be operated on a not-for-profit basis, while others are more liberal and allow for both nonprofit and for-profit institutions to operate and compete freely in the same markets. There has been an emergence of more for-profit institutions across the globe. Typically, but not always, they will serve urban-based middle- to upper-class families, and the tuition fees they charge can vary considerably. These schools are normally registered by public authorities, are subject to socially based regulatory requirements, and in some cases they receive public subsidies. Such is the case in many eastern European countries and South Africa, where subsidies are paid on a sliding scale based on the levels of tuition fees charged to students.

The main difference between the two categories of private schools is that nonprofit entities are not traditionally obliged to pay any taxes on surpluses they may generate, whereas for-profit entities are required to pay taxes on the profits they earn.

In countries where all private schools are required by regulation to be nonprofit entities, it is typical for investors to establish for-profit entities that can *parent,* or own, a school's physical assets and deliver essential services, usually on preferred commercial terms. While the education institution preserves its status by complying with the not-for-profit regulations, the parent entity can operate on a for-profit basis, selectively deriving income from the school's operations on favorable terms. Using these for-profit vehicles, proprietors are generally able to find more flexible mechanisms to minimize the tax impact on their earnings, and at the same time provide satisfactory social and financial returns to investors.

Public-Private Partnerships

Partnerships between the public sector and the private sector have provided a basis for positive collaboration between governments and private-sector interests. In some developed countries where effective decentralization has taken place (e.g., Chile, New Zealand), greater autonomy at the institution level has had a positive impact on institution efficiency and accountability. Depending on the degree of outsourcing in each case, traditional services such as teacher payroll, school transport, financial services, and professional development have been successfully outsourced to the private sector. In cases where sensitivity to privatization exists, governments are actively seeking ways to outsource the design, building, and management of selected facilities, while retaining the ownership and control of all academic operations.

Supply of Textbooks and Ancillary Services

Traditional private-sector supply of textbooks, curriculum, and other learning materials to both public and private schools has been in place for many years. Food service, catering, cleaning, and building and general maintenance services are also typically provided by the private sector.

Public Schools Managed by Private Companies

Private-sector management of publicly owned schools (e.g., in Chile and the United States) under contract to the state has begun to earn public acceptance. Although it is still too early to know whether delivery of curriculum and learning outcomes improve in these situations, professional staff and many of their school communities are known to be supportive of these initiatives, with communities having greater inputs into school operations and development. In 2001, the Edison Schools network in the United States consisted of 136 schools in 53 cities, covering 22 states and serving approximately 75,000 students. This meant that Edison Schools were servicing approximately one out of every 700 K–12 students.

Private Tutoring Services

Across the globe, private tutoring services have developed into a burgeoning industry. They thrive on supplementing the curriculum delivered in public institutions, are often highly skills-based in nature, and are sometimes staffed by teachers or subject specialists as a second job. In Asia alone there is more than U.S. $20 billion spent annually on English lessons.

Accreditation, Quality Reviews, and Inspections

Independent accreditation services for colleges and universities are the norm in the United States. There is also a growing interest in many countries for quality reviews of schools and tertiary institutions to be carried out by the private sector. Many U.S. agencies, for example, are providing accreditation and quality-assurance services internationally. In Oman, a private British group undertakes operational and quality reviews of public schools.

Education on Internet Portals

The private sector also plays an important role in education, improving access to new technologies through the development of resources and services that the public sector would find difficult to sustain. Private-sector interests will continue to dominate the development of information and communications technology (ICT) resources for the education sector throughout the world. Core curriculum materials and programs developed for use with ICT have, in a few cases, remained the preserve of public education. It is in the future interest of ICT development in education in both developed and developing countries that public- and private-sector education interests work in close partnership with private-sector ICT companies for the benefit of future education development. The private sector has the capability of making the significant investments required to keep pace with the continuous technological changes that are happening in the ICT sectors across the globe.

Education sites on the Internet can take on different forms of ownership. Private-sector sites and resources are common in the United States, India, Canada and elsewhere. In New Zealand, the development and management of the public education Internet portal was outsourced to the private sector. But in each case, consultation with the public sector regarding the linking of resources to the local curriculum was important.

Relevant use of the Internet will help democratize education, giving all students, even those in poor communities, access to global libraries and teachers around the world. A majority of the ICT resources developed to support electronic learning, or to add value to the delivery of curriculum into the classroom, have been developed by the private sector.

Education authorities in both developed and developing countries do not have the capability of making the significant investments required to keep pace with the continuous technological changes that are happening in the ICT sectors.

See also: COMMERCE OF EDUCATION; INTERNATIONAL EDUCATION; INTERNATIONAL STUDENTS, *subentry on* THE GLOBAL COMMERCE OF HIGHER EDUCATION.

BIBLIOGRAPHY

BEDI, ARJUN S., and GARG, ASHISH. 2000. "The Effectiveness of Private Versus Public Schools: The Case of Indonesia." *Journal of Development Economics* 61(2):463–494.

FULLER, BRUCE, and ELMORE, RICHARD F., eds. 1996. *Who Chooses? Who Loses? Culture, Institutions, and the Unequal Effects of School Choice.* New York: Teachers College Press.

HEYNEMAN, STEPHEN P. 2000. "Educational Qualifications: The Economic and Trade Issues." *Assessment in Education: Principles, Policy, and Practice* 7(3):417–439 (special issue on "Globalization, Qualifications, and Livelihoods," ed. Angela Little).

HEYNEMAN, STEPHEN P. 2001. "The Growing International Market for Education Goods and Services." *International Journal of Education Development* 21:345–361.

INTERNATIONAL FINANCE CORPORATION. 2001. *Investing in Private Education: IFC's Strategic Directions.* Washington, DC: International Finance Corporation.

KINGDON, GEETA G. 1994. "An Economic Evaluation of Schools Management Types in Urban India: A Case Study of Uttar Pradesh." Ph.D diss., University of Oxford.

LOCKHEED, MARLAINE, and JIMENEZ, EMMANUEL. 1996. "Public and Private Schools Overseas: Contrasts in Organizations and Effectiveness." In *Who Chooses? Who Loses? Culture, Institutions, and the Unequal Effects of School Choice,* ed. Bruce Fuller and Richard F. Elmore. New York: Teachers College Press.

WORLD BANK. 2002. *Tertiary Education: New Challenges.* Washington, DC: Education Group, World Bank Human Development Network.

RONALD F. PERKINSON

INTERNATIONAL ASSESSMENTS

OVERVIEW

International comparisons of student achievement involve assessing the knowledge of elementary and secondary school students in subjects such as mathematics, science, reading, civics, and technology. The comparisons use test items that have been standardized and agreed upon by participating countries. These complex studies have been carried out since 1959 to explicitly compare student performance among countries for students at a common age. To participate in such a comparative study, a country must demonstrate that it has had prior experience in conducting empirical studies of education.

Comparing student achievement between countries has several goals. To policymakers, country-to-country comparisons of student performance help indicate whether their educational system is performing as well as it could. To a researcher of education issues, the studies provide a basis for hypothesizing whether some policies and practices in education are necessary or sufficient for high student performance (such as requiring all teachers to obtain college degrees in the subject area they teach). To teachers and school administrators, international studies provide examples of behavior that may be a source of new forms of practice and self-evaluation.

Types of Study Results

The results of a large international study in 1995 showed that eighth-grade teachers in the United

States are often not involved in decisions about the content areas of their teaching, as teachers are in other nations. U.S. teachers work longer hours than those in most other countries, they do not have as much time during the day to prepare for classes, and their daily classroom teaching is disrupted more often by things such as announcements, band practice, and scheduling changes. Moreover, the organization of curriculum used by elementary and middle schools in the United States appears not to be focused on topics that will propel students toward a more advanced understanding of mathematics. Comparisons with other countries show that U.S. students are just as interested in science and mathematics as other students, they study as long, and they watch just as much television.

Organizational History

Education researchers and policymakers from twelve countries first established a plan for making large-scale cross-national comparisons between countries on student performance in 1958 at the UNESCO Institute for Education in Hamburg, Germany. The first successful large-scale quantitative international study in mathematics was conducted in 1965 by the International Association for the Evaluation of Educational Achievement (IEA) and included Australia, Belgium, England, Finland, France, Germany, Israel, Japan, Netherlands, Scotland, Sweden, and the United States. Since then, studies in fourteen or more countries have been conducted periodically in several subject areas of elementary and secondary education.

Between 1965 and 2001 the IEA sponsored studies of mathematics in 1965, 1982, 1995, and 1999; science in 1970, 1986, 1995, and 1999; reading in 1970, 1991, and 2001; civics in 1970 and 1998; and technology in 1990 and 1999. The Educational Testing Service conducted an International Assessment for Education Progress in science and mathematics in 1990. The Adult Literacy and Lifeskills survey is a large-scale comparative survey designed to identify and measure prose literacy, numeracy, and analytical reasoning in the adult population (those between sixteen and sixty-five years of age). This survey was conducted in 1994 and 2001.

Studies such as these require the development of a set of test items, which are translated into the languages of the participating countries. The translated items are checked for proper translation and they are pretested in each country to determine whether they have misunderstandings or errors that would make the items unsuitable for use in the final study (about three times as many items are written as are finally used). The participating countries collectively agree upon a framework to define critical aspects of the topic area. For example, an elementary mathematics test would include items in numbers, geometry, algebra, functions, analysis, and measurement, and would also have items that represented different aspects of student performance, such as knowing the topic, using procedures, solving problems, reasoning, and communicating. However, no single assessment could cover comprehensively an entire topic for all countries.

The tests are administered to a sample of students in 100 to 200 schools, which are selected to represent all students in the country. An international referee monitors the school selection process to insure that all countries follow correct sampling procedures. The test items are scored according to internationally agreed-upon procedures and are analyzed at an international center to insure cross-national comparability. Countries that do not meet high standards of participation are not included in the comparisons.

Problems of Comparability

Some educators believe that learning is too elusive and culturally specific to be measured in a statistical survey. They believe that the outcomes of education are too diverse, indirect, and unpredictable to be measured in a single instrument. Others believe that comparisons are "odious" because practices that work in one culture may not be appropriate in another culture due to differences in social context and history.

The first IEA study planners were not confident that cross-national comparisons would be valid. They were concerned that the curriculum of different countries would stress different aspects of mathematics, science, or reading, and that any test of student performance might not reflect what students had been taught. To recognize national differences in teaching, the first studies measured the degree to which topics that were emphasized in the school system were actually covered. Curriculum differences were categorized as *intended, implemented,* or *attained* curriculum in order to separate the policies of the school district from classroom presentations and actual student performance. The amount of coverage of a topic became an important explanatory variable for between-school and between-country differences in achievement. The analysis showed that students in every country cover the same topics, but that they were often covered in a different order, and with a different emphasis, thus showing that international comparisons of student achievement do reflect the same content areas as other countries and thus they do make sense.

Education practices in the countries studied have been found to have more similarities than differences. The differences can be studied, however, and give important insights into which practices can be improved. International studies have helped policymakers understand that student performance is strongly determined by how schools articulate the content areas they are responsible for.

For example, a study conducted in 1965 showed significant differences in how countries approached the teaching of mathematics. Subsequent studies showed which topics of mathematics each country considered important, at what age they were introduced, and how the topics were sequenced. These studies led educators to pay closer attention to the underlying curriculum and the training of teachers in the United States. They also led to the earliest efforts by the mathematics education professionals to develop a single set of standards for mathematics teaching.

Studies of writing have had difficulty in achieving standards that permit comparison across countries. After several attempts to develop a standard set of principles for grading the writing of students across countries, the IEA gave up its efforts to evaluate writing across cultures. However, a study of reading achievement was successfully conducted in elementary and middle school grades in 1970, and studies are being conducted by the IEA and the Organisation for Economic Co-operation and Development (OECD). International studies have shown that U.S. elementary school students have a high performance level in reading compared with the rest of the participating countries, but only moderate performance at grade nine. These results indicate that U.S. students begin school with sufficient ability to read and interpret texts.

Forms of Inquiry

Comparative studies of student achievement require carefully designed statistical surveys for the statistical measurement aspect of the comparison. The popula-

tions must be defined in a common way for each country, even though definitions of a grade might differ from country to country. For example, one way to insure comparability is to select a careful sample of all students who attend whatever grade is common for fourteen-year-old students. These surveys involve students taking a test for about an hour and filling in a background questionnaire of their attitudes toward school. Teachers are asked to complete questionnaires about the curriculum topics they cover and their own professional training.

Since the 1990s studies have sometimes involved the use of videotape technology to collect information on teaching practices and student activities. For example, large national samples of mathematics classrooms were videotaped in 1995 in Japan, Germany, and the United States, and classrooms for other subjects were videotaped, in additional countries, in 2000. Videotape methods permit a more careful description of teaching practices than classroom surveys, and they provide a check on the validity of teachers' self-reporting of their practices. Detailed case studies of educational practices in several countries have also provided information about the social context in which students are taught.

International Assessments in the Twentieth Century

The first international studies were carried out by university research centers unaffiliated with government agencies. The results of those studies were published in academic journals, technical volumes, and academic books. During the 1980s these studies influenced policies in American education. Beginning in 1989 government agencies decided that they should have a larger role in organizing and supporting the studies and improving their quality. The National Center for Education Statistics (NCES), an agency of the U.S. Department of Education, and the National Science Foundation provided the leadership and funding support for creating international assessments. The U.S. National Academy of Sciences established an oversight committee called the Board on International Comparative Studies in Education to monitor the progress of these studies.

By 1995 international comparative studies had become an accepted continuing aspect of describing the status of the educational outcomes and were being carried out regularly by the NCES. Many countries originally participated in these studies in order to conduct an analysis of a single subject area in a single year. They have since shifted toward a more strategic plan to develop consistently measured trends in educational achievement with international benchmarks.

International Assessments in the Twenty-First Century

The complexity of conducting standardized comparisons of student achievement in many countries will always challenge researchers, yet they have become institutionalized in many countries. The OECD, which is based in Paris, has gained support from at least twenty-five governments for a continuing series of international comparisons of reading, mathematics, and science. These comparisons began in 2000. Also in 2000 UNESCO established the International Institute of Statistics to further institutionalize a process for improving the use of comparative statistics for policymaking.

Studies on the use of technology in schools are being developed to provide new information on forms of instructional technology that are becoming widespread in schools. Schools all over the world have introduced the use of computers and other forms of technology to classroom instruction, and studies seek to determine how educational practices are being altered by these systems.

See also: ASSESSMENT, *subentry on* NATIONAL ASSESSMENT OF EDUCATIONAL PROGRESS; STANDARDS FOR STUDENT LEARNING; TESTING, *subentry on* INTERNATIONAL STANDARDS OF TEST DEVELOPMENT.

BIBLIOGRAPHY

BLACK, PAUL, and WILIAM, DYLAN. 1998. "Inside the Black Box: Raising Standards through Classroom Assessment." *Phi Delta Kappan* 80(2):139–148.

COMBER, L. C., and KEEVES, JOHN P. 1973. *Science Education in Nineteen Countries: An Empirical Study.* Stockholm: John Wiley.

HARNQVIST, KJELL. 1987. "The IEA Revisited." *Comparative Education Review* 31(1):48–55.

HUSÉN, TORSTEN, ed. 1967. *International Study of Achievement in Mathematics,* Volume 1. New York: John Wiley.

HUSÉN, TORSTEN. 1979. "An International Research Venture in Retrospect: The IEA Surveys." *Comparative Education Review* 23(3):371–385.

HUSÉN, TORSTEN, and POSTLETHWAITE, T. NEVILLE, eds. 1985. *The International Encyclopedia of Edu-* *cation Research and Studies.* Oxford: Pergamon Press.

MULLIS, INA; MARTIN, MICHAEL O.; BEATON, ALBERT E.; GONZALEZ, EUGENIO J.; KELLY, DANA L.; and SMITH, TERESA A. 1998. *Mathematics and Science Achievement in the Final Year of Secondary School: IEA's Third International Mathematics and Science Study (TIMSS).* Boston: Center for the Study of Testing, Evaluation, and Education Policy, Boston College.

ROBITAILLE, DAVID F.; SCHMIDT, WILLIAM H.; RAIZEN, SENTA; McKNIGHT, CURTIS; BRITTON, EDWARD; and NICOL, CYNTHIA. 1993. *Curriculum Frameworks for Mathematics and Science.* Vancouver, BC, Canada: Pacific Educational Press.

SCHMIDT, WILLIAM H., et al. 1996. *Characterizing Pedagogical Flow: An Investigation of Mathematics and Science Teaching in Six Countries.* Dordrecht, Netherlands: Kluwer.

STIGLER, JAMES W.; GONZALES, PATRICK A.; KAWANAKA, TAKAKO; KNOLL, STEFFEN; and SERRANO, ANA. 1999. *The TIMSS Videotape Classroom Study: Methods and Findings from an Exploratory Research Project on Eighth-Grade Mathematics Instruction in Germany, Japan, and the United States.* Washington, DC: National Center for Education Statistics.

SUTER, LARRY. 2001. "Is Student Achievement Immutable? Evidence from International Studies on Schooling and Student Achievement." *Journal for the Review of Educational Research.* 70(4):529–545.

TRAVERS, KENNETH J., and WESTBURY, IAN. 1990. *The IEA Study of Mathematics, I: Analysis of Mathematics Curricula.* Oxford: Pergamon Press.

INTERNET RESOURCES

INTERNATIONAL ORGANIZATION FOR THE EVALUATION OF EDUCATIONAL ACHIEVEMENT (IEA). 2002. <www.iea.nl/>.

NATIONAL CENTER FOR EDUCATION STATISTICS. 2001. <http://nces.ed.gov/surveys/SurveyGroups.asp?Group=06>.

LARRY SUTER

INTERNATIONAL ASSOCIATION FOR EDUCATIONAL ASSESSMENT

The International Association for Educational Assessment (IAEA) was conceived as an international association of measurement agencies in 1974 at a meeting at Educational Testing Service (ETS) in Princeton, New Jersey. Later that same year a preparing committee, representing various geographic regions, met at CITO, the Institute for Educational Measurement in the Netherlands, to formulate the plans for the association.

In 1976 the United Nations Educational, Scientific and Cultural Organization (UNESCO) admitted IAEA to C (information sharing) status as a nongovernmental organization (NGO). In 1981 UNESCO admitted IAEA to B (consultative) status.

Purpose and Objectives

The broad purpose of IAEA is to assist educational agencies in the development and appropriate application of educational assessment techniques to improve the quality of education. IAEA's main objectives are to:

- improve communication among organizations interested in educational assessment through the sharing of professional expertise, conferences, and publications, while providing a framework that includes cooperative research, training, and projects involving educational assessment;

- make expertise in assessment techniques readily available for the solution of problems in the field of educational evaluation;

- cooperate with other organizations and agencies having complementary interests;

- engage in other activities leading to the improvement of assessment techniques and their appropriate use by educational agencies throughout the world.

Membership

IAEA has mainly three groups of membership: primary organizations, affiliate organizations, and individuals. Primary organization members are not-for-profit organizations, often associated in one way or another with ministries of education, which have educational assessment as their primary function. Affiliate organizations are those that make a major use of educational assessment techniques, or financial agencies that devote a large part of their budgets to work involving educational assessment. Individual members are those with a professional interest in assessment who may not be associated with an organization that has educational assessment as a primary concern. An executive committee whose officers and members are elected by the primary organization members governs IAEA. A subscription to the journal *Assessment in Education: Principles, Policy and Practice* is included with membership.

Activities and Projects

IAEA organizes annual conferences on assessment themes of international significance. Rotated on a geographic basis, a primary organization member in a region assumes responsibility for organizing the conference. IAEA has focused on topics such as standard setting, school-based assessment, public examinations, and admission to higher education.

In cooperation with UNESCO, IAEA organizes roundtables on the impact of assessment on education. The roundtables bring experts from designated geographic areas together to share information about topics of mutual interest, such as "The Impact of Evaluation and Assessment on Educational Policy," "The Impact of Examination Systems on Curriculum Development," and "International Comparisons of Student Achievements." Since its inception IAEA has conducted through its members a number of projects for UNESCO and the World Bank.

The executive Secretaryship of IAEA is located at CITO, The Netherlands.

See also: INTERNATIONAL DEVELOPMENT AGENCIES AND EDUCATION, *subentry on* UNITED NATIONS AND INTERNATIONAL AGENCIES.

TON LUIJTEN

INTERNATIONAL ASSOCIATION FOR THE EVALUATION OF EDUCATIONAL ACHIEVEMENT

The International Association for the Evaluation of Educational Achievement (IEA), founded in the late 1950s, conducts international comparative studies in which educational achievement is assessed in relation to student background, teacher, classroom, and school variables. At the time of the IEA's founding, there was a growing awareness among international agencies of the role of formal education in social and economical development while indicators for educational "productivity" were lacking. A group of researchers, among them Torsten Husén and his colleagues, decided in the early 1960s to undertake a first study of mathematics achievement in twelve countries to explore the feasibility of international comparative achievement studies. This first study marked the birth of the IEA.

After starting as a group of researchers, the IEA soon became a cooperative of research institutes with a primarily academic research focus. Since the early 1980s the IEA has begun to focus more specifically on the interests of policymakers, and an increasing number of member countries are represented by their ministry of education and no longer by a leading research institute. The current membership of the IEA comprises almost sixty countries from all regions of the world, and these are represented in a policymaking body, the IEA General Assembly, that is supported by the Secretariat in Amsterdam. Each IEA study is managed by three bodies: the International Coordinating Centre (ICC), which is responsible for the conduct of the research at the international level; the International Steering Committee (ISC), which monitors the quality of the research and is responsible for the general policy directions; and the International Study Committee, which consists of the National Research Coordinators (who are responsible for the study at the national level), the ISC, and the ICC.

Over the years the IEA has conducted many survey studies of basic school subjects. Most of the studies were curriculum driven and measure educational outcomes (the attained curriculum) on the basis of an analysis of the "official" curricula (the intended curricula) of the participating countries. All these studies evaluate school and classroom process variables (the implemented curriculum), as well as teacher and student background variables. Examples are the studies of mathematics and science, reading literacy, civics education, and English and French as foreign languages. The IEA also conducts studies that are not curriculum based, such as the Pre-Primary Project and the Computers in Education study. In a typical IEA study, data are collected in the third and/or fourth grade, the seventh and/or eighth grade, and the final year of secondary schooling, although some studies do not include all three populations. IEA's best-known study is the Third International Mathematics and Science Study (TIMSS),

conducted between 1992 and 1999 for all three populations, in which more than forty countries participated. This study was designed to assess achievement in mathematics and science in the context of national curricula, instructional practices, and the social (and learning) environment of students.

To allow countries a longitudinal international comparative perspective, the IEA in the late 1990s initiated a basic cycle of studies in which the association studies, in alternating years, mathematics and sciences (through TIMSS—now called Trends in Mathematics and Science Study) and reading literacy (through the Progress in International Reading Literacy Study). Additionally, the IEA conducts other studies such as the Civic Education Study, which was completed in 2002, and the Second Information Technology in Education Study, which started in the fall of 1997.

Purposes and Functions of IEA Studies

IEA's mission is to enhance the quality of education. Its studies have two main purposes: (1) to provide policymakers and educational practitioners with information about the quality of their education in relation to relevant reference countries; and (2) to assist in understanding the reasons for observed differences among educational systems.

Given these purposes, the IEA strives for two kinds of comparisons in its studies. The first one consists of straight international comparisons of effects of education in terms of scores (or subscores) on international tests. The second relates to how well a country's official curriculum is implemented in the schools and achieved by students.

As a result, IEA studies have a variety of functions for educational policymakers, practitioners, and researchers:

- describing the national results in an international context
- analyzing the information about the status of the achievement of pupils against the results of one or more other countries or against the results in the country of interest in an earlier study ("benchmarking")
- analyzing data to contribute to recommendations for changes when and where needed ("monitoring")
- analyzing data with the purpose of understanding the reasons for observed performances either in a national context or within an international comparative perspective

• promoting a general "enlightenment"—that is, there is not a direct link to decisions but rather a gradual diffusion of ideas into the sphere of organizational decision-making

Many national and international reports on IEA studies illustrate the usefulness of IEA studies for educational policy and practice. For example, in Australia, Hungary, Ireland, Japan, New Zealand, and the United States, specific curriculum changes have been attributed to IEA findings.

Considerations in Planning IEA Studies

IEA studies are very complex endeavors and are conducted with attention to quality at every step of the way. The first question to be answered in planning an IEA study is "what questions do we want to address through this study." The leading research questions become very compelling because there are a variety of competing perspectives in realizing a study. In order to obtain valid and useful data and indicators, high-level scientific and technical standards have to be met for each component of the study, such as the development of a conceptual framework; determining target populations; curriculum analysis; instrument development (including pilot testing, translation, etc.); sampling; data collection, cleaning and file building; quality control in participating countries of each component; data analysis; and report writing.

Many countries participate in IEA studies (e.g., in TIMSS more than forty countries), and according to its mission the IEA aims to create opportunities for each country to conduct its own cross-national analysis in order to enhance the understanding of the functioning of its educational system at all levels. The varying interests of participating countries contribute to the dilemma between desirability and feasibility (many stakeholders want an array of data, while there are practical limitations in collecting data in schools), and in these types of studies compromises have to be found among the interests of all participating countries. The IEA aims for a design and for instruments that are as equally fair as possible to all participating countries, while also allowing for national options. For example, in the 1999 TIMSS study in South Africa, where the majority of pupils receive instruction in a language other than the home language, a language proficiency test was included to allow for investigating relationships between language and achievement.

A final point that requires careful attention is the organizational and logistical complexities of the IEA studies. For instance, the 1995 TIMSS study involved the following: achievement testing in mathematics and science in forty-five countries; five grade levels (third, fourth, seventh, eighth, and final year of secondary school); more than half a million students; testing in more than thirty languages; more than 15,000 participating schools; nearly 1,000 open-ended questions, generating millions of student responses and performance assessments; questionnaires from students, teachers, and school principals containing about 1,500 questions; and many thousands of individuals to administer the tests and process the data.

Conclusions

IEA studies do not lead to easy answers to complex educational problems, but they contribute to the body of knowledge of how educational systems work and of optimal conditions for teaching and learning. An example can be found in a 1992 report by T. Neville Postlethwaite and Kenneth N. Ross, who determined on the basis of cross-national analysis of the IEA Progress in International Reading Literacy Study that a large number of variables (including school, teacher, teaching, and student variables) influenced reading achievement. Their analyses illustrate how IEA studies can contribute to informed decision-making by policymakers and create an awareness of the rich variety of educational settings and approaches around the world. On the other hand, the types of studies conducted by the IEA have some limitations and also receive criticism. Technical criticisms have largely been addressed in the recent studies, and critiques have become increasingly political.

Finally, reflecting on nearly half a century of IEA activities, a number of developments have occurred and benefits have emerged. IEA studies have moved beyond simply international comparative assessment scores and contextual information. They have contributed to the national and international education community in various ways. They have provided possibilities of addressing regional issues as part of an international comparative study, linking national assessments to international assessments, and for developing countries, in particular, the opportunity to collect baseline data on education. Important benefits of the international comparative IEA studies have been the development of education research capacities in many countries, culminating in the development of a network of researchers and specialists who can be drawn from by both governments and other agencies both nationally and internationally.

See also: INTERNATIONAL ASSESSMENTS, *subentries on* IEA AND OECD STUDIES OF READING LITERACY, IEA STUDY OF TECHNOLOGY IN THE CLASSROOM, IEA THIRD INTERNATIONAL MATHEMATICS AND SCIENCE STUDY, POLITICAL DEMOCRACY AND THE IEA STUDY OF CIVIC EDUCATION.

BIBLIOGRAPHY

BEATON, ALBERT E., et al. 1996a. *Mathematics Achievement in the Middle School Years.* Chestnut Hill, MA: Boston College, TIMSS International Study Center.

BEATON, ALBERT E., et al. 1996b. *Science Achievement in the Middle School Years.* Chestnut Hill, MA: Boston College, TIMSS International Study Center.

BEATON, ALBERT E., et al. 2000. *The Benefits and Limitations of International Educational Achievement Studies.* Paris: International Institute for Educational Planning/International Academy of Education.

HUSÉN, TORSTEN. 1967. *International Study of Achievement in Mathematics: A Comparison of Twelve Countries,* Vols. 1–2. Stockholm, Sweden: Almqvist and Wiksell; New York: Wiley.

HUSÉN, TORSTEN, and POSTLETHWAITE, T. NEVILLE. 1996. "A Brief History of the International Association for the Evaluation of Educational Achievement (IEA)." *Assessment in Education* 3:129–141.

INTERNATIONAL ASSOCIATION FOR THE EVALUATION OF EDUCATIONAL ACHIEVEMENT. 1998. *IEA Guidebook, 1998: Activities, Institutions, and People.* Amsterdam: IEA Secretariat.

KEEVES, JOHN P. 1995. *The World of School Learning: Selected Key Findings from Thirty-Five Years of IEA Research.* Amsterdam: IEA Secretariat.

KELLAGHAN, THOMAS. 1996. "IEA Studies and Educational Policy." *Assessment in Education* 3:143–160.

LOXLEY, WENDY. 1992. "Introduction to Special Volume." *Prospects* 22:275–277.

MARTIN, MICHAEL O.; RUST, KEITH; and ADAMS, RAYMOND, eds. 1999. *Technical Standards for IEA Studies.* Amsterdam: IEA Secretariat.

MARTIN, M. O., et al. 2000. *TIMSS, 1999: International Science Report.* Chestnut Hill, MA: Boston College, Lynch School of Education, IEA TIMSS International Study Center.

MULLIS, INA V. S., et al. 2000. *TIMSS, 1999: International Mathematics Report.* Chestnut Hill, MA: Boston College, Lynch School of Education, IEA TIMSS International Study Center.

PELGRUM, WILLEM J., and ANDERSON, RONALD E., eds. 1999. *ICT and the Emerging Paradigm for Lifelong Learning.* Amsterdam: IEA Secretariat.

POSTLETHWAITE, T. NEVILLE, and ROSS, KENNETH N. 1992. *Effective Schools in Reading: Implications for Planners.* Amsterdam: IEA Secretariat.

SHORROCKS-TAYLOR, DIANE, and JENKINS, EDGAR W. 2000. *Learning from Others.* Dordrecht, Netherlands: Kluwer.

TORNEY-PURTA, JUDITH; LEHMANN, RAINER; OSWALD, HANS; and SCHULZ, WOLFRAM. 2001. *Citizenship and Education in Twenty-Eight Countries.* Amsterdam: IEA Secretariat.

INTERNET RESOURCE

INTERNATIONAL ASSOCIATION FOR THE EVALUATION OF EDUCATIONAL ACHIEVEMENT. 2002. <www.iea.nl/>.

TJEERD PLOMP

IEA AND OECD STUDIES OF READING LITERACY

Globalization, increased worker mobility, and competition between knowledge-based economies have led to a growth in demand for studies to measure and compare the achievement outcomes of education systems. Given its importance in students' educational development and in everyday life, it is not surprising that reading has featured in a number of these studies. Reflecting a concern with functional aspects of learning, the assessment of reading was expanded from one that mainly focused on decoding and comprehension skills to one that addressed the ability to understand and use written language forms required by society and valued by the individual.

The International Association for the Evaluation of Educational Achievement (IEA), a nongovernmental organization, pioneered international assessment studies in the early 1960s. The number of education systems (mostly in the industrialized world) participating in its reading studies increased from fifteen in 1970–1971 to thirty-two in 1991–1992 and to thirty-six in 2001. In the studies assessment instruments were developed by international panels, translated into national languages, and administered to representative samples of nine- or ten-year-old students and thirteen- or fourteen-year-old students in participating countries. A variety of correlates of reading proficiency, including students' opportunity to learn and resources for reading, were identified.

The Organisation for Economic Co-operation and Development (OECD), responding to concern among member governments about the preparedness of young people to enter society and the world of work, has supported the development of the Programme for International Student Assessment (PISA), which is designed to monitor the achievements of fifteen-year-old students in reading literacy (as well as in mathematics and science). Thirty-two countries participated in the first survey in 2000. The ability to comprehend forms of prose organized as continuous and noncontinuous text, such as lists and forms, and to retrieve and evaluate information were assessed.

In the 1990s a number of countries (eventually twenty) joined with Statistics Canada in studies, later involving OECD, to assess the ability of adults (sixteen to sixty-five years old) to understand and employ written information in daily activities at home, at work, and in the community. Reading tasks were based on text from newspapers and brochures, maps, timetables, and charts; basic arithmetic tasks were also included. Proficiency was found to be negatively related to age and, in eighteen countries, respondents' level of education was its strongest predictor.

Although international studies were initially planned to improve understanding of the educational process and to provide information relevant to policymaking and educational planning, the media have generally interpreted their findings in a competitive context, focusing on countries' relative performances, without considering the social, economic, and educational conditions that affect student learning.

See also: INTERNATIONAL ASSESSMENTS, *subentry on* INTERNATIONAL ASSOCIATION FOR THE EVALUATION OF EDUCATIONAL ACHIEVEMENT.

BIBLIOGRAPHY

ELLEY, WARWICK B. 1992. *How in the World Do Students Read?* The Hague, Netherlands: International Association for the Evaluation of Educational Achievement.

INTERNATIONAL ADULT LITERACY SURVEY. 2000. *Literacy in the Information Age: Final Report of the International Adult Literacy Survey.* Paris: Organisation for Economic Co-operation and Development; Ottawa, ON: Statistics Canada.

VINCENT GREANEY
THOMAS KELLAGHAN

IEA STUDY OF TECHNOLOGY IN THE CLASSROOM

Prior to 1980 few teachers utilized information technology (IT) in the classroom. But the global diffusion of personal computers in the 1980s generated considerable interest in educational circles around the world, leading the International Association for the Evaluation of Educational Achievement (IEA) to initiate the first international comparative study of IT or computers in education. This study was named the Computers in Education Study and sometimes called CompEd.

IEA Computers in Education Study

Twenty-two countries participated in the first stage of the Computers in Education Study and in 1989 conducted school surveys, as documented by Pelgrum and Plomp. Surveys were conducted in elementary, lower secondary, and upper secondary schools, and within each school sample, questionnaires were completed by the principal, computer coordinator, and several teachers. In 1992 the second stage of the study repeated the surveys of the first stage and added a student assessment, according to Willem Pelgrum and colleagues and Robert E. Anderson.

An assessment was designed to measure the ability of students to generally understand and use information technology. The performance of students in this assessment depended largely on the extent to which school curricula in each country provided opportunity to learn such skills. A number of countries already had instituted an informatics curriculum at the middle- or upper-secondary levels. Perhaps the most important finding of the study was that teachers in general lacked opportuni-

TABLE 1

The three modules of SITES

Module	Time Frame	Number of Countries	Issue	Data
School Survey (Module 1)	1997–1999	26	What are the main trends?	Surveys of principals and of technology coordinators.
Case Studies (Module 2)	1999–2003	30	What innovative teaching uses technology and what forms does it take?	In-depth case studies of innovative teaching in schools.
Assessment (Module 3)	2001–2005	Not yet known	What are teachers and students able to do with ICT to improve their learning?	Surveys of schools, teachers, and students. Student test and performance assessment.

SOURCE: Courtesy of author.

ties for the type of training that would enable them to integrate technology into their instruction.

The terminology for information technology has changed since the 1980s. Whereas information technology was called computers or IT during that decade, by the late 1990s educators in most countries referred to it as ICT to stand for the phrase *information and communication technology*. However, in some countries, most notably the United States, educators refer to information technology simply by the word *technology*.

Second IEA Study

The rapid diffusion of the Internet and multimedia technology during the mid-1990s generated an interest in a new study that among other things could investigate the changes in the curricula and classrooms since IEA's earlier study. The Second International Technology in Education Study (SITES) was initiated in 1996 by the IEA and school surveys were conducted in 1998. The SITES study consists of three modules as summarized in Table 1.

Although the study was approved by the IEA in 1996, the survey data of module 1 were collected in 1998. The module 2 case study visits to the school sites were conducted during 2000 and 2001, and the reports will be released in 2002 and 2003. Module 3 was launched in 2001, but the data for the surveys and student assessments will be collected during 2004, with the results released in 2005 and 2006. Each of the three modules will be described briefly in turn.

School Survey Module. In 1998 data were collected using a questionnaire survey of principals and one of technology coordinators or their equivalents. Twenty-six countries participated by conducting these surveys in one or more of these three school levels: primary, lower secondary, and upper secondary. As reported by Pelgrum and Anderson, this module produced findings on the following phenomena:

- the extent to which ICT is used (and by whom) in education systems across the globe

- the extent to which education systems have adopted, implemented, and realized the results from objectives that are considered important for education in a knowledge society

- teaching practices that principals consider to be innovative, important, effective, and satisfying

- existing differences in ICT-related practices both within and between education systems and what lessons can be learned from this.

The findings on school Internet access were representative of the heterogeneous pattern of cross-national adoption of new ICT practices. Figure 1 shows that while 100 percent of the schools in Singapore and Iceland had access, some countries had only about a fourth of their schools connected. Most of the other countries had connected more than 50 percent of their schools. What is so remarkable about this pattern is that even in populations that do not speak English—the dominant language of the Internet—most of their countries' schools had been connected and many of the students were using the Internet in school. This rapid connection of schools to the Internet occurred within only about five years or less.

FIGURE 1

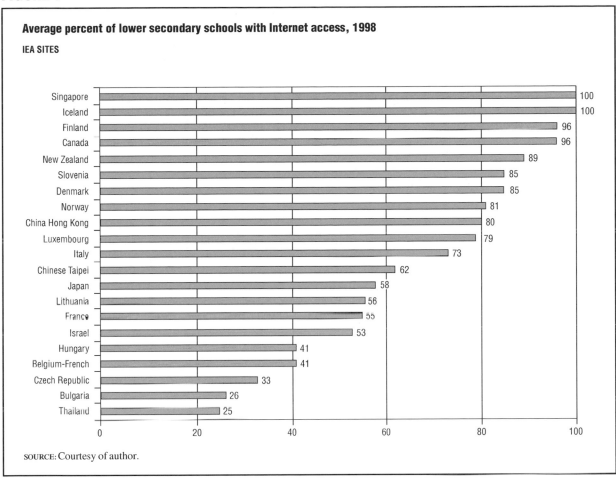

Average percent of lower secondary schools with Internet access, 1998

IEA SITES

Country	Percent
Singapore	100
Iceland	100
Finland	96
Canada	96
New Zealand	89
Slovenia	85
Denmark	85
Norway	81
China Hong Kong	80
Luxembourg	79
Italy	73
Chinese Taipei	62
Japan	58
Lithuania	56
France	55
Israel	53
Hungary	41
Belgium-French	41
Czech Republic	33
Bulgaria	26
Thailand	25

SOURCE: Courtesy of author.

Case Studies Module. Nearly thirty countries conducted in-depth case studies during the last half of 2000 and the first half of 2001. The focus of this qualitative research is innovative pedagogical practices that use technology (IPPUT). The main purposes are to understand what sustains these practices and what outcomes they produce. To accomplish this investigation, each case study describes and analyzes classroom-based processes and their contexts. These case studies are intended to provide policy analysts and teachers with examples of "model" classroom practices and offer policymakers findings regarding the contextual factors that are critical to successful implementation and sustainability of these exemplary teaching practices using ICT.

The twenty-eight countries participating in this module of SITES were Australia, Canada, Chile, China Hong Kong, Chinese Taipei, Czech Republic, Denmark, England, Finland, France, Germany, Israel, Italy, Japan, Korea, Latvia, Lithuania, the Nether-

lands, Norway, Philippines, Portugal, Russian Federation, Singapore, Slovakia, South Africa, Spain (Catalonia), Thailand, and the United States. As each country will conduct four to twelve case studies, the total number of cases for analysis is expected to be more than 150.

One noteworthy preliminary finding was that the students used the Internet as part of nearly every innovative practice selected. Another preliminary finding of perhaps greater importance is that the students involved in these innovative pedagogical practices often engaged in activities that could be considered "knowledge management" in that they frequently constructed knowledge products. Typically such activities were called projects and included the tasks of searching, organizing, and evaluating knowledge. For instance, Germany's first case study found that students "turned into providers of knowledge." Portugal's pilot case reported that the teachers wanted their students to be "constructors rather than receptors of mathematical knowledge." In Norway and the USA the case studies found students working collaboratively with ICT tools to complete projects yielding diverse types of knowledge.

Assessment Module. This module builds upon these findings from the leading-edge classrooms of the case studies. Specifically, the school survey, teacher survey, and student assessment will include indicators to determine the difference between the innovative and the typical learning contexts. The study will measure the ICT-supported knowledge management competencies of students, including their abilities to retrieve, organize, critically evaluate, communicate, and produce knowledge. In addition, the study will determine the readiness of schools and teachers to provide a learning environment where students can develop these abilities. In addition, this module will follow up the school survey module by having a school survey administered to principals and ICT-coordinators to measure trends of technology availability and use in schools.

All countries participating in the assessment module will study fourteen-year old students; the target population will be the grade with the most students of age fourteen. An optional population will be the grade with the most ten-year-old students. Each country will be expected to attain a sample of a minimum of 200 randomly selected schools per population. In at least 100 of these participating schools, one intact class will be sampled from all classes in the target grade. In addition to surveying the teacher of the sampled class, three additional teachers will be sampled and surveyed from those teaching the target grade.

Guiding the development of the student assessment is a framework that considers different types of knowledge management and types of tools. The categories of knowledge and tools are shown in Table 2 with the cells that illustrate sample performance tasks.

In the student assessment there will be a paper-and-pencil assessment administered to all students in the sample, and an optional Internet-based performance assessment given to four students in each class, provided that they are Internet-"literate." Students in the sampled class will be administered a survey questionnaire and a short paper-and-pencil assessment during a single class period. The assessment will include a short Internet screening test.

Students will not be eligible for participation in the performance assessment unless they pass the screening test. If at least half of the students pass the Internet screening test, then the school will be eligible for participation in the performance assessment.

Despite highly diverse national educational systems around the world, almost every country has established policies regarding ICT in education. SITES in its first two modules found many different approaches across countries to the ICT challenge in education. Yet there are common threads such as widespread and rapidly growing access to the Internet. There is every reason to believe that this trend, as well as the large digital divide across countries, will continue in the early twenty-first century. It is anticipated that the assessment module with its focus on knowledge management will capture significant trends in information technology and the changing role of knowledge in society.

See also: INTERNATIONAL ASSESSMENTS, *subentry on* INTERNATIONAL ASSOCIATION FOR THE EVALUATION OF EDUCATIONAL ACHIEVEMENT.

BIBLIOGRAPHY

ANDERSON, RONALD E., ed. 1993. "Computers in American Schools, 1992: An Overview." *IEA Computers in Education Study.* Minneapolis: University of Minnesota, Department of Sociology.

ANDERSON, RONALD E. 2001. "Youth and Information Technology." In *The Future of Adolescent Experience: Societal Trends and the Transition to Adulthood,* ed. Jeylan T. Mortimer and Reed Larson. New York: Cambridge University Press.

PELGRUM, WILLEM J., and ANDERSON, RONALD E., eds. 1999. *ICT and the Emerging Paradigm for Life Long Learning: A Worldwide Educational Assessment of Infrastructure, Goals, and Practices.* Amsterdam: International Association for the Evaluation of Educational Achievement.

PELGRUM, WILLEM J.; JANSSEN REINEN, I. A. M.; and PLOMP, TJEERD. 1993. *Schools, Teachers, Students and Computers: A Cross-National Perspective.* The Hague, Netherlands: International Association for the Educational Evaluation of Educational Achievement (IEA).

PELGRUM, WILLEM J., and PLOMP, TJEERD. 1991. *The Use of Computers in Education Worldwide.* Oxford: Pergamon.

TABLE 2

Knowledge management competencies by ICT tool types with illustrative performance assessment tasks in cells			
ICT Knowledge Management Competency	Tools to find, organize (e.g., browser, database)	Tools to analyze, model (e.g., spreadsheet)	Tools to present, communicate, write (e.g., multimedia presentation)
Knowledge construction	Project with choice of tools and data	Project with choice of tools and data	Project with choice of tools and data
Critical thinking: analyze, interpret data, evaluate evidence	Drill down to highly granular information	Scenario simulation	
Projects and complex problem solving		Using a model to make decisions	
Complete collaborative projects			
Effective presentations and discourse			Develop persuasive web-based presentation
Find, assemble, restructure knowledge	Web search and analysis		
Understand principles including secondary effects			

SOURCE: Courtesy of author.

PLOMP, TJEERD; ANDERSON, ROBERT E; and KONTO-GIANNOPOULOU-POLYDORIDES, GEORGIA. 1996. *Cross National Policies and Practices on Computers in Education.* Dordrecht, Netherlands: Kluwer.

RONALD E. ANDERSON

IEA THIRD INTERNATIONAL MATHEMATICS AND SCIENCE STUDY

The Third International Mathematics and Science Study (TIMSS) is the largest and most ambitious educational assessment ever done under the auspices of the International Association for the Evaluation of Educational Achievement (IEA). The TIMSS data collection in 1995 involved testing more than a half-million students in more than forty educational systems (usually countries) around the world. Students were assessed at five different grade levels, and students, as well as their teachers and principals, were given questionnaires about their backgrounds, attitudes, and practices. The TIMSS data collection in 1999 focused on eighth-grade students in thirty-eight countries.

The TIMSS study resulted in many provocative findings, which are published in the TIMSS international reports. The results showed that the averages of students of participating Asian nations (Hong Kong, Japan, Korea, and Singapore) were higher than those of students of other nations in mathematics at both the elementary and middle school levels. Japan and Korea also did very well in science at these levels, although Australia, Austria, and the United States also performed highly at the elementary level, and the Czech Republic performed well at the middle school level.

Testing was also done at the end of secondary school, where a sample of the total population of students was assessed in mathematical and scientific literacy. In addition, samples of students taking advanced mathematics or physics courses were tested on those subjects. The Asian countries were not among the twenty countries that participated in this assessment. The average scores of the Netherlands, Sweden, Iceland, Norway, and Switzerland were highest in mathematical and scientific literacy; the average achievement in advanced mathematics was highest in France and Russia; and the average physics test scores were highest in Norway, Sweden, and Russia.

The TIMSS results have been widely reported in the press and in numerous public reports. All TIMSS reports, including those cited above, are available on the Internet. TIMSS's website also contains technical reports that contain the details of the TIMSS methodology, and the raw TIMSS data are available at this site for those who would like to use the data to investigate different educational questions or research methodologies.

The study was administered by the International Study Center at Boston College and by the International Coordinating Centre at the University of British Columbia. TIMSS has been funded by the participating countries along with major contributions by the Government of Canada, the National Science Foundation (U.S.), and National Center for Education Statistics (U.S.).

The Aim of TIMSS

The TIMSS was established to improve the teaching and learning of mathematics and science in school systems around the world through a comparison of the curricula and practices of different countries, and to relate this information to the performance of their students. The research questions included not only what students in the participating countries had learned, but also how the curricula varied in different countries and what facilities and opportunities were made available for students to learn what was in their curricula. The relationships of students' performance to their curricula, educational opportunities, and backgrounds were also to be investigated.

IEA Studies of Mathematics and Science

The IEA has been involved in comparing the educational systems of various countries for many years. Four previous IEA studies of mathematics or science led up to TIMSS:

- First International Mathematics Study (FIMS), 1959–1960.
- First International Science Study (FISS), 1970.
- Second International Mathematics Study (SIMS), 1980–1982.
- Second International Science Study (SISS), 1982–1986.

TIMSS, which included both mathematics and science, was conducted in the Northern Hemisphere in 1995 and in the Southern Hemisphere in both 1994 and 1995. A second round of TIMSS, involving only eighth-grade students, was conducted in 1999. A third assessment is planned for 2003.

TIMSS Design

The design of TIMSS grew out of discussions in the late 1980s by many researchers who were involved in SIMS, and these discussions led to the Study of Mathematics and Science Opportunity (SMSO), which explored the curricula and teaching practices of a few countries around the world and initiated the development of the tests and questionnaires for TIMSS. The final design and its instrumentation were developed and approved by the participating countries in conjunction with mathematics and science education specialists and specialists in educational assessment.

Populations and Sampling

TIMSS defined three populations of students for assessment:

- Population 1—all students enrolled in the two adjacent grades that contain the largest proportion of students nine years old at the time of testing. In most participating countries, grades three and four fit this definition.
- Population 2—all students enrolled in the two adjacent grades that contain the largest proportion of students thirteen years old at the time of testing. In most participating countries, grades seven and eight fit this definition.
- Population 3—all students in their final year of secondary education, including students in vocational education programs. In most countries, this was grade twelve. Population 3 included two subpopulations: students taking advanced courses in mathematics and students taking advanced courses in physics.

In Populations 1 and 2, an early decision was made to sample intact mathematics classrooms so that information about teachers and students could be matched and studied. The students who were not enrolled in any mathematics class were treated as a separate classroom, and thus they could be selected for the sample. In Population 3, students were not sampled by classroom, but were classified according to their mathematics and science courses, and then individually sampled for assessment. All participating countries were required to assess Population 2, but assessments of Populations 1 or 3 were optional.

TIMSS Tests and Questionnaires

The TIMSS tests were constructed using mathematics and science frameworks that were agreed upon by the participating countries and subject-matter specialists. TIMSS included multiple-choice, short answer, extended response, and performance items. Countries were not required to administer the performance items.

In order to widen the curriculum coverage of TIMSS, a form of matrix sampling was used in which students in a population received different test items, except for a few items that were common to all booklets. In Populations 1 and 2, there were eight different booklets of items administered along with student questionnaires. Teachers and school questionnaires were also administered. In Population 3, nine test booklets were administered, with the particular booklet to be used dependant on the courses in which a student was enrolled. The teacher questionnaires were omitted because intact classrooms were not sampled. The booklets in Populations 1 and 2 required about an hour of student time, whereas the booklets for Population 3 required about ninety minutes.

Administration and Quality Monitoring

TIMSS was administered by personnel from the participating countries, and the TIMSS administrators were given extensive training to assure the high quality and comparability of the TIMSS data. International quality-control monitors were hired and trained to visit the national research centers and to review their procedures. The translations were also checked centrally to detect and avoid differences in the presentation of assessment questions.

Analysis and Reporting

The basic TIMSS database was constructed in the participating countries and then given extensive statistical scrutiny at the IEA Data Processing Center in Germany. Any unusual occurrences in the database were noted and adjudicated with the participating countries. The data were then sent to Statistics Canada for a review of the sampling and construction of sampling weights. The data also went to the Australian Council for Educational Research for scale development. The scaling was done using a variation of the Rasch model. The scaled database then went to the International Study Center at Boston College for analysis and reporting.

TIMSS was a very complex study that required the cooperation of the many countries and contracting organizations involved. Cooperation was critical to assure that the tests were appropriate for all countries and that the administration of TIMSS was uniform. The coordination required many meetings in which strategy and tactics were discussed and decided. Many training sessions were required to assure that all phases of the TIMSS were carried out successfully. The flow of data from the participating countries to Germany, then Canada, Australia, and

finally to the United States required careful monitoring. Finally, the final reports were designed and approved by the participating countries before the data were available. The details of the procedures are given in the TIMSS technical reports.

See also: INTERNATIONAL ASSESSMENTS, *subentry on* INTERNATIONAL ASSOCIATION FOR THE EVALUATION OF EDUCATIONAL ACHIEVEMENT.

BIBLIOGRAPHY

BEATON, ALBERT E.; MARTIN, MICHAEL O.; MULLIS, INA V. S.; GONZALEZ, EUGENIO J.; SMITH, TERESA A.; and KELLY, DANA L. 1996. *Mathematics Achievement in the Middle School Years: IEA's Third International Mathematics and Science Study (TIMSS)*. Chestnut Hill, MA: Boston College.

BEATON, ALBERT E.; MARTIN, MICHAEL O.; MULLIS, INA V. S.; GONZALEZ, EUGENIO J.; SMITH, TERESA A.; and KELLY, DANA L. 1996. *Science Achievement in the Middle School Years: IEA's Third International Mathematics and Science Study (TIMSS)*. Chestnut Hill, MA: Boston College.

HARMON, MARYELLEN E.; SMITH, TERESA A.; MARTIN, MICHAEL O.; KELLY, DANA L.; BEATON, ALBERT E.; MULLIS, INA V.S.; GONZALEZ, EUGENIO J.; and ORPWOOD, GRAHAM. 1997. *Performance Assessment in IEA's Third International Mathematics and Science Study*. Chestnut Hill, MA: Boston College.

MARTIN, MICHAEL O.; MULLIS, INA V. S.; BEATON, ALBERT E.; GONZALEZ, EUGENIO J.; SMITH, TERESA A.; and, KELLY, DANA L. 1997. *Science Achievement in the Primary School Years: IEA's Third International Mathematics and Science Study (TIMSS)*. Chestnut Hill, MA: Boston College.

MARTIN, MICHAEL O.; MULLIS, INA V. S.; GONZALEZ, EUGENIO J.; GREGORY, KELVIN D.; SMITH, TERESA A.; CHROSTOWSKI, STEVEN J.; GARDEN, ROBERT A.; and O'CONNOR, KATHLEEN M. 2000. *TIMSS 1999: International Science Report*. Chestnut Hill, MA: International Study Center, Lynch School of Education, Boston College.

MULLIS, INA V. S.; MARTIN, MICHAEL O.; BEATON, ALBERT E.; GONZALEZ, EUGENIO J.; KELLY, DANA L.; and SMITH, TERESA A. 1997. *Mathematics Achievement in the Primary School Years:*

IEA's Third International Mathematics and Science Study (TIMSS). Chestnut Hill, MA: Boston College.

MULLIS, INA V. S.; MARTIN, MICHAEL O.; BEATON, ALBERT E.; GONZALEZ, EUGENIO J.; KELLY, DANA L.; and SMITH, TERESA A. 1998. *Mathematics and Science Achievement in the Final Year of Secondary School: IEA's Third International Mathematics and Science Study (TIMSS)*. Chestnut Hill, MA: Boston College.

ROBITAILLE, DAVID F., and GARDEN, ROBERT A., eds. 1996. *TIMSS Monograph No. 2: Research Questions and Study Design*. Vancouver, BC, Canada: Pacific Educational Press.

SCHMIDT, WILLIAM H.; McKNIGHT, CURTIS C.; VALVERDE, GILBERT A.; HOUANG, RICHARD T.; and WILEY, DAVID E. 1997. *Many Visions, Many Aims*, Volume 1: *A Cross-National Investigation of Curricular Intentions in School Mathematics*. Dordrecht, Netherlands: Kluwer.

INTERNET RESOURCES

INTERNATIONAL ASSOCIATION FOR THE EVALUATION OF EDUCATIONAL ACHIEVEMENT. 2002. <www.iea.nl/>.

THIRD INTERNATIONAL MATHEMATICS AND SCIENCE STUDY. 2002. <www.timms.org>.

ALBERT E. BEATON

POLITICAL DEMOCRACY AND THE IEA STUDY OF CIVIC EDUCATION

In examining the contributions of education to political democracy researchers have considered shared decision-making, use of extracurricular activities to promote civic awareness, and policies designed to enhance educational equity. School curricula (especially in history, civics and government, and the social sciences/social studies) and the atmosphere of classroom discussion are also dimensions of education that contribute to students' acquisition of an understanding of and willingness to participate in political democracy. Citing empirical findings from a massive international study of civic education, evidence about these dimensions of education will be examined. The special focus is on how classroom practices contribute to what fourteen-year-old students know and believe about democratic processes and institutions.

The 1999 IEA Civic Education Study

The International Association for the Evaluation of Educational Achievement (IEA), headquartered in Amsterdam, is a consortium of research institutes and agencies in more than fifty countries. Since the late 1950s IEA has carried out nearly twenty large, cross-national studies of educational achievement in various curriculum areas. The 1999 Civic Education Study, the first IEA study in this subject area since 1971, was ambitious both in concept and in scope. About 90,000 fourteen-year-old students from twenty-eight countries as well as approximately 10,000 teachers and thousands of school principals participated in the study.

The countries participating in the test and survey of fourteen-year-olds in 1999 included Australia, Belgium (French-speaking), Bulgaria, Chile, Colombia, Cyprus, the Czech Republic, Denmark, England, Estonia, Finland, Germany, Greece, Hong Kong (SAR), Hungary, Italy, Latvia, Lithuania, Norway, Poland, Portugal, Romania, the Russian Federation, the Slovak Republic, Slovenia, Sweden, Switzerland, and the United States. Fifteen of these countries and Israel surveyed an older population of students, primarily in 2000.

Design of the IEA Civic Education Study

Through an international consensus process involving representatives from the participating countries and reflecting observations from structured national case studies conducted during the first phase of this study, three domains were identified as important topics in civic education across democracies: Democracy, Institutions, and Citizenship; National Identity and International Relations; and Social Cohesion and Diversity. Test and survey items were then written to assess students' knowledge and skills as well as attitudes in these three domains. Specifically, students were tested on their knowledge of democratic processes and institutions and their skills at interpreting political communication (e.g., interpreting the message of a political cartoon and an election leaflet). In addition, students were surveyed on their concepts of democracy and citizenship, their attitudes toward their countries and political institutions, the political rights of women and immigrants, and their expected civic participation. Background information was also collected from the students, including the activities in which they participated both in and out of school, the books available to them at home, and their perceptions of classroom climate.

The test and survey were administered to fourteen-year-olds by national research teams in accordance with IEA technical policies and guidelines. Teachers and school principals were also surveyed. The data provide a rich and complex picture of the civic development of young adolescents and the views of their teachers.

The Importance of Classroom Climate

The extent to which students experience their classrooms as places to discuss issues and express their opinions as well as hear the opinions of their peers has been identified as a vital element of civic education. Because of its importance, a scale was developed to measure students' perceptions of the classroom climate for open discussion in the 1999 IEA Civic Education Study. Students were asked how frequently (never, rarely, sometimes, or often) they were encouraged to make up their own minds about issues, how often they felt free to disagree with their teachers about political and social issues during class, and the extent to which teachers respected student opinions and encouraged their expression during class. Students were also asked how often teachers presented several sides of an issue and whether the students felt free to express opinions even when the issues might be controversial.

The students' responses to these statements proved to be a significant predictor of both student knowledge and attitudes. For example, single level path analyses show that a democratic classroom climate where discussion takes place and teachers encourage multiple points of view was an important predictor of students' knowledge of democratic processes and institutions and skills in interpreting political communication. The only factors more closely related to knowledge were the home literacy resources available to the students and their plans for future education. Classroom climate was also positively associated with students' plans to vote as adults—an essential element of democracy. Furthermore, positive classroom climate was related to students' trust in government institutions, their confidence in school participation, and positive attitudes toward immigrants and women. In short, findings from students tested in 1999 in the IEA Civic Education Study show that when schools model democratic values by providing an open climate for discussing issues, they enhance their effec-

tiveness in promoting students' civic knowledge and engagement.

Although open classroom climate seems to enhance democratic learning and engagement, this classroom approach is not the norm in many countries. Across the twenty-eight countries in the IEA Study, about one-third of the students reported that they were often encouraged to voice their opinions in the classroom, but an almost equal proportion said that this rarely or never occurred (especially when the issues were potentially controversial). Teacher responses confirmed the students' perceptions. They reported that teacher-centered methods of instruction, such as the use of textbooks, recitation, and worksheets were dominant in civic-related classrooms in most of the countries, although there were also opportunities for classroom discussion of issues.

Conclusion

Classrooms where students feel free to express their views on issues, and where multiple perspectives can be heard, seem to foster both knowledge about democratic principles and processes as well as positive attitudes toward civic engagement and the rights of others. Yet, these classroom practices are not the norm in some democratic countries. An emphasis on the transmission of factual knowledge through textbooks and worksheets seems to dominant in many (though certainly not all) classrooms. Research closely tied to the design of professional development programs could help to illuminate the ways in which classrooms might better reflect democratic practices and thereby enhance civic learning and engagement.

See also: INTERNATIONAL ASSESSMENTS, *subentry on* INTERNATIONAL ASSOCIATION FOR THE EVALUATION OF EDUCATIONAL ACHIEVEMENT; SOCIAL CAPITAL AND EDUCATION; SOCIAL COHESION AND EDUCATION.

BIBLIOGRAPHY

ELMORE, RICHARD F. 1990. *Restructuring Schools: The Next Generation of Educational Reform.* San Francisco: Jossey-Bass.

HAHN, CAROLE L. 1998. *Becoming Political: Comparative Perspectives on Citizenship Education.* Albany: State University of New York Press.

TORNEY, JUDITH; OPPENHEIM, ABRAHAM N.; and FARNEN, RUSSELL F. 1975. *Civic Education in*

Ten Countries: An Empirical Study. New York: John Wiley and Sons.

TORNEY-PURTA, JUDITH. 2001. "Civic Knowledge, Beliefs about Democratic Institutions, and Civic Engagement among 14-Year-Olds." *Prospects* 31(3):279–292.

TORNEY-PURTA, JUDITH, and SCHWILLE, JOHN. 2002. *New Paradigms and Recurring Paradoxes in Education for Citizenship.* Oxford: Elsevier Science.

TORNEY-PURTA, JUDITH; LEHMANN, RANIER; OSWALD, HANS; and SCHULZ, WOLFRAM. 2001. *Citizenship and Education in Twenty-Eight Countries: Civic Knowledge and Engagement at Age Fourteen.* Amsterdam: IEA.

TORNEY-PURTA, JUDITH; SCHWILLE, JOHN; and AMADEO, JO-ANN. 1999. *Civic Education across Countries: Twenty-Four National Case Studies from the IEA Civic Education Project.* Amsterdam: IEA.

VERBA, SIDNEY; SCHLOZMAN, KAY LEHMAN; and BRADY, HENRY E. 1995. *Voice and Equality: Civic Voluntarism in American Politics.* Cambridge, MA and London: Harvard University Press.

JUDITH TORNEY-PURTA
JO-ANN AMADEO
JOHN SCHWILLE

INTERNATIONAL ASSOCIATION FOR EDUCATIONAL ASSESSMENT

See: INTERNATIONAL ASSESSMENTS, *subentry on* INTERNATIONAL ASSOCIATION FOR EDUCATIONAL ASSESSMENT.

INTERNATIONAL BACCALAUREATE DIPLOMA

The international baccalaureate (IB) diploma program is a curriculum whose time has come. Growing out of a perceived need in the 1960s, the IB diploma—as it is commonly known—has gone from strength to strength in creating a role for itself as a major player on the world education stage.

The Establishment of the IB Diploma

The IB diploma was first developed in international schools and, in particular, the International School of Geneva. Reportedly the oldest international school in existence, this bilingual (French/English) school was founded in 1924 primarily as a means of providing education for the offspring of employees of the League of Nations. As the number of international schools grew over the following thirty-year period, in response to increasing ease of international travel and global mobility of professional parents, this school remained at the forefront of educational development. In 1951 it took the lead in founding the International Schools Association (ISA), which was set up "to help the growing number of international schools all over the world with their common problems" (Peterson, p. 15). As Peterson describes, one of the most pressing of these problems was that of providing adequate university preparation for their older students, destined as they were to seek university places in many different countries of the world. In 1962 a group of teachers from the International School of Geneva, with a small amount of funding from the United Nations Educational, Scientific, and Cultural Organization (UNESCO), organized a conference of social studies teachers from international schools to investigate the possibility of developing an international social studies program. With sponsorship from the Twentieth-Century Fund and the Ford Foundation, and central involvement of Atlantic College in Wales, the United Nations International School in New York, and Oxford University's department of educational studies in England, the program was launched. Developments led to the setting of a first full examination paper in 1971 and generation of a program that would, on the one hand, provide "an education that would facilitate the admission of students into the universities of their choice in different countries, without having to engage in the lengthy and uncertain process of obtaining equivalence agreements"; and, on the other, have as a major purpose "promoting international understanding and world peace" (Fox, p. 65).

The Early Twenty-First Century

The IB diploma of the early twenty-first century is based on essentially the same structure as was developed originally, which is represented by Figure 1. Students are required to engage in study of six subjects, with at least one selected from each of groups one to five, and a sixth choice, which may be from any of the six groups. Either three or four subjects must be studied at higher level and the others at standard level, while students must also complete a course in the theory of knowledge, write an extended essay of some four thousand words, and engage in the creativity, action, service (CAS) program. The IB diploma program can be shown to have four main characteristics, as follows:

- **Breadth:** By requiring the study of a range of disciplines to pre-university level, the diploma avoids the narrowness of programs such as the English "Advanced" ("A") Level, where students commonly study no more than three or four subjects at the ages of 16 to 18, often in very restricted areas of the curriculum.

- **Depth:** The availability of two levels of study, taken alongside the possibility of studying a second subject from groups one to five and of writing an extended essay in a chosen area of interest, "allows for a specialist element within the context of overall breadth" (Hayden and Wong, p. 351).

- **Coherence:** Two elements at the center of the hexagon model serve to support the notion of the IB diploma as a coherent program, as opposed to simply a collection of subjects. The theory of knowledge program "has often been seen as the 'cement' or 'glue' that binds together the different curricular areas of the IB Diploma hexagon" and has "been viewed as the sort of meta-learning that can give meaning to knowledge acquired in the subjects which students must study" (Mackenzie, p. 46), while the CAS program promotes the affective as well as cognitive dimensions of the student experience.

- **Internationalism:** The mission statement of the International Baccalaureate Organization (IBO) includes reference to strong emphasis being placed upon "the ideals of international understanding and responsible citizenship" (IBO web site), and subject programs are designed to encourage students to consider issues from a number of perspectives as they become "global citizens" (Hill dissertation).

Schools may opt to offer the program in one or more of three working languages (English, French, and Spanish) in which all curriculum materials are produced and examinations are set. All subjects are graded on a scale from one (low) to seven (high), with a further total of three points potentially avail-

FIGURE 1

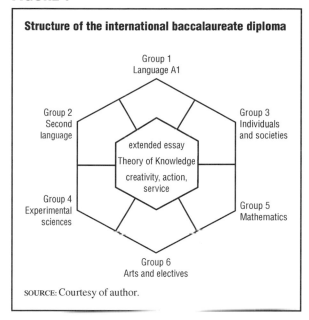

Structure of the international baccalaureate diploma

Group 1
Language A1

Group 2
Second language

Group 3
Individuals and societies

extended essay
Theory of Knowledge
creativity, action, service

Group 4
Experimental sciences

Group 5
Mathematics

Group 6
Arts and electives

SOURCE: Courtesy of author.

able for the theory of knowledge and extended essay, leading to a maximum possible score of forty-five points. A minimum score of twenty-four points with achievement of a number of other conditions (including satisfactory completion of the nonassessed CAS program) leads to the award of the diploma. As an alternative to the diploma, students may elect to register for one or more individual certificates, which are also awarded if conditions for the award of the diploma are not met.

The IBO head office is in Geneva, the Curriculum and Assessment Centre is in Cardiff Wales, and its Research Unit is based at the University of Bath in England. It also has regional offices in New York, Geneva, Buenos Aires, and Singapore. The curriculum is developed by examiners and teachers worldwide, and some 3,400 examiners and assessors for the program are similarly located in many different countries. The number of schools offering the IB diploma program has grown steadily: as of May 2001 some 960 schools in more than one hundred countries were authorized to offer the diploma program, through which some 40,000 students were assessed in 2001.

According to former students, the advantages of studying the IB diploma program include "its breadth-depth balance, its academic rigour and its suitability as a preparation for university-level study . . . (and its) contribution to world peace and understanding" (Hayden and Wong, p. 352). The IB diploma is accepted by universities worldwide, including those in Europe, North America (where advanced placement may be offered for diploma holders), and all other continents.

Issues for the Future

In a relatively short period of time, the IB diploma program has come to satisfy varying needs of different constituencies. Clearly it continues to provide an appropriate curriculum for those international schools worldwide that seek to promote an "international education" that is not associated with a particular national system. Additionally, in more recent years the program has been adopted by a number of schools in national education systems, which are attracted to it for a variety of reasons. Some of those in England and Wales, for instance, undoubtedly favor its breadth compared with the narrowness of the national ("A" level) system. The many American high schools that offer the program are attracted to the combination of an international perspective with the rigor and high academic standards that the IB diploma represents. In some cases it serves as a basis on which to promote programs for particularly able students and in others as a means of assisting state or public schools in their efforts to help students to meet state or provincial standards. Schools in still other systems are undoubtedly influenced by what might be termed *credentialism* where local elites respond to a "stiffening of the local positional competition on the one hand and a globalization of that competition on the other. As more people gain local educational qualifications, those who can afford to do so seek a new competitive edge by taking qualifications that they hope will give them a local advantage" (Lowe, pp. 24–25). A major challenge, then, to the IB diploma in the twenty-first century is the continued development of its attraction to national as well as international schools as it moves from being "a programme for international schools" to being "an international programme for schools" (Hagoort, p. 11).

A further and related challenge is that of determining the appropriate linguistic base for a program that is now so widely used internationally. Forty-five different languages are available as languages A1 (the student's "best language"), each including a study of world literature, and in principle an A1 examination can be set in any language with a sufficient body of written literature. The Eurocentric nature of the IBO's English, French, and Spanish working languages, however, is an issue currently being addressed in terms of how many—and which—working languages a program should offer before it can claim to be truly "international." Although new subjects have been added to the program since its inception, an interesting development is the current trialing of a small number of transdisciplinary subjects, which cross existing subject boundaries. A further important development in recent years has been the extension of the IB organization's provision to younger students by the development of the IB middle-years program (designed for ages eleven to sixteen, added in 1994 with 184 schools authorized to offer the program in May 2001) and the IB primary-years program (designed for ages three to twelve, added in 1997 and offered by fifty-nine authorized schools in May 2001). As a program now catering, therefore, to the entire pre-university age range, which is increasingly being offered within national systems as well as by international schools, the international baccalaureate seems likely to have interesting and challenging times ahead.

See also: ALTERNATIVE SCHOOLING; CURRICULUM, SCHOOL; ELEMENTARY EDUCATION, *subentry on* CURRENT TRENDS; SECONDARY EDUCATION, *subentry on* CURRENT TRENDS.

BIBLIOGRAPHY

DORE, RONALD. 1997. *The Diploma Disease: Education, Qualification and Development,* 2nd edition. London: Institute of Education.

FOX, ELISABETH. 2001. "The Emergence of the International Baccalaureate as an Impetus for Curriculum Reform." In *International Education: Principles and Practice,* ed. Mary C. Hayden and J. Jeff Thompson. London: Kogan Page.

HAGOORT, TOM 1994. "A Message from the President." *IB World* 6:11.

HAYDEN, MARY C., and THOMPSON, J. JEFF, eds. 2000. *International Schools and International Education: Improving Teaching, Management and Quality.* London: Kogan Page.

HAYDEN, MARY C., and THOMPSON J. JEFF, eds. 2001. *International Education: Principles and Practice.* London: Kogan Page.

HAYDEN, MARY C., and WONG, SING DEE. 1997. "The International Baccalaureate: International Education and Cultural Preservation." *Educational Studies* 23(3):349–361.

HILL, IAN. 1994. "The International Baccalaureate: Policy Process in Education." Ph.D. diss., University of Tasmania.

JONIETZ, PATRICIA L., and HARRIS, DUNCAN, eds. 1991. *International Schools and International Education.* London: Kogan Page.

KELLAGHAN, THOMAS, ed. 1995. *Admission to Higher Education: Issues and Practice.* Conference Proceedings of the 18th International Association for Educational Assessment, Dublin, Ireland, 1992. Dublin, Ireland: Educational Research Centre.

LOWE, JOHN A. 2000. "Assessment and Educational Quality: Implications for International Schools." In *International Schools and International Education: Improving Teaching, Management and Quality,* ed. Mary C. Hayden and J. Jeff Thompson. London: Kogan Page.

MACKENZIE, JOHN. 2000. "Curricular Interstices and the Theory of Knowledge." In *International Schools and International Education: Improving Teaching, Management and Quality,* ed. Mary C. Hayden and J. Jeff Thompson. London: Kogan Page

PETERSON, ALEC D. C. 1987. *Schools Across Frontiers: The Story of the International Baccalaureate and the United World Colleges.* La Salle, IL: Open Court.

SPAHN, BLAKE A. 2000. *The Implementation of the International Baccalaureate in the United States, Including a Case Study of Three IB Schools.* D.Phil. thesis, University of Oxford.

INTERNET RESOURCE

INTERNATIONAL BACCALAUREATE ORGANIZATION. 2002. <www.ibo.org>.

MARY C. HAYDEN

INTERNATIONAL CURRICULUM

See: CURRICULUM, INTERNATIONAL.

INTERNATIONAL DEVELOPMENT AGENCIES AND EDUCATION

BILATERAL AGENCIES
Andrew J. Finch

REGIONAL INSTITUTIONS
Andrew J. Finch
Katherine Taylor Haynes
UNITED NATIONS AND INTERNATIONAL AGENCIES
Katherine Taylor Haynes
Andrew J. Finch

BILATERAL AGENCIES

An official bilateral development or aid agency is responsible to a single government. It is usually a ministry or part of a government ministry dedicated to advancing foreign policy goals while contributing to the economic and social development of recipient countries. This discussion will review the history, legacy, importance, and current role of some of the more important bilateral agencies with regard to education.

U.S. Agency for International Development (USAID)

As an agency within the U.S. State Department, the United States Agency for International Development's mandate includes assisting countries with disaster recovery, poverty reduction, and the expansion of democratic reforms. USAID education and training support activities fall within this mandate and cover six major areas: basic education, learning technologies, higher education, workforce development, participant training, and telecommunications reform and applications.

USAID's current efforts in basic education include activities such as the Demographic and Health Surveys Education Data for Decision-Making (DHS EdData), which builds on population-based demographic surveys and provides data for planning and evaluation of education policies worldwide; the Global Education Database (GED), a computer-based database of international statistics; and Basic Education and Policy Support (BEPS). Learning technologies consist of activities such as Global Information Network in Education (GINIE). Higher education includes activities such as the Higher Education Partnerships and Development and Advanced Training for Leadership and Skills (ATLAS). Workforce development entails activities such as Global Workforce in Transition. Participant training includes activities such as Global Training for Development and the Training Resources and Information Network (TraiNet). Telecommunications reform and applications entail activities such as the Telecommunications Leadership Program.

USAID was created by executive order in 1961 when U.S. President John F. Kennedy signed the Foreign Assistance Act. It was the first U.S. foreign assistance organization whose primary emphasis was on long-range economic and social development assistance efforts. The agency faced early criticisms fueled by opposition to the Vietnam War, concern that aid was too focused on short-term military considerations, and concern that aid, particularly development aid, was a giveaway program producing few foreign policy results for the United States. Thus in 1972 and 1973 the Senate rejected the foreign-assistance bill authorizing funds. In 1973 the House Committee on Foreign Affairs restructured aid to focus on "functional categories," including "education and human resources development." Since then, USAID has faced concerns about its administration and structure, and there have been multiple efforts to officially restructure the administration and control of the agency. In 1998 the Foreign Affairs Reform and Restructuring Act placed the agency under the direct authority and foreign policy guidance of the secretary of state. In 2001 the George W. Bush administration reorganized USAID into three spheres of influence: global health, economic growth and agriculture, and conflict prevention and developmental relief. The second sphere captures most education funding.

USAID has continually tried to define its education policy. Policy papers from the mid-1980s established the priorities for USAID funding of "basic education and technical training." First, a 1982 statement proclaimed that "assisting countries to establish more efficient systems of education" was an essential component of an "effective development strategy." These efforts would include raising the levels of basic education and relating technical-training systems more effectively to productive employment. A 1984 paper stated the policy of improving primary education enrollment, program efficiency, and diversification of training. In the 1990s a USAID–higher education community consultation was designed (1) to enhance the U.S. foreign assistance program by incorporating the experience and knowledge of higher education institutions to develop better USAID policies, country and sector strategies, and activity designs and implementation; (2) to collaborate constructively in the delivery of development and humanitarian assistance when interests are compatible; and (3) to increase the transparency of USAID's decision and policymaking processes relevant to higher education institutions. In 1997 the agency released a strategic plan listing seven goals to support USAID's mission, the third of which was "to build human capacity through education and training." Still, the $7.7 billion total 2002 fiscal-year budget request allocated a mere 3 percent to education and training.

Canadian International Development Agency (CIDA)

The Canadian International Development Agency assists in issues from health, education, and agriculture to peace building, governance, human rights, land mines, and information technology. CIDA works with a variety of partners, both inside and outside of Canada, and it supports projects in more than 150 countries. Partners include nongovernmental organizations (NGOs), the private sector, and academic institutions—in Canada and in recipient countries—as well as a number of international organizations and institutions. Some projects are run bilaterally, while others are carried out through multilateral organizations. According to CIDA, its primary objective regarding development assistance is "to support sustainable development in developing countries in order to reduce poverty and contribute to a more secure, equitable, and prosperous world." In funding education projects, CIDA has chosen to define education as "the acquisition of knowledge, skills, and training through formal, non-formal, and informal systems and activities" (Isaac, p. 2).

CIDA has its official origins as Canada's External Aid Office, created in 1960 to reduce poverty and promote growth. The office's primary functions were to administer assistance programs funded by the Department of External Affairs, coordinate operations with other agencies, consult with international agencies and Canadian NGOs, and coordinate Canadian efforts to obtain aid for countries affected by disasters. Edward T. Jackson et al., in a 1996 report, note that most bilateral organizations, such as CIDA, spent the 1950s and 1960s focusing on initiatives to increase national production through industrial growth and paid little attention to income distribution within countries. However, as the spirit of such organizations started to change in the late 1960s, Canada complied with international guidelines and replaced "Office" with "Agency" and "Aid" with "International Development," becoming the Canadian International Development Agency in

1968. Education became more of a focus in the 1970s, as growth was promoted through equity by targeting interventions at the poor and meeting "basic human needs." The 1980s were characterized by structural adjustment policies, forcing developing nations to reduce deficits, privatize and deregulate industry, and promote exports. With the 1990s came an emphasis on "accountability and value-for-money spending." In 1990 Canada co-chaired the United Nations World Summit for Children, and it set a ten-year agenda for improving the well-being of children. Goals included attaining a basic education for all children and achieving at least an 80 percent completion rate of primary education for all boys and girls. However, rising public debt and nationwide unemployment forced Canada to cut social programs in the 1990s and also led the country to emphasize development programs that best served Canadian trade and competitiveness objectives. During this time CIDA faced some criticism for having "no comprehensive, official policy on basic human needs," having out-of-date "sub-priority" policies on areas such as education, having an "underdeveloped" management information system, a tendency to "underestimate, undervalue, or ignore altogether the record of engagement in basic human-need by the nongovernmental sector," and a need to boost accountability assessments (Jackson et al., section 5.25).

In 2001 CIDA released *Social Development Priorities: A Framework for Action,* in which budgetary allocations for social development programs, including education, increased from 19 percent to 38 percent. The plan called for quadrupling funding for basic education to $164 million annually. The additional financial commitment provides support for activities that promote the development and reform of the basic education sector in selected countries, strengthen the integration of locally driven education efforts, and improve the quality of basic education. The two stated goals were to increase gender equality and to achieve universal primary education by 2015. The plan called for improving programming, investing in girls' education, strengthening action against HIV/AIDS, integrating efforts of local communities and NGOs, and strengthening global political commitment.

Swedish International Development Cooperation Agency (SIDA)

The Swedish International Development Cooperation Agency handles Sweden's bilateral international development cooperation and much of its relationship with central and eastern Europe. SIDA attempts to raise the standard of living among poorer populations throughout the world while also addressing geographical concerns, such as security and the environment, through cooperation with countries in central and eastern Europe. Although SIDA contributes financial resources and skill development, it holds partner countries responsible for their own general development and improvement.

SIDA supports development through nine operational areas, including social development that encompasses education. According to the 1997 annual report, SIDA gives priority to programs that have a direct effect on classrooms, particularly textbooks and teacher training. While SIDA's main task is to promote the development of international partners, it also promotes Swedish interests in a variety of ways. First, solving global problems holds direct appeal for both Sweden and its partners. In education, this has included funding primary education in rural areas and building education centers in villages. Second, development cooperation (such as research, business, and volunteerism) helps strengthen relations of value to Swedish society. SIDA has supported the privatization of textbook production in Tanzania and worked with many Swedish university departments to enable Swedish students to perform minor field studies during their senior years. Finally, by contracting with domestic companies and using Swedish goods, SIDA contributes to both the short- and long-term growth of the country. About 300 Swedish NGOs receive support, and 60 percent of SIDA's budget goes ultimately to Swedish companies and foundations in the form of consultancy assignments, higher levels of employment, construction contracts, and sales orders. One-third of SIDA's cooperation is channeled through various multilateral organizations (such as the United Nations agencies and the World Bank).

For many years Swedish aid focused on nations that had advanced the most toward a planned economy. In the first part of the 1990s, total Swedish aid declined, thus affecting development program aid. In 1999 Howard White's *Dollars, Dialogue, and Development: An Evaluation of Swedish Programme Aid* noted SIDA had an excessive bureaucratic burden, which acted as a constraint to SIDA's operations. Also, SIDA supported anti-inflationary policies, which some felt might be "detrimental for long-run growth by undermining investment in human capital" programs, such as education and training. Questions also arose about how well Swedish program aid (which comprised about 12% of total aid in the 1990s) supported policy change in recipient countries.

At the turn of the century, SIDA began to reduce the number of projects by 25 percent in order to maintain quality and efficiency. SIDA also determined that certain countries had developed sufficiently to warrant replacing development grant aid with other types of cooperation. Indeed, the 1997 annual report mentioned phasing out "one-sided giving" in favor of development that "creates mutual benefits and from which all parties gain." According to SIDA, at the center of all development cooperation is developing knowledge and skills, but major efforts in education will not succeed unless other important functions in society, such as public administration, trade, and industry work properly.

The Department for International Development (DFID)

The Department for International Development is the British government entity responsible for promoting development and reducing poverty. DFID has six divisions (Africa, Asia, eastern Europe, western hemisphere, International, and Resources) and seven advisory groups or departments, of which education is one. The majority of DFID's assistance goes to the poorest countries in Asia and sub-Saharan Africa.

The current department was created in 1997, with policy outlined in the *White Paper on International Development.* DFID replaced Britain's Ministry of Overseas Development, which was created in 1964. The transformation was in response to increasing globalization of the world economy and a "review of aspirations." According to the *White Paper,* the 1970s and 1980s had produced inadequate economic policies that benefited only a small portion of the population, and those years produced external factors, such as high oil prices, which particularly affected developing countries.

Thus the new DFID established the goals of contributing to the elimination of poverty in poorer countries through bilateral and multilateral development programs, as well as intergovernmental cooperation. One of the three initial objectives was to improve education, health, and opportunities for poor people. In particular this meant promoting ef-

fective universal primary education, literacy, access to information, and life skills. It created targets based on the United Nations conventions and resolutions, which aimed for universal primary education in all countries by 2015 and the elimination of gender disparity in primary and secondary education by 2005. DFID's stated priority was "to achieve the full participation of all children and adults in quality education at all levels."

DFID focuses its education support on access, quality, retention, and equity. Initial strategies included strengthening and extending partnerships by involving local communities in managing schools, reconstructing school systems in poor countries, and promoting research to improve understanding of how education can contribute to the elimination of poverty. Early spending reviews suggested DFID needed to become more selective and focused on poverty reduction in its assistance.

French Agency for Development (AFD)

The French Agency for Development is a public, industrial, and commercial institution and a component of France's official development assistance. The AFD financially supports public and private job-creating projects in developing countries. Some projects are financed completely by the AFD, while others are cofinanced with partner-funding agencies. In addition, the AFD deploys and administers structural adjustment aid allocated by the French government.

The AFD functions as a group of domestic and foreign entities, including two domestic subsidiaries and fourteen banking, financial, and real estate subsidiaries operating in the overseas departments and territories. Although the AFD itself manages state treasury loans, grants, and other government funding, it has two domestic subsidiaries: the Society of Promotion and Participation for Economic Cooperation (Proparco) and the Center for Finance, Business, and Banking Studies (CEFEB).

Proparco was established in 1977 as a limited company owned by the AFD, and originally it was concerned mainly with risk capital. The AFD converted Proparco to a financial company in 1990, and it currently works entirely with private-sector funding.

CEFEB focuses purely on education and training. Founded in 1963, it is based in Marseilles, France. CEFEB provides continuing education and training for personnel from France and developing countries with current or future careers in senior posts in economic or financial public services, financial development institutions, and public or private enterprises. CEFEB's principal activities are: (1) an annual diploma course for approximately seventy trainees; (2) specialized short-duration seminars in France; and (3) training missions abroad. In addition, in cooperation with the University of Aix-Marseilles or Hautes Etudes Commerciales (HEC), CEFEB runs two master's-level courses for senior executives—one for human resources managers and the other for managers of operational or functional units. Finally, CEFEB is also involved in running in-service training for AFD staff and courses for the Ministry of Foreign Affairs.

The AFD operates in more than eighty countries and has a network of forty-three local offices and agencies around the world. In 1941 General Charles de Gaulle created the Caisse Centrale de la France Libre in London. In 1992 the Caisse Française de Développement was established by decree to succeed the Caisse Centrale de la France Libre, and six years later the name was changed to the Agence Française de Développement, or the French Development Agency. Under a French law established in the 1980s, the AFD is classed as a "specialized financial institution," which is a credit institution with a permanent public-service mission. The AFD's commitments, the terms of those commitments, and the company accounts are submitted for approval to its supervisory board. As a public institution the AFD is subject to control by the French Court of Auditors and, as a specialized financial institution, by the French Banking Commission.

The AFD plays a role in both bilateral and multilateral programs. Bilateral aid is directed mainly toward countries with strong historical and political ties. Countries in Africa and French-speaking countries worldwide have traditionally been given special attention by the AFD and its predecessors. About 75 percent of AFD aid is handled on a bilateral basis. The other 25 percent is handled at a multilateral level, within international and European organizations. As a whole, the AFD has designed its development cooperation to be compatible with other members of the Organisation for Economic Co-operation and Development (OECD) and to have a European context through investments in central and eastern Europe.

The AFD's program activity can be divided into fourteen sectors, of which the educational infrastructure is one. After becoming the AFD in 1998, almost 60 percent of project aid went to sub-Saharan Africa. However, the government directed the agency to expand, and more aid started to move into the Mediterranean region and Lebanon. Still, only about 1 percent of all project aid went to education-specific projects. Conversely, about 50 percent of all project aid at the beginning of the new millennium went to support rural development and urban infrastructure.

Japan International Cooperation Agency (JICA)

The Japan International Cooperation Agency was created in 1974 to handle Japan's bilateral Official Development Assistance (ODA). As Japan's governmental aid agency, JICA has a stated goal of "helping people to help themselves." Japan handles official development assistance through a program devised in 1954 as a part of the Colombo Plan to assist Asian countries. That program has three components: (1) bilateral grants; (2) bilateral loans; and (3) multilateral assistance. JICA is responsible for most of the first component, bilateral grants, which are composed of grant aid and "technical cooperation." The agency also conducts surveys and helps execute a capital-grant assistance program on the part of Japan's Ministry of Foreign Affairs. In addition, JICA has helped create a long-term training program to allow foreign students to obtain academic degrees in Japan as well as a grant-aid program to support foreign students.

One of JICA's education contributions is through this capital-grant assistance program. These projects may hold public value but are not highly profitable, as grant aid involves financial assistance without obligation of repayment and is focused upon basic human needs. There are three types of grant aid: general, aid for fisheries, and aid for increased food production. Education projects are funded through general grant aid, and projects include construction of education-related facilities such as school buildings, expansion of broadcast education services, and training and retraining of educators. Aid is also provided for specific local needs.

In addition, JICA provides for training through technical cooperation activities. In essence, technical cooperation refers to the fostering of human and socioeconomic development through the exchange of technology and knowledge. JICA engages in technical cooperation with developing countries in six basic ways: (1) by providing training in Japan; (2) dispatching Japanese experts to provide training abroad; (3) supplying equipment; (4) providing technical assistance in the development of projects; (5) conducting economic development studies; and (6) dispatching Japanese volunteers to work in developing countries. Training, expert dispatch projects, and volunteer dispatch each have educational elements. Training courses include both group and individual courses, and many group courses have been implemented in the field of education (such as "The Practice of Science Education"). The volunteer dispatch program sends Japan Overseas Cooperation Volunteers (JOCV) to primary and secondary educational institutions. The expert dispatch sends experts to education-related agencies and vocational-training programs in Japan and overseas. Finally, project cooperation is directed at universities through such programs as agriculture, engineering, and medicine.

The Japanese government's interest in assisting developing countries grew after receiving aid from the World Bank in the 1950s for its own reconstruction. In 1954 Japan established Official Development Assistance (ODA), and according to JICA, Japan's development assistance has expanded annually since that time. Initially, Japan focused on funding Asian countries, but toward the end of the twentieth century began expanding aid to eastern and central Europe. By 1992 it was the major donor in twenty-five countries. With the creation of JICA in 1974, Japan's ODA started taking a more country- and issue-specific approach. As the cold war came to a close, certain development issues, such as education, the environment, and population began to receive more global attention, and this was reflected in JICA projects. Beginning with the 1990 World Conference on Education for All in Jomtien, Thailand, Japan adopted the international goals of extending primary education and eliminating gender inequality in education. Consequently, a much larger portion of JICA's contributions have gone to primary schools whereas until 1990 higher education had received greater emphasis.

Norwegian Agency for Development Cooperation (NORAD)

The Norwegian Agency for Development Cooperation aims to assist developing countries in improving political, economic, and social conditions.

Headquartered in Oslo, Norway, NORAD is a Norwegian directorate under Norway's Ministry of Foreign Affairs. NORAD is responsible for bilateral and long-term aid, while the Ministry of Foreign Affairs handles the administration of multilateral projects. The education sector became a higher priority in the late 1980s and 1990s, with funding nearly tripling during that time. Asia receives the most Norwegian educational support.

NORAD focuses on six major areas of development: social development; economic development; peace, democracy, and human rights; environment and natural resource management; humanitarian assistance in the event of conflict or natural disasters; and gender equality. NORAD gives priority to education funding, and most of these six major areas have educational objectives. For example, by providing assistance for multilingual education and cultural diversity, NORAD attempts to support human rights and democracy.

In addition, NORAD invests in knowledge and human resource development in order to assist in the health and education sectors. A variety of programs support the development of knowledge management, research-based planning, support for international involvement in centers of knowledge, institutional development at universities and colleges in partner countries, the development of financial plans for research and higher education, and cooperation in research and education.

Although Norway has been involved in international development activities since the late 1940s, NORAD was created in 1968. Norway's first bilateral education project began in 1952, as a component of the India Fund's "Kerala Project." The project was designed to promote economic and social development of the people of India and had a number of programs, including "fishery colleges." In the 1960s programs extended to other countries in Asia and Africa, and in 1968 NORAD took over aid activities and obtained a broader range of objectives. In essence, NORAD became the sole agency responsible for coordinating and preparing Norway's official development aid. Before 1990 most of NORAD's education aid went to tertiary education. In 1991 a Norwegian white paper endorsed the goals of "education for all," established at the 1990 Jomtien World Declaration of Education for All conference. Since that time, NORAD's orientation to development has evolved from a project approach to more sectorwide programs, such as the Basic Primary Education Project in Nepal, and the Basic Education Sub-Sector Investment Program in Zambia.

Norway conducts annual evaluations, available to the public, of its foreign aid program. Suggestions for NORAD's education programs have included improving donor coordination and ensuring that recipient countries play a stronger role in coordinating aid, improving information management, conducting specific evaluations of education programs, and funding educational research in beneficiary countries.

Netherlands Organization for International Cooperation in Higher Education (Nuffic)

The Netherlands Organization for International Cooperation in Higher Education was created in the 1950s to promote an accurate image of Dutch higher education around the world. Its mission states four major areas of interest: development cooperation, internationalization of higher education, credential evaluation, and positioning Dutch higher education worldwide. Within these four areas, human resource and institutional development receives the most funding, followed by international academic relations, communication, and finally, international credential evaluation.

Higher education in the Netherlands has three branches: (1) the universities of professional education; (2) the remaining universities; and (3) international education institutes. Nuffic's board consists of members appointed by organizations representing each of these branches. Nuffic also has three secretariats: the National Commission for UNESCO, the Netherlands Development Assistance Research Council, and the Steering Committee of the Netherlands Israel Development Research Program. In addition to these three autonomous secretariats, Nuffic began conducting language courses for both foreigners and Dutch people in 1966. Participants in this program include students, foreign employees and their partners, embassy staff, au pairs, and classroom groups.

One of Nuffic's initial programs in the 1950s was international credential evaluation. Essentially, Nuffic offers advice regarding the relative value of foreign higher education diplomas in the Netherlands and vice versa. Nuffic publishes a manual, *Evaluation of Foreign Credentials in the Netherlands,* to help clients in this regard. An Internet resource describing procedures of higher education qualifica-

tions earned within the European Union (EU) and the European Economic Area Countries (EEA) is also maintained. As internationalization grew throughout the world in the mid-1980s, Nuffic assumed a role of encouraging cooperation between Dutch institutions and other industrialized countries. The goal was to improve Dutch higher education and broaden its dimensions. The primary method of promoting internationalization was the exchange of Dutch students and staff, and these efforts were supported by grants and scholarships.

Nuffic's primary source of difficulty has been the confrontation between different academic and cultural traditions, which has resulted in delays and irritation among participants. Nuffic has published various books in an effort to help program participants deal with issues arising from these differences.

Development cooperation represents one of Nuffic's main activities. At the end of the 1990s Nuffic reduced its concentration to a smaller number of countries to install a sectorwide approach, which emphasizes human resource development. This change represents a philosophical shift within the agency in which education is regarded as integral to all areas of development, and thus development cooperation receives the greatest amount of Nuffic's expenditures. Nuffic administers and finances education programs, initiates communication, and helps develop policy in beneficiary countries. Programs are categorized as human resource development, such as fellowships and scholarships, or institutional development, such as the Joint Financing Program for Cooperation in Higher Education (MHO) and Cooperation between the Netherlands and South Africa (CENESA).

In 1999 Nuffic adopted a more succinctly worded mission regarding knowledge export, by stating the goal "to position Dutch higher education on emerging markets." That same year, Nuffic set up the Project Office for Positioning Higher Education, to coordinate and support efforts of Dutch higher education institutions with the goal of recruiting institutional partners and foreign students. Three nations were targeted: Taiwan, China, and Indonesia. In 1998 Nuffic established the Network for the Export of Higher Education, in which nearly forty higher education institutions join to exchange information and coordinate activities.

The German Organization for Technical Cooperation (Deutsche Gesselschaft fur Technische Zusammenarbeit) (GTZ)

The German Organization for Technical Cooperation is owned by the Federal Republic of Germany, and it operates as a service enterprise for international development cooperation. Established in 1975 as a private-sector enterprise with a development-policy mandate, the GTZ supports international development, reform, and technical cooperation on behalf of the Federal German Ministry for Economic Cooperation (BMZ) and other German ministries, partner-country governments, and international organizations. Education represents one of the GTZ's sector-related themes, and it has four major components: educational aids, basic education, vocational training, and universities/scientific and technical institutions.

The first educational area, education aids, operates by the name of the Crystal project. Crystal provides teachers' aids such as textbooks and materials, specialist literature, and consulting. Consulting services are provided for vocational training, work-oriented training, and development cooperation (such as the application of new media and education aids). Services and materials are free to developing countries, and many of them are described in a Crystal catalog.

In the second area of basic education, the GTZ serves in an advisory role. The GTZ advises developing government partners on ways to improve their basic education systems. The suggestions focus upon quality, efficiency, and relevance through the design of programming methods and system structures. The GTZ's educational philosophy supports a decentralized approach utilizing parents and communities. Three major basic education activities include: (1) developing and introducing appropriate curricular elements and relevant learning and teaching materials; (2) institution building; and (3) systems consulting.

Vocational training encompasses the GTZ's third education area. These services are aimed at policymakers, industry, research and planning institutions, state and private training institutions, and in-company training facilities. The GTZ serves a consulting and planning role for the general vocational field as well as individual institutes of further and advanced training and vocational agencies. Specific services include concept design, planning, and evaluation, along with the establishment and commissioning of agencies and staff.

Finally, the GTZ provides consulting for universities and scientific and technical institutions. The goals of this higher education theme are to improve the performance capacity of education and research systems, to boost training performance and research capacity, and to encourage an exchange of ideas and experience at the academic level through international linkages. The GTZ provides services such as developing education and research systems, developing institutions, consulting on program conduct and efficiency, and the promotion of cooperation in training and research.

When the GTZ was developed, most services were conducted out of the head office. Though the head office is still the major interface between the government and project implementation abroad, in an effort to cut costs, the organization began to emphasize decentralization and regionalization in the late 1980s and early 1990s. This shifted responsibility to the field offices in more than sixty partner countries. The GTZ has also focused most heavily on advisory services. The late 1980s figured prominently in the GTZ's development because of German reunification. This required Eastern bloc nations, including the former East Germany, to make the transition to a market economy. Since the changes in Germany both drove and were affected by globalization, the GTZ decided to expand its cooperation with other organizations. In addition, the GTZ took on a larger role in the promotion of democracy worldwide.

Summary

Overall, bilateral agencies have been expanding their education and training goals since the early 1990s. The opening of eastern Europe, the fall of state socialism, and the 1990 Jomtien World Conference on Education for All were among the main factors shaping education policy regarding the geography and the goals of bilateral aid. Still, in the late 1990s, actual overall aid budgets had begun to decline, especially across the member countries of the OECD. Indeed, though policies have had lofty objectives, the reality often has not been as positive. According to Therien and Lloyd, bilateral aid agencies have faced issues such as dwindling resources, the loss of donors and a rationale for aid because of the end of the cold war and the dismantling of the Soviet Union, greater support of domestic aid instead of foreign development assistance, and an overall decrease in public support. As interests of donors have taken precedence over the interests of recipients, development aid has suffered. Other issues facing bilateral agencies include problems working through recipient governments, the inconsistency between economic and social development objectives (which span countries), and inconsistent foreign policy goals (with regard to specific countries). Some examples of these issues include French aid to francophone Africa, U.S. aid to Egypt and Israel, and Nordic aid to its program countries. Furthermore, globalization and development assistance received much scrutiny at the beginning of the new millennium, as groups questioned whether or not programs were actually reducing poverty.

See also: INTERNATIONAL DEVELOPMENT AGENCIES AND EDUCATION, *subentry on* UNITED NATIONS AND INTERNATIONAL AGENCIES; NONGOVERNMENTAL ORGANIZATIONS AND FOUNDATIONS.

BIBLIOGRAPHY

CANADIAN INTERNATIONAL DEVELOPMENT AGENCY. 1976. *Annual Report: 1975–1976.* Hull, Quebec: Canadian International Development Agency.

CANADIAN INTERNATIONAL DEVELOPMENT AGENCY. 2001. *Social Development Priorities: A Framework for Action.* Hull, Quebec: Canadian International Development Agency.

DEUTSCHE GESSELSCHAFT FUR TECHNISCHE ZUSAMMENARBEIT. 1999. *Annual Report, 1998.* Eschborn, Germany: Deutsche Gesselschaft fur Technische Zusammenarbeit.

DEUTSCHE GESSELSCHAFT FUR TECHNISCHE ZUSAMMENARBEIT. 2000. *Annual Report, 1999.* Eschborn, Germany: Deutsche Gesselschaft fur Technische Zusammenarbeit.

HEYNEMAN, STEPHEN P. 1997. "Economic Growth and the International Trade in Education Reform." *Prospects* 37:501–530.

ISAAC, ANNETTE. 1999. *Education and Peacebuilding—A Preliminary Operational Framework.* Hull, Quebec: Canadian International Development Agency Peacebuilding Unit.

JACKSON, EDWARD T.; BEAULIEU, DENISE; GALLANT, MARIELLE; and HODGSON, DWAYNE. 1996. *Learning for Results: Issues, Trends, and Lessons Learned in Basic Human Needs—Literature Review.* Ottawa, Ontario: E.T. Jackson and Associates.

LEXOW, JANNE. 2000. *Norwegian Support to the Education Sector: Overview of Policies and Trends, 1988–1998.* Taastrup, Denmark: Nordic Consulting Group.

NETHERLANDS ORGANIZATION FOR INTERNATIONAL COOPERATION IN HIGHER EDUCATION. 1999. *Building Bridges: Annual Report, 1999.* The Hague, The Netherlands: Netherlands Organization for International Cooperation in Higher Education.

SWEDISH INTERNATIONAL DEVELOPMENT AGENCY. 1998. *Annual Report: 1997.* Stockholm: Swedish International Development Agency.

THERIEN, JEAN PHILIPPE, and LLOYD, CAROLYN. 2000. "Development Assistance on the Brink." *Third World Quarterly* 21(1):21–38.

WHITE, HOWARD. 1999. *Dollars, Dialogue, and Development: An Evaluation of Swedish Programme Aid.* Stockholm, Sweden: Swedish International Development Agency.

INTERNET RESOURCES

AGENCY FOR FRENCH DEVELOPMENT. 2002. <www.afd.fr>.

CANADIAN INTERNATIONAL DEVELOPMENT AGENCY. 2002. <www.acdi-cida.gc.ca>.

DEPARTMENT FOR INTERNATIONAL DEVELOPMENT. 2002. <www.dfid.gov.uk>.

DEUTSCHE GESSELSCHAFT FUR TECHNISCHE ZUSAMMENARBEIT. 2002. <www.gtz.de>.

JAPAN INTERNATIONAL COOPERATION AGENCY. 2002. <www.jica.go.jp>.

NETHERLANDS ORGANIZATION FOR INTERNATIONAL COOPERATION IN HIGHER EDUCATION. 2002. <www.nuffic.nl>.

NORWEGIAN AGENCY FOR DEVELOPMENT COOPERATION. 2002. <www.norad.no>.

SWEDISH INTERNATIONAL DEVELOPMENT COOPERATION AGENCY. 2002. <www.sida.se>.

U.S. AGENCY FOR INTERNATIONAL DEVELOPMENT. 2002. <www.usaid.gov>.

ANDREW J. FINCH

REGIONAL INSTITUTIONS

Official regional development agencies are those whose mandate confines them to serve regional objectives. Some are part of regional governments, such as the European Union (EU), while others are managed by groups of individual national governments with common interests, like the Organisation for Economic Co-operation and Development (OECD). This entry will review the history, legacy, importance, and role of some of the more important regional institutions with regard to education.

Organisation for Economic Co-operation and Development (OECD)

Purpose. Originally founded as the Organisation for European Economic Co-operation (OEEC), OECD was formed to administer American and Canadian aid for the reconstruction of Europe under the Marshall Plan after World War II. In 1961 the organization was renamed the Organisation for Economic Co-operation and Development to promote economic growth and global trade. Since then, its mandate has been to build strong economies in member countries, improve efficiency, hone market systems, expand free trade, and contribute to development in industrialized and developing countries. It also groups the thirty member countries in an organization that provides a setting in which governments develop economic and social policy. Increasingly nongovernmental organizations and civil society are included in policy and thematic discussions. OECD is well known for its publications and statistics, which cover economic and social issues including education, the environment, social policy, and science and technology.

Structure. OECD's internal governance consists of each member country having a permanent representative, usually of ambassadorial rank, who sits on the council, the governance body. The council, meeting in sessions of ministers or permanent representatives, makes all major decisions on budgetary issues and the work programs of each committee.

Projects and activities. OECD does not generate operational development projects, but rather focuses on information-generating projects, such as collecting statistical indicators across OECD countries and writing publications. For example, OECD's Directorate of Education, Employment, Labor, and Social Affairs (DEELSA) undertakes work in the following five areas: (1) education and skills; (2) employment; (3) health; (4) international migration; and (5) social issues.

DEELSA undertakes research and policy work in education as well as other areas. The emphasis with-

in education is on lifelong learning, from early childhood to adulthood, which is considered important for social integration and a tool in the battle against social exclusion, from both society and the labor market. However, the work of DEELSA spans the range from early childhood development to higher education, including adult learning and literacy, education indicators, education policies, finance of lifelong learning, higher education management, human and social capital, information and communication technology (ICT) and the quality of learning, inclusion and equity, knowledge and learning, a program for international student assessment, schooling for tomorrow, and the transition from initial education to working life. The directorate produces host meetings and conferences to discuss these issues and provides online documents, newsletters, and publications pertaining to each area. In addition, the directorate works in close cooperation with the thirty member countries and draws on the expertise of the secretariat and external consultants, who provide advice and guidance through their national delegations and ministerial meetings. The resulting work is intended to meet the needs of member countries and their citizens.

Within DEESLA is the Centre for Educational Research and Innovation (CERI), which carries out studies and promotes an international dialogue about education across OECD countries. It is a source of information and publications on the topic of education. It strives to establish links between research, policy innovation, and practice, to enhance knowledge about educational trends internationally, and to actively engage educational researchers, practitioners, and government officials in cross-national discussions.

Statistical improvements. One of the first efforts to improve education statistics was the creation, in 1990, of the Indicators of National Education Systems (INES) with support in part from the U.S. Department of Education. OECD embraces the importance of statistics as a means of achieving informed policymaking. The INES program responds to the need to standardize the collection of statistics on a given aspect of education. For example, in the area of students with disabilities or learning or behavior problems, each member country uses a different definition for a particular term. The INES program works to establish uniformity in the definition and collection of indicators.

More recently, the World Education Indicator (WEI) project, a joint endeavor of OECD and the United Nations Educational, Scientific and Cultural Organization (UNESCO), has become an important initiative to expand the indicators system beyond OECD countries. Begun in 1997 as a pilot project for a small group of countries invited by OECD and UNESCO, the primary aim of the project is to develop a small but critical mass of policy-oriented education indicators, which measure the current state of education in an internationally valid, timely, and efficient manner. The project received funding from the World Bank for organization and administration, but participating countries provided their own resources for assembling and reporting data.

During the first year, the eleven countries that initially agreed to participate identified common education issues of concern, agreed upon an indicator set and the definitions and classifications to be used in the data collection, and assembled and provided the data. OECD processed the data and results, which were subsequently presented in the annual publication *Education at a Glance*. During the second year of the project, OECD and UNESCO agreed to add a number of countries that had expressed an interest in joining the pilot group, bringing the number of participating countries to sixteen. Indicators prepared from the data submissions over the two-year period served as the basis for a separate WEI report released in 2000. In 2001 the project produced *Teachers for Tomorrow's Schools: Analysis of the World Education Indicators,* a second volume that analyzes education indicators developed through the WEI project.

In addition to the basic data collection to derive the indicators, a number of special-interest groups assembled to research areas requiring data development and make recommendations based on their research of additions to the indicator set. World Bank funding permits pilot projects in six selected countries to develop national education indicators systems that both respond to national policy information needs and are compatible with education indicators used at the international level. The result of these pilot projects is a number of national education indicator publications that are disseminated to policymakers within national ministries and development agencies.

European Union (EU)

Purpose. The European Union, formed by the Maastricht Treaty of 1993, expanded European integration through the establishment of a common foreign and security policy and standards of justice, and improved police protection. A twenty-member European Commission represents the policymaking arm and executive body for the fifteen countries that comprise the EU. The Council of the European Union (not to be confused with the Council of Europe, which is a separate regional institution) is comprised of one representative of ministerial level from each member country, and it represents the legislative body of the EU. Along with the European Parliament, the council makes legislative and budgetary decisions for the EU.

In the formation of the EU, education was suggested to remain a national enterprise. Article 149 of *The Treaty Establishing the European Community* notes, "The Community shall contribute to the development of quality education by encouraging cooperation between Member States and, if necessary, by supporting and supplementing their action, while fully respecting the responsibility of the Member States for the content of teaching and the organization of education systems and their cultural and linguistic diversity." However, although education itself is thus not an official function of the EU mandate, EU literature still claims education and vocational training were "two cornerstones of the Commission's commitment to securing investment in people" ("Education—Training—Youth"). In fact, education programs were inaugurated to improve the prospects of European integration in culture, science, technology, and labor markets.

The EU's education policy has six basic components: (1) education; (2) vocational training; (3) recognition of diplomas and comparability of vocational qualifications; (4) training and mobility; (5) youth; and (6) international cooperation. The education component contains programs dealing with quality, access, and the teaching of languages. There have been four main programs—Tempus, Socrates, Erasmus, and Lingua—and European integration was the rationale for each.

Erasmus program. Erasmus (1987), Lingua (1989), and Tempus (1990) were each established before the official creation of the EU in 1993, as projects of the European Community, a precursor to the EU. The Erasmus program was adopted in June 1987 and amended in December 1989, and its focus was the mobility of university students within the European Community. The steps included establishing a European university network among the member states, the creation of grants to assist with travel and the cost-of-living differential, recognition and mobility of diplomas and periods of study, and the financing of promotional activities to create awareness of work throughout the European Community. In 1994, its final year as an independent program, Erasmus received European Currency Unit (ECU) 96.7 million.

Lingua program. Lingua went into effect in January 1990 and lasted independently for five years. It was an attempt to bolster foreign-language competence within the EU. Specifically, it focused upon Danish, Dutch, English, French, German, Greek, Irish, Italian, Luxembourgish, Portuguese, and Spanish. The program operated at various levels: citizens, teachers, university students, and organizations. The focus was on promotion, increasing learning opportunities, and innovative training. Lingua's budget was set at about 200 million euros. In its five years, Lingua provided services for 120,000 youth through educational projects, 30,000 students through interuniversity cooperation, and 30,000 teachers through training grants. In addition, projects promoting languages in economics and business were established. In 1995 Lingua activities were integrated into other EU programs.

Tempus program. Tempus was first established in May 1990, with a second phase adopted in April 1993, and a third phase adopted in April 1999. The third phase was scheduled to last from 2000 through 2006. Tempus was designed to help develop higher education systems for the "eligible countries" operating as partners with EU member states, and funding was established at ECU 95 to 100 million per year. Eligible countries include a number of republics in central and eastern Europe and central Asia. Its stated objectives were to develop new teaching programs, purchase equipment, encourage mobility of university professors, create periods of study in member states, and promote the learning of European Community languages. The overall goal of each of these objectives was to assist in the transfer to a market economy. The second and third phases added more countries to the list of eligible nations and further refined its features. The third phase aimed to adapt higher education to the socioeconomic and cultural needs of the new democracies. By phase three, the focus had become the reform

of higher education structures, linking training to industry, and strengthening citizenship and democracy.

Socrates program. While Tempus was continually updated as its own program, both Lingua and Erasmus were melded into the Socrates program, the only one of the four to be established first as an EU program. Socrates was inaugurated in March 1995 and moved into a second six-year phase in January 2000. Socrates had a much more general aim to actually create an open European educational area through access, mobility, and language knowledge. It incorporated higher education (Erasmus), school education (Comenius), and adult education initiatives (Grundtvig), as well as language learning (Lingua), distance learning and technology education (Minerva), and information exchanges (Arion and Eurydice). Socrates also extended beyond the member states into some central and eastern European countries and former Soviet republics. Phase two had a budget of 1.85 million euros.

Program evaluation. Criticism and difficulties of the four programs included the divergence among the legacies of the various nations, especially the newly independent states; coordination and communication between nations; and monitoring and evaluation of projects. However, there have also been some indirect side effects, including the improvement of quality, coverage, and content of local and national systems.

The remaining components. Vocational training involves access to training, analyzing qualification requirements, quality of training, and promotion of apprenticeship. The EU has run a variety of programs and organizations to handle vocational training. These have included Comett and Eurotecnet to promote technology and human resource training, IRIS (Inter-Regional Information Society) to promote equality of opportunity, Petra to boost the status of vocational education and encourage transnational cooperation, Force to encourage investment in vocational education, and Leonard da Vinci to promote lifelong learning and EU cooperation.

Recognition of diplomas and qualifications and training and mobility both attempt to facilitate unity with the EU. This has involved creating mechanisms for the recognition of diplomas and the establishment of comparable training. It has also meant the removal of barriers to mobility, such as recognition of training abroad and the continuation of health insurance.

Youth programs have included volunteer service, social inclusion, and youth exchange programs, such as "Youth for Europe." Finally, international cooperation programs have involved the United States and Canada.

The EU has its origins in the European Federalists Union, designed in 1946. The following year, the Marshall Plan was signed, and a variety of unionist movements began, culminating in the International Coordination of Movements for the Unification of Europe Committee in December 1947. Some of those involved in the movement wanted a federation, and others wanted simply cooperation. In 1950 French Foreign Minister Robert Schuman proposed a union of countries to pool coal and steel resources. Six nations (Belgium, France, Germany, Italy, Luxembourg, and the Netherlands) ultimately subscribed to the Schuman Plan, forming the European Coal and Steel Community (ECSC) in 1951. These six nations ratified the Treaty of Rome in 1953, thus officially starting the path toward a European union forty years later. This community developed from a tax, customs, and quantity regulator into a full-fledged political institution, dealing with trade, human rights, labor, economics, agriculture, and energy. In 1967 the ECSC merged with the European Economic Community and Euratom to form the European Communities (EC). In November 1976 a council was held in The Hague, and a statement was published regarding the possible construction of a "European Union." In 1983 the Ministers of Education held their first joint meeting with the Ministers of Employment and Social Affairs. A ruling on non-discriminatory enrollment fees was handed down in 1985. Following the fall of the Berlin Wall and the subsequent opening of eastern Europe, a council held in Maastricht, the Netherlands, drafted a Treaty on the European Union in 1991, which was ratified in 1993 with twelve member nations. Just before ratification, the commission published a green paper on creating a "European dimension of education." In 1995 Austria, Sweden, and Finland joined the EU, bringing the number to fifteen, with a number of eastern European newly independent states awaiting ratification. A council in Brussels in 2001 outlined a ten-year strategic education and training plan with three main objectives: (1) increase quality and effectiveness of education in the EU; (2) facilitate access; and (3) open up education and training systems "to a wider world" through research, mobility, and exchanges.

The Council of Europe (COE)

The Council of Europe is distinct from—and larger than—the European Union. As of 2001 the COE comprised forty-three member states, including all fifteen of the European Union states. Established in 1949 and headquartered in Strasbourg, France, the COE is a regional organization that essentially makes recommendations (through conventions, studies, and activities) to member states. The COE holds no legislative authority over its members, and this allows it to consider a large breadth of issues. The COE has developed programs involving human rights, economics, health, culture, sport, the environment, education, and many others, not including defense. It also tries to ensure that citizens of one nation, who are residents of another, will receive the same social benefits as the nationals. The requirements for membership in the COE are less stringent than the EU, as nations basically must accept "the principle of the rule of law" and guarantee "human rights and fundamental freedoms to everyone under its jurisdiction" (Council of Europe website 2001).

The COE was born from the 1948 Congress of Europe. While some nations favored a European union or federation, others felt more comfortable with basic intergovernmental cooperation. These nations (along with five of the six eventual charter members of the ECSC) formed the COE in 1949. One of the earliest COE conventions included education. In 1950 the ten original member states signed the European Cultural Convention, which established a framework for education, as well as youth, culture, and sport.

With so many nations involved in discussions, the breadth of issues considered by the COE has also stretched the specific area of education. The COE has considered educational projects in primary, secondary, higher, and adult education; research and promoting links and exchanges; recognition of educational qualifications throughout Europe; publishing handbooks for policymakers and educators; and cooperating with European institutions and nongovernmental organizations. In addition, with the opening of central and eastern Europe, educational programs to assist the new democracies took hold in the 1990s. The COE has been active in promoting democratic citizenship and, toward the end of the 1990s, social cohesion.

Regarding higher education, the COE established the Higher Education and Research Committee for the exchanges of views and experience among member-state universities. Other higher education activities have included mobility, recognition of qualifications, lifelong learning, citizenship, cultural heritage, access, research, and social sciences. In 1971 the COE established the European Documentation and Information System for Education (EUDISED), which pools education research from throughout Europe and is available via the Internet. EUDISED is a joint project with the EU's European Commission. In addition, the Legislative Reform Program (LRP) helps new member states reform their higher education laws.

The variety of cultures and languages represented by the COE presents challenges for any cooperative effort, thus language learning and social science have been the focus of many programs, such as the Council for Cultural Cooperation's Modern Language Project and the European Center for Modern Languages. The COE's cultural work has also involved democracy, human rights, minorities, history teaching, and "Europe at School," an annual Europewide competition for school children.

Organization for Security and Cooperation in Europe (OSCE)

The Organization for Security and Cooperation in Europe is the largest regional security organization in the world with fifty-five participating states from Europe, Central Asia, and North America. It is active in early warning, conflict prevention, crisis management, and postconflict rehabilitation.

The OSCE approach to security is comprehensive and cooperative. It deals with a wide range of security-related issues, including arms control, preventive diplomacy, confidence- and security-building measures, human rights, democratization, election monitoring, and economic and environmental security. It is cooperative in the sense that all OSCE participating states have equal status, and decisions are based on consensus.

The OSCE headquarters are located in Vienna, Austria. The organization also has offices and institutions located in Geneva, Switzerland; The Hague, Netherlands; Prague, Czech Republic; and Warsaw, Poland. The organization employs about 4,000 staff in more than twenty missions and field activities located in southeastern Europe, the Caucasus, eastern Europe, and Central Asia. They work "on the ground" to facilitate political processes, prevent or settle conflicts, and promote civil society and the rule of law.

The organization's attention to education is twofold; it comprises (1) internal and external training efforts, and (2) an emphasis on voter and civic education.

Given the considerable increase in the number and size of OSCE field activities in the 1990s, the OSCE's training efforts must be able to adapt to the changing environment. The OSCE participating states regard training as a tool for enhancing the ability of the organization's institutions and missions to carry out their mandate. This is the underlying principle behind the *OSCE Strategy on Capacity-Building and Training* adopted by the OSCE Permanent Council in March 1999. Participating states have acknowledged the need for training in two main spheres: first, training as a component of human resources management within the organization; second, training as an instrument to achieve the goals of the OSCE in conflict prevention, crisis management, and postconflict rehabilitation.

Within the areas of voter and civic education, training is emphasized. The OSCE deems it necessary for election observers to be able to assess the extent and effectiveness of voter and civic education. Sufficient voter and civic education is necessary to ensure that participants in the electoral process are fully informed of their rights and responsibilities as voters. These efforts can also generate knowledge and interest about the election process and build a climate for open debate. Voter education is focused on the particular election and should inform voters of when, how, and where to vote. It is therefore essential that this information be provided in a timely manner, allowing voters sufficient time to make use of the information. Civic education is a long-term process of educating citizens in the fundamentals of democratic society and civic responsibility. It may focus on the choices available to the voter and the significance of these choices within the respective political system.

Although political parties and civic organizations may contribute to voter and civic education efforts, it is ultimately the responsibility of the government and the election authorities to ensure that voters receive objective and impartial information, which should be provided to all eligible voters, including traditionally disenfranchised segments of the population, such as minorities.

Southeast Asian Ministers of Education Organization (SEAMEO)

The Southeast Asian Ministers of Education Organization promotes cooperation in education, science, and culture in Southeast Asia. The SEAMEO was established in 1965 in Bangkok, Thailand, and it has a mission to establish networks and partnerships, to provide a forum for policymakers and experts, and to develop regional "Centers of Excellence" for human resource development. Some specific education project areas include education technology, language, higher education, science and mathematics, vocational and technical education, distance learning, history, and education management.

The SEAMEO has ten member countries from Southeast Asia, six associate member countries from Australia, North America, and Europe, and one donor country, Japan. Each member and associate member assigns a representative to the SEAMEO Council. There are eleven centers that focus upon various sectors.

Each of the centers involves education to some degree. The Center for the Impact on Tropical Biology builds capabilities and provides grants and training. It also is developing a postgraduate degree program in information technology in natural resource management. The Center for the Impact on Educational Innovation and Technology provides training in educational leadership, curriculum and policy development, technology, literacy, nonformal education, and community development. The Center for the Impact on Education in Science and Mathematics provides research and teacher training in science and mathematics instruction. The Center for the Impact on Language Education provides teacher training in language instruction through pedagogy, testing, and textbooks. The Center for the Impact on Higher Education Development promotes recognition of qualification in Southeast Asia and conducts networking and policy development in higher education. The Center for the Impact in Indochina runs a regional training center in Ho Chi Minh City, Vietnam, which provides English training and planning for vocational and technical school directors. The Center for the Impact on Open Learning/Distance Education provides computer resources and training to promote distance learning. The Center for the Impact on Graduate Study and

Research in Agriculture provides graduate study, training, and research, and it adopted an elementary school through the Community Outreach Program. The Center for the Impact on Archaeology and Fine Arts develops theories of standard practices and scholarship on regional culture, arts, archaeology, and heritage. The Center for the Impact of Tropical Medicine and Public Health was established for training and research, and it grew into a forum on policies and sector needs. Finally, the Center for the Impact on Vocational and Technical Education conducts training programs and provides an education database.

SEAMEO emerged from a 1965 meeting between education ministers from Thailand, Singapore, Malaysia, Laos, and the Republic of South Vietnam (now Vietnam). Advisers from UNESCO and the United States were also involved. Indonesia and the Philippines joined in 1968, followed by Cambodia in 1971, Brunei Darussalam in 1984, and Myanmar in 1998. Its first thirty-five years saw numerous challenges within the region in the form of various social and political transitions, some of them violent, and an extreme economic downturn in the 1990s. Also, SEAMEO has faced cultural diversity that has created both tension and programs.

Inter-American Development Bank (IDB)

The Inter-American Development Bank, the oldest and largest regional multilateral development institution, was established in December 1959 to help accelerate economic and social development in Latin America and the Caribbean. The bank's operations cover the entire spectrum of economic and social development. In the past, IDB lending emphasized the productive sectors of agriculture and industry, the physical infrastructure sectors of energy and transportation, and the social sectors of environmental and public health, education, and urban development. Current lending priorities include poverty reduction and social equity, modernization and integration, and the environment.

IDB provides financing for projects in the education sector for the purpose of promoting greater integration of educational activities within the national development strategy of the member countries. The loans and technical cooperation from the bank for education have the following objectives:

- Training of human resources for development to contribute to the formation of technical and scientific skills that enable people to efficiently carry out the occupational tasks of promotion and management needed for the economic and social development of the country.

- Equality of educational opportunities to facilitate national efforts for introducing conditions of fairness in access to education opportunities for the entire population.

- Efficiency of investments in education to stimulate and support national efforts for rational planning of education systems and the essential reforms in content, teaching methods, organization and administration of programs, and institutions and systems, to achieve more positive results within the financial possibilities of the country.

IDB gives preference for financing development projects in the following educational areas:

1. Higher education programs at the professional, postgraduate, and scientific and technological research level and the training of specialized technicians in short-duration courses. The bank will support the role of higher education in the training of management teams needed in the development process and will stimulate the strengthening, at the national and regional levels, of institutions with high academic standards capable of showing the way in critical development areas.

2. Programs on technical education and professional training to turn out skilled workers and middle-level technicians in occupations needed for productive activities and to assure their participation in the social and cultural benefits of their communities, including reform and adaptation of middle-level education programs, which provide training in technical occupations without sacrificing the opportunity of acquiring basic education.

3. Education programs to provide a minimum of social and work skills to young persons and adults who did not have access to formal education, thus equipping them to find employment in rural development programs or rehabilitation of urban areas.

4. Programs to introduce substantive reforms in curriculum, teaching methods, structure, organization, and functioning of basic,

formal, and nonformal education at the primary and secondary level. These programs can include education research, training and retraining of teachers and auxiliary technical staff, nontraditional forms of education, and the design, production, and evaluation of institutional materials, equipment, and communication systems of proven effectiveness. The basic objective of these programs is to improve the quality and efficiency of education activities and to expand the levels of participation without considerable increase in cost.

5. Programs to improve efficiency and fairness in the application of funds intended for financing education and promoting the creation of additional sources of financing by improving student loan systems, social security, business support, scholarships for priority professional fields, and such other systems as appropriate.

Asian Development Bank (ADB)

The Asian Development Bank, a regional multilateral development institution established in 1966, provides loans and investments for developing countries; technical assistance for development projects, programs, and services; facilitation of public and private capital investment for development; and assistance in policy coordination and planning. The ADB has fifty-nine member countries, with Japan and the United States as the largest shareholders (combining for almost one-third of the shares). The ADB has a stated primary goal of reducing poverty in Asia and the Pacific, and its headquarters are in Manila, Philippines.

One of the ADB's objectives is supporting human development, and education is one of the major means to this end. Noting that education is a basic human right recognized in the 1948 Universal Declaration of Human Rights, the ADB states, "Education helps lay the foundation for the three pillars of poverty reduction: human development, equitable economic growth, and good governance" (Asian Development Bank 2001). However, it was not until 1988 that the ADB formally stated in a policy paper that basic education was a human right. According to its own historical accounts, the ADB invested $4.6 billion in education between 1970 and 2000, with about two-thirds of that investment occurring in the 1990s. During its initial years, the ADB followed a "manpower planning" and economic growth philosophy and funded facilities and equipment for vocational and technical education. In 1988 the ADB published its first education sector policy paper, which called for investment in primary and secondary education to foster human and social development. In 1990 the ADB adopted the goals set down by the World Conference on Education for All, held in Jomtien, Thailand, which called for universal education and gender equity. With these goals came an emphasis on basic education, teacher training, and curriculum planning. The ADB also moved deeper into policy, research, and capacity-building activities. However, education represented only about 6 percent of the ADB's total investments during the 1990s.

The ADB's 2001 education policy paper called for the ADB to support programs in literacy and nonformal education, early childhood development, basic education, secondary education, higher education, and skills training. It also called for reducing poverty, enhancing the status of women, and facilitating economic growth.

Critique of the ADB has included a narrow focus on "schooling as opposed to education in the broader sense" (Asian Development Bank 2001), uneven distribution of support (three countries accounted for two-thirds of the total education lending between 1970 and 2000), an early focus on traditional project technical assistance, education as a relatively small proportion of the ADB's overall investment portfolio, sector reform not always guided by clear policy goals and strategies, and overall education investment not reaching its impact potential because of weak sector analysis.

The Economic Commission for Africa (ECA)

The Economic Commission for Africa is a United Nations regional institution designed to foster economic and social development and promote regional integration and cooperation in Africa. Established in 1958, the ECA has its headquarters in Addis Ababa, Ethiopia, and it reports directly to the United Nations Economic and Social Council. The fifty-three African countries comprise the ECA's member states, and it serves four main modal functions: (1) advocacy and policy analysis; (2) convening stakeholders and building consensus; (3) technical cooperation and capacity building; and (4) enhancing the United Nation's role in Africa. In approaching educational and other policy issues, the ECA essentially reports on social situations and influences policy.

Because of Africa's size, political situations, and economic extremes, education in the continent provides a variety of challenges. A 1995 conference of ministers' report (United Nations Economic Commission for Africa 2001) outlined many of the educational issues the ECA has faced and documented during its existence. According to the report, "the crisis in African education" intensified in the 1980s and 1990s, because of rapid population growth and cuts in public spending. Many African countries during this period offered little funding for primary education, and primary school enrollments declined while total enrollment increased. Together with these issues were declining standards, overcrowding, lack of teaching materials, and declining teacher morale. Inadequate facilities and "deteriorating" educational quality also plagued secondary education during the period. Girls were not served at the same level as boys, and fewer girls stayed in school through tertiary education. Higher education as a whole faced low salaries, political issues, lack of materials, student and professor unrest, and university closures. Finally, the number of adult illiterates rose considerably during the last two decades of the twentieth century.

The ECA has served a number of roles in handling educational issues and other sector situations. It helped create the African Development Bank in 1964, and it has assisted in the establishment of a number of other regional organizations and technical institutions. The ECA also helps member nations communicate and cooperate in efforts to tackle issues. Through analyses and reports, the ECA tries to suggest and implement strategical approaches to problem areas, and it also helps evaluate the progress of implemented programs.

As economic development strategies moved away from primarily physical or structural developments and recognized the importance of education and human capital in capacity building, many of the ECA member states adopted international conventions on educational development. A 2001 ECA strategy noted eight "sub-programs," including facilitating economic and social policy analysis, promoting trade and mobilizing finance for development, enhancing food strategy and sustainable development, strengthening development management, harnessing information for development, promoting regional cooperation and integration, promoting the advancement of women, and supporting subregional activities for development.

The African Development Bank (AfDB)

The African Development Bank, a regional multilateral development bank, was established in 1964 and began operations in 1966. The AfDB has seventy-seven shareholder states, including each of the fifty-three African countries and twenty-four nations in Asia, Europe, North America, and South America. As a development bank, the AfDB provides: (1) loans and investments for developing countries; (2) technical assistance for development projects, programs, and services; (3) facilitation of public and private capital investment for development; and (4) assistance in policy coordination and planning. Education is one of the AfDB's major sectors of support, and financing includes specific projects, loans, private-sector support, and cofinancing with bilateral and multilateral institutions.

The AfDB did not support an education project during its first nine years of operation. The first education project occurred in Mali in 1975. From 1975 through 1998, education lending represented 6.7 percent of the total lending to all sectors. During that period, over 80 percent of the AfDB's lending in education went to hardware, such as equipment and furniture. In addition to funding hardware, the AfDB has funded training for teachers, administrators, and planners, and construction and rehabilitation. The AfDB has also supported both regional and national projects.

Three publications/conferences had major effects on AfDB educational policy. First, the AfDB published an *Education Sector Policy Paper* in 1986. Before that time, education accounted for just under 60 percent of the AfDB's social-sector lending. After the policy paper, education accounted for an average of 70 percent of all social-sector spending (from 1985 to 1998). A second milestone was the 1990 Jomtien World Conference on Education for All, which called for gender equality and universal basic education. Prior to 1990 nearly half of all funding went to secondary, general, vocational, and technical education or teacher-training projects. After the Jomtien conference (1991–1998), however, 52.8 percent of the total lending went to basic education.

As Africa's education issues evolved in the last years of the 1990s, the AfDB tried to address challenges, such as globalization, the growth of information technology, the increased role of the private sector, deepening poverty, high unemployment, low human-capital production, extreme population growth, HIV/AIDS and malaria, armed conflicts and population displacement, and unequal access to education. Recognizing that education could both affect and was affected by these issues, the AfDB released a new *Education Sector Policy Paper* in 1999. This paper listed three priority areas: (1) quality education for all; (2) provision of middle- and high-level skills; and (3) organization and management of the education sector. The paper also listed five strategies of improvement: (1) access; (2) equity; (3) quality of instruction and output; (4) management and planning; and (5) financing mechanisms. It also suggested the AfDB's approach would shift from a project-orientation to a sectorwide approach focused on joint financing with governments and institutional partners. Among the areas of interest that had grown since 1986 were girls' education, technology and distance learning, environmental education, population and AIDS education, and peace education.

Some of the areas in need of improvement within education-sector funding, according to the policy paper, included the need to balance qualitative and quantitative approaches, coordinating projects at the community level, participation of beneficiaries and stakeholders, maintenance and sustainability of building and equipment, supervision of projects, and monitoring of evaluations. In addition, Njoki Njoroge Njehû, the director of 50 Years Is Enough: U.S. Network for Global Economic Justice, a coalition "dedicated to the profound transformation of the World Bank and the International Monetary Fund" ("Hearing on U.S. Policy," 2001), noted that the conditions in Africa had not improved substantially during the first thirty-five years of bank lending and that the AfDB, "as it recovers from its management crisis of the 1990s, is losing relevance to most of the people of the continent" by lending to "very few sub-Saharan countries."

See also: INTERNATIONAL DEVELOPMENT AGENCIES AND EDUCATION, *subentry on* UNITED NATIONS AND INTERNATIONAL AGENCIES; INTERNATIONAL EDUCATION STATISTICS; NONGOVERNMENTAL ORGANIZATIONS AND FOUNDATIONS.

BIBLIOGRAPHY

AFRICAN DEVELOPMENT BANK/AFRICAN DEVELOPMENT FUND. 1999. *Education Sector Policy Paper.* Abidjan, Côte d'Ivoire: African Development Bank Group.

ALI, SHEIKH RUSTUM. 1992. *The International Organizations and World Order Dictionary.* Santa Barbara, CA: ABC-CLIO.

ASIAN DEVELOPMENT BANK. 2001. *Education Sector Policy Paper: Draft for Discussion.* Manila, Philippines: Asian Development Bank.

SCHECHTER, MICHAEL G. 1998. *Historical Dictionary of International Organizations.* Lanham, MD: Scarecrow Press.

INTERNET RESOURCES

AFRICAN DEVELOPMENT BANK. 2002. <http://afdb.org>.

ASIAN DEVELOPMENT BANK. 2002. <http://adb.org>.

COUNCIL OF EUROPE. 2002. <www.coe.int>.

EUROPEAN UNION. 2001. "Consolidated Version of the Treaty Establishing the European Community." <http://europa.eu.int/eur-lex/en/treaties/dat/ec_cons_treaty_en.pdf>.

EUROPEAN UNION. 2001. "Education—Training—Youth." <http://europa.eu.int/scadplus/leg/en/cha/c00003.htm>.

EUROPEAN UNION. 2002. <http://europa.eu.int>.

50 YEARS IS ENOUGH NETWORK. 2001. "Hearing on U.S. Policy toward the African Development Bank and African Development Fund, April 25, 2001: Testimony by Njoki Njoroge Njehû, Director of the 50 Years Is Enough Network." <www.50years.org/update/testimony2.html>.

INTER-AMERICAN DEVELOPMENT BANK. 2001. "OP-743 Education." <www.iadb.org/cont/poli/op-743e.htm>.

ORGANISATION FOR ECONOMIC CO-OPERATION AND DEVELOPMENT. 2002. <www.oecd.org>.

SOUTHEAST ASIAN MINISTERS OF EDUCATION ORGANIZATION. 2000. "SEAMEO Annual Report 1998–1999." <www.seameo.org/vl/library/dlwelcome/publications/anrpt98/index.htm>.

SOUTHEAST ASIAN MINISTERS OF EDUCATION ORGANIZATION. 2002. <www.seameo.org>.

UNITED NATIONS ECONOMIC COMMISSION FOR AFRICA. 2001. "Report on the Activities of ECA in the Areas of Human and Social Development as Well as Civil Society: The Years 1997–2001." <www.uneca.org/publications/dmd/old/civil/report.htm>.

UNITED NATIONS ECONOMIC COMMISSION FOR AFRICA. 2001. "Report on the Work of the ECA, 1998–2000." <www.uneca.org/search_home.htm>.

UNITED NATIONS ECONOMIC COMMISSION FOR AFRICA. 2002. <www.uneca.org>.

ANDREW J. FINCH
KATHERINE TAYLOR HAYNES

UNITED NATIONS AND INTERNATIONAL AGENCIES

Official multilateral development agencies are those that are responsible to and governed by representatives of worldwide organizations. The United Nations (UN), a multilateral organization with a variety of institutional mandates, has many organizations under its umbrella. Other organizations have a single mandate but are similarly broad in scope. A distinction should be made between the multilateral development banks—such as the World Bank—whose projects take the form of loans, and the other multilateral development agencies—such as United Nations Educational, Scientific and Cultural Organization (UNESCO)—whose projects take the form of nonreimbursable grants. This entry will describe the history, legacy, importance, and role of international agencies with regard to education.

The World Bank (or the International Bank for Reconstruction and Development)

The World Bank is an international bank established in 1944 to help member nations reconstruct and develop by guaranteeing loans. The organization has members (both donors and borrowers) who own shares in the bank, although each member nation does not have a vote. Rather, the governance structure is representative in nature, such that one representative may vote on issues for a cluster of nations. It provides loans and technical assistance in many sectors—including education—to reduce poverty and advance sustainable economic growth. There are several types of loans: project loans, macropolicy loans, and sector-policy loans. For each project bank staff work carefully with country counterparts to establish a project covenant or loan agreement, which stipulates the government's commitments, to reform, for example. As part of the loan agreement, when the bank and the country meet to negotiate the loan contract, the bank can establish conditionalities or parameters that commit the country to accomplishing certain changes. Should these benchmarks not be reached, then the bank, according to the terms set out in the contract, can take action.

Educational mission. Education is a cornerstone in the bank's overall mission to help countries fight poverty. The World Bank's mission in education is to assist clients to improve access to relevant learning opportunities, use education resources wisely and fairly, and build stronger institutional capacity. More specifically, the bank works with national ministries of education to identify and implement the countries' strategic steps in order to provide access for all to quality education. The institution works in partnership with the client (or government) as well as other stakeholders, including bilateral-aid agencies, nongovernmental organizations (NGOs), and other members of civil society.

The long-term goal in education is to ensure that everyone completes a basic education of adequate quality, acquires foundation skills (literacy, numeracy, reasoning, and social skills such as teamwork) and has further opportunities to learn advanced skills throughout life, in a range of postbasic education settings.

At the beginning of the twenty-first century the bank draws upon four decades of experience in education with approximately 600 projects in 115 countries totaling $26 billion. Although the focus of early projects was on building school infrastructure, increasingly the focus is on improving access to schooling, student attendance, and the quality of education once students are there. Concern for the adequacy of the education has led to greater emphasis on teaching quality and learning achievement. In addition, the concern about a greater demand on limited resources has precipitated a concern about efficiency, including the need for building the institutional capacity required to implement and sustain improvements.

The World Bank made its first loan for education in 1963, and the bank is now the largest single source of external financing for education in developing countries. Since 1980 the total volume of lending for education has tripled, and its share in overall bank lending has doubled. The primary and secondary levels of education are increasingly important; in the fiscal years from 1990 to 1994 these levels represented half of all World Bank lending for education. Early bank lending for education concentrated on Africa, East Asia, and the Middle East, but at the beginning of the twenty-first century lending is significant in all regions. Girls' education is at the forefront, and increasing attention is being given to the educational needs of ethnic minorities and indigenous people. World Bank funds are used less for buildings and more for other educational inputs. The narrow project focus of the past is increasingly giving way to a broad sectoral approach.

The World Bank is strongly committed to continued support for education. However, even though bank funding now accounts for about a quarter of all aid to education, this funding still represents only about 0.5 percent of developing countries' total spending on the sector. Therefore, the World Bank sees its key contribution as advice or technical assistance, designed to help governments develop education policies suitable for the circumstances of their countries. Bank financing will generally be designed to leverage spending and policy change by national authorities. According to World Bank documents, future operations are expected to adopt a more explicit sectorwide policy focus to support changes in educational financing and management. Because of the need to consult key stakeholders, this strategy may increase both the resources and the time needed to prepare projects. In increasingly decentralized contexts, the stakeholders will include not only central governments but also other levels of government, as well as communities, parents, teachers, and employers. Donor cooperation is expected to extend to broad policy advice, as well as investment coordination.

Programs. World Bank programs encourage governments to make education and education reform a higher priority, particularly as economic reform becomes a permanent process. Projects will take more account of outcomes and their relation to inputs, making explicit use of cost–benefit analysis, participatory methods, learning assessments, and improved monitoring and evaluation. The share of basic education in total World Bank lending for education is expected to continue to increase, especially in the poorest countries, which receive International Development Association (IDA) funds. The bank emphasizes a sectoral approach that recognizes the importance of each level of the education system, the interdependencies among levels, and the need to focus bank assistance in areas where the bank can be most useful in the particular circumstances of each country.

At the outset of the twenty-first century, World Bank-supported projects have paid greater attention to equity. This is especially the case in education for girls, for disadvantaged ethnic minorities, and for the poor—and consequently for early childhood education. Projects will support household involvement in school governance and in school choice through an increased emphasis on the regulatory framework for education, on quality-enhancing mechanisms such as outcome monitoring and inspection, on recurrent cost financing, and on demand-side financing mechanisms such as targeted scholarships for the poor, stipends for girls, and student loan schemes for higher education. They will encourage flexible management of instructional resources, complemented by national assessment and examination systems to provide incentives. In all these areas, bank-supported projects are expected to focus more intently on institutional development, including strengthening educational administration and appropriate financial mechanisms, and the bank's staff will pay increased attention to implementation.

Criticism. Criticisms of the World Bank emanate from across the political spectrum, from NGOs as well as committees of the U.S. Congress (e.g., the Meltzer Commission), and are strikingly similar in nature. Critics from the conservative right, such as the Meltzer Commission, argue that institutions such as the World Bank should stop the business of lending and instead serve as development agencies. Critics from the left contend that the bank does not alleviate poverty, but rather condemns citizens of poor nations to chronic debt. Both ends of the political spectrum have registered criticism of the need for reform, restructuring, and revisiting the mission of the bank, an increase in transparency and access to information, and the creation of an independent audit and evaluation unit. Another area of criticism revolves about the issue of conditionalities. The criticisms leveraged by NGOs include mention of the unreasonable restrictions and demands placed on countries by the multilateral development banks, including the World Bank.

The United Nations Children's Fund (UNICEF)

The United Nations Children's Fund is an affiliated agency of the United Nations. It was originally established in 1946 as the United Nations International Children's Emergency Fund. UNICEF is concerned with assisting children and adolescents throughout the world, particularly in devastated areas and developing countries. Unlike most United Nations agencies, UNICEF is financed through voluntary contributions from governments and individuals, rather than by regular assessments. National UNICEF committees collaborate with UNICEF in various projects. UNICEF was awarded the Nobel Peace Prize in 1965.

UNICEF was created at the end of World War II to relieve the suffering of children in war-torn Europe. It continues to respond rapidly in crises, helping recreate a sense of stability and normalcy, reopening schools and establishing safe spaces for children when armed conflict, war, flood, and other disruptions occur.

The mandate of UNICEF confines its activities and operations to projects intended to benefit children and youth. Unrestricted donations to its budget permit UNICEF to provide assistance on a grant basis and to operate wherever it deems most necessary, independent of political or governmental influence. As part of its mission, UNICEF is committed to the notion that the survival, protection, and development of children are universal imperatives, integral to human progress.

UNICEF currently works in more than 160 countries, areas, and territories on solutions to the problems plaguing poor children and their families and on ways to realize their rights. Its activities vary according to the local challenges presented. They include encouraging the care and stimulation that offer the best possible start in life, helping prevent childhood illness and death, making pregnancy and childbirth safe, and combating discrimination and cooperating with communities to ensure that girls as well as boys attend school. UNICEF works on behalf of children's well-being in other ways. It supports National Immunization Days in the global effort to eradicate polio. It encourages young people to prepare for and participate in issues affecting them. It helps youth resist the onslaught of HIV/AIDS. UNICEF is out in the field at the local level and at the fore, bringing ideas, resources, strategies, and support to bear when and where they are needed most.

UNICEF strives through its country programs to promote the equal rights of girls and women and to support their full participation in the political, social, and economic development of their communities.

United Nations Educational, Scientific and Cultural Organization (UNESCO)

United Nations Educational, Scientific and Cultural Organization is the agency charged with instituting and administering programs for cooperative, coordinated action in education, science, and the arts. The agency promotes education for all, cultural development, protection of the world's natural and cultural heritage, press freedom, and communication. The internal governance structure grants each member nation one representative in the decision-making body of UNESCO and one vote.

Within UNESCO is an International Bureau of Education (IBE) that is responsible for holding conferences on both broad and specific topics within education. This includes international, regional, and country-specific work, including research, technical assistance projects, the provision of data banks and publications to be used by professionals in international organizations, NGOs, ministries of education, and others.

The IBE Documentation and Information Unit has two main tasks: (1) the Internet site with its data banks, and (2) the Documentation Center. The unit manages the IBE's website in general and, to increase the relevance of its services to decision-making processes in member states and to the needs of educational practice, has developed several data banks, which are accessible and regularly updated on the website: (1) INNODATA—innovative projects in the fields of educational content, methods, and teacher education; (2) world data on education; (3) educational profiles—descriptions of national education systems; (4) national reports—full texts of reports presented to the International Conference on Education in 1996; and (5) country dossiers—a compilation of various sources on education. The data banks provide wider access to materials gathered and analyzed at the IBE. These materials are available for local consultation in the Documentation Center. UNESCO is heavily involved in numerous education-related endeavors, which include associated schools, the production of basic learning materials, drug-abuse prevention programs, early childhood and family development programs, pro-

motion of Education for All, educational facilities, e-learning, emergency assistance, girls and women in Africa, higher education, HIV/AIDS work, the literacy decade project, poverty eradication, primary education, science and technology, special needs education, street and working children, sustainable future, and technical and vocational education.

In addition, it provides more than half a dozen networks for communication among practitioners, policymakers, and people interested in education-related topics. UNESCO also works to build partnerships among key stakeholders in the education policy process, including intergovernmental organizations (IGOs), NGOs and other UN agencies.

A learning materials project, the Basic Learning Materials Initiative (BLM) is based on the premise that successful materials-development strategies must include mechanisms for generating a wide range of printed materials needed by a reading society. The development of a viable local publishing industry in each country is a necessary element of such strategies. The creation of a well-functioning system for the production and distribution of basic learning materials may be a first step toward creating a literate society and a market for books and other printed materials. This project seeks to address the scarcity of books, magazines, newspapers, and even posters in the developing world and to provide learning materials for the classroom environment, which is often the only place where children encounter words in written form. Textbooks provide the main resource for teachers, enabling them to animate the curricula and give life to the subjects taught in the classroom. The importance of books to the quality of education and rates of educational achievement has been well documented. But the goal of Education for All also involves the development of literate societies in the developing world and cannot be attained solely by providing quality learning materials to schools. If people are to stay literate, they must have access to a wide variety of written materials and continue the habit of reading in their adult lives.

Like any large organization, UNESCO has not been immune to controversy. In the 1980s it suffered accusations of mismanagement, which precipitated the withdrawal of three nations: the United States, the United Kingdom, and Singapore. Although the latter two have returned, UNESCO closed its Washington, DC, office definitively in 2001.

International Labor Organization (ILO)

The ILO formulates policies and programs to improve working conditions and employment opportunities and defines international labor standards as guidelines for governments. It settles labor disputes and establishes guidelines for acceptable labor practices. In the field of education, the ILO is involved in issues regarding teaching personnel, including initial preparation, further education and recruitment of teachers, the conditions of employment and work, and the extent of teacher's participation in decision-making processes of public and private educational authorities that affect teaching and learning. The internal governance structure grants each member nation one representative in the decision-making body of ILO and one vote. The philosophical basis of all ILO operations is the equal tripartite partnership of labor, business, and government, with representatives of all three on most internal commissions.

The ILO established the InFocus Program on Strengthening Social Dialogue to strengthen and promote the practice of social dialogue in ILO-member states as a means of sharing information among labor administrations, trade unions, and employers' associations, as well as developing consensus on policy approaches and practical measures to ensure equitable social and economic development. Social dialogue is understood to include all types of negotiations, consultations, or exchange of information between or among the tripartite and bipartite partners on issues of common interest relating to economic and social policy. As such, it plays a pivotal role in identifying the important labor and social issues of the ILO's constituents and in realizing fundamental principles and rights at work promoted by the ILO.

World Health Organization (WHO)

The World Health Organization is the international directing and coordinating authority for information on international health work, which strives to bring the highest quality health to all people. Health is defined in the WHO constitutions as a state of complete physical, mental, and social well-being, not merely the absence of disease or infirmity. In support of its main goal, the WHO works to promote technical cooperation; assist governments at their behest to strengthen health services, to provide appropriate technical assistance and, in emergencies, necessary aid; to stimulate and advance work on the

prevention and control of epidemic, endemic, and other diseases; and to promote, in cooperation with other specialized agencies, the improvement of nutrition, housing, sanitation, recreation, economic or working conditions, and other aspects of environmental hygiene. The internal governance structure grants each member nation one representative in the decision-making body of WHO and one vote.

As part of an educational mission of sorts, the WHO works to promote and coordinate biomedical and health services research. It also promotes improved standards of teaching and training in health, medical, and related professions.

The WHO conducts numerous health-education programs for the benefit of health care professionals and health care beneficiaries. Such health-education programs include, for example, teaching medical students about diarrheal diseases, programs to prevent and reduce the use of tobacco, and health education in food safety. The role of education at the WHO is to aptly disseminate information about ways to prevent and cure disease.

The WHO serves as a conduit to numerous sources of health and medical information as well as health initiatives. The WHO Global School Health Initiative, for example, seeks to mobilize and strengthen health and education activities at the local, national, regional, and global levels. The initiative is designed to improve the health of students, school personnel, families, and other members of the community through schools. Another example is that of the WHO Healthy Cities Project in which attention is given to the principle that health can be improved by modifying living conditions, that is, the physical, environmental, social, and economic factors that affect or determine people's health. The home, the school, the village, the workplace, or the city are all places or settings where people live and work. Health status is often determined more by the conditions in these settings than by the provision of health care facilities.

The WHO has extended collaboration with a number of organizations. One such example is WHO's collaboration with the Industry Council for Development (ICD) and the International Life Sciences Institute (ILSI), both NGOs in official relations with WHO. Some of their joint activities include (1) the Second Asian Conference on Food Safety; (2) Hazard Analysis Critical Control Point training in several countries; (3) training of nutritionists in food safety in Indonesia; and (4) development of a food safety program in Indonesia.

Food and Agriculture Organization of the United Nations (FAO)

The Food and Agriculture Organization of the United Nations is an intergovernmental, multilateral organization created to boost standards of living through improving nutrition, agricultural productivity, and the conditions of rural populations. This is accomplished through development strategies and projects undertaken in cooperation with both national governments and other organizations. The FAO is the largest of the many specialized organizations in the UN system. The FAO's 180 member states and one member organization, the European Community, form the FAO Conference, which meets every two years to determine policy and approve a budget. Each member nation has one representative at the conference. The conference also elects a council of 49 member nations, which form the executive organ of the organization. The council meets at least three times between each conference session, and each of the 49 member nations has one vote. Council representatives are selected for three-year terms.

Founded in 1945, the FAO moved its headquarters from Washington, DC, to Rome, Italy, in 1951. The FAO has eight departments: Administration and Finance, Agriculture, Economic and Social, Fisheries, Forestry, General Affairs and Information, Sustainable Development, and Technical Cooperation. Education programming falls primarily under the control of the Sustainable Development department.

The Sustainable Development (SD) department has four main components: communication for development, education, extension, and research and technology. According to the FAO, it gives priority to basic education through promoting and supporting initiatives aimed at improving children's health and capacity to learn, using technology and distance education, educating rural girls and women, and promoting lifelong education and skills for life in a rural environment. However, the SD expands beyond basic education to improve the quality of all levels of education by supporting curriculum development and teacher training. The FAO tries to respond to the needs of farmers and rural communities by assisting agricultural universities to better serve farmers and to interact with basic and second-

ary educators. In addition, the SD encourages debate on future trends in education and training in agriculture, rural development, and food security; researches practices and case studies; supports partnerships for education for rural development; and provides technical assistance for the training of policymakers and managers.

Youth programming includes a Youth Network for Food and Security and various exchange programs. The goal is to provide education and training to prepare future farmers and community planners.

The SD agriculture extension service does much of its work through universities and extension-research-education linkages. This involves fostering interaction between academic staff and students, with members of local farming communities, and supporting collaborative problem solving.

The FAO further assists in human-resource capacity building through efforts to improve literacy, health and nutrition, and economic well-being. The FAO Nutrition Education and Training Group works with governments to provide training about nutrition and dietary habits. The Policy Assistance Division assists with capacity building through policymaker training.

A 1997 FAO report available on the FAO Internet site in the SD area titled "Agricultural Education and Training: Issues and Opportunities" outlines some of the changes that have affected agricultural education. These include advances in communications technology, decreasing proportions of economically active populations dependent upon agriculture and an increasing marginalization of agriculture and rural life, population increases, scientific progress, changing market demands and employment opportunities, and the increasing recognition of the roles of women in the sector.

The United Nations High Commissioner for Refugees (UNHCR)

The United Nations High Commissioner for Refugees helps resettle people who have left their home countries due to a fear of persecution and who either do not want to or cannot return to their homelands. The UNHCR has two basic goals. First, it aims to protect refugees, and second, it tries to help refugees normalize their lives again. According to the UNHCR women, children, and the elderly comprise 80 percent of the typical refugee population, and the organization attempts to meet their basic needs. For children, this includes education projects.

The UNHCR views education services as meeting psychological needs; restoring structure to children, families, and communities; and helping prevent conflict by providing alternatives to joining armed groups. The UNHCR funds governments and NGOs to construct, rebuild, and operate schools for children and adolescents. Many of these projects are small-scale, quick-impact projects of building and repairs. Although most of the UNHCR's activities are focused on primary and secondary schools, it also provides for literacy classes and vocational training for adults.

The UNHCR tries to use familiar languages and the curriculum from refugees' home countries. In some instances, refugee status might be long-term, and in those cases the UNHCR combines curriculum from countries of origin and the host countries. In cases where a host country forbids education of refugee youth, the UNHCR negotiates on behalf of the refugees.

Beyond direct assistance to refugees and their teachers, the UNHCR also provides information and curriculum materials for teachers worldwide. These resources are provided with the goal of expanding awareness of historical issues and current refugee situations. These efforts can be preventive and build assistance possibilities.

The UNHCR was established with a three-year mandate in 1950 to help resettle refugees left homeless in Europe following World War II. The UN has extended the mandate every five years. It began as a small agency and gradually expanded to offices in 120 countries. It has faced resistance from some countries either unwilling to provide assistance to fleeing civilians or willing to help only temporarily.

See also: INTERNATIONAL EDUCATIONAL AGREEMENTS; NONGOVERNMENTAL ORGANIZATIONS AND FOUNDATIONS.

BIBLIOGRAPHY

HEYNEMAN, STEPHEN P. 1986. *Investing in Education: A Quarter Century of World Bank Experience.* Washington, DC: World Bank.

HEYNEMAN, STEPHEN P. 1993. "Educational Quality and the Crisis in Educational Research." *International Review of Education* 39:511–517.

HEYNEMAN, STEPHEN P. 1998. "Educational Cooperation between Nations in the Twenty-First Century." In *Education for the Twenty-First Century: Issues and Prospect.* Paris: UNESCO.

HEYNEMAN, STEPHEN P. 1999. "Development Aid in Education: A Personal View." *International Journal of Educational Development* 19:183–190.

HEYNEMAN, STEPHEN P. 1999. "The Sad Story of Education Statistics in UNESCO." *International Journal of Educational Development* 19:65–74.

INTERNET RESOURCES

FOOD AND AGRICULTURE ORGANIZATION OF THE UNITED NATIONS. 1996. "Human Resource and Institutional Capacity Building through Agricultural Education." <www.fao.org/sd/exdirect/exan0015.htm>.

FOOD AND AGRICULTURE ORGANIZATION OF THE UNITED NATIONS. 1999. "Agricultural Education for Sustainable Rural Development: Challenges for Developing Countries in the Twenty-First Century." <www.fao.org/sd/exdirect/exan0025.htm>.

FOOD AND AGRICULTURE ORGANIZATION OF THE UNITED NATIONS. 2001. "Sustainable Development Dimensions." <www.fao.org/sd>.

ORGANIZATION FOR SECURITY AND COOPERATION IN EUROPE. 2001. "General Information." <www.osce.org/general>.

UNITED NATIONS HIGH COMMISSIONER FOR REFUGEES. 2001. <www.unhcr.ch>.

KATHERINE TAYLOR HAYNES
ANDREW J. FINCH

INTERNATIONAL EDUCATION

In the late 1970s a course on international education at the University of Chicago included a series of readings that seemed to fall into the following types of materials. First, there were references to some of the nineteenth-century travelers—Horace Mann, Mathew Arnold, Joseph Kay—who brought back impressions of education in foreign lands for domestic consideration. Second, there were references to some who tried to systematize the results of these kinds of impressions—Michael Sadler, Isaac Kandel, George Bereday. Third, there were references to great minds drawn from philosophy or from the social sciences generally that were of interest to comparative education as well as to many other lines of inquiry—Plato, Leo Tolstoy, Max Weber, Émile

Durkheim, Clifford Geertz, Edward Shils, Stuart Eisenstadt, and David Apter. Either they had thought about education, or they were contributors to compelling theories in which education played a role—in modernization, tradition, center and periphery, economic development, civic culture, and stratification. Fourth, there were references to those who had begun to measure and estimate what it was about education that seemed to make a difference in society—Philip Foster, Torsten Husén, Alex Inkeles, Yuri Bronfenbrenner, Edward Denison, and John McClelland. The purpose of these figures was to study education as though it were like any other social function—religion, law, or medicine, for instance. They were curious about whether education's role and function were similar around the world and why. And last, there were individuals who helped "plan" education's effects—Fredrick Harbison and Charles Myers, Neville Postlethwaite, Benjamin Bloom, Charles Havighurst, James Coleman, C. Arnold Anderson, and Mary Jean Bowman.

Readings by and about these figures constituted "the literature" in the late 1970s. The field, however, was greater. Attending meetings of the Comparative and International Education Society were representatives of various foundations and public agencies who took a keen interest in the field and the society itself. The conferences included scholars from anthropology, political science, public administration, comparative literature, sociology, and regional area studies—Africa, Asia, Latin America, and the Middle East—linked by a common interest in education.

By the early twenty-first century, the major interdisciplinary programs at Stanford University and at the University of Chicago had closed, and the level of international development assistance to education in developing countries continued to decline. Was there less interest in the field than twenty-five years previous? Is international education at risk in the early twenty-first century? Where is international education headed?

International Education: More but Different

There is more written in the early twenty-first century concerning international education than was written in the 1970s. One reference system of public policy issues shows 34 entries on international education in the 1970s and 155 ten years later, a nearly fivefold increase. Another reference system, which includes formal articles and publicly presented papers, shows a substantial level of production of 478 entries in the 1970s, compared to 2,125 ten years later.

Both systems exclude the many and varied internal reports from public agencies, such as the World Bank, the Inter-American Development Bank, the Asian Development Bank, the United Nations Educational, Scientific and Cultural Organization (UNESCO), and the United Nations Children's Fund. There were, for example, 33 World Bank education sector reports produced annually during the 1970s and almost four times that level (123) ten years later, going from 1 in 1972 and 1975, to 10 in 1977, to 12 in 1978, to 17 in 1981 and 1985, to a high of 24 in 1992. The current average is about 20 per year.

The U.S. federal government changed too. Out of more than 3,000 research projects sponsored by the federal government on adolescence and youth in 1974, only one had anything to do with international education. Moreover, the agency sponsoring this particular study (the National Institute of Education) made some effort to underplay its existence for fear of being scrutinized by a congressional committee as being frivolous.

For education, the rise in oil prices in 1974 became a "second *Sputnik.*" Rightly or wrongly it was widely believed that the United States was "behind" in some fundamental way, motivating local demands for more information. These came, for instance, from the offices of state governors in Tennessee, South Carolina, Kentucky, and Washington. Questions about international information began coming from the National School Boards Association, the National Governors Association, the National Educational Association, the American Federation of Teachers, the Council of Chief State School Officers, and the National Association of Manufacturers. This demand for answers to "what's wrong?" led to the 1983 publication of *A Nation at Risk,* a report by the National Commission on Excellence in Education that led to a significant increase in the demand for more international information on education and more reliable information.

The year after the publication of *A Nation at Risk,* there was an acrimonious meeting of the board of directors of the Center for Educational Research and Innovation (CERI). The U.S. delegate pushed for the Organisation for Economic Co-operation and Development (OECD) to be engaged in a project collecting and analyzing statistical education "inputs" and "outcomes"—quantifiable information on curricular standards, costs and sources of finance, learning achievements on common subject matter, employment trends, and the like. The reaction among the staff of CERI was one of shock and suspicion. Many thought that generalizations about education were confined to individual cultures, and hence that it was unprofessional to try and quantify education processes or results. They believed that the process of quantification would oversimplify and misrepresent a nation's educational system. Perhaps more importantly, some suspected that the demand for such information would shift as soon as the political party of the U.S. president changed.

A common European mistake has been to rely primarily on traditional central ministries of education for information. Europeans traveled to the United States to do primary source research on education only sparingly, and they often assumed that the structure and policies were settled in a manner closely resembling their own experience.

The point is that this common European mistake has become less common. Since the 1970s there has been a growth in demand and in sophistication concerning international educational information on both sides of the Atlantic. From the European side, they have learned that the demand for better and more reliable data was not coming exclusively from a single president or a single political party. It was coming, in fact, from educational consumers and grassroots interests, from parts of the society and the educational system over which Washington had no control, and to which political leaders in any democracy had no choice except to respond.

By the early twenty-first century, the OECD's publication on education indicators was being published in French and English and constituted the most widely circulated publication in OECD history. New projects have been launched on academic achievement, adult literacy, and the use of technology in education. Supported by the World Bank and UNESCO, the World Education Indicators project has expanded to include seventeen non-OECD countries, including China, Brazil, and India, allowing the OECD indicators to claim that they are now representative of the majority of the world's education systems.

There have been four Nobel prizes dealing with human capital issues (awarded to Edward Dennison, Jan Tinbergen, T. W. Schultz, and Gary Becker).

There has been a flurry of reports on the status of education issued by international agencies in the early 1980s onward. There have been two meetings of heads of state on international educational issues: the Education for All meeting held in Jomtien, Thailand, in March 1990; and the World Summit for Children, which took place in New York City in September 1990. There are three new educational boards of the U.S. National Academy of Sciences and major new research initiatives from the General Accounting Office, the Office of Technology Assessment, various congressional committees, and the Carnegie, Spencer, Ball, and Soros Foundations. There is an ongoing cooperative effort among the donors to assist African education. This is, of course, in addition to the many new efforts in Europe and Asia. The Japanese initiated an important fund to assist human resources in developing countries. The ministers of education from fourteen nations in Asia and North America have decided to pool resources on projects having to do with curriculum requirements and teacher certification. These resources are not classified as foreign aid; instead, they come out of ministry of education budgets. This is also characteristic of the Dutch CROSS (Coordination Dutch-Russian Cooperation in Education) Program, which is designed to assist Russian education. It is justified on grounds that Dutch educational officials have something significant and unique to offer the Russians in the fields of educational management, educational publishing, and assessments of learning achievement and educational examinations and standardized testing, and that the Dutch can themselves learn equally from the cooperative effort. The British Council is also assisting Russian educators with studies and analytic resources. The British Know How Fund is assisting eastern Europeans with studies of the "textbook sector"; the Swedish and the American academies of sciences are assisting higher education and research capacity in the former Soviet Union, as is the European Union. Perhaps unique, though, is an effort led by the chancellor of the State University of New York to provide high-quality advice in comparative education to the minister of higher education in Russia.

These efforts, and the many publications rapidly emerging from them, are not isolated. From a low point of the National Institute of Education's fear that their one comparative education project would be seen as a waste of resources in 1974 has emerged a new industry of international education initiatives and projects.

Quality of International Education Information

The international education questions coming from public authorities reveal new sophistication. No longer is thinking confined to "Why Johnny cannot read as well as Ivan." No longer are the interests of public officials confined to that of an Olympic finish. This increasing sophistication is not uniform, but the kinds of questions being asked in the early twenty-first century cover a much wider spectrum of comparative educational endeavors. The staff of congressional committees ask increasingly about teaching and organizational techniques, types of salary incentives, and the methods of teaching children racial and ethnic tolerance. Questions concern the arts, the system of finance and management, morals, culture, language, and ethnicity. It is now (almost) normal for U.S. political figures to appreciate that political leaders and educators from other countries are not necessarily interested in the exact same questions and problems that interest Americans. Only infrequently does one find the "marble syndrome" of educational politics (if they are not interested in my game and my rules, I go home); rather, there is an appreciation that educational research and the gathering of educational statistics is a natural and normal part of diplomacy. For example, the United States remained in an (expensive, publicly financed) international study of computer literacy even though it was felt there was not very much to learn from other countries. The reason it remained was because it was felt that other countries wanted to learn from the United States. Similarly, the United States lowered its expectations of international research on educational standards with the Asia-Pacific Economic Conference in lieu of the Asian nations' need to learn about moral education and the teaching of national consensus building. It has become understood that the Japanese may wish to learn about diversified curriculum from the United States, that Russians wish to learn about the teaching of democracy with a heterogeneous school population, and that all societies want to know more about techniques of local management and local finance—all of which are areas in which the United States is not "behind."

Is it possible that Americans are showing signs of international tolerance and understanding in the field of education? Is it possible that Americans are coming out of their long-held tradition of localism and educational isolationism? It may be too early to make firm conclusions. But the diversity and sophistication in the kinds of questions being asked by public authorities has increased so dramatically that at times one has the sense that nearly every social science issue on the comparative education reading list the early 1970s seems to be coming of age and into maturity—civic culture and governance, the complexity of human capital theory, stratification and cultural integration, the need for tradition as well as economic development. In every sense, the new century may be a "golden age" for international education.

Why Interest in International Education Is Growing

Some changes come about suddenly and have an immediate worldwide impact. In 1999 Thomas L. Friedman suggested that this is the case with respect to the Internet. Other changes are glacial in the speed by which they are recognized, yet in terms of impact are no less profound. Such is the case with respect to education issues and their shift from local to international relevance.

Significant shifts have affected the governance of education and, hence, the character of international education. These include: the globalization of social and economic forces; the shift to mass education, including mass higher education; the spread of democracy to new areas of the world; the mismatch between education objectives and fiscal capability; the demands placed on the systems to attract high-level talent in terms of international students and faculty; the urgent demands of technology; the new efforts to systematically provide sources of cross-national statistical information; the pressures to create a level playing field in terms of international trade in education services; and the new demands for education to influence social cohesion.

In the 1970s and 1980s governments often determined economic investments, and foreign aid frequently was the dominant source of development capital for middle- and low-income countries. By the early twenty-first century, transfers of private capital far outstripped public investments. A future computer manufacturing plant might be located in Nashville, Tennessee, Northern Ireland, or southern Italy; a textile plant in Bangalore, India, or Sonora, Mexico; a farm for winter fruit in Florida or Chile. What determines the choice of where to invest? Investment capital flows to one or another location on the basis of many factors—taxation policy, freedom to repatriate profit, labor productivity, labor cost, and social stability. The latter three are heavily influenced by education and by the success of local education systems. Hence, the demands for economic growth and prosperity help determine that pressures on education systems to perform are similar.

In the 1960s the central education representatives were often the sole representatives. Education in the early twenty-first century is frequently a decentralized activity with many new decision makers. Local authorities increasingly drive budgets and policy priorities. This is particularly evident in Brazil, Mexico, India, Russia, Nigeria, and other federal systems; but it is also evident in France, Indonesia, and Malaysia, which had been traditionally centralized. Local states and communities increasingly evaluate their own program innovations, initiate their own research projects, and review their own policies. Local or administrative initiative is often a leading force in centralized education systems as well. Local business and community groups, industries, and nongovernmental organizations increasingly influence policymakers as well as educational authorities. In higher education and private education, where policy decisions are increasingly the responsibility of individual institutions, these institutions are involved in international relations on their own. Educational software companies, publishers, and corporate training firms are ever more active and are demanding new and current information on the size of the educational markets in many countries. Taken together these new categories of participants have deeply affected the vision and the expressed interests of the traditional education authorities.

The Influence of Democracy on Educational Governance

Under autocratic governments, there was little need to explain education policy to the public. Educational policy consisted of edicts of intent and orders for administrative action that may or may not have been carried out effectively. Mechanisms for public debate did not exist. The performance of educational institutions was not open to public scrutiny. Data and other information on program effectiveness were not required. The curriculum was imposed; the goals of civics and history were decided unilaterally. If problems occurred, public officials were not held accountable.

New democracies have emerged in South Africa, Europe and Central Asia, Latin America and the Caribbean, and East Asia. With democracy, the requirements of educational management shift. The effectiveness of educational institutions is open to public scrutiny for the first time, and education policy is the subject of heated public debate. To be effective, policy requires public awareness and consensus prior to any announcements. Institutions have come to be in the position of competing for new resources, new faculty, and new curricula to keep abreast of quickly changing public demands.

Educational systems in the new democracies are faced with problems even more serious than that of efficient management. In many countries, curricular authority has been localized to the region or the local school. In some instances, such as in Bosnia, this has led to serious disagreements over the role of the school itself. Such disagreements have included the content of history and civics, the use of pedagogy counterproductive to interethnic harmony, and the existence of barriers to the equality of educational opportunity for particular ethnic and social groups. In many instances, schools and school systems have been engaged in performing functions exactly the opposite of their traditional intent. Instead of resolving differences across social groups, schools have been used to exacerbate those differences.

The Influence of Financial Austerity on Educational Governance

School systems differ from one country to another, but all share certain characteristics. All school systems share the universal struggle to balance the rapidly changing demands for improvement with the equally problematic realities of fiscal constraints, a permanent and unsolvable dilemma. The demand for mass access, higher levels of equity (for the socially excluded), and higher quality (for everyone) inevitably exceeds financial capacity. These universal demands make all schools and all school systems conscious consumers of educational policy innovations. The key difference in the early twenty-first century, compared to two decades previous, is the growing recognition that relevant innovations may emerge from anywhere; they are not necessarily local or even domestic. This new era in international education is led by the burgeoning realization from active consumers—teachers, school and university managers, and system administrators—that their success may well depend on having the most com-

FIGURE 1

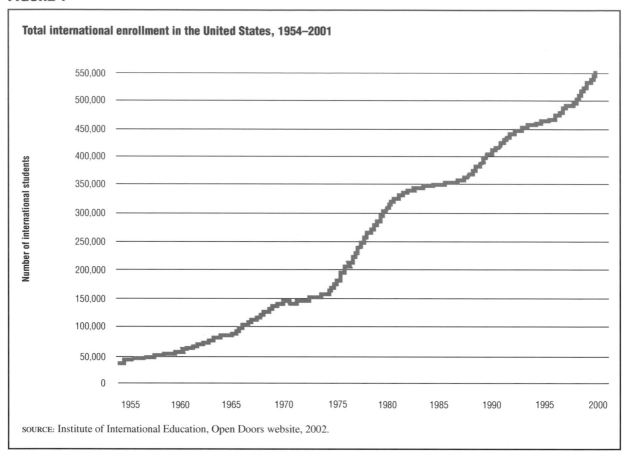

Total international enrollment in the United States, 1954–2001

SOURCE: Institute of International Education, Open Doors website, 2002.

pelling innovations, and that they are quite capable of making their decisions on whether geographical origin is a critical factor or not.

As a result, new policies have become common in widely disparate localities—including such policies as focusing on the quality and relevance of teaching materials that are procured from an open and competitive market; developing a professional force in which more effective teachers receive higher compensations; conducting research that allows for transparent comparisons that are available to the public; and securing financing from multiple sources to maximize local investment without abrogating equity. Educational managers around the world have become focused on common problems such as school-based management, teacher incentives, multicultural education, civic responsibilities, tracking, curriculum depth, individualized instruction, fair testing and assessment, special learning problems, and communications with the public.

Higher education has become mass education—it is no longer only for the elite. In the 1960s, in no

country in western Europe was more than 9 percent of the age cohort enrolled in higher education; by the early twenty-first century, however, no country in the region enrolled fewer than about 35 percent of the age cohort. This shift has been associated with common, if not identical, fiscal and administrative pressures. These in turn have generated demand for creative policy reforms. Demand exists for innovations in institutional efficiency in terms of student–faculty ratios, judicious use of new technologies, efficiency in generating contractual outsourcing of traditional functions, department-based budgeting, marketing of university copyrights, and attention to the problems of international trade in education commerce.

In terms of size, the U.S. education system accounts for less than 5 percent of world enrollment. Together, industrialized countries account for about 17 percent. The remaining 83 percent of the world's enrollments are located in the middle-income and developing countries, with 57 percent enrolled in East and South Asia. Each of these "nonindustrial-

TABLE 1

Source of funds for international students in the United States

Primary Source of Funds	All foreign students (percent)	Under-graduate (percent)	Graduate (percent)	Other (percent)
Personal and family	66.9	80.7	46.9	65.2
U.S. college or university	19.8	8.4	39.9	6.1
Home government/university	4.0	3.6	4.5	3.9
Private U.S. sponsor	2.5	2.8	2.3	1.0
Foreign private sponsor	2.4	2.7	2.1	2.1
Current employment	2.4	0.4	1.4	18.9
Other sources	1.9	0.6	1.4	1.3
U.S. government	0.6	0.4	0.9	0.8
International organization	0.4	0.3	0.5	0.8
Total number of students	547,867	254,429	238,497	54,941

SOURCE: Institute of International Education, Open Doors website, 2002.

ized" countries is changing rapidly. As economies grow, more is spent on students. Unit expenditures across the world doubled between 1980 and 1994, but different regions showed different rates of growth. Expenditures doubled in the United States, but they increased by 135 percent in Europe and 200 percent in East Asia. In terms of challenges and dilemmas, the world's education systems share more than ever before.

These common challenges imply several things. First, the demand for innovative policies in education is growing rapidly, and their source is no longer confined to one country's experience. This is particularly important for the United States, which has a high demand for policy innovation, yet a small portion of the world's education experience from which to draw lessons. To attain excellence today the education profession must keep abreast of relevant innovations and educational experience from wherever they derive.

But these trends imply something else as well. With the common decentralization of decision-making, the client for educational research and policy innovation is not limited to central or public authorities. There are many different demands for good ideas and information, and therefore many different clients to decide what is relevant. Local school officials in Minnesota, for example, have opted to join international studies of academic achievement so they might compare their educational performance with Sweden and Singapore. The American Federation of Teachers has studied the degree to which American high-stakes tests compare with those in Europe and Asia. These examples illustrate

that traditional notions of what is relevant to local school systems are constantly being retested with new information but are also in the hands of an increasingly diverse set of local educational clients and decision makers.

The Influence of International Students on Education Policy

In 1960 there were only 50,000 international students in the United States. The number of international students in the United States rose steadily thereafter, reaching a record high of 549,000 in 2001 (see Figure 1). Final year expenditures on tuition and fees by international students in the United States reached $11 billion in 2001. Of those expenditures, approximately 66 percent were derived from personal and family sources. At the undergraduate level (i.e., for 254,000 students), family support accounted for 81 percent (see Table 1). While American higher education may be expensive by world standards, a large number of families outside the United States can afford it. Because of its potential, international education is now classified as a traded service by the U.S. Department of Commerce and has become the nation's fifth-largest service export.

More than one-half of the foreign students in the United States come from Asia, with students from China and India together accounting for more than 25 percent alone (see Table 2). Most are in the United States to study for utilitarian purposes. The proportion of international students studying humanities is only 2.9 percent; fine arts, 6.2 percent; and social sciences, 7.7 percent. Almost one-half of the foreign students are "crowded" into three fields:

TABLE 2

International students in the United States by leading country of origin

Place of Origin	1999–2001	2000–2001	Percent Change	Scholar Total
World Total	74,571	79,651	6.8	
China	13,229	14,772	11.7	18.5
Japan	5,460	5,905	8.2	7.4
Republic of Korea	5,015	5,830	16.3	7.3
India	4,929	5,456	10.7	6.8
Germany	5,016	5,221	4.1	6.6
Canada	3,578	3,735	4.4	4.7
United Kingdom	2,916	3,352	15.0	4.2
Russia	3,195	3,253	1.8	4.1
France	3,076	3,154	2.5	4.0
Italy	2,108	2,226	5.6	2.8
Spain	1,729	1,706	-1.3	2.1
Brazil	1,273	1,315	3.3	1.7
Australia	1,090	1,212	11.2	1.5
Israel	1,108	1,205	8.8	1.5
Taiwan	1,200	1,196	-0.3	1.5
Netherlands	978	1,037	6.0	1.3
Turkey	898	918	2.2	1.2
Mexico	959	898	-6.4	1.1
Poland	805	862	7.1	1.1
Switzerland	774	767	-0.9	1.0

SOURCE: Institute of International Education, Open Doors website, 2002.

19.4 percent are in business and management, 15.2 percent in engineering, and 12.4 percent in mathematics and computer sciences. Human resources are becoming more popular, with health at 4.1 percent and education at 2.6 percent of the total (see Table 3). Just as demand is growing for students to study in the United States, demand by American students to study abroad, even temporarily, is growing. From 1985 to 1999, the number of American students studying abroad increased from 45,000 to 140,000 (see Figure 2). These figures reflect high demand. But is the demand for higher education institutions in the United States as high as it is for higher education institutions outside the United States? In other words, in terms of attracting international students, does U.S. higher education continue to be competitive with higher education elsewhere?

In fact the trade in higher education outside the United States is growing faster. Since 1990 the share of international students studying within the United States dropped from 40 percent to less than 30 percent. And as a proportion of the overall student population, in 2001 the international student population in the United States (3.9%) was not that much greater than it was in 1954 (1.4%). As a percentage of the overall student population, in fact, the United States

ranked twelfth among OECD countries in 1998. The international student proportion in Switzerland that year was 16 percent; in Australia, more than 12 percent; in Britain, about 11 percent; in Germany, about 8 percent; and in France, about 7 percent (see Figure 3).

These figures suggest that international education has become openly competitive and that the United States does not have as large an advantage as it once did. The figures would also suggest that given their proportion of the overall student population, the "impact" of international students in the United States is modest by comparison to the situation that some of its trading partners face.

Cross-National Sources of Statistical Information

In spite of the inevitable political emphasis on the Olympic nature of cross-national studies, countries are beginning to participate because the lessons derived have proven to be insightful and to stimulate new questions and ideas for improvement. Many have learned that the lessons in one country are not identical to the lessons elsewhere. For example, with respect to the Third International Mathematics and Science Study (TIMSS), Americans drew conclusions about the curriculum being "a mile wide and an inch deep" (Schmidt, p. 3), but Colombians drew conclusions about the range of age within each grade level; Latvians drew conclusions about differences between Latvian and minority students. All countries seemed to draw conclusions about the manner in which subject matter is sequenced. Moreover, it is common to sponsor reanalyses of the datasets, which often result in new insights. For instance, Americans must now ponder why their disadvantaged perform worse than the disadvantaged in other participating countries and why school resources are more inequitably distributed than in other countries.

International standards have been greatly enhanced by the procedures and the results of cross-national studies. Achievement studies around the world have learned from the three different elements used in TIMSS: what one expects to be learned, what has been taught, and what has been learned. The new studies have tried to include case examples and videotape episodes, as well as both cross-sectional and time-series surveys. This experience has helped mitigate the long-standing unproductive battles between quantitative and qualitative evidence; all evidence

TABLE 3

International students in the United States by field of study

Field of Study	1999–2000 Foreign Students	2000–2001 Foreign Students	Percent of Total	Percent Change
Total	514,723	547,867	100.0	6.4
Business and management	103,215	106,043	19.4	2.7
Engineering	76,748	83,186	15.2	8.4
Mathematics and computer sciences	57,266	67,825	12.4	18.4
Other (general studies, communication, law)	53,195	57,235	10.4	7.6
Social sciences	41,662	42,367	7.7	1.7
Physical and life sciences	37,420	38,396	7.0	2.6
Undeclared	32,799	35,779	6.5	9.1
Fine and applied arts	32,479	34,220	6.2	5.4
Intensive English language	21,015	23,011	4.2	9.5
Health professions	21,625	22,430	4.1	3.7
Humanities	16,686	16,123	2.9	-3.4
Education	12,885	14,053	2.6	9.1
Agriculture	7,729	7,200	1.3	-6.8

SOURCE: Institute of International Education, Open Doors website, 2002.

has its strengths and weaknesses, and the principles governing the use of data have become largely understood to be universal. International standards of data collection, reporting, quality control, sampling, the impartiality of questionnaire design, first proposed by the authorities within the United States, have been established and widely accepted, and this has led to questioning and then strengthening of the international institutions that support education data collection and dissemination.

Future Issues

The institutional structure underpinning international education data collection remains fragile. There is no consensus about how financial support for international data collection should be obtained in a fashion that is fair to all countries. Now considered a trade good, education is the source of debate surrounding the World Trade Organization. Are there indeed barriers to the trade in education, or is education a "cultural good" falling within the purview of each nation independently? It is clear that as a separate field of study, international education has shifted. No longer is it viable as an esoteric field of study. Instead, international experience is becoming a normal part of all fields of study—curriculum, administration, human development, and pedagogy. But graduate schools of education, particularly in the United States, are not well-equipped to respond to this new set of demands and will have to undergo a significant, and perhaps painful, adjustment to catch up with the field itself.

See also: DECENTRALIZATION AND EDUCATION; GLOBALIZATION OF EDUCATION; INTERNATIONAL ASSESSMENTS; INTERNATIONAL EDUCATION STATISTICS; INTERNATIONAL ISSUES OF SOCIAL MOBILITY OF UNDERPRIVILEGED GROUPS; INTERNATIONAL STUDENTS; POPULATION AND EDUCATION.

BIBLIOGRAPHY

AMERICAN FEDERATION OF TEACHERS and NATIONAL CENTER FOR IMPROVING SCIENCE EDUCATION. 1994. "What College Bound Students Abroad Are Expected to Know about Biology: Exams from England and Wales, France, Germany, and Japan, Plus a Comparative Look at the United States." Washington, DC: American Federation of Teachers.

BAKER, D. P. 2002. "Should We Be More Like Them? Reflections on Causes of Cross-National High School Achievement Differences and Implications for Education Reform Policy." Paper presented at the Brookings Education Policy Conference, Washington, DC, May 14.

BOYER, ERNEST L. 1983. *High School: A Report on Secondary Education in America.* New York: Carnegie Foundation for the Advancement of Teaching.

CARNOY, MARTIN. 1992. *The Case for Investing in Basic Education.* New York: United Nations Children's Fund.

COMMISSION ON NATIONAL CHALLENGES IN HIGHER EDUCATION. 1988. *Memorandum to the*

FIGURE 2

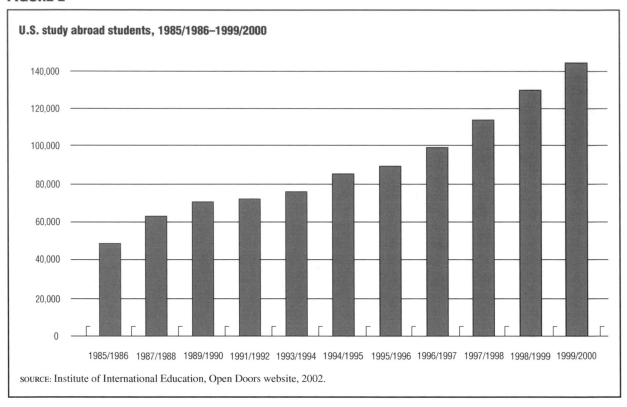

U.S. study abroad students, 1985/1986–1999/2000

SOURCE: Institute of International Education, Open Doors website, 2002.

Forty-First President of the United States. Washington, DC: American Committee on Education.

FRIEDMAN, THOMAS L. 1999. *The Lexus and the Olive Tree: Understanding Globalization.* New York: Farrar, Straus, and Giroux.

GOODLAD, JOHN I. 1984. *A Place Called School: Prospects for the Future.* New York: McGraw-Hill.

GUTHRIE, JAMES W., and HANSEN, JANET S., eds. 1995. *Worldwide Education Statistics: Enhancing UNESCO's Role.* Washington, DC: National Academy of Sciences.

HAWES, HUGH; COOMBE, TREVOR; COOMBE, CAROL; and LILLIS, KEVIN, eds. 1986. *Education Priorities and Aid Responses in Sub-Saharan Africa.* London: Overseas Development Administration.

HEYNEMAN, STEPHEN P. 1974. *Toward Inter-agency Coordination: Annual Report of the Inter-agency Panel for Research and Development on Adolescence.* Washington, DC: George Washington University, Social Research Group.

HEYNEMAN, STEPHEN P. 1993. "Quantity, Quality, and Source of Comparative Education." *Comparative Education Review* 37:372–388.

HEYNEMAN, STEPHEN P. 1995. "Economics of Education: Disappointments and Potential." *UNESCO Prospects* 25:559–583.

HEYNEMAN, STEPHEN P. 1997. "Economic Development and the International Trade in Education Reform." *UNESCO Prospects* 30:501–531.

HEYNEMAN, STEPHEN P. 1999a. "Development Aid in Education: A Personal View." In *Changing International Aid to Education: Global Patterns and National Contexts,* ed. Kenneth King and Lene Buchert. Paris: UNESCO Publishing.

HEYNEMAN, STEPHEN P. 1999b. "The Sad Story of UNESCO's Education Statistics." *International Journal of Education Development* 19:65–74.

HEYNEMAN, STEPHEN P. 2000. "Educational Qualifications: The Economic and Trade Issues." *Assessment in Education: Principles, Policy, and Practice* 3:417–439.

HEYNEMAN, STEPHEN P. 2001. "The Growing International Market for Education Goods and Services." *International Journal of Education Development* 21:345–361.

INTER-AGENCY COMMISSION. 1991. *Final Report. World Conference on Education for All: Meeting*

FIGURE 3

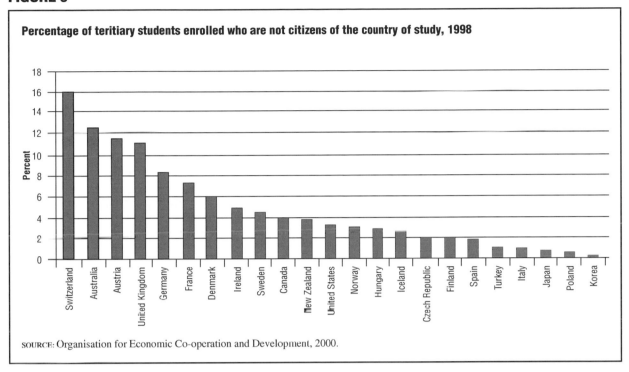

Percentage of teritiary students enrolled who are not citizens of the country of study, 1998

SOURCE: Organisation for Economic Co-operation and Development, 2000.

Basic Learning Needs. New York: Inter-Agency Commission (United Nations Development Programme; United Nations Educational, Scientific and Cultural Organization; United Nations Children's Fund; World Bank).

INTERNATIONAL DEVELOPMENT RESEARCH CENTRE and CANADIAN INTERNATIONAL DEVELOPMENT AGENCY. 1982. *Financing Educational Development.* Ottawa, Ontario, Canada: International Development Research Centre.

INTERNATIONAL LABOR OFFICE. 1989. *International Labour Report.* Geneva, Switzerland: International Labor Office.

NATIONAL ACADEMY OF SCIENCES. 1993. *A Collaborative Agenda for Improving International Comparative Studies in Education.* Washington, DC: National Academy of Sciences.

NATIONAL COMMISSION ON EXCELLENCE IN EDUCATION. 1983. *A Nation at Risk: The Imperative for Educational Reform.* Washington, DC: U.S. Government Printing Office.

NATIONAL SCIENCE BOARD COMMISSION ON PRE-COLLEGE EDUCATION IN MATH, SCIENCE, AND TECHNOLOGY. 1983. *Educating Americans for the Twenty-First Century: A Plan of Action for Improving Mathematics, Science, and Technology*

Education for All American Elementary and Secondary Students so that Their Achievement Is the Best in the World by 1995. Washington, DC: National Science Foundation.

ORGANISATION FOR ECONOMIC CO-OPERATION AND DEVELOPMENT. 1992. *The OECD International Education Indicators: A Framework for Analysis.* Paris: Organisation for Economic Co-operation and Development.

SCHMIDT, WILLIAM H.; MCKNIGHT, CURTIS C.; RAIZEN, SENTA A.; and THIRD INTERNATIONAL MATHEMATICS AND SCIENCE STUDY. 1996. *A Splintered Vision: An Investigation of U.S. Science and Mathematics Education.* Dordrecht, Netherlands: Kluwer Academic.

SINGAPORE, MINISTER OF EDUCATION. 1987. *Towards Excellence in Schools.* Singapore: Ministry of Education.

TASK FORCE ON TEACHING AS A PROFESSION. 1986. *A Nation Prepared: Teachers for the Twenty-First Century.* New York: Carnegie Forum on Education and the Economy.

THROSBY, C. D., and GANNICOTT, KENNETH. 1990. *The Quality of Education in the South Pacific.* Canberra, Australia: National Centre for Development Studies.

UNITED NATIONS CHILDREN'S FUND. 1992. *State of the World's Children, 1992.* New York: United Nations Children's Fund.

UNITED NATIONS CHILDREN'S FUND. TASK FORCE FOR CHILD SURVIVAL. 1990. *Protecting the World's Children: A Call for Action.* New York: Rockefeller Foundation.

UNITED NATIONS DEVELOPMENT PROGRAMME. 1990. *Human Development Report.* New York: Oxford University Press.

UNITED NATIONS EDUCATIONAL, SCIENTIFIC AND CULTURAL ORGANIZATION. 1991. *World Education Report.* Paris: United Nations Educational, Scientific and Cultural Organization.

U.S. CONGRESS, OFFICE OF TECHNOLOGY ASSESSMENT. 1992. *Testing in American Schools: Asking the Right Questions.* Washington, DC: U.S. Government Printing Office.

U.S. DEPARTMENT OF EDUCATION. 1987. *What Works? Research about Teaching and Learning.* Washington, DC: U.S. Government Printing Office.

WORLD BANK. 1988. *Education in Sub-Saharan Africa: Policies for Adjustment, Revitalization, and Expansion.* Washington, DC: World Bank.

WORLD BANK. 1990. *Primary Education Policy Paper.* Washington, DC: World Bank.

WORLD BANK. 1991. *Vocational and Technical Education and Training Policy Paper.* Washington, DC: World Bank.

STEPHEN P. HEYNEMAN

INTERNATIONAL EDUCATION AGREEMENTS

The term *international agreement* refers to an international treaty, declaration, or recommendation adopted by the governments of many different countries in order to set out certain principles or courses of action in a selected field, or set of fields, of mutual interest. Countries sign international agreements on many things, such as travel and health regulations, telecommunications, air and ship navigation, and labor practices. The earliest such agreements in the field of education were adopted in the period between the first and second world wars, and many more have been adopted since then. Most

have their origins in the work of international organizations. In some cases they form part of broader agreements that also cover other fields, as in the case of the Universal Declaration of Human Rights (1948). Broadly speaking, their purposes and scope reflect the context of international relations prevailing at the time they were drawn up.

An analysis of these agreements could take any one of several alternative approaches. A historical approach is used here in order to draw attention to both the accumulation of these agreements over time and the possibility that countries have found it easier to adopt new agreements than to implement old ones. The focus is on agreements that are basically worldwide in scope, and not just confined to countries in a particular geographical region. The full texts of all the agreements specifically mentioned here can be consulted at the websites of the United Nations and the United Nations Educational, Scientific and Cultural Organization (UNESCO).

International Agreements in General

International agreements can be classified according to the level or degree of commitment that countries formally accord each agreement's implementation. The most demanding level is that of an *international treaty*, sometimes referred to as an international *convention* or *covenant*. Treaties typically require a formal signature by representatives of the countries concerned, and they are considered, under international law, to be legally binding on the countries (states) that ratify (accede to) them. The countries that are party to an international treaty normally need to ensure that the terms or provisions of the treaty are reflected in their national legislation.

Certain international treaties have as their purpose the setting up of an intergovernmental organization. An example is the treaty signed in San Francisco in 1945 that set up the United Nations. Another example is the treaty drawn up and adopted by a group of countries in London in 1945 that established UNESCO. Countries that accede to the United Nations and UNESCO treaties undertake to pay dues (assessed financial contributions) to these organizations, and to abide by these organizations' constitutions.

International treaties are normally drawn up and adopted by international conferences of states (so-called diplomatic conferences). They usually come into effect when an agreed number of states in each case has formally ratified them, which can sometimes be several years after the treaty was originally adopted, depending on how rapidly individual states are able to incorporate the treaty in their national legislation. In the case of education, most international treaties since 1945 have been drawn up and adopted by diplomatic conferences convened either by the United Nations or by UNESCO. No international treaty concerning education was adopted before 1945.

International treaties usually include a provision for states to report to a *treaty body* on measures taken to ensure their implementation. In the case of treaties adopted under the auspices of the United Nations, for example, the latter has established committees, such as the Human Rights Committee and the Committee on Economic, Social and Cultural Rights, to serve as treaty bodies.

Diplomatic conferences are also convened from time to time for the purpose of drawing up and adopting less demanding forms of agreement, such as an international *declaration* or *recommendation*. Broadly speaking, declarations tend to focus on principles that should guide action, while recommendations tend to focus on courses of action, although this distinction is not always clearly apparent. The states concerned formally undertake to make their best efforts to abide by the provisions of the declaration or recommendation in question, without necessarily agreeing to adopt specific legislative measures as might be required by a treaty. The declarations, recommendations, and treaties adopted by international conferences of states are generally referred to in diplomatic parlance as international *normative instruments*.

Other types of agreement include resolutions adopted by the member states of international organizations, as well as international declarations and recommendations of an essentially nonformal character that representatives of countries have expressed their support for without formally committing their respective states to abide by. The latter are typically drawn up and adopted by consensus at nondiplomatic conferences that have a mixed composition of participants, often including representatives of international organizations and nongovernmental organizations as well as of governments. Probably the best-known example in the field of education is the World Declaration on Education for All, adopted by the World Conference on Education for All, held in Jomtien, Thailand, in 1990. Such

conferences have also tended to adopt a plan or program of action for implementation of the declaration or recommendation specifying how the various parties concerned will work towards the agreed goals or objectives. In some cases, agreement has also been reached on the establishment of a mechanism to monitor implementation.

The Years between the Wars, 1918–1939

With two or three exceptions, the international education agreements adopted during the period between the two world wars were generally of a nonformal character. The exceptions were in the form of resolutions adopted by the General Assembly of the League of Nations, the forerunner of the United Nations set up by the peace conference that followed World War I. The majority were in the form of recommendations adopted by successive international conferences organized by the International Bureau of Education (IBE), a hybrid nongovernmental/intergovernmental body established in Geneva in 1926.

The idea of governments adopting agreements concerning education emerged from the broader movement of opinion among the leaders of the major industrial countries after World War I in favor of new approaches to the challenge of fostering international understanding and peace. The League of Nations was conceived in this spirit as a permanent mechanism of consultation between states, essentially for the purpose of overcoming misunderstandings and disagreements before they could develop into armed conflict. A key concept of the League was that such consultation should not be just a matter of diplomatic contacts between ministries of foreign affairs, but should also include contacts between the national administrations responsible for matters that were often the basic sources of misunderstanding and disagreement between countries, such as commerce and trade, communications, travel, employment, and health. Various subsidiary organs of the League were established in order to facilitate cooperation between countries in certain of these fields.

Education was not specifically mentioned in the treaty setting up the League, although at the peace conference that drew up the treaty, some countries had favored its inclusion. Others felt that education was mainly an internal matter. Nevertheless, at its first session in 1920 the League's General Assembly adopted a resolution calling for the League's (executive) Council to examine a closely related question, that of "international intellectual co-operation," which the resolution's sponsors (Belgium and France) considered to be highly relevant to the task of developing a spirit of understanding, cooperation, and peace among nations. In the following year the League established an International Commission on Intellectual Co-operation, composed of eminent personalities in the sciences and humanities from different countries and charged with advising the council on measures that governments could take with a view to stimulating international cooperation among scientists, artists, philosophers, writers, and other groups of intellectuals, in furtherance of the League's overall objectives.

This opened a door for the League of Nations to enter somewhat indirectly into educational matters. Thus, one of the early actions taken by the League's General Assembly was its adoption in 1923 of a resolution calling upon countries to encourage the teaching of the goals of the League and the ideals of international cooperation to young people. However, in the absence of a formal mandate in education, the scope for further initiatives by the League in this field was limited. In the years remaining up until the outbreak of World War II, the only other instance of such an agreement being reached by the League's General Assembly was the adoption of a resolution in 1935 calling upon countries to encourage the teaching of history for peaceful purposes.

In the meantime, however, the French government (with the League's blessing, though not its financial support) had set up a body, the International Institute of Intellectual Co-operation, for the purpose of carrying out operational activities in areas of concern to the commission. These indirectly had an educational dimension, if only because international intellectual cooperation partly concerned international cooperation between educational institutions, such as universities, that in most countries were the main centers of intellectual life. The institute became active in promoting exchanges between researchers in different countries, in both the sciences and humanities, and in promoting international cooperation between universities, particularly with regard to teacher and student exchanges and the mutual recognition of degrees and diplomas. Much of this work was to be taken up after World War II by UNESCO.

The absence of a mandate for the League of Nations to get involved in educational matters did not preclude the League's members from showing an interest in another framework of cooperation in this field, which came to be provided by the IBE. The IBE was established in Geneva in 1926 as an offshoot of the University of Geneva's School of Education (Institut Jean-Jacques Rousseau), one of the main centers in Europe of the New Education movement, a body of educational thinking closely associated with the ideas of John Dewey and the Progressive education movement in the United States. Originally conceived as an international nongovernmental clearing-house of educational research and documentation, the IBE revised its statutes in 1929 so as to permit governments to become members, and it was soon discovered that there was widespread latent support for the creation of some kind of forum in which national educational policymakers could exchange views and experiences concerning educational developments in their respective countries.

From 1934, therefore, the IBE undertook to organize an annual conference, the International Conference on Public Education, open to any country that wished to participate. More than thirty countries sent delegations to the first conference, and the attendance increased at subsequent conferences. Delegations were invited to present reports on recent educational developments in their countries, and to participate in a general debate on educational themes selected by the IBE for examination by the conference. The themes (usually three) were selected with a view to addressing current policy issues of concern to conference participants. At the first Conference, for example, the themes were Compulsory Education and the Raising of the School Leaving Age; Admission to Secondary Schools; and Economies in the Field of Public Education. Later conferences examined themes such as The Professional Training of Elementary School Teachers (1935); School Inspection (1937); and The Organization of Preschool Education (1939). In order to give a structure to the debates, the IBE also prepared ahead of the conference a draft recommendation on each theme setting out policies that the conference could consider as likely to help advance the development of education. At the end of its proceedings, the conference would adopt by consensus a final version of each recommendation, taking into account any amendments suggested during the debate.

The spirit that drove the conferences was basically that of the New (or Progressive) Education thinking associated with the IBE: expansion of educational opportunities and the promotion of more child-centered pedagogies. The recommendations were nonformal and purely advisory, and it was accepted that countries would adapt them to their individual circumstances. Their usefulness for participants (generally ministries of education) probably lay in the broad stamp of international approval that they accorded to policies that most countries were inclined to pursue anyway. Significantly, the majority of the recommendations concerned the organizational and administrative aspects of education rather than its contents, which would have been more difficult to handle politically.

Agreements since the End of World War II

The success of the IBE's conferences was probably a factor in the interest among a number of countries, even before the war was over, in the possibility of future international cooperation on educational matters. Towards the end of the war, at the initiative of the British government, a standing Conference of Allied Ministers of Education was formed in London to discuss the tasks of educational reconstruction and cooperation that countries would need to undertake after the war. This body soon coalesced around proposals for establishing an intergovernmental educational and cultural organization, with scientific cooperation being added later. In the meantime, the United States had initiated a process of international negotiations and discussions with a view to setting up the United Nations Organization, the purposes of which were envisaged in Article I of the organization's charter to include, besides the maintenance of "international peace and security" and the development of "friendly relations among nations," the achievement of "international cooperation in solving international problems of an economic, social or humanitarian character, and in promoting and encouraging respect for human rights and for fundamental freedoms for all without distinction as to race, sex, language, or religion." The San Francisco treaty containing the charter came into force in October 1945. The London treaty containing the constitution of UNESCO came into force in November 1946.

Under Article I of its constitution, UNESCO was basically conceived by its founders as complementary to the United Nations:

The purpose of the Organization is to contribute to peace and security by promoting collaboration among the nations through education, science and culture in order to further universal respect for justice, for the rule of law and for the human rights and fundamental freedoms which are affirmed for the peoples of the world, without distinction of race, sex, language or religion, by the Charter of the United Nations.

In accordance with their founding instruments, the United Nations and UNESCO have been responsible for initiating most of the international agreements concerning education that have been adopted since the end of World War II. However, in one important respect their founding instruments were incomplete, because the U.N. Charter in particular (to which the UNESCO Constitution refers) does not actually spell out anywhere what the "human rights and fundamental freedoms" are that the United Nations is mandated "to achieve international cooperation . . . in promoting and encouraging respect for." This task was considered at the time to be too complex for the San Francisco conference to handle, and was therefore deferred until a later date. It was taken up by the United Nations itself shortly after the organization came into being, and was to result in the proclamation of the Universal Declaration of Human Rights by the U.N. General Assembly in December 1948.

In adopting the declaration, the opening words of which affirm that "recognition of the inherent dignity and of the equal and inalienable rights of all members of the human family is the foundation of freedom, justice and peace in the world," countries have accepted a set of principles, covering a vast range of human endeavor, that the organizations of the United Nations system are required under their statutes to encourage member states to put into practice. The principles directly relating to education are set out in the declaration's Article 26:

(1) Everyone has the right to education. Education shall be free, at least in the elementary and fundamental stages. Elementary education shall be compulsory. Technical and professional education shall be made generally available and higher education shall be equally accessible to all on the basis of merit. (2) Education shall be directed towards the full development of the human personality and to the strengthening of respect for human rights and fundamental freedoms. It shall promote understanding, tolerance and friendship among all nations,

racial or religious groups, and shall further the activities of the United Nations for the maintenance of peace. (3) Parents have a prior right to choose the kind of education that shall be given to their children.

Virtually all international agreements concerning education adopted since 1948 have owed at least part of their contents to this article, whether or not the agreement has been specifically focused on human rights or on related questions of international concern such as peace and development.

The agreements fall into two groups: those that deal with education along with several other fields, and those that essentially are confined to education. The former correspond broadly to the agreements adopted under the auspices of the United Nations, and the latter to those adopted under the auspices of UNESCO. A comprehensive listing of the various agreements follows, with brief comments on selected aspects of their contents. Particular attention is given to the treaties, since they represent the strongest degree of commitment by countries.

United Nations agreements. The agreements adopted under the United Nations' auspices are considered first, beginning with the treaties. The three main treaties that contain provisions concerning education are the International Covenant on Economic, Social and Cultural Rights (1966), the Convention on the Elimination of All Forms of Discrimination against Women (1979), and the Convention on the Rights of the Child (1989). Another treaty, the Convention on the Elimination of All Forms of Racial Discrimination (1965), requires the states parties (nations that have ratified a covenant or convention) to eliminate "racial discrimination in all its forms" in regard to "the right to education and training," among several other rights, but does not elaborate further on the matter.

The International Covenant on Economic, Social and Cultural Rights (1966) has a much broader scope than the other treaties. It emerged directly from the process of drawing up the Universal Declaration of Human Rights, following a decision of the United Nations Economic and Social Council that the principles enunciated in the declaration should be transformed into treaty provisions establishing legal obligations on the part of each ratifying state. The prevailing view was that two separate treaties or covenants were needed, one dealing with civil and political rights, and the other with economic, social,

and cultural rights, the rationale being that civil and political rights could, in principle, be secured immediately, whereas economic, social, and cultural rights could be achieved only progressively, according to each state's available resources. The preparation of the International Covenant of Civil and Political Rights and the International Covenant of Economic, Social and Cultural Rights was very laborious, given the legal issues involved for each member state, and took nearly eighteen years. The covenants were adopted in their final form by the General Assembly in December 1966. Another decade was to pass before they came into force. They have substantially influenced all subsequent international treaties relating to human rights.

The Covenant of Civil and Political Rights mentions education in paragraph 4 of its Article 18, which declares that "The States Parties to the present Covenant undertake to have respect for the liberty of parents and moral education of their children in conformity with their own convictions." Article 13 of the Covenant on Economic, Social, and Cultural Rights basically restates paragraph of 4 of Article 18 of the Covenant on Civil and Political Rights. However, there are certain differences. Thus, it provides for "the progressive introduction of free education" in secondary and higher education, and requires the states parties to the covenant "to have respect for the liberty" of parents and guardians "to choose for their children schools, other than those established by the public authorities, that conform to such minimum educational standards as may be laid down or approved by the State." It also requires the states parties to recognize that "the development of a system of schools at all levels shall be actively pursued, an adequate fellowship system shall be established, and the material conditions of teaching staff shall be continuously improved." Under Article 14, the states parties that have not already instituted a system of free and compulsory primary education undertake to do so "within a reasonable number of years." As of February 8, 2002, the covenant had been ratified by 145 states.

The other two treaties mentioned above were intended to focus on particular categories of persons deemed to be especially in need of support and protection. The Convention on the Elimination of All Forms of Discrimination against Women (1979) deals with education in its Article 10. The provisions of this article are based in part on the Covenant on Economic, Social and Cultural Rights, as well as an earlier UNESCO convention (the 1960 Convention against Discrimination in Education), but they enumerate in detail specific conditions that the states parties shall apply in order to "ensure" to women "equal rights with men," such as "the same conditions for career and vocational guidance, for access to studies and for the achievement of diplomas in educational establishments of all categories, . . . access to the same curricula, the same examinations, teaching staff with qualifications of the same standard and school premises and equipment of the same quality, . . . the elimination of any stereotyped concept of the roles of men and women at all levels and in all forms of education," as well as several other conditions of a similar nature. As of February 8, 2002, this convention had been ratified by 168 states.

The Convention on the Rights of the Child (1989) deals with education in Articles 28 and 29. Article 28 is largely a development of Article 13 of the International Covenant on Economic, Social and Cultural Rights, while focusing specifically on the child (essentially defined as a person below eighteen years of age). However, it differs from the covenant by certain omissions and additions. A significant omission is any mention of the "progressive introduction of free education" in respect to higher education. The convention states simply that higher education shall be made "accessible to all on the basis of capacity by every appropriate means." A significant addition is the requirement that states parties take action with a view to achieving the right of the child to education "on the basis of equal opportunity," a notion that first appeared in an international instrument in UNESCO's constitution. Another addition is the requirement that "States Parties shall take all appropriate measures to ensure that school discipline is administered in a manner consistent with the child's human dignity and in conformity with the present Convention." Yet another addition is the requirement that "States Parties shall promote and encourage international cooperation in matters relating to education, in particular with a view to contributing to the elimination of ignorance and illiteracy throughout the world and facilitating access to scientific and technical knowledge and modern teaching methods. In this regard, particular account shall be taken of the needs of developing countries." Article 29 deals mainly with the purposes of education. It basically reiterates the provisions of the covenant, but adds that "States Parties

agree that the education of the child shall be directed to . . . the development of respect for the child's parents, his or her own cultural identity, language and values, for the national values of the country in which the child is living, the country from which he or she may originate, and for civilizations different from his or her own," as well as "the development of respect for the natural environment." As of February 8, 2002, this convention had been ratified by 191 states—all the member states of the United Nations except for Somalia and the United States of America.

The main declarations adopted by the United Nations containing provisions concerning education are the Declaration of the Rights of the Child (1959); the Declaration on the Promotion among Youth of the Ideals of Peace, Mutual Respect and Understanding between Peoples (1965); the Declaration on the Elimination of Discrimination against Women (1967); the Declaration on Social Progress and Development (1969); the Declaration on the Rights of Mentally Retarded Persons (1971); the Declaration on the Rights of Disabled Persons (1975); the Declaration on the Rights of Persons Belonging to National or Ethnic, Religious and Linguistic Minorities (1992); the Declaration and Programme of Action on a Culture of Peace (1999); and the Millennium Declaration (2000). In addition, certain other declarations containing provisions concerning education have been adopted by international conferences of states convened by the United Nations, notably the Proclamation of Teheran adopted by the International Conference on Human Rights (1968); the Rio Declaration on the Environment and Development (1992); the Vienna Declaration and Programme of Action of the World Conference on Human Rights (1993); the Declaration and Programme of Action of the World Summit for Social Development (1995); and the Beijing Declaration and Platform of Action of the Fourth World Conference on Women (1995).

As their titles indicate, the various declarations fall into two broad categories: those focusing on human rights as such and/or the rights of a particular class of persons (e.g., children, women, mentally retarded and disabled persons, persons belonging to various kinds of minorities) deemed to be especially in need of protection and support; and those focusing on particular aspects of the international context (e.g., peace, development, and the environment). Certain of the declarations in the first category were followed up later by treaties (e.g., Rights of the

Child, Elimination of Discrimination against Women). The declarations in the second category have been less amenable to follow-up by treaties, in part because they deal with matters that have been much more open to ideological and political disagreement among countries. Particularly during the cold war, declarations and resolutions of the United Nations concerning peace were open to controversy over the relative priority, if any, to be accorded to peace versus human rights. The declarations relating to the environment and social development, however, have been relatively free of controversy.

The United Nations General Assembly has also from time to time adopted resolutions proclaiming an *International Day, Year,* or *Decade* relating to education, the purpose being to focus world opinion on a particular aspect of education considered to be deserving of attention and support. Examples include International Literacy Day (September 8), World Teachers Day (October 5), International Literacy Year (1990), and United Nations Decade for Human Rights Education (1995–2004).

UNESCO agreements. Turning to the international agreements adopted under UNESCO's auspices, it may first be noted that UNESCO undertook to convene the International Conferences on Public Education jointly with the IBE from 1947 onwards, thus assuming a share of the responsibility for the recommendations adopted by these conferences. The IBE was formally incorporated into UNESCO in 1969, after which the conferences were convened biennially (as International Conferences on Education) up until 1997, and irregularly since then. The International Institute of Intellectual Co-operation, which had been partly involved with education before the war, closed down at the end of 1946.

UNESCO has adopted three international and several regional treaties directly concerning education. The international treaties are the Convention against Discrimination in Education (1960); the Protocol Instituting a Conciliation and Good Offices Commission to Be Responsible for Seeking the Settlement of Any Disputes which may Arise between States Parties to the Convention against Discrimination in Education (1962); and the Convention on Technical and Vocational Education (1989). The regional treaties are agreements relating to the recognition of studies, diplomas, and degrees in higher education.

Two early treaties indirectly relating to education may be noted: the so-called Beirut and Florence Agreements adopted by UNESCO's General Conference at its third and fifth sessions held, respectively, in those two cities. Their titles indicate their nature: the Agreement for Facilitating the International Circulation of Visual and Auditory Materials of an Educational, Scientific and Cultural Character (1948); and the Agreement on the Importation of Educational, Scientific and Cultural Materials (1950). Although both are designed to promote international cooperation in education, science and culture, they are essentially concerned with reducing tariff, tax, currency, and trade obstacles to the international circulation of the materials indicated in their titles, and thus are, in effect, tariff and trade instruments falling within the scope of the World Trade Organization. With the expansion of electronic commerce in education (cross-border distance education), the two instruments are likely to become better known to national educational policymakers in the future.

The Convention against Discrimination in Education (1960) was the first international treaty to be adopted concerning education as such, except for the London treaty that established UNESCO. It was basically designed to transform the principle of nondiscrimination contained in Article 2 of the Universal Declaration of Human Rights into legal obligations pertaining specifically to education, while also taking into account the provisions of the declaration's Article 26 concerning the right to education, as well as the principle of "equality of educational opportunity" affirmed in UNESCO's constitution. The convention influenced the provisions relating to discrimination in education that subsequently came to be included in all international treaties concerned wholly or partly with education, from the Convention on the Elimination of All Forms of Racial Discrimination (1965) down to the Convention on the Rights of the Child (1989). It was also the first international treaty to contain provisions dealing with parental choice and the rights of minorities in education, and in this regard its provisions remain the most comprehensive of any international treaty. As of February 8, 2002, this Convention had been ratified by eighty-four states. The protocol associated with the convention provides for the setting up of a mechanism for dealing with any charges that might be leveled by one country against another accusing it of bad faith in ratifying the convention but not attempting to implement it. As of February 8, 2002, the protocol had been ratified by thirty states.

The Convention on Technical and Vocational Education (1989) is the only international convention ever adopted concerning a specific level or sub-field of education. It was partly inspired by the provision in Article 26 of the Universal Declaration of Human Rights affirming that "technical and professional education shall be made generally available," and partly by an earlier initiative of the International Labour Organization, which in 1975 had adopted a Convention and Recommendation on Vocational Guidance and Vocational Training. At that time, UNESCO had already adopted (in 1974) its Revised Recommendation concerning Technical and Vocational Education, but not yet a convention. Many of the provisions of UNESCO's convention are in the nature of prescriptions or recommendations, rather than actions that the states parties specifically agree to undertake. As of February 8, 2002, this convention had been ratified by twelve states.

Aside from the treaties, and unlike the United Nations, UNESCO has historically tended to adopt recommendations rather than declarations. The main recommendations concerning education adopted by UNESCO's General Conference are the Recommendation concerning the International Standardization of Educational Statistics (1958); the Recommendation against Discrimination in Education (1960; adopted at the same time as the Convention mentioned above); the Recommendation concerning Technical and Vocational Education (1962); the Recommendation concerning the Status of Teachers (1966); the Recommendation concerning Education for International Understanding, Co-operation and Peace and Education relating to Human Rights and Fundamental Freedoms (1974); the Revised Recommendation concerning Technical and Vocational Education (1974); the Recommendation on the Development of Adult Education (1976); the Revised Recommendation concerning the International Standardization of Educational Statistics (1978); the Recommendation on the Recognition of Studies and Qualifications in Higher Education (1993); and the Recommendation concerning the Status of Higher Education Teaching Personnel (1997). The purpose of these recommendations, as of those adopted by the International Conferences on (Public) Education, has essentially been to encourage countries to adopt wise policies and good practices in the relevant fields. Their adoption by UNESCO's General Conference has been intended to give them more weight and validity than the recommendations of the International Conferences on (Public) Education, since the former body is a conference of states, while the latter are basically just conferences of ministers of education. As indicated in the titles of some of the recommendations, it has been understood that the recommended policies and practices might need to be reconsidered later in the light of experience and changes in national and international circumstances.

From time to time UNESCO's General Conference has also adopted resolutions that amount in effect to revised recommendations, though without being formally declared as such. In 1997, for example, it endorsed a new International Standard Classification of Education (ISCED-97) intended to replace an earlier version that had been endorsed by the Revised Recommendation concerning the International Standardization of Educational Statistics (1978).

UNESCO did not issue any recommendations concerning education during the 1980s. This was a period of controversy for the organization, marked by the withdrawal of the United States from the organization at the end of 1984 and the United Kingdom and Singapore at the end of 1985, in protest against what U.S. Secretary of State George Schultz, in his letter of withdrawal, said were "trends in the policy, ideological emphasis, budget and manpower of UNESCO [that] were detracting from the organization's effectiveness [and were leading the organization] away from the original principles of its constitution." A definitive study of the merit of these charges has never been made, although in regard to education it may be noted that after the end of the cold war UNESCO became more active in seeking to collaborate with other international organizations for the purposes of advancing its program in areas such as education for development and education for human rights. Two significant international agreements that were to result from this were the World Declaration on Education for All (1990) and the World Plan of Action on Education for Human Rights and Democracy (1993), adopted by the International Congress on Education for Human Rights and Democracy, held in Montreal. The Salamanca Statement (Declaration) on Special Needs Education (1994), adopted by the World Conference on Special Needs Education (jointly convened by UNESCO and the Spanish government in Salamanca, Spain, in June 1994) may also be noted, as well as a follow-up declaration (the Dakar Declaration on Education for

All) to the Jomtien Declaration mentioned above, adopted by the World Education Forum, an international conference convened by UNESCO jointly with its Jomtien partners in Dakar, Senegal, in April 2000.

Implementation and Impact

A comprehensive study of the implementation and impact of the various international education agreements indicated above has never been undertaken. Since there are so many of these agreements, all of them overlapping to some extent, and all of them having varying degrees of support from the countries of the world, such a study would in any case be an extremely complex undertaking. Although UNESCO, under its constitutional mandate, could undertake such a study, it has largely confined its monitoring activity to the agreements adopted directly under its auspices. Monitoring of the various agreements adopted by the United Nations has been undertaken by the several treaty bodies established by the United Nations for that purpose. Their activities can be consulted at the website of the United Nations High Commissioner for Human Rights.

There are limits to the effectiveness of the existing monitoring mechanisms. The main ones are the dependence of these mechanisms on government-supplied information and the different degrees of readiness and capability of governments to supply information. Indeed, with the growing number of international agreements in education and other fields, there are signs of a *reporting overload* on governments. Thus, questionnaire surveys addressed by the monitoring bodies to the states parties to some of these agreements rarely elicit responses from more than half the countries concerned. Neither the United Nations nor UNESCO can do much about this, since the agreements are, in the last resort, purely voluntary, and both organizations are bound by their constitutions not "to intervene in matters which are essentially within the domestic jurisdiction of any state." It is only in countries with highly developed legal systems, as in western Europe, that ordinary citizens can effectively challenge their governments on questions relating to the implementation of international agreements, whether in education or other fields.

What, then, do they all add up to? Have the agreements had any effect on the worldwide development of education? Probably. The development that has occurred over the years since the Universal Declaration of Human Rights was proclaimed has certainly been dramatic. In the late 1940s, only a minority of the world's young people had access to any kind of formal education, and little more than half the world's adults could read and write a simple passage about their everyday lives. In the early twenty-first century the great majority of the world's young people go to school, with nearly half of them enrolled in formal education beyond the elementary and fundamental stages, while around four out of five of the world's adults (though a larger percentage of men than of women) are estimated to have acquired at least some simple literacy skills. Doubtless much of this development would have occurred without any international agreements concerning education, but it is reasonable to suggest that the steady accumulation of such agreements, constituting, in effect, a broadly coherent body of international opinion committed to the expansion and equalization of educational opportunities, would have reinforced any secular trends (for example, rising income levels) tending to favor such development. The more that such agreements keep coming, each one affirming one or another aspect of the right to education, then the more difficult it becomes morally for countries to disregard this right.

Nevertheless, it is apparent that there is considerable variation among individual agreements in the degree of commitment that countries accord to their implementation, even among the treaties. Compare, for example, the Convention on Technical and Vocational Education (1990), with only twelve ratifications to date, and the Convention on the Rights of the Child, adopted in the same year, with 191 ratifications. It is also apparent that some agreements basically restate long-standing, but not fully implemented, earlier commitments. For example, both the Dakar Declaration on Education for All (2000) and the United Nations' Millennium Declaration (2000) expect universal primary education to be achieved in all countries by the year 2015, although the World Declaration on Education for All (1990) had earlier targeted the year 2000. The danger here is of a progressive devaluation of all education agreements if new ones are too readily adopted ahead of significant progress in implementing earlier ones.

BIBLIOGRAPHY

HOUSE OF COMMONS. 1985. *Fifth Report from the Foreign Affairs Committee, Session 1984–85, United Kingdom Membership of UNESCO, Re-*

port, Together with the Proceedings of the Committee; Minutes of Evidence; and Appendices. London: Her Majesty's Stationary Office.

JOHNSON, M. GLEN., and SYMONIDES, JANUSZ. 1998. *The Universal Declaration of Human Rights: A History of its Creation and Implementation, 1948–1998.* Paris: United Nations Educational, Scientific and Cultural Organization.

RENOLIET, JEAN-JACQUES. 1999. *L'UNESCO oubliée: La Société des Nations et la coopération intellectuelle (1919–1946)* (The forgotten UNESCO: The League of Nations and intellectual cooperation). Paris: Publications de la Sorbonne.

ROSSELLÓ, PEDRO. 1970. "Historical Note." In *UNESCO/IBE, International Conferences on Public Education: Recommendations.* Paris: United Nations Educational, Scientific and Cultural Organization.

SUCHOLDOLSKI, BOGDAN, et al. 1979. *The International Bureau of Education in the Service of National Development.* Paris: United Nations Educational, Scientific and Cultural Organization.

UNITED NATIONS EDUCATIONAL, SCIENTIFIC AND CULTURAL ORGANIZATION. 2000. *World Education Report 2000. The Right to Education: Towards Education for All Throughout Life.* Paris: United Nations Educational, Scientific and Cultural Organization.

UNITED STATES CONGRESS, 98TH SESSION. 1984. *U.S. Withdrawal from UNESCO. Report of a Staff Study Mission, February 10–23, 1984, to the Committee on Foreign Affairs, U.S. House of Representatives.* Washington, DC: U.S. House of Representatives, Committee on Foreign Affairs.

VALDERAMA, FERNANDO. 1995. *A History of UNESCO.* Paris: United Nations Educational, Scientific and Cultural Organization.

INTERNET RESOURCES

UNITED NATIONS. 2002. "United Nations Documents: Research Guide." <www.un.org/Depts/dhl/resguide/resins.htm>.

UNITED NATIONS EDUCATIONAL, SCIENTIFIC AND CULTURAL ORGANIZATION. 2002. "Standard Setting Instruments and Orientation Texts." <www.unesco.org/education/html/norms.shtml>.

UNITED NATIONS HIGH COMMISSIONER FOR HUMAN RIGHTS. 2002. "Conventional Mecha-

nisms (Treaty Monitoring Bodies)." <www.unhchr.ch/html/menu2/convmech.htm>.

JOHN A. SMYTH

INTERNATIONAL EDUCATION STATISTICS

OVERVIEW
  Eugene Owen
  Laura Hersh Salganik
THE USE OF INDICATORS TO EVALUATE THE CONDITION OF EDUCATION SYSTEMS
  Thomas M. Smith
  David P. Baker

OVERVIEW

Comparisons between the education system in the United States and the systems of other countries have become an established element of the public discussion about education policy and practice in the United States. Publications aimed at the education profession often include articles describing approaches in other countries that are relevant to education in the United States, such as a discussion of tuition tax credits in Canada in *Education Week* and a special section in the *Phi Delta Kappan* about early childhood education in Europe.

Why is this information useful? Simply put, countries outside the United States provide something akin to a natural social laboratory in which one can observe education policy, practices, and outcomes under a variety of different conditions and environments. Knowing whether education in one country is the same or different from education in other countries provides a useful perspective for better understanding a country's system, and is also a useful source of ideas. Comparisons of learning outcomes provide a measure of the effectiveness not possible with any other approach. Given the prominent role of statistics and indicators for policymaking in the United States, it is not surprising that statistics have become an important source of information for these comparisons. At the beginning of the twenty-first century rich sources of statistics are available that can be used to compare education in the United States with education in other countries. But this is a relatively new development.

The Demand for International Education Statistics

As is the case for many aspects of history of education in the United States since the mid-1980s, the publication of *A Nation at Risk* in 1983 was a key event for setting the stage for change—in this case for strengthening international education statistics. A steady decline in national test scores during the 1960s and 1970s, coupled with the perception that foreign industrial and consumer products were superior, had led many Americans to question the performance of U.S. schools. An international perspective was central to the argument of *A Nation at Risk,* chief among the many reports prepared to document the problem. Citing the superiority of new manufactured goods from Japan, South Korea, and Germany, as well as the level of worker skill that these foreign products represented, the report proclaimed: "If an unfriendly foreign power had attempted to impose on America the mediocre educational performance that exists today, we might well have viewed it as an act of war" (p. 5). When presenting its list of indicators of the risk facing the country, the poor performance of U.S. students in international studies of achievement was the first item.

A second major event that increased the importance of international comparisons was the adoption of the National Education Goals in 1990. One of the six goals adopted by President George H. W. Bush and the nation's governors was that "by the year 2000, United States students will be first in the world in mathematics and science." Shortly after this announcement, the National Education Goals Panel was created and charged with producing a series of publications aimed at reporting national and state progress toward achieving the goals. This amplified the need to develop performance measures for the U.S. educational system in an international context, particularly in mathematics and science.

During this period, genuine concern about the future of the U.S. economy and the importance of looking outside of the United States for solving problems was a common theme of policy discussions in a variety of arenas. For example, the National Governors Association report *Time for Results* (1986) named global economic competition and poor performance of U.S. students (compared to those of other countries) as reasons why governors should take a more active role in education. *America's Choice: High Skills or Low Wages* (1990), pub-

lished by the National Center on Education and the Economy, presented international comparisons of investment in employment and training policies and called for higher U.S. expenditures in this area.

But in spite of the prominence of international comparisons, it was widely recognized that the data were very weak. The reason that *A Nation at Risk* used studies that were a decade old was that they were the only ones available. Similarly, it was agreed that statistics comparing expenditures for education—which were relevant to perennial questions about costs—were not usable because of their low quality.

Comparability

Why does the international dimension present a particular challenge for statistics of education? The central idea is the notion of comparability. For basic statistics about education at the national level in the United States, there is general agreement about what constitutes the things being measured or counted (e.g., schools, teachers, students, school subjects). Although the decentralization of governance and diversity of approaches and programs require that care be taken when making comparisons among states or local districts, the issue is compounded many times when dealing with making comparisons among countries.

There are many instances in the arena of international education statistics in which differences among countries in fundamental aspects of the system can put statistics in jeopardy of being inaccurate and misleading. In the United States, for example, public schools are financed by public funds and private schools by private funds (at least the vast majority of the funding), whereas many countries in Europe finance privately governed schools with public funds. Thus, counting funding of public schools as a measure of a nation's financial support of education would be misleading. In many countries, it is common for staff considered to be teachers to also function in a position equivalent to a principal in small elementary schools. From the U.S. perspective, counting such staff members as teachers would lead to an overcount of staff resources devoted to teaching, an undercount of resources for administration, and misleading student–teacher ratios. Similarly, achievement tests that do not take differences in curricula and practices associated with testing and test-taking into account may inaccurately represent school learning.

In cases where there are common definitions and concepts, it is of equal importance to collect and process the data in a manner that captures the information desired. This often requires that countries recalculate national statistics based on these common definitions. Issues are even more complex when surveys are involved. For example, countries must agree on common practices for selecting comparable samples, setting acceptable response rates, and calculating response rates and margins of error. Another methodological issue is translation, which requires a high level of understanding of the concepts involved. Translation can even affect the difficulty of test items, a factor requiring attention in the development of international assessments.

During the 1980s, the generally weak comparability of the international education statistics prepared by the United Nations Educational, Scientific and Cultural Organization (UNESCO) and the Organisation for Economic Co-operation and Development (OECD) was well known, and the published works received limited circulation and attention. The comparability of comparative studies of achievement was also routinely questioned. But with the demand created by the introduction of an international aspect to the education policy questions of the day, the need for improvement was clear.

Country Collaboration

The United States was not alone in its interest in improved statistics for comparing education systems. Similar circumstances—particularly pressure on public services to demonstrate their productivity and efficiency and a new awareness of economic competitiveness in a global market—led to a growing interest in education statistics in other OECD countries. The OECD responded to this demand by initiating the Indicators of Education Statistics (INES) program after two preparatory meetings, one hosted by the U.S. Department of Education in 1987, and the other by the French Ministry of Education in 1988.

To improve the quality of international statistics, it was necessary to have the participation of individuals with deep knowledge of their national education systems, access to national data systems, and the motivation and commitment to collaborate on an ongoing basis with those from other countries. The INES project put these elements together. The Netherlands, Scotland, the United States, and Sweden contributed substantial resources to lead working groups on topics such as enrollment in education, finance, learning outcomes, labor force outcomes, school functioning, and attitudes about education. Australia, Austria, and France also made important financial contributions. Meeting at regular intervals, individual delegates, sponsored by their countries, worked through comparability issues and served as contact points in their countries for the preparation and submission of data prepared specifically to meet the international standards. The result was much-improved comparability and a quality-control process that was supported by peer review and the personal commitment of participants in the working groups. In addition, the participants gained expertise that enhanced their countries' resources for interpreting the statistics in a national context.

The OECD had extensive involvement in coordinating the process, collecting the data, and preparing and publishing a series of volumes of indicators under the title *Education at a Glance: OECD Indicators*. The first *Education at a Glance* (1992) was about 150 pages long, with parallel text in French and English, and several of the indicators were designated as provisional because of general questions about their validity or applicability. With succeeding years, new indicators have been added, as well as extensive background information relevant for interpreting the indicators. The 1995 and 1996 editions have annotated charts prepared by each country describing the organization of their education systems, including types and levels of schools and ages of students in each. The 2001 edition is almost 400 pages long, includes data from many non-OECD countries, and is available in English, French, and German. Selected editions of *Education at a Glance* have been translated into Czech, Italian, Japanese, Korean, and Spanish.

The establishment of the Program for International Student Assessment (PISA) highlights the importance of country collaboration in the development of international education statistics. To those working in the INES project, it quickly became clear that there was a lack of coherent data for indicators of student achievement. There was no extant database and no structure designed for governments to collaborate on an ongoing basis for regular data collections. Factors that needed to be overcome included major comparability issues ranging from conceptualization of outcomes to general survey practices; some countries' reluctance to publish indicators of achievement in a limited number of school subjects; and the large cost associated with producing the indicators. After several years of ongoing discussions, a consensus was reached to set up a project in which for the first time, countries shared the central cost of developing and implementing the assessment (countries typically are responsible for the cost of local data collection). The effort is governed by a board composed of representatives of participating countries and managed by the OECD secretariat. It includes assessments at three-year intervals of reading, mathematics, and science literacy, and of selected cross-curricular competencies such as attitudes and approaches related to learning.

Among the many other accomplishments associated with the country collaboration through the INES project, two that stand out are improvements in the comparability of expenditure data and of the categories for different levels of education (e.g., primary, secondary, tertiary). In the case of the levels of education, UNESCO's International Standard Classification of Education (ISCED), developed during the 1970s, was revised to reflect various changes—for example, growth in continuing education and training outside of education institutions and programs that straddle the boundaries between upper secondary and postsecondary education, and a manual was developed to facilitate consistent interpretation of the new system.

Studies conducted by the International Association for the Evaluation of Educational Achievement (IEA) also involve collaboration among governments and researchers. Three studies that have contributed to the data available for international education statistics are the Third International Mathematics and Science Study (TIMSS), the Second Information Technology in Education Study (SITES), and the Civic Education Study (CivEd). The Civic Education Study, working in an area in which different countries have different notions about many of the concepts involved (such as democracy and participation of individuals in democracy), relied heavily on international teams throughout the entire project for identifying common core ideas, developing assessment items, and interpreting results.

What Has Been Learned?

Because of the range and depth of international education statistics, it is impossible to provide more than a very brief summary in this limited space. What follows are a few illustrative highlights taken from publications of the OECD, the IEA, and the U.S. National Center for Education Statistics (NCES). NCES publications include explanatory notes and background information useful for interpreting the material from a U.S. perspective. Readers are encouraged to consult the publications directly to find additional statistics relevant to their particular interests.

Context of education. It is widely recognized that there is a large association between poverty and school achievement. Among a large number of countries participating in one study, the United States had by far the largest percentage of youth who were poor.

Participation in education. Into the 1990s, there was a general impression that the young people remained enrolled in school longer in the United States than in other countries. However, statistics show that the percentage of those fifteen to nineteen years old and those twenty to twenty-nine years old enrolled in education in the United States is quite close to the average percentage among OECD countries.

Expenditures. The United States spends a similar percentage of its gross domestic product (GDP) on education as other countries. On a per pupil basis, its expenditures are among the highest for elementary and secondary education. In higher education, the U.S. also spends considerably more per student than any other OECD country.

Teachers and teaching. Teachers in the United States have the highest number of teaching hours, although teachers in a few other countries put in almost as many hours. The student–teacher ratio in the United States is similar to the average of OECD countries in elementary, secondary, and postsecondary education, with the exception of vocational postsecondary education, where there are fewer students per teacher in the United States than in most other countries.

Learning outcomes for school-age youth. On studies of mathematics and science achievement, U.S. students typically score lower in relation to other countries as they progress through the grades. Performance of fifteen year olds in the United States was similar to the average for countries participating in PISA in reading, mathematics, and science literacy tasks designed to reflect real-life situations (in contrast to school curriculum). Many countries have variation in achievement in the same range as that of the United States, although some have less variation. Some countries with relatively little variation have high achievement, indicating that it is not necessary to "sacrifice" the bottom to have a high average score. Among countries participating in the IEA Civic Education Study, the United States is among the highest in knowledge of civic content among fourteen year olds, as well as the highest in civic skills, such as interpreting information.

States and nations. Because states have primary responsibility for education in the United States and are similar in size to many countries, comparisons between the states and other nations are of special interest to policymakers. Some U.S. states and school districts compare favorably in math and science with the highest-scoring countries, while others have scores in the same range as the lowest-performing ones. This pattern is repeated in other indicators that include both states and nations.

Adult literacy. Variation in adult literacy is strongly associated with income variation—countries that have a wider income distribution also have a higher percentage of adults in both high- and low-literacy groups, with the United States having the highest variation in both income and literacy.

Conclusion

Increased demand in the mid-1980s for data to support solid comparisons among the education systems of different countries fueled major advances in the quality and quantity of international education statistics. These advances would not have been possible without an organizational structure that incorporated collaborative working relationships among statisticians and education professionals from different countries. This model was essential throughout the many phases of the work, including agreeing on common definitions of the concepts to be represented by statistics, developing methodologies for surveys and translation, and generating commitment and adherence to high standards and quality control. It will continue to be important to assure comparability as work proceeds to improve and broaden statistics in areas such as learning outcomes for students and adults, expenditures for education, teachers and teaching, and the relationship between education and the labor market.

See also: INTERNATIONAL ASSESSMENTS; NATIONAL CENTER FOR EDUCATION STATISTICS.

BIBLIOGRAPHY

BALDI, STEPHANIE; PERIE, MARIANNE; SKIDMORE, DAN; GREENBERG, ELIZABETH; and HAHN, CAROLE. 2001. *What Democracy Means to Ninth Graders: U.S. Results from the International IEA Civic Education Study.* Washington, DC: U.S. Government Printing Office.

BARRO, STEPHEN. 1997. *International Education Expenditure Study: Final Report,* Vol. I: *Quantitative Analysis of Expenditure Comparability.* Washington, DC: National Center for Education Statistics.

BOTTANI, NORBERTO. 2001. "Editorial." *Politiques d'Education et de Fromation: Analyses et Comparaisons Internationale* 3(3):7–12.

BOTTANI, NORBERTO, and TUIJNMAN, ALBERT. 1994. "International Education Indicators: Framework, Development, and Interpretation." In *Making Education Count: Developing and Using International Indicators,* ed. Norberto Bottani and Albert Tuijnman. Paris: Organisation for Economic Co-operation and Development.

GUILFORD, DOROTHY, ed. 1993. *A Collaborative Agenda for Improving International Comparative Studies in Education.* Washington, DC: National Academy Press.

HEYNEMAN, STEPHEN P. 1999. "The Sad Story of UNESCO's Education Statistics." *International Journal of Educational Development* 19:65–74.

INTERNATIONAL STUDY CENTER AT BOSTON COLLEGE. 2001. *TIMSS 1999 Benchmarking Highlights.* Boston: International Study Center at Boston College.

LEMKE, MARIANN; BAIRU, GHEDAM; CALSYN, CHRISTOPHER; LIPPMAN, LAURA; JOCELYN, LESLIE; KASTBERG, DAVID; LIU, YUN; ROEY, STEPHEN; WILLIAMS, TREVOR; and KRUGER, THEA. 2001. *Outcomes of Learning: Results from the 2000 Program for International Student Assessment of 15-Year-Olds in Reading, Mathematics, and Science Literacy.* Washington, DC: U.S. Government Printing Office.

LUBECK, SALLY, ed. 2001. "Early Childhood Education and Care in Cross-National Perspective." *Phi Delta Kappan* 83(3):213–254.

MATHESON, NANCY; SALGANIK, LAURA H.; PHELPS, RICHARD P.; PERIE, MARIANNE; ALSALAM, NABEEL; and SMITH, THOMAS M. 1996. *Education Indicators: An International Perspective.* Washington, DC: U.S. Government Printing Office.

MEDRICH, ELLIOTT A., and GRIFFITH, JEANNE E. 1992. *International Mathematics and Science Assessments: What Have We Learned.* Washington, DC: National Center for Education Statistics.

NATIONAL CENTER ON EDUCATION AND THE ECONOMY. 1990. *America's Choice: High Skills or Low Wages! The Report of The Commission on the Skills of the American Workforce.* Washington, DC: National Center on Education and the Economy.

NATIONAL COMMISSION ON EXCELLENCE IN EDUCATION. 1983. *A Nation at Risk.* Washington, DC: U.S. Government Printing Office.

NATIONAL EDUCATION GOALS PANEL. 1999. *The National Education Goals Report: Building a Nation of Learners.* Washington, DC: National Education Goals Panel.

NATIONAL GOVERNORS ASSOCIATION. 1986. *Time for Results: The Governors' 1991 Report on Education.* Washington, DC: National Governors' Association. (ERIC Document Reproduction Service No. ED279603).

ORGANISATION FOR ECONOMIC CO-OPERATION AND DEVELOPMENT. 1999. *Classifying Educational Programmes: Manual for ISCED-97 Implementation in OECD Countries.* Paris: Organisation for Economic Co-operation and Development.

ORGANISATION FOR ECONOMIC CO-OPERATION AND DEVELOPMENT. 2001a. *Education at a Glance: OECD Indicators.* Paris: Organisation for Economic Co-operation and Development.

ORGANISATION FOR ECONOMIC CO-OPERATION AND DEVELOPMENT. 2001b. *Knowledge and Skills for Life: First Results from PISA 2000.* Paris: Organisation for Economic Co-operation and Development.

ORGANISATION FOR ECONOMIC CO-OPERATION AND DEVELOPMENT and STATISTICS CANADA. 2000. *Literacy in the Information Age: Final Report of the International Adult Literacy Survey.* Paris: Organisation for Economic Co-operation and Development.

PHELPS, RICHARD; SMITH, THOMAS M.; and ALSALAM, NABEEL. 1996. *Education in States and Nations: Indicators Comparing U.S. States with Other Industrialized Countries in 1991.* Washington, DC: U.S. Government Printing Office.

SAUVAGEOT, CLAUDE. 2001. "Un outil au service des comparaisons internationale: CITE (ISCED)." *Politiques d'Education et de Formation: Analyses et Comparaisons Internationale* 3(3):95–118.

SHERMAN, JOEL. 1997. *International Education Expenditure Study: Final Report,* Vol. II: *Quantitative Analysis of Expenditure Comparability.* Washington, DC: National Center for Education Statistics.

TORNEY-PURTA, JUDITH; LEHMANN, RAINER; OSWALD, HANS; and SCHULZ, WOLFRAM. 2001. *Citizenship and Education in Twenty-Eight Countries: Civic Knowledge and Engagement at Age Fourteen.* Amsterdam: Eburon.

U.S. DEPARTMENT OF EDUCATION, NATIONAL CENTER FOR EDUCATION STATISTICS. 1998. *The Condition of Education, 1998 (NCES 98-013).* Washington, DC: U.S. Government Printing Office.

U.S. DEPARTMENT OF EDUCATION, NATIONAL CENTER FOR EDUCATION STATISTICS. 2000. *The Condition of Education 2000 (NCES 2000-062).* Washington, DC: U.S. Government Printing Office.

U.S. DEPARTMENT OF EDUCATION, NATIONAL CENTER FOR EDUCATION STATISTICS. 2001a. *The Digest of Education, 2000 (NCES 2001-034),* by T. Snyder. Production Manager, C. M. Hoffman. Washington, DC: U.S. Government Printing Office.

U.S. DEPARTMENT OF EDUCATION, NATIONAL CENTER FOR EDUCATION STATISTICS. 2001b. *The Condition of Education 2001.* Washington, DC: U.S. Government Printing Office.

U.S. DEPARTMENT OF EDUCATION, NATIONAL CENTER FOR EDUCATION STATISTICS. 2002. *The Digest of Education Statistics 2001.* Washington, DC: U.S. Government Printing Office.

INTERNET RESOURCES

INTERNATIONAL ASSOCIATION FOR THE EVALUATION OF EDUCATIONAL ACHIEVEMENT. 2002. <www.iea.nl>.

NATIONAL CENTER FOR EDUCATION STATISTICS. 2002. <www.nces.ed.gov>.

EUGENE OWEN
LAURA HERSH SALGANIK

THE USE OF INDICATORS TO EVALUATE THE CONDITION OF EDUCATION SYSTEMS

The use of widely published *statistical indicators* (also referred to as *social indicators* outside the purely economic realm) of the condition of national education systems has in the early twenty-first century become a standard part of the policymaking process throughout the world. Uniquely different from the usual policy-related statistical analysis, statistical indicators are derived measures, often combining multiple data sources and several statistics, that are uniformly developed across nations, repeated regularly over time, and have come to be accepted as summarizing the condition of an underlying complex process. Perhaps the best known among all statistical indicators is the gross national product, which is derived from a statistical formula that summarizes all of the business activity of a nation's economy into one meaningful number. In the closing decades of the twentieth century, international statistical indicators of educational processes made considerable advances in quantity, quality, and acceptance among policymakers.

These cross-national indicators often have significant impact on both the public and the education establishment. In the United States, for example, the *New York Times* gives high visibility to reports based on indicators of where American students rank in the latest international math or science tests, or those revealing how educational expenditures per student, teacher salaries, or high school dropout rates compare across countries. National education ministries or departments frequently use press releases to put their own spin on statistical indicator reports such as the annual *Education at a Glance* (EAG), published by the Organisation for Economic Co-operation and Development (OECD). The use of indicators for comparisons and strategic mobilization has become a regular part of educational politics. Dutch teachers, for example, used these indicators to lobby for increases in their salaries after the 1996 EAG indicators of teacher salaries showed that they were not paid as well as their Belgian and German neighbors. Similarly, in the United States, comparisons of a statistical indicator of dropout rates across nations were used to highlight comparatively low high school completion rates in 2000. In an extreme, but illustrative, case, one nation's incumbent political party requested that the publication of the EAG be delayed until after parliamentary

election because of the potentially damaging news about how its education system compared to other OECD nations.

These examples of the widespread impact of international education statistical indicators are all the more interesting when one considers that an earlier attempt to set up a system of international statistical indicators of education during the 1970s failed. While attempts to create a national, and then an international, system of social indicators (known as the *social indicators movement*) faltered, early attempts by the OECD to develop statistical indicators on education systems fell apart as idealism about the utility of a technical-functionalist approach to education planning receded.

History of Social Indicators

The social indicators movement, born in the early 1960s, attempted to establish a "system of social accounts," that would allow for cost-benefit analyses of the social components of expenditures already indexed in the National Income and Product Accounts. Many academics and policy makers were concerned about the social costs of economic growth, and social indicators were seen as a means to monitor the social impacts of economic expenditures. *Social indicators* are defined as time series that are used to monitor the social system, which help to identify change and to guide efforts to adjust the course of social change. Examples of social indicators include unemployment rates, crime rates, estimates of life expectancy, health status indices such as the average number of "health days" in the past month, rates of voting in elections, measures of subjective well-being, and education measures such as school enrollment rates and achievement test scores.

Enthusiasm for social indicators led to the establishment of the Social Science Research Council (SSRC) Center for Coordination of Research on Social Indicators in 1972 (funded by the National Science Foundation) and the initiation of several continuing sample surveys, including the General Social Survey (GSS) and the National Crime Survey (NCS). As reporting mechanisms, the Census Bureau published three comprehensive social indicators data and chart books in 1974, 1978, and 1980. The academic community launched the international journal *Social Indicators Research* in 1974. Many other nations and international agencies also produced indicator volumes of their own during this period. In the 1980s, however, federal funding cuts led to the discontinuation of numerous comprehensive national and international social indicators activities, including closing the SSRC Center. Some have argued that a shift away from data-based decision making towards policy based on conservative ideology during the Reagan administration, coupled with a large budget deficit, helped to pull the financial plug on the social indicators movement. While field-specific indicators continue to be published by government agencies in areas such as education, labor, health, crime, housing, science, and agriculture, the systematic public reporting envisioned in the 1960s has largely not been sustained, although comprehensive surveys of the condition of youth have arisen in both the public and private spheres, such as those by the Annie E. Casey Foundation (2001) and the Forum on Child and Family Statistics (2001).

Some of the main data collections that grew out of the social indicators movement, including the GSS and NCS, continue, as do a range of longitudinal and cross-sectional surveys in other social areas. On the academic side, a literature involving social indicators has continued to grow, mostly focused on quality-of-life issues. While education is seen as a component of quality of life, it tends to be used in a fairly rudimentary fashion. For example, out of 331 articles published in *Social Indicators Research* between 1994 and 2000, only twenty-six addressed education with any depth. And although the widely cited Human Development Index compiled by the United Nations Development Programme has education and literacy components, these are limited to basic measures of school enrollments and, arguably, non-comparable country-level estimates of literacy rates, which are often based on census questions about whether someone can read or write. As a subfield of social indicators, however, the collection and reporting of education statistics has expanded rapidly since the early 1980s in the United States, the early 1990s in OECD countries, and, more recently, in developing countries.

State of International Education Statistical Indicators Today

Among the current array of statistical indicators of education within and across nations are some that go far beyond the basic structural characteristics and resource inputs, such as student-teacher enrollment ratios and expenditures per student, found in statistical almanacs. More data-intensive and statistically complex indicators of participation in education, financial investments, decision-making procedures, public attitudes towards education, differences in curriculum and textbooks, retention and dropout rates in tertiary (higher) education, and student achievement in math, science, reading, and civics have become standard parts of indicators reports. For example, the OECD summarizes total education enrollment through an indicator on the average years of schooling that a 5-year-old child can expect under current conditions, which is calculated by summing the net enrollment rates for each single year of age and dividing by one hundred. Unlike the gross enrollment ratios (calculated as total enrollment in a particular level of education, regardless of age, divided by the size of the population in the "official" age group corresponding to that level) that have traditionally been reported in UNESCO statistical yearbooks, the *schooling expectancy* measures reported by the OECD aggregate across levels of education and increase comparability by weighting enrollment by the size of the population that is actually eligible to enroll.

Examples of other indicators that attempt to summarize complex issues into concise numerical indices include measures of individual and societal rates of return of investments in different levels of education, measures of factors contributing to differences in relative statutory teachers' salary costs per student, and *effort indexes* for education funding, which adjust measures of public and private expenditures per student by per capita wealth. Furthermore, the OECD is working to develop assessment and reporting mechanisms to compare students' problem-solving skills, their ability to work in groups, and their technology skills. There are few components of the world education enterprise that statisticians, psychometricians, and survey methodologists are not trying to measure and put into summary indicator forms for public consumption.

High-quality indicators require data that are accurate and routinely available. Behind the creation of so many high-quality indicators of national education systems is the routine collection of a wide array of education data in most industrialized countries. In addition to the costs of gathering data and information for national purposes, a large amount of human and financial investment is made to ensure that the data meet standards of comparability across countries. Country-level experts, whether from statistical or policy branches of governments, frequently convene to discuss the kinds of data that should be collected, to reach consensus on the most methodologically sound means of collecting the data, and to construct indicators.

Growth and Institutionalization of International Data Collections

Numerous international organizations collect and report education data, with the range of data types expanding and the complexity of collection and analysis increasing. Hence, the total cost of these collections has increased dramatically since 1990. Government financial support, and in some cases control, has been a significant component of this growth in both the sophistication of data and the scope of collections. Briefly described here are some of the basic institutional components involved in the creation of a set of international organizations or organizational structures that provide the institutional infrastructure for creating and sustaining international education statistical indicators.

IEA. Collaboration on international assessments began as early as the late 1950s when a group composed primarily of academics formed the International Association for the Evaluation of Educational Achievement (IEA). In 1965, twelve countries undertook the First International Mathematics Study. Since that time, the IEA has conducted fourteen different assessments covering the topics of mathematics, science, reading, civics, and technology. Findings from IEA's Second International Mathematics Study were the primary justification for the finding in the early 1980s that the United States was a "nation at risk." In the 1990s, government ministries of education became increasingly important for both funding and priority setting in these studies.

The results of the Third International Mathematics and Science Study (TIMSS) were widely reported in the United States and served as fuel for the latest educational reform efforts. As governments became increasingly involved in setting the IEA agenda, some key aspects of the research orientation of earlier surveys were no longer funded (e.g., the pre-test/post-test design in the Second International Science Study), while other innovative activities were added. For example, the TIMSS video study conducted in Germany, Japan, and the United States applied some of the most cutting-edge research technology to international assessments. As part of the 1999 repeat of TIMSS (TIMSS-R), additional coun-

tries have agreed to have their teachers videotaped and science classrooms have been added to the mix.

Over time, the IEA assessments have become more methodologically complex, with TIMSS employing the latest testing technology (e.g., item response theory [IRT], multiple imputation). As the technology behind the testing has become more complex, cross-national comparisons of achievement have become widely accepted, and arguments that education is culturally determined or that the tests are invalid, and thus that achievement results cannot be compared across countries, have for the most part disappeared.

OECD. While the IEA has been the key innovator in the area of education assessment, the OECD has led the development of a cross-nationally comparable system of education indicators. After a failed attempt to initiate an ambitious system of data collection and reporting in the early 1970s, the OECD, with strong support from the United States, undertook the development of a new system of cross-nationally comparable statistical indicators in the late 1980s. The ministers of education of OECD countries agreed at a meeting in Paris in November 1990 that accurate information and data are required for sound decision-making, informed debate on policy, and accountability measures. Ministers also agreed that data currently available lacked comparability and relevance to education policy.

Although led by the OECD, the core of the International Indicators of Education Systems (INES) projects was the organization of four country-led developmental networks: Network A on Educational Outcomes, Network B on Student Destinations, Network C on School Features and Processes, and Network D on Expectations and Attitudes towards Education—led by the United States, Sweden, the Netherlands, and the United Kingdom, respectively. The OECD secretariat chairs a technical group on enrollments, graduates, personnel, and finances. These networks—involving up to 200 statisticians, policymakers, and, in some cases, academics—designed indicators, negotiated the definitions for data collections, and supplied data for annual reporting. This model of shared ownership in the development of *Education at a Glance* (which was at first published biennially and later became an annual publication) contributed to its success. Participants in the networks and the technical group invested the time needed to supply high-quality data because they had a stake in the publication's success.

INES was initially a reporting scheme where administrative databases within countries were mined and aggregated, and it has evolved into an initiative that mounts its own cross-national surveys, including school surveys, public attitudes surveys, adult literacy surveys, and surveys of student achievement. The largest and most expensive project to date is the OECD Programme for International Student Assessment (PISA). PISA is an assessment of reading literacy, mathematical literacy, and scientific literacy, jointly developed by participating countries and administered to samples of fifteen-year-old students in their schools. In 2000 PISA was administered in thirty-two countries, to between 4,500 and 10,000 students per country. Expected outcomes include a basic profile of knowledge and skills among students at the end of compulsory schooling, contextual indicators relating results to student and school characteristics, and trend indicators showing how results change over time. With the results of PISA, the OECD will be able to report, for the first time, achievement and context indicators specifically designed for that purpose (rather than using IEA data) for country rankings and comparisons.

UNESCO. The United Nations Educational, Scientific and Cultural Organization (UNESCO) has been the main source of cross-national data on education since its inception near the end of the Second World War. UNESCO's first questionnaire-based survey of education was conducted in 1950 and covered fifty-seven of its member states. In the 1970s UNESCO organized the creation of the International Standard Classification of Education (ISCED), a major step forward towards improving the comparability of education data. Although as many as 175 countries regularly report information on their education systems to UNESCO, much of the data reported is widely considered unreliable. Throughout the 1990s the primary analytical report on education published by UNESCO, the *World Education Report,* based many of its analyses and conclusions on education data collected by agencies other than UNESCO.

Between 1984 and 1996 personnel and budgetary support for statistics at UNESCO declined, and UNESCO's ability to assist member countries in the development of their statistical infrastructure or in the reporting of data was severely limited. In the late 1990s, however, the World Bank and other international organizations, as well as influential member countries such as the Netherlands and the United Kingdom, increased pressure and financial contributions in order to improve the quality of the education data UNESCO collects.

Collaboration between UNESCO and OECD began on the World Bank–financed World Education Indicators (WEI) project, which capitalized on OECD's experience, legitimacy, and status to expand the OECD *Indicators Methodology* to the developing world. Although this project includes only eighteen nations (nearly fifty if OECD member nations are included), it has helped to raise the credibility of indicator reporting in at least some countries in the developing world. Even though this project has in many ways "cherry-picked" countries having reasonably advanced national education data systems, the collaborative spirit imported from OECD's INES project has been quite effective.

A major step for the newly constituted UNESCO Institute for Statistics will be to take this project to a larger scale. Significantly expanding WEI will be quite a challenge, however, as the financial and personnel costs needed to increase both the quality of national data collection and reporting, as well as processing and indicator production on an international level, are likely to exceed the budget and staff capacity of the institute in the short term. The visible success of the WEI project, however, shows that the interest in high-quality, comparable, education indicators expands far beyond the developed countries of the OECD.

Integration of National Resources and Expertise into the Process

Many of the international organizations dedicated to education data collection were in operation well before the renaissance of the statistical indicator in the education sector, but these groups lacked the political power and expertise found in a number of key national governments to make them what they have recently become. A central part of the story of international data and statistical indicators has been the thorough integration of national governments into the process. As technocratic operations of governance, with its heavy reliance on data to measure problems and evaluate policies, became standard in the second half of the twentieth century, wealthier national governments invested in statistical systems and analysis capabilities. As was the case for the IEA and its massive TIMSS project, several key nations lent crucial expertise and legitimization to the process, factors that were clearly missing in earlier attempts. Although this "partnership" has not always been a conflict-free one, it has taken international agencies to new technical and resource levels.

The integration of national experts, often from ministries of education or national statistical offices, into international indicator development teams has improved both the quality of the data collected and the national legitimacy of the data reported. A number of decentralized states, including Canada, Spain, and the United States, have used the international indicators produced by OECD as benchmarks for state/provincial indicators reports. As more national governments build significant local control of education into national systems, this use of international indicators at local levels will become more widespread. In the case of Canada, the internationally sanctioned framework provides legitimacy to a specific list of indicators that might not otherwise have gained a sufficient level of agreement among the provinces involved.

The initial release of results from the PISA project will take this one step further, in that the OECD will provide participating countries reports focused on their national results, in a way similar to how the National Assessment of Educational Progress (NAEP) produces reports for each of the fifty U.S. states. This reporting scheme will allow participating countries to "release" their national data at the same time as the international data release. The same could easily happen with releases of subnational indicators in conjunction with international releases. This form of simultaneous release is seen as an effective way to create policy debate at a number of levels within the American system, as illustrated by the U.S. National Center for Education Statistics' ability to generate public interest in its release of achievement indicators from TIMSS and TIMSS-R. International education indicators provide constituencies within national education systems another vantage point to effect change and reform.

Conclusions

There have been four main trends behind the massive collection of data and the construction of cross-national statistical indicators in the education sector over the past several decades. These trends are: (1) greater coordination and networks of organizations dedicated to international data collection; (2) integration of national governments' statistical expertise and resources into international statistical efforts that lead to statistical indicators; (3) political use of cross-national comparisons across a number of public sectors; and (4) near universal acceptance of the validity of statistical indicators to capture central education processes.

Although examples presented here of each factor focus more on elementary and secondary schooling, the same could be said for indicators of tertiary education. The only difference is that the development of a wide range of international statistical indicators for higher education (i.e., indicators of higher education systems instead of research and development products of higher education) lags behind what has happened for elementary and secondary education. However, there are a number of signs that the higher education section will incorporate similar indicators of instruction, performance, and related processes in the near future. It is clear that international statistical indicators of education will continue to become more sophisticated and have a wider impact on policy debates about improving education for some time to come.

See also: INTERNATIONAL ASSESSMENTS; INTERNATIONAL DEVELOPMENT AGENCIES AND EDUCATION.

BIBLIOGRAPHY

ANNIE E. CASEY FOUNDATION. 2001. *Kids Count Data Book 2001: State Profiles of Child Well-Being.* Washington, DC: Center for the Study of Social Policy.

BOTTANI, NORBERTO, and TUIJNMAN, ALBERT. 1994. "International Education Indicators: Framework, Development, and Interpretation." In *Making Education Count: Developing and Using International Indicators,* ed. Norberto Bottani and Albert Tuijnman. Paris: Organisation for Economic Co-operation and Development.

FEDERAL INTERAGENCY FORUM ON CHILD AND FAMILY STATISTICS. 2001. *America's Children: Key National Indicators of Well-Being, 2001.* Washington, DC: U.S. Government Printing Office.

FERRISS, ABBOTT L. 1988. "The Uses of Social Indicators." *Social Forces* 66(3):601–617.

GUTHRIE, JAMES W., and HANSEN, JANET S., eds. 1995. *Worldwide Education Statistics: Enhancing UNESCO's Role.* Washington DC: National Academy Press.

HEYNEMAN, STEPHEN P. 1986. "The Search for School Effects in Developing Countries: 1966–

1986." Economic Development Institute Seminar Paper No. 33. Washington DC: The World Bank.

Heyneman, Stephen P. 1993. "Educational Quality and the Crisis of Educational Research." *International Review of Education* 39(6):511–517.

Organisation for Economic Co-operation and Development. 1982. *The OECD List of Social Indicators.* Paris: OECD Social Indicator Development Programme.

Organisation for Economic Co-operation and Development. 1992. *High-Quality Education and Training for All,* Part 2. Paris: OECD/CERI.

Organisation for Economic Co-operation and Development. 2000. *Investing in Education: Analysis of the 1999 World Education Indicators.* Paris: OECD/CERI.

Organisation for Economic Co-operation and Development. 2001. *Education at a Glance, OECD Indicators 2001.* Paris: OECD/CERI.

Puryear, Jeffrey M. 1995. "International Education Statistics and Research: Status and Problems." *International Journal of Educational Development* 15(1):79–91.

United Nations. 1975. *Towards a System of Social and Demographic Statistics.* New York: United Nations.

United Nations Educational, Scientific and Cultural Organization. 2000. *World Education Report 2000—The Right to Education: Towards Education for All Throughout Life.* Paris: UNESCO Publishing.

United Nations Educational, Scientific and Cultural Organization and the Organisation for Economic Co-operation and Development. 2001. *Teachers for Tomorrow's Schools: Analysis of the World Education Indicators.* Paris: UNESCO Publishing/UIS/OECD.

INTERNET RESOURCE

Noll, Heinz-Herbert. 1996. "Social Indicators and Social Reporting: The International Experience." Canadian Council on Social Development. <www.ccsd.ca/noll1.html>.

Thomas M. Smith
David P. Baker

INTERNATIONAL GAP IN TECHNOLOGY, THE

At the dawn of the twenty-first century, there was a major gap between industrialized and developing countries in terms of their access to information and communications technology (ICT). This gap has come to be known as the *digital divide* and is illustrative of the vast differences in development among nations resulting from the process of globalization. While most industrialized countries were linked into the global information economy through high speed information networks and computers, the majority of people in the developing world had very little or no access to basic information and communications networks—let alone the new technology of the Internet. Indeed, more than half the people on the planet, mostly in the developing world, had yet to make a telephone call.

There are many ways of measuring the digital divide. One measure is the extent to which people in the industrialized and developing countries have access to the Internet. Table 1 provides a rough estimate of the approximately 500 million worldwide Internet users by region at the beginning of the current century. It shows that the industrialized countries represented some 65 percent of all Internet users.

Another measure is the location of Internet content providers. Here the dominance of the developed world is still more accentuated: the United States shows a ratio of 25.2 Internet domains per thousand population and parts of Europe 15 per thousand, compared to Brazil's 0.5, China's 0.2, and India's 0.1.

The digital divide is far more than a gap in access to ICT, however. It is a major impediment to the social and economic development of poor nations. In the twenty-first century, knowledge and information and a highly skilled labor force are increasingly important determinants of growth in the global economy. Or as Manuel Castells has observed, "Information technology, and the ability to use it and adapt it, is the critical factor in generating and accessing wealth, power, and knowledge in our time" (1998, p. 92). ICT has already revolutionized economic life and business in the industrialized countries and is transforming these societies in equally profound ways. ICT is a key weapon in the war against world poverty. When used properly, it offers huge potential to empower people in developing countries to overcome development obstacles, to address the most important social problems they face, and to strengthen communities, democratic institutions, a free press, and local economies.

According to some, the development of information and communications technology is increasing the gap between the rich and the poor, the knowledgeable and the knowledge deprived, the information rich and the information poor. Instead of closing the divide, the introduction of more ICT exacerbates social and economic divides—not only between rich and poor countries, but also among various socioeconomic groups within countries. Others argue that ICT closes the divide by integrating countries in the global economy and providing them access to global knowledge and information for development. Nonetheless, there are stark differences in access across the world according to gender, geography (i.e., urban versus rural), income, education, age, occupation, and even ethnicity and race. The groups with the greatest access to new information and communications technology are generally well-educated, high income urban males. Poor, illiterate females in rural areas are least likely to have access to ICT.

The Digital Divide in Education

The global dimensions of the digital divide are most prominent in education. At the beginning of the twenty-first century many industrialized countries had begun to gear up their education systems for the knowledge economy by making major investments in computers for classrooms, in networking their schools, and in training teachers to use technology in their teaching. Thus, in the United States the ratio of students to instructional computers reached five to one and 98 percent of schools were connected to the Internet. In the United Kingdom, the ratio of students to computers was twelve to one in primary school and seven to one in secondary school while access to the Internet was virtually universal, as it was in the European Union as a whole. Canada showed similar patterns, as did Australia and New Zealand. In addition, many students either owned their own computers or had access to the Internet outside of school hours. Getting online had also become the buzz of the higher education sector in industrialized countries; most universities had or were acquiring access to both fiber optic and wireless high speed digital networks.

In contrast, most of the developing countries, with few exceptions, were more concerned with very

TABLE 1

Worldwide Internet users by region, 2001

Region	Number of users	Percentage
Africa	4 million	1
Asia/Pacific	144 million	28
Canada and United States	181 million	35
Europe	155 million	30
Latin America	25 million	5
Middle East	5 million	1
World Total	**514 million**	**100%**

SOURCE: Adapted from Nua Internet Surveys. August 2001.

difficult educational issues—low primary and secondary school enrollments, inadequately trained teachers, little or no access to textbooks, and ineffective school management—rather than with improving ICT. The exceptions were a small number of countries in Asia, Latin America, and other parts of the developing world that began introducing computers in classrooms, networking schools, and developing digital content to address the educational requirements of the global knowledge economy.

Among Asian countries, Singapore, Malaysia, Korea, China, and Thailand were making important investments in ICT in higher education and at the primary and secondary levels. Thailand developed the first nationwide, free-access network for education in Southeast Asia, SchoolNet@1509. This program also made Thai content available on the Internet. China's Ministry of Education planned to provide online education services to five million higher education students by 2005. In Latin America, Brazil, Mexico, and Chile were making significant ICT investments. Brazil built high speed data networks for university research and installed large numbers of computers in primary and secondary schools nationwide. Chile had linked 5,000 primary and secondary schools and produced educational software under its Enlaces program. In other parts of the world, Turkey launched a major initiative to install computers in more than 5000 classrooms, and the South African SchoolNet (SchoolNetSA) began providing Internet services to local schools and developed online educational content.

Education and Technology in the Balance

Does access to computers and the Internet give the education systems of industrialized countries an advantage over those in developing countries? Or has technology balanced rich and poor countries, because poor countries now have access to high quality information, data, and research via the Internet they never would have had without technology? The answers to these questions depend in large measure upon how one assesses the impact and cost-effectiveness of ICT on the education systems in the industrialized countries. At the start of the twenty-first century, the educational impact of computers and the Internet was not widely in evidence in many schools, although it is clear that ICT was being widely adopted and used at all levels of education. Moreover, a new "Net Generation" of learners weaned on the Internet was stimulating new approaches to teaching and learning online, initially within the traditional classroom, but increasingly outside that venue, without regard to physical location or time of day.

While there has been good progress in providing access to ICT in schools and universities in industrialized countries, the expected benefits to education, as noted, have been difficult to measure: (1) increasing productive teaching and learning; (2) transforming teaching and learning from traditional textbook lessons to more learner-friendly, student-centered approaches that employ powerful interactive tools and methods; and (3) equipping students with higher order thinking and problem-solving skills that prepare them for life in an information-based society and workplace.

Some researchers, such as James Kulick, have recorded positive outcomes from the use of computers for teaching and learning basic skills and for information and knowledge management. Others, such as Larry Cuban, believe that computers have been oversold and underused; they argue that most educational institutions remain essentially as they were decades ago, despite the availability of technology, and are not reaping enough benefits from technology to justify the investments. Further, others question the cost-effectiveness of computers relative to other inputs for improving the quality of education in the classroom: smaller class sizes, self-paced learning, peer teaching, small group learning, innovative curricula, and in-class tutors.

The experience of the industrialized countries would suggest that access to the Internet and the wealth of knowledge and information it provides does not automatically lead to measurable improvements in the quality of teaching and learning in schools. Rather, such improvements are the result of parallel efforts to enhance the teaching and learning process by training teachers, reducing class size, making textbooks available, and establishing standards of learning. Nonetheless, it is obvious that school systems everywhere, and especially in the developing countries, need to find ways of providing more students with regular and frequent access to information and communications technology and to enable students to acquire the knowledge and skills needed to support a knowledge economy.

Bridging the Digital Divide in Education

The developing countries face massive challenges in bridging the digital divide in education. What are these challenges? And is progress possible? In order to bridge the digital divide in education, developing countries will first need to overcome the key constraints to the development of ICT in general. Too often programs fail to address the problems in a comprehensive and sustainable way. To reduce the technology gap developing countries need to discover ways to expand information infrastructure, increase access by improving markets, and reduce the cost of service, especially for Internet access. A reduction in Internet costs—both telecommunications company charges and Internet service provider charges— in developing countries is necessary for a broadening of the information society there, and for more widespread and cost-effective use of new technologies to improve education.

Even with the best of intentions, however, achieving these goals will not be easy for developing countries. They lack both the funding and the technical expertise to overcome infrastructure and human resource constraints. Many international financial organizations, aid agencies, and private foundations are committed to helping developing countries bridge the digital divide and are being mobilized into action by the United Nations, the World Economic Forum, and other bodies.

Additionally, many feel that advances in technology will help bridge the digital divide between industrial and developing countries. Overall, diffusion of Internet access is expected to be rapid in the first decade of the twenty-first century. Indeed, access to information over the Internet is already being greatly facilitated for consumers in developing countries by the existence of new data caches and innovative networking of servers around the world. The development of wireless telecommunications is also expected to facilitate access to the Internet in remote rural areas where telephone service has been unavailable. And, above all, computers are likely to become both pervasive and affordable, not just on the desk top and as handheld appliances, but embedded in intelligent objects everywhere.

While access to computers and telecommunications networks is necessary to bridge the digital divide, access alone is not sufficient to ensure that education systems in developing countries benefit from the Internet revolution. The governments of these countries also need to: (1) train teachers and trainers to exploit the potential of learning technologies; (2) offer free or inexpensive Internet access to schools; (3) foster capacity to develop content and instructional resources in their own language; (4) build networks and well-maintained facilities for both accessing knowledge and providing affordable lifelong learning and skill upgrading; and (5) preserve the freedom of teachers and students to explore the myriad educational resources on the web without filtering and censorship such as that which exists in China, Saudi Arabia, Iran, and other countries.

Both industrialized and developing countries must also seek to address the digital divide between rich and poor. The United States has made significant progress in bridging the gap, although there are still considerable inequities, especially in instructional practice—that is, in how effectively modern learning technologies are being used with different groups of students. In the developing countries, public policies to promote competition (which lowers prices and improves quality) and to make new technologies more accessible will ultimately influence availability and adoption of technology and access. However, special community-based programs by governments and nongovernmental organizations involving marginalized or rural communities, women, and minorities are also essential for bridging the digital divide.

See also: INTERNATIONAL ASSESSMENTS, *subentry on* IEA STUDY OF TECHNOLOGY IN THE CLASSROOM; TECHNOLOGY EDUCATION; TECHNOLOGY IN EDUCATION.

BIBLIOGRAPHY

CAIRNCROSS, FRANCES. 1997. *The Death of Distance.* Boston: Harvard Business School Press.

CASTELLS, MANUEL. 1998. *End of Millennium.* Malden, MA: Blackwell.

CASTELLS, MANUEL. 2001. *The Internet Galaxy.* New York: Oxford University Press.

CUBAN, LARRY. 2001. *Oversold and Underused: Computers in the Classroom.* Cambridge, MA: Harvard University Press.

INTERNATIONAL ALLIANCE FOR CHILDHOOD. 2001. *Fools Gold: A Critical Look at Computers in Childhood.* College Park, MD: International Alliance for Childhood.

KULICK, JAMES A. 1994 "Meta-Analytic Studies of Findings on Computer-Based Instruction." In *Technology Assessment in Education and Training,* ed. Eva L. Baker and Harold F. O'Neil, Jr. Hillsdale, NJ: Erlbaum.

PRESIDENT'S COMMITTEE OF ADVISORS ON SCIENCE AND TECHNOLOGY, PANEL ON EDUCATIONAL TECHNOLOGY. 1997. *Report to the President on the Use of Technology to Strengthen K–12 Education in the United States.* Washington, DC. Executive Office of the President.

UNITED NATIONS DEVELOPMENT PROGRAM. 2001. *Human Development Report 2001: Making New Technologies Work for Human Development.* New York: Oxford University Press.

U.S. DEPARTMENT OF COMMERCE. 2000. *Falling Through the Net: Toward Digital Inclusion.* Washington, DC: U.S. Department of Commerce.

U.S. DEPARTMENT OF EDUCATION NATIONAL CENTER FOR EDUCATIONAL STATISTICS. 2001. *Internet Access in U.S. Public Schools and Classrooms: 1994–2000.* (NCES 2001–071). Washington, DC: Office of Educational Research and Improvement.

INTERNET RESOURCES

DIGITAL DIVIDE NETWORK. 2002. <http://www.digitaldividenetwork.org/content/sections/index.cfm>.

UNITED KINGDOM DEPARTMENT FOR EDUCATION AND SKILLS. 2001. *Statistics of Education: Survey of Information and Communications Technology in Schools 2001.* <http://www.dfes.gov.uk/statistics/DB/SBU/b0296/sb09-2001.pdf>.

WILSON, ERNEST J., III. 2000. "Closing the Digital Divide: An Initial Review." *Internet Policy Institute.* <http://www.internetpolicy.org/briefing/ErnestWilson0700.html>.

MICHAEL POTASHNIK

INTERNATIONAL ISSUES OF SOCIAL MOBILITY OF UNDERPRIVILEGED GROUPS

Children of lower socioeconomic status (SES) groups tend to perform worse in school than upper SES groups, and they tend to stay in school for a shorter time. In addition, these children tend to be underrepresented in higher education. These patterns exist regardless of region of world, sociopolitical system, and level of economic development of a country. This article examines the universality of these observations. It also discusses exceptions to these general tendencies and promising interventions that enable children of lower socioeconomic groups to overcome barriers to progress in school.

Education, Equality, and Equity

The theme of education and social mobility of underprivileged groups is integrally related to issues of social equality and equity. Equality, according to Martin Bronfenbrenner, refers to the numerical distribution of a good or service (such as income, land, or years of schooling), whereas equity refers to judgments concerning the fairness or justice of that distribution. The sociological study of equality of educational opportunity and outcomes usually focuses on the relationship between stratification—the hierarchical ordering of people on such dimensions as wealth, power, and prestige—and the amount and type of schooling available to different social groups. According to Ann Parker Parelius and Robert James Parelius, it is widely assumed that "'equality of opportunity' exists when each person regardless of such ascribed characteristics as family background, religion, ethnicity, race, or gender, has the same chance of acquiring a favorable socioeconomic position" (p. 264).

It should be noted that equal educational opportunity does not necessarily imply that people will end up equal but simply that an individual's socioeconomic position will be the result of a "fair and open contest—one in which the winners are those who work hardest and demonstrate the most ability" (Parelius and Parelius, p. 264). In the debate over inequality, one critical question concerns the degree to which advantage is passed on from one generation to another. For example, if the social-class standing of a family is high in terms of income, occupational status, and educational attainment, will the family's offspring have greater access to the highest levels of

a school system? And what is the effect of family socioeconomic position on the relationship between level of schooling attained and subsequent income and occupational status? Christopher J. Hurn noted in 1993 that if a society's education system is truly meritocratic (that is, based on ability and not on ascriptive factors such as social class, gender, and ethnicity), then (1) the correlation between individuals' educational attainment (how far one goes in school) and future occupational status should increase over time; (2) the correlation between students' educational attainment and their parents' socioeconomic status should decrease over time; and (3) the correlation between parents' SES and their offspring's SES should also decrease.

Evidence strongly supports the proposition that, around the world, education increasingly is becoming the strongest determinant of occupational status and the type of life chances individuals experience. Evidence does not, however, support the thesis that the relationship between family background and how far one goes in school and what one learns is decreasing over time. Indeed, the relationship between family SES and school success or failure appears to be increasing since the 1980s as the result, in part, of public policies that tend to decentralize and privatize education. While primary education has expanded to near universal coverage of the relevant age group, access to the levels of education that are most important for social mobility and entry into the most modern and competitive sectors of the increasingly globalized economies remain elusive for all but elites. Consequently, the relationship between parents' SES and their children's SES has shown little evidence of changing over time.

Significant Educational Interventions

Moreover, comparative longitudinal studies of factors influencing what is learned in school and level of educational attainment suggest that as societies industrialize and modernize, social class increasingly plays a significant role in determining educational outcomes. This finding does not discount the importance of school-based factors in determining how well students, especially those living in conditions of poverty, fare in school. Well-designed interventions aimed at improving the quality of instruction can make a difference. These include quality preschool and early childhood programs with supplementary nutrition and health care services; more adequate school infrastructure so that poor, rural, and indigenous children have the same amenities (school desks and chairs, electricity, running water, and toilets) enjoyed by their more advantaged peers in urban and private schools; a flexible academic calendar responsive to the socioeconomic context of schools in different regions of a country; sufficient supplies of textbooks and culturally sensitive as well as socially relevant curricular materials in the appropriate languages; teaching guides matched to transformed curricula; student-centered, more active pedagogies that involve collaborative work as well as personalized attention to each child; significantly improved pre-service and in-service teacher education and professional development programs and opportunities; incentive pay for teachers working under difficult conditions and, generally, more adequate remuneration and social recognition of the importance of teaching; and, importantly, greater participation of teachers, parents, and communities in the design of education programs to meet their self-defined needs.

For female students, who are often the most discriminated against with regard to access to schooling and the types of curricula that lead to high-status jobs, a complementary set of interventions would include placement of schools closer to their homes, female teachers and administrators as role models, opportunities to be taught separately where appropriate, academically challenging curricula, waiver of tuition and book fees, and, in some cases, monetary incentives to families to compensate for lost income or opportunity costs borne by them. In some cases, agencies working to promote greater school participation rates by females have employed a variety of outreach activities and media, including extension agents and sociodramas performed in communities, to counter notions that religious doctrine or cultural traditions prohibit the education of daughters.

Intangible factors such as school culture (the values propounded by school personnel and student peer groups) also are significant. Bradley Levinson's ten-year study of a Mexican junior high school, for example, documents how the egalitarian ideology of the 1910 Revolution enters the discourse and practices of school personnel and is appropriated by students. The belief that *Todos Somos Iguales* ("We Are All Equal") strongly shapes interactions between students and, contrary to much U.S. and European social and cultural reproduction theory, overrides the forces that would stratify students by social class, ethnicity, and gender. Elizabeth Cohen and asso-

ciates' research on "equitable classrooms" underscores the importance of multidimensional and complex instruction that demand high levels of performance of all students and encourages the use and evaluation of multiple abilities. In such classrooms, "the interaction among students is 'equal-status,' that is all students are active and influential participants and their opinions matter to their fellow students" (Cohen, p. 276). Similarly, *effective schools* research indicates that an overall ethos of high expectations and a climate of respect have a positive impact on the achievement of lower SES students.

Problematic Reforms: National Standards and High-Stakes Examinations

Along with greater respect accorded to students and the knowledge and values they bring to school, teacher expectations and general curricular standards are important factors in raising student performance. The worldwide trend to establish national standards in core academic subjects and hold schools and individual teachers and students accountable for them through systematic testing may contribute to higher test scores for disadvantaged groups. These efforts, however, are fraught with serious problems and may, instead, lead to greater failure for the intended beneficiaries of these reforms. While standards may be uniformly applied to all students, the resources to accomplish heightened expectations usually are not equally available. The standards themselves may be questioned as to whose knowledge and values are represented; the language in which tests are administered is a particularly significant issue in multilingual, pluralist societies. Generally, there is widespread criticism that the tests constrain the professional autonomy of teachers to determine what is in the best interest of students, often involve a *dumbing down* and narrowing of what is taught, and tend to be a one-size-fits-all strategy for educational improvement.

Cultural and Social Capital

As indicated above, educators concerned with educational interventions that are culturally sensitive and contextually appropriate take into account the so-called cultural and social capital of their students, families, and communities. The term *cultural capital* refers to the knowledge, linguistic skills and speech codes, and modes of behavior that students bring to school, whereas *social capital* refers to the networks of support and resources that families and their children can draw upon to interact successfully with various public agencies such as schools. The failure of students from lower socioeconomic groups and ethnic minorities to succeed in school often resides in the mismatch between the expectations of state curricula and school personnel and what students actually know and value. Education systems must build upon this individual and local knowledge while expanding it so that students, with a heightened sense of their own identity and efficacy, also can participate in the larger society in ways beneficial to themselves and others.

The significance of social capital and how to mobilize it has received substantial attention since the late 1980s. Ways to strengthen the social capital of lower SES families include enabling closer and more systematic involvement of teachers with parents (rather than only when problems arise), arranging for parent-teacher conferences to take place at convenient locations and times, making information about the workings of the education system and individual schools available in the home language, and focusing on the strengths of the children and what they can do. In the absence of other social-service agencies in rural areas and depressed urban neighborhoods, schools necessarily must offer a number of educational and social services, such as extended day care, recreational facilities and sports programs, health programs (including inoculations and birth-control information), and literacy and adult education classes.

Neoliberal Economic and Education Policies

Unfortunately, as noted by such authors as Robert Arnove, Joel Samoff, Fernando Reimers, and Maria Bucur, the full panoply of interventions and reforms is rarely implemented. Reform efforts usually are piecemeal, haphazardly implemented, and inadequately funded. Furthermore, current neoliberal policy initiatives that are being uniformly initiated around the world are likely to widen the gap between academic achievement (what students learn in school) and the educational attainment of the rich and the poor. The term *neoliberal* derives from the neoclassical economic theories expounded by the major international donor agencies, such as the World Bank and the International Monetary Fund, as well as by national governments that pursue economic and social policies that give priority to the workings of market forces. The theories are based on writings of the classical economists Adam Smith

(1723–1790) and David Ricardo (1772–1823), who believed the role of the state consisted in establishing the conditions by which the free play of the marketplace, the laws of supply and demand, and free trade based on competitive advantage would inevitably redound to the benefit of all. Government policies based on these notions have led to a drastic reduction in the state role in social spending, deregulation of the economy, and liberalization of import policies. The educational counterparts of these policies have included moves to decentralize and privatize public school systems.

Initiatives to decentralize national education systems most commonly involve transfer of a number of previously centralized functions (such as hiring of teachers) to local levels of government along with greater responsibility for the financing of education. At the same time, in many countries, a core national curriculum is established, and, increasingly, national standards, systematic testing, and various accountability measures are introduced. In countries with dramatic differences in wealth by regions, these policies tend to exacerbate the availability and quality of schooling. Comparisons of test scores between more-advantaged urban areas and depressed rural areas, and between elite private schools and poor urban schools, reveal a growing gap between children of upper and lower socioeconomic strata. Moreover, cost-recovery measures are usually introduced, which means that previously free services are no longer provided. Parents, for example, must pay for textbooks, school uniforms, special classes, and equipment (usually related to computers and the learning of a foreign language). These fees, in countries where a majority of the population is living in poverty, may drive children out of the school system. Frequently, parents must choose between paying school fees and buying food, clothing, and medicines. Sometimes, the principal incentive for sending children to school is the milk or a hot meal that will be provided. Various measures facilitating the creation and subsidization of private education further widen the gap between the rich and the poor, as well-to-do families are encouraged to send their children to private schools, thereby eroding the base of support for public schooling.

Higher Education and Stratification

At the higher education level, postsecondary education has become so integrally linked to individual economic well-being that it is now deemed one of the "essential components of cultural and socioeconomic development of individuals, communities and nations" (United Nations Development Programme, p. 2). As such, the higher education degree credential, over time, has become the principal entry point into the most modernized sectors of the economy and middle- or upper-class status. Nevertheless, as countries around the globe contend with issues of increased demand for, and access to, higher education institutions, financially sustaining those institutions has become a dilemma for all societies. As a result, while the costs of higher education in many countries traditionally involve no or minimal tuition fees, policy reforms increasingly shift the costs of higher education to students and their families. Ironically, at the very moment when historically marginalized groups have begun to gain access to higher education, the neoliberal move to decentralize and privatize education has become most prominent. Such reform initiatives have frequently led to student as well as faculty seizures of higher education facilities, public protests, and occasionally violent demonstrations.

One reason for this opposition to reform is that despite the diverse histories of, and demands, cultures, and clients for, higher education throughout the world, dissimilar nations are increasingly connected by their policy decisions without sufficient local adaptation. For higher education, the 1990s was a period of financial crisis around the world. These financial pressures have led to surprisingly similar reforms for higher education. Oftentimes, policy solutions of industrialized nations (e.g., the United States, the United Kingdom, and Australia) become the prevailing model used by other nations facing the same fiscal pressures. The most widespread financial reform mechanism involves increasing tuition and fees at the same time that financial-aid systems of grants and student loans are introduced. Student loan programs exist in more than fifty countries. Because student loan programs are costly to administer, they often compete with grants for governmental program support. As loan programs are introduced, grant programs are frequently reduced.

The conflict between student loans, which must be repaid by the student, and outright grants, which do not need to be repaid, is contested by policy analysts. Some researchers support charging students and their families for an increasing share of the cost of higher education because keeping tuition prices low through governmental support mainly benefits high-income students. Other analysts assert that the high cost of tuition discourages minority and low-income students from even considering college attendance. Most researchers agree that the enrollment of high-income students in tertiary education does not change because of price. Shifting the costs of higher education to students and their families has also served to stratify educational opportunities by institution type such that the students from high- and middle-income backgrounds increasingly seek degrees from more prestigious universities, while low-income students increasingly enroll in the less prestigious institutions and vocational institutions.

More than adequate financial support is important for low-income and nontraditional students to succeed in higher education. Equally crucial for student success are a welcoming environment; a variety of support services; adaptation of academic calendars, curricula, and pedagogy to the characteristics of students; and flexible class schedules and modalities for delivering instruction. Taking into account the cultural and social capital of students from diverse backgrounds as well as their financial resources constitutes a major move toward more inclusive and equitable higher education systems.

The Need for Poverty Reduction: International Data

While the association between levels of educational attainment and lifetime earning streams is substantial and becoming stronger, economic policies can alleviate the dramatic wage differences between those who have a higher education and those who do not. Stephen Nickell and Brian Bell note that comparative data (from Germany, the Netherlands, Switzerland, and the United Kingdom) point out that wage policies and efforts made to provide high-level skills to those not receiving a higher education can lead to more equitable systems of income distribution.

Ultimately, public policies related to poverty alleviation are critical to overcoming the gap between the rich and poor within and between countries. Lyle V. Jones draws attention to the strong correlation between poverty levels, school expulsions and suspensions, and achievement scores in the United States, Germany, and Japan to underscore the point "that within every one of the nations that participated, poverty is related to achievement. . . . Based on these findings, there can be little basis for surprise when we discover that the U.S. [with more than double the level of children living in poverty] may lag behind Japan, Germany, and some other countries in average school achievement in mathematics" (p. 8).

Unfortunately, current national development and economic policies based on the application of market forces to the provision of social services, and especially education, have led to an expansion and deepening of poverty not only within countries but also between countries and large regions of the world. While certain countries have successfully integrated into the global economy, many countries have not. Among those excluded from the so-called benefits of international market forces and policies of privatization and decentralization are large sectors of Africa, Latin America, Russia and eastern Europe, and Asia. The poorer the country, the greater is the probability that a higher percentage of children will never even enter or complete primary education. For example, in 1990 Marlaine E. Lockheed and Adriaan M. Verspoor found that in thirteen countries with low gross national product the median dropout rate was 41 percent compared with 14 percent for seven upper-middle-income countries. More recent research, summarized in 2000 by the International Institute of Educational Planning as a ten-year follow-up to the 1990 Jomtien, Thailand, international conference on "Education for All," found that "the lower the national income, the greater the inequalities in education within a country," with "the differences between rich and poor, between center and periphery, between men and women, generally greater . . . the poorer the country" (Hernes, p. 2). While enrollment figures are important indicators of access to schooling, they do not reveal high dropout and repetition rates, especially among disadvantaged groups. Instead, educational attainment and years of schooling have been identified as the key factors in determining subsequent occupational attainment, income, and SES, particularly in highly industrialized countries. Therefore, Table 1 demonstrates the disparity in educational attainment and years of schooling for different regions of the world by income group. Education systems and teachers most frequently bear the brunt in cost reductions in social spending, resulting in the erosion of previous gains for the poorest and most marginalized sectors of the society and an undermining of public schooling relative to that of the private sector.

Conclusions

The relationships among family background, educational achievement and attainment, and subsequent life chances are obviously complex. Research that clarifies these relationships must take into account the interaction among contextual (macro-level) as well as local institutional (micro-level) variables. At the level of national comparisons, promising research needs to be conducted along the lines of explaining how certain countries, such as Finland, that excel in international tests of academic achievement, are able to do a good job with all students.

Over time the meaning of equality of educational opportunity has changed significantly. If one thinks of equal educational opportunity in relation to a race or contest, the initial conceptualization was to ensure that all students started the race on fairly comparable terms and, subsequently, that they would attend schools with similar resources and a common curriculum. Students who were disadvantaged would have early intervention programs to bring them up to par. More recent conceptualizations emphasize the outcomes of the education process—that is, the ability of schools to develop to the fullest the potential of students with different backgrounds and talents. In 1972 Torsten Husén referred to this new definition of equal educational opportunity in these terms: "every student should have an equal opportunity to be treated unequally" (p. 26). What this seemingly paradoxical principle means is that every single student should receive an education that is personally appropriate and beneficial. It also implies that more resources are likely to be required for those who are most disadvantaged—just as more costly, intensive care in a hospital is required to remedy a critical health situation. As John Rawls noted, given the years and decades of neglect and often discrimination faced by lower SES groups, ethnic minorities, and females, principles of redistributive justice would require that greater resources be dedicated to achieving maximum benefits for them. Without such idealism, it is unlikely that current trends toward greater inequalities and inequities in the economic, social, and educational spheres will be reversed.

See also: GENDER ISSUES, *subentry on* INTERNATIONAL; INTERNATIONAL DEVELOPMENT AGENCIES AND EDUCATION; POVERTY AND EDUCATION; SOCIAL CAPITAL IN EDUCATION; TESTING, *subentry on* STANDARDIZED TESTS AND EDUCATIONAL POLICY.

TABLE 1

Highest level of education attained in the percentage of population age twenty-five and over, 1995

	No school (percent)	Primary attainment (percent)	Secondary attainment (percent)	Tertiary attainment (percent)	Average years of schooling in population over 25
World	26.7	32.2	28.0	13.0	6.49
Low and middle income	41.8	33.5	18.3	6.3	4.47
Sub-Saharan Africa	45.6	32.5	19.0	2.6	3.62
East Asia and Pacific	27.1	36.6	26.2	10.1	6.03
South Asia	54.7	26.2	15.2	4.0	3.73
Latin America and Caribbean	19.2	41.8	18.4	10.5	5.38
Middle East and North Africa	43.9	28.7	20.0	7.4	4.46
Transitional economies	1.4	35.9	48.4	14.2	9.72
High income	4.0	28.7	41.4	25.9	9.57

Note: The authors used the International Standard Classification of Education criteria adopted in 1976 as the common criterion for international comparison. This may vary from the criteria used by the United Nations Educational, Scientific and Cultural Organization in its reporting of educational attainment data.

SOURCE: Barro, Robert J., and Lee, Jong-Wha. 2000. "International Data on Educational Attainment: Updates and Implications." Harvard University, Department of Economics. <http://post.economics.harvard.edu/faculty/barro/workpapers.html>.

BIBLIOGRAPHY

ALTBACH, PHILIP G., and JOHNSTONE, D. BRUCE. 1993. *The Funding of Higher Education: International Perspectives.* New York: Garland.

ARNOVE, ROBERT F. 1994. *Education as Contested Terrain: Nicaragua, 1979–1993.* Boulder, CO: Westview Press.

ARNOVE, ROBERT F. 1997a. "Neoliberal Education Policies in Latin America: Arguments in Favor and Against." In *Latin American Education: Comparative Perspectives,* ed. Carlos Alberto Torres and Adriana Puiggros. Boulder, CO: Westview.

ARNOVE, ROBERT F. 1997b. "Sociology and the Study of Education Systems." In *Cultural and Social Foundations of Education: An Interdisciplinary Approach,* ed. Miguel Angel Escotet. Boston: Simon and Schuster.

ARNOVE, ROBERT F., and TORRES, CARLOS ALBERTO, eds. 1999. *Comparative Education: The Dialectic of the Global and the Local.* Lanham, MD: Rowman and Littlefield.

BANKS, JAMES A. 2001. "Citizenship Education and Diversity: Implications for Teacher Education." *Journal of Teacher Education* 52(1):5–16.

BEHRMAN, JERE R., and TAUBMAN, PAUL. 1997. "Family Status and Economic Status." In *International Encyclopedia of the Sociology of Education,* ed. Lawrence Saha. New York: Plenum.

BERMAN, EDWARD H. 1999. "The Political Economy of Educational Reform in Australia, England and Wales, and the United Sates." In *Comparative Education: The Dialectic of the Global and the Local,* ed. Robert F. Arnove and Carlos Alberto Torres. Lanham, MD: Rowman and Littlefield.

BERNSTEIN, BASIL, ed. 1973–1976. *Class, Codes, and Control,* 3 vols. London: Routledge and Kegan Paul.

BOURDIEU, PIERRE, and PASSERON, JEAN-CLAUDE. 1977. *Reproduction.* Beverly Hills, CA: Sage.

BRONFENBRENNER, MARTIN. 1973. "Equality and Equity." *Annals* 409(September):5–25.

BROOKOVER, WILBUR, et al. 1979. *School Social Systems and Student Achievement.* New York: Praeger.

BUCUR, MARIA, and EKLOF, BEN. 1999. "Russia and Eastern Europe." In *Comparative Education: The Dialectic of the Global and the Local,* ed. Robert F. Arnove and Carlos Alberto Torres. Lanham, MD: Rowman and Littlefield.

CARNOY, MARTIN. 1994. *Faded Dreams: The Politics and Economics of Race in America.* Cambridge, Eng.: Cambridge University Press.

CHAPMAN, DAVID W., and SYNDER, CONRAD WESLEY, JR. 2000. "Can High Stakes National Testing Improve Instruction: Reexamining Conventional Wisdom." *International Journal of Educational Development* 20:457–474.

CLEMENTS, MARGARET M. 2000. "An International Comparison of Higher Education Loan Programs." Paper presented at the annual meeting of the Comparative and International Education Society, San Antonio, TX.

CLEMENTS, MARGARET M. 2001. "Planning for Affirmative Loans for Higher Education: A Transformative Possibility?" Paper presented at the annual meeting of the Comparative and International Education Society, Washington, DC.

COHEN, ELIZABETH G. 2000. "Equitable Classrooms in a Changing Society." In *Handbook of the Sociology of Education,* ed. Maureen T. Hallinan. New York: Kluwer Academic/Plenum.

COHEN, ELIZABETH G., and LOTAN, RACHEL A., eds. 1997. *Working for Equity in Heterogeneous Classrooms: Sociological Theory in Practice.* New York: Teachers College Press.

COLEMAN, JAMES S. 1968. "The Concept of Equality of Opportunity." *Harvard Educational Review* 38:7–32.

COLEMAN, JAMES S. 1990. "Social Capital in the Creation of Human Capital." *American Journal of Sociology* 94(supplement):S95–S120.

COLLINS, RANDALL. 1979. *The Credential Society.* New York: Academic Press.

FARRELL, JOSEPH P. 1999. "Changing Conceptions of Equality of Education: Forty Years of Comparative Evidence." In *Comparative Education: The Dialectic of the Global and the Local,* ed. Robert F. Arnove and Carlos Alberto Torres. Lanham, MD: Rowman and Littlefield.

FARRELL, JOSEPH P., and SCHIEFELBEIN, ERNESTO. 1985. "Education and Status Attainment in Chile: A Comparative Challenge to the Wisconsin Model of Status Attainment." *Comparative Education Review* 19:490–506.

FULLER, BRUCE, et al. 1999. "How to Raise Children's Early Literacy? The Influence of Family, Teacher, and Classroom in Northeast Brazil." *Comparative Education Review* 43(1):1–35.

GARDNER, HOWARD. 1999. *Intelligence Reframed: Multiple Intelligences for the Twenty-First Century.* New York: Basic.

HANUSHEK, ERIC A. 1997. "Education Production Functions." In *International Encyclopedia of the*

Sociology of Education, ed. Lawrence Saha. New York: Plenum.

HAWLEY, WILLIS D., and ROLLIE, DONALD L. 2002. *The Keys to Effective Schools: Educational Reform as Continuous Improvement.* Thousand Oaks, CA: Corwin Press.

HERNES, GUDMUND. 2000. "All for Education." *IIEP Newsletter* 18(2):2.

HEYNEMAN, STEPHEN P. 1976. "Influences on Academic Achievement: A Comparison of Results from Uganda and More Industrialized Societies." *Sociology of Education* 49(3):200–211.

HEYNEMAN, STEPHEN P., and LOXLEY, WILLIAM. 1983. "The Effects of Primary School Quality on Academic Achievement across Twenty-Nine High and Low-Income Countries." *American Journal of Sociology* 88:1162–1194.

HURN, CHRISTOPHER J. 1993. *The Limits and Possibilities of Schooling: An Introduction to the Sociology of Education,* 3rd edition. Boston: Allyn and Bacon.

HUSÉN, TORSTEN. 1972. "Equality as an Objective of Educational and Social Policy." In *Social Background and Educational Careers,* ed. Torsten Husén. Paris: Organisation for Economic Cooperation and Development.

JOHNSTONE, D. BRUCE. 1998. *The Financing and Management of Higher Education: A Status Report on World Reforms.* Washington, DC: World Bank.

KIPP, SAMUEL M., III; PRICE, DEREK V.; and WOHLFORD, JILL K. 2002. *Unequal Opportunity: Disparities in College Access among the Fifty States.* Indianapolis, IN: Lumina Foundation for Education.

KOZOL, JONATHAN. 1991. *Savage Inequalities.* New York: Crown.

KOZOL, JONATHAN. 2000. *Ordinary Resurrections: Children in the Years of Hope.* New York: Crown.

LAREAU, ANNETTE. 1989. *Home Advantage: Social Class and Parental Intervention in Elementary Education.* London: Falmer.

LEVIN, HENRY M. 1988. *Accelerated Schools for At-Risk Students.* New Brunswick, NJ: Center for Policy.

LEVINSON, BRADLEY A. U. 2001. *We Are All Equal: Student Culture and Identity at a Mexican Secondary School, 1988–1998.* Durham, NC: Duke University Press.

LEWIN, KEITH M. 1998. "Education in Emerging Asia: Patterns, Policies, and Futures into the Twenty-First Century." *International Journal of Educational Development* 18:81–118.

LOCKHEED, MARLAINE E., and VERSPOOR, ADRIAAN M. 1990. *Improving Primary Education in Developing Countries: A Review of Policy Options.* Washington, DC: Published for the World Bank, Oxford University Press.

MANSKI, CHARLES F. 1993. "Dynamic Choice in Social Settings." *Journal of Econometrics* 58(1–2):121–137.

MCDONOUGH, PATRICIA M. 1997. *Choosing Colleges: How Social Class and School Structure Opportunity.* Albany: State University of New York Press.

NATIONAL CENTER FOR EFFECTIVE SCHOOLS RESEARCH AND DEVELOPMENT. 1989. *A Conversation between James Comer and Ronald Edmonds.* Dubuque, IA: Kendall/Hunt.

NICKELL, STEPHEN, and BELL, BRIAN. 1996. "Changes in Distribution of Wages and Unemployed in OECD Countries." *American Economic Review, Papers and Proceedings* 86:302–314.

PARELIUS, ROBERT JAMES, and PARELIUS, ANN PARKER. 1987. *The Sociology of Education,* 2nd edition. Englewood Cliffs, NJ: Prentice-Hall.

PRAWDA, JUAN. 1993. "Educational Decentralization in Latin America: Lessons Learned." *International Journal of Educational Development* 13:253–264.

RAWLS, JOHN. 1999. *A Theory of Justice,* revised edition. Cambridge, MA: Harvard University Press.

REIMERS, FERNANDO. 2000. *Unequal Schools, Unequal Chances: The Challenges to Equal Opportunity in the Americas.* Cambridge, MA: Harvard University Press.

RUTTER, MICHAEL, et al. 1979. *Fifteen Thousand Hours.* London: Open Books.

SALMI, JOEL. 1999. *Student Loans in an International Perspective: The World Bank Experience.* Washington, DC: World Bank.

SAMOFF, JOEL. 1999. "No Teacher Guide, No Textbooks, No Chairs: Contending with Crisis in African Education." In *Comparative Education: The Dialectic of the Global and the Local,* ed. Robert F. Arnove and Carlos Alberto Torres. Lanham, MD: Rowman and Littlefield.

SHUGURENSKY, DAVID. 1999. "Higher Education Restructuring in the Era of Globalization." In *Comparative Education: The Dialectic of the Global and the Local,* ed. Robert F. Arnove and Carlos Alberto Torres. Lanham, MD: Rowman and Littlefield.

SUTTON, MARGARET. 1998. "Educational Access and Attainment." In *Women in the Third World: An Encyclopedia of Contemporary Issues,* ed. Nelly P. Stromquist. New York: Garland.

TACHIBANAKI, TOSHIAKI. 1997. "Education, Occupation, and Earnings." In *International Encyclopedia of the Sociology of Education,* ed. Lawrence Saha. New York: Plenum, 1997.

TASK FORCE ON HIGHER EDUCATION AND SOCIETY. 2000. *Higher Education in Developing Countries: Peril and Promise.* Washington, DC: World Bank, International Bank for Reconstruction and Development.

UNITED NATIONS DEVELOPMENT PROGRAMME. 1998. *Changing Today's Consumption Patterns—for Tomorrow's Human Development.* New York: United Nations Development Programme.

WHITTY, GEOFF, and POWER, SALLY. 2000. "Marketization and Privatization in Mass Education Systems." *International Journal of Educational Development* 20:93–107.

WOODHALL, MAUREEN. 1992. *Student Loans as a Means of Financing Higher Education: Lessons from International Experience.* Washington, DC: World Bank.

INTERNET RESOURCES

BARRO, ROBERT J., and LEE, JONG-WHA. 2000. "International Data on Educational Attainment: Updates and Implications." Harvard University, Department of Economics. <http://post.economics.harvard.edu/faculty/barro/workpapers.html>.

JONES, LYLE V. 1998. "National Tests and Education Reform: Are They Compatible?" <www.ets.org/research/pic/jones.html>.

ROBERT F. ARNOVE
MARGARET M. CLEMENTS

INTERNATIONAL READING ASSOCIATION

The International Reading Association (IRA) is a nonprofit professional organization that seeks to promote high levels of literacy by improving the quality of reading instruction. The association works to achieve this mission by studying the reading process and teaching techniques, serving as a clearinghouse for the support and dissemination of reading research through conferences and publications, and actively encouraging a lifetime reading habit. The association is concerned with reading at all levels—from the school readiness stage through college and adult learning.

The five organizational goals of the association are: (1) professional development to enhance and improve professional development of reading educators worldwide; (2) advocacy to provide leadership in support of research, policy, and practice that improves reading instruction and supports the best interests of all learners and reading professionals; (3) partnerships to establish and strengthen national and international alliances with a wide range of organizations; (4) research to encourage and support evidence-based policy and practice at all levels of reading and language arts education; and (5) global literacy development to identify, focus, and provide leadership on significant literacy issues.

History and Development

The International Reading Association was established in 1956 through a merger of two existing groups, the National Association for Remedial Teachers and the International Council for the Improvement of Reading Instruction. The membership has increased from about 5,000 in 1956 to nearly 90,000 in 2002. A headquarters office was first established in Chicago, but was moved to Newark, Delaware, in 1961. IRA's Government Relations and International Development divisions are located in Washington, D.C., and an editorial office for the journal *Lectura y vida* is located in Buenos Aires, Argentina.

Projects and Programs

The association publishes six peer-reviewed journals. Issued monthly from October to May are *The Reading Teacher,* which reports on research and practice at the elementary level, and the *Journal of Adolescent and Adult Literacy,* which focuses on information relating to middle school, secondary, college, and adult levels. *Reading Research Quarterly* is oriented toward reading theory and research and is published in both print and electronic formats. *Lectura y vida* is a Spanish language journal published

in Argentina four times per year. *Reading Online* is a free Internet-based interactive journal for literacy educators at all levels. *Peremena* is published quarterly in English and Russian for literacy educators in newly emerging democracies in eastern Europe and elsewhere. The organization's bimonthly newspaper, *Reading Today,* provides coverage of the reading profession and activities of the association. The association's active publishing program, which includes a list of more than 200 print and nonprint publications, produces an average of twenty new books and other resources each year, and supports a full-service online bookstore.

An annual convention is held each spring in either the United States or Canada. This five-day program of scholarly and social events attracts some 18,000 dedicated professionals from throughout the world. The association also sponsors a biennial world congress to promote global cooperation and the dissemination of information. In addition to these regularly scheduled conventions, many regional conferences, seminars, and meetings are held.

The association has embarked on a series of comprehensive projects to expand global literacy in both industrialized nations and developing countries. The Reading and Writing for Critical Thinking (RWCT) Project has grown from nine to twenty-four participating countries since its inception in 1997. This project links educators from North America, Europe, and Australia with those from emerging democracies in central and eastern Europe and the former Soviet Union. The Language to Literacy Project in Africa will help to advance literacy in several African nations through professional networking, community development, and increased access to technology.

Through research, the International Reading Association provides a cornerstone for professional development and influence. This includes the creation and dissemination of position papers, collaboration with a wide range of organizations throughout the world, and the active support of research through grants, awards, and the prestigious annual Reading Research Conference. The association also speaks for its members before many government bodies, which has led to increased funding for reading programs, expanded professional development opportunities for members, and the development of new legislation.

Organizational Structure

The International Reading Association serves members at local, state, provincial, national, and international levels through more than 1,250 councils and forty-two national affiliates. The ultimate governing body of the association is the Delegates Assembly, which convenes each year at the annual convention and is made up of representatives from the councils and affiliates. During the year an elected board of directors, made up of three officers and nine directors, controls the activities of the association. An executive director and a staff of 100 people carry out the daily business of the organization.

Membership in the association is open to any individual interested in the field of reading. Membership options allow members to receive a choice of professional publications and discounts on association publications, conferences, and services.

INTERNET RESOURCE

INTERNATIONAL READING ASSOCIATION 2002. <www.reading.org>.

ALAN E. FARSTRUP

INTERNATIONAL SOCIETY FOR PERFORMANCE IMPROVEMENT

Formerly known as the National Society for Programmed Instruction, the International Society for Performance Improvement (ISPI) is dedicated to improving performance in education and industry through a better understanding and use of evolving technology and methodology. It draws on the expertise of individuals from academia, the military, and industry, aiming for a truly multidisciplinary organization representing a broad range of practical and theoretical perspectives.

Program

The society's members are involved in a wide variety of activities, from research on technological advances and their utility in the educational and work settings to publishing books and journals dealing with technology and performance enhancing initiatives. Its original mission, set forth in its earliest charter, was "to enhance education and training through the collection, development, and diffusion of information concerned with programmed instruction." In the early twenty-first century the concerns of the organization exceed its original focus on the application of technology to education and extend to using technology to improve performance in the workplace as well.

The society carries out its mission through its annual meetings, conferences, seminars, and workshops. It puts out a number of publications dedicated to performance improvement technology, including the *Performance Improvement Journal,* the *Performance Xpress* (formerly titled *News and Notes*), and the *Performance Improvement Quarterly,* as well as books relating to the subject written by distinguished society members.

In addition to these activities, the ISPI, in conjunction with Boise State University, also operates an online, nonprofit educational and research facility called the Human Performance Technology Institute, which offers courses to members and non-members alike. It also sponsors grants ranging from $2,000 to $9,000 for research relating to the field of performance technology.

Organization

The ISPI is governed by a board of directors elected for a year's term by the membership. Serving on the board are the current year's president, vice president, secretary, and treasurer, as well as the president of the previous term and the president-elect for the upcoming term. A board of editors is responsible for the publications arm of the organization. All positions except that of managing editor of the journal are voluntary.

Membership and Support

Members are drawn from the academic community, the professions, the military, and industry. The society has more than 10,000 members in the United States, Canada, and in forty other countries, making it truly international in scope. The society maintains its independence by being fully self-supporting, earning revenues from annual membership dues, subscriptions to its periodicals, the sale of books, and course fees collected from its seminars, workshops, and the Human Performance Technology Institute.

History

The 1950s and early 1960s were a time of rapid technological and methodological innovation. As early

INTERNATIONAL STUDENTS: U.S. COLLEGES AND UNIVERSITIES

as 1954 the potential practical impact of these changes on education was envisioned by noted psychologist B. F. Skinner, who proposed that the practices of scientific inquiry could be profitably applied to what he termed the "art" of teaching. He asserted that educators could use the techniques of the psychology laboratory—techniques designed to elicit desired behaviors—to improve performance in individual students. He called this methodology "programmed instruction."

At the time of these insights, professional educators were becoming increasingly alarmed at what was seen to be the declining performance of the nation's schools. It was not long before the concept of programmed instruction began to be adopted, and it spread rapidly throughout the public school system. Soon an interest in the application of programmed instruction extended beyond the field of education.

In 1961 a group of Air Force training officers began a study of the effectiveness of programmed instruction, and they discovered that the use of this approach generated a 33 percent reduction in the time it took for a student to master a subject and a 9 percent improvement in overall achievement. Inspired by their findings, several of the study's participating officers joined with a group of nonmilitary educators to form the Programmed Learning Society of South Texas in January 1962. Within a month these first seven charter members were joined by twenty-five more, and the group decided to establish a national charter. Remarkably unified in their convictions and principles, the greatest point of contention among these early members appears to have been over the spelling (one *m* or two) of the word *Programmed* in the society's official name.

Over the next eight months the organization grew rapidly, spreading throughout Texas and spilling over into California when the San Diego chapter was formed there in October 1962. By March 1963 the society had more than 600 members, and by 1968 the organization had achieved true national scope, which prompted the board to move its executive offices to Washington, D.C. During the 1970s the growth of the organization was spurred by further technological advances—driven largely by the rapid evolution of the field of computing—and interest in the society spread to the international community.

In its earliest incarnation, ISPI was primarily concerned with applying principles of programmed instruction to the classroom through the incorporation of then-new technologies, such as films, slides, and other innovations as well as the development of formal lesson plans and the use of standard methods by which to measure the progress of individual students. Over time this focus has been enlarged to include the introduction of technology in the workplace, as corporate executives began to recognize the need to provide in-house training programs for their employees. Nonetheless, the society's mission remains consistent with its founding principles: to extend the benefits of instructional technology to the society at large. At the same time, the society is concerned to minimize the problems that arise from the blind adoption of the latest technological fad. To this end it devotes much of its time and energy to training consumers of educational technology in the optimal selection and use of such materials.

INTERNATIONAL SOCIETY FOR PERFORMANCE IMPROVEMENT. 2002. <www.ispi.org>.

SUSAN MEYER MARKLE
Revised by
NANCY E. GRATTON

INTERNATIONAL STUDENTS

U.S. COLLEGES AND UNIVERSITIES
Kathryn Gray Skinner
THE GLOBAL COMMERCE OF HIGHER EDUCATION
Anuradha Shenoy

U.S. COLLEGES AND UNIVERSITIES

Formerly referred to as *foreign* students, *international students* are students from abroad who are enrolled for courses at American schools, colleges, or universities and admitted under a temporary visa. These students' primary intent is to obtain an American undergraduate, graduate, or professional degree and return to their home countries.

The number of international students studying at American colleges and universities is rising. More international students pass through America's doors than those of any other country, making the United States the world's most sought-after and diverse educational region in the world. More than half a million (514,723 in the year 2000) international students, or 3.8 percent of all U.S. higher education students, were enrolled between 1999 and 2000. This 3.8 percent included 2.7 percent of all four-year undergraduates and 12 percent of graduate enrollments. These individuals were admitted expressly for the purpose of study. They did not include recent immigrants, resident aliens, or refugees.

Characteristics of International Students

In 2000 Asian students (from China, Japan, and India) constituted more than half of international enrollments, and Europeans were the second largest regional group, with 15 percent of U.S. enrollments. More than two-thirds (67%) of all international students in the United States receive their primary source of support from non-U.S. sources. These sources include personal and family funds. U.S. colleges and universities provide approximately 19 percent of funds and home governments/universities provide 4 percent.

More than 20 percent of all international students are enrolled in universities and colleges located in just ten U.S. counties in or around New York City, Los Angeles, Boston, and Washington, D.C. International students currently study in areas where there are centers of finance, information, technology, media services, education, and industry, which are crucial to the emerging global economy.

Business and management are the most popular fields of study among international students, followed by engineering, mathematics, and computer science. These students come to America to study fields that are not well developed in their countries. International undergraduates have in the past outnumbered graduates; however, the pattern changed in the late 1980s, when the graduate and undergraduate proportions were roughly equal. Male foreign students have consistently outnumbered female students; however, the proportion of females is rising steadily. More than 2,500 U.S. institutions host international students and the international presence varies widely from institution to institution.

International students, scholars, and faculty enrich American colleges and universities and, eventually, U.S.-based firms. It is the collective responsibility of lawmakers, university administrators, and state government to ensure that the best of them continue to choose the United States for their education. In addition to providing diversity on American campuses, these students and their dependents make an economic contribution of $12.3 billion dollars per year (1999–2000).

Admissions Process for International Students

Admissions offices at universities, which admit large numbers of international students, are well versed in the recruitment and admission of international students. Colleges, which admit smaller numbers of international students, must develop recruitment and admission procedures and often rely on knowledgeable colleagues at nearby universities to answer admission and immigration questions.

Testing. Each U.S. college and university has its own admission standards for admitting international students. Most universities require the Test of English as a Foreign Language (TOEFL), proof of graduation from high school, and either the SAT or ACT Assessment. The question often arises if the SAT and ACT Assessment are appropriate tests to be used for admission of international students into American colleges and universities, as it has been argued they are culturally bound tests (made for American students). Although there is truth to this argument, the SAT and ACT Assessment are the two tests that are most familiar to American universities for admissions decisions. Traditionally, test scores alone are not the sole determinants for university admission. Usually university admissions offices use a composite of international students' high-school course work (its rigor and depth), English-language ability, participation in school and community activities, scores on standardized tests, and commitment to academic purpose in making admissions decisions. International students are often asked to provide a writing sample and are given mathematics and English-language placement tests, once they are admitted, to determine their correct academic placement in classes.

Foreign transcript evaluation. International students seeking to transfer to American universities from foreign universities abroad must have their transcripts evaluated by a transcript-evaluation service in order to determine if their course work taken abroad will transfer (for degree credit) to the American semester or quarter system. Large universities often evaluate foreign credentials in-house, while smaller universities require that international students have their credentials evaluated by a professional evaluation service (specializing in the translation and evaluation of foreign academic credentials) either prior to or during the admissions process.

Entering the United States. International students currently apply to American universities via university websites, through overseas advising centers, by written form, and in person while visiting the United States. The most common visa category for international students is F–1 (student visa) followed by the J–1 (exchange visitor). Visas are obtained abroad in the student's home country once he or she has been fully admitted to an American college or university, and a document—either I–20 (for F–1 students) or IAP–66 (for J–1 students)—has been sent to the student.

Foreign student advisers must determine that each international student has sufficient academic preparation to enter the college or university, appropriate English-language ability (or the student will enroll for English as a second language [ESL] classes prior to pursuing academic credit), and sufficient funding to cover the total cost of tuition, room, board, fees, books, insurance, and so forth, while studying in the United States. Foreign student advisers are the front line for American embassies abroad and their roles are vital in that they are responsible for determining which students possess the academic, linguistic, and financial ability to be admitted to study in the United States. Academic institutions in the United States, which have been designated by the Immigration and Naturalization Service (INS) to offer courses of study, are allowed to admit international students for a specific educational or professional objective. Just because a student has the appropriate academic background, sufficient financial resources, and is issued a Form I–20 or a Form IAP–66 does not always mean that he or she will receive a visa to study in the United States.

U.S. consulates abroad determine which students receive visas. If a visa officer determines that a student does not (in his or her estimation) have the appropriate academic background, sufficient English-language fluency, and the financial means of support, or if the officer determines that the student has intent to immigrate (or has otherwise misinterpreted his or her intent) the visa may be denied. The Immigration and Nationality Act of 1952 (INA) allows a nonimmigrant student to enter the United States, who is a bona fide student qualified to pursue a full course of study and who seeks to enter the United States temporarily and solely for the purpose of pursuing a course of study at an established college, university, seminary, conservatory, academic high school, elementary school, or other academic institution, or in a language-training program.

The school, through the official responsible for admission, accepts the prospective student for enrollment in a "full course of study" that leads to the attainment of a "specific educational or professional objective"(Fosnocht, p. 3). In order to be admitted to an American college or university, the international student's application, transcripts, and all other supporting documents normally necessary to determine scholastic and linguistic eligibility for admission, as well as the student's financial documentation, must be received, reviewed, and evaluated at the school's location in the United States. Newly admitted international applicants should be advised that they are likely to be required to present documentary evidence of financial support at the time they apply for a visa and again to the INS when they arrive in the United States. Close communication during the application and admission process between a prospective international student and the foreign student adviser can prevent most (but not all) unexpected problems and visa denials.

Adjustments for International Students

International students who choose to study in the United States usually are among the brightest and most highly motivated of the student-age population in their home countries. Only students with a high degree of motivation can cope simultaneously with the necessary language learning, travel, and dislocation anxiety necessary to enter American universities. Pierre Casse defines cross-cultural adaptation as the process by which an individual is forced to function effectively, but without alienation, in a setting that does not recognize all or parts of the assumptions and behavioral patterns that the person takes for granted. Culture shock is brought on by the anxiety that results from losing all the familiar signs and symbols of social intercourse.

The challenges. International students often arrive in the United States unaware of the immense hurdles in adjustment they must overcome to be successful in the American educational system. These hurdles include English-language acquisition, adaptation to differences in education systems, differences in philosophy/purpose of education, learning styles, and the challenges of other social, religious, and economic values. International students arrive with their own strategies for coping, studying, and socializing; however, these strategies often do not fit the dominant culture and must be reworked.

A myriad of adaptive behaviors, including cognitive self-awareness, behavior modification, and experimental learning take place. Studies by Jin Abe, Donn M. Talbot, and Robyn J. Geelhoed indicate that social adjustment and institutional attachment are significantly lower for international students than for their U.S. counterparts. In addition noncognitive variables, such as self-confidence, availability of a strong support person, realistic self-appraisal, leadership opportunities, and preference for long-range academic goals all impact international students' academic success and persistence. The pressure for international students created by inadequate language skills, inappropriate study skills and habits, and ineffective coping strategies for being a student reveal themselves in many areas of students' lives. Ongoing organized interactions between international and American students are crucial for successful integration into the campus environment. International students experience a constant adaptational process as they attempt to integrate into the American university system.

Cultural adaptation. According to Carmel Camilleri, there is much tension and many psychological problems that international students face related to difficulties of cultural adaptation. Five areas that give foreign students the most difficulty are: abandonment of important cultural values, compromises to merge modern privileges while preserving traditional values, viewing one's community in a position of inequality with respect to society, inability to make sense of nonverbal communication, and dual roles related to parental issues.

The acquisition of culture for international students occurs inside and outside the classroom. There are the lessons that are taught formally and the lessons that are learned informally. These lessons enable international students to make meaning of their environment. Certain agreed-on values reside within and become part of the international student's cultural repertoire and are used to cope with the student's academic environment.

The process of international students entering and graduating from American colleges and universities is a dynamic one fraught with many chances to fail. It is the collective responsibility of administrators, professors, staff, and community volunteers to attempt to connect international students to their

American higher education experience. Philip G. Altbach states that the presence of a half million international students and scholars from virtually every country in the world is the most important single element of globalization on American campuses.

Services Designed to Assist International Students

International education is growing in importance and as enrollments of international students in the United States increase, the abilities of teachers and administrators on American campuses must increase to meet these students' unique needs. The international dimension is critical to a well-conceived educational program. The internationalization of the university is one of the most significant challenges facing higher education in the twenty-first century.

The foreign student adviser. Typical services for international students at American colleges and universities include visa and immigration services, English as a second language (ESL) classes, orientation programs, and host family programs. Staff in international student services, admissions, and student affairs, and academic advisers and professors all help these international students. The foreign student adviser (in the international office or student services office) has the specialized function of dealing with international students. Skilled counselors, often housed in international offices on large campuses, provide services that include referral, coordination, and a special field of knowledge that deals with international students and their specific problems and needs. Traditionally, foreign student advisers and the staff of international offices help students with academic, immigration/visa, acculturation, language, financial, racial, cultural, religious, and ethnic issues.

The major function of the foreign student adviser is to help international students optimize their American educational experience. From orientation programs at the beginning of an international student's degree program to assistance with résumés as the student prepares to graduate, these advisers are interested in the international student's success. Foreign student advisers are responsible for international students and also to their universities. An odd situation exists in that foreign student advisers do not work for the federal government, yet they represent the federal government as Designated School Official (DSO) and Responsible Officer (RO) for the

U.S. Department of Justice and the State Department in issuing visa paperwork. They are not paid or trained by the U.S. government, relying instead on professional training from organizations, such as NAFSA: Association of International Educators, a nonprofit professional organization, which provides thorough and authoritative sources of information for international educators in the United States.

See also: ADJUSTMENT TO COLLEGE; BILINGUALISM, SECOND LANGUAGE LEARNING, AND ENGLISH AS A SECOND LANGUAGE; RACE, ETHNICITY, AND CULTURE, *subentry on* RACIAL AND ETHNIC MINORITY STUDENTS IN HIGHER EDUCATION.

BIBLIOGRAPHY

ABE, JIN; TALBOT, DONN M.; and GEELHOED, ROBYN J. 1998. "Effects of a Peer Program on International Student Adjustment." *Journal of College Student Development* 39:539–547.

ALTBACH, PHILIP G. 1997. "The Coming Crisis in International Education." *International Educator* 6(2):9, 43.

BOYER, S. PAUL, and SEDLACEK, WILLIAM E. 1987. "Non-cognitive Predictors of Academic Success for International Students: A Longitudinal Study." *University of Maryland Counseling Report.* College Park: University of Maryland Press.

CAMILLERI, CARMEL. 1986. *Cultural Anthropology and Education.* Paris: Kogan Page/UNESCO.

CASSE, PIERRE. 1981. *Training for the Cross-Cultural Mind.* Washington, DC: Society for Intercultural Education, Training, and Research.

CHALMERS, PAUL. 1998. "The Professionalism of the Foreign Student Adviser." *International Educator* (spring):27–31.

DAVIS, TODD. 2000. *Open Doors: Report on International Educational Exchange.* New York: Institute of International Education.

FOSNOCHT, DAVID. 2000. *NAFSA Adviser's Manual for Federal Regulations Affecting Foreign Students and Scholars.* Washington, DC: NAFSA.

JOHNSON, MARLENE. 2000. "Creating an International Education Policy." *International Educator* (fall/winter):2–3.

SOLOMON, LEWIS C., and YOUNG, BETTY J. 1987. *The Foreign Student Factor: Impact on American Higher Education.* New York: Institute of International Education.

KATHRYN GRAY SKINNER

THE GLOBAL COMMERCE OF HIGHER EDUCATION

International students contribute billions of dollars to the economy of the United States every year. The U.S. Department of Commerce recognizes education and training as the fifth largest export of the United States and formally classifies it as an industry. During the 1998–1999 academic year, 490,933 international students studied in the United States and they brought almost $11.7 billion into the economy. During the 1999–2000 academic year, 514,723 international students were studying in the United States and they brought $12.3 billion into the economy, through expenditures on tuition and living expenses. While the number of international students studying at higher education institutions has steadily increased over the years, policymakers, market analysts and advocates have been concerned because U.S. competitiveness in the international student market has been declining. The U.S. share of internationally mobile students seeking higher education at universities outside their country of birth in 1982 was 40 percent. Statistics compiled by the Organisation for Economic Co-operation and Development (OECD) in the year 1998 show that this percentage has now declined to approximately 32 percent.

Recognizing the contribution of international students to their economies, countries such as the United Kingdom, France, and Australia have introduced vigorous recruitment campaigns to compete for international students. The United States, in its bid to remain competitive in this market, is also formulating a series of measures to regain its market share in this industry.

Definition and Distribution

For the purposes of this entry, an international student will be defined as a student who (1) is a citizen or permanent resident of a country other than that in which he or she intends to study; (2) has a legal residence outside the country that he or she intends to study in; and (3) is or proposes to be in the host country solely for educational purposes on a temporary student visa. The United States today uses the term *international student* to describe individuals who fit this description, rather than *foreign student*, as in the past. Other countries still refer to students from other countries as foreign students. In this entry, these terms will be used interchangeably since different sources use either term. Table 1 provides figures for the distribution of foreign students in OECD countries by host country in academic year 1998–1999.

Global Market for International Higher Education

The global market for international higher education may be explained in terms of an interaction between supply-side factors and demand-side factors. It is important to note that the available literature in this area focuses only on students from developing nations choosing to pursue their higher education in developed countries. The literature does not shed light on reasons that students from developed countries choose to study in either developing countries or in other developed countries.

Supply-side factors. Supply-side factors refer to factors that motivate host countries to invite international students to study at their institutions of higher education. Supply-side factors may be classified into economic, political, security, and academic factors. Many of the factors mentioned here are specific to the United States, but may be generalized to other countries as well.

Economic factors. First, as mentioned earlier, international students and their dependents bring money into the economy. International students in Australia contributed more than $1 billion to the Australian economy and foreign students in the United Kingdom contributed approximately $1.8 billion to the economy of the United Kingdom. Second, international graduate students serve as research assistants in labs and projects at universities in the United States, thereby contributing to technological and scientific advancements. Third, in a country like the United States that has a strong tradition of immigration, foreign-born doctoral recipients, especially those in the science and technology fields, often stay on to enter the labor market as academicians or researchers, thereby making positive contributions to the U.S. economy and national interests. Finally, the presence of international students contributes to the creation of new jobs in the field of international educational exchange.

Political and security factors. First, students who study in the United States and then return to

TABLE 1

Distribution of foreign students in OECD countries by host country, 1998–1999	
Country	**Percent**
United States	32
United Kingdom	16
Germany	13
France	11
Australia	8
Japan	3
Canada, Spain, Austria, and Italy	2 each
Other countries	6

SOURCE: Based on data from the Organisation for Economic Co-operation and Development, 2000.

their home countries are seen to go back with a sense of good will towards the United States. This good will benefits both U.S. political interests and business interests globally. Second, educating international students presents an opportunity to shape the future leaders who will guide the political, social, and economic development of their countries. International students in the United States gain an in-depth exposure to American values such as democracy and take those values home to support democracies and free-market economies in their own countries. Third, educating international students plays an important role in American development assistance programs. Students educated in the United States form a cadre of trained professionals that understand the mission of U.S. development agencies such as the U.S. Agency for International Development (USAID). Development activities, while promoting social and economic progress in nations, also help to create a greater demand for American goods and services. Finally, international students provide Americans with an exposure to different cultures and political philosophies that, in addition to its social value, is seen as vital for U.S. security concerns.

Academic factors. First, international students provide cultural diversity to American campuses. Second, since they are often the best and the brightest in their countries, international students often provide a healthy dose of competition to American students, thereby raising the standards at institutions.

Demand-side factors. Demand-side factors refer to factors that motivate international students to seek higher education in countries outside their home countries. Economic models of student mobility have been developed since the mid-1960s by researchers including Everett Lee, Larry Sirowy and Alex Inkeles, Gerald Fry, William Cummings, Vinod B. Agarwal and Donald R. Winkler, and Philip G. Altbach. Most studies analyze demand-side factors that are classified as "push" factors and "pull" factors.

Push factors. The term *push factors* refers to factors that push students to seek higher education in countries other than their host or native countries. These can include poor educational facilities in certain subjects, social discrimination, limited openings at the university level, and an array of political and economic factors at home.

Pull factors. The term *pull factors* refers to incentives that pull students towards host countries. These factors include availability of scholarships, better facilities, political ties, cultural and linguistic similarities with the host country, and finally the hope that a foreign educational credential will help in obtaining a better job on their return to their home country.

Attracting International Students

The 1970s and 1980s saw a set of restrictive mechanisms, including tougher entry requirements and sharply higher tuition costs, come into place to restrict the flow of foreign students into the United States, Britain, France, Germany, Australia, and Canada. Reasons for this development included arguments that enrollments of foreign students damaged chances of students at home, that foreign students concentrated themselves in urban centers, and that foreign students often stayed and obtained employment in the host countries, thereby reducing opportunities for noninternational students in certain fields in those countries. However, recognizing the contributions that foreign students make to the economy, the United States and other countries have started making efforts to attract foreign students again.

Since late in the twentieth century, the United States has been in the process of formulating an international education policy to ease visa requirements, ease prohibitive tuition costs, and increase scholarships for international students.

The United Kingdom, the primary competitor of the United States for international students, has declared a formal international education policy designed to attract international students. The government and the British Council developed a program known as "the U.K. Education Brand" in 1999. The U.K. Education Brand is a research and development program that, according to the British Council, is intended to "re-establish and maintain the United Kingdom's credentials as a world class provider of education and training." In addition to aggressive marketing strategies, Prime Minister Tony Blair proposed a four-point program in 1999 to increase their current market share from 16 percent to 25 percent by 2005. The four point program includes (1) a streamlined visa process for qualified applicants; (2) state-of-the art electronic information systems in other countries to provide information to potential students; (3) removal of work restrictions so that international students can work and pay for school; and (4) 1,000 extra scholarships for international students funded by government and private industries.

Australia and other countries created easy-to-read websites that are inviting to students. Australia has established a comprehensive website that deals with all aspects of international education, sponsored by the government.

France, in 1998, announced a new initiative called EduFrance, jointly created by the French ministry of national education, research, and technology; the ministry of foreign affairs; and the ministry for international cooperation. EduFrance was created with a budget of 100 million French francs for four years and a target of attracting 500,000 students overall.

Japan's government is developing a plan to raise the number of foreign students studying in Japan from approximately 20,000 to 100,000. In 1999 the Japanese ministry of education instituted a simplified testing requirement for foreign students in Japan. Until 1999 students who came to Japan either at their own expense or on private scholarships had to take two tests, the Japanese Language Proficiency Test and the General Examination for Foreign Students. Now they need to take only one. Students interested in studying a liberal arts curriculum take the language proficiency test and students interested in studying science-based subjects take the general examination. Also, the tests are now given in ten overseas locations in Asia and are administered twice a year, compared to the previous system where they were administered only in Japan and only once a year.

Most countries interested in attracting international students are now formulating policies which ease work restrictions and visa requirements and simplify testing procedures.

Implications of September 11, 2001

The events of September 11, 2001, when international terrorists (several of whom had been in the United States under student visas) hijacked and crashed four American passenger planes, do not portend well for the United States as an attractive destination for international students. First, national security concerns have demanded that the United States tighten its immigration and admission procedures. Legislative demands for better tracking of international students could increase the oversight of international students in ways that some may find oppressive. Second, foreign students' own concerns for their personal safety might cause students not to choose the United States as a destination for study. Since neither the nature nor the degree of U.S. and international students' responses to the events of September 11, 2001 are clear at this time, it is too early to gauge the short- or long-term impact of potential changes.

See also: COMMERCE OF EDUCATION; HIGHER EDUCATION, INTERNATIONAL ISSUES; INTERNATIONAL EDUCATION.

BIBLIOGRAPHY

AGARWAL, VINOD B., and WINKLER, DONALD R. 1985a. "Foreign Demand for United States Higher Education: A Study of Developing Countries of the Eastern Hemisphere." *Economic Development and Cultural Change* 33:623–644.

AGARWAL, VINOD B., and WINKLER, DONALD R. 1985b. "Migration of Students to the United States." *Journal of Higher Education* 56:509–522.

ALTBACH, PHILIP G. 1991. "Impact and Adjustment: Foreign Students in Comparative Perspective." *Higher Education* 21(3):305–323.

CHANDLER, ALICE. 1991. *Paying the Bill for International Education: Programs, Purposes, and Possibilities at the Millennium, 1999.* Washington, DC: National Association of International Educators.

CHANDLER, ALICE. 1992. "Behind the Trend Lines: Foreign Student Flows—Policy Lessons for the New Administration." *International Educator* 2(2):26–31.

CUMMINGS, WILLIAMS K. 1984. "Going Overseas for Higher Education: The Asian Experience." *Comparative Education Review* 28:203–220.

CUMMINGS, WILLIAM K. 1993. "Global Trends in International Study." In *International Investment in Human Capital,* ed. Goodwin Craufurd. New York: Institute of International Education.

CUMMINGS, WILLIAM K., and SO, K. 1985. "The Preference of Asian Overseas Students for the United States: An Examination of the Context." *Higher Education* 14(4):403–423.

DUBOIS, CORA. 1956. *Foreign Students and Higher Education in the United States.* Washington, DC: American Council on Education Press.

FRY, GERALD. 1984. "The Economic and Political Impact of Study Abroad." *Comparative Education Review* 28(2):203–220.

GUTEK, GERALD L. 1993. *American Education in a Global Society-Internationalizing Teacher Education.* New York: Longman.

JENKINS, HUGH M., ed. 1983. *Educating Students from Other Nations.* San Francisco: Jossey-Bass.

LAMBERT, RICHARD D. 1993. "The Impact of Foreign Graduate Student Flows on American Higher Education." *NAFSA: Association of International Education Newsletter* 44(3):1–2.

LAMBERT, RICHARD D. 1995. "Foreign Student Flows and the Internationalization of Higher Education." In *International Challenges to American Colleges and Universities—Looking Ahead,* ed. Katherine H. Hanson and Joel W. Meyerson. Phoenix, AZ: Oryx Press and the American Council on Education.

LEE, EVERETT. 1966. "A Theory of Migration." *Demography* 3(1):47–57.

MUNGAZI, DICKSON A. 2001. *Knowledge and the Search for Understanding Among Nations.* Westport, CT: Praeger.

SIROWY, LARRY, and INKELES, ALEX. 1985. "University-Level Student Exchanges: The U.S. Role in Global Perspective." In *Foreign Student Flows: Their Significance for American Higher Education,* ed. Elinor G. Barber. New York: Institute of International Education.

SMITH, ALAN; TEICHLER, ULRICH; and VAN DER WENDE, MARJIK, eds. 1994. *The International Dimension of Higher Education: Setting the Research Agenda.* Vienna, Austria: Rema Print.

INTERNET RESOURCES

ALTBACH, PHILIP G. 1997."The Coming Crisis in International Education in the United States." *International Higher Education* 8:1. <www.bc.edu/bc_org/avp/soe/cihe>.

COMMONWEALTH OF AUSTRALIA. 2002. "Australian Education International." <http://aei.detya.gov.au>.

EDUFRANCE. 2002. "Agence EduFrance: The Gateway to Higher Education in France." <www.edufrance.fr/en>.

INSTITUTE OF INTERNATIONAL EDUCATION. 2001. "Open Doors on the Web." <www.opendoorsweb.org>.

JAPAN INFORMATION NETWORK. 2000. "Come Study in Japan! Government Plans to Attract More Foreign Students."<http://jin.jcic.or.jp/trends00/honbun/tj001201.html>.

NAFSA: ASSOCIATION OF INTERNATIONAL EDUCATORS. 2000. "Towards an International Education Policy for the United States—A White Paper for the President-Elect's Transition Team." <www.nafsa.org/content/PublicPolicy/USIntlEdPolicy/alliancepaper.htm>.

NATIONAL SCIENCE FOUNDATION. 1998. "Statistical Profiles of Foreign Doctoral Recipients in Science and Engineering: Plans to Stay in the United States." <www.nsf.gov/sbe/srs/nsf99304/start.htm>.

SCHNEIDER, MICHAEL. 2000. "Others' Open Doors—How Other Nations Attract International Students. Implications for Educational Exchange." <http://exchanges.state.gov/iep/execsummary.pdf>.

U.K. DEPARTMENT FOR EDUCATION AND SKILLS. 2002. "Information for International Students." <www.dfes.gov.uk/international-students>.

U.S. DEPARTMENT OF COMMERCE. 2001. "Top Ten Service Exports, 2000." <www.ita.doc.gov/td/sif/Charts12012001/0112T10.htm>.

U.S. DEPARTMENT OF STATE AND THE U.S. DEPARTMENT OF EDUCATION. 2000. "International Education Policy—A Joint Partnership." <http://exchanges.state.gov/iep>.

U.S. INFORMATION AGENCY and EDUCATIONAL TESTING SERVICE. 1998. "U.S. Leadership in International Education: The Lost Edge." <http://dosfan.lib.uic.edu/usia/E-USIA/education/sept/lostedge.htm>.

ANURADHA SHENOY

INTERNATIONAL TEACHERS ASSOCIATIONS

A large majority of teachers' unions and associations around the world are represented internationally by one unified organization, Education International (EI). Headquartered in Brussels, Belgium, EI was created by the merger of two major teachers' organizations in 1990. It includes 310 teachers' organizations from 159 countries, with a membership of more than 25 million teachers and other education workers.

The creation of a unified international organization of teachers was the result of several major post–World War II international trends and political developments (e.g., the cold war, the end of European colonization, the expansion of the worldwide movement for civil and human rights, the rise of teacher unionism, the collapse of communism) that brought together two former teachers' internationals and doomed two others.

Ideologies and the International Labor Movement

Following World War II the international labor movement, of which teachers formed a small part, divided into three major strands, each of which was associated with a competing political ideology. These strands were aligned with democratic, communist, and Christian Democratic ideologies.

At the close of the war, there was a short period during which union federations in Europe, North America, and the Soviet Union joined to form a common international confederation of national union federations, the World Federation of Trade Unions (WFTU), as well as corresponding international trade secretariats (ITSs) for unions in common sectors, such as metal workers, textile workers, and government employees. (ITSs actually predate World War II, but were reorganized after the war as part of the family of international labor confederations.)

From the beginning a small minority of national unions questioned the wisdom of creating an international union organization that included organizations from the Soviet Union and communist-controlled Eastern European countries, arguing that such unions were not independent from the state and from controlling communist parties. (For example, in the United States, the American Federation of Labor [AFL] refused to join the new international, while the more leftist Congress of Industrial Organizations [CIO] did join.) However, at that time the impulse to create a workers' international overcame any qualms about the validity of unions in communist-controlled countries.

This brief period of labor unity ended in 1949. Between 1945 and 1948, it became increasingly clear to union leaders in democratic countries that so-called unions in Russia and Eastern Europe were actually front organizations that served the foreign policy interests of the Soviet Union, rather that the legitimate interests of workers. The efforts of these communist-controlled unions to block any criticism of the Soviet role in the 1948 coup in Czechoslovakia proved to be a breaking point.

In 1949 democratic union federations in Western Europe and other parts of the world split from the broad labor international to form, with the AFL, the International Confederation of Free Trade Unions (ICFTU). ITSs that had previously included both communist and noncommunist members also split, and new democratic ITSs were organized. The word *free* in the titles of new international labor organizations signaled that they were democratic internationals (e.g., the International Federation of Free Teacher Unions). Socialist and social democratic unions typically led these international labor organizations. The Soviet Union's internationals were composed of labor fronts from Eastern-bloc nations and communist-dominated unions in Western Europe and other parts of the world.

The third political strand in the international labor world was that of the Christian Democrats. The Christian Democratic political movement, founded by the Catholic Church in the first half of the twentieth century in response to the growth of communist and socialist movements, included the organization of fraternal labor movements at the national and international levels. Christian Democratic teachers' organizations were members of the International Federation of Employees in Public Services (INFEDOP; part of the Christian trade unions family) until 1963, when they split off to form the World Confederation of Teachers (WCT).

The Four Trade Internationals

By the early 1960s there were three international teachers' organizations, each associated with one of these three political strands: the International Federation of Free Teachers' Unions (IFFTU—social democratic), the World Federation of Teachers' Unions (known by its French acronym, FISE—communist), and the World Confederation of Teachers (WCT—Christian Democratic). Then, in 1952, a group of smaller regional and international teachers' organizations that existed before World War II formed a fourth international organization, the World Confederation of Organizations in the Teaching Profession (WCOTP).

The WCOTP differed from the other teacher internationals by its lack of political orientation and, at least originally, any union orientation. It was created at a time when most national teachers' organizations were dominated either by school administrators or by teachers who had little interest in traditional union activity. For example, in the United States, the National Education Association (NEA) was founded as a professional teachers' association and was a founding member of the WCOTP (from 1952 to 1972 the WCOTP office was located in the NEA building in Washington, DC). The American Federation of Teachers was founded as a labor union and was a member of the original AFL, as well as being a founding member of the IFFTU—the social democratic–oriented teachers' international.

The background of member organizations in the IFFTU, the FISE, and the WCT were ideologically related, respectively, to the social democratic, communist, and Christian Democratic political movements. In contrast the WCOTP would accept organizations with any or no political orientation—and with little concern about an organization's independence from government or political parties, as long as it claimed to represent educators.

The ideological identification of the IFFTU did not mean that all its members were affiliated with, or directly connected to, a democratic socialist party. Rather, it indicated that the traditional leadership of the IFFTU unions tended to relate to social democratic movements or with similar parties, such as the Democratic Party in the United States. However, not all European teachers' organizations with social democratic ties affiliated with the IFFTU. For example, most Scandinavian teachers' organizations were affiliated with the WCOTP until the beginning of the 1990s.

With one notable exception, the internationals did not prohibit members from being simultaneously affiliated with other teacher internationals. Generally, teachers' organizations from developed countries did not hold dual affiliations, for economic reasons, among other factors—it was not practical to pay dues to multiple organizations. Many teachers' organizations from poorer countries, however, held more than one affiliation in order to benefit from financial assistance from different international organizations and free participation in international conferences and congresses—while paying little or nothing in membership fees to any international. Each international teachers organization had a dues structure that adjusted dues to take into consideration the per-capita income of different countries.

While WCOTP and the FISE had no such prohibition, the IFFTU constitution restricted its members from holding dual affiliation with the communist teachers' international, the FISE. WCT members generally did not hold dual affiliations. As a result, the WCOTP included organizations that also belonged to either the FISE or the IFFTU. The IFFTU included members that also belonged to the WCOTP, but not to the FISE. This situation simultaneously contributed to and impeded the IFFTU-WCOTP merger movement in the late 1980s.

Competition and Convergence

Throughout the cold war era, there was a constant competition, especially between the IFFTU and the WCOTP, for members, prestige, and recognition. Initially, both the IFFTU and the WCOTP were primarily composed of organizations from Europe and North America. Decolonization in Africa and Asia, and the creation of teachers' associations in newly independent nations, resulted in a major expansion of all the four teacher internationals. During the 1960s the membership of the WCOTP expanded rapidly, with the greatest growth coming from Africa, Latin America, and Asia. The membership growth in the IFFTU lagged behind the WCOTP, but began to catch up in the late 1960s and early 1970s. Much of the new membership in the IFFTU came from organizations that were already members of the WCOTP.

It was always difficult to compare the size of the four international teacher organizations with any degree of accuracy. Membership figures for national affiliates were often unreliable. For example, Indian teachers' unions claimed millions of members, but few of the claimed members paid dues to the national organizations, nor did the national organizations pay more than token dues to the internationals. In general, due to economic hardship, almost no members from developing countries paid more than token dues to international teacher organizations. In addition, the competition between the internationals for members, and therefore to claims of strength on the international stage, made it difficult for an international to pressure members to pay dues for fear of losing those members.

As a result, member organizations from the developed world (Europe, North America, and Japan) were responsible for more than 60 to 70 percent of the core budgets of the WCOTP and the IFFTU. The WCT's and the FISE's core budgets were less transparent. It was assumed that the majority of operating funds for the FISE came from the Soviet government, and that of other communist countries. The WCT received a combination of funding from its major members and from government subsidies in countries with strong Christian Democratic parties.

The Rise of Teacher Unionism

From the 1960s to the 1980s, the WCOTP was the largest international teacher organization—measured by membership, funding, and prestige—in the international education world. In the earlier years, the IFFTU was smaller and financially weaker than the WCOTP. However, the issue of teacher unionism began to change this balance. Teacher unionization was, by and large, a post–World War II phenomenon. Even teachers' organizations that were founded as unions and belonged to union federations, such as the American Federation of Teachers (AFT), only began engaging significantly in traditional union activities, such as collective bargaining and strikes, in the late 1950s.

The first major teachers' strike in the United States took place in New York City in 1967, when the New York City local of the AFT went on strike for fourteen days. This was the beginning of modern teacher unionism in the United States. Eventually all the major locals in the AFT adopted the demand for union representation and collective bargaining rights. The success of this new strategy for teachers also influenced the National Education Association to change from a management-dominated professional association to a union led by teacher representatives. In the 1970s and 1980s this transition from professionalism to unionism was duplicated in most of the developed democracies and in many parts of Africa, Asia, and Latin America.

This trend among members of the IFFTU and the WCOTP, and the accompanying emphasis by both internationals on the right of teachers to unionize, increased the coincidence of interests between the two organizations. A second factor that contributed to the harmonization of the two internationals was the development of the European teachers' unions' organization, the ETUC. The ETUC was created in response to the creation of the European Community (EC) and included all European teachers' organizations, regardless of their international affiliations. While European teachers' organizations were divided between those who were members of the IFFTU and the WCOTP or the WCT, the same organizations worked together at the European level.

Merger

This growing convergence of memberships, interests, and union orientation led to formal merger discussions between the IFFTU and the WCOTP in the late 1980s. After approximately two years of talks, the two organizations reached a merger agreement that was ratified at a joint unity congress held in Stockholm in December 1990. The most significant political requirements of the new organization, Education International, were that its members be independent democratic organizations and not be members of any other international organization of teachers. These two requirements were departures from the practice of the former WCOTP, which had not imposed such qualifications for membership. The impact of these requirements meant that if a national teachers' organization desired membership in the largest, and potentially most influential, teachers' international, it had to give up any affiliation it might have with the two smaller organizations, the FISE and the WCT.

The breakup of the Soviet Union, and the accompanying decline in support of communist movements in other parts of the world in the late 1980s, made this dual membership prohibition somewhat of a moot issue. The FISE closed its Paris offices in the early 1990s and ceased to exist, and the WCT was never as large and influential as either the WCOTP or the IFFTU. In general, the international

Christian Democratic labor movement seems to have withered in terms of numbers and financial support since the 1980s, and the prohibition against EI members holding dual memberships has restricted the membership potential of the WCT. Currently, EI and the WCT are discussing some form of a merger or, short of that, an agreement of cooperation.

New Century, New Challenges

At the start of the twenty-first century the vast majority of national teachers' unions are represented by Education International. The post–World War II ideological conflicts and divisions have faded away, while many traditional issues, such as recognition of union rights for teachers, remain in several parts of the world. At the same time, organized teachers are facing new challenges to public education, to teacher welfare, and to security, as well as a growing concern over national and international equity issues. The unification of the international teacher's movement has created a vehicle for teachers to address these issues in an international environment. The new focus for EI is to develop the flexibility, financial base, and expertise to effectively defend teachers' interests and promote quality education systems for all countries in the context of the globalization of education issues and policies.

See also: AMERICAN FEDERATION OF TEACHERS; NATIONAL EDUCATION ASSOCIATION; TEACHER PREPARATION, INTERNATIONAL PERSPECTIVE.

INTERNET RESOURCES

EDUCATION INTERNATIONAL. 2002. <www.ei-ie.org>.

WORLD CONFEDERATION OF TEACHERS. 2002. <www.wctcsme.org>.

DAVID DORN

INTERNATIONAL TRADE IN EDUCATION PROGRAMS, GOODS, AND SERVICES

Historically, education has provided the medium for transferring knowledge and skills to a global society. Research by the World Bank has demonstrated that education is "essential for civic order and citizenship and for sustained economic growth and the reduction of poverty" (1996, p. 1). As the Independent Commission on Population and the Quality of Life states, "education is one of the keys to social development, and virtually every aspect of the quality of life" (p. 170).

As Stanley Katz explains, the commercialization of education took a large leap forward with the development of the personal computer. From the 1950s through the 1970s, computers were expensive and were therefore used mainly for research, instructional, and administrative purposes. But the computer revolution of the 1980s and 1990s saw the development of cheaper computers, better software programs, and the Internet. This resulted in institutions of higher learning expanding their computer capabilities in order to remain competitive. The technology revolution produced many opportunities for the commercialization of education.

Unfortunately, education is facing difficult times in many countries. There are problems with budget shortfalls, increasing enrollment demands, escalating educational costs, and a reduction in foreign aid. Coupled with this has been the protectionism policies practiced by governments to restrict international trade in education.

General Agreement on Trade and Services

In 1986 a series of trade negotiations was initiated in order to find solutions for these problems. These negotiations, called the Uruguay Round, lasted for seven and a half years with 125 countries, including the United States, as participants. It concluded in 1994 with the formation of the World Trade Organization and the creation of the General Agreement on Trade and Services (GATS).

This pact has been called the most significant agreement ever negotiated by the World Trade Organization. It took effect on January 1, 1995, and is considered to be the first and only collection of multilateral rules governing international trade. Its major goal is to remove or reduce barriers that obstruct international trade. The agreement covers goods, services, and intellectual property. Other major features include procedures for dispute resolution and special treatment guidelines for developing countries. As signatories, governments have made commitments to lower tariffs and other trade barriers, and to open their markets for trade in services to all World Trade Organization members. This is known as *most-favored-nation treatment.*

The trade sectors covered under the agreement include services related to business, communications, construction and related engineering, distribution, environmental, financial, health and social, tourism and travel, recreational, culture and sports, transport, and education. Until the creation of the GATS, such a wide variety of activity had never been recognized in global trade policy.

The trade in services area is important because it is the fastest growing segment of the global economy. According to the World Trade Organization, the trade in services area increased from 17 percent in 1980 to 22 percent in 1995, and service exports expanded by 8.4 percent between 1980 and 1995.

Trade in Education Services

Education services are defined as primary education services, secondary education services, higher or tertiary education services, adult education services, and other education services. The higher education services sector has been subdivided into advanced/theoretical/professional and practical/occupational categories to allow for more accurate statistical reporting. Other education services are related activities that support the educational process, such as educational testing services and student exchange program services.

The implementation of this arrangement for education services and goods is presently limited to member nations whose governments decided in 1994 to incorporate this section into their agreement. This amounts to forty countries out of the 143 World Trade Organization members. The forty countries that have committed to this section may limit the extent of their use of the concepts of most favored nation and national treatment. They can partially control access to their markets from foreign investors and restrict the movement of persons who cross their territorial borders. In addition, these countries are prohibited from creating new restrictions on foreign service providers without compensating those countries affected by the restrictions. At this time, none of the nations have agreed to open their education markets without restrictions.

The benefits of education services liberalization under the compact are numerous. By opening domestic markets to foreign education service providers, countries create competition with their domestic education service providers, which results in greater efficiency, lower prices, improved service, more consumer choices, reduced inequality, and increased employment. A 1994 study by the World Bank found that employment in the telecommunications industry in Asia and Latin America rose by 20 percent in markets in which competition was permitted, but by only 3 percent in monopolized markets.

Martin Rudner points out that international trade in postsecondary education services is rising. He attributes this to a number of factors, including an increasing number of students studying abroad, more international marketing of academic programs, enhanced educational cooperation between institutions, and the development of foreign institution branch campuses. The United States is the largest exporter of education services in the world followed by France, Germany, the United Kingdom, and the Russian Federation. The United Nations Educational, Scientific and Cultural Organization (UNESCO) estimated that in 1996 the United States exported $7 billion in higher education services—its fifth largest service-area export.

As these statistics indicate, the major avenue of trade in educational services is through student exchange. In an effort to reduce this student migration, some governments are partnering with foreign educational institutions to establish local branch campuses. Another commercial educational strategy gaining popularity is the "twinning arrangement." This consists of an educational institution in one country linking up with an educational institution in a foreign county to offer courses leading to a degree from the foreign institution. Sometimes local campus facilities are used in this arrangement. In other instances, the educational programs are "franchised" from the foreign institution so there is little participation at the local level. This approach is particularly popular for distance-education programs.

Trade Barriers to Education Services

The major emphasis of the ongoing trade negotiations for General Agreement on Trade and Services is the reduction of protectionism. Lowering or eliminating barriers to trade will accomplish this goal. But several existing trade barriers continue to provide grist for continuing negotiations. One major hurdle that faces negotiators is governmental use of its immigration laws to restrict not only students from leaving the country to study at foreign institutions and but also the number of foreign teachers employed. These restrictions usually take the form of quotas, nationality requirements, restricted visas, and limitations on financial aid eligibility. To assist in compliance monitoring, all countries are required to publish and make easily accessible all laws and regulations related to trade. Another barrier to trade involves the local recognition of degrees from foreign institutions. This is an important issue for distance-education service providers because students enrolled in distance-education programs from a foreign country need to have their credentials approved in the country where they intend to work.

Educational credentials from unauthorized institutions cannot be used to acquire governmental certifications or licenses needed to secure employment in the professions. Continued negotiations are needed in this area to develop common standards and quality assurance measurements for professional education. Foreign education service providers often have difficulties acquiring governmental authorization or national operating licenses. For example, governments sometimes permit foreign education service providers to enter their markets but will not recognize them as legitimate degree granting institutions. Future negotiations should include the formulation of acceptable global accreditation standards for institutions and programs in order to eliminate this problem.

Trade in Electronic Education Services

Transformation in communication and information technology is changing the institution of education. Technological breakthroughs of the late 1990s provided a world communications network with global capability. Education providers have the potential to offer their programs throughout the world. In 1997, the Clinton administration published a paper promoting the Internet as a "duty-free zone," and calling for keeping trade on the Internet free of all tariffs. If governments decide to impose tariffs on electronic transmissions in the future, it would be difficult to enforce because many online transactions are services and require the creation of a mutually acceptable classification system for the content of the transmission. Therefore, negotiations on the tariff treatment of electronic transmissions should be an integral part of any trade barrier reduction effort.

Trade in Intellectual Property

In addition to the GATS, another significant agreement, the Trade Related Aspects of Intellectual Property Rights (TRIPS), was created during the Uruguay Round. It has major implications for education service providers since the programs that they sell are copyrighted or contain copyrighted material. This agreement requires governments to guarantee enforcement of their intellectual property rights laws and to assure the World Trade Organization that their penalties for violations are severe enough to effectively deter potential offenders.

Objections to the Liberalization of Trade Policies in Education

Philip Altbach maintained that higher education regulated by the World Trade Organization would result in a loss of academic autonomy. According to his theory, individual nations would find it difficult to enforce copyright laws, patent and licensing regulations, and trade regulations on academic institutions, programs, and credentials from foreign education service providers. By providing hard-to-regulate educational programs to less developed nations without regard to the local educational culture, educational service providers may inadvertently supplant that country's educational ideas and practices.

See also: HIGHER EDUCATION, INTERNATIONAL ISSUES; INTERNATIONAL COOPERATION IN EDUCATION, TRENDS AND PROSPECTS; INTERNATIONAL STUDENTS.

BIBLIOGRAPHY

ALTBACH, PHILIP. 2001. "Why Higher Education Is Not a Global Commodity." *Chronicle of Higher Education* May 11.

CARTY, WINTHROP. 1999. "New Markets for Meeting Old Needs: U.S. Distance Education and Developing Countries." Paper presented at annual meeting of EDUCAUSE, October.

CURRIE, JAN, and NEWSON, JANICE. 1998. *Universities and Globalization: Critical Perspectives.* Thousand Oaks, CA: Sage.

INDEPENDENT COMMISSION OF POPULATION AND THE QUALITY OF LIFE. 1996. *Caring for the Future.* Oxford: Oxford University Press.

KATZ, STANLEY. 2001. "In Information Technology, Don't Mistake a Tool for a Goal." *Chronicle of Higher Education* June 15.

LINDSEY, BRINK; GRISWOLD, DANIEL; GROOMBRIDGE, MARK; and LUKAS, AARON. 1999. "Seattle and Beyond: A WTO Agenda for the New Millennium." Washington, DC: Cato Institute.

MARCHESE, TED. 1998. "Not-So-Distant Competitors: How New Providers Are Remaking the Post-Secondary Marketplace." *AAHE Bulletin* May.

OFFICE OF THE PRESIDENT OF THE UNITED STATES. 1997. "Framework for Global Economic Commerce." July 1.

OTTEN, ADRIAN, and WAGER, HANNU. 1996. "Compliance with TRIPS: The Emerging World View." *Vanderbilt Journal of Transactional Law* May:391–413.

RUDNER, MARTIN. 1997. "International Trade in Higher Education Services in the Asia Pacific Region." *World Competition* 21:88–116.

SCOTT. PETER, ed. 1998. *The Globalization of Higher Education.* Buckingham, Eng.: Open University Press.

UNITED NATIONS EDUCATIONAL, SCIENTIFIC AND CULTURAL ORGANIZATION. 1997. *UNESCO Statistical Yearbook.* Lawham, MD: United Nations Educational, Scientific and Cultural Organization and Bernan.

U.S. INTERNATIONAL TRADE COMMISSION. 1995. "General Agreement on Trades and Services: Examination of Major Trading Partners Schedules of Commitments." USITC Publication 2940. Washington, DC: U.S. International Trade Commission.

WORLD TRADE ORGANIZATION. 1997. *International Trade,* Vol. 1. Geneva: World Trade Organization.

INTERNET RESOURCES

WORLD BANK. 1996. "Priorities and Strategies for Education." *HDDFlash.* <http://worldbank.org/html/extdr/hnp/hddflash/issues/00132.html>.

WORLD BANK. 2002. <http://worldbank.org>.

WORLD TRADE ORGANIZATION. 1995. "General Agreement on Trade and Services." <www.wto.org>.

MICHAEL A. OWENS

INTERNSHIPS IN HIGHER EDUCATION

Internships, along with cooperative education, field studies, service-learning, and practica, are part of the field of experiential education. Internships require students to apply classroom learning, theories, and experiences to professional settings. Internships or other forms of practical learning for undergraduate, as well as graduate, students have been part of American higher education since its beginning. The most influential ideas about experiential education are from John Dewey's educational philosophy of Pragmatism, particularly his 1938 book *Experience and Education.*

Goals

All internships have the general goal of having students apply learning. Academic internships, which are characterized by being linked to the undergraduate curriculum in one or more ways, have more specific learning goals and broader outcomes than just career exploration or learning the basics of professional practice. Nonacademic internships for which students do not receive credit are usually limited to work experience for the student; there are no measurable learning outcomes. Part-time internships offer less time at the work site and thus the learning outcomes are limited. Full-time internships, usually defined as thirty-two hours per week, significantly increase the students' learning and enhance intellectual and skill development. Credit-bearing internships are very distinctive because they share common goals and elements with on-campus study. These include reading, writing, critical thinking, and problem solving. While many goals are specific to each internship program or course, the list below is of intended benefits or goals for students that are most commonly found:

- Engaging the intern in the discipline or major
- Causing interaction with a variety of individuals, systems, and organizations
- Improving self confidence
- Using a variety of learning styles and frequently challenging participants to use new ways of learning and thinking
- Improving skills in research, communication in groups, interpersonal communication, and observation
- Improving critical thinking and problem-solving skills
- Personalizing learning, giving it relevance and meaning
- Putting learning into context to improve understanding and retention of concepts

- Providing networking and mentoring opportunities
- Conditioning the participant to adapt to change
- Frequently challenging attitudes and beliefs, which often change
- Helping a participant grow emotionally and learn from failure and success
- Helping an intern become a more motivated life-long learner

Structure

While administrative structures vary across successful internship programs, educational and instructional structures are very important. The crucial structural components include participating in an experiential education seminar, writing a learning plan, engaging in reflection, completing reading and writing assignments, undergoing assessment, and creating a learning portfolio. These structures are rooted in Dewey's argument that for experience to be educative it has to be purposefully structured; these structures include the field part of the experience as well as the reflective learning activities that are part of the curriculum.

A credit-bearing internship seminar is a hallmark of a serious internship program. This seminar assists the student in understanding the process of learning and encourages self-directed learning. The academic components of a seminar include assignments such as preparing a thoughtful learning plan; writing reflective journal entries that include analysis of on-site issues and critical incidents; understanding the stages of the internship; completing an analysis of the organization; writing a reflective essay which serves as part of the final learning portfolio; articulating the learning; and giving a final, formal presentation of the learning portfolio or capstone project associated with the internship.

Special attention should be given to the student's learning plan, which is a tool that allows the student to plan personal learning objectives for the internship. It should include content, activities, and methods of evaluation. The learning plan may have different categories of learning, such as knowledge goals, professional goals, technical goals, and cultural goals. The learning plan provides a framework for the student to use throughout the internship and to use when evaluating the learning at the end of the period. The learning plan has been adopted for internships from the practice of adult education by Malcolm Knowles.

Reflection is an essential element of experiential education and therefore of an internship program. Reflection, or critical reflection as it is sometimes called, is the process of deriving meaning from experience through questioning what is experienced or observed. Typical reflection questions are "What is happening? Why? How could this be so? So what?" Reflection can be done in a variety of ways, including classroom discussion, presentations, journal writing, or structured assignments. The point is to provide students an environment and the tools with which to think about what they are doing and what they are learning. Experience without reflection is just experience. However, experiential learning occurs when there is a fusion of theory, practice, and reflection. Reflection allows students to integrate what they are learning and doing at the internship site with what they have learned in the classroom.

Assessment is another important component of an internship program. Someone with academic credentials who can accurately assess student learning should conduct assessment of the student. In addition, the agency sponsor (site supervisor) should be asked to write an evaluation of the student. A learning portfolio often serves as the culmination of the internship and as the major product for assessment.

Internship program goals will determine which structures are used and at what stages of a student's curriculum. Freshman or sophomore internships may be exploratory in nature and include few project elements. A capstone internship course, like the one required for students in the Human and Organizational Development major at Vanderbilt University, will emphasize cumulative learning. This internship is done in one of the last semesters before graduation and includes a senior project that is assessed for mastery of the content and skills of the major. Other internships are tied to a specific course topic or to mastering the skills of a profession, such as social work. Education majors often do an internship or practicum before they do student teaching at the end of their teacher-training curriculum.

Process

Like other educational processes, internships have identifiable stages or phases. In their very practical manual, *The Experienced Hand: A Student Manual for Making the Most of an Internship*, Timothy Stanton and Kamil Ali outline ten steps to obtaining an internship, beginning with self-assessment of goals and ending with the first day of starting an internship. They argue that students who pay attention to each of the ten steps are more likely to obtain a quality and interesting internship. Preparing students thoroughly for an internship is a key element of the process.

Another view of the internship process comes from a developmental theory perspective where predictable stages can be identified and the challenges and tasks of each stage can be addressed. One model by Marijean Suelzle and Lenore Borzak uses the stages of entry, initiation, competence, and completion. Interns have found it helpful to view the semester-long process through this framework so they can be aware of what they should be learning and how they are doing at each stage. Another model developed by H. Frederick Sweitzer and Mary A. King has five stages of an internship: anticipation, disillusionment, confrontation, competence, and culmination. Sweitzer and King's five stages provide a very useful way for interns to anticipate and understand their journeys to deal with problems that often arise after the excitement of the initial stages has passed. Whichever model one uses, it is important for interns to be aware of their increasing levels of competence and the learning challenges they are mastering.

Standards

There is no set of "Principles of Good Practice" for internships but there is some general agreement in the field that "The Seven Principles for Good Practice in Undergraduate Education" offered by Arthur Chickering and Zelda Gamson are relevant. Educational research supports the need for structure so that learning takes place and is assessed. Because internships lack a standard definition and have few recognized norms for evaluating and comparing different types of internships that students pursue, Mary Ryan, executive director of the Institute for Experiential Learning, in Washington, DC, compiled a list of standards of excellence that gives a succinct statement of what is known about undergraduate education as applied to internships. These principles, summarized below, illustrate the goals, processes, and structures that are discussed above.

> **Enhancing On-Campus Excellence.** The internship program should be integrated with and enhance the college's mission and curriculum.
>
> **Institutional Excellence and Integrity.** For internships away from campus, the

organization offering the internship program should have an appropriate management structure, staff, and policies to support the provision of a sound and high quality internship program that includes concurrent curricula, support services, and housing.

Academic Excellence and Rigor. The internship incorporates a defined project(s) resulting in outcomes and products of benefit to the organization and involving college-level learning on the student's part.

Individual Attention and Involvement. The internship program should provide individualized attention and support for the students and should provide for active involvement of students in their education.

Appropriate Internships. Internships should be designed to support the student's educational program.

Appropriate Course Work. The internship program should provide course work that facilitates the experiential learning process and that supports each student's academic program.

Diversity. The program should introduce the student to participants in the larger world of all ages and nationalities and to a variety of opinions, ideas, and philosophies.

Assessment and Evaluation. The student's progress and learning should be assessed based on learning outcomes, in other words, students should be able to articulate and apply what they have learned. The assessment process should be ongoing throughout the semester.

See also: ACADEMIC MAJOR, THE; EXPERIENTAL EDUCATION; SERVICE LEARNING, *subentry on* HIGHER EDUCATION.

BIBLIOGRAPHY

CHICKERING, ARTHUR, and GAMSON, ZELDA. 1987. "The Seven Principles for Good Practice in Undergraduate Education." Special insert in *The Wingspread Journal.* 9(2).

DEWEY, JOHN. 1938. *Experience and Education.* New York: Collier Books.

EYLER, JANET. 1995. "Graduates' Assessment of the Impact of a Full-time College Internship on Their Personal and Professional Lives." *College Student Journal* 29(2):186–194.

EYLER, JANET; GILES, DWIGHT E., JR.; and SCHMIEDE, ANGELA. 1996. *A Practitioner's Guide to Reflection in Service-Learning.* Nashville, TN: Vanderbilt University.

GILES, DWIGHT E., JR. 1986. "Getting Students Ready for the Field." *Experiential Education* 11(5):1, 6.

KNOWLES, MALCOLM. 1986. *Using Learning Contracts.* San Francisco: Jossey-Bass.

MOORE, DAVID T. 1999. "Behind the Wizard's Curtain: A Challenge to the True Believer." *Experiential Education Quarterly* 25(1):1, 8.

RYAN, MARY, and CASSIDY, JOHN. 1996. "Internships and Excellence." *Liberal Education* 82(3):16–23.

STANTON, TIMOTHY, and ALI, KAMIL. 1994. *The Experienced Hand: A Student Manual for Making the Most of an Internship,* 2nd edition. New York: Caroll Press.

SUELZLE, MARIJEAN, and BORZAK, LENORE. 1981. "Stages of Fieldwork." In *Field Study: A Sourcebook for Experiential Learning,* ed. Lenore Borzak. Beverly Hills, CA: Sage Publications.

SWEITZER, H. FREDERICK, and KING, MARY A. 1999. *The Successful Internship: Transformation and Empowerment.* New York: Brooks/Cole.

DWIGHT E. GILES JR.
MARY RYAN

ISLAM

Islam has, from its inception, placed a high premium on education and has enjoyed a long and rich intellectual tradition. Knowledge (*'ilm*) occupies a significant position within Islam, as evidenced by the more than 800 references to it in Islam's most revered book, the Koran. The importance of education is repeatedly emphasized in the Koran with frequent injunctions, such as "God will exalt those of you who believe and those who have knowledge to high degrees" (58:11), "O my Lord! Increase me in knowledge" (20:114), and "As God has taught him, so let him write" (2:282). Such verses provide a forceful stimulus for the Islamic community to strive for education and learning.

Islamic education is uniquely different from other types of educational theory and practice largely because of the all-encompassing influence of the Koran. The Koran serves as a comprehensive blueprint for both the individual and society and as the primary source of knowledge. The advent of the Koran in the seventh century was quite revolutionary for the predominantly illiterate Arabian society. Arab society had enjoyed a rich oral tradition, but the Koran was considered the word of God and needed to be organically interacted with by means of reading and reciting its words. Hence, reading and writing for the purpose of accessing the full blessings of the Koran was an aspiration for most Muslims. Thus, education in Islam unequivocally derived its origins from a symbiotic relationship with religious instruction.

History of Islamic Education

Thus, in this way, Islamic education began. Pious and learned Muslims (*mu' allim* or *mudarris*), dedicated to making the teachings of the Koran more accessible to the Islamic community, taught the faithful in what came to be known as the *kuttāb* (plural, *katātīb*). The *kuttāb* could be located in a variety of venues: mosques, private homes, shops, tents, or even out in the open. Historians are uncertain as to when the *katātīb* were first established, but with the widespread desire of the faithful to study the Koran, *katātīb* could be found in virtually every part of the Islamic empire by the middle of the eighth century. The *kuttāb* served a vital social function as the only vehicle for formal public instruction for primary-age children and continued so until Western models of education were introduced in the modern period. Even at present, it has exhibited remarkable durability and continues to be an important means of religious instruction in many Islamic countries.

The curriculum of the *kuttāb* was primarily directed to young male children, beginning as early as age four, and was centered on Koranic studies and on religious obligations such as ritual ablutions, fasting, and prayer. The focus during the early history of Islam on the education of youth reflected the belief that raising children with correct principles was a holy obligation for parents and society. As Abdul Tibawi wrote in 1972, the mind of the child was believed to be "like a white clean paper, once anything is written on it, right or wrong, it will be difficult to erase it or superimpose new writing upon it" (p. 38).

The approach to teaching children was strict, and the conditions in which young students learned could be quite harsh. Corporal punishment was often used to correct laziness or imprecision. Memorization of the Koran was central to the curriculum of the *kuttāb*, but little or no attempt was made to analyze and discuss the meaning of the text. Once students had memorized the greater part of the Koran, they could advance to higher stages of education, with increased complexity of instruction. Western analysts of the *kuttāb* system usually criticize two areas of its pedagogy: the limited range of subjects taught and the exclusive reliance on memorization. The contemporary *kuttāb* system still emphasizes memorization and recitation as important means of learning. The value placed on memorization during students' early religious training directly influences their approaches to learning when they enter formal education offered by the modern state. A common frustration of modern educators in the Islamic world is that while their students can memorize copious volumes of notes and textbook pages, they often lack competence in critical analysis and independent thinking.

During the golden age of the Islamic empire (usually defined as a period between the tenth and thirteenth centuries), when western Europe was intellectually backward and stagnant, Islamic scholarship flourished with an impressive openness to the rational sciences, art, and even literature. It was during this period that the Islamic world made most of its contributions to the scientific and artistic world. Ironically, Islamic scholars preserved much of the knowledge of the Greeks that had been prohibited by the Christian world. Other outstanding contributions were made in areas of chemistry, botany, physics, mineralogy, mathematics, and astronomy, as many Muslim thinkers regarded scientific truths as tools for accessing religious truth.

Gradually the open and vigorous spirit of enquiry and individual judgment (*ijtihād*) that characterized the golden age gave way to a more insular, unquestioning acceptance (*taqlīd*) of the traditional corpus of authoritative knowledge. By the thirteenth century, according to Aziz Talbani, the *'ulama'* (religious scholars) had become "self-appointed interpreters and guardians of religious knowledge. . . . learning was confined to the transmission of traditions and dogma, and [was] hostile to research and scientific inquiry" (p. 70). The mentality of *taqlīd* reigned supreme in all matters, and religious scholars condemned all other forms of inquiry and research. Exemplifying the *taqlīd* mentality, Burhän al-Din al-Zarnüji wrote during the thirteenth century, "Stick to ancient things while avoiding new things" and "Beware of becoming engrossed in those disputes which come about after one has cut loose from the ancient authorities" (pp. 28, 58). Much of what was written after the thirteenth century lacked originality, and it consisted mostly of commentaries on existing canonical works without adding any substantive new ideas. The lethal combination of *taqlīd* and foreign invasion beginning in the thirteenth century served to dim Islam's preeminence in both the artistic and scientific worlds.

Despite its glorious legacy of earlier periods, the Islamic world seemed unable to respond either culturally or educationally to the onslaught of Western advancement by the eighteenth century. One of the most damaging aspects of European colonialism was the deterioration of indigenous cultural norms through secularism. With its veneration of human reason over divine revelation and its insistence on separation of religion and state, secularism is anathema to Islam, in which all aspects of life, spiritual or temporal, are interrelated as a harmonious whole. At the same time, Western institutions of education, with their pronounced secular/religious dichotomy, were infused into Islamic countries in order to produce functionaries to feed the bureaucratic and administrative needs of the state. The early modernizers did not fully realize the extent to which secularized education fundamentally conflicted with Islamic thought and traditional lifestyle. Religious education was to remain a separate and personal responsibility, having no place in public education. If Muslim students desired religious training, they could supplement their existing education with moral instruction in traditional religious schools—the *kuttāb*. As a consequence, the two differing education systems evolved independently with little or no official interface.

Aims and Objectives of Islamic Education

The Arabic language has three terms for education, representing the various dimensions of the educational process as perceived by Islam. The most widely used word for education in a formal sense is *ta'līm*, from the root *'alima* (to know, to be aware, to perceive, to learn), which is used to denote knowledge being sought or imparted through instruction and teaching. *Tarbiyah*, from the root *raba* (to increase, to grow, to rear), implies a state of spiritual and ethical nurturing in accordance with the will of God. *Ta'dīb*, from the root *aduba* (to be cultured, refined, well-mannered), suggests a person's development of sound social behavior. What is meant by *sound* requires a deeper understanding of the Islamic conception of the human being.

Education in the context of Islam is regarded as a process that involves the complete person, including the rational, spiritual, and social dimensions. As noted by Syed Muhammad al-Naquib al-Attas in 1979, the comprehensive and integrated approach to education in Islam is directed toward the "balanced growth of the total personality . . . through training Man's spirit, intellect, rational self, feelings and bodily senses . . . such that faith is infused into the whole of his personality" (p. 158). In Islamic educational theory knowledge is gained in order to actualize and perfect all dimensions of the human being. From an Islamic perspective the highest and most useful model of perfection is the prophet Muhammad, and the goal of Islamic education is that people be able to live as he lived. Seyyed Hossein Nasr wrote in 1984 that while education does prepare humankind for happiness in this life, "its ultimate goal is the abode of permanence and all education points to the permanent world of eternity" (p. 7). To ascertain truth by reason alone is restrictive, according to Islam, because spiritual and temporal reality are two sides of the same sphere. Many Muslim educationists argue that favoring reason at the expense of spirituality interferes with balanced growth. Exclusive training of the intellect, for example, is inadequate in developing and refining elements of love, kindness, compassion, and selflessness, which have an altogether spiritual ambiance and can be engaged only by processes of spiritual training.

Education in Islam is twofold: acquiring intellectual knowledge (through the application of reason and logic) and developing spiritual knowledge (derived from divine revelation and spiritual experience). According to the worldview of Islam, provision in education must be made equally for both. Acquiring knowledge in Islam is not intended as an end but as a means to stimulate a more elevated moral and spiritual consciousness, leading to faith and righteous action.

See also: MIDDLE EAST AND NORTH AFRICA.

BIBLIOGRAPHY

ABDULLAH, ABDUL-RAHMAN SALIH. 1982. *Educational Theory: A Qur'anic Outlook.* Makkah, Saudi Arabia: Umm al-Qura University Press.

AL-ALAWNI, TAHA J. 1991. "*Taqlīd* and the Stagnation of the Muslim Mind." *American Journal of Islamic Social Sciences* 8:513–524.

ALI, SYED AUSEF. 1987. "Islam and Modern Education." *Muslim Education Quarterly* 4(2):36–44.

AL-ATTAS, SYED MUHAMMAD AL-NAQUIB. 1979. *Aims and Objectives of Islamic Education.* Jeddah, Saudi Arabia: Hodder and Stoughton.

AL-ATTAS, SYED MUHAMMAD AL-NAQUIB. 1985. *Islam, Secularism, and the Philosophy of the Future.* London: Mansell.

AL-ZARNÜJI, BURHÄN AL-DIN. 1947. *Ta'alim al-Muta'allim: Tariq al-Ta'allum* (Instruction of the student: The method of learning), trans. Gustave Edmund von Grunebaum and Theodora M. Abel. New York: Kings Crown Press.

COOK, BRADLEY J. 1999. "Islamic versus Western Conceptions of Education: Reflections on Egypt." *International Review of Education* 45:339–357.

DODGE, BAYARD. 1962. *Muslim Education in Medieval Times.* Washington, DC: Middle East Institute.

HUSAIN, SYED SAJJAD, and ASHRAF, SYED ALI. 1979. *Crisis in Muslim Education.* Jeddah, Saudi Arabia: Hodder and Stoughton.

LANDAU, JACOB M. 1986. "*Kuttāb.*" In *Encyclopedia of Islam.* Leiden, Netherlands: E.J. Brill.

MAKDISI, GEORGE. 1981. *The Rise of Colleges: Institutions of Learning in Islam and the West.* Edinburgh: Edinburgh University Press.

NASR, SEYYED HOSSEIN. 1984. "The Islamic Philosophers' Views on Education." *Muslim Education Quarterly* 2(4):5–16.

SHALABY, AHMED. 1954. *History of Muslim Education.* Beirut, Lebanon: Dar al-Kashaf.

TALBANI, AZIZ. 1996. "Pedagogy, Power, and Discourse: Transformation of Islamic Education." *Comparative Education Review* 40(1):66–82.

TIBAWI, ABDUL LATIF. 1972. *Islamic Education.* London: Luzac.

BRADLEY J. COOK

J

JAMES, WILLIAM (1842–1910)

William James was the American philosopher whose work in psychology established that science as an important element in the revision of social and philosophical doctrines at the turn of the nineteenth century. Thereafter it was no longer possible to erect systems in purely deductive fashion. All thought must take account of the deliverances of current natural science, and particularly the branch relating to man's mind. This respect for the organized experience of the laboratory inevitably influenced educational theory and practice, then still known by their proper name of *pedagogy*.

But James was not merely a scientist in psychology and a proponent of scientific rigor in moral philosophy, including education. He was a philosophical genius—the greatest that America has produced—who touched upon every department of life and culture and who ranks as a chief architect of the reconstruction in Western thought that took place in the 1890s. In the company of Nietzsche, Dilthey, Renouvier, Bergson, Mach, Vaihinger, and Samuel Butler, he led the revolt against orthodox scientism, Spencerism, and materialism and contributed to that enlargement of outlook that affected the whole range of feeling and opinion and has since earned the name of Neo-Romanticism. Every academic discipline and every art was involved in the change; and, in each, thinkers of uncommon scope laid the foundation for the new systems of ideas on which the twentieth century still lives.

William James was in a favored position for adding something unique to the movement: He possessed the American experience as his birth-right and was early acclimated to European ways, British and Continental. He studied in Germany and was fluent in both German and French, and his family circumstances were propitious. He was the eldest son of Henry James Sr., son of the original William James who had emigrated from Ireland to this country and made a fortune. Henry Sr. could devote himself to study and did so. His original ideas on religion and society won no acceptance in his day, but they have been found important by modern scholars, and they certainly influenced the two geniuses who were his sons, William the philosopher and Henry the novelist.

William James's own intellectual career is marked by his father's easy unconventionality, which as will be seen permitted long exploration before "settling down." Every shift in his own development is caught up in, and contributory to, his mature work. James wanted at first to become a painter, but he had the critical sense to see that his talent was insufficient. Next he took up chemistry at Harvard, went on to study physiology in response to his interest in living things, and wound up preparing for a medical degree. He interrupted his course to spend a highly formative year as one of Louis Agassiz's assistants in the Thayer expedition to Brazil. He then went abroad, where he read literature, attended university lectures, and became acquainted with the new psychology, which the Germans had made experimental and exact. He returned to take his Harvard M.D. in 1869 and after further study abroad began to teach anatomy and physiology.

It was not long before his inquiring spirit led him to offer courses in the relations of psychology to physiology, for which he soon established the first psychology laboratory in America. After the publication of his great book, *The Principles of Psychology,* in 1890, James's work exhibited the flowering of an intellect that had from the beginning been haunted by the enigmas of life and mind: He gave himself exclusively to metaphysics, morals, and religion.

By an oddity of academic arrangements, James was a professor of philosophy four years before he was made a professor of psychology, but nomenclature is irrelevant: His beginnings in the psychology laboratory were very soon followed by his offering of a course in philosophy. In other words, the subjects for him commingled and he was always a philosophical writer and teacher. Those were the great days of the Harvard department of philosophy, and during his thirty-five years of teaching James's direct influence spread over a wide range of students, as disparate as George Santayana and Gertrude Stein.

To the end of the century James, despite his new goals, continued to write and lecture on the subject that had first brought him fame. He pursued his research on the newest topics of abnormal psychology, he read Freud and helped bring him over for a lectureship at Clark University. And what is more to the point of the present entry, between 1892 and 1899, James delivered at a number of places the *Talks to Teachers,* which were an offshoot of the *Psychology* and which constitute his important contribution to educational theory.

In any such theory, the assumptions made about the human mind are fundamental and decisive. If "the mind"—which for this most practical of purposes is the pupil's mind—is imagined as a sensitive plate merely, then teaching can take the simple form of making desired impressions on the plate by attending chiefly to the choice and form of those impressions. The rest is done by setting the child to take these in by rote, by repeating rules, by watching and remembering contrived experiments. In other words, the teacher points the camera and pushes the button for a snapshot or time exposure.

No pedagogy has ever been quite so simple, of course, for the least gifted or attentive teacher is aware that the child must exert *some* effort, be in some way active and not photographically passive, before he can learn the set verses or the multiplication table. So, to start the machinery, a system of rewards and punishments is established, which will by mechanical association strengthen the useful acts of mind or hand and discourage the useless or harmful. In this primitive pedagogy, the pupil's acquirements are deemed a resultant of essentially mechanical

forces, and the teacher serves as the manipulator of a wholly environmentalist scheme.

It is unlikely that any good teacher has ever adhered strictly to that role or thought of himself or herself as operating that sort of invisible keyboard. If it were so, no child would ever have learned much of value from any schooling whatever. But it is also true that educational practice always tends toward the crude mechanics just described. And the reasons are obvious: sheer incompetence in many teachers and weariness in the rest. For the two great limitations on classroom performance under any theory are (1) the scarcity of born teachers; and (2) the strenuousness of able and active teaching (which means that even the best teachers can sustain the effort for only a given number of hours at a time).

The state of affairs which James and other school reformers of the 1890s found and sought to remedy was a result of these several deficiencies. The movement of Western nations toward providing free, public, and compulsory education was, it must be remembered, an innovation of the nineteenth century. The inherent difficulties of this new social and cultural goal were great. It made unprecedented demands—on children, parents, administrative systems, and (most important) on the national resources of teaching talent, which are not expandable at will. Theory, too, was wanting for the supervision and teaching of teachers themselves. The confusion that ensued was therefore to be expected. Only a few points were clear: the older pedagogies were too mechanical in their view of the mind; the number of inadequate teachers was excessive; and the exploitive use of the good ones was a danger to the trying-out of mass education.

It was high time, therefore, that psychology put in its word on the subject it supposedly knew all about—the mind. Unfortunately, the mechanical view of the mind existed in two forms—one, as the view natural to ignorant or indifferent persons and, two, as the view that the prevailing scientific metaphor of the time seemed to justify. The universe, according to the Darwin-Spencer philosophy, was a vast machine, and its elements, living or dead, were also moved by the great push-pull of matter like the parts of a machine. The prophets of science—T. H. Huxley, John Tyndall, John Fiske—held audiences spellbound with illustrations of this principle, which everyone was sure could be demonstrated in the laboratory. The newest science, German born and bred, was psychophysics, a name which alone was enough to show that the operations of the mind bore the universal character of mechanism. Man was no exception to the law exemplified by the collision of billiard balls or (in more refined form) by the effect of light on a photographic plate.

To be sure, these scientific interpreters of nature would not have subscribed to a simplistic pedagogy if they had ever turned the full force of their minds on the problem of teaching. One of them, Herbert Spencer, did write a fairly sensible tract on education. And the psychophysicists did not entirely blot out the influence of earlier and richer pedagogies, notably that of the German psychologist Johann Herbart, who died in 1841. But on the whole the situation of the schools in the decades of the nineteenth century was critical, and the strictures and exhortations of the reformers tell us very precisely in what ways.

James, with his encyclopedic knowledge of psychology, theoretical and experimental, his mastery of the art of teaching, and his genius for diagnosis in the study of human feeling, was in an ideal position for showing up the false principles, old and new, and propounding the true ones. The root of the matter was to consider the pupil as an active being—not merely a mind to be filled, but complex and growing organism, of which the mind was but one feature. That feature, in turn, was not a receptacle, but an agent with interests, drives, powers, resistances, and peculiarities which together defined a unique person. Nothing can be imagined farther removed from this than a machine built to a pattern and responding passively to external prods and prizes.

Rather, as one marks the difference, the familiar outline appears of the child who presides over the child-centered school of the Progressives—the men and women who came to dominate theory and practice thirty years after James. But it is only the outline of that child, for James was much too wise a philosopher to suppose that doing the opposite of whatever is done will correct present abuses. His *Talks to Teachers* (1899) fill but a small volume, yet they contain an extremely subtle and complex set of precepts—precepts, not commandments. To follow the precepts one must—alas—use intelligence and judgment, not because James is not clear and definite, but because the teaching situation is infinitely variable—like its object, the child.

To begin with, James does not reject the associationist principle that was the mainstay of the earlier

pedagogy. It is a sound principle, but it is not simple or automatic as was once thought. Associations impress the mind not in a one-to-one arrangement, but in groups or constellations, some members of which fight or inhibit each other. Moreover, the structure of the particular mind favors or excludes certain kinds and ranges of associations. It follows that to reach—and teach—any mind, the teacher must multiply the number of cues that will bring to full consciousness in the pupil the points he should retain or remember. The reason for this method, which is in fact less a method than a call to exert the imagination, is that the same reality can be cognized by any number of psychic states. It is accordingly a *field theory of thought* that James substitutes for the linear-mechanical and would have the teacher act upon.

Throughout his chapters, James moves back and forth from the schoolroom to the world, where the habits and powers of great minds and dull ones can be observed and turned into examples. The point of the shuttling is that there is or should be no difference in kind between what the child is asked to imagine, perform, remember, or reason out and what the grown man does or fails to do. This soon becomes an important criterion. Meanwhile the difference is in degree, which means that the teacher must be aware of differences in development—crudely measured by the age of the child, more closely measured by his rate of maturing, most delicately marked by what is called native ability.

Any teacher starts with the pupil as a lively bouncing creature in which the body and its needs predominate. The curiosity of the child is indeed a sign that mind is present also, but James knows that the "native interests of children lie altogether in the sphere of sensation" (1899, p. 92). Hence James recommends that until artificial interests develop, children be taught through objects, things that move, events of dramatic quality, anecdotes in place of propositions. Stressing also the link between instinct (which rules these early interests) and action, James strongly favors letting the child handle the means of instruction, build, take apart, try out, *do*.

In this commonsense view that instruction should begin by exploiting native interests (which turn out to be physical and active), James is a forerunner of the Chicago School, of which John Dewey was the instigator and later the idol. But neither James nor Dewey was an innovator in the desert. The European kindergarten movement, the early, scattered elements of the Montessori method, and numerous other reforms of school and preschool instruction were in full swing even before James. Indeed, Rabelais and Rousseau had long since made the identical point about the value for education of having the naturally restless child learn by playing, both because playing is congenial and because it is the fundamental form of learning: trial and error.

That point evidently has to be made over and over again in history. But each time history gives it a special coloring. It was natural that in the period immediately after Darwin, which saw the popular triumph of science, the reminder about the child's activism should be seen as the root of the scientific march of mind; for if play is the germ of trial and error, trial and error is the germ of experimentation. It is this plausible linkage that set Dewey and the Progressives to pursue the scientific analogy to an extreme. For them—at least as educators—the mind is forever facing problems and seeking solutions. Teaching school therefore becomes the art of devising situations that will challenge the problem-solving mind and build up in its child-owner a stronger and stronger capacity to size up, ascertain, verify, and solve.

William James never had to confront this hypothesis head on, but it is clear what form his refutation would have taken. In the first place, not every adult is a scientist, and though it is true that adults who are not scientists encounter problems and resolve them, that activity is but one of many forms that cerebration takes. The poet, the painter, the mystic, the housewife, the salesman, the rabble-rouser, each performs his task differently, even if at times they all resort to "situation analysis" and "problem-solving." We must remember James's assertion that the mind is continuous: it stretches from the kindergarten, where it learns, to the laboratory, where James studies it, just as it stretches from Plato's garden to the London Stock Exchange; which is to say that within the unity of the human mind reigns a great diversity, not reducible to the very special, historically late, and purposely artificial form of scientific reasoning.

According to James, good teaching, therefore, cannot follow a set form; it is not the curing of a weakness, such as the replacement of unreason by reason and superstition by science. Rather, it is the interaction of a practiced or well-filled mind with one on its way to the same state. The contents of any mind at any moment—that which James first called

"the stream of consciousness"—is an ever-flowing rush of objects, feelings, and impulsive tendencies. The art of teaching consists in helping to develop in the child the power to control this stream, to sort out its objects, classify their kinds, observe their relationships, and then multiply their significant associations.

In the abstract, this work may be called *attending;* the power generated is *Attention.* James is particularly valuable on this faculty. He points out that if passive attention is sustained by making subject matter continuously interesting, active attention will not develop. He knows that a good part of any subject for any learner of whatever age is bound to be dull; mastering it is drudgery. Therefore, while he encourages the teacher to arouse the pupil's interest in the dull parts of the work by associating them closely with the more interesting through showing unsuspected facets, by challenging pugnacity to overcome difficulty, by dwelling on the concrete effects of the abstract, and by any other means that ingenuity can supply, he does not lose sight of the goal. All this effort at building up enticing associations is to "lend to the subject . . . an interest sufficient *to let loose the effort*" of deliberate attention (1899, p. 110).

Not the precept alone but its pattern has significance. Throughout his educational doctrine, James is at pains to counteract what he calls the "softer pedagogy" by qualifying its blind zeal. The softer pedagogy is that which, having seized on a good teaching principle, such as "make the work interesting," forgets that it is only a device and reduces the end of education to its means: What we can't make interesting we won't teach—or at least not require; there is a good reason for the pupil's not learning it: it's not interesting. On the contrary, says James, education that works for voluntary attention is "the education par excellence" (1890, p. 424).

The Jamesian correctives spring from a sense of the original *complexity* of the human mind. It is not a machine that mysteriously gets more *complicated.* Thus, when James recommends the use of objects, the indulgence of childish touching, building, and trying out, it is not in order to ingrain a habit of fiddling, but in order to develop mental powers that *transcend* the tangible and even the visual. Again, he refuses to give objects primacy over words or to deride the utility of abstraction: " . . . words . . . are the handiest mental elements we have. Not only are they very *rapidly* revivable, but they are revivable as actual sensations more easily than any other items of our experience" (1890, p. 266). And he goes on to remark that the older men are and the more effective as thinkers, the less they depend on visualization. The implications for educational method, when we consider its evolution since 1890 and are aware that the abandonment of teaching to read has lately been urged on the strength of the visual substitutes at our disposal, deserve our closest attention.

The retreat from the word was already beginning in James's time and he warned against its dangers. He bore incessant witness to the important connection between words and memory and its role in making knowledge secure. "I should say therefore, that constant exercise in verbal memorizing must still be an indispensable feature in all sound education. Nothing is more deplorable than that inarticulate and helpless sort of mind that is reminded by everything of some quotation, case, or anecdote, which it cannot now exactly recollect" (1899, pp. 131–132). The description seems to fit the student mind that does best at "objective" examinations, where the case or quotation is helpfully supplied. To summon it up unaided requires a more athletic type of mind, developed by training in verbal memory.

It is clear that James's standard of performance, for both teacher and pupil, was quite simply *the best mind.* He was in that sense a thorough educational democrat, unwilling to classify and mark down intelligences ahead of time, on the basis of their background or their probable future. Everybody had a chance to rival the greatest; education was the means of finding out who could succeed, while helping all equally in the effort. This assumption and the attitude it dictates is the opposite of competing with oneself alone, setting one's own standards, and pursuing only one's own "needs"—which boil down to one's own momentary wants.

All these limiting, hierarchical ideas were in the air when James wrote and lectured, and he put his finger on their unfortunate cause: "Our modern reformers . . . write too exclusively of the earliest years of the pupil. These lend themselves better to explicit treatment; . . . Yet away back in childhood we find the beginnings of purely intellectual curiosity, and the intelligence of abstract terms" (1899, p. 151). The implication here—and experience justifies it—is that the pupils are often brighter than their teachers: "Too many school children 'see' . . . 'through' the namby-pamby attempts of the softer pedagogy to lubricate things for them."

The absurdity of believing that geography begins and ends with "the school-yard and neighboring hill" is a case in point. The child soon comes to think of all schooling as contemptible make-believe—and James with prophetic vision denounces the Dick-and-Jane reading books as yet unheard of: "School children can enjoy abstractions, provided they be of the proper order; and it is a poor compliment to their rational appetite to think that anecdotes about little Tommies and little Jennies are the only kind of things their minds can digest" (1899, pp. 151—152).

A principal cause of James's impatience with spoon-feeding methods, with educational research and statistics ("those unreal experimental tests, those pedantic elementary measurements"), with theoretical advice, including his own ("a perceptive teacher . . . will be of much more value"), is his awareness of the deadly grip of habit (1899, p. 136). "Could the young but realize how soon they will become mere walking bundles of habits, they would give more heed to their conduct while in the plastic state" (1899, p. 77).

If this is true, how much more to blame are the teachers whose "method" in instruction becomes the mold of a habit imposed on the young mind. For James, a right education is precisely the power to sidestep ruts, to link ideas freely over a wide range, to exert voluntary attention, to be rich in suggestion and invention, and to be prompt in receptivity. He repeatedly contrasts the dry, prosaic mind with the witty and imaginative. And since knowledge and experience alike tell him that this balance of freedom and control which he disiderates depends on a well-furnished and strenuously trained mind, he wants teachers capable of arousing passion in their charges—the "whole mind working together." Native deficiencies in this or that faculty can be overcome or ignored: "In almost any subject your passion for the subject will save you." And at the same time he shows a warm understanding of the non-academic type. The student who cuts a poor figure in examinations may in the end do better than "the glib and ready reproducer," just because of deeper passions and of "combining power less commonplace" (1899, pp. 137, 143).

It comes as no surprise, then, that James ends by defining education not in intellectual terms—though his whole impetus is toward intellect—but in terms that unite emotion and action: education is "the organization of acquired habits of conduct and tendencies to behavior. . . . To think is the moral act:" it "is the secret of will, . . . it is the secret of memory . . . . Thus are your pupils to be saved: first, by the stock of ideas with which you furnish them; second, by the amount of voluntary attention that they can exert in holding to the right ones . . . . ; and, third, by the several habits of acting definitely on these latter to which they have been successfully trained" (1899, pp. 29, 186–188).

The "saving" is of course from the blind compulsion of determinism reinforced by bad habit. James's pronouncements about education rest upon a mass of physiological and psychological facts and are abundantly illustrated by reference to them. The reflex arc is as much a condition of learning as the stream of thought; the individual type of memory (visual, auditory, muscular) as determinative as the hereditary constitution of the neural synapses. But James is not a materialist, for he can find no evidence that these factors which limit or condition thought also produce it. And at the same time he finds in man's power of fixing the mind upon an idea—the power of thinking—a range of freedom to be exploited.

These considerations and conclusions bring us back to the starting point. If the nascent mind to be taught in the schoolroom is not a machine, if it is continuous and unified in kind, but diversified in quality and degree, if its operations are not exclusively analytic and directed at problem-solving, what sort of mind is it, in a single word? And what sort of educational theory will suit its needs? To answer the second question first, psychology can and ought to give the teacher help, but it is a great mistake to think that "the science of the mind's laws" can serve to define "programmes and schemes and methods of instruction for immediate schoolroom use. Psychology is a science, and teaching is an art; and sciences never generate arts directly out of themselves. An intermediary inventive mind must make the application, by using its originality" (1899, pp. 7–8).

In short, no matter which way we turn, we cannot in education get away from the work of the mind or substitute for it an ingenious abstraction. How then does the mind work? The scientific way, we saw, was but a special form of its activity; what is the inclusive mode, or as we just asked, what sort of mind? It is, so to put it, an artistic mind: it is by a kind of artistry that we perceive reality, which is the mind's most inclusive task. True, sensations hold a controlling position commanding our belief in what is real, but not all sensations are "deemed equally real. The more practically important ones, the more permanent ones, and the more aesthetically apprehensible ones are selected from the mass, to be believed in most of all; the others are degraded to the position of mere signs and suggestions of these" (1890, p. 305). This description of the mind's seizing upon reality fairly parallels the operations of the artist upon his materials for the creation of another kind of reality: it is the pragmatic method, which only means human impulse seeking convenience and delight, seeking the permanent and the recognizable, the orderly and the satisfying. All education therefore aims at preparing the mind to fulfill its native tendencies and thereby to grasp and enjoy an enlarged order of multifarious reality.

See also: EDUCATIONAL PSYCHOLOGY; PHILOSOPHY OF EDUCATION.

BIBLIOGRAPHY

ALLEN, GAY WILSON. 1967. *William James: A Biography.* New York: Viking Press.

BAKEWELL, CHARLES M., ed. 1917. *Selected Papers on Philosophy by William James.* Everyman's Library. New York: Dutton.

BARZUN, JACQUES. 1956. "William James and the Clue to Art." In *The Energies of Art: Studies of Authors, Classic and Modern.* New York: Harper.

BLANSHARD, BRAND, and SCHNEIDER, HERBERT W., eds. 1942. *In Commemoration of William James, 1842–1942.* New York: Columbia University Press.

CREMIN, LAWRENCE A. 1961. *The Transformation of the School: Progressivism in American Education, 1876–1957.* New York: Knopf.

DEWEY, JOHN. 1910. *How We Think.* New York: Heath.

HECHINGER, GRACE, and HECHINGER, FRED M. 1963. *Teenage Tyranny.* New York: Morrow.

JAMES, WILLIAM. 1890. *The Principles of Psychology.* American Science Series. Advanced Course. 2 Vols. New York: Holt.

JAMES, WILLIAM. 1892. *Psychology.* American Science Series. Briefer Course. New York: Holt.

JAMES, WILLIAM. 1916. *Talks to Teachers on Psychology, and to Students on Some of Life's Ideals* (1899). New York: Holt.

KALLEN, HORACE M., ed. 1953. *The Philosophy of William James.* Selected from his chief works.

With an introduction by Horace M. Kallen. New York: Modern Library.

KEY, ELLEN K. 1909. *The Century of the Child.* New York and London: Putnam.

PERRY, RALPH BARTON. 1948. *The Thought and Character of William James.* Briefer Version. Cambridge, MA: Harvard University Press.

JACQUES BARZUN

JEANES TEACHERS

African-American supervisors of teachers in the rural south from 1908 to 1968, Jeanes teachers (formally called Jeanes supervising industrial teachers) worked toward improving the communities of schools. They reported to the county school superintendent and the state agent for Negro education.

Jeanes teachers were mostly women and were paid in part from a fund established in 1907 by Anna T. Jeanes, a white Quaker woman who wanted to provide rudimentary education for African Americans who lived in rural areas. Additional funding came from the counties employing Jeanes teachers and the General Education Board (GEB), a private foundation created by John D. Rockefeller in 1902 to support southern education. From 1908 to 1926, Jeanes teachers received an average salary of $45 per month for six to seven months of employment.

The portion of Jeanes teachers' salaries paid by their respective counties was based on the willingness and ability of county school board leaders to pay. County contributions varied, therefore, but until the mid-1920s were typically considerably lower than those provided by the Jeanes fund. Although some counties contributed to the traveling expenses of Jeanes teachers, others did not.

The economic situation affected county contributions as well as the teachers' workload. During the depression, for instance, the North Carolina State Board of Education made all Jeanes teachers work full time as teachers or principals, and perform their Jeanes tasks before and after school, on Saturdays and during vacations. Their salaries were paid in full by the Jeanes fund or other private donations.

History

The first Jeanes teacher was Virginia Estelle Randolph of Henrico County, Virginia, who started to work for the program in 1908. She was born in 1874 to former slaves. In 1890 Randolph passed the county teaching examination at the age of sixteen, beginning a fifty-nine-year teaching career. That Jeanes teachers were expected to be active not just in schools but in the community suited Randolph, who had always been active in her community. Prior to becoming the first Jeanes teacher, she organized a "Willing Workers Club" in Henrico County and a "Patrons Improvement League," composed mainly of women and aimed at improving sanitary and health conditions of homes and schools.

Impressed by Randolph's work, Jackson T. Davis, the superintendent for Negro education in Henrico County, applied for funding from the Jeanes Fund and convinced Randolph to become a Jeanes teacher. Not certain that she wanted to take on additional responsibilities such as supervising teachers in the entire county, Randolph prayed for guidance, then accepted the position. Her concern for the welfare of the entire community became the model for Jeanes teachers. Especially during the first two decades of the program, the trustees promoted Randolph's model by giving broad directions to Jeanes teachers and stressing the need to improve their communities.

By 1910, 129 Jeanes teachers worked in 130 counties in 13 southern states. In 1931 there were 329 teachers, but the figure had dropped to 303 in 1934 because of the states' financial difficulties during the Great Depression. By 1937 the figure had increased again to 426. In 1934 only 17 teachers were men, and 286 teachers were women, 177 of them married or widowed. The dominance of women was no coincidence. Dr. James Hardy Dillard, president of the Anna T. Jeanes Fund from 1908 to 1931, felt that women were better suited for the intensive work that required superb human-relations skills. The fund's administrators also argued that rural women, as opposed to urban, were best suited for the work, and women with a rural background dominated the Jeanes work during the program's first three decades.

Goals and Duties

Jeanes Fund administrators stressed the need for the teachers to adapt to the specific needs of individual communities as well as to promote higher standards of living. Specific duties included school visits to help and encourage schoolteachers to teach sanitation, sewing, cooking, basket making, chair caning, and mat making. Jeanes teachers were to meet with men and women in the communities to form Improvement Leagues or Betterment Associations. These organizations were to elevate living conditions and paint or whitewash schoolhouses, homes, and outhouses. The teachers also had to raise money to build better schoolhouses and lengthen school terms. Furthermore, they had to encourage and organize home and school gardens, tomato clubs, and corn clubs.

The first Jeanes teachers were considered industrial teachers but in 1918 at least two were trained nurses who taught good health and hygiene habits and how to care properly for children and sick people. The work of Jeanes teachers was often influenced by their gender. Women were expected to teach the "fundamental industries of the home." Some women teachers taught sewing or cooking or both to other teachers, students and adults in the community. A few taught washing and ironing. Others were expert dressmakers, milliners, weavers and basket makers. The men, on the other hand, were expected to teach some "sort of bread-winning work." They mainly taught farming and gardening but also carpentry, bricklaying, blacksmithing, shoemaking and repairing. Other male Jeanes teachers included a painter and paper-handler, a mattress-maker, a cook, and a tailor.

Most Jeanes teachers unofficially served as the county superintendent for African-American schools as white superintendents directed most of their energy toward schools for whites. Jeanes teachers encouraged mainly local African Americans and whites to give money and time to black education. They worked with principals and teachers in implementing curricula changes. They served as liaisons between black schools and white county and state school administrators. They also served as liaisons between black schools and state and local government agencies as well as federal agencies such as the U.S. Department of Agriculture.

To encourage African-American students to attend school, Jeanes teachers simultaneously addressed illiteracy and poverty throughout their communities. Jeanes teachers used Homemakers Clubs and other forms of industrial education to improve the rural food supply, health care, and their schools' finances. They raised funds to build and maintain Rosenwald and county training schools. Jeanes teachers participated in and provided leadership for numerous racial uplift organizations such as the Federation of Afro-American Club Women, the National Association of Colored Women, the National Council for Negro Women, and church missionary associations. These organizations all provided avenues for community improvement, to support social welfare institutions such as orphanages and homes for wayward girls, and to set up and maintain recreational facilities. Providing clothing to destitute children and access to health care, along with the teachers' efforts to increase the number of schools and improve existing ones, stimulated attendance. The attendance rate increased by 22 percent between 1900 and 1920; by 1950, 69 percent of southern African-American children attended school.

The Homemakers Clubs

The Homemakers Clubs were a major component of the Jeanes teachers' work and of industrial education for blacks in general during the early part of the twentieth century. They were community groups organized as early as 1913 by Jeanes teachers to instruct the locals mainly but not exclusively in the preservation of food. Homemakers Clubs were to encourage vegetable gardens, home sanitation, food preservation and sewing. The Jeanes teacher made personal visits to schools and homes and gave instruction in planting, cultivating, canning, and so forth. They placed special emphasis on the family garden.

Rosenwald Schools

Jeanes teachers also encouraged people in their communities to become involved in building and maintaining schools. They used the contacts and goodwill they developed through Homemakers Clubs, churches and other organizations. Their success encouraged the GEB to increase funding for black schools. It helped efforts to attract funding for black education in the south from philanthropic organizations other than the Jeanes Fund, such as the the Julius Rosenwald Fund. Rosenwald, president of Sears, Roebuck and Company (1910 to 1924) and later chairman of the board (1925 to 1932), established the Rosenwald Fund for improving rural school buildings in the south through public–private partnerships. Jeanes teachers were directly involved in the construction of Rosenwald schools, and it probably challenged their fundraising, public-relations, and organizing skills more than anything else.

Rosenwald contracts stipulated that African-American communities match or exceed the amount requested from the fund and demanded cooperation between state and county school authorities. The contracts also required that land, equipment and all other property be deeded to the county school. The Rosenwald program stressed industrial education. The first Rosenwald school was built in 1913 in Alabama. In 1936 the fund reported 5,357 schools built in fifteen southern states. North Carolina led the way. The Rosenwald Fund began its funding of schools there in 1915, and between 1915 and 1932 North Carolina built over 800 Rosenwald schools, far more than any other state.

Jeanes teachers worked with local and state officials, professionals such as attorneys and doctors, as well as religious and nonreligious organizations, both black and white, to promote the construction of these schools. They raised funds for equipment, including kitchen equipment. By July 1, 1932, Rosenwald contributions to school construction in the south was $4.3 million. African Americans had contributed $4.7 million, and local governments, $18.8 million. Rosenwald funding increased dramatically during the last four years of the program as it built larger, six-room to seven-room schools.

State agents were important to African-American education, but Jeanes teachers facilitated their success and played the most significant role in the Rosenwald building program. Of the more than 4,000 Rosenwald schools built by the mid-1930s in all fifteen southern states, two-thirds were in counties where Jeanes teachers were employed. Although overlooked by historians, the efforts of Jeanes teachers and other women made the most significance difference in the number and quality of schools for rural African Americans.

Health Care

In addition to providing buildings to facilitate access to education, Jeanes teachers addressed other student needs. During the first three decades of the twentieth century, hookworm disease, tuberculosis, syphilis, and to some extent malaria and pellagra wreaked havoc on southern communities. Most counties could not afford a nurse, and few health institutions existed for African Americans or the poor. As early as 1917 Jeanes teachers were selected by health departments to help combat tuberculosis. Jeanes teachers invited city nurses to talk to parent–teacher associations and organized medical examinations for students. They held preschool clinics during which nurses or doctors checked students'

tonsils, and visited homes in advance to make sure parents brought their children. Jeanes teachers organized "Clean Tooth" campaigns and National Health Week activities. They fumigated school buildings, following the county health officer's instructions.

Contribution

Heavy workloads and high expectations from both the community and the Jeanes teachers themselves often meant that most worked long hours, even though they were not paid for much of their overtime. Some teachers visited three to four schools a week, others five to eight. Teachers sometimes spent a week at a particular school, overseeing industrial training projects, assisting teachers with reading, writing, spelling, and arithmetic instruction, visiting homes, and organizing clubs for home and school improvement.

The sheer size of their mandate and the fact that they had to develop most programs from scratch meant that Jeanes teachers could not fulfill all expectations. Jeanes teachers were allowed considerable freedom and flexibility to decide priorities based on their assessment of a community's need and the resources available. It also allowed them to manipulate a Jim Crow system to provide African Americans with some opportunities and most importantly, hope.

See also: EDUCATION REFORM; MULTICULTURAL EDUCATION.

BIBLIOGRAPHY

JONES, LANCE. 1937. *The Jeanes Teacher in the United States, 1908–1933.* Chapel Hill: University of North Carolina Press.

LITTLEFIELD, VALINDA W. 1999. "'To Do the Next Needed Thing': Jeanes Teachers in the Southern United States 1908–1934." In *Telling Women's Lives,* ed. Kathleen Weiler and Sue Middleton. Philadelphia: Open University Press.

SMITH, ALICE BROWN. 1997. *Forgotten Foundations: The Role of Jeanes Teachers in Black Education.* New York: Vantage Press.

VALINDA LITTLEFIELD

JEWISH EDUCATION, UNITED STATES

Throughout history, the Jewish people have been a minority culture and religion. In times of peace, Judaism thrived; in times of hostility, Jews protected themselves from outside forces. In the United States today, Jews face relatively little hostility. Jews are allowed to live wherever they please, they can study and engage in any profession, and they may practice their religion openly. Fighting anti-Semitism is no longer the rallying cry that it once was for the Jewish community. The state of Israel, another center of Jewish cohesiveness, now stands strong in the Middle East and American Jews no longer worry about Israel's permanence as a nation. Furthermore, most Jewish people in the world today are free to leave their countries and move to Israel. Jews cannot rally around the cries to free Soviet Jewry as they did in the late 1980s. Those Ethiopian Jews who dreamt of immigration to Israel are already being resettled. While small pockets of Jews still live in countries that do not allow them to leave, the vast majority of Jews around the world are free.

The multitude of issues that propelled Jewish communities in the United States to come together—and drew individual Jews to work together for the good of the Jewish people worldwide—no longer have the urgency that they once did. Jews in the United States can live without Judaism; many immerse themselves in their secular lives without feeling the loss of the richness of their Jewish heritage. Many Jewish parents are failing to pass their Jewish religion and heritage to their children. In fact, less than half of all children born to at least one Jewish parent (or a parent who was born Jewish) are being raised as Jews, according to Alice Goldstein and Sylvia Fishman's 1993 study. Furthermore, the rate of intermarriage is at an all time high. Almost 50 percent of American Jews married since 1985 did not marry within the Jewish faith. Thus, the overriding concern for American Jewry in the twenty-first century is Jewish continuity—the continued existence of the Jewish people, its culture, traditions, practices and beliefs.

There are three main denominations in the U.S. Jewish community: the Orthodox, who strictly follow the traditions of Jewish life and the basic code of Jewish law; the Conservative, who embrace the central rituals and laws of Judaism but adapt them to modern life; and the Reform, who preserve the spirit of the law, with the letter of the law as a guidepost for modern decision-making. Across all denominations and movements of Judaism, the response to threats of total assimilation and continuity is education. Jewish education is an important tool as community leaders look to ways to ensure the survival of Judaism for generations to come. Jonathan Sarna maintained in 1998 that "Jewish education serves as the vehicle through which we train successive generations of Jews to negotiate their own way as Jews, in the American arena" (p. 10). This mission is achieved through numerous educational frameworks: day schools, afternoon religious schools, Sunday schools, informal educational programs, university-based programs, and extensive adult education.

Jewish Day Schools

Day schools are private, independent schools that teach Jewish and secular education subjects, similar to other parochial schools in the United States. The Jewish subject matter typically focuses on Hebrew language, prayers, the Bible, customs, ceremonies and rituals, Jewish history, and the state of Israel. Most day schools are not affiliated with any particular congregation or synagogue, although most are connected to one of the three main denominations of Judaism.

Reform and Conservative Jews have long been ardent supporters of public education. Public schools have typically been seen as a place where children of different backgrounds could mix with—and learn about—each other in a safe environment. Jews have often been at the forefront of efforts to oppose educational options that would lead to segregated schools. Furthermore, many Jews have long felt that Jewish day schools are outdated and not appropriate for Jewish children brought up in the modern world. For instance, in 1870, Rabbi Isaac Mayer Wise, a prominent Reform Jewish leader declared, "Education of the young is the duty of the State and that religious instruction . . . is the duty of religious bodies. Neither ought to interfere with the other" (quoted in Sarna, p. 11).

In contrast, for Orthodox Jews, day schools—including yeshivas—where Torah and other religious subjects are the primary curricula, continue to be the sole avenue for educating children. Most Orthodox day schools belong to an umbrella organization called Torah Umesorah that provides curricula, teacher training, placement services, and special education supports to the Orthodox educational community. Some Orthodox day schools continue to use Yiddish as the language of instruction, while most day schools rely heavily upon Hebrew.

At the end of the twentieth century, day school enrollment—including that of non-Orthodox day schools—increased dramatically. A census of Jewish Day Schools in the United States conducted by Marvin Schick in 2000 calculated that 185,000 students were enrolled in Jewish day schools across the United States. About two-thirds of these students were in either New York or New Jersey, which strongly correlates to the large percentage of Orthodox Jews who live in these states. In fact, Orthodox schools accounted for 80 percent of the total enrollment in Jewish day schools during the 1998 to 1999 school year.

In all day schools, enrollment is higher in the younger grades. For Orthodox schools, this is true because of increased—and high—birthrates in their communities. In non-Orthodox day schools many parents believe that better opportunities exist in public or other private, non-Jewish schools for their older children when college admissions becomes a key decision factor. Furthermore, many communities do not have non-Orthodox Jewish high school options.

For Reform and Conservative Jews, day schools are seen as a solution to the multitude of Jewish youth growing up without knowledge or commitment to Judaism or a Jewish identity. Seen as a response to the Jewish continuity crisis, new day schools are cropping up across America. Goldstein and Fishman's 1993 research indicates that youth who receive Jewish day school education are less likely to intermarry and are more likely to raise their children as Jews.

Synagogue Education

While attendance at Jewish day schools increased markedly in the ten years prior to the beginning of the twenty-first century, most non-Orthodox Jewish children still receive the majority of their Jewish education in supplemental religious schools run by local synagogues. This mode of education allowed parents to avoid the fears of "ghettoization" of the day schools. Synagogue religious schools have long been given the task of educating Jewish youth in a wide range of subjects, including history, culture, holidays, Hebrew language, prayer, and Torah. Students in some congregations attend supplementary religious school one day per week, called Sunday school. Other students, especially those affiliated with the Conservative movement, attend approximately six hours per week, one and one-half hours on two days after "regular" school and three hours on Sunday morning. Much of the focus of supplementary school education is on preparing youth for the bar or bat mitzvah at the age of thirteen. Hence, enrollment often declines after bar/bat mitzvah age.

Attendance at synagogue religious school is the central mechanism for children to learn about Judaism. Because of the part-time nature of these educational programs, numerous challenges confront these schools. One is the obvious lack of time and sustained focus available to educators. Children attend with low levels of motivation and commitment after a long day in their secular school. An even bigger challenge is the personnel crisis in Jewish education. These supplementary school classes are often taught by teachers who, although committed Jews, know little about the subjects they teach. A study of Jewish educators in three communities in the United States found that close to 80 percent of the teachers in supplementary schools have neither a degree in Jewish studies nor certification as Jewish educators. In preschools, 10 percent of the teachers are not even Jewish. In one community the figure was as high as 21 percent according to the Council for Initiatives in Jewish Education. Professional development opportunities are relatively scant as well.

However, a new generation of supplemental religious schools is emerging to refocus on both the personnel and continuity crises. Educational efforts are geared toward learners of all ages, including families. Teachers are participating in expanded educational opportunities. Synagogue communities are recognizing that if supplemental education is to be successful it will have to (1) span all age groups and (2) allow students to enter a "Jewish existence that they will recognize to be existentially, intellectually, and spiritually meaningful" (Pekarsyky, p. 39). Successful supplementary schools tend to be housed in synagogues where the educational programs are a high priority for the congregation as a whole, have favored status and commitment from all stakeholders (especially the rabbis and lay leadership), and are linked to the culture and mission of the synagogue.

Informal Education

One of the most important developments in Jewish education is the huge increase in participation in Jewish summer camps, youth groups, organized youth trips to Israel, and family and adult education. Summer camps are places were Jewish youth can interact with one another in uniquely Jewish environments. Camps allow participants to see the value of living as more than cultural Jews. Campers are able to gain respect and appreciation for engaging in daily Jewish ritual. They experience the power of group observance, and gain their own Jewish identity, independent of that of their parents.

Jewish youth groups are also instrumental in giving Jewish children the education they need to be committed Jews. Like camps, youth groups have many purposes beyond that of education. Social, athletic, and community service activities often attract Jewish youth who may not have attended Jewish day schools, supplemental religious schools, or camps. Thus, participation in Jewish youth groups is an important mechanism to reach out to all types of youth, particularly the unaffiliated. Youth groups are often housed in Jewish community centers and other cross-denominational frameworks.

Summer youth trips to Israel are a large part of the "curriculum" of Jewish education. It was estimated by the Commission of Jewish Education in North America in 1990 that approximately 25,000 American youth annually participate in educational trips to Israel. Some supplementary religious schools mandate participation in a class trip to Israel. Many Jewish federations, a community umbrella organization for all Jewish organizations in a city, provide scholarships to make it possible for youth to go to Israel on educational trips. The educational value of trips to Israel is well documented. Those youth who experience Israel firsthand are more committed ideologically to the state of Israel and to Judaism.

Informal adult education programs provide numerous opportunities for Jewish study. Small groups of adults meet together in informal text study groups, attend retreats, and participate in noncredit courses offered by Jewish community centers, local Hebrew colleges and synagogues. Family education is considered one of the newest models of Jewish education. Young and old alike come together as families to focus on Jewish learning, holiday workshops, and cultural events.

Conclusion

The end of the twentieth century saw a revival of interest in Jewish education. Day schools increased in popularity across all denominations. Synagogues refocused on providing quality, meaningful education to both children and adults either in a religious school setting or through adult and family education. Informal educational opportunities for youth expanded. Although it is true that, in part, this is due to the traditional Jewish emphasis on education, the increased financial support by Jewish federations and individual philanthropists was aimed at attacking trends of intermarriage, assimilation, and Jewish continuity. Formal and informal Jewish education is the rallying cry.

See also: CATHOLIC SCHOOLS; ISLAM; PRIVATE SCHOOLING; PROTESTANT SCHOOL SYSTEMS.

BIBLIOGRAPHY

COHEN, BURTON, and SCHMIDA, MIRIAM. 1997. "Informal Education in Israel and North America." *Journal of Jewish Education* 63(2):50–58.

FISHMAN, SYLVIA B., and GOLDSTEIN, ALICE. 1993. *When They Are Grown They Will Not Depart: Jewish Education and the Jewish Behavior of American Adults.* CMJS Research Report 8. Waltham, MA: Maurice and Marilyn Cohen Center for Modern Jewish Studies.

GAMORAN, ADAM, et al. 1998. *The Teachers Report: A Portrait of Teachers in Jewish Schools.* New York: Council for Initiatives in Jewish Education.

GOLDSTEIN, ALICE, and FISHMAN, SYLVIA B. 1993. *Teach Your Children When They Are Young: Contemporary Jewish Education in the United States.* CMJS Research Report 10. Waltham, MA: Maurice and Marilyn Cohen Center for Modern Jewish Studies.

HOLTZ, BARRY W.; DORPH, GAIL Z.; and GOLDRING, ELLEN B. 1997. "Educational Leaders as Teacher Educators: The Teacher Educator Institute: A Case from Jewish Education." *Peabody Journal of Education* 72(2):147–166.

ISAACS, LEORA W., ed. 1994. *Youth Trip to Israel: Rationale and Realization.* New York: Jewish Education Service of North America.

PEKARSYKY, DANIEL. 1997. "The Place of Vision in Jewish Educational Reform." *Journal of Jewish Education* 63:31–40.

REIMER, JOSEPH. 1990. *The Synagogue as a Context for Jewish Education.* Cleveland, OH: The Commission on Jewish Education in North America.

SARNA, JONATHAN D. 1998. "American Jewish Education in Historical Perspective." *Journal of Jewish Education* 64:8–21.

SCHICK, MARVIN. 2000. *A Census of Jewish Schools in the United States.* New York: Avi Chai Foundation.

INTERNET RESOURCE

CENTRAL CONFERENCE OF AMERICAN RABBIS. 2001. "Resolutions Adopted by the CCAR." <www.ccarnet.org/reso>.

ELLEN GOLDRING
ROBERT J. BERK

JOHNS HOPKINS UNIVERSITY

Johns Hopkins University was founded in 1876 by educational pioneers who abandoned the traditional roles of the American college and forged a new era of modern research universities by focusing on the expansion of knowledge, graduate education, and support of faculty research.

Early Years

In 1873 Johns Hopkins, a childless bachelor, bequeathed $7 million to fund a hospital and university in Baltimore, Maryland. At that time this fortune, generated primarily from the Baltimore and Ohio Railroad, was the largest philanthropic gift in the history of the United States. Flush with funds, the new board searched the nation for appropriate models of higher education. Finding none to their liking, they opted for an entirely new model. It was to be a truly national school dedicated to the discovery of knowledge. It owed its inspiration not to America's higher educational system but to modernized Germany. By following the Germanic university example, the board animated a new spirit and structure, which moved higher education in the United States away from a focus on either revealed or applied knowledge to a concentration on the scientific discovery of new knowledge. This made Johns Hopkins the genesis of the modern research university.

The Gilman Period

Johns Hopkins was intended to be national in scope, so it could serve as a balm for a country divided over the sectional strife of the Civil War. As such, the university's official commemoration took on great significance: 1876 was the nation's centennial year and February 22 was George Washington's birthday. Notwithstanding the care taken in selecting this date, the institution's viability depended directly on the board's choice for the first president. They chose wisely. Daniel Coit Gilman, lured away from the presidency of the University of California, helped create Johns Hopkins University and lead American higher education in new directions. In word and sometimes deed, Gilman held to some traditional goals of the denominational college but, nevertheless, he created the first American campus focused on the faculty and their research. To Gilman, Johns Hopkins existed not for the sake of God, the state, the community, the board, the parents, or even the students, but for knowledge. Therefore, faculty who expanded knowledge were rewarded.

Connected with the new university's focus was its concentration on graduate education and the fusion of advanced scholarship with such professional schools as medicine and engineering. It was the national pacesetter in doctoral programs and was the host for numerous scholarly journals and associations. Having a faculty-oriented perspective, the university did not want its professors bogged down in remedial education, but rather wanted to attract serious, prepared students who could genuinely participate in the discovery of new knowledge. Though the opposite is often mistakenly believed, Johns Hopkins has always provided undergraduate education, although Gilman had to be persuaded to include it and other early presidents attempted to eliminate the program. However, whether undergraduate or graduate, Johns Hopkins concentrates on providing research opportunities for all of its students. And its strong ties with John Hopkins Hospital, a teaching and research hospital, attract students from around the nation interested in biomedical engineering and medicine.

Modern Times

The legacy of adroit leadership begun by Gilman has continued. Among the many able presidents, Milton S. Eisenhower, brother of Dwight Eisenhower, led Johns Hopkins during the 1950s and 1960s when the university's income tripled, endowment doubled, ambitious building projects were undertaken, and strong ties with Washington, DC, were developed. Because of his contributions, Eisenhower was one of two men named president emeritus. Steven Muller, who served as president from 1972 until 1990, is the only other one awarded this title—and along with Gilman is one of two to be named president of both the Johns Hopkins hospital and the university.

Though privately endowed, Johns Hopkins University embodies what Clark Kerr called the "federal grant university," as it often tops the nation in federal research and development expenditures. Johns Hopkins University also illustrates the skewed priorities of federal grants, as the school's humanities programs cannot hope to attract research funding commensurate with that attracted by medicine, public health, engineering, and physics. Despite this imbalance, the institution remains committed to professional instruction in conjunction with academic disciplines within a true university setting. The Georgian-style Homewood campus provides an academic atmosphere that allows students to participate in extracurricular activities. In intercollegiate athletics, Johns Hopkins is famous for lacrosse and houses the National Lacrosse Hall of Fame and Museum, a fitting location because the Blue Jays have won thirty-seven national championships. At the same time, its medical school and hospital remain in their historic setting in downtown Baltimore's harbor area. The university's educational presence in Baltimore is supplemented by its economic role as the city's single largest employer. Clearly, the Johns Hopkins University continues to fulfill its mission as a national university and as an academic pioneer.

See also: GRADUATE SCHOOL TRAINING; HIGHER EDUCATION IN THE UNITED STATES, *subentry on* HISTORICAL DEVELOPMENT; RESEARCH UNIVERSITIES.

BIBLIOGRAPHY

HAWKINS, HUGH. 1960. *Pioneer: A History of the Johns Hopkins University, 1874–1889.* Ithaca, NY: Cornell University Press.

RUDOLPH, FREDERICK. 1962. *The American College and University: A History.* New York: Random House.

SCHMIDT, JOHN C. 1986. *Johns Hopkins: Portrait of a University.* Baltimore, MD: Johns Hopkins University.

JASON R. EDWARDS
ERIC MOYEN
JOHN R. THELIN

JOHNSON, MARIETTA PIERCE (1864–1938)

Founder of the School of Organic Education in Fairhope, Alabama, Johnson won international recognition as a child-centered Progressive educator. She was born near St. Paul, Minnesota, and grew up as a twin in a close-knit farming family. After attending public schools in St. Paul and graduating from the state normal school at St. Cloud in 1885, she taught in rural elementary and secondary schools, and served as a training teacher in normal schools. Johnson found success and popularity as a traditional instructor, priding herself on how quickly she could teach first graders to read.

Organic Education

After a decade and a half of classroom work, she suddenly rejected the very methods she practiced and demonstrated so impressively. In 1901, with all the force of a religious conversion experience, Johnson was convinced that her well-intended but misguided teaching methods violated the "order of development of the nervous system. I realized that my enthusiasm was destructive, and the more efficient I was, the more I injured the pupils!" (Johnson 1974, p. 8). The catalyst for this change was a personal reading program that led Johnson from child psychology books into works by Jean Jacques Rousseau, Friedrich Froebel, and John Dewey. Through these readings as well as her own observation, she came to see that children move through distinct stages as they grow and that parents and teachers should key their educational efforts to the developmental process.

Johnson's belief in social reform made her unusually receptive to ideas on educational reform. She and her husband John Franklin were socialists, and in 1902 they moved to the small Gulf Coast village of Fairhope, a utopian community dedicated to the single-tax philosophy of Henry George, author of

Progress and Poverty (1879). At home among former Midwesterners and northeasterners who seemed determined to set an example for the rest of the world, Johnson added an educational dimension to the Fairhope experiment.

Johnson immediately began searching for ways to educate each student as a complete organism—a "whole child," as Progressive educators would soon have it—paying balanced attention to body, mind, and spirit. The School of Organic Education she founded in 1907 became known as the most child-centered progressive school in the nation. Dewey explained in *Schools of To-Morrow* (1915) that he was one of many students and experts who had made pilgrimages to this remote corner of the Deep South to see Johnson's experiment. Dewey pronounced it a "decided success," and his rave review helped catapult Johnson into national prominence. Soon the School of Organic Education was attracting talented teachers and well-to-do boarding students from throughout the country.

Johnson's approach to education was genuinely radical. The once eager teacher now steered students away from books until the age of nine. Younger children, she maintained, were not ready for print. They could learn more through direct experience with the environment. Dewey and other visitors to the school were impressed with the time spent teaching and learning outdoors or in the shop, which Johnson regarded as the "most important place on our campus." Every student did daily handwork in the shop, while students and teachers joined in daily folk dancing. Students did no homework and took no tests until high school; nor did they receive grades or report cards. Such features drew most of the attention so that observers tended to overlook the curriculum, which became more demanding and rigorous as students gained maturity.

Refusing to compare one student to another, Johnson rejected "external, competitive" standards in favor of the "inner, human" standard of simply doing one's best. To critics who charged that the school was a "do-as-you-please" school—a common caricature of child-centered Progressive education—she countered that "children have no basis for judgment [and] do not know what is good for them" (Johnson 1974, p. 95). Teachers and parents, she insisted, were responsible for taking charge and directing young people away from "unwholesome" activities.

Such tough talk notwithstanding, Johnson was anything but authoritarian. She relied instead on personal appeal—a quiet but powerful presence—to convince people to do things her way. She was a charismatic woman who projected self-confidence. She shared some of these qualities with other women founders of early-twentieth-century progressive schools, most of which were elite private institutions. In an era when males imposed a business-oriented, measurement-driven version of progressivism on public schools, a few women opened private schools as child-centered alternatives. But Johnson was less autocratic than most of her peers, and her school also differed in significant ways.

Part of an experimental community, Organic operated as a quasi-public institution that charged local children no tuition. During Johnson's lifetime, one-half to two-thirds of Fairhope's white families chose to send their children to her school, which she hoped would become a model for reforming public education. She worked to create a climate of equal opportunity for females, accommodated disabled students, but reluctantly yielded to community pressure to bar African Americans.

Despite support from local tax revenue, Johnson fought an uphill battle to keep the Organic School solvent, a situation that forced her into a parallel career as a fundraiser. She spent much of her time on the lecture circuit, speaking throughout the United States and in several other countries, recruiting boarding students whose tuition and fees subsidized the attendance of local students. She was especially popular in the New York City area, where a group of socially prominent women organized the Fairhope Educational Foundation to support her efforts, particularly her work as director of the Edgewood School in Greenwich, Connecticut. A cofounder of the Progressive Education Association in 1919, Johnson tried with limited success to use the organization to promote organic education nationwide. Her efforts did inspire the founding of several private child-centered progressive schools, including the Peninsula School in Menlo Park, California, and a school in Rose Valley, Pennsylvania.

New Trends in Education

While the Great Depression of the 1930s wreaked financial havoc on an already unstable Organic School, Johnson's name lost some of its magic within the Progressive education movement, now dominated by social reconstructionists who dismissed her as a "play schooler" despite her longstanding commitment to social reform. Disappointed that few public educators had accepted organic education, she died in poor health in 1938. Without Johnson, the Organic School has drifted far from its educational moorings at times, but unlike many such schools, it continues to offer, in the early twenty-first century, a version of its founder's original vision.

See also: CURRICULUM, SCHOOL; PROGRESSIVE EDUCATION.

BIBLIOGRAPHY

ADSHEAD, MARY LOIS. 2000. "Marietta Johnson, Visionary." *Alabama Heritage* 58:28–35.

DEWEY, JOHN, and DEWEY, EVELYN. 1915. *Schools of To-Morrow.* New York: Dutton.

GASTON, PAUL M. 1984. *Women of Fair Hope.* Athens: University of Georgia Press.

JOHNSON, MARIETTA. 1929. *Youth in a World of Men.* New York: John Day.

JOHNSON, MARIETTA. 1931. "Standards and the Child." *Progressive Education* 8:692–694.

JOHNSON, MARIETTA. 1974. *Thirty Years with an Idea.* Birmingham: University of Alabama Press.

MARIETTA JOHNSON MUSEUM. 1996. *Organic Education: Teaching without Failure.* Montgomery, AL: Communication Graphics.

NEWMAN, JOSEPH W. 1999. "Experimental School, Experimental Community: The Marietta Johnson School of Organic Education in Fairhope, Alabama." In *Schools of Tomorrow, Schools of Today: What Happened to Progressive Education?* ed. Susan F. Semel and Alan R. Sadovnik. New York: Lang.

JOSEPH W. NEWMAN

JOURNALISM EDUCATION ASSOCIATION

When the Journalism Education Association (JEA) celebrated its seventy-fifth anniversary in 1999, it noted that the organization's name and location had changed several times, but the goals are still very similar to those of its founders—to support secondary school journalism teachers and media advisers.

According to its mission, JEA supports free and responsible scholastic journalism by providing resources and educational opportunities, by promoting professionalism, by encouraging and rewarding student excellence and teacher achievement, and by fostering an atmosphere that encompasses diversity yet builds unity.

In 1924 a group of teachers attending the Central Interscholastic Press Association in Madison agreed unanimously to start a national association for high school journalism teachers. The group did not settle on a name and goals until 1929 when it became the National Association of High School Teachers of Journalism (NAHSTJ). Other name changes occurred in 1930 to National Association of Journalism Advisers (NAJA), in 1935 to National Association of Journalism Directors (NAJD), and in 1939 it became a department of the National Education Association with an advisory council. After World War II the group pushed for increased membership and by late 1949 had 800 members.

The current name, Journalism Education Association, was created in November 1963. At that time, a forward-looking curriculum commission chair, Sr. Ann Christine Heintz, oversaw the publication of several booklets for teachers, including ones that went beyond JEA's previous focus on newspapers and yearbooks to include broadcast media, classroom teaching methods, and publication trends. In 1966 the journal *Communication: Journalism Education Today* (C:JET) was established, evolving into a quarterly publication about mass media in secondary schools. When two JEA members participated in the Robert F. Kennedy Commission of Inquiry into High School Journalism, the organization embraced a new concern. The commission's findings, which included the pervasive presence of censorship in high school media, sparked JEA's increased support of free student expression.

With a membership topping 2,000 in 1999, JEA is the only independent national scholastic journalism organization for teachers and advisers. A volunteer organization, its elected board consists of current or retired journalism teachers. In addition to its president, vice president, secretary, and immediate past president, who acts as parliamentarian and convention coordinator, the board has regional directors and commission chairs. These commissions represent the areas of interest and concern for JEA and, as of 2002, were Scholastic Press Rights, Certification, Multicultural, Development/Curriculum, and Junior High/Middle School. A national headquarters at Kansas State University serves as a clearinghouse for programs and activities, maintains the JEA Bookstore and membership records, and is the office of JEA's executive director.

To achieve its mission, JEA hosts two conventions per year with the National Scholastic Press Association. These spring and fall meetings offer on-site contests, break-out sessions, media tours, hands-on training, and keynote speeches from media professionals. By 2002 attendance at these four-day conventions often topped 5,000.

Other activities include a voluntary certification program; awards, including High School Journalist of the Year, Future Journalism Teacher, and High School Yearbook Adviser of the Year; Adviser Institute summer training; an Internet site; and a member listserv, JEAHELP, which offers immediate connection and support between members.

See also: JOURNALISM, TEACHING OF.

INTERNET RESOURCE

JOURNALISM EDUCATION ASSOCIATION. 2002. <www.jea.org>.

CANDACE PERKINS BOWEN

JOURNALISM, TEACHING OF

Journalism in American secondary schools began at approximately the same time journalism programs appeared in colleges. The first known high school journalism class was in Salina, Kansas, in 1912. But student newspapers are not always tied to a class, so not surprisingly they appeared long before this date. The first recorded one, *The Student Gazette,* was handwritten by the students of William Penn Charter School in Philadelphia in June 1777. The first known printed school paper, *The Literary Journal,* was published at Boston Latin School on May 9, 1829.

The growth of journalism as part of the high school curriculum became significant in the 1920s. By the mid-1920s a number of state and national organizations had been founded to support secondary school journalism teachers and publications advisers. During the ensuing half century, substantial interest grew in such organizations as the Columbia

Scholastic Press Association, headquartered at Columbia University; the Quill and Scroll Society, an honorary organization of high school journalists at the University of Iowa; the National Scholastic Press Association, based at the University of Minnesota; and the Journalism Education Association, the only organization solely for teachers, which had several names and locations but in 1987 settled at Kansas State University.

Teachers indicate that support from such organizations is vital because a majority of journalism teachers have little specific media training and because keeping current in such a quickly changing field is difficult. Certification or licensing to teach journalism is not required at all in roughly half the states, and many others have only minimal formal academic demands, according to Marilyn Weaver of Ball State University, who conducted a 1993 survey reported in *Death By a Cheeseburger* (1994). By the end of the twentieth century, some states, such as Ohio and Oregon, offered licenses in Integrated Language Arts, which include journalism but require virtually no course work in it. The number one field of licensure among journalism teachers and advisers is English (80%). Journalism is next (26.2%), followed by social studies and speech or drama, according to respondents to a 1998 national survey reported by Jack Dvorak.

Because state requirements vary so greatly, voluntary "certification" became an option in 1990 when the Journalism Education Association launched its Certified Journalism Educator/Master Journalism Educator program. Although it is not designed to replace state licensure where it does exist, the JEA's program offers teachers a variety of ways to earn these designations and indicate their knowledge of the field, including combinations of course work, years in the classroom, tests, and projects. By 1998, 500 teachers had been named CJEs, and by 1999, 100 were MJEs.

Curriculum and Teaching Standards

Teachers tap into state and national organizations to get help with curriculum, which changed significantly in the late twentieth century. Journalism programs range from those that offer English credit and allow students a variety of choices—from Journalistic Writing to Newspaper Production to Photojournalism—to those with only a yearbook staff meeting after school. However, a 1998 national study of the status of journalism in the nation's high schools revealed that nearly 97 percent of them have at least one media-related activity—a journalism course for credit, a yearbook, a newspaper, a newsmagazine, or a television or radio station. More than 77 percent of the journalism educators who participated in the survey reported that at least one journalism class was offered at the school. About 90 percent of the schools offered a media laboratory for student journalists who work on newspaper, yearbook, or broadcast facilities. Projected onto the high school population in the United States, these percentages mean that about 453,576 students were enrolled in a course called "Journalism," and nearly half a million students served on school media staffs in the late 1990s, as estimated by Dvorak's research.

Course objectives and curriculum vary widely, but by the 1980s, teachers groups worked to emphasize the academic respectability of journalism. Some administrators who grew up in an era when high school publications were filled with jokes and puzzles question the educational value of the course. To combat this, the Dow Jones Newspaper Fund launched a project that offered workshops on various university campuses to train teachers for Intensive Journalistic Writing courses at their schools. The high school students in the classes they taught then took the College Board's Advanced Placement English Language and Composition Examinations. Results since then have shown a higher percentage of journalism students than Advanced Placement English students passing the examination. This result motivated a group of JEA officers and college journalism educators to ask the College Board to create a course and corresponding test for Advanced Placement Journalism. By 2002 the College Board had surveyed educators at both the high school and college levels and was considering this.

Standards. National standards for journalism became a concern in the 1990s. Since so many programs are part of the English curriculum, a group of educators sought to show the parallels between the two disciplines. *Standards for the English Language Arts,* published in 1996 by the International Reading Association and the National Council of Teachers of English, established twelve standards for all language arts courses "to ensure that all students are knowledgeable and proficient users of language." By 2002, *NCTE Standards in Practice as They Apply to Journalism* presented a series of lesson plans and vignettes to illustrate the way media and media-related projects also help teachers meet these standards.

In 2001 a committee of high school and college educators began developing national standards for journalism teacher education. Basing its work on newly created standards from Indiana, Michigan, and Kansas, the group prefaced its national standards with the following: "Educators who teach secondary school journalism must have a broad range of knowledge and performance abilities. Although their courses are frequently placed in a school's English Department, their teaching responsibilities go beyond what most English or language arts curriculum requires. Therefore, these standards reflect their need to be skilled in teaching writing, listening, speaking, leadership skills, cooperative processes, press law and ethics, and media design and production. The combination of these helps them prepare their students as knowledgeable media producers and consumers who are essential to our democracy."

An increasing amount of support for high school journalism came from the professional press in the late 1990s. Such groups as the Dow Jones Newspaper Fund and the Newspaper Association of America, which had sponsored programs for more than twenty years, were joined by the American Society of Newspaper Editors, which funded university training for more than 200 teachers each summer, and the Radio and Television News Directors Foundation, seeking to help advisers of all electronic media forms.

Digital and Electronic Media in the Curriculum

The media that students study and produce shifted dramatically with the growth of digital technology in the 1990s, and teachers found the changes challenging. Instead of typing articles and pasting them on large sheets of paper as their predecessors did, students began using computers. First this was just for word processing, but soon research tools included e-mail for communication and the Internet for information gathering. Meanwhile, production switched to desktop publishing with specialized software and graphics programs, scanners, and digital cameras. By the beginning of the twenty-first century, students at a growing number of schools were creating online publications with timely updates of breaking news, reader response capabilities, and even video and audio clips of local events. Some student staffs collaborated with schools across town, across the country, or around the world to write related articles and share photos from events that would interest a wide teen audience.

In the 1990s many schools across the country found ways to acquire free broadcast equipment, so launching television stations became an option, as well. While some students merely delivered morning announcements, others hosted talk shows and created in-depth video packages for weekly viewing on area cable channels. Student-managed electronic media nearly doubled between 1991 and 1998.

Law and Ethics

A final area of concern for journalism educators has been law and ethics. In 1974 the Robert F. Kennedy Commission produced *Captive Voices: The Report of the Commission of Inquiry into High School Journalism*. Among the findings of the 22-member commission was the extent of censorship in high school media: "(S)tudent rights are routinely denied, with little or no protest of the students." One result of the Commission was the formation of the Student Press Law Center in Washington, D.C. The SPLC is an advocate for student free-press rights and provides information, advice, and legal assistance at no charge to students and the educators who work with them. More than 2,000 of them contact the SPLC each year to get advice and support in producing media that allows free student expression and teaches journalism students the rights and responsibilities they have in a democracy.

Concern that student journalists were not learning about the First Amendment and how to apply it in their programs led a coalition of media organizations to launch the Let Freedom Ring Award in 2000. The Journalism Education Association, National Scholastic Press Association, Columbia Scholastic Press Association, Quill and Scroll, and the Freedom Forum's First Amendment Center developed a program to recognize and applaud schools that support all parts of the First Amendment in their student publications and their teaching.

See also: ENGLISH EDUCATION, *subentries on* PREPARATION OF TEACHERS, TEACHING OF; JOURNALISM EDUCATION ASSOCIATION; LANGUAGE ARTS, TEACHING OF; SECONDARY EDUCATION, *subentries on* CURRENT TRENDS, HISTORY OF; WRITING, TEACHING OF.

BIBLIOGRAPHY

DVORAK, JACK; LAIN, LARRY; and DICKSON, TOM. 1994. *Journalism Kids Do Better.* Bloomington, IN: ERIC Clearinghouse on Reading, English, and Communication.

DVORAK, JACK. 1998. "Journalism Student Performance on Advanced Placement Exams." *Journalism and Mass Communication Educator* 53(3):4–12.

THE FREEDOM FORUM. 1994. *Death By Cheeseburger: High School Journalism in the 1990s and Beyond.* Arlington, VA: The Freedom Forum.

NELSON, JACK, ed. 1974. *Captive Voices: The Report of the Commission of Inquiry into High School Journalism.* New York: Schocken Books.

INTERNET RESOURCE

DVORAK, JACK. 1998. "Status of Journalism and News Media in the Nation's Secondary Schools." Website of Indiana High School Journalism Institute, Bloomington, IN. <www.journalism.indiana.edu/workshops/HSJI/>.

CANDACE PERKINS BOWEN

JUNIOR HIGH SCHOOLS
See: MIDDLE SCHOOLS.

JUVENILE JUSTICE SYSTEM

HISTORY OF JUVENILE COURTS
  William Wesley Patton
CONTEMPORARY JUVENILE JUSTICE SYSTEM AND
  JUVENILE DETENTION ALTERNATIVES
  William Wesley Patton
JUVENILE CRIME AND VIOLENCE
  Dewey G. Cornell
  Daniel C. Murrie

HISTORY OF JUVENILE COURTS

The juvenile court and its philosophy of treating minors who violate the criminal law differently than adults is barely a century old. Historically, juvenile criminals were treated the same as adult criminals.

The Law Prior to the Creation of the Juvenile Court

Punishment was the central criminal law philosophy in English common law. A conclusive presumption that children under seven could not form criminal intent eliminated the youngest from the criminal justice system. Children between the ages of seven and fourteen were presumed incompetent to form the requisite criminal intent; the prosecutor, however, could rebut that presumption by demonstrating that the child knew the difference between right and wrong. Children over age fourteen were presumed to have the capacity to form criminal intent. There were no special courts for children, and they were treated as adult criminals. Minors were arrested, held in custody, and tried and sentenced by a court that had discretion to order the child imprisoned in the same jail as adult criminals. Although children received the same punishment as adults, they were not provided with many of the due process protections accorded adult criminals. For instance, minors did not have a right to "bail, indictment by grand jury, [and] right to a public trial" (Conward, p. 41).

Although the early American colonies adopted the English common laws regarding child criminals, from 1825 until 1899 several reform movements initiated significant changes both in philosophy and in treatment of juvenile delinquents. Quaker reformers spurred the New York Legislature in 1824 to pass legislation creating a House of Refuge, which separated poor children and juvenile delinquents from adult criminals. The goal of the House of Refuge movement was both to prevent predelinquents from becoming criminals and to reform those who had already committed crimes. The judge had discretion to determine which juvenile delinquents might properly benefit from the House of Refuge; child criminals unlikely to reform were maintained in adult prisons.

The First Juvenile Court

Progressive reformers in Illinois persuaded the legislature to pass the 1899 Illinois Juvenile Court Act creating America's first juvenile court. The act adopted the early English common law *parens patriae* philosophy in providing that "the care, custody and discipline of a child shall approximate as nearly as may be that which should be given by its parents." Several unique features characterized the early juvenile court. First, because reformation was the goal, the system focused more on the individual child rather than on the nature of the criminal offense. Second, because the time within which reformation could be accomplished varied with the child, indeterminate sentences often exceeded the determinate sentences that adult criminals received for committing the identical criminal act. Third, juvenile delinquents were separated from adult criminals be-

cause they were different in kind. Adult criminals were morally blameworthy; children were merely the products of their environment and therefore retributive punishment was not warranted. Fourth, because juvenile court proceedings were not criminal, children were not entitled to the full panoply of due process protections accorded adult criminals. Informality permitted the court to consider all facts relevant to determining the child's reformation plan. Petitions replaced criminal complaints, summons replaced warrants, custody replaced arrest, detention replaced confinement, initial hearings replaced arraignments, and delinquency replaced conviction. Fifth, juvenile courts had broad discretion to fashion innovative rehabilitation programs not always available in adult courts, such as release upon informal voluntary probation conditions. Sixth, technical evidentiary rules were inapplicable in juvenile court because they impeded the judge from determining all facts necessary to determine the individualized treatment necessary to rehabilitate the minor.

Although the goals of the juvenile court were laudable, many historians have bemoaned the system's realities. In 1970 the harshest critic, Sanford Fox, termed the reformers' legislation "a colossal failure" (p. 1224). It became apparent that the informal procedures and almost unbridled discretion of juvenile court judges often supplied minors with less-fair procedures and treatment than adults received. In a famous 1839 Pennsylvania case, *Ex parte Crouse,* the court expressed the general view of American courts that because the goal of juvenile justice is rehabilitation, not punishment, the due process protections afforded adult criminals need not be provided to juveniles: "The House of Refuge is not a prison, but a school. Where reformation, and not punishment is the end" the formalities of the criminal court are not required. In addition, the juvenile court's goal of individualized treatment often lacked objective criteria and conflicted with notions of justice. By the 1960s critics spoke of the demise of the juvenile court, and they "raised questions about the effect on juveniles of the lack of due process procedures and protection of individual rights" (Sarri, p. 5).

In re Gault and the Constitution

The assault on the reform movement began with a 1966 case in the U.S. Supreme Court, *Kent v. United States,* which held that under a District of Columbia statute the informal process of determining whether a juvenile should be tried in juvenile or in adult court failed to provide sufficient due process protection for children. The Court held that before a minor is transferred to adult court the child is entitled to an informal hearing where the trial court must articulate the reasons for the transfer so that the child can have an adequate record for appellate review. Additionally, in response to the state's position that juvenile cases were civil, not criminal, the Court responded, "There is evidence, in fact, that there may be grounds for concern that the child receives the worst of both worlds; that he gets neither the protections accorded to adults nor the solicitous care and regenerative treatment postulated for children." The Court thereby rejected the reform movement's justification for informality in juvenile delinquency cases. And a year later in *In re Gault,* the Court set the due process boundaries between adult criminal procedure and juvenile delinquency trials. First, the Court rejected the reformers' claims that the juvenile justice system accurately and fairly determined children's criminal responsibility: "Under our Constitution, the condition of being a boy does not justify a kangaroo court." Second, although *Gault* rejected the argument that the Fourteenth Amendment due process clause requires identical due process procedures for adults and juveniles, the Court determined that juveniles must at least receive alternative equivalents. Thus, in a juvenile delinquency trial, children are entitled to: (1) notice of the charges, (2) a right to counsel, (3) a right to confrontation and cross-examination, and (4) a privilege against self-incrimination. The U.S. Supreme Court quickly followed the *Kent* and *Gault* cases with the 1970 case *In re Winship,* which held that juvenile delinquency requires the "beyond a reasonable doubt" adult standard of proof, and the 1971 case *McKiever v. Pennsylvania,* which held that juveniles charged with a criminal law violation are not entitled to a jury trial because the Sixth Amendment right to jury trial applies only to criminal actions and because juries would substantially eviscerate the beneficial aspects of the juvenile court's "prospect of an intimate, informal protective proceeding."

The U.S. Supreme Court's juvenile delinquency due process cases ushered in a period of reform in state juvenile court systems that lasted almost a decade. In 1974 the President's Commission on Law Enforcement and Administration of Justice was established to study the deficiencies in the juvenile delinquency system. The commission urged more nonjudicial service agency intervention for predelinquents and recommended limitations on the confinement of minors.

Increased and More Serious Juvenile Crime

From the mid-1980s to the early 1990s the national juvenile crime rate rose dramatically; "property crime by juveniles increased 11 percent nationally between 1983 and 1992, [and] violent crime increased by 57 percent" (Feld, pp. 976–977). During this same period, media coverage of juvenile crime dramatically increased. Even though the frequency and content of news coverage often exaggerated the rise in youth crime, the coverage had an enormous impact on the public's call for more protection for citizens and for harsher treatment of juveniles committing serious criminal acts. In reality, during the decade 1987–1997 only 6 percent of American juveniles were arrested and fewer than 0.5 percent were arrested for violent crimes. Nevertheless, state legislatures quickly responded to the public's fear of rising juvenile crime rates by substantially modifying the juvenile court process.

All fifty states modified their juvenile law codes to provide that, under certain circumstances, juveniles could be tried as adults in criminal court. These procedures fall into three distinct types: (1) judicial discretion to transfer a minor from juvenile court to adult court; (2) prosecutorial discretion to decide in which court the child will be tried; and (3) legislative mandates requiring juveniles who commit certain offenses to be tried in adult court. A second statutory change lowered the age at which children were eligible to be transferred to adult court. According to Elizabeth S. Scott, writing in 2000, "Between 1992 and 1995, eleven states lowered the age for transfer; twenty-four states added crimes to automatic/legislative waiver statutes, and ten states added crimes to judicial waiver statutes" (p. 585, fn. 145). A third major juvenile law modification was the development of blended sentences, which involve lengthy juvenile law confinements coupled with the transfer of the juvenile upon reaching the age of majority to serve the remainder of the sentence in adult prison. Finally, juvenile courts have opened their proceedings to the public in cases that involve certain specified serious crimes, and legislatures have substantially reduced minors' right to seal juvenile delinquency court records.

Both liberal and conservative experts and organizations have called for the elimination of the juvenile court either because it is a too lenient response to the perception of increasing serious juvenile crime or because it unfairly treats poor and minority children. It is uncertain whether the public's clamor for change will be quelled by the reduction in juvenile crime that began in the mid-1990s.

See also: JUVENILE JUSTICE SYSTEM, *subentries on* CONTEMPORARY JUVENILE JUSTICE SYSTEM AND JUVENILE DETENTION ALTERNATIVES, JUVENILE CRIME AND VIOLENCE; VIOLENCE, CHILDREN'S EXPOSURE TO.

BIBLIOGRAPHY

CONWARD, CYNTHIA. 1998. "The Juvenile Justice System: Not Necessarily in the Best Interests of Children." *New England Law Review* 33:39–80.

COUPET, SACHA M. 2000. "What to Do with the Sheep in Wolf's Clothing: The Role of Rhetoric and Reality about Youth Offenders in the Constructive Dismantling of the Juvenile Justice System." *University of Pennsylvania Law Review* 148:1303–1346.

FELD, BARRY C. 1995. "Violent Youth and Public Policy: A Case Study of Juvenile Justice Law Reform." *Minnesota Law Review* 79:965–1022.

FOX, SANFORD J. 1970. "Juvenile Justice Reform: An Historical Perspective." *Stanford Law Review* 22:1187–1239.

MACK, JULIAN W. 1909. "The Juvenile Court." *Harvard Law Review* 23:104–122.

MELLI, MARYGOLD S. 1996. "Juvenile Justice Reform in Context." *Wisconsin Law Review* 1996:375–398.

RENDLEMAN, DOUGLAS R. 1971. "*Parens Patriae:* From Chancery to the Juvenile Court." *South Carolina Law Review* 23:205–259.

SARRI, ROSEMARY, and HASENFELD, YEHESKEL. 1976. *Brought to Justice? Juveniles, the Courts, and the Law.* Ann Arbor: National Assessment of Juvenile Corrections, University of Michigan.

SCHWARTZ, IRA M.; WEINER, NEIL ALAN; and ENOSH, GUY. 1998. "Nine Lives and Then Some: Why the Juvenile Court Does Not Roll Over and Die." *Wake Forest Law Review* 33:533–552.

SCOTT, ELIZABETH S. 2000. "The Legal Construction of Adolescence." *Hofstra Law Review* 29:547–598.

SHEPHERD, ROBERT E., JR. 1999. "The 'Child' Grows Up: The Juvenile Justice System Enters Its Second Century." *Family Law Quarterly* 33:589–605.

THOMAS, MASON P. 1972. "Child Abuse and Neglect, Part I: Historical Overview, Legal Matrix, and Social Perspectives." *North Carolina Law Review* 50:293–349.

U.S. DEPARTMENT OF JUSTICE. OFFICE OF JUSTICE PROGRAMS. OFFICE OF JUVENILE JUSTICE AND DELINQUENCY PREVENTION. 2000. "Annual Report." Washington, DC: U.S. Department of Justice, Office of Justice Programs, Office of Juvenile Justice and Delinquency Prevention.

WILLIAM WESLEY PATTON

CONTEMPORARY JUVENILE JUSTICE SYSTEM AND JUVENILE DETENTION ALTERNATIVES

The juvenile justice system under English common law and early American colonial law did not differentiate between legally competent minors and adults regarding criminal sanctions. Juveniles aged seven or older who had sufficient criminal capacity were tried in adult courts and sentenced to adult institutions. In the United States from about 1825 until 1899 a reform movement ushered in dramatic changes in the philosophy toward juveniles in the criminal law system. Children were seen not as sinners but rather as immature, malleable, and developing individuals who were very different from adults. Rather than applying the retributive justice of the adult criminal system, the reformers argued that children should be educated and nurtured so that they could become productive members of society rather than being housed with adult criminals who would further mold them into hardened recidivists. By 1899 a separate juvenile court was established in Chicago. The reformers argued that in order for a judge to properly determine the specialized care necessary for each juvenile who came before the court, the formal due process structure of the criminal court must be abandoned so that judges could assess all relevant data.

By the middle of the twentieth century it became clear that the good intentions of the reformers had never materialized and that children in the juvenile court were receiving neither the specialized care nor the due process necessary for the public to have confidence in juvenile court determinations. From the mid-1960s through the mid-1970s the U.S. Supreme Court on several occasions held that the informal structures of the nineteenth century juvenile court denied juveniles due process of law under the Fourteenth Amendment of the U.S. Constitution. Except for the right to a jury trial and bail, the Court held that juveniles were entitled to a panoply of due process protections, including the right to timely notice of the charges, confrontation, and cross-examination; proof beyond a reasonable doubt; and the privilege against self-incrimination.

During the 1980s the public perceived an escalation in juvenile crime, and a new reform movement developed that aimed to make the juvenile justice system more responsive to public safety and to assure personal responsibility by juvenile delinquents. States experimented with mandatory juvenile sentences, mandatory transfer of serious juvenile offenders to adult criminal court, modification of confidentiality of juvenile records, active participation by victims, mandatory victim restitution, and new correctional alternatives for dangerous juvenile offenders.

Experts have identified a juvenile justice cycle that has continued to revolve since the nineteenth century. The initial cycle starts when the public perceives a dramatic increase in juvenile crime and that the juvenile justice system is providing too lenient dispositions and too little public protection. The system responds with harsher treatment of juvenile delinquents and a reduction in informal resolution processes. Then, according to a 2000 article by Sacha M. Coupet, "following a period of extreme harshness and largely punitive policies, when the level of juvenile crime remains exceptionally high, 'justice officials . . . are forced to choose [once again] between harshly punishing juvenile offenders and doing nothing at all'" (p. 1329). From 1990 to the early twenty-first century, the American public has viewed juvenile crimes as constantly escalating in number and severity. By the early twenty-first century, U.S. society was at that point in the cycle where retributive justice had substantially overtaken the nineteenth century reformers' notions of rehabilitation and individualized treatment of juvenile delinquents.

The Reality of Juvenile Crime Statistics

There is a substantial disconnect between the public's perceptions of juvenile crime and the reality of juvenile crime statistics. Although juvenile crime is still a major social problem, contrary to the impres-

sion portrayed by the media regarding the explosion in youth crime, the juvenile crime rate began decreasing in 1995. In 1999 juveniles comprised only 17 percent of all arrests and 12 percent of all violent crime arrests. In 1999 the juvenile murder arrest rate fell 68 percent, to the lowest level since the 1960s, and juvenile arrests for violent crime dropped 23 percent from 1995 to 1999.

Many have argued that the most significant factor in the public's misinformation is the distortion of juvenile crime by the news media. A comprehensive examination of crime in the news conducted by Lori Dorfman and Vincent Schiraldi in 2001 found that: (1) the press reported juvenile crime out of proportion to its actual occurrence; (2) violent crime, although representing only 22 to 24 percent of juvenile crime from 1988 to 1997, dominated the media's coverage of juvenile offenses; (3) the media presented crimes without an adequate contextual base for understanding why the crime occurred; (4) press coverage unduly connected race and crime; and (5) juveniles were rarely covered by the news other than to report on their violent criminal acts.

Significant changes in the demographics of juvenile crime occurred between 1988 and 1998. Not only did the number of juvenile delinquency court cases increase, but also many changes in the age, sex, and race of delinquents altered the landscape of juvenile offenders. In 1988 the juvenile courts processed 1.2 million cases; by 1997 the total had increased to 1.8 million. According to a November 2001 fact sheet issued by the U.S. Department of Justice's Office of Juvenile Justice and Delinquency Prevention, a study of California delinquency cases found that "a small percentage (8%) of the juveniles were arrested repeatedly . . . and were responsible for 55 percent of repeat cases." The most important types of cases and trends during the period from 1988 to 1998 included violent juvenile crime, juvenile property offenses, juvenile drug offenses, and juvenile gangs.

Violent juvenile crime. In 1988, 24 percent of juvenile court cases involved crimes of violence against a person. Of those violent crimes, 20 percent were committed by females and 62 percent by children under age sixteen. White children represented 56 percent of violent delinquents while African-American children represented 40 percent. In 1998, by contrast, 23 percent of the juvenile court caseload involved crimes of violence, females committed 28 percent of the violent crimes, children under age sixteen accounted for 64 percent, and 62 percent were committed by white youth and 35 percent by African-American children. Thus the juvenile population of violent offenders in 1998 was comprised of more females, more white children, and younger juveniles than in 1988. The percentage of violent crimes among children, however, remained relatively constant. The dispositions for juvenile offenses also changed during that same period. In 1989, 33 percent of juveniles found in court to have committed a violent crime were placed outside the home, compared to 27 percent in 1998. Also, in 1989, 54 percent were placed on probation, compared to 58 percent in 1998. During the period between 1988 and 1997, the number of adjudicated cases resulting in out-of-home placement increased more for African-American children (60%) than for white children (52%).

Juvenile property offenses. From 1988 through 1994 the juvenile arrest rate for property offenses was relatively stable. Between 1994 and 1999, however, the juvenile arrest rate for property offenses dropped 30 percent to the lowest level since the 1960s. The disposition of sustained property offense petitions in 1988 resulted in out-of-home placement in 28 percent of juvenile cases; by 1997, however, the rate had dropped to 26 percent. In addition, in 1988 property offenses comprised 52 percent of all juvenile court out-of-home dispositions, but that number dropped to 42 percent in 1997, reflecting a softening juvenile court attitude toward property offenses in relation to other juvenile crimes.

Juvenile drug offenses. Several dramatic shifts in the numbers and demographics of juveniles arrested for drug offenses occurred between 1988 and 1999. Drug abuse violation arrests were relatively constant from the 1980s until 1993. From 1993 and 1998, however, the number of drug offenses more than doubled. In 1994 drug offenses comprised 8 percent of all delinquency cases, and in 1998 the rate increased to 11 percent. Although the number of formally processed juvenile drug cases increased by more than 50 percent from 1994 until 1998, the percentage of out-of-home placements for drug offenses decreased from 36 percent in 1989 to 23 percent in 1998. This decline has been credited to an inadequate number of out-of-home placements and/or to a shift in juvenile court attitude regarding the seriousness of drug offenses in relation to violent person offenses. The age of juveniles arrested for drug cases remained relatively constant. In 1989

children age fourteen and younger comprised 18 percent of arrested juveniles compared with 19 percent in 1998. There was a dramatic shift, however, in the race of arrested juveniles. In 1989 whites represented 58 percent of those arrested for drug offenses and African Americans comprised 40 percent. In 1998 whites represented 68 percent and African Americans only 29 percent of all juvenile drug cases. Finally, the percentage of drug arrests for girls increased from 14 percent in 1989 to 16 percent in 1998. The drug arrest rate for both sexes was twice the average of the rate in the 1980s.

Juvenile gangs. Juvenile gang crime was a significant social issue during the last quarter of the twentieth century. The number of cities reporting youth gang activity rose from 300 in the 1970s to nearly 2,500 in 1998. In the 1970s only nineteen states reported gang problems, but in the 1990s all fifty states reported gang crimes. In 1999 there were approximately 26,000 gangs and 840,500 gang members in the United States. Compared to the figures for 1998, these numbers represented a decrease in gangs of 9 percent and an increase in gang members of 8 percent. Also, the average age of gang members increased; gang members aged fifteen to seventeen decreased 8 percent from 1996 to 1999. In addition, the number of girl youth gang members increased greatly from the 1970s through the 1990s. It is estimated that in the 1970s girls comprised only 10 percent of juvenile gangs; in the 1990s, however, girls made up between 8 and 38 percent of many gangs. Female youth gang members are arrested most frequently for drug offenses, and arrests for prostitution increased from 0.8 percent in 1993 to 9.8 percent in 1996. Youth gangs continue to be a major problem that the juvenile justice system has not yet begun to control.

An Increasing Emphasis on Juvenile Crime Prevention

Even though the 1990s and early twenty-first century have ushered in a new era of retributive juvenile justice, federal government policies still emphasize a juvenile crime prevention model formally established in 1974 when the president and the U.S. Congress created the Office of Juvenile Justice and Delinquency Prevention (OJJDP) as part of the U.S. Department of Justice's Office of Justice Programs. The goal of the OJJDP, according to its 2000 annual report, is "to provide national leadership in addressing the issues of preventing and controlling delinquency and improving the juvenile justice system." The OJJDP operates a host of juvenile delinquency crime prevention programs and research in the following areas: gangs, girls, mental health, safe schools, state coordination, drug education, juvenile mentoring, national youth network, violence in the media, truancy reduction, very young offenders, child development, gun violence, children's advocacy centers, and Internet crimes.

A unique and very controversial juvenile crime prevention policy of the latter part of the 1990s and the early twenty-first century is a partnership between police departments and public schools to identify, treat, and punish juvenile delinquents. This partnership is the result of four different intersecting juvenile problems. The first is the nexus between truancy and juvenile delinquency, drug abuse, gang activity, and adult crime and poverty. According to a 2001 bulletin by Myriam L. Baker, Jane Nady Sigmon, and M. Elaine Nugent, "adults who were frequently truant as teenagers are much more likely than those who were not to have poorer health and mental health, lower paying jobs, an increased chance of living in poverty, more reliance on welfare support, children who exhibit problem behaviors, and an increased likelihood of incarceration" (p. 1). Research conducted in 2000 determined that 60 percent of juvenile crime occurs between 8 A.M. and 3 P.M. when children should be in school. The most common truancy delinquency prevention programs include a sharing of data between schools and police and prosecutors, holding parents criminally responsible for their children's truancy, assessing parents fines, and requiring parents to attend parent training classes.

A second partnership between public schools and law enforcement was spurred by a few high-profile multiple-victim homicides involving teenagers that occurred between 1993 and 1998. Because of the media attention on these very few high-profile school violence cases, parents pressured school districts to develop serious school violence prevention programs. In reality, according to a 2001 article by Margaret Small and Kellie Dressler Tetrick, "school-associated violent deaths are rare . . . less that 1 percent of the more than 1,350 children who were murdered in the first half of the 1998–99 school year . . . were killed at school" (p. 4). Public schools responded, in part, by using law enforcement as references in designing preventative and emergency response programs and in monitoring and investigating suspicious student activity.

Third, after empirical studies demonstrated that the adult criminal conviction rate of children who bullied other children in school was almost twice as high as the rate for those children who did not engage in bullying, public schools began focusing on less-violent aggressive student behavior. A 2000 study by the National Institute of Child Health and Human Development found that 1.6 million children in grades six through ten were bullied at least once a week. Many schools have instituted "zero tolerance" programs that expel students after one sustained finding of bullying. These children are also often referred to law enforcement for consideration of juvenile justice intervention.

Finally, because research has demonstrated a correlation between abused children and high rates of juvenile delinquency, schools and law enforcement have partnered in establishing programs that identify, treat, and prosecute child abusers. All states mandate that teachers report suspected child abuse to either law enforcement or to children's services workers.

Modern Juvenile Law Disposition Alternatives

Because rehabilitation is no longer the central goal of the juvenile justice system, new forms of placement have developed to assure community safety and juvenile responsibility to victims. Traditional juvenile delinquency dispositions involved individualized indeterminate terms based upon the needs of the child for rehabilitation. During the 1990s the model shifted to a determinate sentence length based not on the child's needs but rather on the seriousness and frequency of criminal law violations, with a goal of deterrence and retribution. Further, the trend in the early twenty-first century is to shift sentencing discretion in cases of violent crime from the juvenile court judge to the legislature. In 1997 Congress enacted the Innovative Local Law Enforcement and Community Policing Program, requiring those states that accept federal funds to create accountability-based dispositions that balance the interests of the community, victim, and offender. Therefore, juveniles whose delinquency hearings are litigated in juvenile court usually face one of the following disposition alternatives. If the child committed a minor offense and does not have a prior delinquency record, it is likely that the juvenile trial judge can grant a form of probation termed a "home of parent custody" order in which the child agrees to abide by relevant probation conditions; a violation of a probation condition, however, can lead to institutionalization. In 1998, 665,500 children were under probation supervision, an increase of 56 percent since 1989. Some juveniles are released home upon the condition that they wear electronic monitoring equipment, which limits the child's freedom without the necessity of formal incarceration. If the crime charged is minor, but the juvenile has a prior delinquency record, the judge usually has discretion to order the child detained out of home in an institutional setting until the child reaches the age of majority in that jurisdiction. If the minor commits a serious offense, a modern trend is developing for the legislature to create a mandatory minimum sentence that may also involve a "blended sentence" in which the juvenile upon reaching the age of majority is transferred to an adult institution to serve the remainder of the mandatory minimum sentence. Prior to the blended sentence movement, juvenile courts did not have discretion to hold children accountable beyond the age of majority.

Because many juveniles are being transferred to adult courts, the adult correctional systems have responded with a new variety of sentencing schemes. The total number of juvenile delinquency cases transferred to adult criminal court peaked in 1994, and the number of children tried in adult courts increased 33 percent in 1998. In 2000 approximately 14,500 children were incarcerated in adult facilities; 9,100 were housed in adult jails and 5,400 in adult prisons. There was a 366 percent increase in the number of juveniles confined in adult jails from 1983 to 1998. Juveniles are more likely to be violently victimized and five times as likely to be sexually assaulted if they are placed in an adult rather than a juvenile facility. There are fewer sentencing alternatives in adult court than in juvenile court. In "straight adult incarceration" jurisdictions, juveniles are sentenced like adults with little or no differentiation in the terms of the confinement. In "graduated incarceration" models, juveniles receive adult sentences, but they are housed in juvenile or separate wings in an adult institution and are transferred to the adult wing upon reaching a defined age. In "segregated incarceration" models, juveniles are sentenced as adults but are housed in special young offender units that have many of the rehabilitative services available to delinquents in juvenile correctional facilities.

In order to reduce cost and recidivism, some states are experimenting with community-based programs in which the child's family can participate in necessary therapy to cure or control the conditions that led to the child's delinquency. Another innovation involves community-based aftercare programs that provide juveniles released from secure confinement facilities intensive supervision upon release. Ironically, these aftercare programs are based upon the rehabilitation model rejected by the contemporary retributive juvenile delinquency model. In exchange for intensive monitoring by a probation officer, mandatory drug testing, and the imposition of a curfew, the juvenile receives individualized analyses of the conditions that initially led to delinquency, including assessments of the juvenile's relationships with family, peers, and the community. The goal is to reduce recidivism by mixing intensive services and surveillance. Whether this new juvenile model of "punishment first/rehabilitation second" will be effective is yet to be determined.

See also: JUVENILE JUSTICE SYSTEM, *subentries on* HISTORY OF JUVENILE COURTS, JUVENILE CRIME AND VIOLENCE; VIOLENCE, CHILDREN'S EXPOSURE TO.

BIBLIOGRAPHY

AUSTIN, JAMES; JOHNSON, KELLEY DEDEL; and GREGORIOU, MARIA. 2000. *Juveniles in Adult Prisons and Jails: A National Assessment.* Washington, DC: Bureau of Justice Assistance.

BAKER, MYRIAM L.; SIGMON, JANE NADY; and NUGENT, M. ELAINE. 2001. *Truancy Reduction: Keeping Students in School.* Bulletin. Washington, DC: U.S. Department of Justice, Office of Justice Programs, Office of Juvenile Justice and Delinquency Prevention.

BELLINGER, M. E., and ARON, WENDY. 2000. *Analysis and Interpretation of Proposition 21 and Its Impact on Delinquency Court Proceedings.* Los Angeles: Los Angeles Superior Court.

BUTTS, JEFFREY, and ADAMS, WILLIAM. 2001. *Anticipating Space Needs in Juvenile Detention and Correctional Facilities.* Washington, DC: U.S. Department of Justice, Office of Justice Programs, Office of Juvenile Justice and Delinquency Prevention.

CONWARD, CYNTHIA. 1998. "The Juvenile Justice System: Not Necessarily in the Best Interests of

Children." *New England Law Review* 33(1):39–80.

COTHERN, LYNN. 2000. *Juveniles and the Death Penalty*. Washington, DC: Coordinating Council on Juvenile Justice and Delinquency Prevention.

COUPET, SACHA M. 2000. "What to Do with the Sheep in Wolf's Clothing: The Role of Rhetoric and Reality about Youth Offenders in the Constructive Dismantling of the Juvenile Justice System." *University of Pennsylvania Law Review* 148:1303–1346.

DORFMAN, LORI, and SCHIRALDI, VINCENT. 2001. *Off Balance: Youth, Race, and Crime in the News*. Washington, DC: Berkeley Media Studies Group, Public Health Institute and Justice Policy Institute.

FINKELHOR, DAVID, and ORMROD, RICHARD. 2001. *Homicides of Children and Youth*. Washington, DC: U.S. Department of Justice, Office of Justice Programs, Office of Juvenile Justice and Delinquency Prevention.

GERAGHTY, THOMAS F., and DRIZIN, STEVEN A. 1997. "Forward—The Debate over the Future of Juvenile Courts: Can We Reach Consensus?" *Journal of Criminal Law and Criminology* 88:1–13.

GINSBURG, NANCY. 2001. "Girls and the Juvenile Justice System." *Practicing Law Institute* 187:131–144.

KELLY, KATHLEEN. 2000. "The Education Crisis for Children in the California Juvenile Court System." *Hastings Constitutional Law Quarterly* 27:757–773.

MILLER, WALTER B. 2001. *The Growth of Youth Gang Problems in the United States, 1970–1998*. Washington, DC: U.S. Department of Justice, Office of Justice Programs, Office of Juvenile Justice and Delinquency Prevention.

MOORE, JOAN, and HAGEDORN, JOHN. 2001. *Female Gangs: A Focus on Research*. Washington, DC: U.S. Department of Justice, Office of Justice Programs, Office of Juvenile Justice and Delinquency Prevention.

OSOFSKY, JOY D. 2001. *Addressing Youth Victimization*. Washington, DC: Coordinating Council on Juvenile Justice and Delinquency Prevention Action Plan Update.

PETERSON, ERIC. 1996. *Juvenile Boot Camps: Lessons Learned*. Washington, DC: Juvenile Justice Clearinghouse.

ROBERTS, DOROTHY E. 2001. "Criminal Justice and Black Families: The Collateral Damage of Over-Enforcement." *U.C. Davis Law Review* 34:1105–1028.

SCHWARTZ, IRA M.; WEINER, NEIL ALAN; and ENOSH, GUY. 1998. "Nine Lives and Then Some: Why the Juvenile Court Does Not Roll Over and Die." *Wake Forest Law Review* 33:533–552.

SCHWARTZ, IRA M.; WEINER, NEIL ALAN; and ENOSH, GUY. 1999. "Myopic Justice? The Juvenile Court and Child Welfare Systems." *Annals of the American Academy of Political and Social Science* 564:126–141.

SMALL, MARGARET, and TETRICK, KELLIE DRESSLER. 2001. "School Violence: An Overview." *Journal of Juvenile Justice and Delinquency Prevention* 8(1):1–12.

SNYDER, HOWARD N., and SICKMUND, MELISSA. 1999. *Juvenile Offenders and Victims: 1999 National Report*. Washington, DC: U.S. Department of Justice, Office of Justice Programs, Office of Juvenile Justice and Delinquency Prevention.

TORBET, PATRICIA; GABLE, RICHARD; HURST, HUNTER, IV; MONTGOMERY, IMOGENE; SZYMANSKI, LINDA; and THOMAS, DOUGLAS. 1996. *State Responses to Serious and Violent Juvenile Crime*. Washington, DC: U.S. Department of Justice, Office of Justice Programs, Office of Juvenile Justice and Delinquency Prevention.

U.S. DEPARTMENT OF JUSTICE. OFFICE OF JUSTICE PROGRAMS. OFFICE OF JUVENILE JUSTICE AND DELINQUENCY PREVENTION. 1996–2001. "Fact Sheets." Washington, DC: U.S. Department of Justice, Office of Justice Programs, Office of Juvenile Justice and Delinquency Prevention.

U.S. DEPARTMENT OF JUSTICE. OFFICE OF JUSTICE PROGRAMS. OFFICE OF JUVENILE JUSTICE AND DELINQUENCY PREVENTION. 2000. "Annual Report." Washington, DC: U.S. Department of Justice, Office of Justice Programs, Office of Juvenile Justice and Delinquency Prevention.

WASSERMAN, GAIL A.; MILLER, LAURIE S.; and COTHERN, LYNN. 2000. *Prevention of Serious and Violent Juvenile Offending*. Washington, DC: U.S. Department of Justice, Office of Justice Programs, Office of Juvenile Justice and Delinquency Prevention.

WIEBUSH, RICHARD G.; MCNULTY, BETSIE; and LE, THAO. 2000. *Implementation of the Intensive*

Community-Based Aftercare Program. Washington, DC: U.S. Department of Justice, Office of Justice Programs, Office of Juvenile Justice and Delinquency Prevention.

WILLIAM WESLEY PATTON

JUVENILE CRIME AND VIOLENCE

Juvenile crime is a perennial public concern, although public perceptions of juvenile crime are often shaped by misconceptions and unwarranted fears rather than by objective facts. For example, in 1996 the cover of a national magazine (*Newsweek*, March 10) made the alarming claim that "Juvenile violence is soaring—and it's going to get worse." In contrast, a 1999 federal report by Howard Snyder and Melissa Sickmund cited national arrest statistics and other data showing that violent juvenile crime peaked in 1993 and began a steady decline. From 1995 to 1999, juvenile arrests for violent crime declined 23 percent, and homicides declined an astonishing 56 percent, despite an 8 percent increase in the population of juveniles. The murder rate for juveniles in 1999 was the lowest since 1966. Yet in 1999, public anxiety over a series of school shootings skyrocketed when two teenage boys murdered twelve classmates and a teacher at Columbine High School in Colorado.

The Surgeon General's Report on Youth Violence, released by the U.S. Department of Health and Human Services in 2000, identified numerous public myths about youth violence. Among these misconceptions were: (1) the belief that the United States was threatened by a new, violent breed of young super-predators; (2) nothing works in treating or preventing juvenile violence; and (3) juvenile crime could be curbed by prosecuting juvenile offenders as adults. In fact, there was no evidence that young offenders in 2000 were more vicious or callous than previous generations, only that the availability of cheaper, more lethal firearms resulted in more homicides. Further, controlled scientific studies found that well-run prevention and intervention programs do reduce violent behavior and criminal recidivism among the young. And finally, studies found no crime reduction associated with transferring juveniles to adult court; in contrast, youths tried as adults were more likely to be physically and sexually victimized in adult institutions, and were more likely to commit additional offenses upon release to the community.

Scope and Prevalence of Juvenile Crime

Juvenile crime traditionally refers to criminal acts committed by persons under age eighteen. If one includes status offenses, such as consuming alcohol, smoking, being truant from school, running away, and violating curfews, that are crimes only because the person committing them is underage, then the majority of youth in the United States might at some point be classified as delinquent offenders! Nonstatus offenses are much less common. According to Snyder and Sickmund's 1999 report only about 5 percent of juveniles are ever arrested, and more than 90 percent of the arrests are for nonviolent crimes. Of course, arrest statistics undercount the true numbers of offenses, since an unknown number of offenses committed by juveniles go undetected. Self-report studies generally reveal higher prevalence rates; for example, among high school seniors, the annual prevalence of committing an assault with injury to the victim was 10 to 15 percent and the prevalence of robbery with a weapon was 5 percent.

Juveniles account for only about 16 percent of serious violent crimes, but nearly one-third (32%) of property crimes, according to FBI arrest statistics from the Uniform Crime Reports. Juveniles are involved in the majority (54%) of arson arrests and disproportionate numbers of vandalism (42%), motor vehicle theft (35%), and burglary (33%) arrests. Of the 2.5 million juvenile arrests in 1999, the most frequent charges were larceny-theft, simple assaults, drug abuse violations, curfew and loitering, disorderly conduct, and liquor law violations. Arrest statistics are difficult to interpret, because they do not correspond directly with the number of youth arrested or the number of crimes committed; several youths might be arrested for the same crime, a single youth might be arrested multiple times in the same year, or a youth might be arrested once, but charged with multiple offenses. Nevertheless, comparisons of adult and juvenile offenders, again as summarized by Snyder and Sickmund, indicate that juveniles are generally not predisposed to crime, and although they commit a disproportionate number of minor crimes, they are much less likely than adults, especially young adults, to commit serious violent crimes.

Crime in Schools

Highly publicized episodes of gun violence at schools raised national concern that schools were not safe environments. Homicides at school, though tragic, are fortunately quite rare. In a 2001 report, the National School Safety Center concluded that less than one percent of all juvenile homicides occur in school, and that the number of homicide deaths in schools declined from forty-two in the 1993–1994 school year to eleven in 1999–2000.

Schools are not crime-free sanctuaries, however, and crime rates in schools correlate with the crime rate of the surrounding community. A 1998 study by the National Center for Education Statistics found that approximately 21 percent of high schools, 19 percent of middle schools, and 4 percent of elementary schools experienced at least one serious violent crime (primarily aggravated assaults) per year, including crimes committed by nonstudents. Nevertheless, most juvenile crime takes place in the hours immediately after school, when students are less likely to be supervised.

Property crimes are three times more prevalent than violent crimes at school (including travel to and from school). According to the National Center for Education Statistics's 1998 report on school crime and safety, approximately 12 percent of students reported thefts of their personal property in a six-month period, whereas only 4 percent reported violent crimes, defined as physical attacks or robbery with threat of violence. The annual rate of serious violent crimes (sexual assault, robbery, and aggravated assault) at school is less than half the rate away from school.

According to noted Norwegian researcher Dan Olweus, as well as reports by the U.S. National School Safety Center, bullying is increasingly recognized as a serious and pervasive problem in schools, although it is often overlooked or disregarded by parents and teachers. Common bullying behaviors, such as pushing and shoving, verbal harassment, and threats of violence, would be regarded as crimes if they took place in an adult workplace, but often go undetected or unpunished in schools. Studies indicate that most students have been bullied at some time and that bullying is most common in the middle school grades, where more than 10 percent of students may be victims of chronic bullying.

Juvenile Offenders

There is no single profile or adequate characterization of the diverse group of youth who come to be identified as juvenile offenders. Most youths who commit crimes as juveniles desist in early adulthood, and most who come to juvenile court never return on a new referral. However, a small group of juveniles is prone to continued offending. Marvin Wolfgang's classic 1972 study of a Philadelphia birth cohort of 10,000 boys found that about 6 percent of the boys were responsible for more than fifty percent of the crimes committed by the entire sample. Subsequent studies, summarized by Snyder and Sickmund in 1995, found that 5 to 16 percent of all referrals to juvenile court are youths with five or more arrests, and these youths account for 50 to 80 percent of all juvenile offenses.

Why do youth commit acts of violence and other crimes? Theories abound, but there is general agreement that there are multiple developmental pathways associated with different contributory factors. Youth whose onset of problem behavior begins before puberty commit more frequent and more violent crimes in adolescence, and are more likely to persist in violent offending in adulthood, than youth with later onset.

Family factors. Many factors increase the risk that a juvenile will engage in criminal or violent behavior, but no single factor is necessary or sufficient. For example, poverty and single parent family status are widely recognized risk factors, but most poor children raised by single parents in low-income homes do not become criminals. Global factors such as poverty and parent marital status are too broad to specify the precise problems in the child's family environment. A single mother working long hours for low wages may not be able to provide supervision for her children, she may be under too much stress to maintain a warm, supportive relationship with her children, and she may be inconsistent in disciplining them. In contrast, there are many examples of poor, single parents who nevertheless manage to provide excellent care for their children. Risk factors might be buffered by protective factors such as a mentoring relationship, religious convictions, special talents, or strong motivation to achieve.

More intensive studies reveal patterns of inconsistent or inappropriate parental discipline, as well as poor monitoring and supervision, in families of children who develop conduct problems. In one common pattern, parents fail to respond to their child's misbehavior, or when they do respond, it is often with excessive force or harsh emotion. Such parents tend to threaten, hit, grab, or yell to coerce children into compliance. Not surprisingly, their children then respond similarly (e.g. yelling, stomping, or hitting) when parents try to limit their behavior. The parents intermittently overlook or acquiesce to their children's misbehavior, thereby reinforcing it and rendering it even more resistive to discipline. Other important family risk factors include child abuse, exposure to domestic violence, and parental substance abuse.

Social factors. Parental influences diminish markedly in adolescence and are often superceded by peer influences. Youths who associate with delinquent peers adopt more antisocial attitudes and engage in more delinquent behavior. Youths who are unpopular with conventional peers are especially likely to seek friendships with less conventional, more antisocial youths.

As youths spend increasing amounts of time unsupervised outside the home, they become more vulnerable to the negative influence of communities characterized by a high level of social disorganization—high residential turnover, high unemployment and few job opportunities, frequent crime, drug trafficking, gang activities, and a relative lack of recreational opportunities. Youths who feel endangered in the community are more likely to carry weapons and seek protection from gang affiliation, which ironically increases the risk of involvement in violent or criminal activities. Access to handguns is particularly problematic and was linked to a three-fold increase in juvenile homicide arrests from 1984 to 1993.

Adolescents are highly influenced by the entertainment industry. As noted by the 2001 Surgeon General's Report and many other authorities, more than forty years of research demonstrates that even brief exposure to film violence causes short-term increases in aggressive behavior, including physical aggression, in youth. Longitudinal studies show small but consistent correlations between childhood television viewing and young adult aggression, even after controlling for other factors such as socioeconomic status and parental discipline. The impact of violent music and video games has not been extensively studied, but early studies show similar effects. Advocates for the entertainment industry point out that many other factors influence the development of aggressive behavior, and that the link to serious violent crime is less clear.

Individual factors. Social toxins like poverty, neighborhood crime, and entertainment violence do not have the same impact on all children; individual dif-

ferences in personality, temperament, and aptitude play an important role in ways not fully understood. Children with attention problems, impulsivity, and low verbal intelligence are more likely to engage in violent and criminal behavior in adolescence and adulthood. A 2001 study by Linda Teplin found that as many as two-thirds of youth involved in the juvenile justice system have one or more diagnosable mental or substance abuse disorders.

Violence and crime can be regarded fundamentally as learned behaviors, and youth involvement in such behaviors may reflect a multitude of different learning experiences. Nevertheless, children can learn alternatives to crime and violence as well. Controlled outcome studies, described in the Surgeon General's report and by Rolf Loeber and David Farrington, demonstrate that many prevention efforts—preschool family services, social competence training and structured recreational programs for at-risk children, and multisystemic family therapy or multidimensional treatment foster care for juvenile offenders—are successful and cost-effective.

See also: AGGRESSIVE BEHAVIOR; JUVENILE JUSTICE SYSTEM, *subentries on* CONTEMPORARY JUVENILE JUSTICE SYSTEM AND JUVENILE DETENTION ALTERNATIVES, HISTORY OF JUVENILE COURTS; VIOLENCE, CHILDREN'S EXPOSURE TO.

BIBLIOGRAPHY

FEDERAL BUREAU OF INVESTIGATION. 2000. *Crime in the United States: 1999 Uniform Crime Reports.* Washington, DC: U.S. Department of Justice.

LOEBER, ROLF, and FARRINGTON, DAVID P., eds. 1998. *Serious and Violent Juvenile Offenders: Risk Factors and Successful Interventions.* Thousand Oaks, CA: Sage.

NATIONAL CENTER FOR EDUCATION STATISTICS. 1998. *Indicators of School Crime and Safety.* Washington, DC: U.S. Departments of Education and Justice.

NATIONAL SCHOOL SAFETY CENTER. 1999. *School Safety Update: Bullying: Peer Abuse in Schools.* Westlake Village, CA: National School Safety Center.

NATIONAL SCHOOL SAFETY CENTER. 2001. *School Associated Violent Deaths.* Westlake Village, CA: National School Safety Center.

OLWEUS, DAN. 1993. *Bullying at School: What We Know and What We Can Do.* New York: Blackwell.

SNYDER, HOWARD N., and SICKMUND, MELISSA. 1995. *Juvenile Offenders and Victims: 1995 National Report.* Washington, DC: Office of Juvenile Justice and Delinquency Prevention.

SNYDER, HOWARD N., and SICKMUND, MELISSA. 1999. *Juvenile Offenders and Victims: 1999 National Report.* Washington, DC: Office of Juvenile Justice and Delinquency Prevention.

TEPLIN, LINDA. 2001. *Assessing Alcohol, Drug, and Mental Disorders in Juvenile Detainees.* Washington, DC: Office of Juvenile Justice and Delinquency Prevention.

U.S. DEPARTMENT OF HEALTH AND HUMAN SERVICES. 2001. *Youth Violence: A Report of the Surgeon General.* Rockville, MD: U.S. Department of Health and Human Services.

WOLFGANG, MARVIN E.; FIGLIO, ROBERT M.; and SELLIN, JOHAN T. 1972. *Delinquency in a Birth Cohort.* Chicago: University of Chicago Press.

DEWEY G. CORNELL
DANIEL C. MURRIE

K

KANDEL, ISAAC L. (1881–1965)

A pioneer in the field of comparative education, Isaac Leon Kandel conducted extensive studies of educational systems around the world. Kandel was born in Botosani, Romania, to English parents. He attended the Manchester Grammar School and earned his B.A. in classics in 1902 and M.A. in education in 1906 at the University of Manchester. From 1906 to 1908 he taught classics at the Royal Academical Institute in Belfast, Ireland. After summer study with William Rein at the University of Jena, Kandel enrolled at Teachers College, Columbia University, completing his Ph.D. in 1910. Kandel served there as instructor and then as associate professor until 1923, when he became professor of education and an associate in the Teachers College International Institute until 1946. He then taught at the University of Manchester from 1947 to 1949. From 1924 until 1944, he edited the Teachers College International Institute's Educational Yearbook, the journal *School and Society* from 1946 to 1953, and *Universities Quarterly* from 1947 to 1949.

Over his long and prolific career, Kandel received many honors, including honorary doctorates from the University of North Carolina and the University of Melbourne, and the title of Chevalier of the Legion of Honor from France. Kandel's principal scholarly contributions were in the areas of the history of education, educational theory, and, notably, comparative and international education.

History of Education

Kandel's *History of Secondary Education* (1930) represents his major contribution to the history of education. For Kandel, history should inform efforts to resolve contemporary problems. As he put it, the historical study of education should be based upon

> the sincere conviction that progress in any social field, and especially in education, is possible only with a clear understanding of the factors that have brought about the present situation, and with an intelligent appreciation of the forces that must be analyzed in order to construct a new philosophy or a new body of principles to guide in its further reconstruction. (p. x)

Accordingly, as he traced the history of secondary education, he devoted his greatest attention to developments that had the most direct bearing on the problems of his day.

Kandel identified liberal education as the "central tradition" in secondary education in Europe and the United States. He traced its foundations in ancient Rome and Greece and its development during the Middle Ages, Renaissance, and Enlightenment periods, and detailed the emergence of systems of secondary education in France, Germany, England, and the United States, emphasizing the latter two. He also devoted special attention to the education of girls. Kandel examined the impact of contemporary developments, including knowledge expansion, new social and economic circumstances wrought by the industrial revolution, and the widening acceptance of democratic ideals, on the tradition of liberal education in the secondary school.

Specifically, Kandel discerned among recent trends in secondary education in industrial democracies a recognition of the role of education in promoting national welfare and economic growth and an increasing respect for achieving the full development of the individual regardless of social origins. Kandel identified the potential conflict between provision of educational opportunity to all individuals and selection for social and economic roles as a central problem of secondary education.

Comparative and International Education

Kandel's approach to comparative education comprised more than sheer description of administrative, curricular, and instructional practices in particular countries. Such descriptions and the compilation of data pertaining, for example, to national expenditures, per pupil costs, enrollment figures, and dropout rates were necessary but insufficient tasks for understanding educational systems. He presciently warned of the limitations of comparative use of statistical measures of student achievement to determine educational purposes and standards of student performance. Kandel maintained that the sociopolitical milieu exerted a greater impact on school practice than educational theories. Kandel conceived comparative education as the study of the ways particular countries addressed educational problems in the context of their respective social, political, and cultural traditions. Comparative studies of education were therefore premised upon an understanding of the social and economic life of the culture under study.

In his most important work in the field, *Comparative Education* (1933), Kandel stated, "The chief value of a comparative approach to [educational] problems lies in an analysis of the causes which have produced them, in a comparison of the differences between the various systems and the reasons underlying them, and, finally, a study of the solutions attempted" (p. xix). Kandel viewed each national education system as a "laboratory" in which solutions to educational problems were tested and implemented. Kandel hoped that comparative education, by distilling common principles from variegated national contexts, would contribute to the development of a philosophy of education, that is, an educational theory, based not merely on metaphysical and ethical ruminations, but on practical, empirical grounds as well. Additionally, Kandel sought through comparative study of national education systems to promote international understandings and sympathies.

Educational Theory

Kandel's work in the area of educational theory largely took the form of a critique of Progressive education. He wrote his most significant work in this area, *The Cult of Uncertainty* (1943), in a tone and temper marked by a vehemence uncharacteristic of his scholarship on educational history and comparative education. In this work Kandel detected "the American traditions of rootlessness, of practicality, and of desire for new sensations" manifest both in the philosophy of pragmatism and in Progressive education (p. 90). Kandel rejected the tendency of child-centered Progressives to advocate a "nothing-fixed-in-advance" approach to curriculum in which education began and ended with the individual student's present interests and inclinations. Kandel advocated inculcating "common understanding, common knowledge, common ideals, and common values" through liberal education (p. 126). Although Kandel advanced an incisive critique of the excesses of child-centered forms of Progressivism, his overgeneralization of his criticisms to all Progressive education (exclusive only of John Dewey and Boyd Bode, both of whom he evoked to attack other Progressives), undermined his argument.

An avowed essentialist, Kandel viewed subject matter not as potential evidence for the resolution of social problems, but as a stable source of values to guide social behavior. He criticized science as overly relativistic and touted the primacy of the liberal arts curriculum. Scholars have argued that Kandel's commitment to traditional liberal arts education contradicted his recognition of the need for reform engendered by changing social, economic, and political values and conditions. Indeed, Kandel's principal, if not sole, concession to Progressive education involved a recognition of its value for improving "traditional methods of instruction," although he gave principal credit for that to psychology (p. 94). Although he viewed essentialism as occupying a sort of educational middle ground between traditionalism and Progressivism, he held little hope for a synthesis of the two approaches.

See also: EDUCATION REFORM; INTERNATIONAL EDUCATION; SECONDARY EDUCATION.

BIBLIOGRAPHY

BRICKMAN, WILLIAM W. 1951. "I. L. Kandel: International Scholar and Educator." *The Educational Forum* 15:389–412.

CREMIN, LAWRENCE A. 1966. *Isaac Leon Kandel (1881–1965): A Biographical Memoir.* Chicago: National Academy of Education.

KANDEL, ISAAC LEON. 1930. *History of Secondary Education.* Boston: Houghton Mifflin.

KANDEL, ISAAC LEON. 1933. *Comparative Education.* Boston: Houghton Mifflin.

KANDEL, ISAAC LEON. 1943. *The Cult of Uncertainty.* New York: Macmillan.

KANDEL, ISAAC LEON. 1955. *The New Era in Education.* Boston: Houghton Mifflin.

POLLACK, ERWIN W. 1989. "Isaac Leon Kandel: A Pioneer in Comparative and International Education." Ph.D. diss., Loyola University of Chicago.

TEMPLETON, ROBERT G. 1956. "Isaac L. Kandel's Contributions to the Theory of American Education." Ph.D. diss., Harvard University.

WILLIAM G. WRAGA

KEPPEL, FRANCIS C. (1916–1990)

Educational leader and administrator, Francis C. Keppel was born in New York City. He was raised in an atmosphere of liberal reform; his father, Frederick P. Keppel, served as a dean at Columbia University and in 1923 was appointed president of the Carnegie Corporation of New York. Among the elder Keppel's many interests was the role of education in achieving social equality, and one of his most important decisions was to sponsor Gunner Myrdal's groundbreaking study of racial inequality, leading to Myrdal's publication of *An American Dilemma* in 1944. Francis Keppel was educated at Groton before entering Harvard in 1934, and apparently inherited many of his father's liberal proclivities, helping to cultivate a vision of equality that came to influence the course of American education.

After earning a B.A. in English literature in 1938 and being elected to Phi Beta Kappa, Keppel decided to pursue an abiding interest in sculpture, spending a year at the American Academy in Rome. In this regard Keppel exhibited a sensibility he may have acquired from his grandfather, an art dealer. Finding that his talents did not match his aspirations, however, Keppel returned to Harvard to take a position as assistant dean of admissions, marking the beginning of a long association with that institution. After several years of service as an officer in the U.S. Army's Information and Education Division during World War II, Keppel returned once again to Harvard to become assistant to the provost. It was in this capacity, through his efforts to locate candidates to lead the university's Graduate School of Education, that he caught the eye of Harvard President James Bryant Conant. Keppel so impressed Conant, who was unsettled at the lack of suitable candidates, that he appointed him to the job. Thus, at age thirty-two Keppel became the youngest dean at Harvard.

Conant's choice turned out to be judicious. Keppel was an energetic, imaginative, and effective leader for the Harvard Graduate School of Education, helping to transform it from a small concern focused on training administrators into a dynamic center of innovation and reform. During his fourteen years as dean, the school more than quadrupled in size, applications increased tenfold, and the endowment swelled. The school grew in influence as well. The thrust of Keppel's efforts at Harvard was in keeping with his liberal disposition: improving the quality of teaching, testing reform ideas, and suggesting innovations for practice. He expanded the master of arts in teaching program, an avenue for talented college graduates interested in becoming teachers. He also promoted experiments in team teaching, programmed learning, curricular reform, and educational television. Although most of these ideas had little long-term impact on educational practice, they reflected a spirit of innovation and originality that set Harvard apart from other education schools. At the same time, the school became an important center of education scholarship, and Keppel helped to forge ties to other departments in the social sciences and humanities at Harvard. He was a widely respected leader nationally as well, serving on a number of important committees, task forces and councils during his tenure as a dean.

In 1962 U.S. President John F. Kennedy appointed Keppel to the post of U.S. commissioner of education, the start of a four-year term in federal service. It was in this capacity that Keppel's liberal predilections and his abilities as a leader exerted their greatest influence. He was an aggressive proponent of civil rights, and threatened to withhold federal funds from racially segregated school districts under provisions for equal educational opportunity in the Civil Rights Act of 1964. It was this posture of assertive enforcement that many observers believe led southern schools to begin complying with desegregation directives in the 1960s.

In addition to this, Keppel generally is credited with being a major force behind the drafting and passage of the Elementary and Secondary Education Act (ESEA) of 1965, which substantially increased the federal role in public education. Working closely with President Lyndon Johnson and legislative leaders, Keppel helped to craft provisions leading to the establishment of Title I of the act, providing funds for schools serving poor children. He was a strong believer in providing educational opportunities to all children, declaring that education "must make good on the concept that no child within our society is either unteachable or unreachable." When the cabinet-level office of Health, Education and Welfare was established in 1965, Keppel became assistant secretary for education.

Keppel also played a leading role in the establishment of the National Assessment of Educational Progress (NAEP), which was intended to be a means of comparing the performance of schools in different parts of the country and helping to raise academic standards. He helped to secure the passage of groundbreaking federal legislation in the areas of higher education, workforce training, and library services. In each of these instances, the federal role in general education was expanded significantly.

Keppel's reform propensities eventually landed him in trouble, and he departed Washington under a cloud of controversy. In 1965 he threatened to withhold some $32 million in funds from the Chicago Public Schools in response to charges that the system was illegally segregated by race, a decision based largely on an investigation conducted by the U.S. Civil Rights Commission. This was a volatile issue in Chicago, where local leaders were under intense public criticism for inequities between schools attended by black and white students. Exercising his considerable political clout, Chicago Mayor Richard J. Daley made a decisive phone call to the White House that eventually resulted in a number of changes in the administration of federal funds. As a consequence, Chicago's schools received their federal monies, and shortly thereafter Keppel left government service. Ultimately, responsibility for supervising withholding actions was shifted from the Office of Education to the Justice Department.

After leaving Washington, Keppel became chief executive officer of the General Learning Corporation, a publishing and broadcasting venture. In 1974 he became director of the Aspen Institute for Humanistic Studies for a Changing Society for several years before returning to Harvard in 1977 as a senior lecturer in the Graduate School of Education. He also served on a number of boards in these years, including those of Harvard, the City University of New York, the International Development Research Centre in Ottawa, and Lincoln Center for the Performing Arts, as well as education reform commissions in New York and elsewhere. During the 1980s he continued to provide commentary on the state of American education from his post at Harvard, giving a final interview in tandem with his longtime colleague Harold Howe just before his death in 1990.

Equipped only with a B.A. in English literature, Francis Keppel enjoyed a career as one of the nation's leading educational figures in the twentieth century. He helped to establish a prominent graduate school of education, and contributed directly to one of the greatest eras of educational expansion and reform in American history. An energetic proponent of expanding the federal role in education, he lived to see these ideas fall out favor toward the end of his life. Even this, however, cannot diminish the magnitude of his accomplishments, and the considerable imprint he has left on the schools of the early twenty-first century.

See also: ASSESSMENT, *subentry on* NATIONAL ASSESSMENT OF EDUCATIONAL PROGRESS; FEDERAL EDUCATIONAL ACTIVITIES, *subentry on* HISTORY.

BIBLIOGRAPHY

HOFFMAN, NANCY, and SCHWARTZ, ROBERT. 1990. "Remembrances of Things Past: An Interview with Francis Keppel." *Change Magazine* 22(2):52–57.

KEPPEL, FRANCIS. 1961. *Personnel Policies for Public Education.* Pittsburgh, PA: University of Pittsburgh.

KEPPEL, FRANCIS. 1965. *How Should We Educate the Deprived Child? Three Addresses by Francis Keppel, Calvin E. Gross [and] Samuel Shepard.* Washington, DC: Council for Basic Education.

KEPPEL, FRANCIS. 1966. *The Necessary Revolution in American Education.* New York: Harper and Row.

KEPPEL, FRANCIS. 1976. *Educational Policy in the Next Decade.* Palo Alto, CA: Aspen Institute for Humanist Studies.

MIECH, EDWARD J. 2000. "The Necessary Gentleman: Francis Keppel's Leadership in Getting Education's Act Together." Ph.D. diss., Harvard University.

JOHN L. RURY

KERSCHENSTEINER, GEORG (1854–1932)

A dominating figure in the German Progressive education movement, Georg Kerschensteiner gained an international reputation as promoter of activity schools, civic instruction, and vocational education.

Born into an impoverished merchant family, Kerschensteiner taught at elementary schools (*Volksschule*) before he attended gymnasium and university, passed the state examination for secondary school teachers (1881), and earned the Ph.D. degree at the University of Munich (1883). In 1895, after twelve years of teaching at a gymnasium, he was elected school superintendent of Munich, a position he held until his retirement in 1919. In this capacity, he devoted his energies to a reorganization of elementary and vocational education, implementing in particular two innovations: the "activity school" (*Arbeitsschule*) and the "continuation school" (*Fortbildungsschule*). To the activity school, Kerschensteiner introduced workshops, kitchens, laboratories, and school gardens for the upper grades of the elementary school, and developed a kind of project method, with the intent to increase and elevate the students' learning motivation, their problem-solving capacities, their self-esteem, and their moral character. Kerschensteiner's continuation school was a mandatory part-time school for all boys and girls between the ages of fourteen and seventeen who had finished the compulsory eight-year elementary school and were working. As apprentices and young laborers they received eight to ten hours of instruction weekly; in addition to practical training they attended classes in religion, composition, mathematics, and civics—subjects that were taught in close connection with their specific trades.

In this way Kerschensteiner tried to foster their liberal education and further their social advancement; he stressed, however, that the main aim of education had to be citizenship (*staatsbürgerliche Erziehung*). The activity school and the continuation school were to make useful and purposeful citizens: first, by guiding the student to his proper life work; second, by planting the idea that each vocation had its place in serving society; and third, by teaching the student that through a vocation society grew to a more perfect community. Kerschensteiner appealed to the students' practical bent by building the learning process upon their active participation in work projects and extracurricular activities chosen in accordance with their own interests. Participation and project work were to convert the school from a place of individual and intellectual singularity into a place of practical and socially serviceable plurality.

His work brought him high recognition, making Munich the "pedagogical Mecca" for educators from all over the world. He received invitations to lecture in Europe, Russia, and America; his books were even translated into Turkish, Chinese, and Japanese. An admirer of John Dewey and his foremost interpreter in Germany, Kerschensteiner toured the United States in 1910 on behalf of the National Society for the Promotion of Industrial Education. By this he hastened the most vigorous debate of the Progressive era with Dewey, David Snedden, Charles Prosser, Charles McCarthy as protagonists, resulting in the Munich system of vocational education (e.g. dual control and continuation schools) becoming in part the model for Wisconsin's Cooley Bill of 1911 and the Federal Smith-Hughes Act of 1917.

In England, Switzerland, and Japan his concept of compulsory continuing education had a similar impact on school reform and legislation. From 1912 to 1918 Kerschensteiner was, on the liberal ticket, member of the German Parliament (Reichstag) in Berlin. After his retirement, from 1918 to 1930, he served as professor of education at the University of Munich, publishing numerous books and articles, among them *Die Seele des Erziehers und das Problem der Lehrerbildung* (1921; The soul of the educator and the problem of teacher education), *Theorie der Bildung* (1926; Theory of culture), and *Theorie der Bildungsorganisation*, (1933; Theory of the educational system).

Kerschensteiner's philosophy of education was influenced by contemporary Neoidealists and opposed to the classical ideal of culture as conceived by Wilhelm von Humboldt. Whereas Humboldt (and Dewey for that matter) claimed that general education had to precede specific education, Kerschensteiner maintained that vocational, not general, education was to be the focal center of teaching and the "golden gate to culture and humanity." Only the individual, he claimed, who finds himself through his work can, in the course of his development, become a truly cultivated person. Having worked his way up from humble beginnings, Kerschensteiner based all his educational innovations on a democratic impetus that was designed to overcome the rigid caste structure of German society, break up its inflexible school system, and increase the occupational opportunities for talented youth from the lower classes.

Apart from *Die Entwicklung der zeichnerischen Begabung* (1905; The development of talent for drawing) and *Wesen und Wert des naturwissenschaftlichen Unterrichts* (1914; Nature and value of science instruction), his most important books and articles published before World War I are available in English: *Education for Citizenship* (1911; *Die staatsbürgerliche Erziehung der deutschen Jugend* [1901]); *Three Lectures on Vocational Education* (1911: *A Comparison of Public Education in Germany and in the United States* (1913); *The Idea of an Industrial School* (1913; *Begriff der Arbeitsschule* [1912]); *The Schools and the Nation* (1914; *Grundfragen der Schulorganisation* [1907]).

See also: PROGRESSIVE EDUCATION; VOCATIONAL AND TECHNICAL EDUCATION.

BIBLIOGRAPHY

BENNETT, CHARLES A. 1937. *History of Manual and Industrial Education, 1870–1917.* Peoria, IL: Manual Arts Press.

KNOLL, MICHAEL. 1993. "Dewey versus Kerschensteiner. Der Streit um die Einführung der Fortbildungsschule in den USA, 1910–1917." *Pädagogische Rundschau* 47:131–145.

LINTON, DEREK S. 1997. "American Responses to German Continuation Schools during the Progressive Era." In *German Influences on Education in the United States to 1917,* ed. Henry Geitz, et al. Cambridge, Eng.: Cambridge University Press.

SIMONS, DIANE. 1966. *Georg Kerschensteiner. His Thought and Its Relevance Today.* London: Methuen.

TOEWS, EMIL O. 1955. "The Life and Professional Works of Georg Michael Kerschensteiner, 1854–1932." Ph.D. diss., University of California, Los Angeles.

WEGNER, ROBERT A. 1978. "Dewey's Ideas in Germany. The Intellectual Response, 1901–1933." Ph.D. diss., University of Wisconsin, Madison.

MICHAEL KNOLL

KILPATRICK, WILLIAM H. (1871–1965)

Progressive educational philosopher and interpreter of John Dewey's work, William Heard Kilpatrick was born in White Plains, Georgia, the son of a Baptist minister. Educated in village schools, he graduated from Mercer University in Macon, Georgia, moving on to do graduate work in mathematics at Johns Hopkins University. Kilpatrick served as a public school principal in Georgia before returning to his alma mater to teach and briefly serve as Mercer's acting president. In 1906 he became embroiled in a series of controversies with the institution's president that resulted in the board of trustees holding a "heresy" trial, after which Kilpatrick resigned. In 1908 he moved to New York City to begin his doctoral studies at Teachers College, Columbia University, where John Dewey, one of his major professors, called him the best student he ever had. His dissertation, which he defended in 1911, was a history of colonial Dutch schools in New York. Beginning his work at Teachers College as a part-time administrator in the Appointment Office and a history of education instructor, Kilpatrick eventually attained a full-time teaching appointment in the philosophy of education, which he held from 1912 to 1937.

Kilpatrick's meteoric rise in educational circles began with the publication in 1918 of his article "The Project Method" in the Teachers College *Record.* In that article Kilpatrick provided a practical approach to implementing John Dewey's educational philosophy. Drawing on Dewey's earlier work, *Interest and Effort,* he attempted to demonstrate how students could engage in purposeful activity at the intellectual, physical, and affective levels. The inclusion of projects matched the child-centered approach advocated by Progressive educators at this time. The emphases that projects placed on individual learning, on reflective activity, and on the development of the whole child struck a resonant chord with teachers of the period. "The Project Method" was an immediate bestseller among educators and launched Kilpatrick's national public career.

Other reasons for Kilpatrick's rising influence in American education were his effective teaching and charismatic public-speaking ability. Often teaching classes in excess of 600 students, he was able to use group work, discussion, and summary lectures to enrich the educational experience for his students. Kilpatrick was known for his cultured Georgian accent, his thick mane of white hair, and his perceptive blue eyes, all contained within a small, energetic frame. His popularity was such that the New York City press gave him the moniker "Columbia's Million Dollar Professor." Although his salary never approached that figure, the tuition his classes generated for the coffers of Columbia University did exceed that amount during his quarter century of service to Teachers College.

Kilpatrick's career at Teachers College came to a close amid controversy. Dean William Russell decided to enforce the institution's mandatory retirement age, and his action set off a national firestorm among educators when Kilpatrick was the ruling's first casualty. It became a cause célèbre at several national conferences during 1936, with John Dewey wading into the controversy to support Kilpatrick's continued appointment. Kilpatrick's final class in 1937 consisted of 622 students, bringing to 35,000 the number of students he had taught at Teachers College. Living almost another three decades, Kilpatrick was active in his retirement, leading the New York Urban League, the Progressive Education Association, and the John Dewey Society as its first president. He continued writing and speaking in addition to teaching summer school classes at such universities as Stanford, Northwestern, and Minnesota. His involvement in organizations often brought him into conflict with the major conservatives of the day, including Robert Hutchins, Father Charles Coughlin, and William Randolph Hearst. Kilpatrick's activities also placed him within the ranks of influential liberals in post–World War II America, including Eleanor Roosevelt, Ralph Bunche, and Bayard Rustin.

Kilpatrick's consistent Progressive message was that schools needed to be more child-centered, democratic, and socially oriented. After World War II, critics attacked many of the ideas and practices of Progressive education. They saw a curriculum that lacked rigor and students who were academically unprepared to compete with in a global economy. Specific criticism aimed at Kilpatrick emerged in the school reform literature of the 1980s and 1990s. Sup-porters of a traditional curriculum, such as E.D. Hirsch and Diane Ravitch, viewed the Progressive philosophy that Kilpatrick had espoused as the principal cause for what, in their opinion, was a decline in the academic standards of American schools. Over the same period, though, numerous Progressive-oriented pedagogies were implemented in the nation's classrooms. These innovations included cooperative learning, team teaching, individualization of instruction, and the experiential elements of the middle school movement. These student-centered practices, along with Kilpatrick's unswerving commitment to democratic principals in the schools, form the bedrock of his legacy. In one of his final statements, John Dewey said that Kilpatrick's works "form a notable and virtually unique contribution to the development of a school society that is an organic component of a living, growing democracy" (Tenenbaum, p. x).

See also: CURRICULUM, SCHOOL; DEWEY, JOHN; INSTRUCTIONAL STRATEGIES; PHILOSOPHY OF EDUCATION; PROGRESSIVE EDUCATION.

BIBLIOGRAPHY

BEINEKE, JOHN A. 1998. *And There Were Giants in the Land: The Life of William Heard Kilpatrick.* New York: Lang.

KILPATRICK, WILLIAM HEARD. 1923. *Source Book in the Philosophy of Education.* New York: Macmillan.

KILPATRICK, WILLIAM HEARD. 1925. *Foundations of Method.* New York: Macmillan.

KILPATRICK, WILLIAM HEARD. 1941. *Selfhood and Civilization: A Study of the Self-Other Process.* New York: Macmillan.

KILPATRICK, WILLIAM HEARD. 1951. *Philosophy of Education.* New York: Macmillan.

TENENBAUM, SAMUEL. 1951. *William Heard Kilpatrick: Trail Blazer in Education.* New York: Harper.

VAN TIL, WILLIAM. 1996. "William Heard Kilpatrick: Respecter of Individuals and Ideas." In *Teachers and Mentors: Profiles of Distinguished Twentieth-Century Professors of Education,* ed. Craig Kridel, Robert V. Bullough, and Paul Shaker. New York: Garland.

JOHN BEINEKE

KINDERGARTEN

See: EARLY CHILDHOOD EDUCATION.

KNOWLEDGE BUILDING

In what is coming to be called the "knowledge age," the health and wealth of societies depends increasingly on their capacity to innovate. People in general, not just a specialized elite, need to work creatively with knowledge. As Peter Drucker put it, "innovation must be part and parcel of the ordinary, the norm, if not routine." This presents a formidable new challenge: how to develop citizens who not only possess up-to-date knowledge but are able to participate in the creation of new knowledge as a normal part of their work lives.

There are no proven methods of educating people to be producers of knowledge. Knowledge creators of the past have been too few and too exceptional in their talents to provide much basis for educational planning. In the absence of pedagogical theory, learning-by-doing and apprenticeship are the methods of choice; but this does not seem feasible if the "doing" in question is the making of original discoveries, inventions, and plans. Rather, one must think of a *developmental trajectory* leading from the natural inquisitiveness of the young child to the disciplined creativity of the mature knowledge producer. The challenge, then, will be to get students on to that trajectory. But what is the nature of this trajectory and of movement along it? There are three time-honored answers that provide partial solutions at best. Knowledge building provides a fourth answer.

One approach emphasizes foundational knowledge: First master what is already known. In practice this means that knowledge creation does not enter the picture until graduate school or adult work, by which time the vast majority of people are unprepared for the challenge.

A second approach focuses on subskills. Master component skills such as critical thinking, scientific method, and collaboration; later, assemble these into competent original research, design, and so forth. Again, the assembly—if it occurs at all—typically occurs only at advanced levels that are reached by only a few. Additionally, the core motivation—advancing the frontiers of knowledge—is missing, with the result that the component skills are pursued as ends

in themselves, lacking in authentic purpose. Subskill approaches remain popular (often under the current banner of "twenty-first century skills") because they lend themselves to parsing the curriculum into specific objectives.

A third approach is associated with such labels as "learning communities," "project-based learning," and "guided discovery." Knowledge is socially constructed, and best supported through collaborations designed so that participants share knowledge and tackle projects that incorporate features of adult teamwork, real-world content, and use of varied information sources. This is the most widely supported approach at present, especially with regard to the use of information technology. The main drawback is that it too easily declines toward what is discussed below as shallow constructivism.

Knowledge building provides an alternative that more directly addresses the need to educate people for a world in which knowledge creation and innovation are pervasive. Knowledge building may be defined as the production and continual improvement of ideas of value to a community, through means that increase the likelihood that what the community accomplishes will be greater than the sum of individual contributions and part of broader cultural efforts. Knowledge building, thus, goes on throughout a knowledge society and is not limited to education. As applied to education, however, the approach means engaging learners in the full process of knowledge creation from an early age. This is in contrast to the three approaches identified above, which focus on kinds of learning and activities that are expected to lead eventually to knowledge building rather than engagement directly in it.

The basic premise of the knowledge building approach is that, although achievements may differ, the *process* of knowledge building is essentially the same across the trajectory running from early childhood to the most advanced levels of theorizing, invention, and design, and across the spectrum of knowledge creating organizations, within and beyond school. If learners are engaged in process only suitable for a school, then they are not engaged in knowledge building.

Learning and Knowledge Building: Important Distinctions

An Internet search turned up 32,000 web pages that use the term "knowledge building." A sampling of these suggests that business people use the term to connote knowledge creation, whereas in education it tends to be used as a synonym for learning. This obscures an important distinction. Learning is an internal, unobservable process that results in changes of belief, attitude, or skill. Knowledge building, by contrast, results in the creation or modification of public knowledge—knowledge that lives "in the world" and is available to be worked on and used by other people. Of course creating public knowledge results in personal learning, but so does practically all human activity. Results to date suggest that the learning that accompanies knowledge building encompasses the foundational learning, subskills, and socio-cognitive dynamics pursued in other approaches, along with the additional benefit of movement along the trajectory to mature knowledge creation. Whether they are scientists working on an explanation of cell aging, engineers designing fuel-efficient vehicles, nurses planning improvements in patient care, or first graders working on an explanation of leaves changing color in the fall, knowledge builders engage in similar processes with a similar goal. That goal is to advance the frontiers of knowledge as they perceive them. Of course, the frontiers as perceived by children will be different from those perceived by professionals, but professionals may also disagree among themselves about where the frontier is and what constitutes an advance. Dealing with such issues is part of the work of any knowledge building group, and so students must learn to deal with these issues as well. Identifying the frontier should be part of their research, not something preordained. The knowledge building trajectory involves taking increasing responsibility for these and other high-level, long-term aspects of knowledge work. This distinguishes knowledge building from collaborative learning activities. Keeping abreast of advancing knowledge is now recognized as essential for members of a knowledge society. Knowledge building goes beyond this to recognize the importance of creating new knowledge. The key distinction is between learning—the process through which the rapidly growing cultural capital of a society is distributed—and knowledge building—the deliberate effort to increase the cultural capital of society.

Shallow versus Deep Constructivism

"Constructivism" is a term whose vagueness beclouds important distinctions. Knowledge building is clearly a constructive process, but most of what goes on in the name of constructivism is not knowledge building. To clarify, it is helpful to distinguish between shallow and deep forms of constructivism. The shallowest forms engage students in tasks and activities in which ideas have no overt presence but are entirely implicit. Students describe the activities they are engaged in (e.g., planting seeds, measuring shadows) and show little awareness of the underlying principles these tasks are to convey. In the deepest forms of constructivism, people are advancing the frontiers of knowledge in their community. This purpose guides and structures their activity: Overt practices such as identifying problems of understanding, establishing and refining goals based on progress, gathering information, theorizing, designing experiments, answering questions and improving theories, building models, monitoring and evaluating progress, and reporting are all directed by the participants themselves toward knowledge building goals.

Most learner-centered, inquiry-based, learning community, and other approaches labeled "constructivist" are distributed somewhere between these extremes of shallow and deep constructivism. Participants in this middle ground are engaged to a greater or lesser extent with ideas and they have greater or lesser amounts of responsibility for achieving goals, but the over-arching responsibility and means for advancing the frontiers of knowledge are either absent or remain in the hands of the teacher or project designer. The idea of "guided discovery" suggests this middle ground. Middle-level constructivist approaches are best categorized as constructivist learning rather than knowledge building. Knowledge building calls for deep constructivism at all educational levels; it is the key to innovation.

Knowledge Building Environments

In knowledge building, ideas are treated as real things, as objects of inquiry and improvement in their own right. Knowledge building environments enable ideas to get out into the world and onto a path of continual improvement. This means not only preserving them but making them available to the whole community in a form that allows them to be discussed, interconnected, revised, and superseded.

Threaded discourse, which is the predominant Internet technology for idea exchange, has limited value for this purpose. Typically, ideas are lodged within conversational threads, contributions are unmodifiable, and there is no way of linking ideas in different threads or assimilating them into larger wholes. By contrast, CSILE/Knowledge Forum, a technology designed specifically to support knowledge building, has these required provisions and scaffolding supports for idea development, graphical means for viewing and reconstructing ideas from multiple perspectives, means of joining discourses across communities, and a variety of other functions that contribute to collaborative knowledge building. Contributions to a community knowledge base serve to create shared intellectual property, and give ideas a life beyond the transitory nature of conversation and its isolation from other discourses. Thus the environment supports sustained collaborative knowledge work, integral to the day-to-day workings of the community, as opposed to merely providing a discussion forum that serves as an add-on to regular work or study.

A shared workspace for knowledge building enables a self-organizing system of interactions among participants and their ideas and helps to eliminate the need for externally designed organizers of work. Advances within this communal space continually generate further advances, with problems reformulated at more complex levels that bring a wider range of knowledge into consideration. Thus there is a compounding effect, much like the compounding of capital through investment. Supporting such compounding and social responsibility for the collective work is the main challenge in the principled design of knowledge building environments.

In keeping with the belief that the process of knowledge building is fundamentally the same at beginning and advanced levels, and across sectors and cultures, Knowledge Forum is used from grade one to graduate school, and in a variety of knowledge-based organizations in countries around the world.

Social Aspects of Knowledge Building

Educational approaches of all kinds are subject to what is called the "Matthew effect": The rich get richer. The more you know the more you can learn. This is as close to a law of nature as learning research has come. It can be used to justify loading the elementary curriculum with large quantities of content. However, another potent principle is that knowledge needs to be of value to people in their current lives, not merely banked against future needs. This is part of the justification for activity and project-based methods where work is driven by students' own interests. In knowledge building this Deweyean principle is carried a step farther: Advances in understanding produce conceptual tools to achieve further advances in understanding. Thus there is a dynamism to knowledge building that can be a powerful motivator.

The Matthew effect foretells a widening gap between haves and have-nots in education, one that may already be manifesting itself in the widening income gap between the more and the less well-educated. No educational approach can be expected to solve the related equity problems, but knowledge building offers signal advantages. The knowledge building trajectory offers value all along its course, not just at its upper reaches. At all stages people are building authentic knowledge that is immediately useful to themselves and their community in making sense of their world. They are also developing skills and habits of mind conducive to lifelong learning. It is not assumed that everyone will come out equal in the end, but possibilities for continual advancement remain open for all.

From a social standpoint, the ability to connect discourses within and between communities opens new possibilities for barrier-crossing and mutual support. Successful knowledge-building communities establish socio-cognitive norms and values that all participants are aware of and work toward. These include contributing to collective knowledge advances, constructive and considerate criticism, and continual seeking of idea improvements. Grade one students, participants with low-literacy levels, and workers in knowledge-creating organizations can all adopt such norms, which then serve as a basis for cooperation across the developmental trajectory and among culturally diverse groups.

Knowledge building has been shown to yield advantages in literacy, in twenty-first century skills, in core content knowledge, in the ability to learn from text, and in other abilities. However, it is the fact that knowledge building involves students directly in creative and sustained work with ideas that makes it especially promising as the foundation for education in the knowledge age.

See also: CURRICULUM, SCHOOL, *subentry on* CORE KNOWLEDGE CURRICULUM; LEARNING THEORY, *subentry on* CONSTRUCTIVIST APPROACH; TEACHING, *subentry on* KNOWLEDGE BASES OF.

BIBLIOGRAPHY

BEREITER, CARL. 2002. *Education and Mind in the Knowledge Age.* Mahwah, NJ: Erlbaum.

DRUCKER, PETER. 1985. *Innovation and Entrepreneurship: Practice and Principles.* New York: Harper and Row.

HOMER-DIXON, THOMAS. 2000. *The Ingenuity Gap: Facing the Economic, Environmental, and Other Challenges of an Increasingly Complex and Unpredictable World.* New York: Knopf.

SCARDAMALIA, MARLENE. 2002. "Collective Cognitive Responsibility for the Advancement of Knowledge." In *Liberal Education in a Knowledge Society,* ed. Barry Smith. Chicago: Open Court.

SCARDAMALIA, MARLENE; BEREITER, CARL; and LAMON, MARY. 1994. "The CSILE Project: Trying to Bring the Classroom into World 3." In *Classroom Lessons: Integrating Cognitive Theory and Classroom Practice,* ed. Kate McGilley. Cambridge, MA: Massachusetts Institute of Technology Press.

STANOVICH, KEITH E. 1986. "Matthew Effects in Reading: Some Consequences in Individual Differences in Reading in the Acquisition of Literacy." *Reading Research Quarterly* 21:360–406.

MARLENE SCARDAMALIA
CARL BEREITER

KNOWLEDGE MANAGEMENT

Due to the wealth of information, the knowledge explosion, and the rapid development of information and communication technologies at the start of the twenty-first century, it is essential to handle complex information and knowledge intelligently and responsibly. Therefore, it is necessary to manage knowledge on an individual as well as on an organizational level. Knowledge management basically encompasses the deliberate and systematic handling of knowledge and the precise use of knowledge in organizations (companies, schools, universities etc.). However, if knowledge management is to be established as a long-term strategy, it must address the following factors simultaneously: *individual, organization,* and *technology.*

In most cases an organization's involvement with knowledge management is not the end in itself but connected to specific goals, that can be deduced from the organization's superordinate goals, either directly or indirectly. In other words, to be economically justifiable, knowledge management has to contribute added value to the organization's efforts to meet its overacting goals. This "value added" must be specific and measurable in relationship to organizational goals and their achievement.

Basics of Knowledge Management

The formulation of knowledge goals is the starting point of knowledge management on an individual as well as on an organizational level. The process of knowledge evaluation can be seen as the end of the knowledge management processes. There is a feedback look from evaluation to goals in that the results of the evaluation may lead to changes in the knowledge goals. A wide range of possible tasks and processes are relevant between goal setting and evaluation. These can be grouped into four kinds of processes that are closely connected and interactive: *knowledge representation, knowledge communication, use of knowledge,* and *development of knowledge.* These categories describe the knowledge management processes on an individual as well as on an organizational level.

Knowledge goals. The formulation and identification of knowledge goals is necessary to provide the initial direction for the knowledge management activities. Carefully planned knowledge management processes are the basis of knowledge goals on an individual as well as on an organizational level.

Evaluation. Evaluation can be seen as the final stage of the four knowledge management processes. On both an individual as well as on an organizational level it is necessary in evaluation to estimate if the knowledge goals have been reached within this context.

Knowledge representation. Knowledge representation describes the process of knowledge identification, preparation, documentation and actualization. The main goal of this category is to transform knowledge into a format which enhances the distribution and exchange of knowledge.

Knowledge communication. In knowledge communication, processes are combined which concern the distribution of information and knowledge, the mediation of knowledge, knowledge sharing, and the co-construction of knowledge, as well as knowledge-based cooperation. These activities necessitate two or more people communicating directly, indirectly face-to-face, or in a virtual environment.

Development of knowledge. The development of knowledge includes not only processes of external knowledge procurement (i.e. through cooperative efforts, consultants, new contacts, etc.) or the creation of specific knowledge resources like research and development departments. The formation of personal and technical knowledge networks are also part of the development of knowledge.

Use of knowledge. Use of knowledge focuses on the *de facto* transformation of knowledge to products and services. This category is of special interest because it shows the effectiveness of the preceding actions in the range of the categories such as knowledge representation, knowledge communication and development of knowledge.

Knowledge Management in the Organization

With the goal of knowledge management to develop the potential for learning of individuals and organizations by developing, exchanging, and using knowledge, knowledge management can be seen as a prerequisite for innovations in organizations.

In this context knowledge management is often regarded as a concept and instrument for the realization of the metaphor of the learning organization. Concepts regarding the learning organization emphasize almost the same goals as knowledge management; but in actuality knowledge management can be regarded as a prerequisite for the creation and maintenance of a learning organization. If an organization (company, school, university etc.) is able to handle its knowledge resources well, it can react to shifts in the marketplace faster and more flexibly. Thus it demonstrates its capability to learn. The learning ability of employees provides a major competitive advantage in the framework of the increasing market pressure. In this context, individual and team-based learning are as important as the documentation and distribution of knowledge within an organization.

Knowledge Management and the Individual

The individual as the initial point of knowledge management has been neglected, especially as knowledge management has become a topic important in the business world. Most companies at first relied on technology-based knowledge management, which has mostly led to the implementation of databases.

On the basis of an intensive analysis of the subject of knowledge management, the conclusion can be drawn that most attempts to manage the resource of knowledge have failed. Today it is clear that knowledge management approaches can only be successful if the individual plays a major role in the process. But it is the individual acting as a member of a community that is critical. Etienne Wenger introduced the idea of communities of practice in the workplace as providing added value to companies. According to Wenger, a *community of practice* is a community in which the members are informally bound by what they do together and by what they have learned through mutual engagement in these activities. Communities are highly self-organized, and it is the responsibility of the members to control the community and distribute the work among its members. Thus self-management, communication skills, the capacity for teamwork and the handling of knowledge are valuable skills for the members of communities. These individual knowledge management competencies are not only important in the range of communities but also for life in a knowledge society. To be able to cope with the new challenges of a knowledge society these skills become core competencies of every individual.

Knowledge Management in Formal Education

It is the task of schools and universities to provide students with basic knowledge management skills needed for life in a rapidly changing society. However, the traditional system of schools and universities does not meet the requirements of a knowledge society. Schools and universities should be transformed into learning organizations where knowledge management comes to life. The core aim should be the mediation of deep understanding of topics and the development of individual knowledge management skills. This new orientation requires a holistic change process in schools. In schools the analog of communities of practice is learning communities. Learning communities offer multifaceted possibilities for the integration of knowledge-management processes in schools and universities. Communities can be developed among the learners within the school. Thus long-term and deep engagement with a topic, interdisciplinary learning, and the development of social skills can be facilitated. At the same time, the exchange of knowledge between the teachers can be stimulated by implementing communities among teachers. In this context the initiation of a community that reaches out over the school boundaries can further enhance this process of knowledge sharing and mutual learning.

Issues in Implementation

In this context the question arises of how the implementation of knowledge management processes to organizations can be facilitated. Within the field of knowledge management, research activities are still limited primarily to case studies. On the basis of several case studies with focus on small and medium-sized companies, six critical success factors for the implementation of knowledge management processes have been found. These factors can also be applied to different kinds of organizations (companies, schools, universities, etc.).

> **Corporate culture.** Successful implementation of knowledge management is closely related to the corporate culture. However, these cultural changes need time. In the context of the implementation of knowledge management activities, it is important to know how knowledge management initiatives interact with the culture and to determine how the culture should be changed.

> **Qualification of employees.** The competencies and motivation of employees strongly influence the success of knowledge management. Thus human resource development and the design of incentive-systems are highly important.

> **Learning culture.** The implementation of knowledge management can be seen as a step-by-step learning process which has to be nurtured.

> **Management support.** Knowledge management activities only have the opportunity to be successful if they are supported by the executive board.

> **Integration of knowledge processes to organization's processes.** It is important to connect knowledge management closely to the organization's processes in order to gain acceptance and for reasons of economical legitimacy.

> **New information and communication technologies.** The implementation of knowledge management does not necessarily have to be connected to an investment in new information and communication technologies. The potential for such technologies evolves only if the cultural and organizational conditions exist.

To confirm and empirically verify these findings further research—basic as well as applied research—is needed in the field of knowledge management. Basic and applied research should be closely connected. Moreover, research questions should be oriented on authentic and current problems. Research initiatives on knowledge management should be designed to be interdisciplinary and extremely precise. Furthermore they should be based on a wide range of methods.

See also: LEARNING, *subentry on* KNOWLEDGE ACQUISITION, REPRESENTATION, AND ORGANIZATION; SCIENCE LEARNING, *subentry on* KNOWLEDGE ORGANIZATION AND UNDERSTANDING; TEACHING, *subentry on* KNOWLEDGE BASES OF.

BIBLIOGRAPHY

BIELACZYC, KATERINE, and COLLINS, ALLAN M. 1999. "Learning Communities in Classrooms: A Reconceptualization of Educational Practice." In *Instructional Design Theories and Models. Volume II: A New Paradigm of Instructional Theory,* ed. Charles M. Reigeluth. Mahwah, NJ: Erlbaum.

DAVENPORT, THOMAS H., and PRUSAK, LAWRENCE. 1998. *Working Knowledge: How Organizations Manage What They Know.* Boston: Harvard Business School.

GIBBONS, MICHAEL; LIMOGES, CAMILLE; NOWOTNY, HELGA; SCHWARTZMAN, SIMON; SCOTT, PETER; and TROW, MARTIN. 1994. *The New Production of Knowledge: The Dynamics of Science and Research in Contemporary Societies.* London: Sage.

GOLDMAN, SUSAN R.; BRAY, MELINDA H.; GAUSE-VEGA, CYNTHIA L.; and ZECH, LINDA K. 1999. "A Learning Communities Model of Professional Development." Paper presented at the 8th Conference of the European Association for Research on Learning and Instruction, Göteborg, Sweden.

SCARDAMALIA, MARLENE, and BEREITER, CARL. 1999. "Schools as Knowledge-Building Organizations." In *Developmental Health and the Wealth of Nations: Social, Biological, and Educational Dynamics,* ed. Daniel P. Keating and Clyde Hertzman. New York: Guilford.

WENGER, ETIENNE. 1999. *Communities of Practice: Learning, Meaning and Identity.* Cambridge, Eng.: Cambridge University Press.

HEINZ MANDL
KATRIN WINKLER

KOHLBERG, LAWRENCE
(1927–1987)

Lawrence Kohlberg virtually developed the fields of moral psychology and moral education through his pioneering cognitive developmental theory and research. Kohlberg's work grew out of a lifelong commitment to address injustice. After graduating from high school at the end of World War II, he volunteered as an engineer on a ship that was smuggling Jewish refugees from Europe to Palestine through the British blockade. He was captured, interred in Cyprus, escaped, fled to a kibbutz in Palestine, and made his way back to the United States where he joined another crew transporting refugees.

A passionate reader of the Great Books throughout his life, Kohlberg completed his undergraduate degree from the University of Chicago in one year. In 1958 he received his doctoral degree in psychology after writing a dissertation on developmental changes in children's moral thinking. This dissertation, which evaluated children's responses to the fictional dilemma of an impoverished man who steals an expensive drug for his dying wife, became one of the most cited unpublished dissertations ever. Kohlberg taught briefly at Yale, then at the University of Chicago, and finally at Harvard's Graduate School of Education, where he established the Center for Moral Education.

When Kohlberg began his graduate studies, American psychologists, who were for the most part behaviorists, did not even use the word *moral.* Kohlberg's broad intellectual pursuits, which embraced philosophy, sociology, and psychology, led him to challenge mainstream thinking. In his dissertation and subsequent research, he drew on a moral philosophical tradition extending from Socrates to Kant that focused on the importance of moral reasoning and judgment. Although Kohlberg was heavily influenced by Jean Piaget's research and played a major role in advancing Piaget's cognitive developmental paradigm in the United States, James Mark Baldwin, John Dewey, and George Herbert Mead also significantly affected Kohlberg's thinking.

Kohlberg's empirical research yielded an original and fecund description of moral development. In his dissertation, he presented a cross-section of children and adolescents with a set of moral dilemmas and asked them to justify their judgments with a series of probing questions. Using an abductive "bootstrapping" method, he derived a sequence of moral types, which became the basis for his well-known six stages of moral judgment.

Stages of Moral Judgment

Kohlberg modified his descriptions of the stages and method for coding them from the time of his dissertation to the publication of the *Standard Issue Scoring Manual* in 1987. Stage one is characterized by blind obedience to rules and authority and a fear of punishment. Stage two is characterized by seeking to pursue one's concrete interests, recognizing that others need to do the same, and a calculating instrumental approach to decision-making. Stage three is characterized by trying to live up to the expectations of others for good behavior, by having good motives, and by fostering close relationships. Stage four is characterized by a concern for maintaining the social system in order to promote social order and welfare. Stage five is characterized by judging the moral worth of societal rules and values insofar as they are consistent with fundamental values, such as liberty, the general welfare or utility, human rights, and contractual obligations. Stage six is characterized by universal principles of justice and respect for human autonomy.

Kohlberg hoped that his stages could provide a framework for moral education. He noted, however, that one could not simply assume that a higher stage was a better stage; one had to make a philosophical argument that the higher stages were more adequate from a moral point of view. It was only then that educators could find a warrant for pursuing moral development as an aim of education. In his provocative essay, "From Is to Ought: How to Commit the Psychological Fallacy and Get Away with It in the Study of Moral Development," Kohlberg demonstrated a parallelism between psychological descriptive and philosophical-normative analyses of the stages, a parallelism, which, he contended, led to a complementarity and even convergence of the two analyses.

In addition to the moral hierarchy of the stages, Kohlberg made four other fundamental claims for his moral stage approach that are directly relevant to moral education. First, he, like Piaget, conceived of the stages as constructed and reconstructed by individuals through interacting with their social environment. Kohlberg sharply distinguished his constructivist/interactionist approach from approaches which emphasize primarily the environment (socialization approaches) or the individual (maturationist approaches). Second, he posited that the stages of moral development are universal. Third, he held that the stage formed an invariant sequence of development without skips or reversals. Finally, he maintained that his stages were holistic structures or organized patterns of moral reasoning. Kohlberg and his colleagues attempted to support these claims through twenty years of longitudinal and cross-cultural research.

Moral Education

When he turned his attention to moral psychology to moral education, Kohlberg was faced with the objection that any form of teaching virtue involved the imposition of an arbitrary personal or religious belief. Kohlberg appealed to the U.S. Constitution to demonstrate the principles of justice upon which the American government is based are, in fact, the very principles at the core of his highest stages. For Kohlberg civic and moral development are one and the same. Kohlberg endorsed Dewey's view that development (intellectual as well as moral) ought to be the aim of education and that schools ought to provide an environment conducive to development. As a constructivist, Kohlberg advocated that schools provide an environment that encouraged active exploration rather than passive learning. Later Kohlberg would put these ideas into practice when he instituted the just community first in prisons and later in schools.

Kohlberg's first research-based contribution to moral education was the moral discussion approach. He started working on the approach in 1967 after his graduate student, Moshe Blatt, had found that the discussion of moral dilemmas led to a modest but significant development in moral reasoning. The moral discussion approach offered educators a way of promoting moral development while avoiding the Scylla of indoctrination and Charybdis of values relativism. The key to the moral discussion approach was to stimulate a lively exchange of points of view that would lead to the disequilibrium necessary for cognitive development. The discussion leader acted

as a facilitator and Socratic questioner, encouraging students to consider the perspective of others and to examine the adequacy of their own arguments.

The moral discussion approach should not be confused with the values clarification approach that was very prevalent in the 1960s and 1970s. The values clarification approach, which started with the assumption that values were a matter of individual preference, represented the extreme of individual relativism. According to this approach, the role of the teacher was limited to helping individual students to become aware of their own values and to tolerate the values of others.

Kohlberg saw the moral discussion approach as one way of promoting development to higher stages of moral reasoning through thoughtful and critical dialogue about moral issues. He was concerned that traditional approaches to character education with their emphasis on exhortation and role-modeling oversimplified the process of moral development and encouraged conformity. Kohlberg wanted an approach to moral education that could address the social issues of his day, such as racism and social inequality. He also wanted an approach to moral education that went beyond cultural relativism. Moral education, he believed, ought to be about fostering universal principles of justice, not transmitting the values of one's particular culture or subculture.

Kohlberg's abiding concern for building a more just society through moral education led him to question whether the moral discussion approach was sufficient. Classroom moral discussions focused on hypothetical dilemmas or problems in history and literature, but not the problems that students encountered in school. Dilemma discussions stopped at individual students' moral reasoning and did not address the school environment. Kohlberg challenged schools to take a more radical approach and become "little republics" ruled not by an aristocracy of philosopher-teachers but by a democracy of teachers and students, engaged in philosophical deliberation about the good of their community.

Kohlberg's most significant contribution to moral education was the just community approach, which he developed over the last thirteen years of his life by working closely with teachers and students in three alternative high schools. The just community approach has two major features: direct-participatory democracy and a commitment to building community, characterized by a strong sense of unity. Direct participatory democracy not only involves students in moral discussions about problems in school, but also helps students to feel responsible for solving those problems. The role of democracy in the just approach cannot be understood, however, apart from the role that community plays in providing a goal for the democracy and shared expectations for student participation.

Kohlberg's view of community was heavily influenced by his observations of a kibbutz high school in Israel and his appropriation of Émile Durkheim's collectivist theory of moral education. Kohlberg believed that American schools were too focused on individual achievement and failed to offer students an opportunity to become attached to a group that could offer them a rich social and moral experience. He urged that teachers become advocates of community in democratic meetings by challenging students to commit themselves to upholding shared values of caring, trust, and collective responsibility. While asking teachers and students to devote themselves to promoting the welfare of the community, he established procedures for checking the power of the group over the individual. Kohlberg believed that the just community approach was needed not only to promote moral development but also to revitalize a sense of democratic civic engagement in a culture that had become excessively focused on private interest.

See also: AFFECT AND EMOTIONAL DEVELOPMENT; EDUCATIONAL PSYCHOLOGY; MORAL DEVELOPMENT.

BIBLIOGRAPHY

COLBY, ANNE, et al. 1987. *The Measurement of Moral Judgment:* Vol 1, *Theoretical Foundations and Research Validation.* New York: Cambridge University Press.

KOHLBERG, LAWRENCE. 1981. *Essays on Moral Development:* Vol. 1, *The Philosophy of Moral Development.* San Francisco: Harper and Row.

KOHLBERG, LAWRENCE. 1984. *Essays on Moral Development:* Vol. 2, *The Psychology of Moral Development.* San Francisco: Harper and Row.

KUHMERKER, LISA; GIELEN, UWE; and HAYES, RICHARD L. 1994. *The Kohlberg Legacy for the Helping Professions.* Birmingham, AL: Doxa.

MODGIL, SOHAN, and MODGIL, CELIA, eds. 1986. *Lawrence Kohlberg, Consensus and Controversy.* Philadelphia: Falmer.

POWER, F. CLARK; HIGGINS, ANN; and KOHLBERG, LAWRENCE. 1989. *Lawrence Kohlberg's Approach to Moral Education.* New York: Columbia University Press.

REED, DONALD R. C. 1997. *Following Kohlberg : Liberalism and the Practice of Democratic Community.* Notre Dame, IN: University of Notre Dame Press.

REIMER, JOSEPH; PAOLITTO, DIANA PRITCHARD; and HERSH, RICHARD H. 1983. *Promoting Moral Growth from Piaget to Kohlberg.* New York: Longman.

F. CLARK POWER

L

LABRANT, LOU L. (1888–1991)

Lou L. LaBrant served as a language arts teacher and a Progressive-education leader from 1906 through 1971. Born in Hinkley, Illinois, LaBrant began her teaching career in public high schools and experimental schools throughout the Midwest during the first two decades of the twentieth century. She completed an undergraduate degree in Latin at Baker University (1911) and, after making a final commitment to education, pursued an M.A. from the University of Kansas (1925), followed by a Ph.D. from Northwestern University (1932). Her professional career spanned eight decades: She was a founding staff member of the University School of Ohio State University (1932–1942), a professor of education at New York University (1942–1953), president of the National Council of Teachers of English (1953–1954), and head of the humanities division at Dillard University (1958–1971), where she implemented the nationally recognized pre-freshman program for African-American students.

Teaching Reading and Writing

An early and consistent proponent of Deweyan progressivism, LaBrant championed holistic and child-centered approaches to teaching reading and writing. She stood at the beginning of the nearly century-long debate between isolated and integrated instructional strategies for language arts classes. Throughout her career LaBrant focused on student choice in reading instruction. From her first years in teaching LaBrant both promoted and practiced free reading programs at experimental schools and major universities. John Dewey (1859–1952) had argued that educators could not know the exact needs of students in their lives, and consequently LaBrant believed teachers had to provide students with conceptual understanding that could be applied in chaotic and unpredictable situations. Essentially, she argued that the reading process was far more important than the specific works students read. She rejected movements such as Great Books and traditional approaches to the canon of required works of literature.

From a late-twentieth-century perspective, LaBrant also spoke for holistic approaches to writing instruction. Isolated grammar instruction, a traditional approach (often taught through text or workbook exercises), had proved to have little or no transfer to student writing, LaBrant emphasized; thus students needed to choose their own topics and writing forms that would be polished after the piece was written—and if the content warranted polishing. LaBrant often chastised teachers who had students correct surface features of empty, mechanical writing. Her ultimate, though not simple, stance was that students learned to write by writing and grew as readers by reading.

Educational Leader

As a writer, editor (*Journal of Educational Method*, 1939–1943), and educational leader (notably as president of the National Council of Teachers of English), LaBrant voiced her support for integrated language arts methodologies; further, she took a variety of stances on the many issues facing education and humanity through much of the her career. Paradoxically, she always believed that reading and writing instruction should not be a separate course, traditionally called English, but an integrated part of all content areas. At the center of many of her beliefs was her contention that language contributed directly to mental health; she warned repeatedly against belief in "word magic"—that saying something could make it happen or be true. Her focus on language instruction was a direct attack on provincialism. She offered, as many Progressives did, the scientific method as the touchstone for growing as a learned individual—a focus she contributed to and carried from her years at the University School of Ohio State University.

Further, she advocated experimental education, especially experimental schools that worked to move students toward content instead of imposing content on the student. As a member of the University School's faculty at Ohio State University, she was directly involved in the eight-year study concerning Progressive education. Her interest in experimentalism included a call for educational methods to be research-based and child-centered. Since she lived through several back-to-basics movements, she also hoped that progressive measures would curb the many moves to standardized education: in her mind, an approach that stifles students' abilities. Her work in research-based and child-centered educational methodologies places her in the constructivist camp of learning theory and in opposition to the traditional behaviorist slant of public education.

A more subtle contribution from LaBrant was her work with disenfranchised and minority students over her career. She applied her progressive methodologies to Native American students in the Midwest, Hispanic and multiethnic classes in New York (P.S. 65), and African-American students entering Dillard University. Her body of work helps to show that traditional education often failed minority students, and Progressive education could and did help bridge the gap left by traditional schooling.

Teaching Teachers

LaBrant was characterized by those who knew her as a demanding person—a teacher with the highest of standards. Many recognized a rigidness and arrogance in LaBrant. She challenged teachers, especially when training them in the teaching of reading and writing.

Whether in her graduate courses or during her many lectures, LaBrant promoted research-based progressive ideas, presenting them assertively, even perhaps excessively so. She appeared to care little for feelings hurt, and was driven to seek and apply the best practices known at that time to ensure that each student receive the most fulfilling and lasting education possible. In the wake of the advocate LaBrant were devoted followers and a sprinkling of angered opponents.

See also: LANGUAGE ARTS, TEACHING OF; LITERACY AND READING.

BIBLIOGRAPHY

ENGLAND, DAVID A., and WEST, B. JANE. 1991. "Lou LaBrant: A Challenge and a Charge." In *Missing Chapters: Ten Pioneering Women in NCTE and English Education,* ed. Jeanne Marcum Gerlach and Virginia R. Monseau. Urbana, IL: National Council of Teachers of English.

LaBRANT, LOU L. 1946. "Teaching High-School Students to Write." *English Journal* 35(3):123–128.

LaBRANT, LOU L. 1951. *We Teach English.* New York: Harcourt, Brace.

LaBRANT, LOU L. 1952. "New Bottles for New Wine." *English Journal* 41(7):341–347.

LaBRANT, LOU L. 1961. "The Use of Communication Media." In *The Guinea Pigs after Twenty Years,* ed. Margaret Willis. Columbus: Ohio State University Press.

THOMAS, P. L. 1999. "The Paradoxes of Lou LaBrant: Choreographer of the Learner's Mind." *Vitae Scholasticae* 18(2):35–54.

THOMAS, P. L. 2000. "Blueprints or Houses? Looking Back at Lou LaBrant and the Writing Debate." *English Journal* 89(3):85–89.

THOMAS, P. L. 2001. *Lou LaBrant: A Woman's Life, A Teacher's Life.* Huntington, NY: Nova Science Publishers.

P. L. THOMAS

LAND-GRANT COLLEGES AND UNIVERSITIES

America's land-grant colleges and universities were brought into being through the Morrill Act of 1862. This unprecedented federal legislation supported a new vision for higher education flowing from a confluence of agricultural, industrial, scientific, political and educational interests in the years before the U.S. Civil War.

By 1873, 26 land-grant colleges and universities were in operation; by 1900, 65; by 1975, 72; and by 2000, 106 (see Table 1). As these institutions developed, they influenced American higher education (and its more than 4,000 postsecondary institutions) well out of proportion to their number. According to the scholar Clark Kerr, the grant movement had a profound effect on the modern American university system and shaped its development throughout the late nineteenth and twentieth centuries.

By the beginning of the twenty-first century, U.S. land-grant colleges and universities had become a model for developing nations seeking to harness their own institutions of higher learning to promote economic development and higher standards of living. The motives typically attributed to the land-grant college movement include the democratization of higher education to serve the working class; the development of an educational system designed to meet utilitarian and "useful" ends; and a desire to emphasize the emerging applied sciences, particularly agricultural science and engineering.

New scholarship has shown that before the Civil War a number of American colleges had begun to accommodate these emerging needs. But these institutions were local in orientation and lacked the collective ability to call attention to the ways in which they were adapting to the demands of a growing nation. By contrast, the land-grant colleges were the outgrowth of a movement that culminated in conscious, organized action to affect federal and state policy. What made the land-grant colleges unique in American higher education was their exclusive relationship with the federal government and a shared set of obligations to their sponsoring states.

The 1850s saw unrelated efforts by Jonathan B. Turner, a professor at Illinois College, and U.S. Senator Justin S. Morrill of Vermont to champion bills calling for federally sponsored agricultural or industrial colleges, but these initiatives failed. Morrill's penultimate bill passed Congress in 1859, but it was vetoed by President James Buchanan—largely on the grounds that a federal role in education was unconstitutional.

The Morrill Act of 1862, signed by President Abraham Lincoln, granted vast holdings of federal lands to states based on the size of their congressional delegations. The lands were to be sold to provide an endowment for the establishment of "at least one college where the leading object shall be, without ex-

cluding other scientific and classical studies and including military tactics, to teach such branches of learning as related to agriculture and the mechanic arts . . . in order to promote the liberal and practical education of the industrial classes in the several pursuits and professions in life." Most states did a poor job of selling their lands, however. The meager profits used for the endowments were insufficient to sustain these growing educational institutions, which offered free tuition but had yet to receive any state funds.

The first institutions to function as land-grant colleges during the Civil War were two agricultural schools that had been chartered by their respective states in 1855: Michigan Agricultural College (now Michigan State University) and the Agricultural College of Pennsylvania (now The Pennsylvania State University). By 1873, twenty-four land-grant institutions enrolled 2,600 students—about 13 percent of the total U.S. collegiate population. Despite this early success, the quarter-century following the Civil War was a dismal period for land-grant colleges. Their facilities were sparse and primitive, and critics began to marshal their forces. Congress launched an investigation, which vindicated the schools. The farmers' organization, the Grange, launched a similar inquest, condemning the colleges for their failure to attract agricultural students. Well into the twentieth century, engineering—not agriculture—was the most popular course of study at land-grant schools.

Land-grant colleges turned the corner from struggle to stability around 1890, chiefly because of two federal acts. The Hatch Act of 1887 established and annually funded agricultural experiment (research) stations at land-grant colleges. Then came the Morrill Act of 1890, best known for giving states the right to designate "separate-but-equal" land-grant colleges for blacks. Soon after this, seventeen such schools were operating in Southern and border states. But the act's main purpose was to create annual federal appropriations to support general educational programs, from English to engineering. This dependable flow of funds provided the long-sought financial foundation the colleges needed and encouraged state governments to make annual appropriations as well. The pivotal figure in these legislative victories was George W. Atherton, president of The Pennsylvania State College. When his lobbying force of land-grant college presidents and agricultural scientists congealed in 1887 into the Association of American Agricultural Colleges and Experiment

TABLE 1

The 106 U.S. land-grant colleges and universities, 2000

Alabama
Alabama A&M University
Auburn University
Tuskegee University

Alaska
University of Alaska System

American Samoa
American Samoa Community College

Arizona
Diné College
University of Arizona

Arkansas
University of Arkansas, Fayetteville
University of Arkansas at Pine Bluff

California
D-Q University
University of California (original 1862 campus: Berkeley)

Colorado
Colorado State University

Commonwealth of the Northern Marianas Islands
Northern Marianas College

Connecticut
Connecticut Agricultural Experiment Station
University of Connecticut

Delaware
Delaware State University
University of Delaware

District of Columbia
University of the District of Columbia

Federated States of Micronesia
College of Micronesia

Florida
Florida A&M University
University of Florida

Georgia
Fort Valley State University
University of Georgia

Guam
University of Guam

Hawaii
University of Hawaii

Idaho
University of Idaho

Illinois
University of Illinois (original 1862 campus: Urbana-Champaign)

Indiana
Purdue University

[continued]

Iowa
Iowa State University

Kansas
Haskell Indian Nations University
Kansas State University

Kentucky
Kentucky State University
University of Kentucky

Louisiana
Louisiana State University System (original 1862 campus: Baton Rouge)
Southern University and A&M College System

Maine
University of Maine (original 1862 campus: Orono)

Maryland
University of Maryland, College Park
University of Maryland Eastern Shore

Massachusetts
Massachusetts Institute of Technology (engineering)
University of Massachusetts (original 1862 campus for agriculture: Amherst)

Michigan
Bay Mills Community College
Michigan State University

Minnesota
Fond Du Lac Tribal and Community College
Leech Lake Tribal College
University of Minnesota, Twin Cities

Mississippi
Alcorn State University
Mississippi State University

Missouri
Lincoln University
University of Missouri System (original 1862 campus: Columbia)

Montana
Blackfeet Community College
Dull Knife Memorial College
Fort Belknap Community College
Fort Peck Community College
Little Big Horn College
Montana State University
Salish Kootenai College
Stone Child College

Nebraska
Little Priest Tribal College
University of Nebraska (original 1862 campus: Lincoln)

Nevada
University of Nevada, Reno

New Hampshire
University of New Hampshire

New Jersey
Rutgers, the State University of New Jersey

TABLE 1 [CONTINUED]

The 106 U.S. land-grant colleges and universities, 2000

New Mexico
Crownpoint Institute of Technology
Institute of American Indian Arts
New Mexico State University
Southwestern Indian Polytechnic Institute

New York
Cornell University

North Carolina
North Carolina A&T University
North Carolina State University

North Dakota
Fort Berthold Community College
Little Hoop Community College
North Dakota State University
Sitting Bull College
Turtle Mountain Community College
United Tribes Technical College

Ohio
The Ohio State University

Oklahoma
Langston University
Oklahoma State University

Oregon
Oregon State University

Pennsylvania
The Pennsylvania State University

Puerto Rico
University of Puerto Rico

Rhode Island
University of Rhode Island

South Carolina
Clemson University
South Carolina State University

South Dakota
Oglala Lakota College
Sinte Gleska University
Sisston Wahpeton Community College
Si Tanka College
South Dakota State University

Tennessee
Tennessee State University
University of Tennessee (original 1862 campus: Knoxville)

Texas
Prairie View A&M University
Texas A&M University

Utah
Utah State University

Vermont
University of Vermont

Virgin Islands
University of the Virgin Islands

Virginia
Virginia Polytechnic Institute and State University
Virginia State University

Washington
Northwest Indian College
Washington State University

West Virginia
West Virginia State College
West Virginia University

Wisconsin
College of the Menominee Nation
Lac Courte Oreilles Ojibwa Community College
University of Wisconsin–Madison

Wyoming
University of Wyoming

SOURCE: Courtesy of author.

Stations—the first formal organization of peer higher education institutions in America—Atherton was elected its first president.

Since 1900, land-grant institutions have been strengthened by more than a dozen federal acts. For example, the Smith-Lever Act of 1914 established the Cooperative Extension Service in agriculture and home economics, to be carried out by land-grant institutions in connection with U.S. Department of Agriculture. Eighty years later, in 1994, the Elementary and Secondary Education Reauthorization Act conferred land-grant status on twenty-nine Native American colleges.

The major land-grant universities are powerhouses of research and graduate education. Of the top twenty institutions in total research-and-development spending for fiscal 1998, eleven (55%) were land-grant universities, according to the National Science Foundation. Of the top twenty institutions awarding the most earned doctorates in fiscal 1998, twelve (60%) were land-grant institutions. The fruits of these research and graduate programs have profoundly benefited the world. The production of pure uranium, pioneering developments in television and the transistor, advances in meteorology, the field ion microscope and the cyclotron, the isolation of helium, new plant strains resistant to disease and insects—these and much more have come from land-grant institutions.

The land-grant college movement has forged an enduring legacy. Egalitarianism and educational populism, practical or useful education, applied science and research, public service and outreach, and, perhaps most importantly, the idea that the federal government has a key role to play in educational policy—these tenets have become generalized throughout the whole of American higher education.

See also: HIGHER EDUCATION IN THE UNITED STATES, *subentries on* HISTORICAL DEVELOPMENT, SYSTEM.

BIBLIOGRAPHY

ANDERSON, G. LESTER, ed. 1976. *Land-Grant Universities and Their Continuing Challenge.* East Lansing: Michigan State University Press.

CROSS, COY F., II. 1999. *Justin Smith Morrill: Father of the Land-Grant Colleges.* East Lansing: Michigan State University Press.

EDDY, EDWARD D., JR. 1957. *Colleges for our Land and Time: The Land-Grant Idea in American Education.* New York: Harper.

EDMOND, JOSEPH B. 1978. *The Magnificent Charter: The Origin and Role of the Morrill Land-Grant Colleges and Universities.* Hicksville, NY: Exposition Press.

GEIGER, ROGER L., ed. 2000. *The American College in the Nineteenth Century.* Nashville, TN: Vanderbilt University Press.

KERR, CLARK. 1982. *The Uses of the University,* 3rd edition. Cambridge, MA: Harvard University Press.

MARCUS, ALAN I. 1985. *Agricultural Science and the Quest for Legitimacy: Farmers, Agricultural Colleges, and Experiment Stations, 1870–1890.* Ames: Iowa State University Press.

NEVINS, ALLAN. 1962. *The State Universities and Democracy.* Urbana: University of Illinois Press.

ROSS, EARLE D. 1942. *Democracy's College: The Land-Grant Movement in the Formative Stage.* Ames: Iowa State College Press.

WILLIAMS, ROGER L. 1991. *The Origins of Federal Support for Higher Education: George W. Atherton and the Land-Grant College Movement.* University Park: Pennsylvania State Press.

ROGER L. WILLIAMS

LANGUAGE ACQUISITION

Almost every human child succeeds in learning language. As a result, people often tend to take the process of language learning for granted. To many, language seems like a basic instinct, as simple as breathing or blinking. But language is not simple at all; in fact it is the most complex skill that a human being will ever master. That nearly all people succeed in learning this complex skill demonstrates how well language has adapted to human nature. In a very real sense, language is the complete expression of what it means to be human.

Linguists in the tradition of Noam Chomsky tend to think of language as having a universal core from which individual languages select out a particular configuration of features, parameters, and settings. As a result, they see language as an instinct that is driven by specifically human evolutionary adaptations. In their view, language resides in a unique mental organ that has been given as a "special gift" to the human species. This mental organ contains rules, constraints, and other structures that can be specified by linguistic analysis.

Psychologists and those linguists who reject the Chomskyan approach often view language learning from a very different perspective. To the psychologist, language acquisition is a window on the operation of the human mind. The patterns of language emerge not from a unique instinct but from the operation of general processes of evolution and cognition. For researchers who accept this emergentist approach, the goal of language acquisition studies is to understand how regularities in linguistic form emerge from the operation of low-level physical, neural, and social processes. Before considering the current state of the dialog between the view of language as a hard-wired instinct and the view of language as an emergent process, it will be useful to review a few basic facts about the shape of language acquisition and some of the methods that are used to study it.

The Basic Components of Human Language

Human language involves both receptive and productive use. Receptive language use occurs during the comprehension or understanding of words and sentences. Productive language use involves idea generation and the articulation of words in speech. Both reception and production utilize the four basic structural components of language:

1. Phonology: The system of the sound segments that humans use to build up words. Each language has a different set of these segments or phonemes, and children quickly come to recognize and then produce the speech segments that are characteristic of their native language.

2. Semantics: The system of meanings that are expressed by words and phrases. In order to serve as a means of communication between people, words must have a shared or conventional meaning. Picking out the correct meaning for each new word is a major learning task for children.

3. Grammar: The system of rules by which words and phrases are arranged to make meaningful statements. Children need to learn how to use the ordering of words to mark grammatical functions such as subject or direct object.

4. Pragmatics: The system of patterns that determine how humans can use language in particular social settings for particular conversational purposes. Children learn that conversations customarily begin with a greeting, require turn taking, and concern a shared topic. They come to adjust the content of their communications to match their listener's interests, knowledge, and language ability.

These four basic systems can be extended and elaborated when humans use language for special purposes, such as for poetry, song, legal documents, or scientific discourse. The literate control of language constructs additional complex social, cognitive, and linguistic structures that are built on top of the four basic structural components.

Methods for Studying Language Acquisition

The methods used to study language development are mostly quite straightforward. The primary method involves simply recording and transcribing what children say. This method can be applied even from birth. Tape recordings become particularly interesting, however, when the child begins systematic babbling and the first productions of words. Using videotape, researchers can link up the child's use of verbal means with their use of gesture and nonlinguistic cries to draw attention to their desires and interests.

Methods for studying comprehension are a bit more complicated. During the first year, researchers can habituate the infant to some pattern of sounds and then suddenly change that pattern to see if the infant notices the difference. From about nine months onward, children can be shown pictures of toys along with their names, and then researchers can measure whether the children prefer these pictures to some unnamed distracter pictures. Later on, children can be asked to answer questions, repeat sentences, or make judgments about grammar. Researchers can also study children by asking their parents to report about them. Parents can record the times when their children first use a given sound or word or first make some basic types of child errors. Each of these methods has different goals, and each also has unique possibilities and pitfalls associated with it. Having obtained a set of data from children or their parents, researchers next need to group these data into measures of particular types of language skills, such as vocabulary, sentences, concepts, or conversational abilities.

Phases in Language Development

William James (1890) described the world of the newborn as a "blooming, buzzing confusion." It is now known, however, that, on the auditory level at least, the newborn's world is remarkably well structured. The cochlea (in the inner ear) and the auditory nerve (which connects the inner ear with the brain) provide extensive preprocessing of signals for pitch and intensity. In the 1970s and 1980s, researchers discovered that human infants were specifically adapted at birth to perceive contrasts in sounds such as that between /p/ and /b/, as in the words *pit* and *bit*. Subsequent research showed that even chinchillas are capable of making this distinction. This suggests that much of the basic structure of the infant's auditory world can be attributed to fundamental processes in the mammalian ear. Moreover, there is evidence that some of these early perceptual abilities are lost as the infant begins to acquire the distinctions actually used by the native language. Beyond this basic level of auditory processing, it appears that infants have a remarkable capacity to record and store sequences of auditory events. It is as if the infant has a tape recorder in the brain's auditory cortex that records input sounds, replays them, and accustoms the ear to their patterns.

Children tend to produce their first words sometime between nine and twelve months. One-year-olds have about 5 words in their vocabulary on average, although individual children may have none or as many as thirty; by two years of age, average vocabulary size is more than 150 words, with a range among individual children from as few as 10 to as many as 450 words. Children possess a vocabulary of about 14,000 words by six years of age; adults have an estimated average of 40,000 words in their working vocabulary at age forty. In order to achieve such a vocabulary, a child must learn to say at least a few new words each day from birth.

One of the best predictors of a child's vocabulary development is the amount and diversity of input the child receives. Researchers have found that verbal input can be as great as three times more available in educated families than in less educated families. These facts have led educators to suspect that basic and pervasive differences in the level of social support for language learning lie at the root of many learning problems in the later school years. Social interaction (quality of attachment; parent responsiveness, involvement, sensitivity, and control style) and general intellectual climate (providing enriching toys, reading books, encouraging attention to surroundings) predict developing language competence in children as well. Relatively uneducated and economically disadvantaged mothers talk less frequently to their children compared with more educated and affluent mothers, and correspondingly, children of less educated and less affluent mothers produce less speech. Socioeconomic status relates to both child vocabulary and to maternal vocabulary. Middle-class mothers expose their children to a richer vocabulary, with longer sentences and a greater number of word roots.

Whereas vocabulary development is marked by spectacular individual variation, the development of grammatical and syntactic skills is highly stable across children. Children's early one-word utterances do not yet trigger the need for syntactic patterns, because they are still only one-word long. By the middle of the second year, when children's vocabularies grow to between 50 and 100 words, they begin to combine words in what has been termed "telegraphic speech." Utterances typical of this period include forms such as "where Mommy," "my shoe," "dolly chair," and "allgone banana."

At this same time, children are busy learning to adjust their language to suit their audience and the situation. Learning the pragmatic social skills related to language is an ongoing process. Parents go to great efforts to teach their children to say "please" and "thank you" when needed, to be deferential in speaking to adults, to remember to issue an appropriate greeting when they meet someone, and not to interrupt when others are speaking. Children fine-tune their language skills to maintain conversations, tell stories, ask or argue for favors, or tattle on their classmates. Early on, they also begin to acquire the metalinguistic skills involved in thinking and making judgments about language.

As children move on to higher stages of language development and the acquisition of literacy, they depend increasingly on broader social institutions. They depend on Sunday school teachers for knowledge about Biblical language, prophets, and the geography of the Holy Land. They attend to science teachers to gain vocabulary and understandings about friction, molecular structures, the circulatory system, and DNA. They rely on peers to understand the language of the streets, verbal dueling, and the use of language for courtship. They rely on the media for role models, fantasies, and stereotypes. When they enter the workplace, they will rely on their coworkers to develop a literate understanding of work procedures, union rules, and methods for furthering their status. By reading to their children, telling stories, and engaging in supportive dialogs, parents set the stage for their children's entry into the world of literature and schooling. Here, again, the parent and teacher must teach by displaying examples of the execution and generation of a wide variety of detailed literate practices, ranging from learning to write through outlines to taking notes in lectures.

Special Gift or Emergence?

Having briefly covered the methods used to study language acquisition and the basic phases in development, it is now possible to return to this question: Is language development best characterized as the use of a "special gift" or as an emergent result of various cognitive, neural, physiological, and social pressures? There are good arguments in favor of each position.

The special gift position views language as an instinct. People are often overpowered by the "urge to speak." Young children must feel this urge when they interact with others and have not yet learned how to use words correctly. It is important to recognize, however, that crickets, birds, snakes, and many other species can be possessed by a similar urge to produce audible chirps, songs, and rattling. In themselves, these urges do not amount to a special gift for language learning. Better evidence for the special gift comes from the study of children who have been cut off from communication by cruel parents, ancient Pharaohs, or accidents of nature. The special gift position holds that, if the special gift for language is not exercised by some early age, perhaps six or seven, it will be lost forever. None of the isolation experiments that have been conducted, however, can be viewed as providing good evidence for this claim. In many cases, the children are isolated because they are brain-injured. In other cases, the isolation itself produces brain injury. In a few cases, children as old as six to eight years of age have successfully acquired language even after isolation. Thus, the most that can be concluded from these experiments is that it is unlikely that the special gift expires before age eight.

The second form of evidence in favor of the notion of a special gift comes from the observation that children are able to learn some grammatical structures without apparent guidance from the input. The argumentation involved here is sometimes rather subtle. For example, Chomsky noted that children would never produce "Is the boy who next in line is tall?" as a question deriving from the sentence "The boy who is next in line is tall." Instead, they will inevitably produce the question as, "Is the boy who is next in line tall?" That children always know which of the forms of the verb *is* to move to the front of the sentence, even without ever having heard such a sentence from their parents, indicates to Chomsky that language must be a special gift.

Although the details of Chomsky's argument are controversial, his basic insight here seems solid. There are some aspects of language that seem so fundamental that humans hardly need to learn them. Nevertheless, the specific structures examined by linguistic theory involve only a small set of core grammatical features. When looking more generally at the full shape of the systems of lexicon, phonolo-

gy, pragmatics, and discourse, much greater individual variation in terms of overall language proficiency appears.

To explain these differences, it is necessary to view language learning as emerging from multiple sources of support. One source of support is the universal concept all humans have about what language can be. A second source of support is input from parents and peers. This input is most effective when it directly elaborates or expands on things the child has already said. For example, if the child says "Mommy go store," the parent can expand the child's production by saying "Yes, Mommy is going to the store." From expansions of this type, children can learn a wide variety of grammatical and lexical patterns. A third source of support is the brain itself. Through elaborate connections among auditory, vocal, relational, and memory areas, humans are able to store linguistic patterns and experiences for later processing. A fourth source of support are the generalizations that people produce when they systematize and extend language patterns. Recognizing that English verbs tend to produce their past tense by adding the suffix *-ed,* children can produce overgeneralizations such as "goed" or "runned." Although these overgeneralizations are errors, they represent the productive use of linguistic creativity.

Individual children will vary markedly in the extent to which they can rely on these additional sources of support. Children of immigrant families will be forced to acquire the language of the new country not from their parents, but from others. Children with hearing impairments or the temporary impairments brought on by otitis media (ear infections) will have relatively less support for language learning from clear auditory input. Blind children will have good auditory support but relatively less support from visual cues. Children with differing patterns of brain lesions may have preserved auditory abilities, but impaired ability to control speech. Alternatively, other children will have only a few minor impairments to their short-term memory that affect the learning of new words.

Because language is based on such a wide variety of alternative cognitive skills, children can often compensate for deficits in one area by emphasizing their skills in another area. The case of Helen Keller is perhaps the best such example of compensation. Although Keller had lost both her hearing and her vision, she was able to learn words by observing how her guardian traced out patterns of letters in her hand. In this way, even when some of the normal supports are removed, children can still learn language. The basic uses of language are heavily over-determined by this rich system of multiple supports. As a child moves away from the basic uses of language into the more refined areas of literacy and specific genres, progress can slow. In these later periods, language is still supported by multiple sources, but each of the supports grows weaker, and progress toward the full competency required in the modern workplace is less inevitable.

See also: BILINGUALISM, SECOND LANGUAGE LEARNING, AND ENGLISH AS A SECOND LANGUAGE; CATEGORIZATION AND CONCEPT LEARNING; LANGUAGE AND EDUCATION; LITERACY AND READING.

BIBLIOGRAPHY

ASLIN, RICHARD N.; PISONI, D. B.; HENNESSEY, B. L.; and PEREY, A. J. 1981. "Discrimination of Voice Onset Time by Human Infants: New Findings and Implications for the Effects of Early Experience." *Child Development* 52:1135–1145.

CHOMSKY, NOAM. 1982. *Some Concepts and Consequences of the Theory of Government and Binding.* Cambridge, MA: MIT Press.

FENSON, LARRY, et al. 1994. *Variability in Early Communication Development.* Chicago: University of Chicago Press.

FLETCHER, PAUL, and MacWHINNEY, BRIAN, eds. 1995. *The Handbook of Child Language.* Oxford: Blackwell.

HART, BETTY, and RISLEY, TODD R. 1995. *Meaningful Differences in the Everyday Experience of Young American Children.* Baltimore: Brookes.

HUTTENLOCHER, JANELLEN; HAIGHT, W.; BRYK, ANTHONY; SELTZER, M.; and LYONS, T. 1991. "Early Vocabulary Growth: Relation to Language Input and Gender." *Developmental Psychology* 27:236–248.

JAMES, WILLIAM. 1890. *The Principles of Psychology.* New York: Holt, Rinehart and Winston.

KEIL, FRANK C. 1989. *Concepts, Kinds, and Cognitive Development.* Cambridge, MA: MIT Press.

LENNEBERG, ERIC H. 1967. *Biological Foundations of Language.* New York: Wiley.

MacWHINNEY, BRIAN. 2000. *The CHILDES Project: Tools for Analyzing Talk.* Mahwah, NJ: Erlbaum.

McCARTHY, D. 1954. "Manual of Child Psychology." In *Language Development in Children,* ed. L. Carmichael. New York: Wiley.

PIATELLI-PALMARINI, MASSIMO. 1980. *Language and Learning: The Debate between Jean Piaget and Noam Chomsky.* Cambridge, MA: Harvard University Press.

PINKER, STEVEN. 1994. *The Language Instinct.* New York: Morrow.

SAFFRAN, JENNY; ASLIN, RICHARD; and NEWPORT, ELISSA. 1996. "Statistical Learning by Eight-Month-Old Infants." *Science* 274:1926–1928.

TEMPLIN, MILDRED. 1957. *Certain Language Skills in Children.* Minneapolis: University of Minnesota Press.

van IJZENDOORN, MARINUS H.; DIJKSTRA, J.; and BUS, A. G. 1995. "Attachment, Intelligence, and Language: A Meta-analysis." *Social Development* 4:115–128.

WERKER, JANET F. 1995. "Exploring Developmental Changes in Cross-Language Speech Perception." In *An Invitation to Cognitive Science,* Vol. 1: *Language,* ed. Lila Gleitman and Mark Liberman. Cambridge, MA: MIT Press.

BRIAN MacWHINNEY

LANGUAGE AND EDUCATION

In discussions of language and education, language is usually defined as a shared set of verbal codes, such as English, Spanish, Mandarin, French, and Swahili. But language can also be defined as a generic, communicative phenomenon, especially in descriptions of instruction. Teachers and students use spoken and written language to communicate with each other—to present tasks, engage in learning processes, present academic content, assess learning, display knowledge and skill, and build classroom life. In addition, much of what students learn is language. They learn to read and write (academic written language), and they learn the discourse of academic disciplines (sometimes called academic languages and literacies). Both definitions of language are important to understanding the relationship between language and education.

As suggested by M. A. K. Halliday, the relationship between language and education can be divided into three heuristic categories: (1) learning language, (2) learning through language, and (3) learning about language.

Learning Language

In their early years, children are learning both spoken and written language. They are developing use of complex grammatical structures and vocabulary; communicative competence (rules for the appropriate and effective use of language in a variety of social situations); comprehension of spoken and written language; and ways to express themselves.

Educational programs for young children often emphasize curriculum and instruction to facilitate language learning. With regard to spoken language, instructional programs may emphasize opportunities to comprehend a variety of genres from directions to narratives and opportunities to experiment with modes of expression. With regard to written language, classrooms for young children provide opportunities to learn alphabetic symbols, graphophonemic relationships (letter-sound relationships), basic sight vocabulary, and comprehension strategies; and also feature the reading of stories designed for young children. Young children may also have opportunities to learn how to express themselves through written language, including opportunities to form letters, words, sentences, and text structures, and opportunities to learn how to put together a written story.

There is debate about the extent to which classrooms for young children's language learning should provide didactic, teacher-centered instruction or student-centered instruction. Those who support a didactic approach argue that children whose language performance is below that of their peers need explicit instruction to catch up. These advocates argue that the home and community environments do not provide all children with the experiences needed to be proficient and effective users of language and that direct instruction with grammatical forms, vocabulary, and pronunciation can help certain students catch up with their peers. A similar argument is made for the didactic instruction of written language. Written language, it is argued, is sufficiently different from spoken language as to require explicit instruction. Research noting the importance of phonological awareness to reading development is cited as rationale for a parts (letters and sounds) to whole (fluent oral reading) curriculum.

The alternative argument is that children are inherently *wired* as language learners and that providing them with a stimulating, rich language environment supplies them with the tools they need for further developing their spoken and written language abilities. Although teachers may provide instruction, the instruction should follow the student's needs and interests rather than being prescribed in a predetermined manner. The complexity of language processes requires that children be allowed to engage in complete or whole-language activities rather than in isolated skill instruction activities that distort language processes by stripping them of their complexity (and also making them harder to learn). The learning of written language is not viewed as being much different from the learning of spoken language, and thus learning processes similar to those used in learning spoken language are advocated for the learning of written language.

In the United States another set of debates surrounds language learning by children whose native language is other than English. First, there are debates with regard to goals. Some educators advocate for a sole emphasis on the learning of English, whereas others advocate for continued language growth in English and in the child's native language. Arguments focus on the role of the public school in providing a common language that can produce national unity. Although few argue against the importance of learning English, questions are raised about whether national unity depends on English only as opposed to English plus additional languages. With regard to the learning of English, one side advocates for an immersion approach that prohibits use of the child's native, first language. Immersion is believed to provide the child with motivation and language input for becoming a fluent English speaker. The other side argues that stripping children of their native language also strips them of their culture and heritage. Further, these advocates point to studies that show that learning English is not inhibited by continued language growth in a native language or by bilingual educational programs. Learning to read in one's native language has been shown by research studies to provide a useful foundation for students learning to read in English.

At the secondary and postsecondary level, students learn the language of a broad range of disciplines. They must learn how to argue in discipline-specific ways and to read and write discipline-specific texts each with their own set of language conventions. Studies have suggested, however, that in some classrooms and schools there is little difference in the texts or written assignments across disciplines. In both science and social studies, for example, students may encounter the same pattern of reading a textbook chapter and answering end-of-chapter questions.

Learning through Language

Learning in classrooms is primarily accomplished through language. Teachers lecture, ask questions, orchestrate discussions, and assign reading and writing tasks. Students engage in academic tasks through reading, writing, exploring the Internet, giving verbal answers to teacher questions, listening to teacher lectures and student presentations, participating in whole-class and instructional peer group discussions, memorizing written text and vocabulary, and so on. A major thrust of classroom research since the 1970s has focused on the following question: What forms of classroom language practice facilitate what kinds of learning?

One classroom language practice of interest to educational researchers has been *scaffolding*. Scaffolding is the process through which teachers and students interact with each other by building on each other's immediately previous statement or utterance. For example, after making a statement, a teacher might ask a student a question intended to help the student elaborate or probe the academic topic a bit further. The student, building on the teacher's question or comment, produces a statement with more depth, complexity, or insight. The teacher might then ask another question to scaffold the learning even further, and so on. Through scaffolding, teachers may be able to help students explore and understand academic issues beyond what they are able to do on their own. Scaffolding can occur between teachers and students and also among students.

Another classroom language practice that has received a great deal of attention from educational researchers has been the teacher initiation–student response–teacher feedback/evaluation sequence (known as I-R-F). It is also referred to as the asking of known-information questions and recitation questioning. Of concern to researchers and educators are the constraints that such a conversational structure places on academic learning. I-R-F sequences rarely provide students with opportunities to provide long or in-depth responses, and the

knowledge displayed is contextualized by feedback or evaluation that subsequently comes from the teacher. I-R-F sequences rarely allow opportunities to explore explanations or to debate issues. The teacher always generates the topics, and thus students do not have opportunities to ask questions. Further, I-R-F sequences provide students with few opportunities to practice the creation of extended spoken text. Research on I-R-F sequences has also shown, however, that they may be more complex and malleable than previously recognized. For example, instead of just providing an evaluation of the correctness of a student response, a teacher might provide additional information and *revoice* a student response in a way that models for students how to phrase the statement in the academic jargon. Such revoicings can be considered a kind of scaffolding. I-R-F sequences may also be useful to display to the whole class what counts as the knowledge for which they are accountable. And I-R-F sequences may also be used by teachers as a classroom management tool, ensuring that students complete assignments and that they are paying attention.

A third classroom language practice that has received a lot of attention has been sharing time (also known as show-and-tell). Sharing time provides an opportunity for young children to develop narrative performance skills such as topic coherence, sequencing of events, structuring narrative events, and adjusting a narrative to an audience. Research shows that how students construct a narrative during sharing time may reflect narrative practices from their own families and communities. In such cases, the narrative produced by the child may differ from the narrative models that a teacher is using to evaluate the child's language performance, and as a result the teacher may negatively evaluate the child. The research on sharing time and similar classroom language practices shows that there is great variation in the narrative models, structures, and devices used across cultures and that children may experiment with many different types of narratives. Children adopt and adapt narrative models from a broad range of sources. In addition to suggesting the need for educators to be sensitive to cultural variation in narrative performance and in assessment of children's language abilities, the studies of sharing time show the close connections among education, language, and cultural variation.

Beyond questions about the effectiveness of various classroom language practices are questions about who is able to engage in what language practices and language processes, when, and where. In other words, what constitutes equitable classroom language practices? Research on turn-taking practices has shown that a broad range of factors influence who gets a turn to talk during classroom conversations and who is less likely to get a turn. These factors may include race, gender, class, native language, and where the student is seated, among others. Some students may get or seek few turns to talk. Those students who do not get or seek turns to talk and who feel alienated from the classroom are sometimes referred to as having been *silenced*. Although students can be silenced by the behavior of the teacher or of other students, more often silencing involves a deeper social process whereby a student is inhibited from bringing into the classroom his culture, language, heritage, community, personal experience, and so on.

Learning about Language

Perhaps the most obvious classroom practice for learning about language is through the study of grammar and spelling. As linguists point out, the grammar taught in school is a prescriptive grammar and is not what linguists mean by grammar (they mean a descriptive grammar). For those students who use Standard American English, prescriptive grammar is often very close to the language they speak. But for students who speak a variation of English other than Standard English or who speak African-American Language (which is also referred to as African-American English, Black Dialect, and Ebonics, among others), the teaching and learning of prescriptive grammar does not necessarily map onto the language they speak, and thus they are learning about a language different from the language they speak.

Another typical classroom practice for learning about language is the instruction of a second language. Learning a second language can mean one of two things: the learning of a foreign language (such as the learning of Latin, French, and Spanish in the United States) or the learning of English by those in the United States whose native language is not English. It is often the case that the teaching of a second language includes coverage of the grammar, vocabulary structures, and history of the language.

Beyond the teaching of prescriptive grammar and the explicit teaching of a second language, there is very little taught about language in K–12 class-

rooms. Although there have been experimental and one-off programs in K–12 schools that have taught students the practices of linguists, engaged them in sociolinguistic studies, helped them develop language autobiographies, and sensitized students and teachers to language variation, there exists no broad-based trend.

African-American Language and Classroom Education

The lack of education about language and about language variation may explain, in part, the strong popular reaction to the issue of African-American Language and classroom education. In Ann Arbor, Michigan, and in Oakland, California, the issue of African-American Language and education created controversy. Despite substantial linguistic evidence as to its nature and characteristics, some observers characterized African-American Language as a non-language, as slang, or as sloppy English. As stated by a federal court in Ann Arbor in 1978 (in the case of *King v. Board of Education*), teachers sometimes negatively evaluated students' academic abilities and potential because they spoke African-American Language. The court offered a remedy designed to provide educators with the knowledge they needed to make appropriate assessments of students' academic abilities. In the popular press and in the general public there was a great deal of misunderstanding about the issues involved in the court case, with many mistakenly assuming that recognition of African-American Language as a language was either an attempt to force teachers to teach in African-American Language or an attempt to not teach African-American students to use Standard English effectively.

A similar problem occurred in 1996 when the Oakland School Board created a policy that recognized Ebonics as a language. It was widely assumed by the public that the board was recommending the use of African-American Language as a medium of instruction, and hence was abandoning African-American students to what was assumed to be a second-rate curriculum. Again popular views included mistaken assumptions: that African-American Language was not a language, that the Oakland School Board would not provide instruction in the effective use of Standard English, and that speakers of African-American Language would never be successful in the workplace. Both in the documents on which the resolution was based and in their response to the controversy, however, the Oakland School Board made clear that their resolution was an attempt to focus attention on the educational needs of those students who spoke African-American Language and to provide them with effective instructional programs for reading, writing, academic subjects, and the learning of Standard English. The members of the board pointed out that their resolution was built on established linguistic principles and knowledge and on proven educational practices. In 1997 the Linguistic Society of America passed a resolution supporting the resolution of the Oakland School Board. That resolution pointed out that African-American Language was not slang, sloppy, or incorrect and asserted the importance of the maintenance of what the society termed "vernacular" languages.

The controversy over African-American Language in education points to the complex of relationships among language, education, national politics, and cultural politics. The languages that are spoken in schools, the languages that are taught, the use of language for learning and instruction, are all more than simple matters of pedagogical effectiveness. The definition and use of language and language education in schools are part of broader cultural and political debates about how the nation will be defined and about the structure of power relations among various ethnic, racial, economic, and linguistic groups.

See also: Bilingualism, Second Language, and English as a Second Language; Foreign Language Education; Language Acquisition; Language Arts, Teaching of; Language Minority Students; Literacy and Culture.

BIBLIOGRAPHY

Egan-Robertson, Ann, and Bloome, David, eds. 1998. *Students as Researchers of Culture and Language in Their Own Communities.* Cresskill, NJ: Hampton Press.

Goodman, Yetta. 1984. "The Development of Initial Literacy." In *Awakening to Literacy,* ed. Hillel Golman, Antoinette Oberg, and Frank Smith. Exeter, NH: Heinemann.

Green, James Paul. 1983. "Exploring Classroom Discourse: Linguistic Perspectives on Teaching-Learning Processes." *Educational Psychologist* 18:180–199.

Halliday, M. A. K. 1979/1980. "Three Aspects of Children's Language Development: Learning Language, Learning through Language, Learning about Language." *Oral and Written Language Development: Impact on Schools. Proceedings from the 1979 and 1980 IMPACT Conferences,* ed. Yetta Goodman, Myna Hausser, and Dorothy Strickland. Urbana, IL: International Reading Association and National Council of Teachers of English.

Heath, Shirley. 1982. "What No Bedtime Story Means: Narrative Skills at Home and at School." *Language in Society* 11:49–76.

Mercer, Neil. 1995. *The Guided Construction of Knowledge: Talk amongst Teachers and Learners.* Clevedon, Eng.: Multilingual Matters.

Michaels, Sarah. 1986. "Narrative Presentations: An Oral Preparation for Literacy with First Graders." In *The Social Construction of Literacy,* ed. Jenny Cook-Gumperz. Cambridge, Eng.: Cambridge University Press.

O'Conner, Mary Catherine, and Michaels, Sarah. 1993. "Aligning Academic Task and Participation Status through Revoicing: Analysis of a Classroom Discourse Strategy." *Anthropology and Education Quarterly* 24:318–335.

Perry, Theresa, and Delpit, Lisa, eds. 1998. *The Real Ebonics Debate: Power, Language, and the Education of African-American Children.* Boston: Beacon Press.

Smitherman, Geneva. 1981. "'What Go Round Come Round': King in Perspective." *Harvard Educational Review* 51:40–56.

Street, Brian. 1998. "New Literacies in Theory and Practice: What Are the Implications for Language in Education." *Linguistics and Education* 10:1–34.

Vygotsky, Lev S. 1962. *Thought and Language.* Cambridge, MA: MIT Press.

Wells, Gordon. 1986. *The Meaning Makers: Children Learning Language and Using Language to Learn.* Portsmouth, NH: Heinemann.

David Bloome

LANGUAGE ARTS, TEACHING OF

Language arts is the term typically used by educators to describe the curriculum area that includes four modes of language: listening, speaking, reading, and writing. Language arts teaching constitutes a particularly important area in teacher education, since listening, speaking, reading, and writing permeate the curriculum; they are essential to learning and to the demonstration of learning in every content area. Teachers are charged with guiding students toward proficiency in these four language modes, which can be compared and contrasted in several ways. Listening and speaking involve oral language and are often referred to as *primary* modes since they are acquired naturally in home and community environments before children come to school. Reading and writing, the written language modes, are acquired differently. Although children from literate environments often come to school with considerable knowledge about printed language, reading and writing are widely considered to be the school's responsibility and are formally taught.

A different way of grouping the language modes is according to the processing involved in their use. Speaking and writing require constructing messages and conveying them to others through language. Thus they are "expressive" modes. Listening and reading, on the other hand, are more "receptive" modes; they involve constructing meaning from messages that come from others' language. (For those who are deaf, visual and spatial language modes—watching and signing—replace oral language modes.)

When one considers how children learn and use language, however, all of these divisions become somewhat artificial. Whatever we label them, all modes involve communication and construction of meaning. In effective language arts teaching, several modes are usually used in each activity or set of related activities. For example, students in literature groups may read literature, discuss it, and write about it in response journals. In 1976 Walter Loban published a study of the language growth of 338 students who were observed from kindergarten through grade twelve. He found positive correlations among the four language modes both in terms of how students developed competency in each, and of how well students ultimately used them. His study demonstrated the inter-relationships among the four language modes and influenced educators to address and more fully integrate all four of them in classrooms.

Models of Language Arts Instruction

Many changes in language arts instruction have taken place in American schools since 1980. To understand these changes, one must be conversant with the three basic models that have given rise to variations in language arts curriculum over the years: the heritage model, the competencies model, and the process or student-centered model. Each model constitutes a belief system about the structure and content of instruction that leads to certain instructional approaches and methods. The *heritage model,* for example, reflects the belief that the purpose of language arts instruction is to transmit the values and traditions of the culture through the study of an agreed-upon body of literature. It also focuses on agreed-upon modes and genres of writing, to be mastered through guided writing experiences. The *competencies model,* on the other hand, emanates from the belief that the chief purpose of language arts instruction is to produce mastery of a hierarchy of language-related skills (particularly in reading and writing) in the learner. This model advocates the teaching of these skills in a predetermined sequence, generally through use of basal readers and graded language arts textbooks in which the instructional activities reflect this orientation. The majority of adults in this country probably experienced elementary level language arts instruction that was based in the competencies model, followed by high school English instruction that primarily reflected the heritage model. Instruction in both of these models depends heavily on the use of sequenced curricula, texts, and tests.

The third model of language arts instruction, the *process model,* is quite different from the other two models. The curriculum is not determined by texts and tests; rather, this model stresses the encouragement of language processes that lead to growth in the language competencies (both written and oral) of students, as well as exposure to broad content. The interests and needs of the students, along with the knowledge and interests of the teacher, determine the specific curriculum. Thus reading materials, writing genres and topics, and discussion activities will vary from classroom to classroom and even from student to student within a classroom.

"Authentic" assessment is the rule in these classrooms, that is, assessment that grows from the real language work of the students rather than from formal tests. Clearly the process model leads to more flexible and varied curriculum and instruction than the other two models. While the heritage and competencies models have come under criticism for being too rigid and unresponsive to student differences, the process model has been criticized as too unstructured and inconsistent to dependably give all students sufficient grounding in language content and skills. In actuality, teachers of language arts generally strive to help their students develop proficiency in language use, develop understanding of their own and other cultures, and experience and practice the processes of reading and writing. Thus it seems that the three models are not mutually exclusive. They do, however, reflect different priorities and emphases, and most teachers, schools, and/or school systems align beliefs and practices primarily with one or another model.

Focus on Outcomes

From a historical perspective, marked shifts in language arts instruction have taken place. In the early twentieth century, textbooks and assigned readings, writing assignments, and tests came to dominate the language arts curriculum. Instruction was characterized by a great deal of analysis of language and texts, on the theory that practice in analyzing language and drill in "correct" forms would lead students to improved use of language and proficiency in reading, writing, and discourse. Instruction was entirely teacher-driven; literature and writing topics were selected by the teacher; spelling, grammar, and penmanship were taught as distinct subjects; and writing was vigorously corrected but seldom really taught in the sense that composition is often taught today. In the 1980s a shift toward the process model emerged in the works of many language arts theorists and the published practices of some influential teachers including Donald Graves, Lucy M. Calkins, and Nancie Atwell. In 1987 the National Council of Teachers of English and the Modern Language Association sponsored a Coalition of English Associations Conference. Educational leaders from all levels came together at the conference to discuss past and present language arts teaching and to propose directions and goals to guide the teaching of language arts in the years leading up to and moving into the twenty-first century. The conference report specified the ideal outcomes of effective language arts instruction, in terms of the language knowledge, abilities, and attitudes of students. These outcomes were largely process oriented, as illustrated by the following examples of outcomes for students leaving the elementary grades, as reported by William Teale in *Stories to Grow On* (1989):

- *They will be readers and writers,* individuals who find pleasure and satisfaction in reading and writing, and who make those activities an important part of their everyday lives.

- *They will use language to understand themselves and others and make sense of their world.* As a means of reflecting on their lives, they will engage in such activities as telling and hearing stories, reading novels and poetry, and keeping journals.

Principles to guide curriculum development evolved from the conference participants' agreed upon student outcomes, and, like the outcomes, the principles were broad and process-focused. For example, two of the original principles are: *Curriculum should evolve from a sound research knowledge base* and *The language arts curriculum should be learner-centered.* Elaborations on these and other curriculum goals deviated from earlier recommendations in that they included classroom-based ethnographic research, or action research, as well as traditional basic research in the knowledge base that informs the teaching of language arts. There was also agreement that textbooks serve best as resources for activities, but that the most effective language arts curricula are not text driven; rather they are created by individual teachers for varying communities of students.

Language Arts Standards

During the 1990s a movement toward greater accountability in education gained momentum, leading to the development of articulated standards. Standards grow from the endeavor to link curriculum and instruction with specific outcomes—what students can demonstrate they know and are able to do. In response to this movement, the National Council of Teachers of English (NCTE) and the International Reading Association (IRA), two of the leading professional organizations in the language arts field, joined in developing a common set of national standards for the English Language Arts. These standards are more specific, detailed, and comprehensive than the guidelines from the earlier coalition conference, although that work provided a starting point for the development of the national standards. Advances in technology and communication have been rapid since 1987. In the national standards, the definition of English language arts includes viewing and visually representing as well as reading, writing, listening, and speaking. Perhaps the factor that has had the greatest impact on American schools is the immigration that has led to steadily increasing linguistic and cultural diversity in the population. The changing demographics of school populations are reflected in the newer national standards; students for whom English is not the first language are explicitly considered in the goals and recommendations.

IRA/NCTE Standards for the English Language Arts

The following standards are taken from *Standards for the English Language,* published in 1996 by the National Council of Teachers of English.

> Students read a wide range of print and nonprint texts to build an understanding of texts, of themselves, and of the cultures of the United States and the world; to acquire new information; to respond to the needs and demands of society and the workplace; and for personal fulfillment. Among these texts are fiction and nonfiction, classic and contemporary works.

> Students read a wide range of literature from many periods in many genres to build an understanding of the many dimensions (e.g., philosophical, ethical, aesthetic) of human experience.

> Students apply a wide range of strategies to comprehend, interpret, evaluate, and appreciate texts. They draw on their prior experience, their interactions with other readers and writers, their knowledge of word meaning and of other texts, their word identification strategies, and their understanding of textual features (e.g., sound-letter correspondence, sentence structure, context, graphics).

> Students adjust their use of spoken, written, and visual language (e.g., conventions, style, vocabulary) to communicate effectively with a variety of audiences and for different purposes.

> Students employ a wide range of strategies as they write and use different writing process elements appropriately to communicate with different audiences for a variety of purposes.

> Students apply knowledge of language structure, language conventions (e.g., spelling and punctuation), media techniques, figurative language, and genre to create, critique, and discuss print and non-print texts.

> Students conduct research on issues and interests by generating ideas and questions, and by posing problems. They gather, evaluate, and synthesize data from a variety of sources (e.g., print and non-print texts, artifacts, people) to communicate their discoveries in ways that suit their purpose and audience.

> Students use a variety of technological and informational resources (e.g., libraries, databases, computer networks, video) to gather and synthesize information and to create and communicate knowledge.

> Students develop an understanding of and respect for diversity in language use, patterns, and dialects across cultures, ethnic groups, geographic regions, and social roles.

> Students whose first language is not English make use of their first language to develop competency in the English language arts and to develop understanding of content across the curriculum.

> Students participate as knowledgeable, reflective, creative, and critical members of a variety of literacy communities.

> Students use spoken, written, and visual language to accomplish their own purposes (e.g., for learning, enjoyment, persuasion, and the exchange of information).

Evolving Issues

Evolving issues in language arts pedagogy hark back to the three models of instruction described earlier. The IRA/NCTE standards are process oriented, for the most part. Many individual state departments of education have developed their own language arts standards for students at various grade levels; these range from rigidly imposed standards and controlled curricula in the tradition of the skills-based model to process oriented standards and a good deal of local control over the curriculum. Educators are left with the task of reconciling such differences and designing curriculum and assessments that reflect their highest priorities. Issues similar to those in the United States have led to reforms in England—a leader, for many years, in the implementation of meaning-based instruction in reading and writing. Recent reforms in England and Ireland maintain an emphasis on integrating language arts in instruction, while recommending increasingly structured curriculum and assessments geared toward student achievement of specified outcomes.

Large-scale immigration, one of the most important social developments of the late twentieth and early twenty-first centuries, is a global phenomenon, as noted in *Children of Immigration* (2001). As a result, increasing numbers of districts, schools, and educators in other countries as well as in the United States are faced with the necessity of adjusting the curriculum and the use of standards to make them appropriate for students of multiple language and cultural backgrounds. The tension between students' individual backgrounds and developmental levels on the one hand, and universal achievement goals in the language arts as reflected in standards on the other, provide the largest challenges to language arts teachers of the early twenty-first century.

See also: CHILDREN'S LITERATURE; INTERNATIONAL READING ASSOCIATION; NATIONAL COUNCIL OF TEACHERS OF ENGLISH; READING, *subnentry on* TEACHING OF; SPELLING, TEACHING OF; STANDARDS FOR STUDENT LEARNING; WRITING, TEACHING OF.

BIBLIOGRAPHY

ATWELL, NANCIE. 1987. *In the Middle*. Portsmouth, NH: Heinemann.

CALKINS, LUCY M. 1986. *The Art of Teaching Writing*. Portsmouth, NH: Heinemann.

CAMBOURNE, BRIAN. 1987. "Language, Learning, and Literacy." In *Towards a Reading/Writing Classroom*, ed. Andrea Butler and Jan Turbill. Portsmouth, NH: Heinemann.

FARRELL, EDMUND J. 1991. "Instructional Models for English Language Arts." In *Handbook of Research on Teaching the English Language Arts*, ed. James Flood, Julie M. Jensen, Diane Lapp, and James R. Squire. New York: Macmillan.

FARSTRUP, ALAN, and MYERS, MILES. 1996. *Standards for the English Language Arts*. Urbana, IL: National Council of Teachers of English.

GOODMAN, KENNETH, and SHANNON, PATRICK. 1994. *Basal Readers: A Second Look*. Katonah, NY: Richard C. Owen.

GRAVES, DONALD. 1983. *Writing: Teachers and Children at Work*. Portsmouth, NH: Heinemann.

LOBAN, WALTER. 1976. *Language Development: Kindergarten through Grade Twelve*. Urbana, IL: National Council of Teachers of English.

MANDEL, BARRETT J. 1980. *Three Language Arts Curriculum Models*. Urbana, IL: National Council of Teachers of English.

SHIEL, GERRY. 2002. "Reforming Reading Instruction in Ireland and England." *The Reading Teacher* 55(4):372–374.

SUAREZ-OROZCO, CAROLA, and SUAREZ-OROZCO, MARCELO M. 2001. *Children of Immigration*. Cambridge, MA: Harvard University Press.

TEALE, WILLIAM. 1989. "Language Arts for the 21st Century." In *Stories to Grow On*, ed. Julie M. Jensen. Portsmouth, NH: Heinemann.

WOOD, MARGO. 1999. *Essentials of Elementary Language Arts*. Boston: Allyn and Bacon.

MARGO WOOD

LANGUAGE MINORITY STUDENTS

SCOPE
Reynaldo F. Macías
IMPACT ON EDUCATION
Reynaldo F. Macías

SCOPE

Some nations across the globe are becoming more linguistically diverse as a result of the transnational migration of peoples. Others are experiencing an increase in their language diversity as a result of differential growths of their populations, resurgence of language and ethnic nationalism, language revitalization movements, and the official recognition and promotion of multiple languages. Governments may be recognizing the needs of regional or immigrant populations within their borders, or they may be recognizing the fruits of foreign language programs in their nations. This increase in linguistic diversity is taking place at the same time that the estimated total number of different languages in the world is decreasing. While most nations have a multilingual history they recognize as part of their heritage, some view themselves as predominantly monolingual in a dominant language—the United States is one such country. Language diversity in the United States is not a new phenomenon, but language minorities begrudgingly receive recognition and continue to struggle for acceptance.

Who Are Language Minorities?

Around the world, defining language minorities often sparks controversy. What constitutes a language? How big must a group be to be identified and recognized? In the United States there are some generally accepted definitions and concepts for describing these populations. Within the national population, there are groups of individuals who may be called *language minorities* or *non-English-language background* populations. These individuals are people who speak a language other than English, whether or not they also speak English, and/or they may have grown up, or lived in, an environment where a non-English language was present and influential (whether they were born in the United States or any of its jurisdictions, or because they were born and raised in a different country). It also includes the deaf and hearing-impaired. Often, there is also an ethnic dimension to these groups where language helps define identity. They are referred to as "minorities" not only because they are not a numerical majority in the nation (although they may be at more local levels), but also because they often wield little influence or power within the country. American Indians may be considered language minorities even if they speak only English because their history includes a non-English language and repressive language and cultural policies by the U.S. federal government, so that their current use of English was affected by that history.

Very often there is a concern for a subgroup of the language minority population that does not speak, understand, read, or write the dominant language—English—well enough to participate effectively in an English-only classroom. This group has been referred to in many government documents and academic studies as persons who are *non–English proficient* or *limited English proficient*. Beginning in 2000, some states have changed their official definitions for language minority students who do not know enough English to participate effectively in an English-only classroom and have begun to refer to them as *English language learners*. There is some controversy over whether this new label is sufficiently descriptive to be adequate and whether it is distinctive enough, because all school students in the United States are required to learn and master En-

glish throughout their schooling, whether or not they knew English when they entered the schools, and thus are also English language learners.

The Size and Diversity of the Language Minority Population

In 2000 there were nearly 45 million people in the United States, about 17.6 percent of the national population (not including outlying jurisdictions such as Puerto Rico and Guam) over the age of five years, who spoke a language other than English at home. This was an increase of more than 14 million (41.1%) from the total in 1990. The largest single language spoken in the United States, after English, was Spanish, with about 26.8 million speakers (almost 60 percent of all persons who spoke a language other than English; see Table 1). The proportion of persons who spoke a language other than English who were approximately school-age (five to seventeen years of age) was just over one-fifth (21.7%) in 2000.

Three-fourths of the people who could speak a language other than English also reported that they could speak English very well or well, reflecting a high degree of bilingualism (see Table 2). This proportion varied slightly by language groups, with almost 72 percent of Spanish speakers, 86.8 percent of those who spoke another Indo-European language, 77.3 percent of those who spoke an Asian or Pacific Islander language, and 90.2 percent of those who spoke other non-English languages being able to speak English very well or well.

The number of language minority students in the public schools who were not proficient enough in English to participate effectively in an English-only classroom is more difficult to estimate than the total language minority population. The estimate for the fifty states and the District of Columbia of limited English proficient (LEP) students for 2000 was about 3.7 million. This represented about 8 percent of the total public school K–12 enrollment for the nation (46.6 million) and was an increase of about 10 percent over 1997–1998.

The largest numbers of LEP students were in the larger population states—California (about 1.5 million LEP students representing 24.9 percent of the state's public school enrollment), Texas (555,000; 13.9%), Florida (235,000; 9.9%), New York (229,000; 8%), and Illinois (144,000; 7.1%).

In addition to the LEP students in the fifty states and the District of Columbia, there were about

TABLE 1

Non-English-speaking population, 1980 to 2000, United States, by language and age

	1980 Total		1990 Total		2000 Total	
	Number	Percent	Number	Percent	Number	Percent
Non-English						
language speakers	22,973,410	100.0	31,844,979	100.0	44,945,452	100.0
5–17 years	4,529,098	19.7	6,322,934	19.9	9,769,120	21.7
18+ years	18,444,312	80.3	25,522,045	80.1	35,176,332	78.3
Spanish	11,117,606	100.0	17,345,064	100.0	26,771,035	100.0
5–17 years	2,947,051	26.5	4,167,653	24.0	6,650,575	24.8
18+ years	8,170,555	73.5	13,177,411	76.0	20,120,460	75.2
Other	11,855,804	100.0	14,499,915	100.0	18,174,417	100.0
5–17 years	1,582,047	13.3	2,155,281	14.9	3,118,545	17.2
18+ years	10,273,757	86.7	12,344,634	85.1	15,055,872	82.8

SOURCE: Courtesy of author.

685,600 LEP students in the seven outlying U.S. jurisdictions (Guam, Marshall Islands, Micronesia, Northern Mariana Islands, Palau, Puerto Rico, and the Virgin Islands). In four of these U.S. jurisdictions (Marshall Islands, Micronesia, Palau, and Puerto Rico), the entire public school enrollment was reported as limited in their English proficiency. Every state and jurisdiction in the United States included LEP students in their public schools in 2000, ranging from just under 1 percent to 100 percent.

The language backgrounds of these LEP students was fairly stable over the 1990s. The largest language background reported for the public school enrollment by the states in 2000 was Spanish (76.6 percent of all students with limited proficiency in English), followed by Vietnamese (2.3%), Hmong (2.2%), Haitian and French Creole (1.1%), Korean (1.1%), and Cantonese (1%). All other languages were represented with less than 1 percent of LEP students.

Regarding the literacy abilities of the national population, data from 1992 indicated that 89 percent of the national adult population, sixteen years and older (191.3 million), reported being literate (able to read and write very well or well) in English only, 7 percent biliterate in English and another language, and 3 percent literate only in a language other than English. About 1 percent reported they were not literate in any language.

While all of these data provide a profile of the language and literacy diversity of the United States, the data describe an even more diverse population. Many of these students were foreign born and immigrants or refugees from different parts of the world.

Many more were children of immigrant or refugee parents, and a smaller number were native born of native-born parents. The number and proportion of limited English proficient students tended to coincide with those groups who have a large proportion of foreign-born members—Latinos and Asian Americans in particular. Immigration from Mexico, Latin America, and Asia was relatively high in the 1980s and 1990s—representing, during the 1990s, 27.7 percent, 13.5 percent, and 22.5 percent, respectively, of all immigration (in comparison, immigrants from Europe and Canada represented 11.4 percent and 1.7 percent, respectively, of all immigrants during the 1990s). This reflects, in part, the reversal of the explicitly selective and restrictive immigration policy priorities favoring northern and western Europe in force between 1917 and 1965. It also reflects the foreign policies of the federal government in receiving refugees from Cuba beginning in the 1960s, Vietnam in the 1970s, and Communist Eastern Europe in the 1980s, and its involvement in the civil wars of El Salvador and Nicaragua during the 1980s and 1990s.

Aside from the association with immigration, language diversity is also correlated with low academic achievement—primarily as a result of the inability of the public school systems in the country to meet the communicative and learning needs of these students. There is much controversy over whether to teach limited English proficiency students using English alone as the language of instruction or to allow the use of languages other than English for communicative, informational, and instructional purposes in the classroom—despite evidence domestically and

TABLE 2

Non-English-speaking populations, United States, 2000, by English ability

Language	Total		English ability of non-English-language speakers (percent)				
	Number	Percent	Total	Very well	Well	Not well	Not at all
Population, 5+ years	254,762,736	100.0	—	—	—	—	—
Speak English only	209,817,283	82.4	—	—	—	—	—
Speak a non-English language	44,945,452	100.0	100.0	56.6	20.1	16.0	7.4
Spanish	26,771,035	59.6	100.0	53.4	18.5	18.0	10.1
Indo-European language	9,493,791	21.1	100.0	67.2	19.6	10.4	2.8
Asian Pacific Islander language	6,884,637	15.3	100.0	50.5	26.8	17.7	5.0
Other languages	1,795,989	4.0	100.0	70.5	19.7	7.5	2.2

SOURCE: Courtesy of author.

globally that bilingual instruction can work well. This is complicated by the lack of adequate numbers of teachers able and credentialed to teach bilingually. In addition, a nativist English-only movement begun in the early 1980s has targeted bilingual education and the public and private uses of non-English languages for elimination through efforts to make English the official languages of jurisdictions, to mandate English as the dominant or exclusive language of instruction, or to otherwise officially regulate or prohibit the use of non-English languages. This movement has aligned itself with restrictive immigration groups and policies and has created a chilling climate for the use of languages other than English by individuals in schools as well as in workplaces.

Language Trends

The changes in the numbers of speakers of languages across generations is known as language shift or maintenance. There are many reasons for each of these changes. Research involving European immigrants revealed that the dominant pattern established in the United States during the first half of the twentieth century was a three-generation immigrant process: the immigrant generation was monolingual or dominant in their non-English language, the children born and raised in this country tended to be bilingual in their heritage language and English, and their children were often monolingual in English. This research did not take into account the different intergenerational language patterns of indigenous language minorities, such as American Indian communities/nations, nor did it take into account those colonial language groups incorporated into the

country through war, such as Mexicans in the southwest, or the people of Puerto Rico.

More recent research indicates that the language shift from the non-English heritage language to English takes place much more quickly today—some even argue within a single generation—as a result of the more universal schooling and the much longer time spent in schools than in the beginning of the twentieth century. This change also seems to be a result of the increasing influence of the communications media, which are dominated by monolingual English networks and programming; the chilling atmosphere created by the English-only movement and other nativist activities; and other factors. Most of these studies have been short-term studies of individual language change or para-longitudinal in design. They have not been life-cycle studies or even biographical retrospectives of individuals that reflect different language uses at different times of a person's life.

One often-stated situation that results from these changes involves the interactions between parents who are dominant or exclusive speakers of a language other than English and their children who begin to acquire English, especially through the schools, and whose acquisition and development of the non-English language is arrested. In the case of many of these non-English languages, minority children often refuse to speak the non-English language with their parents and sometimes are unable to do so, thereby disrupting the natural and nurturing interactions within these families. This situation also results from the recognition of the low status that many non-English languages have in the country and the advice of many well-meaning but uninformed and ill-advised teachers who believe that one must give up the heritage language in order to acquire English, and so they advise the students and their families to stop using the non-English language.

What these complex processes of language change mean is that the number of English monolinguals increases among language minorities across generations, at the same time that the numbers of speakers of these non-English languages increases in the country, fed by immigration, cross-generational language sharing, and language revitalization efforts.

See also: BILINGUALISM, SECOND LANGUAGE LEARNING, AND ENGLISH AS A SECOND LANGUAGE; LANGUAGE AND EDUCATION; LITERACY AND CULTURE; RACE, ETHNICITY, AND CULTURE.

BIBLIOGRAPHY

CAMAROTA, STEVEN. 2001. *Immigrants in the United States, 2000: A Snapshot of America's Foreign Born Population.* Washington, DC: Center for Immigration Studies.

GREENBERG, ELIZABETH; MACÍAS, REYNALDO F.; RHODES, DAVID; and CHAN, TSE. 2001. *English Literacy and Language Minorities in the United States.* Washington, DC: U.S. Department of Education, National Center for Education Statistics.

MACÍAS, REYNALDO F. 2001. "Minority Languages in the United States, with a Focus on Spanish in California." In *The Other Languages of Europe,* ed. Dürk Gorter and Guus Extra. Clevedon, Eng.: Multilingual Matters Press.

NATIONAL CLEARINGHOUSE FOR BILINGUAL EDUCATION. 2002. *Survey of the States' Limited English Proficient Students and Available Educational Programs and Services, 1999–2001 Summary Report.* Washington, DC: National Clearinghouse for Bilingual Education.

REYNALDO F. MACÍAS

IMPACT ON EDUCATION

In 2000, the number of school-age persons (five to seventeen years of age) who spoke a language other than English in the United States was 9,769,120, or about one out of every five students (the national enrollment of public school students in 2000 was 46,857,321). This assumes, for the sake of argument, that all of these school-age language minority children and youths were in the public schools. About 8 percent (3.7 million students) of the national public-school enrollment in 1999–2000 consisted of language minority students who were not able to use English well enough to participate effectively in an English-only classroom. The proportion of the total enrollment varies by state: In California, 25 percent of the public-school enrollment in 1999–2000 was *limited English proficient* (LEP), while the proportion was 24 percent in New Mexico, 15 percent in Alaska and Arizona, 14 percent in Texas, and 12 percent in Nevada. LEP students represent nearly 100 percent of the total public-school enrollment in the outlying areas of the United States (Marshall Islands, Micronesia, Palau, and Puerto Rico).

The diversity of students with limited ability in English is great. Some of these students are foreign-born immigrants to the United States—some with and some without prior schooling. Some of them are literate in their native language. They came to the United States at different ages and for different reasons—some to escape civil war or strife and political persecutions, while some were attracted to the opportunities in the United States, and still others drawn by its various programs of refuge and asylum. Most LEP students, however, are born in the United States to immigrant parents, and they start school with a native language other than English and with varying degrees of speaking ability in English (and so are increasingly referred to as *English language learners,* or ELLs).

The responses of the public schools to this language diversity vary, but they are generally neither comprehensive nor adequate. There are many reasons this is the case, not the least of which is the mismatch between the needs of the students and the resources and expectations of the school systems. A second reason is the ideologically based resistance to meeting language minority student needs promoted by the ethnocentric English-only movement and pro-assimilation groups throughout the country. These groups influence public and educational policy, curriculum and instruction, and school reform. The issues facing language minority students in the public schools are thus varied. Those faced by students with limited proficiency in English are particularly salient—involving the acquisition and development of English, access to the core curriculum, and high-stakes assessments.

Learning English

Many surveys of immigrants to the United States have concluded that learning English is one of three priorities they have immediately after arriving in the country—along with gaining employment and finding a place to live. Parents of native-born language minority students also respond that they see learning English as a high priority for their children, even while they desire their children to keep their heritage languages. Unfortunately, despite the increasing numbers and proportions of language minority LEP students, most schools are neither prepared nor equipped to meet the needs of these students in teaching them English, or in providing them access to the core curriculum in other subject areas. Often the schools will sacrifice access to the core curriculum in favor of first teaching English to these students.

Students who speak a language other than English will often learn to speak and understand English before learning to read and write it, in and out of school. Much of this English-language acquisition and development depends on the age of their arrival in U.S. schools. The earlier they arrive, the more they are exposed to English—and the earlier and more easily they acquire a native-like pronunciation of the language. However, the older they are in age when they arrive, the more easily they are able to develop vocabulary in English (and the more likely they are to acquire English pronunciation with an accent). How much prior schooling students have received in their country of origin is also a factor affecting English-language acquisition. The more schooling they have had before they enter U.S. schools, the quicker they are able to adjust and excel. The more literate they are in their native language, the easier it is to learn to read and write English and succeed in U.S. schools. In addition, the kind of program students receive when they enter U.S. public schools can affect the learning of English.

Language minority students will often learn a conversational form of English before they learn an academic form of the language. It may take a relatively short time (one to three years) to gain fluency in conversational English, but it will take longer (five to seven years) to be proficient in academic English, assuming adequate instruction.

The acquisition and development of English reading and writing for language minority students who are limited in their English proficiency depends as well on whether the students have already learned to read and write in their non-English language. If these students have learned to read in their native language first (*mother-tongue,* or *native-language, literacy*), then much of the general knowledge about reading (e.g., one can make sense of print) can be transferred to learning English reading and writing (*second-language literacy*). If a student's native language uses a phonemic or alphabetic system of writing, then additional knowledge about the writing system can also be transferred to second-language literacy in English.

It is a more difficult task for a language minority student who is not proficient in English to learn how to read and write initially in English. These students must develop their oral English-language abilities *and* learn how to read and write English. The older the student, the more frequently this is required by the schools to be done simultaneously rather than sequentially (oral language development before literacy). This is more difficult for these language minority students than for native English speakers because it is being done in a more compressed time period and includes learning more language skills at one time than what is required of native English speakers (who bring to elementary school a fully-developed ability in English).

Language of Instruction

Most language minority students with limited English abilities receive their instruction entirely through English. While there is not much good data on the services that LEP students receive in the schools, some generalizations can be made based on several national surveys. In 1993, less than 50 percent of elementary school students limited in their English proficiency received at least a quarter of their instruction in their native language. In middle schools, the percentage was 28 percent, and in high schools, 25 percent. This study also indicated that LEP students of Spanish-language background were more apt to receive this instruction in their heritage language than LEP students of other language backgrounds. In 1998, twenty-six states (which included about 40 percent of the national LEP student enrollment for that year), provided information to the federal government on the language of instruction used to teach these students. They reported that almost 26 percent of all LEP students received some of their instruction in the non-English language through bilingual education (academic instruction through

English and a non-English language); while 14 percent received all of their instruction in English only—through various forms of English-as-a-second-language programs. About 12 percent of these students received no special instructional services at all. The language of instruction was not reported for the other 48 percent of LEP students.

The size of the language minority LEP enrollment with a common language background seems to be a good predictor of the use of a non-English language for instruction. In a 1998 survey of big city school districts, the use of a non-English language (along with English) as the language of instruction was found to be more frequent for the largest language group of students of the district (usually Spanish, except for two school districts in Minnesota, which reported Hmong language LEP students as their largest group), and usually in the elementary grades. Otherwise, the preferred language of instruction was exclusively English through some form of an English-as-second-language program.

California enrolls about 40 percent of all of the LEP students in the country. The language of instruction for the great majority of these students has been exclusively English since the adoption of an initiative in 1998 that mandated the language of instruction for the state to be English and the default program for LEP students to be structured English immersion (a form of English-as-second-language instruction in which English is used exclusively or predominantly for instruction). In the spring of 2001, California school districts reported that 46.6 percent of the 1,511,299 LEP students in the state were receiving all of their instruction in English; another 26.6 percent were receiving almost all of their instruction in English, but with a small amount of the non-English language used for communication support; and 5.4 percent were receiving no special instructional services at all. Only 11.1 percent of California's LEP students were receiving bilingual education—academic instruction in both languages—as compared to 30 percent prior to the adoption of the 1998 initiative.

While most language minority students with limited English abilities are receiving some special instructional services, it is clear that almost all of these services use English as the medium of instruction. The most successful model of bilingual instruction—two-way bilingual immersion—was used in only 260 programs in twenty-three states in 2001. In addition, only half of the those enrolled in these programs were LEP students—hardly a major impact on the instructional services received by this population.

Access to the Core Curriculum

The single most difficult aspect of the schooling of language minority LEP students is providing them adequate access to the core curriculum. Most school districts have opted to enforce a policy of learning English first—before these students can be taught other subject matter. This puts language minority LEP students in a precarious academic situation. Many schools are beginning to require special preparation, professional development, and even licensing for their teachers to instruct these students in English. Many language minority students who enter the schools early in their life can sometimes catch up academically with native English speakers when they work harder than these peers. However, the concentrations of language minority students are in high-minority, high-poverty schools, which are often under-resourced and struggle with hiring a fully credentialed and qualified teaching workforce. Receipt of adequate instruction is the exception, not the rule, for language minority students.

School–Home Communication

The absence of teachers and other school staff who can communicate with parents of language minority students is also a problem in informing parents about the academic performance of their children, about the activities of the schools, or even about the expectations of the teachers. As language minority students, especially children, acquire some English, they often abandon the use of their heritage language. This creates another communication difficulty between children and parents in these homes that strains the quality of family interactions.

High-Stakes Testing

During the 1990s the amount and frequency of high-stakes, standardized testing of students increased dramatically. Much of this testing was used as an accountability measure to identify unsuccessful schools and to measure progress towards educational standards set by the states and the federal government. These tests were given exclusively in English to all students. Language minority students with limited English abilities were often excused from this testing in the early 1990s, but increasingly were included throughout the decade and into the first decade of the new millennium. This practice increased despite the fact that LEP students could not understand the language of the tests (which made the results invalid), despite the ethical concerns about such high-stakes testing, and despite the apparent violation of the Office for Civil Rights regulations on language minority testing. In contrast, local school districts tend to use a variety of tests for identification, classification, and reclassification of LEP students, and a set of multiple criteria for these administrative decisions.

See also: BILINGUALISM, SECOND LANGUAGE LEARN-ING, AND ENGLISH AS A SECOND LANGUAGE; LAN-GUAGE AND EDUCATION; LITERACY AND CULTURE; TESTING, *subentry on* STANDARDIZED TESTS AND HIGH-STAKES ASSESSMENT.

BIBLIOGRAPHY

AUGUST, DIANE, and HAKUTA, KENJI, eds. 1998. *Educating Language-Minority Children.* Washington, DC: National Academy Press.

COUNCIL OF THE GREAT CITY SCHOOLS. 2001. *Educating English Language Learners in the Nation's Urban Schools.* Washington, DC: Council of the Great City Schools.

FLEISCHMAN, HOWARD, and HOPSTOCK, PAUL. 1993. *Descriptive Study of Services to Limited English Proficient Students,* Vol. 1: *Summary of Findings and Conclusions.* Arlington, VA: Development Associates.

NATIONAL CENTER FOR EDUCATION STATISTICS. 2001. *Statistics in Brief: Public School Student, Staff, and Graduate Counts by State, School Year 1999–2000.* (NCES-2001-326r). Washington, DC: National Center for Education Statistics.

NATIONAL CLEARINGHOUSE FOR BILINGUAL EDUCA-TION (NCBE). 1998. *Summary Report of the Survey of the States' Limited English Proficient Students and Available Educational Programs and Services, 1996–97.* Washington, DC: National Clearinghouse for Bilingual Education.

OFFICE FOR CIVIL RIGHTS. 1970. *Identification of Discrimination and Denial of Services on the Basis of National Origin.* Washington, DC: Department of Health, Education, and Welfare.

REYNALDO F. MACÍAS

LATCHKEY CHILDREN

Latchkey child was a term coined to describe children who wore or carried house keys to school so that they could let themselves into their home when they returned from school. Those children were at home without adult supervision until their parents returned from work, school, or other occupations away from home.

Currently, the term *self care* is used to refer to elementary and middle school children who are without adult supervision during the after-school hours whether they are at home, at friends' houses, or in public places. Preschool children usually have not been included in studies measuring self care because it is considered inappropriate for preschool children to be unsupervised for any amount of time. However, one national study that included preschool children found that 67,000 (less than 1 percent of the preschool population) spent some time in self care. Adolescents attending high school also have not been included in studies of self care because researchers and the public consider it developmentally appropriate for high school students to care for themselves after school without direct adult supervision.

Several studies of large nationally representative samples in the United States have measured how many children are in self care by surveying parents about their children's after school care. Those studies have found that a very small percentage of families use self care as the main arrangement for their elementary and middle school age children. For example, researchers estimate that, overall, 12 percent of children between the ages of five and twelve years old care for themselves at least one afternoon per week. That report is probably an underestimate for several reasons. For one, parents have an interest in underreporting self care. Although very few states have laws governing self care, many people do not perceive self care as an optimal arrangement. For another, most families depend on a patchwork of arrangements during the week. The evidence indicates that self care is used for part of the after-school hours either regularly or on occasion by far more than 12 percent of families with elementary school children. For example, a study in one U.S. city found that approximately 33 percent of the third-grade children, 44 percent of the fourth-grade children, and slightly more than half of the fifth-grade children spent some part of the after school hours in self care. A recent estimate of the time lag between when schools are dismissed and when parents return from work suggests that time can amount to twenty to twenty-five hours per week. Self care is one type of arrangement that fills in part of that time for the many families struggling to maintain supervision of their children during the after school hours.

Parental discretion is important in determining when and how much self care children experience. In determining when children can be unsupervised, parents often consider age, emotional maturity, and competence of the child. In general, time spent in self care increases with the age of the child. Most parents gradually transition their children to self care. Families usually start using self care by having their children spend short amounts of time unsupervised after school. As children demonstrate that they are mature enough to handle those short bouts of time alone, most parents increase the frequency and duration of self care about the time that children are entering middle school. Often, children of about ten years of age begin to desire greater autonomy than is afforded by many formal after-school programs. At about that age, children sometimes lobby their parents for more time in self care, especially if the children are dissatisfied with available after-school programs.

More boys than girls experience self care during elementary school, probably because parents tend to be more protective of daughters than sons. However, according to the findings of a large nationally representative study, boys and girls are equally likely to be unsupervised after school during eighth grade.

Family and neighborhood characteristics also are factors affecting when and how often children experience self care. Single parents employed full-time use self care more than dual parent families or than families with part-time adult workers or unemployed adults. Contrary to popular belief, children from families with higher incomes spend more time in self care than children from families with lower incomes. The reason for this is probably related to safety considerations because those families with higher incomes usually live in suburban neighborhoods that the parents rate as being safe. Indeed, urban children are in self care less often than suburban and rural children.

Researchers who have studied self care have described variations in the situations unsupervised children are in after school. Some children are alone,

others are with siblings, and yet others are with peers. Generally, children who are with siblings less than fourteen years of age have been considered to be in self care because they are unsupervised by an adult. Some self care children are at home after school. Others are out and about in their neighborhoods and communities. For example, a national study of public libraries found that the vast majority of librarians reported that latchkey children regularly used their libraries as a place to be after school. Other studies in local areas have found that some young adolescents who are unsupervised after school "hang out" with friends at shopping malls, video arcades, parks, and other such public locations.

Teachers and principals have expressed concern about their students who care for themselves after school. Those educators believe that the self-care children are not safe and that the children are at risk for academic and social emotional problems. There is some indication from surveys that the public agrees with them that self-care children are at risk developmentally. Researchers have been interested in investigating the developmental consequences of self care to determine whether those children who experienced self care suffer negative consequences. Surprisingly, despite the concern of educators and the public about safety, few studies have examined the physical dangers of self care. One report from the early 1980s found that self-care children were more likely than supervised children to be injured. No recent studies were found estimating the number of injuries from accidents, fire, or crime when children were unsupervised. Studies from the 1970s and 1980s appeared to report contradictory results about academic, behavioral, and social emotional development associated with self care. Some studies reported that there were no negative effects of self care for children's academic and social emotional adjustment. Other studies reported poorer academic and social-emotional adjustment of children experiencing self care. Since that time, a number of studies described below that were conducted in the 1990s have found that the effects of self care depend on the type and amount of self care, characteristics of the children in self care, and the circumstances in which the children live. Most of the available studies, however, have used small, nonrepresentative samples in one city or state. So, the findings of those studies must be interpreted cautiously.

Characteristics of the children themselves have been found to contribute to outcomes of self care.

The Child Development Project conducted in Tennessee and Indiana by Gregory Pettit and his colleagues investigated the associations between self care during first grade or third grade and developmental outcomes in sixth grade. That longitudinal study of 466 children from economically diverse circumstances took children's previous behavioral functioning into account in analyzing the effects of first-grade self care on sixth-grade functioning. The researchers found that, for children who were well adjusted in kindergarten, there was virtually no relationship between self care experienced during first grade and the children's behavior problems in sixth grade. However, sixth-grade children who experienced self care in first grade and who were above average in aggression and acting out behavior in kindergarten had far higher scores on aggression and acting out behavior problem scales than those children who experienced no self care in first grade.

Researchers from the Child Development Project also considered the child's age as a factor. They found that more self care in either first or third grade (second-grade self care was not measured) was associated with negative academic and social development in sixth grade. Children who experienced more self care during the primary grades received lower grades, lower achievement test scores, and lower teacher ratings of social competence in sixth grade than did children who experienced less than three hours of self care per week in first or third grade.

Deborah Lowe Vandell and Jill Posner followed 216 low-income urban children living in a Midwestern industrial city from third grade through fifth grade and examined the adjustment of the children by the children's age and the type of self care children experienced. They found that the amount of time children spent alone in third grade predicted children's behavior problems in both third and fifth grade. However, the amount of time alone in fifth grade did not predict subsequent behavior problems.

Posner and Vandell also investigated the effect of unsupervised time with peers. The amount of unsupervised time children spent with peers predicted behavior problems at home and school as well as lower academic functioning. Like Posner and Vandell, Michele Goyette-Ewing investigated the association between types of self care and developmental consequences. She studied the after-school experiences of suburban seventh graders. Those unsupervised children who were "hanging out" with peers were more likely to report behavior problems, alcohol use, susceptibility to negative peer pressure, and lower school achievement than were children who were at home alone or with siblings. Laurence Steinberg found that, among unsupervised middle school students, those who hung out with peers at malls and other public locations were more susceptible to peer pressure than the students who were at a friend's house or at home. Another study of sixth graders conducted by Nancy Galambos and Jennifer Maggs found that girls who hung out with peers after school were more likely to report engaging in problem behaviors than were boys who hung out with peers after school. Taken together, these studies suggest that unsupervised time with peers is detrimental to both the academic and behavioral adjustment of children throughout elementary and middle school.

The amount of time young adolescents spend in self care has been related to their academic, behavioral, and social emotional functioning. The Michigan Middle Start study included 46,000 young adolescents who reported how often and how many hours they were without adult supervision after school. The researchers found that the amount of self care each day mattered a great deal in predicting outcomes. Those young adolescents who experienced self care for less than three hours at a time did not differ from young adolescents who were supervised at all times on depression, self-esteem, behavior problems, or academic success. However, young adolescents who were in self care more than three hours at a time had dramatically lower adjustment scores on all measures when compared to young adolescents who experienced less than three hours of self care. A study of middle school students by Peter Mulhall and his colleagues found that young adolescents in self care more than two days per week used alcohol far more often than young adolescents who were always supervised by an adult after school. Those young adolescents who were not monitored two or more days per week got drunk after school four times more often than their supervised peers. Yet another study, by researchers in Southern California, found that those young adolescents who were unsupervised more than eleven hours per week were truant from school 1.5 times more often than young adolescents who were not unsupervised after school. Researchers who analyzed data from the National Educational Longitudinal Study (NELS) of 1988, a large nationally representative sample of more than 20,000 eighth-grade students, examined associations between amount of self care and the academic performance and after school activities of those students. Those eighth graders who were unsupervised for more than one hour at a time had lower academic achievement than students who were supervised more often.

One reason that self care might contribute to problematic development is that there are limited activities available for children when they are home alone. For example, the NELS study found that television watching was related to the amount of self care such that more hours spent unsupervised after school predicted more hours of television watching. Television watching has been related to self care in several other studies, as well. There have been many studies on the consequences of watching television for children's academic achievement and aggression. In her longitudinal qualitative study of children in Boston, Deborah Belle found that the children were more likely to be lonely, bored, afraid, and unengaged in productive activities during the time they spent in self care than when supervised. Those negative feelings might be related to rules parents establish for safety purposes such as requiring children to stay in the house alone.

Family and neighborhood characteristics have been related to whether self care is problematic for children. Self care has been associated consistently with problematic adjustment among children who live in distressed circumstances such as low-income families and dangerous inner city neighborhoods. However, self care has not been shown to be detrimental to the development of children from middle class families who live in rural or suburban communities. The Child Development Project investigated associations between self care during first grade and developmental outcomes in sixth grade. The researchers found that the relationships between first-grade self care and sixth-grade externalizing behavior problems (aggression and delinquency) as reported by their teachers (who used a standardized checklist of behavior problems) were more pronounced for children from low-income families than for children from middle-income families. Nancy Marshall and her colleagues studied the after school arrangements of 206 urban first- through fourth-grade children in a multiracial sample in Boston. The children's families ranged in socioeconomic status from low to middle income. The researchers asked parents to report about their children's externalizing and internalizing behavior problems using

scales developed for that purpose. Externalizing behavior problems were measured by parent reports about the conduct disorders, restlessness, disorganization, and hyperactivity of the children; internalizing behavior problems were measured by parent report about the anxiety-shyness and psychosomatic symptoms of the children. Time spent in self care was associated with externalizing behavior problems for the children from lower but not middle income families. Internalizing problems were not related to self care among children from either lower- or middle-income families.

In cross-cultural studies of children conducted in traditional societies, some anthropologists have described developmental benefits for children who care for younger siblings. There have been few investigations of possible developmental benefits of self care in the United States. Goyette-Ewing did investigate that question and failed to find any developmental benefits associated with self care. Self-care children were not found to be more competent or mature than their counterparts who were supervised.

In conclusion, the developmental impact of self care appears to depend on the circumstances. Research findings suggests that child characteristics, type and amount of self care, and family circumstances are factors in the outcomes of self care. Younger children and children who were experiencing behavior problems before self care began appear to be more adversely affected by it. Children and young adolescents who hang out with peers and who spend long amounts of time unsupervised also seem to experience more negative outcomes than other children. Children from low-income urban families also appear to be at greater risk from self care.

See also: FAMILY, SCHOOL, AND COMMUNITY CONNECTIONS; PARENTING.

BIBLIOGRAPHY

BELLE, DEBORAH. 1997. "Varieties of Self-Care: A Qualitative Look at Children's Experiences in the After School Hours." *Merrill Palmer Research Quarterly* 43:478–496.

BELLE, DEBORAH. 1999. *The After School Lives of Children: Alone and with Others While Parents Work.* Mahwah, NJ: Erlbaum.

DOWD, FRANCES. 1992. *Library Latchkey Children.* ERIC Digest (ERIC Document Reproduction Service ED 343687).

GALAMBOS, NANCY, and MAGGS, JENNIFER. 1991. "Out-of-School-Care of Young Adolescents and Self-Reported Behavior." *Developmental Psychology* 27:644–655.

GOYETTE-EWING, MICHELE. 2000. "Children's After-School Arrangements: A Study of Self-Care and Developmental Outcomes." *Journal of Prevention and Intervention in the Community* 20:55–67.

KERREBROCK, NANCY, and LEWIT, EUGENE. 1999. "Children in Self-Care." In *The Future of Children* 9, ed. Richard Behrman. Los Altos, CA: The David and Lucille Packard Foundation.

MARSHALL, NANCY, et al. 1997. "After-School Time and Children's Behavioral Adjustment." *Merrill Palmer Research Quarterly* 43:497–514.

MERTENS, STEVEN, and FLOWERS, NANCY. 1998. "The Effects of Latchkey Status on Middle-Grade Students: New Research Findings." Paper presented at the annual conference of the Middle School Association, Denver, CO.

MILLER, BETH. 1995. "Out-of-School Time: Effects on Learning in the Primary Grades." *Action Research Paper #4.* Wellesley, MA: Center for Research on Women.

MULHALL, PETER. 1996. "Home Alone: Is It a Risk Factor for Middle School Youth and Drug Use?" *Journal of Drug Education* 26:39–48.

MULLER, CHANDRA. 1991. "Latch-key Children in the Late 80's: Family Composition, Working Mothers, and After School Supervision." Paper presented at the annual meeting of the American Educational Research Association, Chicago IL (ERIC Document Reproduction Service ED 338357).

PETTIT, GREGORY S., et al. 1997. "Patterns of After-School Care in Middle Childhood: Risk Factors and Developmental Outcomes." *Merrill-Palmer Quarterly* 43:515–538.

PETTIT, GREGORY S., et al. 1999. "The Impact of After-School Peer Contact on Early Adolescent Externalizing Problems Is Moderated by Parental Monitoring, Perceived Neighborhood Safety and Prior Adjustment." *Child Development* 70:768–778.

POSNER, JILL K., and VANDELL, DEBORAH L. 1999. "After-School Activities of Low-Income Urban Children: A Longitudinal Study." *Developmental Psychology* 35: 868–879.

STEINBERG, LAURENCE. 1986. "Latchkey Children and Susceptibility to Peer Pressure." *Developmental Psychology* 22:433–439.

VANDELL, DEBORAH, and SHUMOW, LEE. 1999. "After-School Child Care Programs." In *The Future of Children* 9, ed. Richard Behrman. Los Altos, CA: The David and Lucille Packard Foundation.

LEE SHUMOW

LATIN AMERICA AND THE CARIBBEAN

Countries in Latin America and the Caribbean (LAC) that are undergoing (or expecting to undergo) rapid economic growth are in need of better-trained workers, but the education system in these countries is still far behind the developed world. Latin American nations have tried hard to advance toward universal education and to increase enrollments in secondary and higher education, but they have not been able to improve the quality levels. While universal coverage in primary education is close to being a reality, quality levels in primary and secondary education are rather low and unequally distributed. Higher education has also increased at a fast pace—25 percent of college-age individuals were enrolled in postsecondary institutions in 2001. However, the quality of the higher education faculty is poor, and there is a need for an effective agenda for action.

The 12 billion dollars invested in LAC nations in the 1990s, with the support of the World Bank (WB) and the Inter-American Development Bank (IADB), has been instrumental in providing universal access to primary education (showing that the region really wants to improve its education). The famous Jomtein meeting of 1990 generated the International Education for All program to be implemented in the 1990–2000 decade. A world meeting in Dakkar in 2000 discussed a World Report, in which the Education for All evaluation for Latin America shows that 95 percent of each age group eventually enrolls in primary school, but only 33 percent gets some type of infant or preschool education. In addition, socioeconomic factors drastically reduce enrollment in secondary and higher education.

Comparative information on learning in the region—made available through the UNESCO Regional Office for Latin America and the Caribbean (OREALC) regional study on learning in third and fourth grades—shows that the average student in eleven Latin American countries answered about 50 percent of the questions of the UNESCO test correctly, compared to about 85 percent for Cuban students. The study also shows that student scores in rural areas are lower that in urban areas; capital-city scores are better than in smaller urban areas; and private-school scores are better than in public schools. The Third International Mathematics and Science Study (TIMSS 99) confirmed the OREALC findings by that eighth grade Chilean students had lower achievement levels than students in OECD-member countries.

Development Expectations and Quality Education

Demands for better quality education in the LAC region are supported by a growing awareness of the role education played in successful economic changes in East Asia, as well as by recent research on the multiple impacts of education and international comparisons of educational achievement. The experience of East Asian nations has been widely commented on in the LAC region. Mass media and academic groups have noted that better education and reduced inequality contributed to economic growth in East Asia and how, in turn, economic growth contributed to investment in education. Mass media also paid attention to the World Economic Forum's World Competitiveness Report, which showed that the weakest aspect of LAC countries was related to their human resources. This was confirmed by a 2000 report on functional literacy published by the Organization for Economic Co-operation and Development (OECD).

The International Adult Literacy Survey (ILAS) carried out by OECD in 2000 showed that 80 percent of Chilean workers were not able to perform at the minimum levels required to participate in the labor market of a developed country. Given that Chilean students perform above the regional average, the ILAS report confirmed the need to raise the quality of all levels of education. In spite of the low quality of education, the rates of return obtained on the amount of money invested in one additional school year generated by salaries (before the economic crisis of the late 1990s) were near 20 percent for primary

and secondary education and more than 10 percent for higher education. In spite of these important incentives for general training, market salaries have not provided enough incentives for further technical training.

Universal Education

Since the 1960s remarkable progress has been made in LAC countries in expanding access to education and increasing the number of days students attend per year. However little has changed in most classroom processes (e.g., group work, reading and discussion, interviews, visits, formative evaluation, types of questions), and "scores on national and international exams are alarmingly low," according to Partnership for Educational Revitalization in the Americas. More children than ever are involved in the educational system, and access to basic education is almost universal. Primary school access jumped from 60 percent in the early 1960s to more than 90 percent in the 1990s, with enrollment for nine-year-olds close to 95 percent.

In the early twenty-first century, more than two-thirds of eligible children attend secondary school. In addition, between 1960 and 1990, higher education enrollment ratios increased from 6 percent to 25 percent in LAC nations. However, while several countries have established a comprehensive structure for advanced training, the actual research produced by universities has had very little impact on the economies of these countries.

Scholastic productivity is low in LAC nations. Students attend, on average, more than six years of schooling, but students generally pass only four grades. Income inequality has not been a constraint for enrolling in primary education, but it has played a role in the ability to achieve minimal levels of learning and enrollment in secondary education. The majority of public schools have not been able to deliver adequate education on a sustained basis, and research productivity is low in Latin American universities. On the other hand, there are enough successful education projects to suggest that effective reform can be implemented.

Quality of Education

In spite of the expansion of student enrollments and multiple reform attempts, both the quality and relevance of the education that students receive are inadequate in most countries of the region. In addition to lineal expansion (more of the same educational policies and methods), countries have: (1) enacted curricular reforms and constitutional provisions for minimum budgets or free education; (2) launched educational radio and TV programs and adult literacy campaigns; (3) organized nuclear groupings of schools and created comprehensive secondary schools; (4) instituted on-the-job training of teachers; (5) decentralized decisions and changed administrative structures; and (6) launched testing programs. However, the testing programs have shown that students are learning at roughly half the expected levels (those achieved by students in good private schools), and that only half of the students in the fourth grade are able to understand what they read. Furthermore, only in the elite private schools do students perform close to the average of students in developed countries. International comparisons carried out by the International Association for the Evaluation of Educational Achievement (IEA) show that cognitive achievement in Trinidad and Tobago and Venezuela—which are representative of the best systems in the LAC region—is closer to the levels of Africa than East Asia. In addition, there are serious equity problems. Even in the case of Chile, which has improved most inputs (e.g., teacher time, books, rooms, libraries, remedial training, buses, food) and effectively implemented structural reforms, achievement scores remained constant between 1982 and 2000 for every socioeconomic group.

As detected in the IEA study, achievement scores of students in marginal urban public schools and in rural primary schools (especially among indigenous populations) are usually equivalent to half the scores of wealthy students. Poor public schools also have a shorter school year and daily schedule, which, in many cases, give students less that 800 hours per year of potential learning opportunities (compared with 1200 or more hours offered to students in good private schools, a figure close to the average in developed countries). This limited amount of time for learning is usually due to using public school space in double shifts, and to a lack of teachers' time, even though this is mainly related to poor allocation of the public teaching staff in countries with a student/teacher ratio below thirty to one. In poor schools, a substantial amount of the time available for learning is, in fact, wasted in unproductive activities such as silence (discipline), roll call, and disruptions.

Possible Causes of the Low Quality of Education

These poor regional results seem to be linked to the lack of formal evaluations of most of the implemented projects, and to poor professional review of the strategies included in each project. Most of these educational investments were made on the basis of untested or partially tested assumptions about the cost-effectiveness of particular interventions. This is because current knowledge about cost-effectiveness in education is extraordinarily inadequate, especially considering the amount of money that goes into education. In fact, education projects implemented in this region in the 1990s did not include the three highest cost-effective strategies suggested by a group of ten world experts (M. Carnoy and H. Levin, Stanford; N. McGinn and F. Reimers, Harvard; C. Moura Castro, Inter-American Development Bank; S. Heyneman, H. Martinez, and E. Velez, World Bank; J. Velez, PREAL; and J.C. Tedesco, UNESCO). According to their estimations, countries should start by undertaking interventions that do not cost much but do have an impact. For example, the best teacher should be assigned to the first grade in order to help students to learn to read as well as possible (this is particularly relevant in Latin America, where there is such a poor reading and writing record). These experts also highlighted the need for students to have enough time to learn, and they suggest that the official length of school year should be enforced. The third priority was given to a policy not to switch the classroom teacher during the year. It appears that not a single project undertaken during the 1990s in LAC countries supported these strategies.

It is also puzzling that the approaches and methodologies used in a successful Colombian program, *Escuela Nueva,* have not been adapted in education projects designed to develop basic education in other Latin American countries. In spite of being one of the few programs successfully evaluated in the region, it has only been used by the U.S. Agency for International Development (USAID) to improve primary education in Guatemala and Nicaragua.

Above all, the poor quality of the public education system in LAC countries is linked to a vicious circle, perpetuated by complex social factors resistant to reform. Few high school graduates are interested in a teaching career, as low salary levels and poor student achievement levels have created a low level of professional satisfaction. Therefore, most teachers select the profession not due to its intrinsic interest, but because they are not accepted in more prestigious careers. The difference between the required and actual levels of training tends to raise demands for salaries because all teachers assume they meet the required standards. There are, in fact, no effective methods for assessing the individual ability of teachers. Salary demands are also affected by gender and by time schedules. More than two-thirds of all teachers are female, and all teachers have a part-time schedule, but the expected salary level is the salary of a full-time male teacher.

The problem in the public system is more serious because the best teachers tend to move to good private schools, where salaries may be five times higher that in the public system. Thus, there is continuous pressure for better salaries in the public sector. The pressure also involves annual strikes, because public school teachers make up a large share of the civil servants, which are organized in powerful unions and backed by congress members and political leaders. In addition, some teachers are leading local figures who play a critical role in elections. Even though salaries have not increased, strikes have eroded achievements levels and unions have not tried to improve teaching methods.

Most teachers use a *frontal*, or *whole-class*, teaching method, neglecting the needs of individual learners and distorting key educational objectives. Some 80 percent of Chilean secondary school teachers dictate their classes to students. Furthermore, frontal teaching implies an acceptance of an authoritarian teaching structure, the need to learn by rote, a single correct answer (and no opportunity to discuss divergent answers), lack of peer group discussion, and failure to link teaching with the local context.

There is consensus that improving primary and secondary education requires better educated teachers, but change strategies cannot rely on additional voluntary time spent by teachers or recruitment of better trained replacements. Since most teachers in these countries have poor training (there are few "good" teachers available for hire), teachers must be upgraded and provided with relevant tools such as learning guides. In addition, to get an extra effort from present teachers they must be paid more (e.g., one extra hour per day would increase the total cost by 20 to 25 percent). These tough conditions have been fulfilled in only a few successful projects. In these cases, suitable textbooks have played a key role in helping teachers to complement frontal teaching with other teaching models that support an active

role for students. However, evaluations of textbooks in several countries have shown that they: (1) do not suggest activities that students should carry out to grasp the main concepts; (2) contain no instructions for effective group work; (3) present no options for the student to make decisions about how to engage in the learning experience; (4) give few instructions for writing conclusions or reporting the work carried out; (5) do not include activities to be carried out with the family; and (6) provide limited opportunity (in the book) for students to self-evaluate their work. Usage of traditional books is constrained by the inability of teachers to change the predominant frontal teaching method used during their training.

Teacher Training

Basic inputs are a required condition for learning, but they are not the only required condition. Without basic inputs, little learning may occur, but basic inputs do not necessarily generate expected achievement levels. Key inputs include classroom activities, the amount of time available for learning, materials for students to carry out their work (paper, pencils, learning guides and textbooks, and computers), and, of course, buildings. In addition, food and health programs are important, especially for deprived students. However, provision of these (and other) basic inputs does not guarantee that learning will improve, as observed in Chile. On the other hand, multigrade teaching without learning guides—learning materials with clear instructions for the students and teacher to generate an interesting learning experience—will be a failure. Without these guides, which complement the learning process, learning will be drastically reduced.

Even in LAC countries where more time, computers, and learning materials have been provided, no improvements have been measured, mostly due to the traditional frontal teaching style. Forty percent of students repeat the first grade, a fact that can only be explained in terms of poor teaching techniques. Lack of student discussions, learning tasks that are not related to context or expectations, few opportunities for composition writing, and lack of formative evaluation of students' writing and homework are all related to the lack of suitable training of teachers. In fact, it has been determined that while most training institutions provide theoretical training (e.g., structural grammar, linguistic, or learning models), they do not train teachers with specific strategies for teaching. In LAC countries, "teachers are poorly trained, poorly managed, and poorly paid. Superior teaching is seldom recognized, supported, or rewarded" according to Partnership for Educational Revitalization in the Americas. The training of future teachers is not likely to change as long as those doing the training continue using the frontal techniques now prevalent in teacher training institutions.

Effects of Higher Education

Higher education has expanded the supply of teachers (mainly through private programs) and increased tuitions in professional careers, but less than one-fifth of the faculty has training in doctoral programs. Net enrollment rates of those between eighteen and twenty-two years of age increased from less than 4 percent in 1960 to nearly 25 percent in the late 1990s. Unfortunately, this rapid expansion of undergraduate enrollment was not preceded by an increase in graduate training. Therefore, graduates from undergraduate programs (those training for professional careers) were recruited to fill the additional higher education faculty positions.

Poor training in secondary education and professional careers starting in the first year of postsecondary studies are linked to high dropout and repetition rates in the first years of higher education, and to transfers to other programs. Some universities are trying out one or two years of college (similar to community colleges in the United States) to reduce the wastage of time and tuitions and the high levels of disappointment and rage found among the student population.

Master's degree programs in certain areas, particularly those sought by private business, are being offered by joint ventures of local and foreign universities. Some distance education or visiting professors are usually included in the training packages. The Technological Institute of Monterrey (Mexico) is one of the leading institutions in this area, and has students all over Latin America. But improving the quality of the higher-education staff requires doctoral training linked with research. During the 1990s less than 20 percent of the higher education faculty had completed training in doctoral programs. Furthermore, there are few doctoral programs available for academic personnel willing to improve their training; salaries do not provide incentives for faculty with doctoral degrees; almost no scholarships are available for potential candidates; and few research grants are available for preparing the doctoral thesis required for graduating. However, some advances were made in the 1990s in the allocation of research grants.

Lack of Relevant Research

UNESCO and the OAS recommend that financing of research should be increased to reach at least 1 percent of gross domestic product (GDP), which for many LAC countries would be a twofold increase. In the past, the additional funds provided to universities were not channeled to research, but to many competing objectives. Therefore, present trends to allocate grants through competitive research contests should be reinforced, and contributions by private business (with some reduction in taxes) should be explored in order to link research activities with the problems faced by the private sector.

In some areas more public support seems to be required. For example not enough time has been devoted to identifying, understanding, and defining key educational problems, especially those that happen at the classroom level in primary and secondary education and those related to the development of a tradition of empirical research at the university level. Conventional wisdom has prevailed, however, and too much time has been spent in addressing irrelevant problems (e.g., class size, outdated curricula, labs, and libraries). According to research findings (for example, Gene Glass), class size is not related to achievement. Labs have been provided in most LAC countries through loans, but most of them are used as regular classrooms. Libraries are not used in primary and secondary education. All these elements are used when teachers have been trained in a different way. There is a lack of analysis of the real nature and causes of the poor quality of education observed in LAC countries, and of the probable effects of reforms (in most cases reform means gradual, complex changes, rather than drastic simple changes). Even though everything seems to have been tried in LAC education, the effective fight for quality reform has yet to start.

Lack of Relevant Incentives

The staffs of ministries of education and of development cooperation agencies (and their children) are enrolled in private schools—they do not use the public schools they are managing and thus are not affected by the classroom impact of their projects, nor are their professional careers. They therefore have limited incentives for searching out better strategies to improve the performance of the education system. Fortunately, personal commitment often compensates for this lack of built-in incentives.

The learning process is affected by the gap between the educational background of decision makers and the education delivered to students in rural areas or in urban marginal schools of developing countries. The gap is so wide that policymakers or lending and project officials have problems understanding the key elements of the educational development process. Furthermore, these leaders, who enroll their children in private schools, are not going to be affected by the final outcomes of the recommended strategies or projects, so the effort spent in the design of good education projects only depends on their personal values and commitment. The lack of incentives for educational leaders to do their utmost to achieve success with their policies seems to be sadly reflected in poor educational outcomes.

The lack of evaluation of the impact of projects in students' achievement (and, ideally, in the personal development of students) and the lack of good estimations of the cost-effectiveness of specific strategies, constrain professional judgment and tend to support old approaches focused on traditional goals or on timely implementation of disbursements. Therefore, progress in a teacher's professional career is not related to student improvement. Educational policies have thus been detached from improvement of human resources in the LAC region.

See also: INTERNATIONAL DEVELOPMENT AGENCIES AND EDUCATION; INTERNATIONAL EDUCATION; HIGHER EDUCATION, INTERNATIONAL ISSUES; TEACHER EDUCATION, *subentry on* INTERNATIONAL PERSPECTIVE.

BIBLIOGRAPHY

ALTBACH, PHILIP G. 1996. *The International Academic Profession.* Princeton, NJ: The Carnegie Foundation for the Advancement of Teaching.

BIRDSALL, NANCY; ROSS, DAVID; and SABOT RICHARD. 1994. "Inequality and Growth Reconsidered: Lessons from East Asia." *World Bank Economic Review* 9:477–508.

CASASSUS, JUAN, et al. 1998. *Primer Estudio Internacional Comparativo: Laboratorio de Evaluación de la Calidad de la Educación.* Santiago, Chile: UNESCO Regional Office for Latin America and the Caribbean.

ELLEY, WARWICK B. 1992. *How in the World Do Students Read?* The Hague: International Association for the Evaluation of Educational Achievement.

INTER-AMERICAN DEVELOPMENT BANK. 2001. *Primary Education in Latin America: The Unfinished Agenda.* Washington, DC: Inter-American Development Bank.

INTERNATIONAL ASSOCIATION FOR THE EVALUATION OF EDUCATIONAL ACHIEVEMENT. 2000. *International Student Achievement in Mathematics.* The Hague: International Association for the Evaluation of Educational Achievement.

LUNA, EDUARDO, and WOLFE, RICHARD. 1993. *A Feasibility Report on the Assessment of Mathematics and Sciences Education in Latin America.* Toronto: Institute for Studies in Education.

MALO, SALVADOR, and MORLEY, SAMUEL. 1996. *La Educacion Superior en America Latina.* Washington DC: Inter-American Development Bank.

OLIVEIRA, JOAO. 1989. *Educational Reform in Latin America: Towards a Permanent Agenda.* Washington, DC: The Economic Development Institute of the World Bank.

ORGANIZATION FOR ECONOMIC CO-OPERATION AND DEVELOPMENT. 2000. *Literacy in the Information Age: Final Report of the International Adult Literacy Survey.* Paris: Organization for Economic Co-operation and Development.

PARTNERSHIP FOR EDUCATIONAL REVITALIZATION IN THE AMERICAS (PREAL). 2001. *Lagging Behind: A Report Card on Education in Latin America.* Washington, DC: Inter-American Dialogue.

REIMERS, FERNANDO. 2000. *Unequal School, Unequal Chances: The Challenges to Equal Opportunity in the Americas.* Boston: David Rockefeller Center for Latin American Studies, Harvard University.

SCHIEFELBEIN, ERNESTO; CORVALÁN, ANA MARIA; PERUZZI, SONIA; HEIKKINEN, SEPP; and HAUSMANN, ISABEL. 1995. *Quality of Education, Equity, and Poverty in the Region, 1980–1994.* Santiago, Chile: UNESCO Regional Office of Education.

SCHIEFELBEIN, ERNESTO, and TEDESCO, JUAN CARLOS. 1995. *Una Nueva Oportunidad.* Buenos Aires, Argentina: Santillana.

SCHIEFELBEIN, ERNESTO; WOLFF, LAURENCE; and SCHIEFELBEIN, PAULINA. 1998. *Cost-*

Effectiveness of Education Policies in Latin America: A Survey of Expert Opinion. Washington, DC: Inter-American Development Bank.

SCHLEICHER, ANDREAS, and YIP, JEAN. 1994. *Indicators of Between-School Differences in Reading Achievement.* Amsterdam, The Netherlands: International Association for the Evaluation of Educational Achievement.

TEDESCO, JUAN CARLOS. 1994. *Present Trends of Educational Reforms.* Santiago, Chile: UNESCO Regional Office for Latin America and the Caribbean.

TORO, BERNARDO, and RODRÍGUEZ, MARIELA. 2001. *La Comunicación y la Movilización Social en la Construcción de Bienes Públicos.* Bogotá, Colombia: Banco Interamericano de Desarrollo.

UNESCO. 2000. *Education for All: Status and Trends 2000.* Paris: International Consultative Forum on Education for All.

UNESCO REGIONAL OFFICE FOR LATIN AMERICA AND THE CARIBBEAN. 1993. *Reading Comprehension in Children from Rural and Urban Areas.* Santiago, Chile: UNESCO Regional Office for Latin America and the Caribbean.

UNESCO REGIONAL OFFICE FOR LATIN AMERICA AND THE CARIBBEAN. 1995. *The State of Education in Latin America, 1980–1991.* Santiago, Chile: UNESCO Regional Office for Latin America and the Caribbean.

UNESCO REGIONAL OFFICE FOR LATIN AMERICA AND THE CARIBBEAN. 1998. *UNESCO and Education in Latin America and the Caribbean 1987–1997.* Santiago, Chile: UNESCO Regional Office for Latin America and the Caribbean.

UNITED NATIONS ECONOMIC COMMISSION FOR LATIN AMERICA AND THE CARIBBEAN. 1992. *Education and Knowledge: Basic Pillars of Changing Production Patterns with Social Equity.* Santiago, Chile: United Nations Economic Commission for Latin America and the Caribbean.

WOLFF, LAURENCE; SCHIEFELBEIN ERNESTO; and VALENZUELA, JORGE. 1993. *Improving the Quality of Primary Education in Latin America: Towards the 21st Century.* Washington, DC: World Bank.

WORLD BANK. 1994. *Priorities and Strategies for Education.* Washington, DC: World Bank, Education and Social Policy Department.

WORLD BANK. 2000. *Higher Education in Developing Countries: Peril and Promise.* Washington, DC: World Bank, Task Force on Education and Society.

WORLD ECONOMIC FORUM. 1994. *The World Competitiveness Report, 1994.* Lausanne, Switzerland: World Economic Forum.

ERNESTO SCHIEFELBEIN
PAULINA SCHIEFELBEIN

LATIN IN SCHOOLS, TEACHING OF

Since it was first instituted as a formal course of study—first for Roman children, and then for members of the ever-expanding Roman Empire—Latin has been a staple of formal curricula. And for almost all of that time, controversy has swirled around the methodologies that should be used to teach Latin, its precise role in the curricula, and the aims and goals of teaching Latin. As the arguments and counterarguments have evolved, definite (and cyclical) trends have emerged.

Enrollments

At the turn of the twentieth century, more than 50 percent of the public secondary-school students in the United States were studying Latin. Until 1928 Latin enrollments in U.S. secondary schools were greater than enrollments in all other foreign languages combined, and in the mid-1930s the number of Latin students rose to 899,000. This is not surprising, since Latin was commonly required for admission to college and was seen as the mark of an educated individual. Latin continued to be the front-runner for about another twenty years, until Spanish took the lead. Still, over the next ten years, Latin enrollments generally kept pace, rising 46 percent, compared to 56 percent for Spanish and 90 percent for French. Despite a sudden postwar drop in Latin studies (the number of students fell to about 429,000), Latin was fairly secure in the curriculum, and the numbers grew steadily thereafter.

In 1958 in response to a national concern in the United States over the nation's global status in mathematics and science, Congress passed the National Defense Education Act, which omitted support for all Latin, except at the graduate level. Latin soon began a gradual decline, though it retained much of its old cachet. This would soon change, however. In

1962 there were 702,000 students enrolled in Latin classes in U.S. secondary schools. By 1976 the number had dropped 79 percent, to 150,000, largely due to pressure for more relevant and elective courses at all education levels. The classics profession began a swift counteroffensive, and by 1978 enrollments were on the rise once more. More recent data suggest a slight leveling off at grades nine through twelve, with a total enrollment of 188,833 students in 1994, representing some 1.6 percent of the total enrolled population. New growth areas include middle-school Latin, with more than 25,349 enrolled in grades seven and eight, and 4,265 elementary students of Latin.

At the college level, the overall number of Latin students has changed less dramatically, with 39,600 reported in 1965 and 25,897 in 1995. But given the surge in college enrollments, this represents a percentage drop from .669 percent in 1965 to only .180 percent in 1995. While hard data are not readily available, it is fair to say that the 1980s and 1990s saw a definite decline in traditional classics majors (concentrating in Latin and Greek language study) and an increasing move toward those minoring, and majoring, in classical civilization or classical studies, a curriculum that demands only the rudimentary study of the actual languages. As a result, while K–12 Latin enrollments have increased slightly, an aging population of Latin teachers is facing retirement, with an inadequate number of qualified teachers available to take their place.

Latin is also taught at the junior college level, but with no regularity. Here also, courses in classical civilization, history, and mythology are far more common than the actual study of the languages themselves. It is also worth noting that Latin retained its special status in countries such as England and Germany far longer than it did in the United States. But recent curricular reforms in these countries have put Latin at risk there as well.

Teaching Methods and Textbooks

Few methodologies have been both as traditional and as innovative as those associated with Latin. For the Romans themselves, the goal of learning Latin was totally utilitarian—to learn, as Quintilian put it, "the ability to speak Latin properly and to elucidate the poets" (*recte loquendi scientiam et poetarum enarrationem*) (Marrou, p. 274). In its higher forms, of course, it aimed at the proper use of the language in the fine art of rhetoric, for the way to success in the

Roman world was through the effective use of oratory. What we know of the way in which Romans taught their children Latin would not stand the scrutiny of twenty-first-century educational theorists for very long, for there was a heavy emphasis on rote memorization and corporal punishment. Once the students had the rudiments down, they moved on to the grammar school, where, from roughly age six through age twelve, they began the acquisition of Latin grammar under the tutelage of the appropriately named *grammaticus*. Historian Henri Marrou carefully defines the subject matter as a dull analysis of each word in a text from as many perspectives as possible.

But the ultimate goal of Roman education was the *enarratio poetarum*, and to this day most claim that the sole aim of studying Latin is to acquire a proper appreciation of the Latin classics. Roman students were expected to be able to read, aloud and with expression, a given passage from the works of a poet. Then they were grilled, line by line and word by word, on the many intricacies of the grammar, rhetorical figures, and mythological allusions. Advanced students went on to rhetorical studies to prepare them for public life.

In the Middle Ages Latin continued to be taught as a living tongue. Though no country had Latin as its language, the ability to speak, read, and write Latin was still essential for advancement in church or state circles. Thus, in the elementary schools, "the chief objective and emphasis of teachers and pupils was the ability to speak Latin with ease. Success in this almost automatically entailed ability to read and write it as well" (Ganss, p. 122). A well-written survey of teaching methods, some of them rather innovative, remains to written for this and subsequent periods.

Much has been made about the emphasis on the study of Latin and Greek in early America. To be sure, any educated American needed Latin and Greek to enter college, but Latin was commonly charged with being irrelevant, poorly taught, and dull. Throughout the nineteenth century, and until 1924, the *grammar/translation* method held sway. In this method the grammar was laid out in orderly charts for the student to memorize. Only after endings and forms were memorized and usage had been thoroughly explained was the new material to be applied to practice sentences and, finally, to translation from the Latin. This method traditionally exposed the student to all the basic grammar in Latin in one year. The second year was traditionally given over to reading Caesar, the third to Cicero, and the fourth to Virgil. In these courses the emphasis was on accurate translation and meticulous grammatical explication of the text. Under this methodology, it was found that in the mid-1920s only about 30 percent of students continued beyond the second year, and only 15 percent beyond the third. In 1924 the American Classical League commissioned a study of the teaching of Latin. The so-called Advisory Committee published its *Classical Investigation,* in which it recommended some forward-thinking reforms for Latin teaching, such as adding cultural materials to be read in English, a change from the traditional grammar/translation paradigm (and a move to have students read Latin more naturally as Latin), and the inclusion of other authors in the curriculum. The report was farsighted, but largely ignored. As Judith Sebesta has shown, textbooks remained essentially unchanged until well after the sharp decline in enrollments of the 1960s and 1970s. Several of these grammar/translation texts are still in use in the early twenty-first century (e.g., Wheelock, Jenney) and other, newer texts, still follow their essential format (e.g., Goldman and Nyenhuis, Johnson).

A major break with this tradition was in response to the theories of behaviorism and structural linguistics, which led to Waldo Sweet's text based on *programmed learning,* where the student is allowed to acquire forms at the student's own pace. Glenn Knudsvig's *Latin for Reading* (1986) was influenced by Sweet and relied heavily on linguistic theory to help the student learn how to read Latin in a less rigid and more flowing fashion.

Cognitive psychology and the theories of Noam Chomsky led to the creation of a series of textbooks generally referred to as *reading method* texts. These texts have as their main goal enabling students to read extensive passages in Latin with relative ease. They are marked by their lack of formal grammar explication, use of stories with a connected plot written for the volumes, little if any use of authentic texts in the earlier volumes, and a reliance on illustrations to help students grasp new concepts. Only after a student has seen a new construction used several times is the construction explained. These textbooks are widely used at all levels today, and similar textbooks have been created for special use at the elementary and middle school levels.

Trends, Issues, and Controversies

Latin has made a remarkable comeback in U.S. schools at the start of the twenty-first century. In many districts it ranks as the second most popular language—second only to Spanish. Yet the continued presence of Latin in K–12 curricula depends on the profession's prompt attention to many different forces at work in education. The first problem is a direct result of the profession's aggressive promotion of Latin in the face of the dramatic decline in Latin study during the 1960s and 1970s. The United States is facing an increasingly severe shortage of Latin teachers. Many school districts drop Latin programs each year for lack of teachers, and each year the standard placement services show many more openings for Latin teachers than job applicants.

The placement services also show an increasing call for Latin teachers who can teach one other language, most commonly Spanish. Since Spanish is closely related to Latin it represents a natural alliance that has had great success in pilot programs combining the two languages. Further, as Latin continues to expand at the elementary and middle school levels, the field will be increasingly called upon to devise further curricula and materials suitable for these levels.

Many national initiatives have influenced Latin in the K–12 curriculum. For example, both block scheduling and the International Baccalaureate (which initially did not accommodate the study of Latin) have, over recent years, caused Latin professionals once more both to mount proactive campaigns and to modify outdated teaching methodologies. Such change is facilitated by alliances between such national groups as The American Classical League (ACL; traditionally a K–12 organization) and the American Philological Association (APA; traditionally a college and university organization). As such alliances increase, insularity among Latin teacher groups is becoming a thing of the past. Likewise, the national classics organizations have increasingly allied themselves with modern language groups such as The American Council for the Teaching of Foreign Languages (ACTFL) and the Modern Language Association (MLA). As a result, Latin is routinely included whenever issues affecting all languages are discussed.

This was never more evident than in the matter of the national standards movement. The resurgence of Latin occurred along several tracks at once, with markedly different goals and target audiences. The profession first took note of the disparity among curricula in the late 1980s and early 1990s. This insight was spurred on by ACTFL's *Standards for Foreign Language Learning: Preparing for the Twenty-First Century* and a broad coalition of classicists from all levels gathered to produce *Standards for Classical Language Learning,* which was jointly published by the ACL and APA and has become the accepted standard in its field.

The future of Latin in the schools is somewhat unclear at present. The president of a major state university, looking back at the "good old days" put it well: "I do not know, of course, what is to become of classical study in this country, but personally I should regard it as a great blow to the development of some of the finest and most important sides of American life if the study of Greek and Latin should fall to the relatively unimportant place now occupied by the study of Assyrian and Babylonian, as some people think it is bound to do" (West, p. 188). This nervous statement, however, was made in 1917 by Edmund J. James of the University of Illinois. The study of Latin, it seems, will always have its challenges, and its doubters, but if the past is any indication, it will rise to meet the future as well as it has the past.

See also: CURRICULUM, SCHOOL; FOREIGN LANGUAGE EDUCATION; INTERNATIONAL BACCALAUREATE DIPLOMA; SECONDARY EDUCATION, *subentries on* CURRENT TRENDS, HISTORY OF.

BIBLIOGRAPHY

ABBOTT, MARTHA GORDON. 1991. "Priority: Classics—Critical Instructional Issues in the Classics for American Schools." *Foreign Language Annals* 24:27–37.

BELL, BARBARA. 2000. *Minimus: Starting Out in Latin.* Cambridge, Eng.: Cambridge University Press.

GANSS, GEORGE, S.J. 1956. *Saint Ignatius' Idea of a Jesuit University.* Milwaukee, WI: Marquette University Press.

GEORGE, ED. 1998. "Latin and Spanish: Roman Culture and Hispanic America." In *Latin for the 21st Century: From Concept to Classroom,* ed. Richard LaFleur. Glenville, IL: Scott Foresman-Addison Wesley.

GOLDMAN, NORMA, and NYENHUIS, JACOB. 1982. *Latin Via Ovid: A First Course,* 2nd edition. Detroit, MI: Wayne State University Press.

JENNEY, CHARLES, JR., et al. 1990. *First Year Latin* and *Second Year Latin.* Englewood Cliffs, NJ: Prentice-Hall.

JOHNSON, PATRICIA A. 1988. *Traditio: An Introduction to the Latin Language and Its Influence.* New York: Macmillan.

KITCHELL, KENNETH F. 1998. "The Great Latin Debate: The Futility of Utility?" In *Latin for the 21st Century: From Concept to Classroom,* ed. Richard LaFleur. Glenview, IL: Scott Foresman-Addison Wesley.

KITCHELL, KENNETH F. 2000. "The Latin Teacher Shortage: A Call to Action." *Classical Outlook* 78:1–18.

KNUDSVIG, GLENN M., et al. 1986. *Latin for Reading: A Beginner's Textbook with Exercises,* 2nd edition. Ann Arbor: University of Michigan Press.

KNUDSVIG, GLENN M., and ROSS, DEBORAH PENNELL. 1998. "The Linguistic Perspective." In *Latin for the 21st Century: From Concept to Classroom,* ed. Richard LaFleur. Glenview, IL: Scott Foresman-Addison Wesley.

LAFLEUR, RICHARD A. 1985. "1984: Latin in the United States Twenty Years After the Fall." *Foreign Language Annals* 18(4): 341–347.

LAFLEUR, RICHARD A. 1987. *The Teaching of Latin in American Schools: A Profession in Crisis.* Decatur, GA: Scholars Press.

LAFLEUR, RICHARD A. 1997. "*Latina Resurgens:* Classical Language Enrollments in American Schools and Colleges." *Classical Outlook* 74(4):125–130.

LAFLEUR, RICHARD A., ed. 1998. *Latin for the 21st Century: From Concept to Classroom.* Glenview, IL: Scott Foresman-Addison Wesley.

LAWALL, GILBERT, et al. 1994. *Ecce Romani: A Latin Reading Program,* 2nd edition. Glenview IL: Scott Foresman-Addison Wesley.

MARROU, HENRI. 1982. *A History of Education in Antiquity,* tr. George Lamb (1956). Madison: University of Wisconsin Press.

PHINNEY, ED, and BELL, PATRICIA. 1988. *The Cambridge Latin Course.* Units 1–4, 3rd. edition. Cambridge, Eng.: Cambridge University Press.

POLSKY, MARION. 1998. *First Latin: A Language Discovery Program,* 2nd edition. Glenview, IL: Scott Foresman-Addison Wesley.

SEBESTA, JUDITH LYNN. 1998. "*Aliquid Semper Novi: New Challenges, New Approaches.*" In *Latin for the 21st Century: From Concept to Classroom,* ed. Richard LaFleur. Glenview, IL: Scott Foresman-Addison Wesley.

SWEET, WALDO. 1957. *Latin: A Structural Approach.* Ann Arbor: University of Michigan Press.

SWEET, WALDO. 1966. *Artes Latinae.* Wauconda, IL: Bolchazy-Carducci.

WEST, ANDREW F., ed. 1917. *Value of the Classics.* Princeton, NJ: Princeton University Press.

WHEELOCK, FREDERICK M. 1995. *Wheelock's Latin,* 5th edition, ed. Richard LaFleur. New York: HarperCollins.

KENNETH F. KITCHELL JR.

LAW EDUCATION

The law deals with all aspects of human life in its individual and collective expression, searching for economic and social justice, addressing past injustice, and ruling on divisive issues. As dynamic as the society it represents, the law changes as the zeitgeist or spirit of the times reflects emerging interests and concerns. Those interested in a career in law will find it a route to understanding American culture in all its dimensions.

A career in law requires dedication, persistence, and the analytical skills that are essential for interpreting past and current legal decisions. Liberal arts undergraduate programs or degree programs that have a concentration on critical thinking skills, along with a number of advanced courses—such as logic, English literature, foreign language, business and/or education law, sociology, and philosophy—prepare students for law school. Pre-law school advisers are available on campuses to assist students in planning for a career in law and choosing law schools. Mentoring services are available in most law schools.

Each law school has its own unique culture and admissions process. Although law schools differ in many aspects, a common goal is training well-qualified graduates to represent the highest ideals of the profession in practice. Prospective students are encouraged to review the specifics of individual law school policies and procedures through campus visits and/or websites that are comprehensive and detailed. All law schools now have websites with information about admissions processes.

Criteria for Admission to Law School

Law schools are highly competitive and selective, and there is a wide range of criteria used for admissions. Students can find a law school whose admissions acceptance rates meet their individual profiles.

Although some law schools admit students from the third year of undergraduate studies, most require a bachelor's degree. Since applying to law schools is a time-consuming and costly process, students are encouraged to use a centralized processing agency (Law School Data Assembly Service, or LSDAS), which for a fee will assist them in preparing multiple applications. Law school admission review boards examine a student's GPA (grade point average), Law School Admission Test (LSAT) score, plus a variety of other factors including extracurricular experiences such as leadership activities, debate clubs, foreign language, and travel. A student's résumé should include volunteer service, work experience, and extracurricular activities together with the LSAT test score, also a personal statement about long-term and short-term goals, reasons for choosing law as a profession, and any other information that candidates wish to share. Three or four personal recommendations should be included. It is very important to carefully proofread materials submitted to assure accuracy and grammatical correctness. Admissions offices are inundated with applications; those not correctly filled out may be discarded.

There is no specific formula for admission to law school beyond a good academic record and LSAT score, along with experiences that show a commitment toward community improvement. Students who have low grades in first-year undergraduate courses but who show marked improvement in later studies demonstrate improved achievement and often the review committee will review these applicants favorably. Students need to apply to several law schools to ensure their admission. Applications a year or a year and half before matriculation dates are advised, except for students transferring from other law schools at home or abroad, who should apply earlier than regular law students. Law school admissions officers must receive letters of good standing from previous law schools. Law schools differ in the time frame but applying for the fall term should take place from October through February.

Law schools are interested in having a faculty and student body representative of the larger society.

To ensure ethnic and cultural diversity in enrollment the Council on Legal Education Opportunity, the Association of American Law Schools, the National Bar Association, and the American Bar Association (ABA) support special programs, mentors, individual and group tutors, and remedial courses in reading, writing, and grammar together with practice examinations. In addition, efforts to fund students' tuition costs based on financial need are continuing.

The American Bar Association's list of approved schools provides detailed information about a number of factors important to review prior to submitting applications. Some of these include the credentials of part-time and full-time law school faculty, percentages of dropouts through the three or four years, advanced and joint degree offerings, professional associations program approval, library and special facilities, gender and minority enrollment statistics, costs including available grants, loans, job assistance for spouses, and availability of housing and costs.

Applying to Law School

Students interested in applying to a law school should engage in networking to learn about the school's culture, history, and curriculum. It is helpful to contact current and former students to discuss the admission process as well as to learn about the campus, instructional methods, competitive ranking, and the quality of students, faculty, and administrators. Applying to three or four law schools can give students a range of options from highly competitive institutions with international reputations to "safe schools," or those that have a broader range of admissions acceptance. Study guides and tutorial programs are available to aid in preparation for the LSAT, which is a multiple-choice test given four times a year at strategic sites throughout the country. The Law School Admission Council offers publications such as *The Right Law School for You* and *Financing Your Law School Education.*

Curriculum and Degrees

Full time students are expected to complete a three-year program, while part-time students often take four or more years for completion. Both full-time and part-time students complete their degree more quickly by taking summer school courses. The first year of law school is the most challenging, with the greatest dropout rate. Law schools with the fewest dropouts have very selective admissions processes. Although there are a number of students who drop out at the second year, generally most students who complete the first year of law school complete the degree requirements. Few drop out in the third and fourth year of law school.

A typical first-year law school curriculum includes contracts, criminal law, constitutional law, civil procedure, civil law, property, and torts. Second and third year courses offer students a variety of concentrations such as business and tax law, commercial law, constitutional law, labor and employment law, civil liberties and civil rights, and environmental law. Generally there is no formal second and third year curriculum, but some law schools require legal research and writing courses.

There are a variety of law degrees, including the most common J.D. (Juris doctor), LL.M (Master of Laws), and S.J.D. (Doctor of Juridical Science). Joint degrees are available, including the J.D./M.B.A. (Master of Business Administration), J.D./M.Ed. (Master of Education), and the J.D./Ph.D. (Doctor of Philosophy). Non-ABA-accredited law degree programs offer J.D. degrees. They are often accredited by state agencies. In many states practicing lawyers are required to have graduated from an ABA-accredited school.

Online law schools are available for individuals who are place bound, those who enjoy studying at their own pace, or those who have other needs requiring flexibility in time and place. Online law programs provide unlimited access to faculty and law resources twenty-four hours per day, seven days per week. As in other professions, so in law, online degree programs with their nontraditional formats have challenged accreditation agencies. Accreditation of these programs will be under review as accrediting agencies work through the challenge of innovative, emerging models for legal education. Concord University, one of the first online law degree programs, is accredited by the Distance Education Learning Council and a Committee of Bar Examiners in California.

In a litigious society, well-prepared, well-qualified lawyers will continue to be in demand. Law provides a career well worth a prospective student's best efforts.

See also: LAW SCHOOL ADMISSION TEST.

BIBLIOGRAPHY

DALY, STACY A., ed. 1997. *REA's Authoritative Guide to Law Schools.* Piscataway, NJ: Research and Education Association.

DOUGHTY, HAROLD R. 1999. *The Penguin Guide to American Law Schools.* New York: Pengiun.

LAMMERT-REEVES, RUTH. 2000. *Law School Admissions Adviser.* New York: Simon and Schuster.

MARTINSON, THOMAS H., and WALDHERR, DAVID P. 1998. *Getting into Law School Today.* Stamford, CT: ARCO.

MORGAN, RICK L., and SNYDER, KURT, eds. 2000. *Official American Bar Association Guide to Approved Law Schools.* New York: Macmillan.

MUNNEKE, GARY A. 2001. *How to Succeed In Law School.* Hauppauge, NY: Barron's Educational Series.

OWENS, ERIC. 2001. *The Princeton Review Complete Book of Law Schools.* New York: Random House.

INTERNET RESOURCES

AMERICAN BAR ASSOCIATION. 2002. <www.aba.org>.

LAW SCHOOL ADMISSION COUNCIL. 2002. <www.lsac.org>.

JAMES J. VAN PATTEN

LAW SCHOOL ADMISSION TEST

The Law School Admission Test (LSAT) is the half-day, standardized entrance exam required by the 198 law schools (184 in the United States and 15 in Canada) that constitute the membership of the Law School Admission Council (LSAC) as of July 2001. The LSAC, a nonprofit corporation located in Newton, Pennsylvania, is the sole administering body of the LSAT. The LSAT is administered to large groups of individuals four times per year (February, June, October, and December) at numerous test centers. Approximately 107,000 individuals took the LSAT in 2000.

History

During the first half of the twentieth century the generic intelligence test and its various offspring gained popularity. The use of intelligence tests during World War I by the U.S. military was followed quickly by the introduction in 1920 of the National Intelligence Test for American school children and in 1926 with the Scholastic Aptitude Test. The first LSAT was administered twenty-two years later in 1948. Although the methodology used to score the LSAT has undergone changes over time, the general format and substance of the LSAT has remained relatively constant.

Format

The 2001 LSAT is representative of the contemporary examination. It consists of five multiple-choice sections of thirty-five minutes each and an additional, non-scored thirty-minute writing sample. Two of the test sections focus on logical reasoning by testing the ability of the test-taker to perceive logical fallacies in statements. Another section focuses on analytical reasoning skills by challenging the test-taker to solve complex puzzles based on systems of relationships. The final section is a high-level reading comprehension exercise that examines the individual's ability to digest complex passages of text and identify the author's purpose. An additional fifth experimental section may be any of the other three types and is used to pilot questions for future LSAT exams. The experimental section does not contribute to the individual's score.

Scoring

The LSAT score reported for an individual is a *scaled score* that is generated using a mathematical conversion formula unique for each particular version of the exam. The *raw score,* on the other hand, is a direct representation of the number of test questions the individual answered correctly. With a total of approximately 101 questions on each LSAT, an individual receives a single raw point score for each correctly answered question. The raw score is then converted to a scaled score that falls between 120, the minimum LSAT score, and 180, the maximum LSAT score.

Role of the LSAT in Legal Education

The LSAT is the primary vehicle through which individuals gain entrance to the system of legal education officially approved by the American Bar Association (ABA). The LSAT is analogous to the Medical College Admission Test (MCAT) and the Graduate Management Admission Test (GMAT); it is the standardized mechanism used by a professional school in evaluating applicants for potential ability within the professional school setting and, thus, for possible entry into the profession itself. The impact of the LSAT as the gatekeeper to the legal profession cannot be overstated.

The LSAT is used to make important decisions about the path of law school applicants' lives. It seems unavoidable under these circumstances that the test itself has become a source of ongoing controversy. Questions persist as to whether the LSAT measures the ability to succeed in the modern law school and as to the proper weight to give to LSAT scores during the admissions process. Accordingly, criticisms abound regarding a number of aspects of the LSAT.

The LSAT score is the most heavily weighted criteria considered by those involved in the law school admissions decision-making process. The most common criticism associated with the process is that those making the admissions decisions rely on LSAT scores as an obvious indicator of those who will succeed in law school. Critics argue that the LSAT is not conclusive in its predictive ability of academic performance in law school. They point out the impact of other factors, including support systems, financial demands, and individual motivation, as important in determining the long-term success of a student in law school. The Law School Admission Council itself, however, has always urged law school admissions professionals to resist the urge to make the LSAT score the sole criteria used in the admissions process.

Concerns about the validity of the LSAT bring serious issues of fairness and equity into the dialogue concerning the law school admissions process. The debate surrounding gender, racial, and ethnic bias in the LSAT system generates the majority of the academic literature about the test and supports a flow of legal cases over admissions decisions. Various studies have offered data suggesting that the LSAT serves as a barrier to the admission of women and ethnic applicants into a professional system that has traditionally been dominated by white males. The underlying rationale for the use of the LSAT, however, is to avoid the biases that come with more arbitrary methods of selection. Standardized testing theoretically offers a mechanism for the selection of students based on academic ability rather than more subjective characteristics, such as social standing.

The predictive accuracy of the LSAT will remain under question. Logic demands continued and con-

scious attention to the standardized test that provides admittance to a modern legal education. Indeed, the baseline justification behind using the LSAT in the admission process is the assumption that the test is a strong predictor of performance during the first year of law school. Regardless of the various concerns regarding the test, the LSAT remains the best measure of academic ability developed to date to aid in the law school admissions process.

See also: LAW EDUCATION.

BIBLIOGRAPHY

BROWN, DOROTHY A. 1998. "The LSAT Sweepstakes." *Journal of Gender, Race and Justice* 2:59–75.

KIDDER, WILLIAM C. 2000. "The Rise of Testocracy: An Essay on the LSAT, Conventional Wisdom, and the Dismantling of Diversity." *Texas Journal of Women and Law* 9:167–218.

KIDDER, WILLIAM C. 2000. "Unmasking Gender Bias on the LSAT and Its Relationship to Racial Diversity in Legal Education." *Yale Journal of Law and Feminism* 12:1–42.

SACKS, PETER. 2001. "How Admissions Tests Hinder Access to Graduate and Professional Schools." *Chronicle of Higher Education* June 8.

SHELTON, PHILIP D. 2001. "Admissions Tests: Not Perfect, Just the Best Measures We Have." *Chronicle of Higher Education* July 6.

SUBOTNIK, DAN. 2000. "Goodbye to the SAT, LSAT? Hello to Equity by Lottery? Evaluating Lani Guinier's Plan for Ending Race Consciousness." *Howard Law Journal* 43:141–170.

INTERNET RESOURCE

LAW SCHOOL ADMISSION COUNCIL. 2002. <www.lsac.org>.

MADISON GRAY

LEADERSHIP

See: EDUCATIONAL LEADERSHIP.

LEARNING

ANALOGICAL REASONING

Analogy plays an important role in learning and instruction. As John Bransford, Jeffrey Franks, Nancy Vye, and Robert Sherwood noted in 1989, analogies can help students make connections between different concepts and transfer knowledge from a well-understood domain to one that is unfamiliar or not directly perceptual. For example, the circulatory system is often explained as being like a plumbing system, with the heart as pump.

The Analogical Reasoning Process

Analogical reasoning involves several sub-processes: (1) retrieval of one case given another; (2) mapping between two cases in working memory; (3) evaluating the analogy and its inferences; and, sometimes, (4) abstracting the common structure. The core process in analogical reasoning is mapping. According to structure-mapping theory, developed by Dedre Gentner in 1982, an analogy is a mapping of knowledge from one domain (the base or source) into another (the target) such that a system of relations that holds among the base objects also holds among the target objects. In interpreting an analogy, people seek to put the objects of the base in one-to-one correspondence with the objects of the target so as to obtain the maximal structural match. The corresponding objects in the base and target need not resemble each other; what is important is that they hold like roles in the matching relational structures. Thus, analogy provides a way to focus on relational commonalities independently of the objects in which those relations are embedded.

In explanatory analogy, a well-understood base or source situation is mapped to a target situation that is less familiar and/or less concrete. Once the two situations are aligned—that is, once the learner has established correspondences between them—then new inferences are derived by importing connected information from the base to the target. For example, in the analogy between blood circulation and plumbing, students might first align the known facts that the pump *causes* water *to flow through* the pipes with the fact that the heart *causes* blood *to flow through* the veins. Given this alignment of structure, the learner can carry over additional inferences: for example, that plaque in the veins forces the heart to work harder, just as narrow pipes require a pump to work harder.

Gentner and Phillip Wolff in 2000 set forth four ways in which comparing two analogs fosters learning. First, it can highlight common relations. For example, in processing the circulation/plumbing analogy, the focus is on the dynamics of circulation, and other normally salient knowledge—such as the red color of arteries and the blue color of veins—is suppressed. Second, it can lead to new inferences, as noted above. Third, comparing two analogs can reveal meaningful differences. For example, the circulation/plumbing analogy can bring out the difference that veins are flexible whereas pipes are rigid. In teaching by analogy, it is important to bring out such differences; otherwise students may miss them, leading them to make inappropriate inferences. Fourth, comparing two analogs can lead learners to form abstractions, as amplified below.

What Makes a Good Analogy

As Gentner suggested in 1982, to facilitate making clear alignments and reasonable inferences, an analogy must be structurally consistent—that is, it should have one-to-one correspondences, and the relations in the two domains should have a parallel structure. For example, in the circulation/plumbing system analogy, the pump cannot correspond to both the veins and the heart. Another factor influencing the quality of an analogy is systematicity: Analogies that convey an interconnected system of relations, such as the circulation/pumping analogy, are more useful than those that convey only a single isolated fact, such as "The brain looks like a walnut." Further, as Keith Holyoak and Paul Thagard argued in 1995, an analogy should be goal-relevant in the current context.

In addition to the above general qualities, several further factors influence the success of an explanatory analogy, including base specificity, transparency, and scope. Base specificity is the degree to which the structure of the base domain is clearly understood. Transparency is the ease with which the correspondences can be seen. Transparency is increased by similarities between corresponding objects and is decreased by similarities between noncorresponding objects. For example, in 1986 Gentner and Cecile Toupin found that four- to six-year-old children succeeded in transferring a story to new characters when similar characters occupied similar roles (e.g., squirrel → chipmunk; trout → salmon), but they failed when the match was cross-mapped, with similar characters in different roles (e.g., squirrel → salmon; trout → chipmunk). The same pattern has been found with adults. Transparency also applies to relations. In 2001 Miriam Bassok found that students more easily aligned instances of "increase" when both were continuous (e.g., speed of a car and growth of a population) than when one was discrete (e.g., attendance at an annual event). Finally, scope refers to how widely applicable the analogy is.

Methods Used to Investigate Analogical Learning

Much research on analogy in learning has been devoted to the effects of analogies on domain understanding. For example, in 1987 Brian Ross found that giving learners analogical examples to illustrate a probability principle facilitated their later use of the probability formula to solve other problems. In classroom studies from 1998, Daniel Schwartz and John Bransford found that generating distinctions between contrasting cases improved students' subsequent learning. As reported in 1993, John Clement used a technique of bridging analogies to induce revision of faulty mental models. Learners were given a series of analogs, beginning with a very close match and moving gradually to a situation that exemplified the desired new model.

Another line of inquiry focuses on the spontaneous analogies people use as mental models of the world. This research generally begins with a questionnaire or interview to elicit the person's own analogical models. For example, Willet Kempton in 1986 used interviews to uncover two common analogical models of home heating systems. In the (incorrect) valve model, the thermostat is like a faucet: It controls the rate at which the furnace produces heat. In the (correct) threshold model, the thermostat is like an oven: It simply controls the goal temperature, and the furnace runs at a constant rate. Kempton then examined household thermostat records and found patterns of thermostat settings corresponding to the two analogies. Some families constantly adjusted their thermostats from high to low temperatures, an expensive strategy that follows from the valve model. Others simply set their thermostat twice a day—low at night, higher by day, consistent with the threshold model.

Analogy in Children

Research on the development of analogy shows a relational shift in focus from object commonalities to relational commonalities. This shift appears to result from gains in domain knowledge, as Gentner and Mary Jo Rattermann suggested in 1991, and perhaps from gains in processing capacity as suggested by Graeme Halford in 1993. In 1989 Ann Brown showed that young children's success in analogical transfer tasks increased when the domains were familiar to them and they were given training in the relevant relations. For example, three-year-olds can transfer solutions across simple tasks involving familiar relations such as stacking and pulling, and six-year-olds can transfer more complex solutions. In 1987 Kayoko Inagaki and Giyoo Hatano studied spontaneous analogies in five- to six-year-old children by asking questions such as whether they could keep a baby rabbit small and cute forever. The children often made analogies to humans, such as "We cannot keep the baby the same size forever because he takes food. If he eats, he will become bigger and bigger and be an adult." Children were more often correct when they used these personification analogies than when they did not. This suggests that children were using humans—a familiar, well-understood domain—as a base domain for reasoning about similar creatures.

Retrieval of Analogs: The Inert Knowledge Problem

Learning from cases is often easier than learning principles directly. Despite its usefulness, however, training with examples and cases often fails to lead to transfer, because people fail to retrieve potentially useful analogs. For example, Mary Gick and Holyoak found in 1980 that participants given an insight problem typically failed to solve it, even when they had just read a story with an analogous solution. Yet, when they were told to use the prior example, they were able to do so. This shows that the prior knowledge was not lost from memory; this failure to access prior structurally similar cases is, rather, an instance of "inert knowledge"—knowledge that is not accessed when needed.

One explanation for this failure of transfer is that people often encode cases in a situation-specific manner, so that later remindings occur only for highly similar cases. For example, in 1984 Ross gave people mathematical problems to study and later gave them new problems. Most of their later remindings were to examples that were similar only on the surface, irrespective of whether the principles matched. Experts in a domain are more likely than novices to retrieve structurally similar examples, but even experts retrieve some examples that are similar only on the surface. However, as demonstrated by Laura Novick in 1988, experts reject spurious remindings more quickly than do novices. Thus, especially for novices, there is an unfortunate dissociation: While accuracy of transfer depends critically on the degree of structural match, memory retrieval depends largely on surface similarity between objects and contexts.

Analogical Encoding in Learning

In the late twentieth century, researchers began exploring a new technique, called analogical encoding, that can help overcome the inert knowledge problem. Instead of studying cases separately, learners are asked to compare analogous cases and describe their similarities. This fosters the formation of a common schema, which in turn facilitates transfer to a further problem. For example, in 1999 Jeffrey Loewenstein, Leigh Thompson, and Gentner found that graduate management students who compared two analogical cases were nearly three times more likely to transfer the common strategy into a subsequent negotiation task than were students who analyzed the same two cases separately.

Implications for Education

Analogies can be of immense educational value. They permit rapid learning of a new domain by transferring knowledge from a known domain, and they promote noticing and abstracting principles across domains. Analogies are most successful, however, if their pitfalls are understood. In analogical mapping, it is important to ensure that the base domain is understood well, that the correspondences are clear, and that differences and potentially incorrect inferences are clearly flagged. When teaching for transfer, it is important to recognize that learners tend to rely on surface features. One solution is to minimize surface features by using simple objects. Another is to induce analogical encoding by asking learners to explicitly compare cases. The better educators understand analogical processes, the better they can harness them for education.

See also: LEARNING, *subentry on* TRANSFER OF LEARNING; LEARNING THEORY, *subentry on* HISTORICAL OVERVIEW.

BIBLIOGRAPHY

BASSOK, MIRIAM. 2001. "Semantic Alignments in Mathematical Word Problems." In *The Analogical Mind: Perspectives from Cognitive Science,* ed. Dedre Gentner, Keith J. Holyoak, and Biocho N. Kokinov. Cambridge, MA: MIT Press.

BRANSFORD, JOHN D.; FRANKS, JEFFREY J.; VYE, NANCY J.; and SHERWOOD, ROBERT D. 1989. "New Approaches to Instruction: Because Wisdom Can't Be Told." In *Similarity and Analogical Reasoning,* ed. Stella Vosniadou and Andrew Ortony. New York: Cambridge University Press.

BROWN, ANN L. 1989. "Analogical Learning and Transfer: What Develops?" In *Similarity and Analogical Reasoning,* ed. Stella Vosniadou and Andrew Ortony. New York: Cambridge University Press.

BROWN, ANN L., and KANE, MARY JO. 1988. "Preschool Children Can Learn to Transfer: Learning to Learn and Learning from Example." *Cognitive Psychology* 20:493–523.

CHEN, ZHE, and DAEHLER, MARVIN W. 1989. "Positive and Negative Transfer in Analogical Problem Solving by Six-Year-Old Children." *Cognitive Development* 4:327–344.

CLEMENT, JOHN. 1993. "Using Bridging Analogies and Anchoring Intuitions to Deal with Students' Preconceptions in Physics." *Journal of Research in Science Teaching* 30:1241–1257.

GENTNER, DEDRE. 1982. "Are Scientific Analogies Metaphors?" In *Metaphor: Problems and Per-*

spectives, ed. David S. Miall. Brighton, Eng.: Harvester Press.

GENTNER, DEDRE. 1983. "Structure-Mapping: A Theoretical Framework for Analogy." *Cognitive Science* 7:155–170.

GENTNER, DEDRE, and RATTERMANN, MARY JO. 1991. "Language and the Career of Similarity." In *Perspectives on Thought and Language: Interrelations in Development,* ed. Susan A. Gelman and James P. Brynes. London: Cambridge University Press.

GENTNER, DEDRE; RATTERMANN, MARY JO; and FORBUS, KENNETH D. 1993. "The Roles of Similarity in Transfer: Separating Retrievability from Inferential Soundness." *Cognitive Psychology* 25:524–575.

GENTNER, DEDRE, and TOUPIN, CECILE. 1986. "Systematicity and Surface Similarity in the Development of Analogy." *Cognitive Science* 10:277–300.

GENTNER, DEDRE, and WOLFF, PHILLIP. 2000. "Metaphor and Knowledge Change." In *Cognitive Dynamics: Conceptual Change in Humans and Machines,* ed. Eric Dietrich and Arthur B. Markman. Mahwah, NJ: Erlbaum.

GICK, MARY L., and HOLYOAK, KEITH J. 1980. "Analogical Problem Solving." *Cognitive Psychology* 12:306–355.

GICK, MARY L., and HOLYOAK, KEITH J. 1983. "Schema Induction and Analogical Transfer." *Cognitive Psychology* 15:1–38.

GOSWAMI, USHA. 1992. *Analogical Reasoning in Children.* Hillsdale, NJ: Erlbaum.

HALFORD, GRAEME S. 1993. *Children's Understanding: The Development of Mental Models.* Hillsdale, NJ: Erlbaum.

HOLYOAK, KEITH J., and KOH, K. 1987. "Surface and Structural Similarity in Analogical Transfer." *Memory and Cognition* 15:332–340.

HOLYOAK, KEITH J., and THAGARD, PAUL R. 1995. *Mental Leaps: Analogy in Creative Thought.* Cambridge, MA: MIT Press.

INAGAKI, KAYOKO, and HATANO, GIYOO. 1987. "Young Children's Spontaneous Personification as Analogy." *Child Development* 58:1013–1020.

KEMPTON, WILLET. 1986. "Two Theories of Home Heat Control." *Cognitive Science* 10:75–90.

KOLODNER, JANET L. 1997. "Educational Implications of Analogy: A View from Case-Based Reasoning." *American Psychologist* 52:(1)57–66.

LOEWENSTEIN, JEFFREY; THOMPSON, LEIGH; and GENTNER, DEDRE. 1999. "Analogical Encoding Facilitates Knowledge Transfer in Negotiation." *Psychonomic Bulletin and Review* 6:586–597.

MARKMAN, ARTHUR B., and GENTNER, DEDRE. 2000. "Structure Mapping in the Comparison Process." *American Journal of Psychology* 113:501–538.

NOVICK, LAURA R. 1988. "Analogical Transfer, Problem Similarity, and Expertise." *Journal of Experimental Psychology: Learning, Memory, and Cognition* 14:510–520.

PERFETTO, GREG A.; BRANSFORD, JOHN D.; and FRANKS, JEFFREY J. 1983. "Constraints on Access in a Problem Solving Context." *Memory and Cognition* 11:24–31.

REED, STEVE K. 1987. "A Structure-Mapping Model for Word Problems." *Journal of Experimental Psychology: Learning, Memory, and Cognition* 13:124–139.

ROSS, BRIAN H. 1984. "Remindings and Their Effects in Learning a Cognitive Skill." *Cognitive Psychology* 16:371–416.

ROSS, BRIAN H. 1987. "This Is Like That: The Use of Earlier Problems and the Separation of Similarity Effects." *Journal of Experimental Psychology: Learning, Memory, and Cognition* 13:629–639.

ROSS, BRIAN H. 1989. "Distinguishing Types of Superficial Similarities: Different Effects on the Access and Use of Earlier Problems." *Journal of Experimental Psychology: Learning, Memory, and Cognition* 15:456–468.

SCHANK, ROGER C.; KASS, ALEX; and RIESBECK, CHRISTOPHER K., eds. 1994. *Inside Case-Based Explanation.* Hillsdale, NJ: Erlbaum.

SCHWARTZ, DANIEL L., and BRANSFORD, JOHN D. 1998. "A Time for Telling." *Cognition and Instruction* 16:475–522.

SPIRO, RAND J.; FELTOVICH, PAUL J.; COULSON, RICHARD L.; and ANDERSON, DANIEL K. 1989. "Multiple Analogies for Complex Concepts: Antidotes for Analogy-Induced Misconception in Advanced Knowledge Acquisition." In *Similarity and Analogical Reasoning,* ed. Stella Vosniadou and Andrew Ortony. New York: Cambridge University Press.

DEDRE GENTNER
JEFFREY LOEWENSTEIN

CAUSAL REASONING

A doorbell rings. A dog runs through a room. A seated man rises to his feet. A vase falls from a table and breaks. Why did the vase break? To answer this question, one must perceive and infer the causal relationships between the breaking of the vase and other events. Sometimes, the event most directly causally related to an effect is not immediately apparent (e.g., the dog hit the table), and conscious and effortful thought may be required to identify it. People routinely make such efforts because detecting causal connections among events helps them to make sense of the constantly changing flow of events. Causal reasoning enables people to find meaningful order in events that might otherwise appear random and chaotic, and causal understanding helps people to plan and predict the future. Thus, in 1980 the philosopher John Mackie described causal reasoning as "the cement of the universe." How, then, does one decide which events are causally related? When does one engage in causal reasoning? How does the ability to think about cause–effect relations originate and develop during infancy and childhood? How can causal reasoning skills be promoted in educational settings, and does this promote learning? These questions represent important issues in research on causal reasoning

Causal Perceptions and Causal Reasoning

An important distinction exists between causal perceptions and causal reasoning. Causal perceptions refer to one's ability to sense a causal relationship without conscious and effortful thought. According to the philosopher David Hume (1711–1776), perceptual information regarding contiguity, precedence, and covariation underlies the understanding of causality. First, events that are temporally and spatially contiguous are perceived as causally related. Second, the causal precedes the effect. Third, events that regularly co-occur are seen as causally related. In contrast, causal reasoning requires a person to reason through a chain of events to infer the cause of that event. People most often engage in causal reasoning when they experience an event that is out of the ordinary. Thus, in some situations a person may not know the cause of an unusual event and must search for it, and in other situations must evaluate whether one known event was the cause of another. The first situation may present difficulty because the causal event may not be immediately apparent. Philosophers have argued that causal reasoning is based on an assessment of criteria of necessity and sufficiency in these circumstances. A necessary cause is one that must be present for the effect to occur. Event A is necessary for event B if event B will not occur without event A. For example, the vase would not have broken if the dog had not hit the table. A cause is sufficient if its occurrence can by itself bring about the effect (i.e., whenever event A occurs, event B always follows). Often, more than one causal factor is present. In the case of multiple necessary causes, a set of causal factors taken together jointly produces an effect. In the case of multiple sufficient causes, multiple factors are present, any one of which by itself is sufficient to produce an effect.

The Development of Causal Perception and Causal Reasoning Skills

Causal perception appears to begin during infancy. Between three and six months of age, infants respond differently to temporally and spatially contiguous events (e.g., one billiard ball contacting a second that begins to roll immediately) compared to events that lack contiguity (e.g., the second ball begins to roll without collision or does not start to move until half a second after collision). Thus, the psychologist Alan Leslie proposed in 1986 that infants begin life with an innate perceptual mechanism specialized to automatically detect cause–effect relations based on contiguity. However, psychologists Leslie Cohen and Lisa Oakes reported in 1993 that familiarity with role of a particular object in a causal sequence influence ten-month-old infants' perception of causality. Therefore, they suggest that infants do not automatically perceive a causal connection when viewing contiguous events. The question of whether infants begin with an innate ability to automatically detect causality, or instead gradually develop casual perception through general learning processes remains a central controversy concerning the origins of causal thought.

Although infants perceive causal relationships, complex causal reasoning emerges during early childhood and grows in sophistication thereafter. Thus, information about precedence influences causal reasoning during childhood. When asked to determine what caused an event to occur, three-year-olds often choose an event that preceded it, rather than one that came later, but understanding of precedence becomes more consistent and general beginning at five years of age. Unlike contiguity and precedence, information about covariation is not available from a single casual sequence, but requires repeated experience with the co-occurrence of a cause and effect. Children do not begin to use co-variation information consistently in their casual thinking before eight years of age. Because the various types of information relevant to causality do not always suggest the same causal relation, children and adults must decide which type of information is most important in a particular situation.

In addition to the perceptual cues identified by Hume, knowledge of specific causal mechanisms plays a central role in causal reasoning. By three years of age, children expect there to be some mechanism of transmission between cause and effect, and knowledge of possible mechanisms influences both children's and adults' interpretation of perceptual cues. For instance, when a possible causal mechanism requires time to produce an effect (e.g., a marble rolling down a lengthy tube before contacting another object), or transmits quickly across a distance (e.g., electrical wiring), children as young as five years of age are more likely to select causes that lack temporal spatial contiguity than would otherwise be the case. Because causal mechanisms differ for physical, social, and biological events, children must acquire distinct conceptual knowledge to understand causality in each of these domains. By three to four years of age, children recognize that whereas physical effects are caused by physical transmission, human action is motivated internally by mental states such as desires, beliefs, and intentions, and they begin to understand some properties of biological processes such as growth and heredity. Furthermore, conceptual understanding of specific causal mechanisms may vary across cultures and may be learned through social discourse as well as through direct experience.

A fundamental understanding of causality is present during early childhood; however, prior to adolescence children have difficulty searching for causal relations through systematic scientific experimentation. Preadolescents may generate a single causal hypothesis and seek confirmatory evidence, misinterpret contradictory evidence, or design experimental tests that do not provide informative evidence. In contrast, adolescents and adults may generate several alternative hypotheses and test them by systematically controlling variables and seeking both disconfirmatory and confirmatory evidence. Nevertheless, even adults often have difficulty designing valid scientific experiments. More generally, both children and adults often have difficulty identifying multiple necessary or sufficient causes.

Teaching Causal Reasoning Skills

The psychologist Diane Halpern argued in 1998 that critical thinking skills should be taught in primary, secondary, and higher educational settings. Casual reasoning is an important part of critical thinking because it enables one to explain and predict events, and thus potentially to control one's environment and achieve desired outcomes.

Three approaches to teaching causal reasoning skills may be efficacious. First, causal reasoning skills can be promoted by teaching students logical deduction. For example, teaching students to use counterfactual reasoning may help them assess whether there is a necessary relationship between a potential cause and an effect. Counterfactual reasoning requires student to imagine that a potential cause did not occur and to infer whether the effect would have occurred in its absence. If it would occur, then there is no causal relationship between the two events.

Second, causal reasoning skills can be promoted by teaching students to generate informal explanations for anomalous events or difficult material. For instance, learning from scientific texts can be particularly challenging to students, and often students have the misconception that they do not have adequate knowledge to understand texts. The psychologist Michelene Chi demonstrated in 1989 that students who use their general world knowledge to engage in causal, explanatory reasoning while reading difficult physics texts understand what they read considerably better than do students who do not draw upon general knowledge in this way. Furthermore, in 1999 the psychologist Danielle McNamara developed a reading training intervention that promotes explanatory reasoning during reading. In this program, students were taught a number of strategies to help them to use both information in the text and general knowledge to generate explanations for difficult material. Training improved both comprehension of scientific texts and overall class performance, and was particularly beneficial to at-risk students.

Third, the psychologist Leona Schauble demonstrated in 1990 that causal reasoning skills can be promoted by teaching students the principles of scientific experimentation. A primary goal of experimentation is to determine causal relationships among a set of events. Students may be taught to identify a potential cause of an effect, manipulate the presence of the cause in a controlled setting, and assesses whether or not the effect occurs. Thus, students learn to use the scientific method to determine whether there are necessary and sufficient relationships between a potential cause and an effect. Because the principles of science are often difficult for students to grasp, teaching these principles would provide students with formal procedures for evaluating causal relationships in the world around them.

See also: LEARNING, *subentry on* REASONING; LEARNING THEORY, *subentry on* HISTORICAL OVERVIEW; LITERACY, *subentry on* NARRATIVE COMPREHENSION AND PRODUCTION; READING, *subentries on* COMPREHENSION, CONTENT AREAS.

BIBLIOGRAPHY

BULLOCK, MERRY; GELMAN, ROCHEL; and BAILLARGEON, RENEE. 1982. "The Development of Causal Reasoning." In *The Developmental Psychology of Time,* ed. William J. Friedman. New York: Academic Press.

CHI, MICHELENE T. H., et al. 1989. "Self-Explanation: How Students Study and Use Examples in Learning to Solve Problems." *Cognitive Science* 13:145–182.

COHEN, LESLIE B., and OAKES, LISA M. 1993. "How Infants Perceive a Simple Causal Event." *Developmental Psychology* 29:421–433.

EPSTEIN, RICHARD L. 2002. *Critical Thinking,* 2nd edition. Belmont, CA: Wadsworth.

HALPERN, DIANE F. 1998. "Teaching Critical Thinking for Transfer across Domains." *American Psychologist* 53:449–455.

HUME, DAVID. 1960. *A Treatise on Human Nature* (1739). Oxford: Clarendon Press.

KUHN, D.; AMSEL, ERIC; and O'LOUGHLIN, MICHAEL. 1988. *The Development of Scientific Thinking Skills.* San Diego, CA: Academic Press.

LESLIE, ALAN M. 1986. "Getting Development off the Ground: Modularity and the Infant's Perception of Causality." In *Theory Building in Developmental Psychology,* ed. Paul Van Geert. Amsterdam: North-Holland.

MACKIE, JOHN L. 1980. *The Cement of the Universe.* Oxford: Clarendon Press.

McNAMARA, DANIELLE S., and SCOTT, JEREMY L. 1999. *Training Reading Strategies.* Hillsdale, NJ: Erlbaum.

SCHAUBLE, LEONA. 1990. "Belief Revision in Children: The Role of Prior Knowledge and Strategies for Generating Evidence." *Journal of Experimental Child Psychology* 49:31–57.

SEDLAK, ANDREA J., and KURTZ, SUSAN T. 1981. "A Review of Children's Use of Causal Inference Principles." *Child Development* 52:759–784.

WELLMAN, HENRY M., and GELMAN, SUSAN A. 1998. "Knowledge Acquisition in Foundational Domains." In *Handbook of Child Psychology: Cognition, Perception, and Language,* 5th edition, ed. Deanna Kuhn and Robert Siegler. New York: Wiley.

WHITE, PETER A. 1988. "Causal Processing: Origins and Development." *Psychological Bulletin* 104:36–52.

JOSEPH P. MAGLIANO
BRADFORD H. PILLOW

CONCEPTUAL CHANGE

The term *conceptual change* refers to the development of fundamentally new concepts, through restructuring elements of existing concepts, in the course of knowledge acquisition. Conceptual change is a particularly profound kind of learning—it goes beyond revising one's specific beliefs and involves restructuring the very concepts used to formulate those beliefs. Explaining how this kind of learning occurs is central to understanding the tremendous power and creativity of human thought.

The emergence of fundamentally new ideas is striking in the history of human thought, particularly in science and mathematics. Examples include the emergence of Darwin's concept of evolution by natural selection, Newton's concepts of gravity and inertia, and the mathematical concepts of zero, negative, and rational numbers. One of the challenges of education is how to transmit these complex products of human intellectual history to the next generation of students.

Although there are many unresolved issues about how concepts are mentally represented, conceptual-change researchers generally assume that explanatory concepts are defined and articulated within theory-like structures, and that conceptual change requires coordinated changes in multiple concepts within these structures. New concepts that have arisen in the history of science are clearly part of larger, explicit theories. Making an analogy between the organization of concepts in scientists and children, researchers have proposed that children may have "commonsense" theories in which their everyday explanatory concepts are embedded and play a role. These theories, although not self-consciously held, are assumed to be like scientific theories in that they consist of a set of interrelated concepts that resist change and that support inference making, problem solving, belief formation, and explanation in a given domain. The power and usefulness of this analogy is being explored in the early twenty-first century.

A challenge for conceptual-change researchers is to provide a typology of important forms of conceptual change. For example, conceptual differentiation is a form of conceptual change in which a newer (descendant) theory uses two distinct concepts where the initial (parent) theory used only one, and the undifferentiated parent concept unites elements that will subsequently be kept distinct. Examples of conceptual differentiation include: Galileo's differentiation of average and instantaneous velocity in his theory of motion, Black's differentiation of heat and temperature in his theory of thermal phenomena, and children's differentiation of weight and density in their matter theory. Conceptual differentiation is not the same as adding new subcategories to an existing category, which involves the elaboration of a conceptual structure rather than its transformation. In that case, the new subcategories fit into an existing structure, and the initial general category is still maintained. In differentiation, the parent concept is seen as incoherent from the perspective of the subsequent theory and plays no role in it. For example, an undifferentiated weight/density concept that unites the elements *heavy* and *heavy-for-size* combines two fundamentally different kinds of quantities: an extensive (total amount) quantity and an intensive (relationally defined) quantity.

Another form of conceptual change is *coalescence,* in which the descendant theory introduces a new concept that unites concepts previously seen to be of fundamentally different types in the parent theory. For example, Aristotle saw circular planetary and free-fall motions as natural motions that were fundamentally different from violent projectile motions. Newton coalesced circular, planetary, free-fall,

and projectile motions under a new category, *accelerated motion.* Similarly, children initially see plants and animals as fundamentally different: animals are behaving beings that engage in self-generated movement, while plants are not. Later they come to see them as two forms of "living things" that share important biological properties. Conceptual coalescence is not the same as simply adding a more general category by abstracting properties common to more specific categories. In conceptual coalescence the initial concepts are thought to be fundamentally different, and the properties that will be central to defining the new category are not represented as essential properties of the initial concepts.

Different forms of conceptual change mutually support each other. For example, conceptual coalescences (such as uniting free-fall and projectile motion in a new concept of accelerated motion, or plants and animals in a new concept of living things) are accompanied by conceptual differentiations (such as distinguishing uniform from accelerated motion, or distinguishing dead from inanimate). These changes are also supported by additional forms of conceptual change, such as re-analysis of the core properties or underlying structure of the concept, as well as the acquisition of new specific beliefs about the relations among concepts.

Mechanisms of Conceptual Change

One reason for distinguishing conceptual change from belief revision and conceptual elaboration is that different learning mechanisms may be required. Everyday learning involves knowledge enrichment and rests on an assumed set of concepts. For example, people use existing concepts to represent new facts, formulate new beliefs, make inductive or deductive inferences, and solve problems.

What makes conceptual change so challenging to understand is that it cannot occur in this way. The concepts of a new theory are ultimately organized and stated in terms of each other, rather than the concepts of the old theory, and there is no simple one-to-one correspondence between some concepts of the old and new theories. By what learning mechanisms, then, can scientists invent, and students comprehend, a genuinely new set of concepts and come to prefer them to their initial set of concepts?

Most theorists agree that one step in conceptual change for both students and scientists is experiencing some form of *cognitive dissonance*—an internal state of tension that arises when an existing conceptual system fails to handle important data and problems in a satisfactory manner. Such dissonance can be created by a series of unexpected results that cannot be explained by an existing theory, by the press to solve a problem that is beyond the scope of one's current theory, or by the detection of internal inconsistencies in one's thinking. This dissonance can signal the need to step outside the normal mode of *applying* one's conceptual framework to a more meta-conceptual mode of *questioning, examining, and evaluating* one's conceptual framework.

Although experiencing dissonance can signal that there is a conceptual problem to be solved, it does not solve that problem. Another step involves active attempts to invent or construct an understanding of alternative conceptual systems by using a variety of heuristic procedures and symbolic tools. Heuristic procedures, such as analogical reasoning, imagistic reasoning, and thought experiments, may be particularly important because they allow both students and scientists to creatively extend, combine, and modify existing conceptual resources via the construction of new models. Symbolic tools, such as natural language, the algebraic and graphical representations of mathematics, and other invented notational systems, allow the explicit representation of key relations in the new system of concepts.

In analogical reasoning, knowledge of conceptual relations in better-understood domains are powerful sources of new ideas about the less-understood domain. Analogical reasoning is often supported by imagistic reasoning, wherein one creates visual depictions of core ideas using visual analogs with the same underlying relational structure. These depictions allow the visualization of unseen theoretical entities, connect the problem to the well-developed human visual-spatial inferencing system, and, because much mathematical information is implicit in such depictions, facilitate the construction of appropriate mathematical descriptions of a given domain. Thought experiments use initial knowledge of a domain to run simulations of what should happen in various idealized situations, including imagining what happens as the effects of a given variable are entirely eliminated, thus facilitating the identification of basic principles not self-evident from everyday observation.

Case studies of conceptual change in the history of science and science education reveal that new intellectual constructions develop over an extended period of time and include intermediate, bridging constructions. For example, Darwin's starting idea of evolution via directed, adaptative variation initially prevented his making an analogy between this process and artificial selection. He transformed his understanding of this process using multiple analogies (first with wedging and Malthusian population pressure, and later with artificial selection), imagistic reasoning (e.g., visualizing the jostling effects of 100,000 wedges being driven into the same spot of ground to understand the tremendous power of the unseen force in nature and its ability to produce species change in a mechanistic manner), and thought experiments (e.g., imagining how many small effects might build up over multiple generations to yield a larger effect). Each contributed different elements to his final concept of natural selection, with his initial analogies leading to the bridging idea of selection acting in concert with the process of directed adaptive variation, rather than supplanting it.

Constructing a new conceptual system is also accompanied by a process of evaluating its adequacy against known alternatives using some set of criteria. These criteria can include: the new system's ability to explain the core problematic phenomena as well as other known phenomena in the domain, its internal consistency and fit with other relevant knowledge, the extent to which it meets certain explanatory ideals, and its capacity to suggest new fruitful lines of research.

Finally, researchers have examined the personal, motivational, and social processes that support conceptual change. Personal factors include courage, confidence in one's abilities, openness to alternatives, willingness to take risks, and deep commitment to an intellectual problem. Social factors include working in groups that combine different kinds of expertise and that encourage consideration of inconsistencies in data and relevant analogies. Indeed, many science educators believe a key to promoting conceptual change in the classroom is through creating a more reflective classroom discourse. Such discourse probes for alternative student views, encourages the clarification, negotiation, and elaboration of meanings, the detection of inconsistencies, and the use of evidence and argument in deciding among or integrating alternative views.

Educational Implications

Conceptual change is difficult under any circumstances, as it requires breaking out of the self-perpetuating circle of theory-based reasoning, making coordinated changes in a number of concepts, and actively constructing an understanding of new (more abstract) conceptual systems. Students need signals that conceptual change is needed, as well as good reasons to change their current conceptions, guidance about how to integrate existing conceptual resources in order to construct new conceptions, and the motivation and time needed to make those constructions. Traditional education practice often fails to provide students with the appropriate signals, guidance, motivation, and time.

Conceptual change is a protracted process calling for a number of coordinated changes in instructional practice. First, instruction needs to be grounded in the consideration of important phenomena or problems that are central to the experts' framework—and that challenge students' initial commonsense framework. These phenomena not only motivate conceptual change, but also constrain the search for, and evaluation of, viable alternatives. Second, instruction needs to guide students in the construction of new systems of concepts for understanding these phenomena. Teachers must know what heuristic techniques, representational tools, and conceptual resources to draw upon to make new concepts intelligible to students, and also how to build these constructions in a sequenced manner.

Third, instruction needs to be supported by a classroom discourse that encourages students to identify, represent, contrast, and debate the adequacy of competing explanatory frameworks in terms of emerging classroom epistemological standards. Such discourse supports many aspects of the conceptual-change process, including making students aware of their initial conceptions, helping students construct an understanding of alternative frameworks, motivating students to examine their conceptions more critically (in part through awareness of alternatives), and promoting their ability to evaluate, and at times integrate, competing frameworks.

Finally, instruction needs to provide students with extended opportunities for applying new systems of concepts to a wide variety of problems. Repeated applications develop students' skill at applying a new framework, refine their understanding of the framework, and help students appreciate its greater power and scope.

See also: CATEGORIZATION AND CONCEPT LEARNING; LEARNING, *subentry on* KNOWLEDGE ACQUISITION, REPRESENTATION, AND ORGANIZATION.

BIBLIOGRAPHY

CAREY, SUSAN. 1999. "Sources of Conceptual Change." In *Conceptual Development: Piaget's Legacy,* ed. Ellin K. Scholnick, Katherine Nelson, Susan A. Gelman, and Patricia H. Miller. Mahwah, NJ: Erlbaum.

CHI, MICHELINE. 1992. "Conceptual Change within and across Ontological Categories: Examples from Learning and Discovery in Science." In *Cognitive Models of Science,* ed. Ronald N. Giere. Minnesota Studies in the Philosophy of Science, Vol. 15. Minneapolis: University of Minnesota Press.

CHINN, CLARK A., and BREWER, WILLIAM F. 1993. "The Role of Anomalous Data in Knowledge Acquisition: A Theoretical Framework and Implications for Science Instruction." *Review of Educational Research* 63(1):1–49.

CLEMENT, JOHN. 1993. "Using Bridging Analogies and Anchoring Intuitions to Deal with Students' Preconceptions in Physics." *Journal of Research in Science Teaching* 30(10):1241–1257.

DUNBAR, KENNETH. 1995. "How Scientists Really Reason: Scientific Reasoning in Real-World Laboratories." In *The Nature of Insight,* ed. Robert J. Sternberg and Janet E. Davidson. Cambridge, MA: MIT Press.

GENTNER, DEDRE; BREM, SARAH; FERGUSON, RONALD; MARKMAN, ARTHUR; LEVIDOW, BJORN; WOLFF, PHILLIP; and FORBUS, KENNETH. 1997. "Analogical Reasoning and Conceptual Change: A Case Study of Johannes Kepler." *Journal of the Learning Sciences* 6(1):3–40.

LAURENCE, STEPHEN, and MARGOLIS, ERIC. 1999. "Concepts and Cognitive Science." In *Concepts: Core Readings,* ed. Eric Margolis and Stephen Laurence. Cambridge, MA: MIT Press.

LEHRER, RICHARD; SCHAUBLE, LEONA; CARPENTER, SUSAN; and PENNER, DAVID. 2000. "The Interrelated Development of Inscriptions and Conceptual Understanding." In *Symbolizing and Communicating in Mathematics Classrooms: Perspectives on Discourse, Tools, and Instructional Design,* ed. Paul Cobb, Erna Yackel, and Kay McClain. Mahwah, NJ: Erlbaum.

MILLMAN, ARTHUR B., and SMITH, CAROL L. 1997. "Darwin's Use of Analogical Reasoning in Theory Construction." *Metaphor and Symbol* 12(3):159–187.

NERCESSIAN, NANCY J. 1992. "How Do Scientists Think? Capturing the Dynamics of Conceptual Change in Science." In *Cognitive Models of Science*, ed. Ronald N. Giere. Minnesota Studies in the Philosophy of Science, Vol. 15. Minneapolis: University of Minnesota Press.

PINTRICH, PAUL R.; MARX, RONALD W.; and BOYLE, ROBERT A. 1993. "Beyond Cold Conceptual Change: The Role of Motivational Beliefs and Classroom Contextual Factors in the Process of Conceptual Change." *Review of Educational Research* 63(2):167–199.

POSNER, GERALD; STRIKE, KENNETH; HEWSON, PETER; and GERTZOG, W. A. 1982. "Accommodation of a Scientific Conception: Toward a Theory of Conceptual Change." *Science Education* 66:211–227.

SMITH, CAROL; MACLIN, DEBORAH; GROSSLIGHT, LORRAINE; and DAVIS, HELEN. 1997. "Teaching for Understanding: A Study of Students' Pre-instruction Theories of Matter and a Comparison of the Effectiveness of Two Approaches to Teaching about Matter and Density." *Cognition and Instruction* 15(3):317–393.

VAN ZEE, EMILY, and MINSTRELL, JIM. 1997. "Using Questioning to Guide Student Thinking." *Journal of the Learning Sciences* 6:227–269.

VOSNIADOU, STELLA, and BREWER, WILLIAM F. 1987. "Theories of Knowledge Restructuring in Development." *Review of Educational Research* 57:51–67.

WHITE, BARBARA. 1993. "ThinkerTools: Causal Models, Conceptual Change, and Science Instruction." *Cognition and Instruction* 10:1–100.

WISER, MARIANNE, and AMIN, TAMIR. 2001. "'Is Heat Hot?' Inducing Conceptual Change by Integrating Everyday and Scientific Perspectives on Thermal Phenomena." *Learning and Instruction* 11(4–5):331–355.

CAROL L. SMITH

KNOWLEDGE ACQUISITION, REPRESENTATION, AND ORGANIZATION

Knowledge acquisition is the process of absorbing and storing new information in memory, the success of which is often gauged by how well the information can later be remembered (retrieved from memory). The process of storing and retrieving information depends heavily on the representation and organization of the information. Moreover, the utility of knowledge can also be influenced by how the information is structured. For example, a bus schedule can be represented in the form of a map or a timetable. On the one hand, a timetable provides quick and easy access to the arrival time for each bus, but does little for finding where a particular stop is situated. On the other hand, a map provides a detailed picture of each bus stop's location, but cannot efficiently communicate bus schedules. Both forms of representation are useful, but it is important to select the representation most appropriate for the task at hand. Similarly, knowledge acquisition can be improved by considering the purpose and function of the desired information.

Knowledge Representation and Organization

There are numerous theories of how knowledge is represented and organized in the mind, including rule-based production models, distributed networks, and propositional models. However, these theories are all fundamentally based on the concept of *semantic networks*. A semantic network is a method of representing knowledge as a system of connections between concepts in memory.

Semantic Networks

According to semantic network models, knowledge is organized based on meaning, such that semantically related concepts are interconnected. Knowledge networks are typically represented as diagrams of nodes (i.e., concepts) and links (i.e., relations). The nodes and links are given numerical weights to represent their strengths in memory. In Figure 1, the node representing DOCTOR is strongly related to SCALPEL, whereas NURSE is weakly related to SCALPEL. These link strengths are represented here in terms of line width. Similarly, some nodes in Figure 1 are printed in bold type to represent their strength in memory. Concepts such as DOCTOR and BREAD are more memorable because they are

FIGURE 1

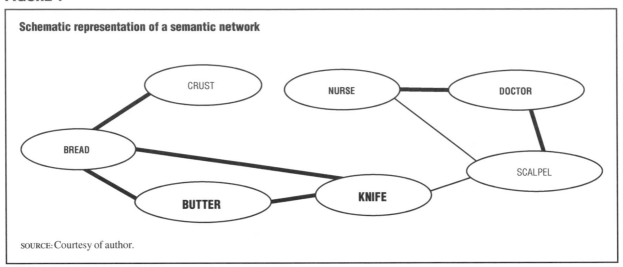

Schematic representation of a semantic network

SOURCE: Courtesy of author.

more frequently encountered than concepts such as SCALPEL and CRUST.

Mental excitation, or activation, spreads automatically from one concept to another related concept. For example, thinking of BREAD spreads activation to related concepts, such as BUTTER and CRUST. These concepts are *primed,* and thus more easily recognized or retrieved from memory. For example, in David Meyer and Roger Schvaneveldt's 1976 study (a typical semantic priming study), a series of words (e.g., BUTTER) and nonwords (e.g., BOTTOR) are presented, and participants determine whether each item is a word. A word is more quickly recognized if it follows a semantically related word. For example, BUTTER is more quickly recognized as a word if BREAD precedes it, rather than NURSE. This result supports the assumption that semantically related concepts are more strongly connected than unrelated concepts.

Network models represent more than simple associations. They must represent the ideas and complex relationships that comprise knowledge and comprehension. For example, the idea "The doctor uses a scalpel" can be represented as the proposition USE (DOCTOR, SCALPEL), which consists of the nodes DOCTOR and SCALPEL and the link USE (see Figure 2). Educators have successfully used similar diagrams, called concept maps, to communicate important relations and attributes among the key concepts of a lesson.

Types of Knowledge

There are numerous types of knowledge, but the most important distinction is between *declarative* and *procedural* knowledge. Declarative knowledge refers to one's memory for concepts, facts, or episodes, whereas procedural knowledge refers to the ability to perform various tasks. Knowledge of how to drive a car, solve a multiplication problem, or throw a football are all forms of procedural knowledge, called *procedures* or *productions.* Procedural knowledge may begin as declarative knowledge, but is proceduralized with practice. For example, when first learning to drive a car, you may be told to "put the key in the ignition to start the car," which is a declarative statement. However, after starting the car numerous times, this act becomes automatic and is completed with little thought. Indeed, procedural knowledge tends to be accessed automatically and require little attention. It also tends to be more durable (less susceptible to forgetting) than declarative knowledge.

Knowledge Acquisition

Listed below are five guidelines for knowledge acquisition that emerge from how knowledge is represented and organized.

Process the material semantically. Knowledge is organized semantically; therefore, knowledge acquisition is optimized when the learner focuses on the meaning of the new material. Fergus Craik and Endel Tulving were among the first to provide evidence for the importance of semantic processing. In their studies, participants answered questions con-

FIGURE 2

Schematic representation of ideas (propositions) in a semantic network

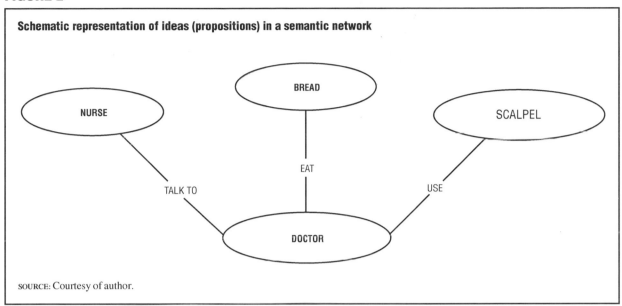

SOURCE: Courtesy of author.

cerning target words that varied according to the depth of processing involved. For example, semantic questions (e.g., Which word, *friend* or *tree*, fits appropriately in the following sentence: "He met a ____ on the street"?) involve a greater depth of processing than phonemic questions (e.g., Which word, *crate* or *tree*, rhymes with the word *late*?), which in turn have a greater depth than questions concerning the structure of a word (e.g., Which word is in capital letters: *TREE* or *tree*?). Craik and colleagues found that words processed semantically were better learned than words processed phonemically or structurally. Further studies have confirmed that learning benefits from greater semantic processing of the material.

Process and retrieve information frequently. A second learning principle is to test and retrieve the information numerous times. Retrieving, or self-producing, information can be contrasted with simply reading or copying it. Decades of research on a phenomenon called the *generation effect* have shown that passively studying items by copying or reading them does little for memory in comparison to self-producing, or *generating*, an item. Moreover, learning improves as a function of the number of times information is retrieved. Within an academic situation, this principle points to the need for frequent practice tests, worksheets, or quizzes. In terms of studying, it is also important to break up, or *distribute* retrieval attempts. Distributed retrieval can include studying or testing items in a random order,

with breaks, or on different days. In contrast, repeating information numerous times sequentially involves only a single retrieval from long-term memory, which does little to improve memory for the information.

Learning and retrieval conditions should be similar. How knowledge is represented is determined by the conditions and context (internal and external) in which it is learned, and this in turn determines how it is retrieved: Information is best retrieved when the conditions of learning and retrieval are the same. This principle has been referred to as *encoding specificity*. For example, in one experiment, participants were shown sentences with an adjective and a noun printed in capital letters (e.g. The CHIP DIP tasted delicious.) and told that their memory for the nouns would be tested afterward. In the recognition test, participants were shown the noun either with the original adjective (CHIP DIP), with a different adjective (SKINNY DIP), or without an adjective (DIP). Noun recognition was better when the original adjective (CHIP) was presented than when no adjective was presented. Moreover, presenting a different adjective (SKINNY) yielded the lowest recognition. This finding underscores the importance of matching learning and testing conditions.

Encoding specificity is also important in terms of the questions used to test memory or comprehension. Different types of questions tap into different levels of understanding. For example, recalling information involves a different level of understanding, and different mental processes, than recognizing information. Likewise, essay and open-ended questions assess a different level of understanding than multiple-choice questions. Essay and open-ended questions generally tap into a conceptual or situational understanding of the material, which results from an integration of text-based information and the reader's prior knowledge. In contrast, multiple-choice questions involve recognition processes, and typically assess a shallow or text-based understanding. A text-based representation can be impoverished and incomplete because it consists only of concepts and relations within the text. This level of understanding, likely developed by a student preparing for a multiple-choice exam, would be inappropriate preparation for an exam with open-ended or essay questions. Thus, students should benefit by adjusting their study practices according to the expected type of questions.

Alternatively, students may benefit from reviewing the material in many different ways, such as recognizing the information, recalling the information, and interpreting the information. These latter processes improve understanding and maximize the probability that the various ways the material is studied will match the way it is tested. From a teacher's point of view, including different types of questions on worksheets or exams ensures that each student will have an opportunity to convey their understanding of the material.

Connect new information to prior knowledge. Knowledge is interconnected; therefore, new material that is linked to prior knowledge will be better retained. A driving factor in text and discourse comprehension is prior knowledge. Skilled readers actively use their prior knowledge during comprehension. Prior knowledge helps the reader to fill in contextual gaps within the text and develop a better global understanding or situation model of the text. Given that texts rarely (if ever) spell out everything needed for successful comprehension, using prior knowledge to understand text and discourse is critical. Moreover, thinking about what one already knows about a topic provides connections in memory to the new information—the more connections that are formed, the more likely the information will be retrievable from memory.

Create cognitive procedures. Procedural knowledge is better retained and more easily accessed. Therefore, one should develop and use cognitive procedures when learning information. Procedures can include shortcuts for completing a task (e.g., using *fast 10s* to solve multiplication problems), as well as memory strategies that increase the distinctive meaning of information. Cognitive research has repeatedly demonstrated the benefits of memory strategies, or *mnemonics,* for enhancing the recall of information. There are numerous types of mnemonics, but one well-known mnemonic is the *method of loci.* This technique was invented originally for the purpose of memorizing long speeches in the times before luxuries such as paper and pencil were readily available. The first task is to imagine and memorize a series of distinct locations along a familiar route, such as a pathway from one campus building to another. Each topic of a speech (or word in a word list) can then be pictured in a location along the route. When it comes time to recall the speech or word list, the items are simply *found* by mentally traveling the pathway.

Mnemonics are generally effective because they increase semantic processing of the words (or phrases) and render them more meaningful by linking them to familiar concepts in memory. Mnemonics also provide ready-made, effective cues for retrieving information. Another important aspect of mnemonics is that mental imaging is often involved. Images not only render information more meaningful, but they provide an additional route for finding information in memory. As mentioned earlier, increasing the number of meaningful links to information in memory increases the likelihood it can be retrieved.

Strategies are also an important component of *meta-cognition,* which is the ability to think about, understand, and manage one's learning. First, one must develop an awareness of one's own thought processes. Simply being aware of thought processes increases the likelihood of more effective knowledge construction. Second, the learner must be aware of whether or not comprehension has been successful. Realizing when comprehension has failed is crucial to learning. The final, and most important stage of meta-cognitive processing is fixing the comprehension problem. The individual must be aware of, and use, strategies to remedy comprehension and learning difficulties. For successful knowledge acquisition to occur, all three of these processes must occur. Without thinking or worrying about learning, the student cannot realize whether the concepts have been successfully grasped. Without realizing that information has not been understood, the student cannot engage in strategies to remedy the situation. If nothing is done about a comprehension failure, awareness is futile.

Conclusion

Knowledge acquisition is integrally tied to how the mind organizes and represents information. Learning can be enhanced by considering the fundamental properties of human knowledge, as well as by the ultimate function of the desired information. The most important property of knowledge is that it is organized semantically; therefore, learning methods should enhance meaningful study of new information. Learners should also create as many links to the information as possible. In addition, learning methods should be matched to the desired outcome. Just as using a bus timetable to find a bus-stop location is ineffective, learning to recognize information will do little good on an essay exam.

See also: LEARNING, *subentry on* CONCEPTUAL CHANGE; READING, *subentry on* CONTENT AREAS.

BIBLIOGRAPHY

ANDERSON, JOHN R. 1982. "Acquisition of a Cognitive Skill." *Psychological Review* 89:369–406.

ANDERSON, JOHN R., and LEBIÈRE, CHRISTIAN. 1998. *The Atomic Components of Thought.* Mahwah, NJ: Erlbaum.

BRANSFORD, JOHN, and JOHNSON, MARCIA K. 1972. "Contextual Prerequisites for Understanding Some Investigations of Comprehension and Recall." *Journal of Verbal Learning and Verbal Behavior* 11:717–726.

CRAIK, FERGUS I. M., and TULVING, ENDEL. 1975. "Depth of Processing and the Retention of Words in Episodic Memory." *Journal of Experimental Psychology: General.* 194:268–294.

CROVITZ, HERBERT F. 1971. "The Capacity of Memory Loci in Artificial Memory." *Psychonomic Science* 24:187–188.

GLENBERG, ARTHUR M. 1979. "Component-Levels Theory of the Effects of Spacing of Repetitions on Recall and Recognition." *Memory and Cognition* 7:95–112.

GUASTELLO, FRANCINE; BEASLEY, MARK; and SINATRA, RICHARD. 2000. "Concept Mapping Effects on Science Content Comprehension of Low-Achieving Inner-City Seventh Graders." *RASE: Remedial and Special Education* 21:356–365.

HACKER, DOUGLAS J.; DUNLOSKY, JOHN; and GRAESSER, ARTHUR C. 1998. *Metacognition in Educational Theory and Practice.* Mahwah, NJ: Lawrence Erlbaum.

JENSEN, MARY BETH, and HEALY, ALICE F. 1998. "Retention of Procedural and Declarative Information from the Colorado Drivers' Manual." In *Memory Distortions and their Prevention,* ed. Margaret Jean Intons-Peterson and Deborah L. Best. Mahwah, NJ: Lawrence Erlbaum.

KINTSCH, WALTER. 1998. *Comprehension: A Paradigm for Cognition.* Cambridge, Eng.: Cambridge University Press.

LIGHT, LEAH L., and CARTER-SOBELL, LINDA. 1970. "Effects of Changed Semantic Context on Recognition Memory." *Journal of Verbal Learning and Verbal Behavior* 9:1–11.

McNAMARA, DANIELLE S., and KINTSCH, WALTER. 1996. "Learning from Text: Effects of Prior Knowledge and Text Coherence." *Discourse Processes* 22:247–287.

MELTON, ARTHUR W. 1967. "Repetition and Retrieval from Memory." *Science* 158:532.

MEYER, DAVID E., and SCHVANEVELDT, ROGER W. 1976. "Meaning, Memory Structure, and Mental Processes." *Science* 192:27–33.

PAIVIO, ALLEN. 1990. *Mental Representations: A Dual Coding Approach.* New York: Oxford University Press.

RUMELHART, DAVID E., and McCLELLAND, JAMES L. 1986. *Parallel Distributed Processing: Explorations in the Microstructure of Cognition,* Vol. 1: *Foundations.* Cambridge, MA: MIT Press.

SLAMECKA, NORMAN J., and GRAF, PETER. 1978. "The Generation Effect: Delineation of a Phenomenon." *Journal of Experimental Psychology: Human Learning and Memory* 4:592–604.

TULVING, ENDEL, and THOMPSON, DONALD M. 1973. "Encoding Specificity and Retrieval Processes in Episodic Memory." *Psychological Review* 80:352–373.

YATES, FRANCIS A. 1966. *The Art of Memory.* Chicago: University of Chicago Press.

DANIELLE S. MCNAMARA
TENAHA O'REILLY

NEUROLOGICAL FOUNDATION

Learning is mediated by multiple memory systems in the brain, each of which involves a distinct anatomical pathway and supports a particular form of memory representation. The major aim of research on memory systems is to identify and distinguish the different contributions of specific brain structures and pathways, usually by contrasting the effects of selective damage to specific brain areas. Another major strategy focuses on localizing brain areas that are activated, that is, whose neurons are activated during particular aspects of memory processing. Some of these studies use newly developed functional imaging techniques to view activation of brain areas in humans performing memory tests. Another approach seeks to characterize the cellular code for memory within the activity patterns of single nerve cells in animals, by asking how information is represented by the activity patterns within the circuits of different structures in the relevant brain systems.

Each of the brain's memory systems begins in the vast expanse of the cerebral cortex, specifically in the so-called cortical association areas (see Figure 1). These parts of the cerebral cortex provide major inputs to each of three main pathways of processing in subcortical areas related to distinct memory functions. One system mediates *declarative memory,* the memory for facts and events that can be brought to conscious recollection and can be expressed in a variety of ways outside the context of learning. This system involves connections from the cortical association areas to the hippocampus via the parahippocampal region. The main output of hippocampal and parahippocampal processing is back to the same cortical areas that provided inputs to the hippocampus, and are viewed as the long-term repository of declarative memories.

The other two main pathways involve cortical inputs to specific subcortical targets that send direct outputs that control behavior. One of these systems mediates *emotional memory,* the attachment of affiliations and aversions towards otherwise arbitrary stimuli and modulation of the strength of memories that involve emotional arousal. This system involves cortical (as well as subcortical) inputs to the amygdala as the nodal stage in the association of sensory inputs to emotional outputs effected via the hypothalamic-pituitary axis and autonomic nervous system, as well as emotional influences over widespread brain areas. The second of these systems mediates

procedural memory, the capacity to acquire habitual behavioral routines that can be performed without conscious control. This system involves cortical inputs to the striatum as a nodal stage in the association of sensory and motor cortical information with voluntary responses via the brainstem motor system. An additional, parallel pathway that mediates different aspects of sensori-motor adaptations involves sensory and motor systems pathways through the cerebellum.

The Declarative Memory System

Declarative memory is the "everyday" form of memory that most consider when they think of memory. Therefore, the remainder of this discussion will focus on the declarative memory system. Declarative memory is defined as a composite of episodic memory, the ability to recollect personal experiences, and semantic memory, the synthesis of the many episodic memories into the knowledge about the world. In addition, declarative memory supports the capacity for conscious recall and the flexible expression of memories, one's ability to search networks of episodic and semantic memories and to use this capacity to solve many problems.

Each of the major components of the declarative memory system contributes differently to declarative memory, although interactions between these areas are also essential. Initially, perceptual information as well as information about one's behavior is processed in many dedicated neocortical areas. While the entire cerebral cortex is involved in memory processing, the chief brain area that controls this processing is the prefrontal cortex. The processing accomplished by the prefrontal cortex includes the acquisition of complex cognitive rules and concepts and *working memory,* the capacity to store information briefly while manipulating or rehearsing the information under conscious control. In addition, the areas of the cortex also contribute critically to memory processing. Association areas in the prefrontal, temporal, and parietal cortex play a central role in cognition and in both the perception of sensory information and in maintenance of short-term traces of recently perceived stimuli. Furthermore, the organization of perceptual representations in cerebral cortical areas, and connections among these areas, are permanently modified by learning experiences, constituting the long term repository of memories.

The parahippocampal region, which receives convergent inputs from the neocortical association areas and sends return projections to all of these areas, appears to mediate the extended persistence of these cortical representations. Through interactions between these areas, processing within the cortex can take advantage of lasting parahippocampal representations, and so come to reflect complex associations between events that are processed separately in different cortical regions or occur sequentially in the same or different areas.

These individual contributions and their interactions are not conceived as sufficient to link representations of events to form episodic memories or to form generalizations across memories to create a semantic memory network. Such an organization requires the capacity to rapidly encode a sequence of events that make up an episodic memory, to retrieve that memory by re-experiencing one facet of the event, and to link the ongoing experience to stored episodic representations, forming the semantic network. The neuronal elements of the hippocampus contain the fundamental coding properties that can support this kind of organization.

However, interactions among the components of the system are undoubtedly critical. It is unlikely that the hippocampus has the storage capacity to contain all of one's episodic memories and the hippocampus is not the final storage site. Therefore, it seems likely that the hippocampal neurons are involved in mediating the reestablishment of detailed cortical representations, rather than storing the details themselves. Repetitive interactions between the cortex and hippocampus, with the parahippocampal region as intermediary, serve to sufficiently coactivate widespread cortical areas so that they eventually develop linkages between detailed memories without hippocampal mediation. In this way, the networking provided by the hippocampus underlies its role in the organization of the permanent memory networks in the cerebral cortex.

See also: BRAIN-BASED EDUCATION.

BIBLIOGRAPHY

EICHENBAUM, HOWARD. 2000. "A Cortical-Hippocampal System for Declarative Memory." *Nature Reviews Neuroscience* 1:41–50.

EICHENBAUM, HOWARD, and COHEN, NEAL J. 2001. *From Conditioning to Conscious Recollection: Memory Systems of the Brain.* Upper Saddle River, NJ: Oxford University Press.

FIGURE 1

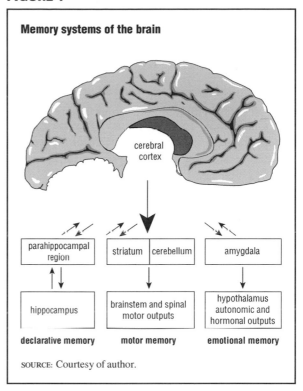

Memory systems of the brain

SOURCE: Courtesy of author.

SCHACTER, DANIEL L., and TULVING, ENDEL, eds. 1994. *Memory Systems 1994.* Cambridge, MA: MIT Press.

SQUIRE, LARRY R., and KANDEL, ERIC R. 1999. *Memory: From Mind to Molecules.* New York: Scientific American Library.

SQUIRE, LARRY R.; KNOWLTON, BARBARA; and MUSEN, GAIL. 1993. "The Structure and Organization of Memory." *Annual Review of Psychology* 44:453–495.

HOWARD EICHENBAUM

PERCEPTUAL PROCESSES

As Eleanor Gibson wrote in her classic text *Principles of Perceptual Learning and Development,* perceptual learning results in changes in the pickup of information as a result of practice or experience. Perception and action are a cycle: People act in order to learn about their surroundings, and they use what they learn to guide their actions. From this perspective, the critical defining features of perception include the exploratory actions of the perceiver and the knowledge of the events, animate and inanimate objects, and surrounding environment gained while engaged in looking, listening, touching, walking, and other forms of direct observation. Perception often results in learning information that is directly relevant to the goals at hand, but sometimes it results in learning that is incidental to one's immediate goals.

Perception becomes more skillful with practice and experience, and perceptual learning can be thought of as the education of attention. Perceivers come to notice the features of situations that are relevant to their goals and not to notice the irrelevant features. Three general principles of perceptual learning seem particularly relevant. First, unskillful perceiving requires much concentrated attention, whereas skillful perceiving requires less attention and is more easily combined with other tasks. Second, unskillful perceiving involves noticing both the relevant and irrelevant features of sensory stimulation without understanding their meaning or relevance to one's goals, whereas skillful perceiving involves narrowing one's focus to relevant features and understanding the situations they specify. And third, unskillful perceiving often involves attention to the proximal stimulus (that is, the patterns of light or acoustic or pressure information on the retinas, cochleae, and skin, respectively), whereas skillful perceiving involves attention to the distal event that is specified by the proximal stimulus.

Different Domains

Perceptual learning refers to relatively durable gains in perception that occur across widely different domains. For example, at one extreme are studies demonstrating that with practice adults can gain exquisite sensitivity to vernier discriminations, that is, the ability to resolve gaps in lines that approach the size of a single retinal receptor. At the opposite extreme, perceptual learning plays a central role in gaining expertise in the many different content areas of work, everyday life, and academic pursuits.

In the realm of work, classic examples include farmers learning to differentiate the sex of chickens, restaurateurs learning to differentiate different dimensions of fine wine, airplane pilots misperceiving their position relative to the ground, and machinists and architects learning to "see" the three-dimensional shape of a solid object or house from the top, side, and front views.

In the realm of everyday life, important examples include learning to perceive emotional expres-

sions, learning to identify different people and understand their facial expressions, learning to differentiate the different elements of speech when learning a second language, and learning to differentiate efficient routes to important destinations when faced with new surroundings.

In "nonacademic" subjects within the realm of academic pursuits, important examples involve music, art, and sports. For example, music students learn to differentiate the notes, chords, and instrumental voices in a piece, and they learn to identify pieces by period and composer. Art students learn to differentiate different strokes, textures, and styles, and they learn to classify paintings by period and artist. Athletes learn to differentiate the different degrees of freedom that need to be controlled to produce a winning "play" and to anticipate what actions need to be taken when on a playing field.

Finally, perceptual learning plays an equally broad role in classically academic subjects. For example, mathematics students gain expertise at perceiving graphs, classifying the shapes of curves, and knowing what equations might fit a given curve. Science students gain expertise at perceiving laboratory setups. These range widely across grade levels and domains, including the critical features of hydrolyzing water in a primary school general science setting, molecular structures in organic chemistry and genetics, frog dissections in biology, the functional relation of the frequency of waves and diffraction in different media in physics, and the critical features of maps in geology.

The borders separating perceptual learning from conceiving and reasoning often become blurred. And indeed, people perceive in order to understand, and their understanding leads to more and more efficient perception. For example, Herbert A. Simon elaborated on this in 2001 in his discussion of the visual thinking involved in having an expert understanding of the dynamics of a piston in an internal combustion engine. When experts look at a piston or a diagram of a piston or a graph representing the dynamics of a piston, they "see" the higher order, relevant variables, for example, that more work is performed when the combustion explosion moves the piston away from the cylinder's base than when the piston returns toward the base. The ability to "see" such higher-order relations is not just a question of good visual acuity, but it instead depends on content knowledge (about energy, pressure, and work) and on an understanding of how energy acts in the context of an internal combustion engine. In a 2001 article, Daniel Schwartz and John Bransford emphasized that experience with contrasting cases helps students differentiate the critical features when they are working to understand statistics and other academic domains. In a 1993 article, J. Littlefield and John Rieser demonstrated the skill of middle school students at differentiating relevant from irrelevant information when attempting to solve story problems in mathematics.

Classical Issues in Perceptual Learning and Perceptual Development

Perceptual development involves normative age-related changes in basic sensory sensitivities and in perceptual learning. Some of these changes are constrained by the biology of development in well-defined ways. For example, the growth in auditory frequency during the first year of life is mediated in part by changes in the middle ear and inner ear. Growth in visual acuity during the first two years is mediated in several ways: by changes in the migration of retinal cells into a fovea, through increasing control of convergence eye movements so that the two eyes fixate the same object, and through increasing control of the accommodate state of the lens so that fixated objects are in focus. The role of physical changes in the development of other perceptual skills, for example, perceiving different cues for depth, is less clear.

Nativism and empiricism are central to the study of perception and perceptual development. Stemming from philosophy's interest in epistemology, early nativists (such as seventeenth-century French mathematician and philosopher René Descartes and eighteenth-century German philosopher Immanuel Kant) argued that the basic capacities of the human mind were innate, whereas empiricists argued that they were learned, primarily through associations. This issue has long been hotly debated in the field of perceptual learning and development. How is it that the mind and brain come to perceive three-dimensional shapes from two-dimensional retinal projections; perceive distance; segment the speech stream; represent objects that become covered from view? The debate is very lively in the early twenty-first century, with some arguing that perception of some basic properties of the world is innate, and others arguing that it is learned, reflecting the statistical regularities in experience. Given that experience plays a role in some forms of perceptual learning, there is evidence that the timing of the experience can be critical to whether, and to what degree, it is learned effectively.

The "constancy" of perception is a remarkable feat of perceptual development. The issue is that the energy that gives rise to the perception of a particular object or situation varies widely when the perceiver or object moves, the lighting changes, and so forth. Given the flux in the sensory input, how is it that people manage to perceive that the objects and situations remain (more or less) the same? Research about perceptual constancies has reemerged as an important topic as computer scientists work to design artificial systems that can "learn to see."

Intersensory coordination is a major feature of perception and perceptual development. How is it, for example, that infants can imitate adult models who open their mouths wide or stick out their tongues? How is it that infants can identify objects by looking at them or by touching them and can recognize people by seeing them or listening to them?

The increasing control of actions with age is a major result of perceptual learning, as infants become more skillful at perceiving steps and other features of the ground and learn to control their balance when walking up and down slopes.

In 1955 James Gibson and Eleanor Gibson wrote an important paper titled "Perceptual Learning: Differentiation or Enrichment?" By differentiation they meant skill at distinguishing smaller and smaller differences among objects of a given kind. By enrichment they meant knowledge of the ways that objects and events tend to be associated with other objects and events. Their paper was in part a reaction to the predominant view of learning at the time: that learning was the "enrichment" of responses through their association with largely arbitrary stimulus conditions. The authors provided a sharp counterpoint to this view. Instead of conceiving of the world as constructed by add-on processes of association, they viewed perceivers as actively searching for the stimuli they needed to guide their actions and decisions, and in this way coming to differentiate the relevant features situated in a given set of circumstances from the irrelevant ones.

See also: ATTENTION; LEARNING THEORY, *subentry on* HISTORICAL OVERVIEW.

BIBLIOGRAPHY

ACREDOLO, LINDA P.; PICK, HERB L.; and OLSEN, M. 1975. "Environmental Differentiation and Familiarity as Determinants of Children's Memory for Spatial Location." *Developmental Psychology* 11:495–501.

ADOLPH, KAREN E. 1997. *Learning in the Development of Infant Locomotion.* Chicago: University of Chicago Press.

ARNHEIM, RUDOLPH. 1974. *Art and Visual Perception: A Psychology of the Creative Eye.* Berkeley: University of California Press.

ASLIN, RICHARD N. 1998. "Speech and Auditory Processing during Infancy: Constraints on and Precursors to Language." In *Handbook of Child Psychology,* 5th edition, ed. William Damon, Vol. 2: *Cognition, Perception, and Language,* ed. Deanna Kuhn and Robert S. Siegler. New York: Wiley.

BAHRICK, LORRAINE E., and LICKLITER, ROBERT. 2000. "Intersensory Redundancy Guides Attentional Selectivity and Perceptual Learning in Infancy." *Developmental Psychology* 36:190–201.

BAILLARGEON, RENEE. 1994. "How Do Infants Learn about the Physical World?" *Current Directions in Psychological Science* 3:133–140.

BARSALOU, LAWRENCE W. 1999. "Perceptual Symbol Systems." *Behavior and Brain Sciences* 22:577–660.

BRANSFORD, JOHN D., and SCHWARTZ, DANIEL L. 2000. "Rethinking Transfer: A Simple Proposal with Multiple Implications." *Review of Research in Education* 24:61–100.

BRYANT, PETER, and SOMERVILLE, S. 1986. "The Spatial Demands of Graphs." *British Journal of Psychology* 77:187–197.

DODWELL, PETER C., ed. 1970. *Perceptual Learning and Adaptation: Selected Readings.* Harmondsworth, Eng.: Penguin.

DOWLING, W. JAY., and HARWOOD, DANE L. 1986. *Music Cognition.* New York: Academic Press.

EPSTEIN, WILLIAM. 1967. *Varieties of Perceptual Learning.* New York: McGraw-Hill.

FAHLE, MANFRED, and POGGIO, TOMASO, eds. 2000. *Perceptual Learning.* Cambridge, MA: MIT Press.

GARLING, TOMMY, and EVANS, GARY W. 1991. *Environment, Cognition, and Action: An Integrated Approach.* New York: Oxford University Press.

GIBSON, ELEANOR J. 1969. *Principles of Perceptual Learning and Development.* Englewood Cliffs, NJ: Prentice-Hall.

GIBSON, ELEANOR J., and PICK, ANNE D. 2000. *An Ecological Approach to Perceptual Learning and Development.* New York: Oxford University Press.

GIBSON, ELEANOR J., and WALK, RICHARD D. 1961. "The 'Visual Cliff.'" *Scientific American* 202:64–71.

GIBSON, JAMES J., and GIBSON, ELEANOR J. 1955. "Perceptual Learning: Differentiation or Enrichment?" *Psychological Review* 62:32–41.

GOLDSTONE, ROBERT L. 1998. "Perceptual Learning." *Annual Review of Psychology* 49:585–612.

GOODNOW, JACQUELINE J. 1978. "Visible Thinking: Cognitive Aspects of Change in Drawings." *Child Development* 49:637–641.

GRANRUD, CARL E. 1993. *Visual Perception and Cognition in Infancy.* Hillsdale, NJ: Erlbaum.

HABER, RALPH N. 1987. "Why Low-Flying Fighter Planes Crash: Perceptual and Attentional Factors in Collisions with the Ground." *Human Factors* 29:519–532.

JOHNSON, JACQUELINE S., and NEWPORT, ELISSA L. 1989. "Critical Period Effects in Second Language Learning: The Influence of Maturational State on the Acquisition of English as a Second Language." *Cognitive Psychology* 21:60–99.

JOHNSON, MARK. 1998. "The Neural Basis of Cognitive Development." In *Handbook of Child Psychology,* 5th edition, ed. William Damon, Vol. 2: *Cognition, Perception, and Language,* ed. Deanna Kuhn and Robert S. Siegler. New York: Wiley.

JUSCZYK, PETER W. 2002. "How Infants Adapt Speech-Processing Capacities to Native Language Structure." *Current Directions in Psychological Science* 11:15–18.

KELLMAN, PHILIP, and BANKS, MARTIN S. 1998. "Infant Visual Perception." In *Handbook of Child Psychology,* 5th edition, ed. William Damon, Vol. 2: *Cognition, Perception, and Language,* ed. Deanna Kuhn and Robert S. Siegler. New York: Wiley.

LITTLEFIELD, J., and RIESER, JOHN J. 1993. "Semantic Features of Similarity and Children's Strategies for Identifying Relevant Information in Mathematical Story Problems." *Cognition and Instruction* 11:133–188.

McLeod, Peter; Reed, Nick; and Diences, Zoltan. 2001. "Toward a Unified Fielder Theory: What We Do Not Yet Know about How People Run to Catch a Ball." *Journal of Experimental Psychology: Human Perception and Performance* 27:1347–1355.

Postman, Leo. 1955. "Association Theory and Perceptual Learning." *Psychological Review* 62:438–446.

Quinn, Paul C.; Palmer, Vanessa; and Slater, Alan M. 1999. "Identification of Gender in Domestic Cat Faces with and without Training: Perceptual Learning of a Natural Categorization Task." *Perception* 28:749–763.

Rieser, John J.; Pick, Herb L.; Ashmead, Daniel H.; and Garing, A. E. 1995. "Calibration of Human Locomotion and Models of Perceptual-Motor Organization." *Journal of Experimental Psychology: Human Perception and Performance* 21:480–497.

Saarni, Carolyn. 1998. "Emotional Development: Action, Communication, and Understanding." In *Handbook of Child Psychology,* 5th edition, ed. William Damon, Vol. 3: *Social, Emotional, and Personality Development,* ed. Nancy Eisenberg. New York: Wiley.

Saffran, Jenny R.; Aslin, R. N.; and Newport, E. L. 1996. "Statistical Learning by Eight-Month-Old Infants." *Science* 274:1926–1928.

Saffran, Jenny R., and Griepentrog, G. J. 2001. "Absolute Pitch in Infant Auditory Learning: Evidence for Developmental Reorganization." *Developmental Psychology* 37:74–85.

Schwartz, Daniel L., and Bransford, John D. 2001. "A Time for Telling." *Cognition and Instruction* 16:475–522.

Simon, Herbert A. 2001. "Observations on the Sciences of Science Learning." *Journal of Applied Developmental Psychology* 21:115–121.

Tighe, L. S., and Tighe, T. J. 1966. "Discrimination Learning: Two Views in Historical Perspective." *Psychological Bulletin* 66:353–370.

von Hofsten, Claes. 1994. "Planning and Perceiving What Is Going to Happen Next." In *The Development of Future-Oriented Processes,* ed. Marshall M. Haith, Janette B. Benson, and Ralph J. Roberts. Chicago: University of Chicago Press.

Walk, Richard D. 1966. "Perceptual Learning and the Discrimination of Wines." *Psychonomic Science* 5:57–58.

Walker-Andrews, Arlene, and Bahrick, Lorraine E. 2001. "Perceiving the Real World: Infants' Detection of and Memory for Social Information." *Infancy* 2:469–481.

Welch, Robert B. 1978. *Perceptual Modification: Adapting to Altered Sensory Environments.* New York: Academic Press.

John J. Rieser

PROBLEM SOLVING

Cognitive processing aimed at figuring out how to achieve a goal is called *problem solving.* In problem solving, the problem solver seeks to devise a method for transforming a problem from its current state into a desired state when a solution is not immediately obvious to the problem solver. Thus, the hallmark of problem solving is the invention of a new method for addressing a problem. This definition has three parts: (1) problem solving is *cognitive*—that is, it occurs internally in the mind (or cognitive system) and must be inferred indirectly from behavior; (2) problem solving is a *process* it involves the manipulation of knowledge representations (or carrying out mental computations); and (3) problem solving is *directed*—it is guided by the goals of the problem solver.

The definition of problem solving covers a broad range of human cognitive activities, including educationally relevant cognition—figuring out how to manage one's time, writing an essay on a selected topic, summarizing the main point of a textbook section, solving an arithmetic word problem, or determining whether a scientific theory is valid by conducting experiments.

A *problem* occurs when a problem solver has a goal but initially does not know how to achieve the goal. This definition has three parts: (1) the *current state*—the problem begins in a given state; (2) the *goal state*—the problem solver wants the problem to be in a different state, and problem solving is required to transform the problem from the current (or given) state into the goal state, and (3) *obstacles*—the problem solver does not know the correct solution and an effective solution method is not obvious to the problem solver.

According to this definition a problem is personal, so that a situation that is a problem for one person might not be a problem for another person. For example, "3 + 5 = ___" might be a problem for a six-year-old child who reasons, "Let's see. I can take one from the 5 and give it to the 3. That makes 4 plus 4, and I know that 4 plus 4 is 8." However, this equation is not a problem for an adult who knows the correct answer.

Types of Problems

Routine and nonroutine problems. It is customary to distinguish between routine and nonroutine problems. In a routine problem, the problem solver knows a solution method and only needs to carry it out. For example, for most adults the problem "589 x 45 = ___" is a routine problem if they know the procedure for multicolumn multiplication. Routine problems are sometimes called exercises, and technically do not fit the definition of *problem* stated above. When the goal of an educational activity is to promote all the aspects of problem solving (including devising a solution plan), then nonroutine problems (or exercises) are appropriate.

In a nonroutine problem, the problem solver does not initially know a method for solving the problem. For example, the following problem (reported by Robert Sternberg and Janet Davidson) is nonroutine for most people: "Water lilies double in area every twenty-four hours. At the beginning of the summer, there is one water lily on the lake. It takes sixty days for the lake to be completely covered with water lilies. On what day is the lake half covered?" In this problem, the problem solver must invent a solution method based on working backwards from the last day. Based on this method, the problem solver can ask what the lake would look like on the day before the last day, and conclude that the lake is half covered on the fifty-ninth day.

Well-defined and ill-defined problems. It is also customary to distinguish between well-defined and ill-defined problems. In a well-defined problem, the given state of the problem, the goal state of the problem, and the allowable operators (or moves) are each clearly specified. For example, the following water-jar problem (adapted from Abrahama Luchins) is an example of a well defined problem: "I will give you three empty water jars; you can fill any jar with water and pour water from one jar into another (until the second jar is full or the first one is empty); you can fill and pour as many times as you like. Given water

jars of size 21, 127, and 3 units and an unlimited supply of water, how can you obtain exactly 100 units of water?" This is a well-defined problem because the given state is clearly specified (you have empty jars of size 21, 127, and 3), the goal state is clearly specified (you want to get 100 units of water in one of the jars), and the allowable operators are clearly specified (you can fill and pour according to specific procedures). Well-defined problems may be either routine or nonroutine; if you do not have previous experience with water jar problems, then finding the solution (i.e., fill the 127, pour out 21 once, and pour out 3 twice) is a nonroutine problem.

In an ill-defined problem, the given state, goal state, and/or operations are not clearly specified. For example, in the problem, "Write a persuasive essay in favor of year-round schools," the goal state is not clear because the criteria for what constitutes a "persuasive essay" are vague and the allowable operators, such as how to access sources of information, are not clear. Only the given state is clear—a blank piece of paper. Ill-defined problems can be routine or nonroutine; if one has extensive experience in writing then writing a short essay like this one is a routine problem.

Processes in Problem Solving

The process of problem solving can be broken down into two major phases: *problem representation*, in which the problem solver builds a coherent mental representation of the problem, and *problem solution*, in which the problem solver devises and carries out a solution plan. Problem representation can be broken down further into *problem translation*, in which the problem solver translates each sentence (or picture) into an internal mental representation, and *problem integration*, in which the problem solver integrates the information into a coherent mental representation of the problem (i.e., a mental model of the situation described in the problem). Problem solution can be broken down further into *solution planning*, in which the problem solver devises a plan for how to solve the problem, and *solution execution*, in which the problem solver carries out the plan by engaging in solution behaviors. Although the four processes of problem solving are listed sequentially, they may occur in many different orderings and with many iterations in the course of solving a problem.

For example, consider the butter problem described by Mary Hegarty, Richard Mayer, and Christopher Monk: "At Lucky, butter costs 65 cents per stick. This is two cents less per stick than butter at Vons. If you need to buy 4 sticks of butter, how much will you pay at Vons?" In the problem translation phase, the problem solver may mentally represent the first sentence as "Lucky = 0.65," the second sentence as "Lucky = Vons − 0.02," and the third sentence as "4 x Vons = ___." In problem integration, the problem solver may construct a mental number line with Lucky at 0.65 and Vons to the right of Lucky (at 0.67); or the problem solver may mentally integrate the equations as "4 x (Lucky + 0.02) = ___." A key insight in problem integration is to recognize the proper relation between the cost of butter at Lucky and the cost of butter at Vons, namely that butter costs more at Vons (even though the keyword in the problem is "less"). In solution planning, the problem solver may break the problem into parts, such as: "First add 0.02 to 0.65, then multiply the result by 4." In solution executing, the problem solver carries out the plan: 0.02 + 0.65 = 0.67, 0.67 x 4 = 2.68. In addition, the problem solver must monitor the problem-solving process and make adjustments as needed.

Teaching for Problem Solving

A challenge for educators is to teach in ways that foster meaningful learning rather than rote learning. Rote instructional methods promote retention (the ability to solve problems that are identical or highly similar to those presented in instruction), but not problem solving transfer (the ability to apply what was learned to novel problems). For example, in 1929, Alfred Whitehead used the term *inert knowledge* to refer to learning that cannot be used to solve novel problems. In contrast, *meaningful instructional methods* promote both retention and transfer.

In a classic example of the distinction between rote and meaningful learning, the psychologist Max Wertheimer (1959) described two ways of teaching students to compute the area of a parallelogram. In the rote method, students learn to measure the base, measure the height, and then multiply base times height. Students taught by the $A = b \times h$ method are able to find the area of parallelograms shaped like the ones given in instruction (a retention problem) but not unusual parallelograms or other shapes (a transfer problem). Wertheimer used the term *reproductive thinking* to refer to problem solving in which one blindly carries out a previously learned procedure. In contrast, in the meaningful method, students learn by cutting the triangle from one end of

a cardboard parallelogram and attaching it to the other end to form a rectangle. Once students have the insight that a parallelogram is just a rectangle in disguise, they can compute the area because they already know the procedure for finding the area of a rectangle. Students taught by the insight method perform well on both retention and transfer problems. Wertheimer used the term *productive thinking* to refer to problem solving in which one invents a new approach to solving a novel problem.

Educationally Relevant Advances in Problem Solving

Recent advances in educational psychology point to the role of domain-specific knowledge in problem solving—such as knowledge of specific strategies or problem types that apply to a particular field. Three important advances have been: (1) the teaching of problem-solving processes, (2) the nature of expert problem solving, and (3) new conceptions of individual differences in problem-solving ability.

Teaching of problem-solving processes. An important advance in educational psychology is cognitive strategy instruction, which includes the teaching of problem-solving processes. For example, in Project Intelligence, elementary school children successfully learned the cognitive processes needed for solving problems similar to those found on intelligence tests. In Instrumental Enrichment, students who had been classified as mentally retarded learned cognitive processes that allowed them to show substantial improvements on intelligence tests.

Expert problem solving. Another important advance in educational psychology concerns differences between what experts and novices know in given fields, such as medicine, physics, and computer programming. For example, expert physicists tend to store their knowledge in large integrated chunks, whereas novices tend to store their knowledge as isolated fragments; expert physicists tend to focus on the underlying structural characteristics of physics word problems, whereas novices focus on the surface features; and expert physicists tend to work forward from the givens to the goal, whereas novices work backwards from the goal to the givens. Research on expertise has implications for professional education because it pinpoints the kinds of domain-specific knowledge that experts need to learn.

Individual differences in problem-solving ability. This third advance concerns new conceptions of intellectual ability based on differences in the way people process information. For example, people may differ in cognitive style—such as their preferences for visual versus verbal representations, or for impulsive versus reflective approaches to problem solving. Alternatively, people may differ in the speed and efficiency with which they carry out specific cognitive processes, such as making a mental comparison or retrieving a piece of information from memory. Instead of characterizing intellectual ability as a single, monolithic ability, recent conceptions of intellectual ability focus on the role of multiple differences in information processing.

See also: CREATIVITY; LEARNING, *subentry on* ANALOGICAL REASONING; MATHEMATICS LEARNING, *subentry on* COMPLEX PROBLEM SOLVING.

BIBLIOGRAPHY

CHI, MICHELENE T. H.; GLASER, ROBERT; and FARR, MARSHALL J., eds. 1988. *The Nature of Expertise.* Hillsdale, NJ: Erlbaum.

DUNKER, KARL. 1945. *On Problem Solving.* Washington, DC: American Psychological Association.

FEUERSTEIN, REUVEN. 1980. *Instrumental Enrichment.* Baltimore: University Park Press.

HEGARTY, MARY; MAYER, RICHARD E.; and MONK, CHRISTOPHER A. 1995. "Comprehension of Arithmetic Word Problems: Evidence from Students' Eye Fixations." *Journal of Educational Psychology* 84:76–84.

HUNT, EARL; LUNNEBORG, CLIFF; and LEWIS, J. 1975. "What Does It Mean to Be High Verbal?" *Cognitive Psychology* 7:194–227.

LARKIN, JILL H.; MCDERMOTT, JOHN; SIMON, DOROTHEA P.; and SIMON, HERBERT A. 1980. "Expert and Novice Performance in Solving Physics Problems." *Science* 208:1335–1342.

LUCHINS, ABRAHAMA S. 1942. *Mechanization in Problem Solving: The Effect of Einstellung.* Evanston, IL: American Psychological Association.

MAYER, RICHARD E. 1992. *Thinking, Problem Solving, Cognition,* 2nd edition. New York: Freeman.

MAYER, RICHARD E. 1999. *The Promise of Educational Psychology.* Upper Saddle River, NJ: Prentice-Hall.

NICKERSON, RAYMOND S. 1995. "Project Intelligence." In *Encyclopedia of Human Intelligence,* ed. Robert J. Sternberg. New York: Macmillan.

PRESSLEY, MICHAEL J., and WOLOSHYN, VERA. 1995. *Cognitive Strategy Instruction that Really Improves Children's Academic Performance.* Cambridge, MA: Brookline Books.

STERNBERG, ROBERT J., and DAVIDSON, JANET E. 1982. "The Mind of the Puzzler." *Psychology Today* 16:37–44.

STERNBERG, ROBERT J., and ZHANG, LI-FANG, eds. 2001. *Perspectives on Thinking, Learning, and Cognitive Styles.* Mahwah, NJ: Erlbaum.

WERTHEIMER, MAX. 1959. *Productive Thinking.* New York: Harper and Row.

WHITEHEAD, ALFRED NORTH. 1929. *The Aims of Education.* New York: Macmillan.

RICHARD E. MAYER

REASONING

Reasoning is the generation or evaluation of claims in relation to their supporting arguments and evidence. The ability to reason has a fundamental impact on one's ability to learn from new information and experiences because reasoning skills determine how people comprehend, evaluate, and accept claims and arguments. Reasoning skills are also crucial for being able to generate and maintain viewpoints or beliefs that are coherent with, and justified by, relevant knowledge. There are two general kinds of reasoning that involve claims and evidence: formal and informal.

Formal Reasoning

Formal reasoning is used to evaluate the form of an argument, and to examine the logical relationships between conclusions and their supporting assertions. Arguments are determined to be either *valid* or *invalid* based solely on whether their conclusions necessarily follow from their explicitly stated premises or assertions. That is, if the supporting assertions are true, must the conclusion also be true? If so, then the argument is considered valid and the truth of the conclusion can be directly determined by establishing the truth of the supporting assertions. If not, then the argument is considered invalid, and the truth of the assertions is insufficient (or even irrelevant) for establishing the truth of the conclusion. Formal reasoning is often studied in the context of *categorical syllogisms* or *"if-then" conditional proofs*. Syllogisms contain two assertions and a conclusion.

An example of a logically valid syllogism is: *All dogs are animals; all poodles are dogs; therefore poodles are animals.* A slight change to one of the premises will create the invalid syllogism: *All dogs are animals; some dogs are poodles; therefore all poodles are animals.* This argument form is invalid because it cannot be determined with certainty that the conclusion is true, even if the premises are true. The second premise does not require that all poodles are dogs. Thus, there may be some poodles who are not dogs and, by extension, some poodles who are not animals. This argument is invalid despite the fact that an accurate knowledge of dogs, poodles, and animals confirms that both the premises and the conclusion are true statements. This validity-truth incongruence highlights the important point that the conceptual content of an argument or the real-world truth of the premises and conclusion are irrelevant to the logic of the argument form.

Discussions of formal reasoning may sometimes refer to the rules of logic. It is common for formal reasoning to be described as a set of abstract and prescriptive rules that people must learn and apply in order to determine the validity of an argument. This is the oldest perspective on formal reasoning. Some claim that the term *formal reasoning* refers directly to the application of these formal rules.

However, many theorists consider this perspective misguided. Describing formal reasoning as the evaluation of argument forms conveys a more inclusive and accurate account of the various perspectives in this field. There are at least four competing theories about how people determine whether a conclusion necessarily follows from the premises. These theories are commonly referred to as *rule-based perspectives, mental models, heuristics,* and *domain-sensitive theories.* People outside the rule-based perspective view the rules of logic as descriptive rules that simply give labels to common argument forms and to common errors or fallacies in logical reasoning. These theories are too complex to be detailed here, and there is currently no consensus as to which theory best accounts for how people actually reason. A number of books and review articles provide comprehensive discussions of these theories and their relative merits; one example is *Human Reasoning: The Psychology of Deduction* by Jonathan Evans, Stephen Newstead, and Ruth Byrne.

There is a consensus that human reasoning performance is poor and prone to several systematic errors. Performance on formal reasoning tasks is generally poor, but can be better or worse depending upon the particular aspects of the task. People perform worse on problems that require more cognitive work, due to excessive demands placed on their limited processing capacity or working memory. The required cognitive work can be increased simply by having more information, or by the linguistic form of the argument. Some linguistic forms can affect performance because they violate conventional discourse or must be mentally rephrased in order to be integrated with other information.

In addition, people's existing knowledge about the concepts contained in the problem can affect performance. People have great difficulty evaluating the logical validity of an argument independent of their real-world knowledge. They insert their knowledge as additional premises, which leads them to make more inferences than is warranted. Prior knowledge can also lead people to misinterpret the meaning of premises. Another common source of error is *belief bias,* where people judge an argument's validity based on whether the conclusion is consistent with their beliefs rather than its logical relationship to the given premises.

The systematic errors that have been observed provide some insights about what skills a person might develop to improve performance. Making students explicitly aware of the likely intrusion of their prior knowledge could facilitate their ability to control or correct such intrusions. Students may also benefit from a detailed and explicit discussion of what logical validity refers to, how it differs from real-world truth or personal agreement, and how easy it is to confuse the two. Regardless of whether or not people commonly employ formal rules of logic, an understanding and explicit knowledge of these rules should facilitate efforts to search for violations of logical validity. Theorists of informal reasoning such as James Voss and Mary Means have made a similar argument for the importance of explicit knowledge about the rules of good reasoning. Errors attributed to limited cognitive resources can be addressed by increasing reasoning skill, and practice on formal reasoning tasks should increase proficiency and reduce the amount of cognitive effort required. Also, working memory load should be reduced by external representation techniques, such as Venn diagrams.

Informal Reasoning

Informal reasoning refers to attempts to determine what information is relevant to a question, what conclusions are plausible, and what degree of support the relevant information provides for these various conclusions. In most circumstances, people must evaluate the justification for a claim in a context where the information is ambiguous and incomplete and the criteria for evaluation are complex and poorly specified. Most of what is commonly referred to as "thinking" involves informal reasoning, including making predictions of future events or trying to explain past events. These cognitive processes are involved in answering questions as mundane as "How much food should I prepare for this party?" and as profound as "Did human beings evolve from simple one-celled organisms?" Informal reasoning has a pervasive influence on both the everyday and the monumental decisions that people make, and on the ideas that people come to accept or reject.

Informal and formal reasoning both involve attempts to determine whether a claim has been sufficiently justified by the supporting assertions, but these types of reasoning differ in many respects. The vast majority of arguments are invalid according to formal logic, but informal reasoning must be employed to determine what degree of justification the supporting assertions provide. Also, the supporting assertions themselves must be evaluated as to their validity and accuracy. Formal reasoning involves making a binary decision based only on the given information. Informal reasoning involves making an uncertain judgment about the degree of justification for a claim relative to competing claims—and basing this evaluation on an ill-defined set of assertions whose truth values are uncertain.

Based on the above characterization of informal reasoning, a number of cognitive skills would be expected to affect the quality of such reasoning. The first is the ability to fully comprehend the meaning of the claim being made. Understanding the conceptual content is crucial to being able to consider what other information might bear on the truth or falsehood of a claim. Other cognitive processes involved in reasoning include the retrieval of relevant knowledge from long-term memory, seeking out new relevant information, evaluating the validity and utility of that information, generating alternatives to the claim in question, and evaluating the competing claims in light of the relevant information.

Successful reasoning requires the understanding that evidence must provide information that is independent of the claim or theory, and that evidence must do more than simply rephrase and highlight the assumptions of the theory. For example, the assertion "Some people have extrasensory perception" does not provide any evidence about the claim "ESP is real." These are simply ways of restating the same information. Evidence must be an assertion that is independent of the claim, but that still provides information about the probable truth of the claim. An example of potential evidence for the claim that "ESP is real" would be "Some people know information that they could not have known through any of the normal senses." In other words, evidence constitutes assertions whose truth has implications for, but is not synonymous with, the truth of the claim being supported.

Without an understanding of evidence and counterevidence and how they relate to theories, people would be ineffective at identifying information that could be used to determine whether a claim is justified. Also, lack of a clear distinction between evidence and theory will lead to the assimilation of evidence and the distortion of its meaning and logical implications. This eliminates the potential to consider alternative claims that could better account for the evidence. People will also fail to use counterevidence to make appropriate decreases in the degree of justification for a claim.

Discussions of informal reasoning, argumentation, and critical thinking commonly acknowledge that a prerequisite for effective reasoning is a belief in the utility of reasoning. The cognitive skills described above are necessary, but not sufficient, to produce quality reasoning. The use of these skills is clearly effortful; thus, people must believe in the importance and utility of reasoning in order to consistently put forth the required effort. The epistemology that promotes the use of reasoning skills is the view that knowledge can never be absolutely certain and that valid and useful claims are the product of contemplating possible alternative claims and weighing the evidence and counterevidence. Put simply, people use their reasoning skills consistently when they acknowledge the possibility that a claim may be incorrect and also believe that standards of good reasoning produce more accurate ideas about the world.

Inconsistent, selective, and biased application of reasoning skills provides little or no benefits for learning. Greater reasoning skills are assumed to aid in the ability to acquire new knowledge and revise one's existing ideas accordingly. However, if one contemplates evidence and theory only when it can be used to justify one's prior commitments, then only supportive information will be learned and existing ideas will remain entrenched and unaffected. The development of reasoning skills will confer very little intellectual benefit in the absence of an epistemological commitment to employ those skills consistently.

General Reasoning Performance

Reports from the National Assessment of Educational Progress and the National Academy of Sciences consistently show poor performance on a wide array of tasks that require informal reasoning. These tasks span all of the core curriculum areas of reading, writing, mathematics, science, and history.

Some smaller-scale studies have attempted to paint a more detailed picture of what people are doing, or failing to do, when asked to reason. People demonstrate some use of informal reasoning skills, but these skills are underdeveloped and applied inconsistently. Children and adults have a poor understanding of evidence and its relationship to theories or claims. Only a small minority of people attempt to justify their claims by providing supporting evidence. When explicitly asked for supporting evidence, most people simply restate the claim itself or describe in more detail what the claim means. It is especially rare for people to generate possible counter-evidence or to even consider possible alternative claims.

The inconsistent application of informal reasoning skills could have multiple causes. Some theorists suggest that reasoning skills are domain specific and depend heavily on the amount of domain knowledge a person possesses. Alternatively, underdeveloped or unpracticed skills could lead to their haphazard use. A third possibility is that people's lack of explicit knowledge about what good reasoning entails prevents them from exercising conscious control over their implicit skills.

Inconsistent use of informal reasoning skills may also arise because people lack a principled belief in the utility of reasoning that would foster a consistent application of sound reasoning. People have extreme levels of certainty in their ideas, and they take this certainty for granted. In addition, the applica-

tion of reasoning skills is not random, but is selective and biased such that prior beliefs are protected from scrutiny. This systematic inconsistency cannot be accounted for by underdeveloped skills, but can be accounted for by assuming a biased motivation to use these skills selectively. Regardless of whether or not people have the capacity for sound reasoning, they have no philosophical basis that could provide the motivation to override the selective and biased use of these skills.

Development of Reasoning Skills

There is only preliminary data about how and when informal reasoning skills develop. There is preliminary support that the development of reasoning takes a leap forward during the preadolescent years. These findings are consistent with Piagetian assumptions about the development of *concrete operational thinking,* in other words, thinking that involves the mental manipulation (e.g., combination, transformation) of objects represented in memory. However, younger children are capable of some key aspects of reasoning. Thus, the improvement during early adolescence could result from improvements in other subsidiary skills of information processing, from meta-cognitive awareness, or from an increase in relevant knowledge.

A somewhat striking finding is the lack of development in informal reasoning that occurs from early adolescence through adulthood. Some evidence suggests that college can improve reasoning, but the overall relationship between the amount of postsecondary education and reasoning skill is weak at best. The weak and inconsistent relationship that does exist between level of education and reasoning is likely due to indirect effects. Students are rarely required to engage in complex reasoning tasks. However, the spontaneous disagreements that arise in the classroom could expose them to the practice of justifying one's claim. Also, engagement in inquiry activities, such as classroom experiments, could provide implicit exposure to the principles of scientific reasoning.

There are relatively few programs aimed at developing informal reasoning skills; hence, there is little information about effective pedagogical strategies. Where they do exist, curricula are often aimed at developing general reasoning skills. Yet, many believe that effective reasoning skills are domain- or discipline-specific. Nevertheless, given the pervasive impact of reasoning skills on learning in general, it is clear that more systematic efforts are needed to foster reasoning skills at even the earliest grade levels. Of the approaches that have been attempted, there is some evidence for the success of *scaffolding*, which involves a teacher interacting with a student who is attempting to reason, and prompting the student to develop more adequate arguments. Another approach is to explicitly teach what *good reasoning* means, what *evidence* is, and how evidence relates to theories. This approach could be especially effective if classroom experiments are conducted within the context of explicit discussions about the principles of scientific reasoning. Also, if reasoning skills are discussed in conjunction with the content of the core subject areas, then students may develop an appreciation for the pervasive utility and importance of reasoning for the progress of ideas.

A number of theorists have suggested that debate between students with opposing views could foster the basic skills needed for informal reasoning. Debates could give students practice in having to consider opposing viewpoints and having to coordinate evidence and counterevidence in support of a claim. Also, providing justification for one's positions requires some cognitive effort, and the norms of social dialogue could provide the needed motivation. However, interpersonal debates are most commonly construed as situations in which individuals are committed to a position ahead of time, and in which their goal is to frame the issue and any evidence in a manner that will persuade their opponent or the audience that their own position is correct. Students' reasoning is already greatly impaired by their tendency to adopt a biased, defensive, or non-contemplative stance. Debate activities that reinforce this stance and blur the difference between defending a claim and contemplating a claim's justification may do more harm than good. To date, there is no empirical data that compare the relative costs and benefits of using interpersonal debate exercises to foster critical reasoning skills.

See also: LEARNING, *subentry on* CAUSAL REASONING; LEARNING THEORY, *subentry on* HISTORICAL OVERVIEW.

BIBLIOGRAPHY

BARON, JONATHAN. 1985. *Rationality and Intelligence.* Cambridge, Eng.: Cambridge University Press.

BARON, JONATHAN. 1988. *Thinking and Deciding.* Cambridge, Eng.: Cambridge University Press.

BOYER, ERNEST L. 1983. *High School: A Report on Secondary Education in America.* New York: Harper and Row.

CARY, SUSAN. 1985. "Are Children Fundamentally Different Thinkers and Learners Than Adults?" In *Thinking and Learning Skills: Current Research and Open Questions,* Vol. 2, ed. Susan Chipman, Judith Segal, and Robert Glaser. Hillsdale, NJ: Erlbaum.

EVANS, JONATHAN ST. B. T.; NEWSTEAD, STEPHEN E.; and BYRNE, RUTH M. J. 1993. *Human Reasoning: The Psychology of Deduction.* Hillsdale, NJ: Erlbaum.

JOHNSON-LAIRD, PHILIP N., and BYRNE, RUTH M. J. 1991. *Deduction.* Hillsdale, NJ: Erlbaum.

KUHN, DEANNA. 1991. *The Skills of Argument.* Cambridge, Eng.: Cambridge University Press.

MEANS, MARY L., and VOSS, JAMES F. 1996. "Who Reasons Well? Two Studies of Informal Reasoning Among Children of Different Grade, Ability, and Knowledge Levels." *Cognition and Instruction* 14:139–178.

NICKERSON, RAYMOND S. 1991. "Modes and Models of Informal Reasoning: A Commentary." In *Informal Reasoning and Education,* ed. James F. Voss, David N. Perkins, and Judith W. Segal. Hillsdale, NJ: Erlbaum.

PERLOMS, DAVID N. 1985. "Postprimary Education Has Little Impact on Informal Reasoning." *Journal of Educational Psychology* 77:562–571.

STEIN, NANCY L., and MILLER, CHRISTOPHER A. 1991. "I Win–You Lose: The Development of Argumentative Thinking." In *Informal Reasoning and Education,* ed. James F. Voss, David N. Perkins, and Judith W. Segal. Hillsdale, NJ: Erlbaum.

VOSS, JAMES F., and MEANS, MARY L. 1991. "Learning to Reason via Instruction and Argumentation." *Learning and Instruction* 1:337–350.

VYGOTSKY, LEV S. 1978. *Mind in Society: The Development of Higher Psychological Processes,* ed. Michael Cole. Cambridge, MA: Harvard University Press.

THOMAS D. GRIFFIN

TRANSFER OF LEARNING

Imagine that every time that people entered a new environment they had to learn how to behave without the guidance of prior experiences. Slightly novel tasks, like shopping online, would be disorienting and dependant on trial-and-error tactics. Fortunately, people use aspects of their prior experiences, such as the selection of goods and subsequent payment, to guide their behavior in new settings. The ability to use learning gained in one situation to help with another is called *transfer.*

Transfer has a direct bearing on education. Educators hope that students transfer what they learn from one class to another—and to the outside world. Educators also hope students transfer experiences from home to help make sense of lessons at school. There are two major approaches to the study of transfer. One approach characterizes the knowledge and conditions of acquisition that optimize the chances of transfer. The other approach inquires into the nature of individuals and the cultural contexts that transform them into more adaptive participants.

Knowledge-Based Approaches to Transfer

There are several knowledge-based approaches to transfer.

Transferring out from instruction. Ideally, the knowledge students learn in school will be applied outside of school. For some topics, it is possible to train students for the specific situations they will subsequently encounter, such as typing at a keyboard. For other topics, educators cannot anticipate all the out-of-school applications. When school-based lessons do not have a direct mapping to out-of-school contexts, memorization without understanding can lead to inert knowledge. Inert knowledge occurs when people acquire an idea without also learning the conditions of its subsequent application, and thus they fail to apply that idea appropriately. Memorizing the Pythagorean formula, for example, does not guarantee students know to use the formula to find the distance of a shortcut.

Knowing when to use an idea depends on knowing the contexts in which the idea is useful. The ideas that people learn are always parts of a larger context, and people must determine which aspects of that context are relevant. Imagine, for example, a young child who is learning to use the hook of a candy cane to pull a toy closer. As the child learns the action,

there are a number of contextual features she might also learn. There are incidental features—it is Christmas; there are surface features—the candy is small and striped; and there are deep features—the candy cane is rigid and hooked. Instruction for transfer must help the child discern the deep features. This way the child might subsequently use an umbrella handle to gather a stuffed animal instead of trying a candy-striped rope.

When people learn, they not only encode the target idea, they also encode the context in which it occurs, even if that context is incidental. For a study published in 1975, Gooden and Baddeley asked adults to learn a list of words on land or underwater (while scuba diving). Afterwards, the adults were subdivided; half tried to remember the words underwater and half on land. Those people who learned the words underwater remembered them better underwater than on land, and those people who learned the words on land remembered them better on land than underwater. This result reveals the context dependency of memory. Context dependency is useful because it constrains ideas to appear in appropriate contexts, rather than cluttering people's thoughts at odd times. But context dependency can be a problem for transfer, because transfer, by definition, has to occur when the original context of learning is not reinstated—when one is no longer in school, for example.

Surface features, which are readily apparent to the learner, differ from incidental features, because surface features are attached to the idea rather than the context in which the idea occurs. Surface features can be useful. A child might learn that fish have fins and lay eggs. When he sees a new creature with fins, he may decide it is a fish and infer that it too lays eggs. Surface features, however, can be imperfect cues. People may overgeneralize and exhibit *negative transfer.* For example, the child may have seen a dolphin instead of a fish. People may also undergeneralize and fail to transfer. A child might see an eel and assume it does not lay eggs. Good instruction helps students see beneath the surface to find the deep features of an idea.

Deep features are based on structures integral to an idea, which may not be readily apparent. To a physicist, an inclined plane and scissors share the same deep structure of leverage, but novices cannot see this similarity and they fail to use a formula learned for inclined planes to reason about scissors.

Analogies are built on deep features. For example, color is to picture as sound is to song. On the surface, color and sound differ, as do pictures and song. Nonetheless, the relation of *used to create* makes it possible to compare the common structure between the two. Analogy is an important way people discover deep features. In the 1990s, Kevin Dunbar studied the laboratory meetings of cell biologists. He found that the scientists often used analogies to understand a new discovery. They typically made transfers of *near* analogies rather than *far* ones. A far analogy transfers an idea from a remote body of knowledge that shares few surface features, as might be the case when using the structure of the solar system to explain the structure of an atom. A near analogy draws on a structure that comes from a similar body of knowledge. The scientists in Dunbar's study used near analogies from biology because they had precise knowledge of biology, which made for a more productive transfer.

Instruction can help students determine deep features by using analogous examples rather than single examples. In a 1983 study, Mary Gick and Keith Holyoak asked students how to kill a tumor with a burst of radiation, given that a strong burst kills nearby tissue and a weak burst does not kill the tumor. Students learned that the solution uses multiple weak radiation beams that converge on the tumor. Sometime later, the students tried to solve the problem of how a general could attack a fortress: If the general brought enough troops to attack the fortress, they would collapse the main bridge. Students did not propose that the general could split his forces over multiple bridges and then converge on the fortress. The students' knowledge of the convergence solution was inert, because it was only associated with the radiation problem. Gick and Holyoak found they could improve transfer by providing two analogous examples instead of one. For example, students worked with the radiation problem and an analogous traffic congestion problem. This helped students abstract the convergence schema from the radiation context, and they were able to transfer their knowledge to the fortress problem.

Transferring in to instruction. In school, transfer can help students learn. If students can *transfer in* prior knowledge, it will help them understand the content of a new lesson. A lesson on the Pythagorean theorem becomes more comprehensible if students can transfer in prior knowledge of right triangles.

Otherwise, the lesson simply involves pushing algebraic symbols.

Unlike transfer to out-of-school settings, which depends on the spontaneous retrieval of relevant prior knowledge, transfer to in-school settings can be directly supported by teachers. A common approach to help students recruit prior knowledge uses *cover stories* that help students see the relevance of what they are about to learn. A teacher might discuss the challenge of finding the distance of the moon from the earth to motivate a lesson on trigonometry. This example includes two ways that transferring in prior knowledge can support learning. Prior knowledge helps students understand the problems that a particular body of knowledge is intended to solve—in this case, problems about distance. Prior knowledge also enables learners to construct a mental model of the situation that helps them understand what the components of the trigonometric formulas refer to.

Sometimes students cannot transfer knowledge to school settings because they do not have the relevant knowledge. One way to help overcome a lack of prior knowledge is to use contrasting cases. Whereas pairs of analogies help students abstract deep features from surface features, pairs of contrasting cases help students notice deep features in the first place. Contrasting cases juxtapose examples that only differ by one or two features. For example, a teacher might ask students to compare examples of acute, right, and obtuse triangles. Given the contrasts, students can notice what makes a right triangle distinctive, which in turn, helps them construct precise mental models to understand a lesson on the Pythagorean theorem.

Person-Based Approaches to Transfer

The second approach to transfer asks whether person-level variables affect transfer. For example, do IQ tests or persistence predict the ability to transfer? Person-based research relevant to instruction asks whether some experiences can transform people in general ways.

Transferring out from instruction. An enduring issue has been whether instruction can transform people into better thinkers. People often believe that mastering a formal discipline, like Latin or programming, improves the rigor of thought. Research has shown that it is very difficult to improve people's reasoning, with instruction in logical reasoning being notoriously difficult. Although people may learn to reason appropriately for one situation, they do not necessarily apply that reasoning to novel situations. More protracted experiences, however, may broadly transform individuals to the extent that they apply a certain method of reasoning in general, regardless of situational context. For example, the cultural experiences of American and Chinese adults lead them to approach contradictions differently.

There have also been attempts to improve learning abilities by improving people's ability to transfer. Ann Brown and Mary Jo Kane showed young children how to use a sample solution to help solve an analogous problem. After several lessons on transferring knowledge from samples to problems, the children spontaneously began to transfer knowledge from one example to another. Whether this type of instruction has broad effects—for example, when the child leaves the psychologist's laboratory—remains an open question. Most likely, it is the accumulation of many experiences, not isolated, short-term lessons, that has broad implications for personal development.

Transferring in to instruction. When children enter school, they come with identities and dispositions that have been informed by the practices and roles available in their homes and neighborhoods. Schools also have practices and roles, but these can seem foreign and inhospitable to out-of-school identities. Na'ilah Nasir, for example, found that students did not transfer their basketball "street statistics" to make sense of statistics lessons in their classrooms (nor did they use school-learned procedures to solve statistics problems in basketball). From a knowledge approach to transfer, one might argue that the school and basketball statistics were analogous, and that the children failed to see the common deep features. From a person approach to transfer, the cultural contexts of the two settings were so different that they supported different identities, roles, and interpretations of social demands. People can view and express themselves quite differently in school and nonschool contexts, and there will therefore be little transfer.

One way to bridge home and school is to alter instructional contexts so children can build identities and practices that are consistent with their out-of-school personae. Educators, for example, can bring elements of surrounding cultures into the classroom. In one intervention, African-American students learned literary analysis by building on their linguistic practice of signifying. These children brought their cultural heritage to bear on school subjects, and this fostered a school-based identity in which students viewed themselves as competent and engaged in school.

Conclusion

The frequent disconnect between in-school and out-of-school contexts has led some researchers to argue that transfer is unimportant. In 1988, Jean Lave compared how people solved school math problems and best-buy shopping problems. The adults rarely used their school algorithms when shopping. Because they were competent shoppers and viewed themselves as such, one might conclude that school-based learning does not need to transfer. This conclusion, however, is predicated on a narrow view of transfer that is limited to identical uses of what one has learned or to identical expressions of identity.

From an educational perspective, the primary function of transfer should be to prepare people to learn something new. So, even though shoppers did not use the exact algorithms they had learned in school, the school-based instruction prepared them to learn to solve best-buy problems when they did not have paper and pencil at hand. This is the central relevance of transfer for education. Educators cannot create experts who spontaneously transfer their knowledge or identities to handle every problem or context that might arise. Instead, educators can only put students on a trajectory to expertise by preparing them to transfer for future learning.

See also: LEARNING, *subentries on* ANALOGICAL REASONING, CAUSAL REASONING, CONCEPTUAL CHANGE.

BIBLIOGRAPHY

BOALER, JO, and GREENO, JAMES G. 2000. "Identity, Agency, and Knowing in Mathematical Worlds." In *Multiple Perspectives on Mathematics Teaching and Learning,* ed. Jo Boaler. Westport, CT: Ablex.

BRANSFORD, JOHN D.; FRANKS, JEFFREY J.; VYE, NANCY J.; and SHERWOOD, ROBERT D. 1989. "New Approaches to Instruction: Because Wisdom Can't Be Told." In *Similarity and Analogical Reasoning,* ed. Stella Vosniadou and Andrew Ortony. Cambridge, Eng.: Cambridge University Press.

Bransford, John D., and Schwartz, Daniel L. 1999. "Rethinking Transfer: A Simple Proposal with Multiple Implications." In *Review of Research in Education,* ed. Asghar Iran-Nejad and P. David Pearson. Washington, DC: American Educational Research Association.

Brown, Ann L., and Kane, Mary Jo. 1988. "Preschool Children Can Learn to Transfer: Learning to Learn and Learning from Example." *Cognitive Psychology* 3(4):275–293.

Ceci, Stephen J., and Ruiz, Ana. 1993. "Transfer, Abstractness, and Intelligence." In *Transfer on Trial,* ed. Douglas K. Detterman and Robert J. Sternberg. Stamford, CT: Ablex.

Chi, Michelene T.; Glaser, Robert; and Farr, Marshall J. 1988. *The Nature of Expertise.* Hillsdale, NJ: Erlbaum.

Dunbar, Kevin. 1997. "How Scientists Think: Online Creativity and Conceptual Change in Science." In *Creative Thought,* ed. Thomas B. Ward, Stephen M. Smith, and Jyotsna Vaid. Washington DC: APA.

Gentner, Dedre. 1989. "The Mechanisms of Analogical Reasoning." In *Similarity and Analogical Reasoning,* ed. Stella Vosniadou and Andrew Ortony. Cambridge, Eng.: Cambridge University Press.

Gick, Mary L., and Holyoak, Keith J. 1983. "Schema Induction and Analogical Transfer." *Cognitive Psychology* 15(1):1–38.

Godden, D. R., and Baddeley, A. D. 1975. "Context-Dependent Memory in Two Natural Environments: On Land and Under Water." *British Journal of Psychology* 66(3):325–331.

Lave, Jean. 1988. *Cognition in Practice.* Cambridge, Eng.: Cambridge University Press.

Lee, Carol. 1995. "A Culturally Based Cognitive Apprenticeship: Teaching African-American High School Students Skills of Literary Interpretation." *Reading Research Quarterly* 30(4):608–630.

Moll, Luis C., and Greenberg, James B. 1990. "Creating Zones of Possibilities: Combining Social Contexts for Instructions." In *Vygotsky and Education,* ed. Luis C. Moll. Cambridge, Eng.: Cambridge University Press.

Nisbett, Richard E.; Fong, Geoffrey T.; Lehman, Darrin R.; and Cheng, Patricia W. 1987. "Teaching Reasoning." *Science* 238(4827):625–631.

Novick, Laura R. "Analogical Transfer, Problem Similarity, and Expertise." *Journal of Experimental Psychology: Learning, Memory, and Cognition* 14(3):510–520.

Peng, Kaiping, and Nisbett, Richard E. 1999. "Culture, Dialectics, and Reasoning about Contradiction." *American Psychologist* 54(9):741–754.

Schwartz, Daniel L., and Bransford, John D. 1998. "A Time for Telling." *Cognition and Instruction* 16(4):475–522.

Daniel L. Schwartz
Na'ilah Nasir

LEARNING COMMUNITIES AND THE UNDERGRADUATE CURRICULUM

Educational observers have long argued that student involvement is important to student education. Indeed a wide range of studies, in a variety of settings and of a range of students, have confirmed that academic and social involvement, sometimes referred to as academic and social integration, enhances student development, improves student learning, and increases student persistence. Simply put, involvement matters. But getting students involved can be difficult. This is especially true for the majority of college students who commute to college, who work while in college, or have substantial family responsibilities beyond college. Unlike students who reside on campus, these students have few, if any, opportunities to engage others beyond the classroom.

For that reason an increasing number of universities and colleges, both two- and four-year, have turned their attention to the classroom—the one place, perhaps the only place, where students meet each other and the faculty. Researchers have asked how that setting can be altered to better promote student involvement and in turn improve student education. In response, schools have begun to institute a variety of curricular and pedagogical reforms ranging from the use of cooperative and problem-based learning to the inclusion of service learning in the college curriculum. One reform that is gaining attention, that addresses both the need for student involvement and the demands for curricular coherence, is the use of learning communities.

Learning communities, in their most basic form, begin with a kind of co-registration or block scheduling that enables students to take courses together, rather than in isolation. In some cases, learning communities will help students make connections with linked courses—tying two courses together, typically a course in writing with a course in selected literature or current social problems. In other cases, it may mean sharing the entire first-semester curriculum so that students in the learning community study the same material throughout the semester. In some large universities such as the University of Oregon and the University of Washington, the twenty-five to thirty students in a learning community may attend lectures with 200 to 300 other students but stay together for a smaller discussion section, often called the Freshman Interest Group, led by a graduate student or upperclassman. In still other cases, students will take all their classes together either as separate, but linked, classes (Cluster Learning Communities) or as one large class that meets four to six hours at a time several times per week (Coordinated Studies). Figure 1 shows examples of these learning community models.

The courses in which students co-register are not coincidental or random. They are typically connected by an organizing theme that gives meaning to their linkage. The point of doing so is to engender a coherent interdisciplinary or cross-subject learning that is not easily attainable through enrollment in unrelated, stand-alone courses. For example, a Coordinated Studies Program at Seattle Central Community College is titled "Body and Mind." It links courses in human biology, psychology, and sociology, and asks students to consider how the connected fields of study pursue a singular piece of knowledge, namely how and why humans behave as they do.

As described by Faith Gabelnick and her colleagues in their 1990 book *Learning Communities: Creating Connections among Students, Faculty, and Disciplines,* many learning communities do more than co-register students around a topic. They change the manner in which students experience the curriculum and the way they are taught. Faculty have reorganized their syllabi and their classrooms to promote shared, collaborative learning experiences among students across the linked classrooms. This form of classroom organization requires students to work together in some form of collaborative groups and to become active, indeed responsible, for the learning of both group and classroom peers. In

this way students are asked to share not only the experience of the curriculum, but also of learning within the curriculum.

Learning Communities as Curriculum Structure

Although the content may vary, nearly all learning communities have three things in common. One is *shared knowledge.* By requiring students to take courses together and organizing those courses around a theme, learning communities seek to construct a shared, coherent curricular experience that is not just an unconnected array of courses in, say, composition, calculus, history, Spanish, and geology. In doing so they seek to promote higher levels of cognitive complexity that cannot easily be obtained through participation in unrelated courses.

The second common element is *shared knowing.* Learning communities enroll the same students in several classes so they get to know each other quickly and fairly intimately and in a way that is part and parcel of their academic experience. By asking students to construct knowledge together, learning communities seek to involve students both socially and intellectually in ways that promote cognitive development as well as an appreciation for the many ways in which one's own knowing is enhanced when other voices are part of that learning experience.

The third common thread is *shared responsibility.* Learning communities ask students to become responsible to each other in the process of trying to know. They participate in collaborative groups that require students to be mutually dependent on one another so that the learning of the group does not advance without each member doing her or his part.

As a curricular structure, learning communities can be applied to any content and any group of students. Most often they are designed for the needs of beginning students. In those instances, one of the linked courses becomes a Freshman Seminar. Increasingly they are also being adapted to the needs of undecided students and students who require developmental academic assistance. In these cases one of the linked courses may be a career exploration or developmental advising course or, in the latter case, a "learning to learn" or study skills course.

In residential campuses some learning communities have moved into the residence halls. These "living learning communities" combine shared courses with shared living. Students, typically those beginning their first semester of college, enroll in a

FIGURE 1

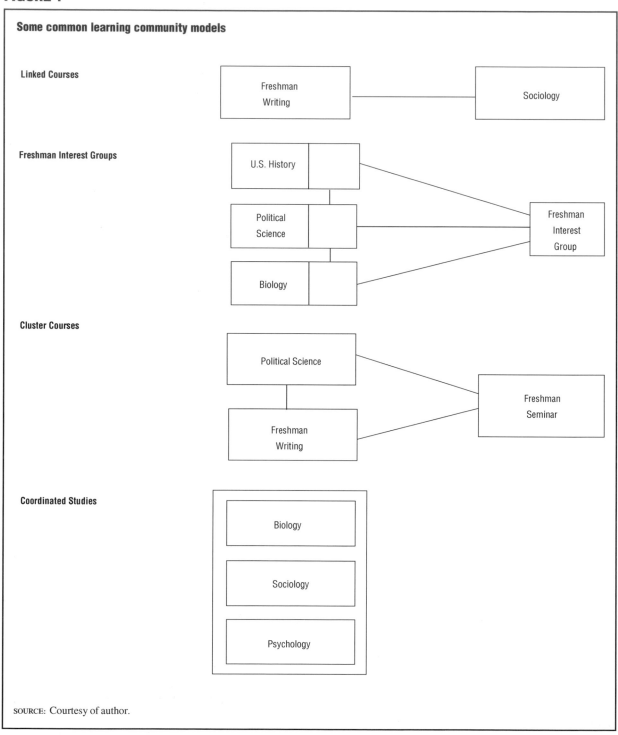

Some common learning community models

SOURCE: Courtesy of author.

number of linked courses and live together in a reserved part of a residence hall.

More recently a number of institutions have used community service as a linking activity or theme for learning communities. The Evergreen State College, Portland State University, St. Lawrence University, and colleges in the Maricopa Community College District have added service learning to one or more of their linked courses. As an extension of traditional models of community service and experiential learning, service learning combines intentional educational activities with service experience to meet critical needs identified by the communities being served. Unlike voluntarism, notes Barbara Jacoby in her 1996 book on the topic, *service learning* is a pedagogical strategy; an inductive approach to education grounded in the assumption that thoughtfully organized experience is the foundation for learning. When connected to learning communities and the collaborative pedagogy that underlies them, service learning becomes a shared experience in which students and faculty are able to engage in time-intensive, interdisciplinary study of complex social problems that may be used to apply and test theory learned in the classroom or to generate knowledge from experience. In either case service learning in a collaborative setting seems to promote not only the acquisition of course content, but also enhanced intellectual development and a shared sense of responsibility for the welfare of others.

Faculty and Staff Collaboration

When applied to particular groups of students, as described above, the faculty of the learning community almost always includes both academic and student affairs professionals. Such learning communities call for, indeed require, the collaborative efforts of both parties. This is the case because the staff of student affairs are typically the only persons on campus who possess the skills and knowledge needed to teach some of the linked courses. Take the case of learning communities for students requiring developmental assistance. In Cluster Learning Communities, for example, the faculty of the learning community may consist of a faculty person who teaches a regular introductory course in economics and two members of a learning support center who teach developmental writing and mathematics.

To be effective such learning communities require their faculty, that is the academic and student affairs professionals who staff the learning community, to collaborate on both the content and pedagogy of the linked courses. They must work together, as equal partners, to ensure that the linked courses provide a coherent shared learning experience. One of the many benefits of such collaboration, where all voices are heard, is that the academic staff often discover the wealth of knowledge that student affairs professionals bring to the discourse about teaching and learning. Furthermore, in leaving, at least momentarily, their respective "silos," both come to discover the many benefits of looking at one's work from fresh eyes.

Benefits to Students

There is now ample evidence that learning communities enhance student learning and persistence in both two- and four-year institutions. Program assessments and multi-institution studies indicate that learning communities promote student achievement in a variety of ways. Though intentionally limited in scope, studies of learning communities have yielded a number of important insights into the impact of learning communities on student learning and persistence. First, students in learning communities tended to form their own self-supporting groups that extended beyond the classroom. Learning community students spent more time together out of class than did students in traditional, unrelated stand-alone classes and they did so in ways that students saw as supportive. Indeed, some students at the urban community colleges saw those groups as critical to their ability to continue in college.

Second, learning community students became more actively involved in classroom learning, even after class. They spent more time learning together both inside and outside the class. In this way, learning communities enabled students to bridge the divide between academic classes and student social conduct that frequently characterizes student life. They tended to learn and make friends at the same time. And as students spent more time together learning, they learned more.

Third, participation in the learning community seemed to enhance the quality of student learning. By learning together, everyone's understanding and knowledge was, in the eyes of the participants, enriched. At the same time, students in the learning community programs perceived themselves as having made significantly greater intellectual gains over the course of the semester than did similar students in the comparison classes.

Fourth, as students learned more and saw themselves as more engaged both academically and socially, they persisted at a higher rate than did comparable students in the traditional curriculum. At Seattle Central Community College, for example, learning community students continued at a rate approximately twenty-five percentage points higher than did students in the traditional curriculum.

Finally, student participants' stories highlighted powerful messages about the value of collaborative learning settings in fostering what could be called "the norms of educational citizenship," that is to say norms that promote the notion that individual educational welfare is tied inexorably to the educational welfare and interests of other members of the educational community. Students in these programs reported an increased sense of responsibility to participate in the learning experience, and an awareness of their responsibility for both their learning and the learning of others.

Learning communities do not represent the final answer to student learning. As with any other pedagogy, there are limits to their effectiveness. Some students do not like learning with others and some faculty find collaborating with other faculty and staff difficult. Nevertheless, like other efforts to enhance student involvement in learning, such as cooperative learning and service learning, there is ample evidence to support the contention that their application enhances student learning and persistence and enriches faculty professional lives. It is no surprise then that so many institutions have initiated learning communities and a number of foundations have established programs to support their development.

See also: ADJUSTMENT TO COLLEGE; COLLEGE AND ITS EFFECT ON STUDENTS; COLLEGE STUDENT RETENTION; CURRICULUM, HIGHER EDUCATION; GENERAL EDUCATION IN HIGHER EDUCATION; LIVING AND LEARNING CENTER RESIDENCE HALLS; RESIDENTIAL COLLEGES.

BIBLIOGRAPHY

ASSOCIATION OF AMERICAN COLLEGES. 1985. *Integrity in the Curriculum: Report to the Academic Community.* Washington DC: Association of American Colleges.

ASTIN, ALEXANDER. 1987. *Achieving Educational Excellence.* San Francisco: Jossey-Bass.

ASTIN, ALEXANDER. 1993. *What Matters in College.* San Francisco: Jossey-Bass.

BOYER, ERNEST. 1987. *College: The Undergraduate Experience in America.* New York: Harper and Row.

CROSS, PATRICIA. 1998. "Why Learning Communities, Why Now?" *About Campus* July/August:4–11.

ENDO, JEAN J., and HARPEL, RON L. 1982. "The Effect of Student-Faculty Interaction on Students' Educational Outcomes." *Research in Higher Education* 16:115–135.

GABELNICK, FAITH; MACGREGOR, JEAN; MATTHEWS, ROBERTA S.; and SMITH, BARBARA LEIGH. 1990. *Learning Communities: Creating Connections among Students, Faculty, and Disciplines.* San Francisco: Jossey-Bass.

HURTADO, SYLVIA, and CARTER, DEBORAH FAYE. 1996. "Latino Students' Sense of Belonging in the College Community: Rethinking the Concept of Integration on Campus." In *College Students: The Evolving Nature of Research,* ed. Francis Stage, Guadalupe Anaya, John Bean, Don Hossler, and George Kuh. Needhman Heights, MA: Simon and Schuster.

JACOBY, BARBARA. 1996. *Service Learning in Higher Education: Concepts and Practices.* San Francisco: Jossey-Bass.

KUH, GEORGE. 1995. "The Other Curriculum: Out-of-Class Experiences Associated with Student Learning and Personal Development." *Journal of Higher Education* 66:123–155.

MEIKLEJOHN, ALEX. 1932. *The Experimental College.* New York: Harper and Row.

MURGUIA, EDWARD; PADILLA, RAYMOND V.; and PAVEL, MICHAEL. 1991. "Ethnicity and the Concept of Social Integration in Tinto's Model of Institutional Departure." *Journal of College Student Development* 32:433–439.

NATIONAL INSTITUTE OF EDUCATION. 1984. *Involvement in Learning: Realizing the Potential of American Higher Education.* Washington, DC: U.S. Department of Education.

PASCARELLA, ERNEST, and TERENZINI, PATRICK. 1991. *How College Affects Students.* San Francisco: Jossey-Bass.

SHAPIRO, NANCY, and LEVINE, JODI. 1999. *Creating Learning Communities: A Practical Guide to Winning Support, Organizing for Change, and Implementing Programs.* San Francisco: Jossey-Bass.

TERENZINI, PATRICK, and PASCARELLA, ERNEST. 1977. "Voluntary Freshman Attrition and Patterns of Social and Academic Integration in a University: A Test of a Conceptual Model." *Research in Higher Education* 6:25–43.

TINTO, VINCENT. 1975. "Dropout from Higher Education: A Theoretical Synthesis of Recent Research." *Review of Educational Research* 65 (winter):89–125.

TINTO, VINCENT. 1987. *Leaving College: Rethinking the Causes and Cures of Student Attrition.* Chicago: University of Chicago Press.

TINTO, VINCENT. 1995. "Learning Communities, Collaborative Learning, and the Pedagogy of Educational Citizenship." *American Association of Higher Education Bulletin* 47:11–13.

TINTO, VINCENT. 1997. "Classrooms as Communities: Exploring the Educational Character of Student Persistence." *The Journal of Higher Education* 68:599–623.

TINTO, VINCENT; GOODSELL, ANNE; and RUSSO, PAT. 1993. "Building Community among New College Students." *Liberal Education* 79:16–21.

TUSSMAN, JOSEPH. 1969. *Experiment at Berkeley.* London: Oxford University Press.

VOLKWEIN, JAMES FREDERICK; KING, MARGARET; and TERENZINI, PATRICK. 1986. "Student-Faculty Relationships and Intellectual Growth among Transfer Students." *Journal of Higher Education* 57:413–430.

VINCENT TINTO
CATHERINE ENGSTROM

LEARNING DISABILITIES, EDUCATION OF INDIVIDUALS WITH

The term *learning disability* was first introduced in the early 1960s. Up until that time, children with relatively normal intelligence who experienced learning difficulties were referred to as *minimally brain injured, slow learners, dyslexic,* or *perceptually disabled.* Despite their learning problems, these children had not received special attention in schools. Parents' unyielding efforts to get their children's educational needs addressed played a major role in the United States federal government's recognition of *specific learning disability* as a special education category in the late 1960s. The learning disability category has since become the largest category of special education in the United States, accounting for over half of all students identified by public schools as needing special education services.

Since the formal inception of the learning disability category in the 1960s, those working in that field have grappled with issues of definition, identifi-

cation, treatment, and placement. A definition of learning disabilities that provides unambiguous identification criteria does not yet exist; however, there is growing consensus regarding some aspects of a definition (e.g., presumption of central nervous system dysfunction; association with underachievement and psychological process disorders; variance within and among individuals). In practice, the principal method for determining identification is discrepancy: the difference between ability—usually measured by standardized intelligence tests—and achievement—usually measured by standardized achievement tests. Many authorities, however, object to the reliance on discrepancy because of invalid assumptions and unreliable scores.

Students with learning disabilities, like other students with disabilities, receive special education services under the Individuals with Disabilities Education Act (originally passed in 1975 as the Education for All Handicapped Children Act). Early attempts (i.e., in the mid-1960s to early 1970s) to alleviate the academic problems of students with learning disabilities involved a focus on perceptual motor training (e.g., tracing embedded figures, connecting dots) in isolation of academic skills. Most teachers no longer use these types of exercises, as research failed to demonstrate their effectiveness. The end result of individuals' and organizations' capitalizing on the appeal of "quick fixes" and "cures" is the emergence of other questionable treatments. In the 1980s, tinted lenses and the Neural Organization Technique—the manual manipulation of the skull—were purported to be effective treatments for severe reading problems.

Notwithstanding some ineffective methods, much progress has been made to identify effective means of addressing the learning needs of students with disabilities. Extensive research syntheses summarized by Sharon Vaughn, Russell Gersten, and David J. Chard indicate that students with learning disabilities learn best when they are taught in small groups (i.e., six or fewer), wherein teachers control tasks to ensure high levels of student success and use procedures to teach students self-questioning (e.g., What do I think this story is about? What mathematical operation should I use to solve this problem?). Best practices in writing instruction, for example, include explicit teaching of the steps in the writing process, explicit teaching of the structure of various types of writing, and guided feedback. Unfortunately, many special educators are inadequately trained to meet the needs of exceptional students; as a result, many instructional practices validated by research are not reaching students.

The most appropriate setting in which to provide special education services is an issue of considerable debate. For most students with learning disabilities, services are provided in general education classrooms as a result of the controversial trend toward policies of inclusion (i.e., placing students with disabilities in general-education classrooms for most or all of the school day). Advocates of full inclusion, such as the Association for Persons with Severe Handicaps, declare that all students, regardless of disability, belong in general education classrooms; others, including the Learning Disabilities Association of America, advocate that decisions regarding placement should be made on an individual basis to optimize academic and social gains for students with disabilities. In accordance with the Individuals with Disabilities Education Act, a full continuum of alternative placements, ranging from general-education classrooms to home instruction, must be available to students with disabilities. To date, evidence indicates that the preservation of the continuum of placements is in the best interest of students with learning disabilities. As special educators of the twenty-first century improve teacher training and refine and replicate research efforts, the educational needs of students with learning disabilities will be met by the most qualified teachers, through the most effective means, in the most appropriate settings.

See also: COUNCIL FOR EXCEPTIONAL CHILDREN; SPECIAL EDUCATION, *subentries on* CURRENT TRENDS, HISTORY OF.

BIBLIOGRAPHY

HALLAHAN, DANIEL P., and KAUFFMAN, JAMES M. 2000. *Exceptional Learners: Introduction to Special Education,* 8th edition. Boston: Allyn and Bacon.

HALLAHAN, DANIEL P.; KAUFFMAN, JAMES M.; and LLOYD, JOHN W. 1999. *Introduction to Learning Disabilities,* 2nd edition. Boston: Allyn and Bacon.

KAUFFMAN, JAMES M. 1999. "Commentary: Today's Special Education and Its Message for Tomorrow." *The Journal of Special Education* 32:244–254.

KAVALE, KENNETH A., and FORNESS, STEVEN R. 2000. "What Definitions of Learning Disability Say and Don't Say." *Journal of Learning Disabilities* 33:239–256.

KIRK, SAMUEL A. 1962. *Educating Exceptional Children.* Boston: Houghton Mifflin.

VAUGHN, SHARON; GERSTEN, RUSSELL; and CHARD, DAVID J. 2000. "The Underlying Message in LD Intervention Research: Findings from Research Syntheses." *Exceptional Children* 67:99–114.

WORRALL, RUSSELL S. 1990. "Detecting Health Fraud in the Field of Learning Disabilities." *Journal of Learning Disabilities* 23:207–212.

ELIZABETH A. MARTINEZ
DANIEL P. HALLAHAN

LEARNING THEORY

HISTORICAL OVERVIEW
Diane F. Halpern
Beth Donaghey
CONSTRUCTIVIST APPROACH
Mary Lamon
SCHEMA THEORY
William F. Brewer

HISTORICAL OVERVIEW

Learning theories are so central to the discipline of psychology that it is impossible to separate the history of learning theories from the history of psychology. Learning is a basic psychological process, and investigations of the principles and mechanisms of learning have been the subject of research and debate since the establishment of the first psychological laboratory by Wilhelm Wundt in Leipzeig, Germany, in 1879. *Learning* is defined as a lasting change in behaviors or beliefs that results from experience. The ability to learn provides every living organism with the ability to adapt to a changing environment. Learning is an inevitable consequence of living—if we could not learn, we would die.

The evolution of learning theories may be thought of as a progression from broad theories developed to explain the many ways that learning occurs to more specific theories that are limited in the types of learning they are designed to explain. Learning theories are broadly separated into two perspectives. The first perspective argues that learning can be studied by the observation and manipulation of stimulus-response associations. This is known as the *behaviorist* perspective because of its strict adherence to the study of observable behaviors. This perspective was first articulated in 1913 by John Watson, who argued that psychology should be the study of observable phenomena, not the study of consciousness or the mind. Watson believed that objective measurement of observable phenomena was the only way to advance the science of psychology.

The second type of learning theory argues that intervening variables are appropriate and necessary components for understanding the processes of learning. This perspective falls under the broad rubric of *cognitive learning theory,* and it was first articulated by Wilhem Wundt, the acknowledged "father of psychology," who used introspection as a means of studying thought processes. Although proponents of these two perspectives differ in their view of how learning can be studied, both schools of thought agree that there are three major assumptions of learning theory: (1) behavior is influenced by experience, (2) learning is adaptive for the individual and for the species, and (3) learning is a process governed by natural laws that can be tested and studied.

Behavior Theory

The behaviorist perspective dominated the study of learning throughout the first half of the twentieth century. Behaviorist theories identified processes of learning that could be understood in terms of the relationships between the *stimuli* that impinge on organisms and the way organisms *respond,* a view that came to be referred to as *S-R theories.* A central process in S-R theories is *equipotentiality.* Equipotential learning means that learning processes are the same for all animals, both human and nonhuman. By studying learning in nonhuman animals, the early behaviorists believed they were identifying the basic processes that are important in human learning. They also believed that learning could only be studied by observing events in the environment and measuring the responses to those events. According to the behaviorists, internal mental states are impossible topics for scientific inquiry, and thus are not necessary in the study of learning. For behaviorists, a change in behavior is the only appropriate indicator that learning has occurred. According to this view, all organisms come into the world with a blank mind, or, more formally, a *tabula rasa* (blank slate), on which the environment writes the history of learning for that organism. Learning, from the behaviorist perspective, is what happens to an organism as a result of its experiences.

Types of behavioral learning. There are two main types of learning in the behaviorist tradition. The first is *classical conditioning,* which is associated with the work of Ivan Pavlov (1849–1936), a Russian physiologist who studied the digestive processes of dogs. Pavlov noticed that dogs salivated in the absence of food if a particular stimulus was present that had previously been paired with the presentation of food. Pavlov investigated the way in which an association between a neutral stimulus (e.g., a lab technician who fed the dogs), an unconditioned stimulus (food), and an unconditioned reflex (salivation) was made. Pavlov's classic experiment involved the conditioning of salivation to the ringing of a bell and other stimuli that were not likely to make a dog salivate without a previously learned association with food.

In the initial stages of the classical conditioning paradigm, an unconditioned response (UCR; in this case, salivation) is elicited by the presentation of an unconditioned stimulus (UCS; in this case, food). If a neutral stimulus (one that does not elicit the UCR, such as a bell) is paired with the presentation of the UCS over a series of trials, it will come to elicit a *conditioned* response (CR; also salivation in this example), even when the UCS (food) is absent. In the paradigm of classical conditioning, the previously neutral stimulus (bell) becomes a conditioned stimulus (CS), which produces the conditioned response (CR) of salivation. In other words, the animal in the experiment learns to associate the bell with the opportunity to eat and begins to salivate to the bell in the absence of food. It is as though the animal came to think of the bell as "mouthwatering," although behaviorists never would have used terms like *think of,* because thinking is not a directly observable behavior.

Even though the original work on classical conditioning was performed using nonhuman animals, this type of learning applies to humans as well. Learned taste aversions and the development of specific phobias are examples of classical conditioning in humans. For example, the first time a person hears a drill at a dentist's office, it probably will not cause the palms to sweat and the heart rate to quicken. However, through the pairing of the sound with the unpleasant sensation of having a cavity drilled, the sound itself may come to elicit symptoms of fear and anxiety, even if one is not in the dentist's chair. Feelings of fear and anxiety may generalize so that the same fear response is elicited by the sight of the dentist's lab coat or the dental chair.

The second type of learning that is categorized in the behaviorist tradition is *instrumental* or *operant,* conditioning. The main difference between instrumental conditioning and classical conditioning is that the emphasis is on behavior that is voluntary (emitted), not reflexive (elicited). The target behavior (e.g., a peck at a lever if one is studying birds) comes before the conditioning stimulus (e.g., food), as opposed to the classical model, which presents the conditioning stimulus (e.g., bell) prior to the target behavior (e.g., salivation).

In the instrumental paradigm, behaviors are learned as a result of their consequences. Edward Thorndike (1874–1949) was a pioneer in instrumental conditioning, although he resisted the label of *behaviorist.* In his view, the consequences of behaving in a particular way controlled learning. Behavior was instrumental in obtaining a goal, and the consequences of the behavior were responsible for the tendency to exhibit (and repeat) a behavior. Thorndike named this principle of instrumental conditioning the *law of effect.* He argued that if a behavior had a positive consequence or led to a satisfying state of being, the response (behavior) would be strengthened. If, on the other hand, a behavior had a negative consequence, the response would be weakened. Thorndike developed the principles of instrumental conditioning using a puzzle box that required that an animal exhibit a certain behavior (push a latch) to obtain a goal (open a door for access to food). The animal was given the opportunity, through trial and error, to discover the required behavior, and the behavior was reinforced through the opening of the door and access to food. With practice, the animal decreased the time that it needed to open the door. In the instrumental paradigm, the animal learned an association between a given situation and the response required to obtain a goal.

Operant conditioning and reinforcement. B. F. Skinner (1904–1990) is credited with the development of the operant-conditioning paradigm. Similar to instrumental conditioning, operant conditioning requires that an organism operate on the environment to achieve a goal. A behavior is learned as a function of the consequences of the behavior, according to a schedule of reinforcement or punishment. Unlike Thorndike, who used the concept of reward and satisfying states, Skinner emphasized the influence of *reinforcers.* Reinforcers are events that follow a response and increase the likelihood that the response will be repeated, but they do not suggest the operation of a cognitive component such as reward (or pleasure). Learning is influenced according to the schedules of reinforcement in the operant paradigm. Skinner tested the operant theory by carefully controlling the environment to study behavior and the effects of reinforcement.

According to Skinner, operant conditioning has two laws. The first is the *law of conditioning,* which states that reinforcement strengthens the behavior that precedes it, which makes it more likely that the behavior will be repeated. The second is the *law of extinction,* which states that lack of reinforcement for a behavior will make that behavior less likely to reoccur. Reinforcement consists of two types of events, those that are *positive,* which means that when they are presented (e.g., present tasty food) the probability of a behavior occurring is increased (e.g., press a lever to get the tasty food), and those that are *negative,* which means that when they are removed (e.g., stop a loud sound or painful shock) the probability of a behavior occurring is increased (e.g., press a lever to stop a loud sound or painful shock). Punishment is defined as an event that weakens the tendency to make a response. Punishment could involve presenting an aversive stimulus (e.g., presenting a loud sound or painful shock), or it could involve removing access to a positive stimulus (e.g., removing a tasty food when a lever is pressed).

Skinner also experimented with different reinforcement schedules, and he found that different schedules produced different patterns of responding. Continuous schedules of reinforcement deliver a reinforcer every time the target behavior is exhibited. These schedules are effective in establishing the target behavior, but the behavior disappears quickly if the contingency is not met. Intermittent schedules of reinforcement deliver the reinforcer on a ratio schedule. For example, an experimenter may decide to reinforce every fourth response that an animal makes, or a reinforcer may be presented after a fixed or random time interval. The two types of intermittent schedules that maintain a high rate of responding and are very resistant to extinction are variable ratio and variable interval schedules.

Strict adherence to the behaviorist tradition excluded analysis of mental or internal events. However, Skinner acknowledged the role of thought. He maintained that thought was caused by events in the environment, and therefore a theory of learning that was concerned with the influence of the environment was appropriate. Like Pavlov and Thorndike, Skinner's work was primarily conducted with non-human animals, but the principles of operant conditioning can be applied to humans as well, and they are widely used in behavior therapy and education.

Cognitive Theories

Although behaviorism was a prolific and dominant theory in learning through the early decades of the twentieth century, certain concerns and observations led to a resurgence of interest in cognitive theories of learning. One area of concern was the distinction between performance and learning—that is, does behaviorism describe the factors that influence performance of learned behavior, rather than the act of learning itself? Within the behaviorist literature, evidence of cognitive elements like expectation and categorization exist. Under an intermittent reinforcement schedule, for example, animals increase their rate of response immediately before a reinforcer is delivered, thus acting as though they expect it. Similarly, animals can be trained to distinguish between types of stimuli that belong to different classes. Learning this type of distinction seems to involve classification, which is a cognitive process. Most importantly, scientists who studied learning recognized that the behaviorist theories could not account for all types of learning. Humans and animals can learn something without exhibiting what they have learned, meaning that performance does not always reflect what has been learned.

Cognitive theories grew from the concern that behavior involves more than an environmental stimulus and a response, whether it be voluntary or reflexive. These theories are concerned with the influence of thinking about and remembering experiences or behavior. The assumptions about learning under cognitive theories are not the same as those for behaviorist theories, because thinking and remembering are internal events. Inferences about the internal events such as thinking and remembering can be made as long as they are paired with careful observation of behavior. Cognitive theorists assume that some types of learning, such as language learning, are unique to humans, which is another difference between these two perspectives. Cognitive theories also focus on the organism as an active processor of information that modifies new experiences, relates them to past experiences, and organizes this information for storage and retrieval. Cognitive psy-

chologists also recognize that learning can take place in the absence of overt behavior.

Edward Tolman (1886–1959) was among the first psychologists to investigate the organization of behavior and learning. He conducted research in the behaviorist tradition (objective research on nonhuman species), but he introduced cognitive elements to his explanation of learning. In Tolman's theory, however, the cognitive elements were based on observed behavior, not on introspection. He believed that learning involved more than stimulus and response events; it involved the development of an organized body of knowledge or expectations about a given situation. Tolman conducted many of his learning experiments using rats whose learning task was to run through a maze. By varying the conditions in the maze, he came to the conclusion that learning involved an understanding about events and their consequences, and this led to purposive, goal-directed behavior. Tolman emphasized the role of expectation and its reinforcing influence on the repetition of behavior. He popularized the concept of cognitive maps, which represent an organism's understanding of the relationship between parts of the environment, as well as the organism's relationship to the environment.

In a clear break with behaviorists, Tolman noted that reinforcement was not a necessary component of learning, and that organisms could demonstrate *latent learning*. Latent learning is displayed only when an organism is motivated to show it. Tolman was also concerned with differences in behavior that might be attributed to internal states of the organism, a consideration that had been largely rejected by earlier theorists. In identical learning paradigms, two organisms can show different behaviors based on their different moods, physiology, or mental states.

Social learning theory. Social learning theory focuses on the sort of learning that occurs in a social context where modeling, or observational learning, constitutes a large part of the way that organisms learn. Social learning theorists are concerned with how expectations, memory, and awareness influence the learning process. Both humans and nonhumans can learn through observation and modeling. Consider, for example, the acquisition of sign language by the offspring of language-trained apes who learn to sign by watching their trained parents. Children learn many behaviors through modeling. A classic experiment by Albert Bandura (1961) allowed one group of children to observe an adult who aggressively pounded on a bobo doll (an inflatable doll used for punching), while another group watched a nonaggressive model and a third group had no model at all. The children who saw the aggressive adult often modeled (imitated) this behavior when given an opportunity to play with the same doll. The children who saw the nonaggressive model showed the least amount of aggressive play when compared to the other two groups. Social learning theorists retain the behaviorist principles of reinforcement and response contingencies, but they also extend the area of inquiry for learning to include components of cognitive processing such as attention, remembering, the processing of information about the environment, and the consequences of behavior.

Appreciation of the cognitive components of learning focused attention on the need to remember an experience over various time intervals. Information-processing theories developed from the cognitive perspective and involve the processes of coding, storing, and retrieving information about the environment. Information processing is used to study the processes of memory, a central cognitive component in modern learning theories. Theories of information processing are a by-product of the computer revolution, and they use the language of computers (e.g., sequential processing stages, input, output) to describe the processes of learning and memory. According to a human information-processing perspective, learning occurs in sequential stages, beginning with *encoding* information from the environment. Encoding of information involves the process by which information from the environment is translated into usable information. The next stage is *storage*, which involves keeping the information that has been encoded. Stored information builds the "database" of past learning. The final stage in the information-processing approach is *retrieval*, which involves accessing the stored information so that it can be used to perform a task. Organisms are seen as active participants in the information-processing model. They do not experience the environment passively or simply absorb information, but instead they seek out certain information, and then manipulate, modify, and store it for later use.

Learning theories have often been used to provide a guide for education. Earlier applications were concerned with the use of appropriate rewards and punishment, concerns that mirrored the major tenets of behaviorist theories. More recently, cognitive perspectives have shaped the field of education, and there has been more concern with learning methods that enhance long-term retention and the transfer of information and skills that are learned in schools to novel problems in out-of-school settings. For example, variability in encoding (learning material in different ways, e.g. video and text) produces more durable long-term retention, even though it is a more effortful (and generally less enjoyable) way to learn. In addition, students can become better thinkers when they receive specific instruction in thinking skills—and when the instruction is designed to enhance transfer. Teaching strategies that enhance transfer include spaced practice (viewing material over time versus cramming), using a variety of examples so learners can recognize where a concept is applicable, and practice at retrieval (repeatedly remembering material over time) with informative feedback.

Learning theories are facing new challenges as people grapple with increases in the amount of available information that needs to be learned, rapidly changing technologies that require new types of responses to new problems, and the need to continue learning throughout one's life, even into old age. Contemporary learning theories supported by empirical research offer the promise of enhanced learning and improved thinking—both of which are critical in a rapidly changing and complex world.

See also: SKINNER, B. F.; THORNDIKE, EDWARD; WATSON, JOHN B.

BIBLIOGRAPHY

BANDURA, ALBERT. 1977. *Social Learning Theory.* Englewood Cliffs, NJ: Prentice-Hall.

BENJAMIN, LUDY T. 1988. *A History of Psychology: Original Sources and Contemporary Research.* New York: McGraw-Hill.

DE WINSTANLEY, PATRICIA A., and BJORK, ROBERT A. 2002. "Successful Lecturing: Presenting Information in Ways That Engage Effective Processing." In *New Directions for Teaching and Learning,* ed. Diane F. Halpern and Milton D. Hakel. San Francisco: Jossey-Bass.

DONAHOE, JOHN W., and WESSELLS, MICHAEL G. 1980. *Learning, Language, and Memory.* New York: Harper and Row.

HALPERN, DIANE F. 1997. "Sex Differences in Intelligence: Implications for Education." *American Psychologist* 52(10):1091–1102.

MOWRER, ROBERT R., and KLEIN, STEPHEN B. 1989. "Contemporary Learning Theories: Pavlovian Conditioning and the Status of Traditional Learning Theory." In *Traditional Learning Theory and the Transition to Contemporary Learning Theory,* ed. Stephen B. Mowrer and Robert R. Klein. Hillsdale, NJ: Erlbaum.

ORMROD, JEANNE E. 1999. *Human Learning,* 3rd edition. Upper Saddle River; NJ: Prentice-Hall.

SKINNER, B. F. 1938. "A System of Behavior." In *A History of Psychology: Original Sources and Contemporary Research,* ed. Ludy T. Benjamin. New York: McGraw-Hill.

THORNDIKE, EDWARD. L. 1913. "The Laws of Learning in Animals." In *A History of Psychology: Original Sources and Contemporary Research,* ed. Ludy T. Benjamin. New York: McGraw-Hill.

TOLMAN, EDWARD C. 1948. "Cognitive Maps in Rats and Men." In *A History of Psychology: Original Sources and Contemporary Research,* ed. Ludy T. Benjamin. New York: McGraw-Hill.

WATSON, JOHN B. 1913. "Psychology As the Behaviorist Views It." In *A History of Psychology: Original Sources and Contemporary Research,* ed. Ludy T. Benjamin. New York: McGraw-Hill.

WESTEN, DREW. 1996. *Psychology: Mind, Brain, and Culture.* New York: John Wilcy and Sons.

DIANE F. HALPERN
BETH DONAGHEY

CONSTRUCTIVIST APPROACH

Constructivism is an epistemology, or a theory, used to explain how people know what they know. The basic idea is that problem solving is at the heart of learning, thinking, and development. As people solve problems and discover the consequences of their actions—through reflecting on past and immediate experiences—they construct their own understanding. Learning is thus an active process that requires a change in the learner. This is achieved through the activities the learner engages in, including the consequences of those activities, and through reflection. People only deeply understand what they have constructed.

A constructivist approach to learning and instruction has been proposed as an alternative to the objectivist model, which is implicit in all behaviorist and some cognitive approaches to education. Objectivism sees knowledge as a passive reflection of the external, objective reality. This implies a process of "instruction," ensuring that the learner gets correct information.

History of Constructivism

The psychological roots of constructivism began with the developmental work of Jean Piaget (1896–1980), who developed a theory (the theory of genetic epistemology) that analogized the development of the mind to evolutionary biological development and highlighted the adaptive function of cognition. Piaget proposed four stages in human development: the sensorimotor stage, the preoperational stage, the concrete operational stage, and the formal operational stage. For Piaget, the development of human intellect proceeds through adaptation and organization. Adaptation is a process of assimilation and accommodation, where external events are assimilated into existing understanding, but unfamiliar events, which don't fit with existing knowledge, are accommodated into the mind, thereby changing its organization.

Countless studies have demonstrated—or tried to discredit—Piaget's developmental stages. For example, it has become clear that most adults use formal operations in only a few domains where they have expertise. Nonetheless, Piaget's hypothesis that learning is a transformative rather than a cumulative process is still central. Children do not learn a bit at a time about some issue until it finally comes together as understanding. Instead, they make sense of whatever they know from the very beginning. This understanding is progressively reformed as new knowledge is acquired, especially new knowledge that is incompatible with their previous understanding. This transformative view of learning has been greatly extended by neo-Piagetian research.

The Russian psychologist Lev Vygotsky's (1896–1934) relevance to constructivism derives from his theories about language, thought, and their mediation by society. Vygotsky held the position that the child gradually internalizes external and social activities, including communication, with more competent others. Although social speech is internalized in adulthood (it becomes thinking), Vygotsky contended that it still preserves its intrinsic collaborative character.

In his experiments, Vygotsky studied the difference between the child's reasoning when working independently versus reasoning when working with a more competent person. He devised the notion of the *zone of proximal development* to reflect on the potential of this difference. Vygotsky's findings suggested that learning environments should involve guided interactions that permit children to reflect on inconsistency and to change their conceptions through communication. Vygotsky's work has since been extended in the *situated approach* to learning.

Vygotsky and Piaget's theories are often contrasted to each other in terms of individual cognitive constructivism (Piaget) and social constructivism (Vygotsky). Some researchers have tried to develop a synthesis of these approaches, though some, such as Michael Cole and James Wertsch, argue that the individual versus social orientation debate is overemphasized. To them, the real difference rests on the contrast between the roles of cultural artifacts. For Vygotsky, such artifacts play a central role, but they do not appear in Piaget's theories.

For the American philosopher and educator John Dewey (1859–1952), education depended on action—knowledge and ideas emerge only from a situation in which learners have to draw out experiences that have meaning and importance to them. Dewey argued that human thought is practical problem solving, which proceeds by testing rival hypotheses. These problem-solving experiences occur in a social context, such as a classroom, where students join together in manipulating materials and observing outcomes. Dewey invented the method of progressive education in North America. The Fostering Communities of Learners (FCL) program, devised by Ann Lesley Brown and Joseph Campione, is a current attempt to put Dewey's progressive education theory to work in the classroom.

In summary, Piaget contributed the idea of transformation in learning and development; Vygotsky contributed the idea that learning and development were integrally tied to communicative interactions with others; and Dewey contributed the idea that schools had to bring real world problems into the school curriculum.

Constructivist Processes and Education

There are a number of competing constructivist views in education. Constructivists tend to celebrate complexity and multiple perspectives, though they do share at least a few educational prescriptions.

Prior knowledge. Constructivists believe that prior knowledge impacts the learning process. In trying to solve novel problems, perceptual or conceptual similarities between existing knowledge and a new problem can remind people of what they already know. This is often one's first approach towards solving novel problems. Information not connected with a learner's prior experiences will be quickly forgotten. In short, the learner must actively construct new information into his or her existing mental framework for meaningful learning to occur.

For example, Rosalind Driver has found that children's understanding of a phenomenon (interpretations that fit their experiences and expectations) differ from scientific explanations. This means that students distinguish school science from their "real world" explanations. Studies of adult scientific thinking reveal that many adults hold nonnormative scientific explanations, even though they have studied science. This is what the philosopher Alfred Whitehead (1861–1947) referred to as *inert knowledge.* Asking students what they already know about a topic and what puzzles them affords an opportunity to assess children's prior knowledge and the processes by which they will make sense of phenomena.

Real and authentic problems. Constructivist learning is based on the active participation of learners in problem-solving and critical thinking—given real and authentic problems.

In *anchored instruction,* for example, as advanced in the work of the Cognition and Technology Group at Vanderbilt University, learners are invited to engage in a fictitious problem occurring in a simulated real-world environment. Rich and realistic video contexts are provided—not only to provide relevant information for solving the problem, but also to create a realistic context. If the students buy in to the proposed problems, they will be engaged in problem solving similar to what the people in the video are engaged in.

There are also many examples of project-based learning in which students take on tasks such as building a vehicle that could cross Antarctica. It is unclear whether these constitute authentic problems—or what students learn from project-based learning.

Constructivist curriculum. A constructively oriented curriculum presents an emerging agenda based on what children know, what they are puzzled by, and the teachers' learning goals. Thus, an important part of a constructivist-oriented curriculum should be the negotiation of meaning. Maggie Lampert, a mathematics teacher, guides students to make sense of mathematics by comparing and resolving discrepancies between what they know and what seems to be implied by new experience.

In constructivist classrooms, curriculum is generally a process of digging deeper and deeper into big ideas, rather than presenting a breadth of coverage. For example, in the Fostering Communities of Learners project where students learn how to learn, in knowledge-building classrooms where students seek to create new knowledge, or in Howard Gardner's classrooms where the focus is on learning for deep understanding, students might study endangered species, island biogeography, or the principles of gravity over several months. As students pursue questions, they derive new and more complex questions to be investigated. Building useful knowledge structures requires effortful and purposeful activity over an extended period.

Cognitive conflict and social context. According to Dewey, "Reflection arises because of the appearance of incompatible factors within an empirical situation. Then opposed responses are provoked which cannot be taken simultaneously in overt action" (p. 326). To say this in another way, cognitive conflict or puzzlement is the stimulus for learning, and it determines the organization and nature of what is being learned. Negotiation can also occur between individuals in a classroom. This process involves discussion and attentive listening, making sense of the points of views of others, and comparing personal meanings to the theories of peers. Justifying one position over another and selecting theories that are more viable leads to a better theory. Katerine Bielaczyc and Allan Collins have summarized educational research on learning communities in classrooms where the class goal is to learn together, to appreciate and capitalize on distributed expertise, and to articulate the kinds of cognitive processes needed for learning.

Constructivist assessment. Assessment of student learning is of two types: formative and summative. Formative assessment occurs during learning and provides feedback to the student. It includes evaluations of ongoing portfolios, and demonstrations of work in progress. Student collaboration also provides a form of formative assessment. In FCL, for example, students report to each other periodically on their research. In knowledge-building classrooms, students can read and comment on each other's

work with the Knowledge Forum software. Formative assessment rarely occurs in classrooms.

Summative assessment occurs through tests and essays at the end of a unit of study. Summative assessments provide little specific feedback. From a constructivist perspective, formative assessments are more valuable to the learner, but with the recent emphasis in North America on standards, and due to the poor alignment of constructivist approaches and standards, it is very difficult to harmonize formative and summative assessments.

Technology and constructivism. Cognitive research has uncovered successful patterns in tutorial, mentoring, and group discussion interactions. However, typical Internet chat and bulletin-board systems do not support a constructivist approach to learning and instruction. During the 1990s, researchers created tools such as Knowledge Forum, the Knowledge Integration Environment, and CoVis to more fully address constructivist principles. Each of these tools invites collaboration by structuring the kinds of contributions learners can make, supporting meaningful relationships among those contributions, and guiding students' inquiries. Teachers who use information and communication technologies in their classrooms are more likely to have a constructivist perspective towards learning and instruction. Additionally, sophisticated information and technology communications tools can capture the cognitive processes learners engage in when solving problems. This affords teacher reflection and coaching to aid deeper learning. It also affords teachers the chance to learn from each other.

The teacher's role. The teacher's role in a constructivist classroom isn't so much to lecture at students but to act as an expert learner who can guide students into adopting cognitive strategies such as self testing, articulating understanding, asking probing questions, and reflection. The role of the teacher in constructivist classrooms is to organize information around big ideas that engage the students' interest, to assist students in developing new insights, and to connect them with their previous learning. The activities are student-centered, and students are encouraged to ask their own questions, carry out their own experiments, make their own analogies, and come to their own conclusions. Becoming a constructivist teacher may prove a difficult transformation, however, since most instructors have been prepared for teaching in the traditional, objectivist manner. It "requires a paradigm shift," as well as "the willing abandonment of familiar perspectives and practices and the adoption of new ones" (Brooks and Brooks, p. 25).

A constructivist approach to education is widely accepted by most researchers, though not by all. Carl Bereiter argues that constructivism in schools is usually reduced to project based learning, and John Anderson, Lynn Reder, and Herbert Simon claim that constructivism advocates very inefficient learning and assessment procedures. In any event, the reality is that constructivism is rarely practiced in schools.

See also: KNOWLEDGE BUILDING; PIAGET, JEAN; VYGOTSKY, LEV.

BIBLIOGRAPHY

ANDERSON, JOHN R.; REDER, LYNN; and SIMON, HERBERT A. 1996. "Situated Learning and Education." *Educational Researcher* 25(4): 5–96.

BEREITER, CARL. 2002. *Education and Mind for the Knowledge Age.* Mahwah, NJ: Erlbaum.

BEREITER, CARL, and SCARDAMALIA, MARLENE. 1989. "Intentional Learning As a Goal of Instruction." In *Knowing, Learning, and Instruction: Essays in Honor of Robert Glaser,* ed. Lauren B. Resnick. Hillsdale NJ: Erlbaum.

BRANSFORD, JOHN D.; BROWN, ANN L.; and COCKING, RODNEY. 1999. *How People Learn: Brain, Mind, Experience, and School.* Washington, DC: National Academy Press.

BROOKS, JACQUELINE G., and BROOKS, MARTIN G. 1993. *In Search of Understanding: The Case for Constructivist Classrooms.* Alexandria, VA: Association for Supervision and Curriculum Development.

BROWN, ANN L., and CAMPIONE, JOSEPH C. 1994. "Guided Discovery in a Community of Learners." In *Classroom Lessons: Integrating Cognitive Theory and Classroom Practice,* ed. Kate McGilly. Cambridge, MA: MIT Press/Bradford Books.

BROWN, JOHN SEELY; COLLINS, ALLAN; and DUGUID, PAUL. 1989. "Situated Cognition and the Culture of Learning." *Educational Researcher* 18(1):32–42.

CASE, ROBBIE. 1985. *Intellectual Development: Birth to Adulthood.* Orlando, FL: Academic Press.

COBB, PAUL. 1994. "Where Is the Mind? Constructivist and Sociocultural Perspectives on Mathematical Development." *Educational Researcher* 23:13–20.

COGNITION AND TECHNOLOGY GROUP AT VANDERBILT. 1997. *The Jasper Project: Lessons in Curriculum, Instruction, Assessment, and Professional Development.* Mahwah, NJ: Erlbaum.

DRIVER, ROSALIND. 1989. "Changing Conceptions." In *Adolescent Development and School Science,* ed. Philip Adey. London: Falmer.

GARDNER, HOWARD. 1999. *The Disciplined Mind: What All Students Should Understand.* New York: Simon and Schuster.

JOHNSON-LAIRD, PHILIP N. 1983. *Mental Models.* Cambridge, MA: Harvard University Press.

LAMPERT, MAGDELEINE. 1986. "Knowing, Doing, and Teaching Multiplication." *Cognition and Instruction* 3:305–342.

LAVE, JEAN, and WENGER, ETIENNE. 1991. *Situated Learning: Legitimate Peripheral Participation.* New York: Cambridge University Press.

PIAGET, JEAN. 1952. *The Origins of Intelligence in Children,* trans. Margaret Cook. New York: International Universities Press.

PIAGET, JEAN. 1971. *Biology and Knowledge.* Chicago: University of Chicago Press.

RAVITZ, JASON; BECKER, HANK J.; and WONG, YANTIEN T. 2000. *Constructivist-Compatible Beliefs and Practices among U.S. Teachers: Teaching, Learning, and Computing.* Center for Research on Information Technology and Organizations, University of California, Irvine, and University of Minnesota.

SCARDAMALIA, MARLENE; BEREITER, CARL; and LAMON, MARY. 1994. "Bringing the Classroom into World III." In *Classroom Lessons: Integrating Cognitive Theory and Classroom Practice.* ed. Kate McGilly. Cambridge, MA: MIT Press.

SIEGLER, ROBERT S. 1981. "Developmental Sequences within and between Concepts." *Monographs of the Society for Research in Child Development* 46(2).

VYGOTSKY, LEV S. 1987. *Collected Works of L. S. Vygotsky,* Vol. 1: *Problems of General Psychology,* trans. Norris Minick. New York: Plenum.

WERTSCH, JAMES V. 1991. *Voices of the Mind: A Sociocultural Approach to Mediated Action.* Cambridge, MA: Harvard University Press.

WHITEHEAD, ALFRED N. 1929. *The Aims of Education.* New York: Macmillan.

INTERNET RESOURCES

COLE, MICHAEL, and WERTSCH, JAMES V. 2002. "Beyond the Individual-Social Antimony in Discussions of Piaget and Vygotsky." <www.massey.ac.nz/~alock/virtual/colevyg.htm>.

DEWEY, JOHN. 1916. *Democracy and Education: An Introduction to the Philosophy of Education.* New York: Free Press. <www.ilt.columbia.edu/publications/dewey.html>.

MARY LAMON

SCHEMA THEORY

Schemata are psychological constructs that have been proposed as a form of mental representation for some forms of complex knowledge.

Bartlett's Schema Theory

Schemata were initially introduced into psychology and education through the work of the British psychologist Sir Frederic Bartlett (1886–1969). In carrying out a series of studies on the recall of Native American folktales, Bartlett noticed that many of the recalls were not accurate, but involved the replacement of unfamiliar information with something more familiar. They also included many inferences that went beyond the information given in the original text. In order to account for these findings, Bartlett proposed that people have *schemata,* or unconscious mental structures, that represent an individual's generic knowledge about the world. It is through schemata that old knowledge influences new information.

For example, one of Bartlett's participants read the phrase "something black came out of his mouth" and later recalled it as "he foamed at the mouth." This finding could be accounted for by assuming that the input information was not consistent with any schema held by the participant, and so the original information was reconstructed in a form that was consistent with one of the participant's schemata. The schema construct was developed during the period when psychology was strongly influenced by behaviorist and associationistic approaches; because the schema construct was not compatible with these worldviews, it eventually faded from view.

Minsky's Frame Theory

In the 1970s, however, the schema construct was reintroduced into psychology though the work of the computer scientist Marvin Minsky. Minsky was attempting to develop machines that would display human-like abilities (e.g., to perceive and understand the world). In the course of trying to solve these difficult problems, he came across Bartlett's work. Minsky concluded that humans were using their stored knowledge about the world to carry out many of the processes that he was trying to emulate by machine, and he therefore needed to provide his machines with this type of knowledge if they were ever to achieve human-like abilities. Minsky developed the *frame* construct as a way to represent knowledge in machines. Minsky's frame proposal can be seen as essentially an elaboration and specification of the schema construct. He conceived of the frame knowledge as interacting with new specific information coming from the world. He proposed that fixed generic information be represented as a frame comprised of slots that accept a certain range of values. If the world did not provide a specific value for a particular slot, then it could be filled by a default value.

For example, consider the representation of a generic (typical) elementary school classroom. The frame for such a classroom includes certain information, such as that the room has walls, a ceiling, lights, and a door. The door can be thought of as a slot which accepts values such as wood door or metal door, but does not accept a value such as a door made of jello. If a person or a machine is trying to represent a particular elementary school classroom, the person or machine *instantiates* the generic frame with specific information from the particular classroom (e.g., it has a window on one wall, and the door is wooden with a small glass panel). If, for some reason, one does not actually observe the lights in the classroom, one can fill the lighting slot with the default assumption that they are fluorescent lights. This proposal gives a good account of a wide range of phenomena. It explains, for example, why one would be very surprised to walk into an elementary classroom and find that it did not have a ceiling, and it accounts for the fact that someone might recall that a certain classroom had fluorescent lights when it did not.

Modern Schema Theory

Minsky's work in computer science had a strong and immediate impact on psychology and education. In 1980 the cognitive psychologist David Rumelhart elaborated on Minsky's ideas and turned them into an explicitly psychological theory of the mental representation of complex knowledge. Roger Schank and Robert Abelson developed the *script* construct to deal with generic knowledge of sequences of actions. Schema theory provided explanations for many experiments already in the literature, and led to a very wide variety of new empirical studies. Providing a relevant schema improved comprehension and recall of opaquely written passages, and strong schemata were shown to lead to high rates of inferential errors in recall.

Broad versus Narrow Use of Schema

In retrospect, it is clear that there has been an ambiguity in schema theory between a narrow use and a broad use of the term *schema*. For example, in Rumelhart's classic 1980 paper, he defined a schema as "a data structure for representing the generic concepts stored in memory" (p. 34). Yet he went on to state that "there are schemata representing our knowledge about all concepts: those underlying objects, situations, events, sequences of events, actions and sequences of actions" (p. 34). Thus, schemata are frequently defined as the form of mental representation for generic knowledge, but are then used as the term for the representation of all knowledge.

There are severe problems with the use of the term *schema* to refer to all forms of complex knowledge. First, there is no need for a new technical term, since the ordinary term *knowledge* has this meaning. In addition, if schema theory is used to account for all knowledge, then it fails. A number of writers have pointed out that schema theory, as presently developed, cannot deal with those forms of knowledge that do not involve old generic information. Thus, schema theory provides an account for the knowledge in long-term memory that the state of Oklahoma is directly above the state of Texas. However, schema theory does not provide an account of the new representation one develops of a town as one travels through it for the first time.

Therefore it seems best to use the term *schema* in the narrower usage, as the form of mental representation used for generic knowledge. However, if one adopts the narrower usage one has to accept that schemata are only the appropriate representations for a subset of knowledge and that other forms of mental representation are needed for other forms of knowledge. For example, *mental models* are needed to represent specific nonschematic aspects of knowledge, such as the layout of an unfamiliar town, while *naive theories* or *causal mental models* are needed to represent knowledge of causal/mechanical phenomena.

Schema Theory in Education

Richard Anderson, an educational psychologist, played an important role in introducing schema theory to the educational community. In a 1977 paper Anderson pointed out that schemata provided a form of representation for complex knowledge and that the construct, for the first time, provided a principled account of how old knowledge might influence the acquisition of new knowledge. Schema theory was immediately applied to understanding the reading process, where it served as an important counterweight to purely bottom-up approaches to reading. The schema-theory approaches to reading emphasize that reading involves both the bottom-up information from the perceived letters coming into the eye and the use of top-down knowledge to construct a meaningful representation of the content of the text.

Broad versus Narrow Use of Schema in Education

The problem with the broad and narrow use of the term *schema* surfaced in education just as it had in cognitive psychology. For example, in Anderson's classic 1977 paper on schemata in education, he clearly takes the broad view. He attacks the narrow view and says that it is impossible "that people have stored a schema for every conceivable scene, event sequence, and message" (p. 421), and that "an adequate theory must explain how people cope with novelty" (p. 421). However in a paper written at roughly the same time (1978), Anderson states that "a schema represents generic knowledge" (p. 67), and he adopts the narrow view systematically throughout the paper. In a 1991 paper on terminology in education, Patricia Alexander, Diane Schallert, and Victoria Hare note that the systematic ambiguity between the narrow and broad views has made it very difficult to interpret a given writer's use of the term *schema* in the education literature.

Instructional Implications of Schema Theory

A number of writers have derived instructional proposals from schema theory. They have suggested that relevant knowledge should be activated before reading; that teachers should try to provide prerequisite knowledge; and that more attention should be given to teaching higher-order comprehension processes. Many of these proposals are not novel, but schema theory appears to provide a theoretical and empirical basis for instructional practices that some experienced teachers were already carrying out.

Impact of Schema Theory on Education

Schema theory has provided education with a way to think about the representation of some forms of complex knowledge. It has focused attention on the role old knowledge plays in acquiring new knowledge, and has emphasized the role of top-down, reader-based influences in the reading process.

See also: LEARNING, *subentry on* CAUSAL REASONING; LITERACY, *subentry on* NARRATIVE COMPREHENSION AND PRODUCTION; READING, *subentries on* COMPREHENSION, CONTENT AREAS.

BIBLIOGRAPHY

ADAMS, MARILYN J., and COLLINS, ALLAN. 1979. "A Schema-Theoretic View of Reading." In *New Directions in Discourse Processing,* Vol. 2: *Advances in Discourse Processes,* ed. Roy O. Freedle. Norwood, NJ: Ablex.

ALEXANDER, PATRICIA A.; SCHALLERT, DIANE L.; and HARE, VICTORIA C. 1991. "Coming to Terms: How Researchers in Learning and Literacy Talk about Knowledge." *Review of Educational Research* 61:315–343.

ANDERSON, RICHARD C. 1977. "The Notion of Schemata and the Educational Enterprise: General Discussion of the Conference." In *Schooling and the Acquisition of Knowledge,* ed. Richard C. Anderson, Rand J. Spiro, and William E. Montague. Hillsdale, NJ: Erlbaum.

ANDERSON, RICHARD C. 1978. "Schema-Directed Processes in Language Comprehension." In *Cognitive Psychology and Instruction,* ed. Alan M. Lesgold, James W. Pellegrino, Sipke D. Fokkema, and Robert Glaser. New York: Plenum.

ANDERSON, RICHARD C. 1984. "Role of the Reader's Schema in Comprehension, Learning, and Memory." In *Learning to Read in American Schools: Basal Readers and Content Texts,* ed. Richard C. Anderson, Jean Osborn, and Robert J. Tierney. Hillsdale, NJ: Erlbaum.

ANDERSON, RICHARD C., and PEARSON, P. DAVID. 1984. "A Schema-Theoretic View of Basic Processes in Reading Comprehension." In *Handbook of Reading Research,* ed. P. David Pearson. New York: Longman.

BARTLETT, FREDERIC C. 1932. *Remembering.* Cambridge, Eng.: Cambridge University Press.

BRANSFORD, JOHN D., and JOHNSON, MARCIA K. 1973. "Considerations of Some Problems of Comprehension." In *Visual Information Processing,* ed. William G. Chase. New York: Academic.

BREWER, WILLIAM F. 1987. "Schemas Versus Mental Models in Human Memory." In *Modelling Cognition,* ed. Peter Morris. Chichester, Eng.: Wiley.

BREWER, WILLIAM F. 1999. "Scientific Theories and Naive Theories as Forms of Mental Representation: Psychologism Revived." *Science and Education* 8:489–505.

BREWER, WILLIAM F. 2000. "Bartlett's Concept of the Schema and Its Impact on Theories of Knowledge Representation in Contemporary Cognitive Psychology." In *Bartlett, Culture and Cognition,* ed. Akiko Saito. Hove, Eng.: Psychology Press.

BREWER, WILLIAM F., and NAKAMURA, GLENN V. 1984. "The Nature and Functions of Schemas." In *Handbook of Social Cognition,* Vol. 1, ed. Robert S. Wyer, Jr. and Thomas K. Srull. Hillsdale, NJ: Erlbaum.

HACKER, CHARLES J. 1980. "From Schema Theory to Classroom Practice." *Language Arts* 57:866–871.

JOHNSON-LAIRD, PHILIP N. 1983. *Mental Models.* Cambridge, MA: Harvard University Press.

MINSKY, MARVIN. 1975. "A Framework for Representing Knowledge." In *The Psychology of Computer Vision,* ed. Patrick H. Winston. New York: McGraw-Hill.

RUMELHART, DAVID E. 1980. "Schemata: The Building Blocks of Cognition." In *Theoretical Issues in Reading Comprehension,* ed. Rand J. Spiro, Bertram C. Bruce, and William F. Brewer. Hillsdale, NJ: Erlbaum.

SCHANK, ROGER C., and ABELSON, ROBERT P. 1977. *Scripts, Plans, Goals and Understanding.* Hillsdale, NJ: Erlbaum.

WILLIAM F. BREWER

LEARNING TO LEARN AND METACOGNITION

Since the time of the Greek philosopher Socrates, educators have realized that teachers cannot possibly teach students everything they need to know in life. Thus, a major goal of educational systems has been to prepare students for a lifetime of learning. To this end, a large part of the educational endeavor involves teaching general skills and strategies that can be applied to a variety of problems and learning situations.

Although strategy instruction has been shown to improve learning, knowledge of strategies may not be sufficient to produce higher levels of learning. For instance, in 1973 Earl C. Butterfield, Clark Wambold, and John M. Belmont taught learning disabled students a strategy for learning a list of items. When these students used the strategy, their performance reached the level of normal achieving students— however, the learning disabled students did not spontaneously use it. To obtain higher levels of performance, learning disabled students had to be told when to use the strategy.

Similarly, young children may have knowledge of strategies but fail to use them. Michael Pressley, John G. Borkowski, and Julia T. O'Sullivan suggested in 1984 that strategy instruction should therefore provide students information about the utility of the strategy and when and how to use it. Put differently, strategy instruction should also include a metacognitive component.

Metacognition broadly defined is knowledge that a person has of his own cognitive processes. In 1979 John H. Flavell proposed that metacognitive knowledge consists of three components: (1) knowledge of self (e.g., knowing that one learns better when studying in a quiet setting than in front of the television); (2) knowledge of task (e.g., knowing that it's easier to prepare for a multiple-choice test than an essay test); and (3) knowledge of strategies (e.g., when and how to use them).

There is a significant relation between learning outcomes and knowledge of specific strategies. For instance, when strategy-training programs include assessing knowledge of the strategy and the utility of the strategy being taught, test performance is greater for children with more knowledge of the strategy than for children with less knowledge. Thus, knowing about a strategy is important. It is also important to know when to use one strategy versus another.

Ideally, children will be able to monitor the effectiveness of a particular strategy in a given situation and change strategies if necessary. To do this, they must accurately monitor their own learning (the degree to which material has been learned). Models of self-regulated learning provide a theoretical framework for understanding the role of metacognition in learning.

These models suggest that a person begins study by setting a learning goal (desired state of learning). As a person studies, she monitors how well the material has been learned. If this monitoring indicates that the goal has been reached, the person will terminate study. By contrast, if the learning goal has not been reached, the person will adjust her study (e.g., selecting a different study strategy or allocating more study time to the material).

According to this framework, accurate metacognitive monitoring is necessary for effective regulation of study, and these together contribute to more optimal learning. Thus, if a person does not accurately monitor his current state of learning, the person may fail to regulate study effectively. For instance, if a person inaccurately assesses progress toward a learning goal, he may prematurely stop studying or may continue using a less-effective strategy when another would be more effective. Therefore, accurately monitoring learning is critical.

A number of factors affect how accurately learning is monitored and how well this information is used to regulate study. Age-related differences are perhaps most relevant to educators. The capability to monitor the effectiveness of one strategy versus another develops with age. Adults discover the utility of a strategy spontaneously by using the strategy and through experiences with tests, and they will use this information to regulate subsequent study—selecting more effective strategies. Older children, although less accurate than adults, also monitor the utility of a particular strategy by using it and gaining feedback through tests; however, they fail to use this information to regulate study without explicit feedback regarding test performance. Young children do not appear to accurately monitor the utility of a strategy even when given an opportunity to monitor their test performance.

One approach to improving the accuracy of monitoring strategy effectiveness is to provide strategy-monitoring training. Marguerite Lodico and colleagues in 1983 trained young children to monitor their performance while using different strategies and to explain how the strategy influenced their performance. Throughout this training, the children received feedback regarding their answers. Children who received this training were better able to derive the utility of the strategies and, in subsequent study, more frequently chose to use the more effective strategy.

The capability to monitor learning during study (prior to test) also develops with age. Annette Dufresne and Akira Kobasigawa showed that children as young as third grade recognized that it was easier to learn related items (e.g., bat and ball) than unrelated items (e.g., frog and table), whereas first graders fail to monitor the difference between these items. This difference in monitoring accuracy influenced regulation of study. Older children chose to restudy the more difficult items, whereas younger children appeared to randomly select items for restudy.

In some cases, adults quite accurately monitor their own learning (e.g., when monitoring associative learning after a delay). That is, in these situations, adults accurately discriminate better-learned material from less-learned material. However, in other cases, such as attempting to monitor comprehension of texts, even adult's monitoring accuracy is less than remarkable. Nonetheless, adults use this monitoring to guide subsequent study, typically opting to restudy material perceived as less well learned over material perceived as better learned. Moreover, monitoring accuracy is related to learning—higher accuracy is associated with greater test performance.

These findings regarding the importance of monitoring lead to the question of how educators can improve monitoring accuracy. First, they can encourage students to assess their own learning. As noted above, strategy-monitoring training involves giving students practice at monitoring the effectiveness of strategies. With practice, students also become more accurate at discriminating better-learned material from less-learned material. Second, they can frequently test student learning and provide explicit feedback on performance. Tests and feedback related to performance helps at least older students monitor the effectiveness of strategies. Tests also help students monitor their learning.

Learning to learn requires that students accurately monitor the effectiveness of their study and problem-solving behavior. Higher-achieving stu-

dents engage in more self-assessment than lower-achieving students. By encouraging self-assessment and developing monitoring skills in students, teachers can provide students with skills that will help them well after they leave the classroom.

See also: LEARNING, *subentry on* CONCEPTUAL CHANGE; READING, *subentries on* COMPREHENSION, CONTENT AREAS.

BIBLIOGRAPHY

BUTTERFIELD, EARL C.; WAMBOLD, CLARK; and BELMONT, JOHN M. 1973. "On the Theory and Practice of Improving Short-Term Memory." *American Journal of Mental Deficiency* 77:654–669.

CAMPIONE, JOSEPH C.; BROWN, ANN L.; and FERRARA, R. A. 1982. "Mental Retardation and Intelligence." In *Handbook of Human Intelligence*, ed. Robert J. Sternberg. Cambridge, Eng.: Cambridge University Press.

DUFRESNE, ANNETTE, and KOBASIGAWA, AKIRA. 1989. "Children's Spontaneous Allocation of Study Time: Differential and Sufficient Aspects." *Journal of Experimental Child Psychology* 47:274–296.

DUNLOSKY, JOHN; RAWSON, KATHERINE A.; and MCDONALD, SUSAN L. 2001. "Influence of Practice Tests on the Accuracy of Predicting Paired Associates, Sentences and Text Material." In *Applied Metacognition*, ed. Timothy J. Perfect and Bennett L. Schwartz. Cambridge, Eng.: Cambridge University Press.

FLAVELL, JOHN H. 1979. "Metacognition and Cognitive Monitoring: A New Area of Cognitive-Developmental Inquiry." *American Psychologist* 34:906–911.

HACKER, DOUGLAS J.; DUNLOSKY, JOHN; and GRAESSER, ARTHUR C. 1998. *Metacognition in Educational Theory and Practice.* Mahwah, NJ: Erlbaum.

LODICO, MARGUERITE G., et al. 1983. "The Effects of Strategy Monitoring Training on Children's Selection of Effective Memory Strategies." *Journal of Experimental Child Psychology* 35:263–277.

MAKI, RUTH H. 1998. "Test Predictions over Text Material." In *Metacognition in Educational Theory and Practice*, ed. Douglas J. Hacker, John Dunlosky, and Arthur C. Graesser. Mahwah, NJ: Erlbaum.

NELSON, THOMAS O., and DUNLOSKY, JOHN. 1991. "When People's Judgments of Learning (Jols) Are Extremely Accurate at Predicting Subsequent Recall: The 'Delayed JOL Effect.'" *Psychological Science* 2:267–270.

NELSON, T. O., and NARENS, L. 1990. "Metamemory: A Theoretical Framework and New Findings." In *The Psychology of Learning and Motivation*, Vol. 26, ed. Gordon H. Bower. New York: Academic Press.

PRESSLEY, MICHAEL; BORKOWSKI, JOHN G.; and O'SULLIVAN, JULIA T. 1984. "Memory Strategy Instruction Is Made of This: Metamemory and Durable Strategy Use." *Educational Psychologist* 19:94–107.

PRESSLEY, MICHAEL; LEVIN, JOEL R.; and GHATALA, ELIZABETH S. 1984. "Memory Strategy Monitoring in Adults and Children." *Journal of Verbal Learning and Verbal Behavior* 23:270–288.

SON, LISA K., and METCALFE, JANET. 2000. "Metacognitive and Control Strategies in Study-Time Allocation." *Journal of Experimental Psychology: Learning, Memory, and Cognition* 26:204–221.

THIEDE, KEITH W. 1999. "The Importance of Accurate Monitoring and Effective Self-Regulation during Multitrial Learning." *Psychonomic Bulletin and Review* 6:662–667.

WEINSTEIN, CLAIRE E.; GOETZ, ERNEST T.; and ALEXANDER, PATRICIA A. 1988. *Learning and Study Strategies: Issues in Assessment, Instruction, and Evaluation.* San Diego, CA: Academic Press.

ZIMMERMAN, BARRY J., and MARTINEZ-PONS, MANUEL. 1988. "Construct Validation of a Strategy Model of Student Self-Regulated Learning." *Journal of Educational Psychology* 80:284–290.

KEITH THIEDE

LESBIAN, GAY, BISEXUAL, TRANSGENDERED STUDENTS

See: SEXUAL ORIENTATION.

LIABILITY OF SCHOOL DISTRICTS AND SCHOOL PERSONNEL FOR NEGLIGENCE

A tort is a civil wrong—a violation of a duty—that causes harm. In the U.S. judicial system, an individual who is injured by a breach of duty can sue the other person to collect compensation for that injury. There are basically three types of civil wrongs.

- **Intentional torts** include trespass, assault, battery and defamation.
- **Unintentional torts** include negligence and strict liability. Strict liability is when someone is held liable, even though they are not at fault. It is often used when an individual is engaged in an ultrahazardous activity.
- **Constitutional torts** occur when a government agent has violated an individual's constitutional rights.

Some intentional torts also can be crimes, and a tortfeasor can be required by a civil court to pay money damages to compensate the injured person and also be required by a criminal court to pay a fine or suffer imprisonment.

Negligence differs from these in that it is an unintentional tort. It occurs when one person unintentionally causes an injury to another through a breach of a duty or violation of a general standard of care. The general standard of conduct is conduct that reasonable people may expect others to observe as they go about their daily lives. Negligence is the failure to exercise due care when carrying out a duty or subjecting another to a risk that causes harm. A negligent tort is a tort that, although not intended, was committed in disregard of the rights or reasonable expectations of another person. This is the area of tort law that has given rise to the most litigation.

The money a tort-feasor must pay to compensate the accuser for the harm the accuser has sustained is called damages. Factors for which money damages are awarded in a tort case include property damage, medical expenses, pain and suffering, and lost wages. If the conduct of the tort-feasor is a particularly outrageous or offensive violation of the reasonable standard of conduct expected, the civil court will add to its award of regular damages to the injured person and amount of money known as exemplary, or punitive, damages. The damages constitute a civil, or private, fine against the tort-feasor and are analogous to the fines imposed by a criminal court.

The sixth edition of *Black's Law Dictionary* defines *negligence* as "the omission to do something which a reasonable man, guided by those ordinary considerations which ordinarily regulate human affairs, would do, or the doing of something which a reasonable or prudent man would not do."

Schools and their employees are not automatically responsible for every injury that may occur within the school. In order to be held liable for negligence, the following four questions must be answered in the affirmative:

1. Did the defendant owe a duty to the plaintiff?

2. Did the defendant breach that duty?

3. Was the plaintiff injured?

4. Was the breach the proximate cause of the injuries?

Further, there can be no defenses to the action. Generally speaking, to recover damages, it must be shown that the defendant owes a duty to the injured person, that the behavior fell short of that required, that this caused a real injury to the person, and that the injured person was not responsible for causing the injury.

Duty

There is a duty of due care that the law recognizes one person owes to another. This duty may arise from a contract, a statute, common sense, or a special relationship the parties have to one another. Regarding students, the courts have found that schools and their employees have the duty to supervise students, provide adequate and appropriate instruction prior to commencing an activity that may pose a risk of harm, and provide a safe environment. Usually, that duty extends to students while they are in the custody or control of the school. Schools may have a duty to supervise students off school grounds when they have caused them to be there such as while on field trips or extracurricular events.

Schools may have a duty to supervise students on school grounds before and after school when they have caused them to be there, for example, when the bus drops them off. A duty can be extended if a person assumes additional responsibilities, such as assuming the duty to supervise students before and after school. Schools may acquire a duty to supervise when they have, by their previous actions, assumed the duty to supervise at this time such as when some staff has supervised intermittently or consistently before official time to arrive.

Schools also have a duty to warn of known dangers even when they do not have a duty to supervise. In the general workforce, a supervisor, and ultimately the company, is responsible for the negligent acts of employees under the doctrine of *respondeat supe-*

rior. However, in education, generally no one is automatically responsible for the acts of another. School administrators are not automatically responsible for the negligent acts of teachers. In school situations, usually a plaintiff must find a separate duty on the part of each defendant.

Breach of Duty

Once a duty has been established, the injured individual must show that the duty was breached. The duty has been breached when the individual unreasonably fails to carry out the duty.

In carrying out duties, one is expected to act as an ordinary, prudent, and reasonable person considering all of the circumstances involved. The court or jury makes a determination of how the reasonable person would have acted; if the individual did less, he or she is found negligent.

The standard varies for professionals; for example, a reasonable teacher or principal. Defendants who are professionals will be held to a standard based on the skills or training they should have acquired for that position. Thus, the question to be answered is: What would the reasonable professional have done under the same or similar circumstances?

The standard varies also with the individual circumstances of the situation. Each situation gives rise to a unique set of circumstances. Some of the factors which may be considered in determining the standard of care include the following:

- Age and maturity
- Nature of the risk
- Precautions taken to avoid injury
- Environment and context (including characteristics of students, location, physical characteristics, and so forth)
- Type of activity
- Previous practice and experience

In determining negligence, children are not held to the same standard of care as adults; instead their actions must be reasonable for a child of similar age, maturity, intelligence, and experience. Some states further classify children according to a presumption of capabilities. In those states, children under seven are not held responsible for negligence or unreasonable acts. The noted exception, however, is that a child may be held to an adult standard of care when engaged in an adult activity, for example, driving a car or handling a weapon.

Injury

The plaintiff must show an actual loss or real damage, for instance a physical bodily injury or a real loss. Compensation may include direct monetary damages for medical expenses, replacement of property, lost wages, and so forth.

The plaintiff may recover also for intangible injuries, such as pain and suffering, and emotional distress. In some situations an intangible injury is sufficient for recovery. However, there are states that require at least a physical manifestation of an injury if there are no tangible injuries.

Causation

To recover for an injury, the plaintiff must show that the defendant's negligence was the cause of the injury. If the accident would have occurred anyway, there can be no liability.

The defendant's negligent act must be a continuous and active force leading up to the actual harm. When there is a lapse of time between the defendant's negligence and the injury, other contributing causes and intervening factors may be the actual cause of the injury.

When there is a series of events leading up to an injury, the person starting that chain of events may be liable for the resultant injury if it was a foreseeable result of his negligence. If the injury at the end of the chain of events was not a logical (foreseeable) result of the negligence, there is no liability.

When another independent act occurs in between the defendant's negligent act and the plaintiff's injury, it may cut off the liability. In other words, someone else's actions may have been the cause of the injury. Intervening acts will not cut off liability when those intervening acts were foreseeable.

Defenses

Once the basic elements have been established, the court looks to the possibility of defenses before a damage award is granted. Defenses vary greatly between states; the most common defenses being governmental immunity; assumption of the risk; and comparative or contributory negligence.

In states that still have strict governmental immunity, an individual may not bring legal action against the state. In these states, immunity is a complete bar to an action. Governmental immunity has greatly eroded in recent years, generally allowing an individual to recover for injuries, but not allowing an action that would undermine the state's decision-making power when carrying out its state or official functions. Governmental actions are those the state undertakes as a policymaker. Thus, an individual is not allowed to sue the school for an injury caused by a policy decision such as making a curriculum choice or setting the date and time for school to start. Some states have abrogated sovereign immunity up to a particular dollar limit or to the extent of insurance coverage. These states usually have strict notice and pleading requirements at the outset of a legal action.

Assumption of the risk is also an affirmative defense that, if successful, presents a complete bar to plaintiff's recovery. This defense is based on the idea that if the plaintiff knowingly and voluntarily accepted the risks of an activity, he or she should not be allowed to recover for injuries caused by those known risks. For knowing acceptance to occur, it is important that all risks inherent in an activity are apparent or explained and that they are voluntarily assumed.

Students in athletic activities are asked to assume the risk of playing that sport. It must be shown that the plaintiff understood how the specific activity was dangerous and nonetheless voluntarily engaged in it. Students should be told of the risks of injury during the regular course of play; therefore if an injury were to occur, the school would not be responsible.

Many people mistakenly believe that parents assume all risks for their children when they sign permission slips. While the parents may assume the normal risks associated with the activity, they do not waive their rights for any and all injuries that may occur. They cannot assume risks of which they have no knowledge. In sum, some permission slips are worthless in terms of waiving liability. They often only serve to provide parents an opportunity to opt their children out of certain activities.

The defenses of contributory and comparative negligence offer a complete bar or a reduction in the damage award due to the plaintiff being partially responsible for his or her own injuries. Making this determination is similar to making the determination of the defendant's negligence—did the plaintiff fail to exercise reasonable care, which resulted in the injury. Contributory negligence is a total bar from recovery. Under contributory negligence, if the plaintiff is responsible for the injuries sustained in any way, no matter how slight, he or she cannot be awarded any damages. Recognizing that this all-or-nothing approach often results in severe consequences, most states have moved to the less severe system of comparative negligence.

In comparative negligence, the damage award is apportioned depending on the degree of fault or contribution to the injuries. Comparative negligence is distinguished between pure and modified forms. Pure comparative negligence allows the plaintiff to recover any amount of damages for which the defendant was negligent. In states that have adopted a modified comparative negligence, damages are awarded only if the defendant's negligence is greater than that of the plaintiff. In the early twenty-first century, a majority of states operate within some type of comparative negligence system.

Malpractice

As in medical malpractice, the term *educational malpractice* refers to negligence on the part of a professional. However, the courts have not recognized educational malpractice as a cause of action for damages. The seminal case is *Peter W. v. San Francisco Unified School District* (1976). Here the student was graduated from high school while still being illiterate. The court found no legal duty on which to base an action against the school district. Further, it concluded that there was no workable standard of care for teaching against which the defendant's actions could be judged. Finally, the court noted that the degree of certainty that the plaintiff had suffered any injury, the extent of the injury, and the establishment of a causal link between defendant's conduct and the plaintiff's injuries were uncertain. The primary motive for courts not recognizing educational malpractice as a cause of action is generally public policy. The concern typically expressed is that recognition of this cause of action would require the courts to make judgments on the validity of educational policies. Additionally, court have noted there are other, more appropriate avenues of relief if an individual is dissatisfied with the public schools, such as individual administrative review and school board elections.

See also: PRINCIPAL, SCHOOL; SCHOOL BOARDS; SPORTS, SCHOOL.

BILIOGRAPHY

ALEXANDER, KERN, and ALEXANDER, M. DAVID. 2001. *American Public School Law*, 5th edition. Belmont, CA: West/Thomson Learning.

McCARTHY, MARTHA M., and CAMBRON-McCABE, NELDA H. 1992. *Public School Law: Teachers' and Students' Rights.* Boston: Allyn and Bacon.

UNDERWOOD, JULIE K. 2000. "Negligence." In *A School Law Primer—Part II,* ed. National School Boards Association Council of School Attorneys. Alexandria, VA: NSBA Council of School Attorneys

JULIE K. UNDERWOOD

LIBERAL ARTS COLLEGES

Rather than emphasizing a specific course of study or professional training, liberal arts colleges aim to expose students to a wide breadth of courses in the humanities and both physical and social sciences. Although the curriculum varies from college to college, a student's coursework at a liberal arts school would include many or all of the following subjects: history, philosophy, religion, literature, physical sciences (e.g., biology, chemistry, physics), social sciences (e.g., psychology, sociology, economics, politics), the arts (e.g., theater, music, art), languages, and mathematics. Liberal arts colleges tend to stress the importance of teaching by faculty and usually have smaller enrollments.

The Carnegie Classification of Institutions of Higher Education is a typology of colleges and universities in America that orders colleges and universities by category. Within the Carnegie Classification system there is a separate and distinct category for liberal arts colleges called "Baccalaureate Colleges–Liberal Arts." Baccalaureate Colleges–Liberal Arts are identified as institutions that "are primarily undergraduate colleges with major emphasis on baccalaureate programs. During the period studied, they awarded at least half of their baccalaureate degrees in liberal arts fields" (Carnegie Foundation for the Advancement of Teaching website). There are 228 liberal arts institutions, which comprise 15.4 percent of all colleges and universities in the United States. Of these 228 colleges and universities twenty-six are public institutions, comprising 15 percent of this category, and 202 are private not-for-profit institutions, comprising 88.6 percent of this category. There are no private for-profit liberal arts institutions. Clearly, private liberal arts colleges outnumber public liberal arts colleges in the United States.

History of Liberal Arts Colleges

American universities began with the founding of Harvard in 1636, which was modeled after Emmanuel College at Cambridge University. After the founding of Harvard and into the early 1800s, several colleges were founded. These colleges, like Harvard, were small, religiously affiliated institutions. Appropriate curriculum for these colleges became widely debated in the early part of the nineteenth century. As science and technology became more prevalent and began to shape the world, American society called upon its colleges to provide coursework that suited the new era. In reply to these demands, Yale President Jeremiah Day organized a committee to address the aforementioned debates. The resultant document was "The Yale Report of 1828."

"The Yale Report of 1828" called for breadth in curriculum as the writers of the document doubted "whether the powers of the mind can be developed, in their fairest proportions, by studying languages alone, or mathematics alone, or natural or political science alone" (p. 173). The document further states that "the course of instruction which is given to undergraduates in the college is not designed to include professional studies. Our object is not to teach what is peculiar to any one of the professions; but to lay the foundation which is common to them all" (p. 173). Since its publication, "The Yale Report of 1828" has become the classic argument for a liberal education and liberal arts colleges in the United States.

In the mid-nineteenth century, Americans began traveling to Germany to obtain their Ph.D.s. The influx of German-educated scholars into to the United States bought a new model for the American college, and created what is now the research university. During this same time, land-grant colleges and technical schools began to develop in the United States. All three of these new types of colleges were focused on specific training, and therefore were antithetical to the liberal arts college. Many of the colleges that were founded on ideals closer to those of liberal arts colleges (e.g. Harvard, Yale, Princeton) became research universities. Other colleges purposefully chose to remain small and committed to a liberal education.

Over time the American liberal arts college has become a small part of the American higher education system. Yet the liberal arts college is flourishing at the beginning of the twenty-first century. Perhaps this is because the liberal arts college is unique in character or perhaps because of the unique character of the students that the liberal arts college produces.

Characteristics of Liberal Arts Colleges

At the heart of the liberal arts colleges are their missions. Most mission statements of liberal arts colleges endeavor to educate the whole student and emphasize education for its own sake rather than for job preparation. Liberal arts colleges tend to be small and private. Many liberal arts colleges have total enrollments of less than 2,000 students with low student-to-teacher ratios. They are also usually residential and value the idea of community. The liberal arts college is invested in teaching, and students and professors often collaborate with one another in the learning process. Oscar Paige, the president of Austin College, characterized the liberal arts college by saying:

> The residential nature of our college and of many liberal arts colleges is unique and adds to the value of the educational experience. The liberal arts community is a community that encourages inquiry and investigation and as a result students are challenged to think "outside the box" more on this type of campus then in other settings. Critical thinking, innovation, interdisciplinary curriculum and personal interaction with faculty all characterize this type of institution. (personal communication with author)

Most liberal arts colleges in the United States were founded by various religious dominations. For example, there are colleges founded by Lutherans (e.g., St. Olaf College, Luther College), Baptists (e.g., Arkansas Baptist College), and Presbyterians (e.g., Rhodes College, St. Andrews Presbyterian College). Many of these colleges have maintained strong religious affiliations into the twenty-first century. Many others maintain links with the church that founded the institution, but have a limited religious presence on campus. Some liberal arts colleges have abandoned all former religious ties.

Liberal arts colleges are often innovative in their programs. In fact, there are many distinct types of liberal arts colleges because of their unique programs. At Colorado College and Cornell College students can take one course at a time. At St. John's College, students study the Great Books. Another special program at several liberal arts colleges is the 4–1–4 semester. Students take four classes in the fall semester, one in-depth class in the month of January, and four classes in the spring semester. Austin College, Calvin College, and Eckerd College are examples of colleges that have 4–1–4 programs. At some colleges students get to design their own program (e.g., Marlboro College). One liberal arts college, Virginia Military Institute, is a military college. Another liberal arts college, Reed College, provides students with written assessments for their complete coursework rather than grades.

Some liberal arts colleges focus on serving particular populations. There are all-women's colleges. Smith College and Mills College are two such liberal arts colleges. Among the nation's historically black colleges and universities are liberal arts colleges (e.g., Morehouse College, Spelman College). One of the few all-men's colleges left in the United States, Walbash College, is a liberal arts institution.

Role of Liberal Arts Colleges in the U.S. System

Liberal arts colleges serve students who wish to become educated citizens and productive members of society. The liberal arts college strives to produce thoughtful, well-rounded citizens of the world. The promise of a liberal arts education is well summed up by Michele Myers, president of Sarah Lawrence College, when she notes that liberal arts colleges provide "an education in which students learn how to learn, an education that emphasizes the forming rather than filling of minds, an education that renders our graduates adaptive to any marketplace, curious about whatever world is around them, and resourceful enough to change with the times."

See also: ACADEMIC DISCIPLINES; CARNEGIE CLASSIFICATION SYSTEM, THE; HIGHER EDUCATION IN THE UNITED STATES.

BIBLIOGRAPHY

BRUBACHER, JOHN S., and RUDY, WILLIS. 1999. *Higher Education in Transition: A History of American Colleges and Universities,* 4th edition. New Brunswick, NJ: Transaction.

FRANEK, ROBERT, et al. 2001. *The Best 331 Colleges.* New York: Princeton Review.

KOBLIK, STEVEN. 1999. "Foreword." *Daedalus* 128(1):13.

LUCAS, CHRISTOPHER J. 1994. *American Higher Education: A History.* New York: St. Martin's Griffin.

MYERS, MICHELE T. 2001. "Preparing Students for an Uncertain Future." *Liberal Education* 87 (3):22–26.

"The Yale Report of 1828." 1989. In *ASHE Reader on the History of Higher Education,* ed. Lester F. Goodchild and Harold S. Wechsler. Needham Heights, MA: Ginn.

INTERNET RESOURCE

CARNEGIE FOUNDATION FOR THE ADVANCEMENT OF TEACHING. 2002. "Category Definitions." <www.carnegiefoundation.org>.

STACY A. JACOB

LIBRARIES, SCHOOL
See: SCHOOL LIBRARIES.

LICENSING AND CERTIFICATION
See: TEACHER EVALUATION.

LIFE EXPERIENCE FOR COLLEGE CREDIT

As higher education continues to attract an increasing number of adult students, many colleges and universities are developing programs to meet their distinctive needs. These students, age twenty-five and over, comprise 38 percent of the undergraduate population, according to the U.S. Bureau of the Census in 1999, and bring with them rich clusters of college-level knowledge gleaned from a variety of sources. They provide challenges to higher education not seen with traditional-age college students, including financial concerns, time constraints, and a distinct desire not to repeat learning what they have already gained from their professional or life experience. As a result, the practice of awarding college credit for learning from life experience has become a popular effort to attract and retain adult students.

Although the awarding of such credit is a legitimate academic process to some, it is not without controversy. The idea of granting college credit for learning that takes place outside the classroom challenges the very foundation of higher education. Some look upon the practice as a radical doctrine of giving away credit or of granting credit just for living, and it may seem inappropriate for the carefully regulated university setting. If the assumption is made that learning takes place everywhere, and that higher education is a part of a larger system of human learning that includes family, church, school, media, social institutions, and the work place, the rationale behind the practice may become more apparent.

Advocates of the practice find support in the teachings of John Dewey, who asserted that "all genuine education comes about through experience." Such experience is not limited to the classroom; in fact, the academy has no monopoly on learning. If learning takes place, it should not matter how it is accomplished, as long as the outcome is realized. If the outcome is college-level learning, then the awarding of college credit for the experience can be justified.

The granting of college credit for learning outside the classroom is not a new practice. As early as 1942 the American Council on Education (ACE) worked with branches of the military to evaluate service members' learning through military education and training. The resulting *Guide to the Evaluation of Educational Experiences in the Armed Services* documents secondary and postsecondary credit equivalencies, and has grown from one volume in its first printing in 1946 to three volumes covering all branches of the military and the U.S. Department of Defense in 2000.

Formalized testing programs as a means of assessing prior learning first made their appearance in the mid-1960s. Standardized examinations, designed by various national organizations, are intended to be applicable to large populations and to measure levels of accomplishment in many subjects.

A program to evaluate the in-house training that was sponsored by business and industry was begun in 1974. The Program on Noncollegiate Sponsored Instruction (PONSI) began by evaluating training courses offered by eight major corporations and recommending college credit when the learning experiences were found to be at the college level. In

the process, a model-reviewing system was designed, which resulted in the publication of *A Guide to Educational Programs in Noncollegiate Organizations*. Replaced in 1985 by *College Credit Recommendations,* the 2000 edition serves nearly 300 organizations across the nation and evaluates more than 5,000 training courses and programs.

At about the same time, the Educational Testing Service (ETS) began a research and development project designed to establish procedures for academic recognition of noncollege learning. Known in 1974 as the Cooperative Assessment of Experiential Learning (CAEL), the project focused on gathering data about prior learning assessment practices throughout the country. As a result, faculty and student handbooks were published for the first time that documented the practice of portfolio assessment. By 1979 ACE, the Council on Postsecondary Accreditation (COPA), and the American Association of College Registrars and Admissions Officers (AACRAO) endorsed the assessment of noncollege learning with the understanding that it would be conducted according to CAEL standards. Now known as the Council for Adult and Experiential Learning, CAEL is an independent organization recognized as a premier authority in the field. CAEL has established and disseminated standards for the awarding of credit for noncollege learning, training faculty evaluators, and implementing research on the outcomes of these efforts. The organization maintains a quality assurance program to monitor and evaluate current assessment programs throughout the nation.

Standards of Assessment

As institutions determine their level of commitment to the practice of granting credit for noncollege learning, a number of standards must be addressed to ensure legitimacy. ACE, PONSI, and CAEL have developed guidelines based upon national practices and research studies. These guidelines are available to any institution for adoption or modification. Colleges and universities can also initiate their own internal processes if they are willing to invest money, time, and resources. In either case, the institution must be aware that credit should only be granted for the learning that accompanies the experience, not for the experience itself. In addition, criteria must be determined for what constitutes college-level learning. Previous research has suggested that college-level learning must exhibit the following characteristics, being (1) demonstrable in some form; (2) conceptual as well as practical; (3) applicable outside the setting in which it was learned; (3) related to an academic field; (4) reasonably current; and (4) traditionally taught at the college level.

Methods of Assessment

For the purpose of determining if college-level learning has taken place in a noncollegiate setting, a prior learning assessment must be conducted. This can be accomplished in a number of ways, including the process of standardized examinations; course challenge or departmental examinations; ACE recommendations on military education and training; PONSI recommendations on corporate education and training programs; and individualized programs, including portfolio assessment, oral interviews, and competence demonstrations.

Standardized examinations may include the College-Level Examination Program (CLEP), the Defense Activity for Nontraditional Educational Support (DANTES), the Student Occupational Competency Achievement Test (SOCAT), Advanced Placement (AP) examinations, and others. They may cover a variety of subject areas and are available at testing centers across the country. Each individual institution must develop policies and practices for acceptance of learning indicated by examination results.

Course challenge or departmental examinations are designed by the institution, the department, or the faculty member responsible for the course for which the student is seeking credit. Challenge examinations are not standardized and may not be available for all subject areas. Credit granted for challenge examinations is subject to university and/or departmental discretion, regulations, and fees.

Military personnel often complete college-level courses while in the service. These include service school courses, monitored correspondence courses, Department of Defense (DoD) courses, and occupation specialty training. A record of completed training appears on a service member's discharge papers and may be assessed with the aid of the ACE *Guide to the Evaluation of Educational Experiences in the Armed Services.* No test or examination is necessary to receive credit through this method.

The National Program on Noncollegiate Sponsored Instruction (PONSI) evaluates courses and programs offered by corporations, unions, govern-

ment agencies, health care organizations, and professional groups and publishes equivalencies in its annual *College Credit Recommendations* series. Again, no test or examination is necessary to receive credit through this method.

Often learning outside the classroom is accumulated over an extended period or in a number of different situations. In such a case documentation may be difficult to provide. Individualized assessment is often the method of choice in such a situation because it is a more flexible means of allowing the student to explain the learning and give evidence of its validity. Individual assessment is designed at the institutional level and may include portfolio evaluation, oral interview, competence demonstration, or any combination of these methods. Although extensive guidelines are available through such advisory services as CAEL, each college or university must adopt its own set of procedures for assessment.

The portfolio is a document compiled by the learner in support of the request for credit. It typically consists of an essay describing background, goals and prior learning, a description of the learnings for which credit is requested, an explanation of how the learnings were acquired, a body of evidence documenting that the learnings are valid, and a request for specific equivalent credit. Often, institutions require that the learner enroll in a portfolio preparation course to provide structure to the process of negotiating for credit. The instructor is a trained faculty member who assists the learner in preparation of the portfolio, conducts interviews and demonstrations as necessary, and makes recommendations for the awarding of credit. Interaction with other faculty with content expertise is also necessary to ensure concurrence with credit recommendations.

Further Considerations

For institutions that adopt the practice of granting credit for learning from life experience, there are other considerations which must be addressed. Financial commitments, faculty training, fee assessment, accreditation outcomes, transcript notations, and transfer issues are just a few of the university processes that may be affected. Just as adult students have changed the face of the early-twenty-first-century university, so does the very practice of assessing the learning that they bring with them.

See also: ASSESSMENT, *subentry on* PORTFOLIO ASSESSMENT; CURRICULUM, HIGHER EDUCATION, *sub-*

entry on Innovations in the Undergraduate Curriculum; Distance Learning in Higher Education; Lifelong Learning.

BIBLIOGRAPHY

American Council on Education. 2000. *Guide to the Evaluation of Educational Experiences in the Armed Services.* Westport, CT: American Council on Education.

Dewey, John. 1938. *Experience and Education.* New York: Collier.

Knapp, Joan, and Gardiner, Marianne. 1981. "Assessment of Prior Learning: As a Model and in Practice." *In New Directions for Experiential Learning: Financing and Implementing Prior Learning Assessment,* No. 14, ed. Joan Knapp. San Francisco: Jossey-Bass.

Lamdin, Lois. 1997. *Earn College Credit for What You Know,* 3rd edition. Chicago: The Council for Adult and Experiential Learning.

Mandell, Alan, and Michelson, Elana. 1990. *Portfolio Development and Adult Learning: Purposes and Strategies.* Chicago: The Council for Adult and Experiential Learning.

McCormick, Donald W. 1993. "College-Level Learning and Prior Experiential Learning Assessment." *Adult Learning* 4(3):20–22.

National Program on Noncollegiate Sponsored Instruction. 2000. *College Credit Recommendations: The Directory of the National Program on Noncollegiate Sponsored Instruction.* Albany, NY: National Program on Noncollegiate Sponsored Instruction.

U.S. Bureau of the Census. 2001. *School Enrollment in the United States: Social and Economic Characteristics of Students, 1999.* Current Population Reports. Washington, DC: U.S. Government Printing Office.

Whitaker, Urban. 1989. *Assessing Learning: Standards, Principles and Procedures.* Philadelphia: Council for Adult and Experiential Learning.

Zucker, Brian J.; Johnson, Chantell C.; and Flint, Thomas A. 1998. *Prior Learning Assessment: A Guidebook to American Institutional Practices.* Chicago: The Council for Adult and Experiential Learning.

INTERNET RESOURCES

American Council on Education (ACE). 2002. <www.acenet.edu>.

Council for Adult and Experiential Education (CAEL). 2002. <www.cael.org>.

National Program on Noncollegiate Sponsored Instruction (PONSI). 2002. <www.nationalponsi.org>.

Nell Northington Warren

LIFELONG LEARNING

Lifelong learning is a broad, generic term that is difficult to define with specificity. Its overlap, or its interchangeable use, with other closely related concepts, such as lifelong, permanent, recurrent, continuing, or adult education; learning organizations; and the learning society (society in which learning is pervasive), makes this even more true. For some it includes learning from childhood and early schooling, while others treat it in terms of the adult learning process. It has grown to a global concept, with differing manifestations that vary with national political and economic priorities, and with cultural and social value systems.

Lifelong learning is used here in an inclusive sense that accommodates this heterogeneity. A statement resulting from a collaboration of the European Lifelong Learning Initiative and the American Council on Education provides a workable expression of this broader acceptance:

> Lifelong learning is *the development of human potential* through *a continuously supportive process* which *stimulates and empowers individuals to acquire all the knowledge, values, skills, and understanding* they will require *throughout their lifetimes* and *to apply them* with *confidence, creativity and enjoyment* in *all roles, circumstances, and environments.* (Longworth and Davies, p. 22)

This definition includes several basic elements of the lifelong learning ideal: (1) a belief in the idea of lifetime human potential and the possibility of its realization; (2) efforts to facilitate achievement of the skills, knowledge, and aptitudes necessary for a successful life; (3) recognition that learning takes place in many modes and places, including formal educational institutions and nonformal experiences such as employment, military service, and civic participation and informal self-initiated activity; and (4) the need to provide integrated supportive systems adapted to individual differences that encourage and facilitate individuals to achieve mastery and self-direction. Society should make these systems available to learners with flexibility and diversity.

Evolution of the Lifelong Learning Movement

Lifelong learning crystallized as a concept in the 1970s as the result of initiatives from three international bodies. The Council of Europe advocated *permanent education,* a plan to reshape European education for the whole life span. The Organisation for Economic Co-operation and Development (OECD) called for *recurrent education,* an alternation of full-time work with full-time study similar to sabbatical leaves. The third of these initiatives, a United Nations Educational, Scientific and Cultural Organization (UNESCO) report, *Learning to Be* (1972), drew most attention and had the broadest influence. Commonly known as the Faure Report, this was a utopian document that used the term *lifelong education* instead of lifelong learning, and it foresaw lifelong education as a transformative and emancipatory force, not only in schools, but in society at large. One commentator, Charles Hummel, called the UNESCO concept a Copernican revolution in education.

U.S. educational and political leaders took note of these ideas. Usually, they adopted the term *lifelong learning* (rather than lifelong education) and applied it to adult education, leaving initial and secondary education to the existing system. The American discussion tended to be more pragmatic than visionary, addressing specific categories of educational need rather than proposing systems. The Mondale Lifelong Learning Act of 1976 included in its scope a laundry list of nearly twenty areas, ranging from adult basic education to education for older and retired persons, a charge that proved too diffuse to address with public policy. European and American policy interest in lifelong learning waned after the early 1980s, although interest continued among educational institutions and nongovernmental organizations.

Interest in lifelong learning revived in the early 1990s, both in Europe and the United States. A fresh round of studies and reports popularized the idea of lifelong learning, and it became part of national policy discussion, particularly as global competition and economic restructuring toward knowledge-based industries became more prevalent. In a full-employment economy, corporations perceived a benefit from investment in human capital, while a new workforce of *knowledge technologists* expected their employers to maintain their employability by investing in their education. The focus on learning thus shifted from personal growth to human resource development. Meanwhile, education and training approaches became central to a transition away from unemployment and welfare dependency.

Implementation of Lifelong Learning

Adult participation rates suggest that a mass population has embraced lifelong learning and that the learning society may have arrived. U.S. data for 1998–1999 show that an estimated 90 million persons (46% of adults) had enrolled in a course during the preceding twelve months, an increase from 32 percent in 1991. There are indications that large increases also occurred in other developed countries. Field called this a "silent explosion" that makes the most of the people inhabiting learning societies.

The U.S. figures stated above include only formal courses led by an instructor, divided into six categories: (1) English as a second language (ESL), (2) adult basic education and high school completion courses, (3) postsecondary credential programs, (4) apprenticeship programs, (5) work-related courses, and (6) personal development courses. The largest categories of participation during the twelve-month period were work-related and personal development courses. Informal learning was not included.

To serve such a vast population, and to absorb a nearly 50 percent rate of increase in less than a decade, implies a major increase in providers and services. An exhaustive discussion is not possible in this brief space, but some indications of change can be suggested. Public schools and community colleges in large measure serve ESL, adult basic education, and high school completion needs, especially preparation for the General Educational Development (GED) examination. Data on dropouts who have attained high school equivalency by age twenty-four indicate that these institutions are being successful in this mission. Many community colleges have increased their ESL programs to serve new immigrant populations, and a large number of voluntary and community organizations have joined them, especially in literacy programs.

Programs related to employment come from several sources: apprenticeship programs, work-related courses, and credential programs. An interesting development has been the collaboration between different providers attempting to enhance credentials by offering joint curricula; such as the collaboration between community colleges and corporations to offer apprenticeships and training in conjunction with the associate degree. Work-related courses touch on a broad range of content, providers, and delivery settings. They may be freestanding, self-contained experiences of a single course, or they may include sustained, interrelated courses that lead to a certificate or other qualification. Many sustained programs focus less on technical skills and more on the general education needed in the knowledge-based workforce. In some cases, largely depending on their size and commitment to workforce development, corporations may create their own internal *corporate universities* to offer extensive programs designed for their own needs. Others prefer to access the resources and experience of external providers, such as higher education institutions or professional education and training organizations. Community colleges have foreseen a major role for themselves in this work.

Around 1970 colleges and universities began to attract greater numbers of adult, nontraditional learners—this population increased from 27.7 percent of all higher education enrollments in 1970 to a range between 42 and 44 percent in the mid-1990s. Many programs adapted their practices and created new programs in response. A generation of innovation in higher education has opened many opportunities for adult learners. Changes have included greater flexibility in admissions and in time and place of instruction, more individualization of curricula, assessment for credit of previous courses and informal learning, transformation of faculty from teacher experts into mentors or facilitators, and provision of more intensive adult-oriented student services, including services responsive to the unpredictable exigencies of adult learners' lives.

Two other developments have attracted considerable attention. One is the rapid growth in the number of for-profit degree-granting institutions, which usually offer high-demand career-related curricula in cohort formats, providing learners with predictability in their time-to-degree and cost commitments. The record of accreditation at these institutions has established a reputation for quality. The other novelty is high-level for-profit certificate programs in information technology. These programs maintain quality through self-regulation, but they stand outside the usual quality-control systems. There is a fear, however, that they may draw lifelong learners away from institutions of higher education.

Personal development courses, which made up 23 percent of the 1998–1999 adult enrollments, are even more heterogeneous than work-related courses, both in their content and their providers. This may be the sector where lifelong learning serves its richest menu, ranging from health and fitness to recreation and hobbies, civic and political engagement, travel and cultural experiences, and religious and Bible studies. It can include every level of interest and every age or stage of development. For instance, major areas of growth have occurred in areas of interest to older learners. Organizations such as Institutes of Learning in Retirement and Elderhostel have played a role in this growth.

Ongoing Issues in Lifelong Learning

Despite a generation of discussion of the concept, a number of questions divide lifelong educators and policymakers. Several still prefer the term *lifelong education* because it implies a more explicitly intentional learning than the casual, unintended learning implied by *lifelong learning*. To many observers, lifelong learning itself is a contested concept with varying meanings and values. Some believe the broad humanistic and democratic idealism of the Faure Report has been sacrificed to an instrumental goal of human capital development, thus weakening the commitment to personal enrichment, civic participation, and social capital development.

Early advocates of lifelong learning not only regarded it as extending to the end of life, but also commencing in the earliest years. In practice, most innovation has come in programs conceived specifically for adults. By 2000, however, appeals to engage early schools in the lifelong learning enterprise began to reappear.

Finally, lifelong learning (and the creation of autonomous, self-directed individuals) implies a risk to learners and to social cohesion. Such emancipated persons can become less likely to defer to established institutions or to be guided by common social and cultural norms, adopting instead an analytical stance that isolates them from others and fragments society. The freedom of choice rests with them, but so also does the burden of responsibility in what some call critically reflective societies.

Conclusion

Few, if any, of the comprehensive, integrated lifelong learning systems envisioned by the Council of Europe and the Faure Report in the 1970s have been realized. On the other hand, observers cannot deny how closely linked learning and well-being have become in the twenty-first century—and how pervasive both awareness of and participation in lifelong learning activities are among contemporary populations. Numerous questions remain, not least among them the inequality of opportunity between well-educated persons and the less advantaged in given societies, and between developed and developing countries. Lifelong learning advocates can only hope that enough of the early fervor and optimism of the movement remain to find solutions to these issues.

See also: CONTINUING PROFESSIONAL EDUCATION; CORPORATE COLLEGES; DISTANCE LEARNING IN HIGHER EDUCATION; EXPERIENTIAL EDUCATION.

BIBLIOGRAPHY

ADELMAN, CLIFFORD. 2000. *A Parallel Postsecondary Universe: The Certification System in Information Technology.* Washington, DC: U. S. Department of Education, Office of Educational Research and Improvement.

ASPIN, DAVID N., and CHAPMAN, JUDITH D. 2000. "Lifelong Learning: Concepts and Conceptions." *International Journal of Lifelong Education* 19(1):2–19.

BOSHIER, ROGER. 1998. "Edgar Faure after 25 Years: Down but Not Out." In *International Perspectives on Lifelong Learning,* ed. John Holford, Peter Jarvis, and Colin Griffin. London: Kogan Page.

DRUCKER, PETER. 2001. "The New Workforce." *The Economist* November 3: 8–11.

FAURE, EDGAR, et al. 1972. *Learning to Be: The World of Education Today and Tomorrow.* Paris: UNESCO.

FIELD, JOHN. 2000. *Lifelong Learning and the New Educational Order.* Sterling, VA: Trentham.

FIELD, JOHN. 2001. "Lifelong Education." *International Journal of Lifelong Education* 20(1/2):3–15.

HOLFORD, JOHN, and JARVIS, PETER. 2000. "The Learning Society." In *Handbook of Adult and Continuing Education,* ed. Arthur L. Wilson and Elizabeth R. Hayes. San Francisco: Jossey-Bass.

HOULE, CYRIL O. 1973. *The External Degree.* San Francisco: Jossey-Bass.

HOULE, CYRIL O. 1992. *The Literature of Adult Education: A Bibliographic Essay.* San Francisco: Jossey-Bass.

HUMMEL, CHARLES. 1977. *Education Today for the World of Tomorrow.* Paris: United Nations Educational, Scientific and Cultural Organization.

KIM, KWANG, and CREIGHTON, SEAN. 1999. *Participation in Adult Education in the United States, 1998–1999.* Statistics in Brief Report No. 2000-027. Washington, DC: National Center for Education Statistics.

KNAPPER, CHRISTOPHER K., and CROPLEY, ARTHUR J. 2000. *Lifelong Learning in Higher Education,* 3rd edition. Sterling, VA: Stylus.

LAMDIN, LOIS, and FUGATE, MARY. 1997. *Elderlearning: New Frontier in an Aging Society.* Phoenix, AZ: Oryx Press.

LONGWORTH, NORMAN, and DAVIES, W. KEITH. 1996. *Lifelong Learning: New Vision, New Implications, New Roles for People, Organizations, Nations and Communities in the 21st Century.* London: Kogan Page.

MAEHL, WILLIAM H. 2000. *Lifelong Learning at its Best: Innovative Practices in Adult Credit Programs.* San Francisco: Jossey-Bass.

NATIONAL CENTER FOR EDUCATIONAL STATISTICS. 2001. *Dropout Rates in the United States: 2000.* Washington, DC: National Center for Education Statistics.

PETERSON, RICHARD E., et al. 1979. *Lifelong Learning in America.* San Francisco: Jossey-Bass.

RICHARDSON, PENELOPE L. 1987. "The Lifelong Learning Project Revisited: Institutionalizing the Vision." *Educational Considerations* 14(2/3):2–4.

RUCH, RICHARD S. 2001. *Higher Education, Inc.: The Rise of the For-Profit University.* Baltimore: Johns Hopkins University Press.

TITMUS, COLIN. 1999. "Concepts and Practices of Education and Adult Education: Education and Lifelong Learning." *International Journal of Lifelong Education* 18(5):343–354.

ZEISS, TONY, et al. 1997. *Developing the World's Best Workforce: An Agenda for America's Community Colleges.* Washington, DC: Community College Press.

WILLIAM H. MAEHL

LINCOLN SCHOOL

The Lincoln School (1917–1940) of Teachers College, Columbia University, was a university laboratory school set up to test and develop and ultimately to promulgate nationwide curriculum materials reflecting the most progressive teaching methods and ideas of the time. Originally located at 646 Park Avenue in New York, one of the most expensive pieces of real estate in the city, the Lincoln School was also a training ground for New York City's elite, including the sons of John D. Rockefeller, Jr., who provided the funding for the school. Among the school's chief architects were Charles W. Eliot, a former president of Harvard University and an influential member of the New England Association of Colleges and Secondary Schools; his protégé Abraham Flexner, a member of the controversial Rockefeller philanthropy, the General Education Board; Otis W. Caldwell, a professor of science education at Teachers College and the school's first director; and the dean of Teachers College, James E. Russell.

In the 1920s and 1930s the Lincoln School was the most closely watched experimental school in the educational world, making solid contributions in the work of laboratory schools. It provided a select number of Teachers College students with clinical teaching experience, engaged in curriculum design and development, and provided an observation and demonstration site for teachers from around the United States and abroad. Its own experimental research institute promoted staff development and student teaching, and it distributed its printed materials in national journals and in mass mailings to schools throughout the United States.

Caldwell and his staff constructed an interactive or "experience" curriculum designed to relate classroom materials to the realities of everyday urban-industrial as well as agricultural life. Science and mathematics courses emphasized the practical application of these subjects to life in the contemporary world. Students learned through nonacademic community resources—the fire department, markets, churches, transportation and communication facilities—that were used as models for the reorganization of school life, and through music, language, art, and social studies where students imbibed principles that, in the language of the school's literature, were "foundational to effective and upright living."

Experiences were rarely spontaneous, however, in classrooms where carefully planned experiments guided every phase of the work and where teachers used modern laboratory methods of collection, organization, and interpretation of data. In keeping with the dual purpose of the school—experimental curriculum development and character training in new forms of social responsibility—children were led through a sequence of avowedly "modern" courses. "Modern" meant practical and useful, with a direct bearing upon the everyday work of the world in finance, industry, agriculture, government and the arts. It also meant a great deal more science and mathematics instruction than one found in the traditional curriculum. Science teaching, according to Caldwell, a biologist, and Harold Rugg, his colleague in mathematics, was valuable because it taught good citizenship defined as "the increased respect which the citizen should have for the expert." This was in an age which had become "amazingly complicated [and] incalculably difficult to understand" and in which the salient feature was "the political and economic ignorance and indifference of the common man."

The classical defenders of liberal culture found much to hate in the program of the Lincoln School, which they regarded as devoid of emotion, imagination, poetry, beauty, and art. Critics also worried about the involvement of the General Education Board and the powerful industrial statesmen who headed it, pointing to the ambiguous position of the charitable trust in a democratic society.

What kind of a school was it, historians still want to know, that could combine cultural epoch theory, the doctrine of interest, and parvenu notions of social efficiency with the relatively remote, patrician sensibilities of founders and supporters like Eliot and the Rockefellers? What kind of a school was it that would teach vocational math and science to its upper and upper-middle class students, but not Greek and Latin, the traditional foundations of elite culture? The School itself could never quite decide what it was: An experiment in progressive practices? A hedge against those practices when they shifted dangerously toward bureaucratic centralism? Or the harbinger of something entirely new and novel and distinctly modern? This last possibility was allowed to die early, a sacrifice to child-centeredness, to subject-matter fetishism, and to an experimental tradition that controlled for these factors but otherwise ignored them for larger, correlative and integrative purposes. In 1940 the Lincoln School collapsed under the weight of its own contradictions. A Special Committee of the Board of Trustees of Teachers College in the interest of both intellectual and practical economy recommended its amalgamation with the larger and less research-intensive Horace Mann School.

See also: ELEMENTARY EDUCATION, *subentry on* HISTORY OF; INSTRUCTIONAL DESIGN; NEWLON, JESSE; PROGRESSIVE EDUCATION.

BIBLIOGRAPHY

CALDWELL, OTIS W. 1921. "Contributions of Biological Sciences to Universal Secondary Education." *School Science and Mathematics* 21:103–115.

ELIOT, CHARLES W. 1918. "The Modern School." *Education* 38:662–663.

FLEXNER, ABRAHAM. 1917. *The Modern School.* New York: General Education Board.

HEFFRON, JOHN M. 1999. "The Lincoln School of Teachers College: Elitism and Educational Democracy." In *Schools of Tomorrow, Schools of Today: What Happened to Progressive Education?* ed. Susan F. Semel and Alan R. Sadovnik New York: Peter Lang.

HOPKINS, L. THOMAS. 1937. *Integration: Its Meaning and Application.* New York: D. Appleton-Century.

KRUG, EDWARD A. 1961. *Charles W. Eliot and Popular Education.* New York: Teachers College Bureau of Publications.

RUGG, HAROLD. 1925. "Curriculum Making: The Lincoln School Experiment in the Social Sciences." *Lincoln School of Teachers College Publications* 1:1–24.

RUSSELL, JAMES E. 1925. "To the General Education Board." James E. Russell Papers. Teachers College, Columbia University.

SHOREY, PAUL. 1917. *The Assault on Humanism.* Boston: Atlantic Monthly.

JOHN M. HEFFRON

LINDQUIST, E. F. (1901–1978)

One of the foremost applied statisticians and educational testing pioneers of the 1900s, Everet Franklin Lindquist received his Ph.D. from the University of Iowa in 1927 and was a member of the faculty there from 1927 until his retirement in 1969. During his long professional career, he made substantial contributions to the field of education in the areas of test development, test-scoring technology, measurement theory, and research methodology. His textbooks on design of experiments and statistical analysis had considerable influence on educational and psychological research.

Test Development

As director of Iowa Testing Programs at the University of Iowa, Lindquist was responsible for the development of the first editions of both the Iowa Tests of Basic Skills (ITBS) and the Iowa Tests of Educational Development (ITED). In the 1940s he served as an advisor to the United States Armed Forces Institute and to the American Council on Education (ACE). He played a major role in formulating policies with respect to granting academic credit for general educational growth during military service. These policies resulted in the development of the General Educational Development Test (GED). Lindquist oversaw the creation of the initial forms of the GED, which were modeled after the ITED. In the late 1950s Lindquist also was responsible for the design and construction of the first forms of the National Merit Scholarship Qualifying Test (NMSQT). In 1959 Lindquist and Ted McCarrel, registrar at the University of Iowa, cofounded the American College Testing Program (ACT) as an alternative to the College Entrance Examination Board. Lindquist was personally responsible for the design and development of the early editions of the ACT tests.

All of these tests continue to be published and used in the early twenty-first century. Although the tests have evolved over the years, it is a tribute to Lindquist's vision and creativity that he recognized the need for such tests and that the philosophy underlying them continues to be reflected in recent editions.

Test-Scoring Technology

In the late 1940s the Iowa tests developed under Lindquist's direction were being administered to large numbers of students in Iowa and throughout the nation. The demand to have the answer sheets of these tests scored at a central agency was growing. It became apparent to Lindquist that this demand would require a more efficient way of processing the answer sheets than the hand-scoring procedures then being used. Although crude scoring machines were available, they were not adequate for large-scale testing. Thus, in the early 1950s Lindquist undertook a major project to design a high-speed electronic scoring machine. He and his colleagues at the University of Iowa succeeded in building such a machine in the mid-1950s. The original version scored at the rate of 4,000 sheets per hour. They developed faster machines fairly quickly, and by 1970 the scoring machine could scan 40,000 sheets per hour. Without question, the availability of such scoring machines had a significant impact on testing practices in the United States.

Measurement Theory

Lindquist's major contributions to the field of measurement theory occurred primarily through two publications. The first of these was the influential volume *Educational Measurement* (1951), for which he served as general editor. Eighteen of the most distinguished measurement experts, including Lindquist himself, wrote chapters for this landmark publication. It served as the major reference for the educational measurement community until the second edition was published twenty years later.

Lindquist's second major contribution, and perhaps his most technical work in measurement, was published as the last chapter in his textbook *Design and Analysis of Experiments in Psychology and Education* (1953). In this chapter, "Estimation of Variance Components in Reliability Studies," Lindquist explicated techniques, which were not new in the statistical sense. But their relevance to educational and psychological measurement had not been appreciated. Lindquist saw these tools as a significant improvement over traditional methods of estimating measurement error variance and hit-or-miss methods of designing efficient, cost-effective measures. In essence, he provided the foundations for an area known as generalizability theory ten years before the first publications of Lee Cronbach et al. on this approach appeared in the literature of educational and psychological measurement.

Research Methodology

Lindquist's influence in the field of educational research occurred primarily through his textbooks. Early in his career, he concluded that a textbook constituted a more valuable vehicle than journal articles or conference presentations in reaching the ed-

ucational research community. Thus many of his innovative ideas and original insights were published in his books. In *Statistical Analysis in Educational Research* (1940), he assumes the role of statistical translator for the educational research community. He was concerned about the slow adoption of the techniques of analysis of variance and covariance, including factorial designs, in the behavioral sciences. The implications of the work of Ronald A. Fisher had made little impression on educational and psychological researchers. Lindquist perceived this failure to be the result of a widespread inability of research workers to read the relevant literature and to translate terms such as *blocks, plots, treatments,* and *yields* into *schools, classes* or *pupils, educational methods,* and *test scores.* In this 1940 text, he undertook to facilitate this translation.

In a second influential book, published in 1953, *Design and Analysis of Experiments in Psychology and Education,* Lindquist again had the goal of translating statistical analyses developed in other fields into language understandable to researchers in psychology and education. However, he soon recognized that the adaptation of certain designs developed for use in industry and agriculture was by no means straightforward. The educational and psychological researcher's alternatives with respect to the choice of the unit of analysis often had no obvious analog in the original industrial and agricultural contexts. The phenomenon of repeated measurements on the experimental units took on a unique character in the behavioral sciences. Certain designs, such as Latin square designs, were seen to be potentially useful in the behavioral sciences. But their purposes and implementation differed significantly from the classical applications. The entire area of multidimensional, repeated-measurements designs had to be reworked. Analyses appropriate to factorial experiments that involve independent groups on some dimensions and repeated measurements on others had to be formulated almost without helpful precedent from other sciences. Thus his 1953 book represented far more than a statistical translation. It incorporated a number of original insights and formulations, particularly in the area of "mixed" designs involving both independent and dependent measurements. In sum, Lindquist's ability to bridge the statistical gap between education and other areas enabled him to exert a significant influence on educational research from the 1940s through the 1970s.

BIBLIOGRAPHY

FELDT, LEONARD S. 1979. "Everet F. Lindquist 1901–1978: A Retrospective Review of His Contributions to Educational Research." *Journal of Educational Statistics* 4:4–13.

LINDQUIST, EVERET F. 1940. *Statistical Analysis in Educational Research.* Boston: Houghton Mifflin.

LINDQUIST, EVERET F., ed. 1951. *Educational Measurement.* Washington, DC: American Council on Education.

LINDQUIST, EVERET F. 1953. *Design and Analysis of Experiments in Psychology and Education.* Boston: Houghton Mifflin.

LINDQUIST, EVERET F. 1970. "The Iowa Testing Programs—A Retrospective View." *Education* 91:7–24.

PETERSON, JULIA J. 1983. *The Iowa Testing Programs: The First Fifty Years.* Iowa City: University of Iowa Press.

LEONARD S. FELDT
ROBERT A. FORSYTH

LINGUISTICS AND LANGUAGE LEARNING

See: LANGUAGE AND EDUCATION.

LITERACY

EMERGENT LITERACY

William Teale and Elizabeth Sulzby coined the term *emergent literacy* in 1986 from Mary Clay's dissertation title, "Emergent Reading Behavior" (1966). Their term designated new conceptions about the relationship between a growing child and literacy information from the environment and home literacy practices. The process of becoming literate starts before school intervention.

Important changes took place around 1975 to 1985 in the way researchers approached young children's attempts at reading and writing, which were influenced by previous language acquisition studies of children actively engaged in learning oral language.

In English-speaking countries, literacy acquisition was traditionally focused on acquisition of reading. Writing was considered an activity undertaken after reading. Carol Chomsky's 1971 article "Write Now, Read Later" was for this reason provocative. It is worth noting that these two opposite views (reading before writing or writing before reading) are alien to other cultural traditions. For instance, in the Spanish school tradition both activities have been traditionally considered as complementary.

Teale and Suzby maintained that "in the schools, the reading readiness program and the notion of the need to teach prerequisites for reading became fixed. Furthermore, using reading readiness programs in the kindergarten literacy curriculum became a widespread practice. The reading readiness program which became so firmly entrenched during the 1960s remains extremely prevalent in the 1980s" (p. xiii).

The concept of emergent literacy was intended to indicate a clear opposition with the then prevailing notion of "reading readiness." This new concept arises from changes in the research paradigm, mainly in developmental psycholinguistics, and not in the practical educational field.

The Original Meaning of the Concept

Several pioneering researchers (among them Clay in New Zealand, Yetta Goodman and Sulzby in the United States, and Emilia Ferreiro in Latin American countries) share several main ideas that can be summarized as follows:

1. Before schooling, a considerable amount of literacy learning takes place, provided that

children are growing in literate environments (homes where reading and writing are part of daily activies; urban environments where writing is everywhere—in the street, in the markets, on all kinds of food containers or toys—as well as on specific objects like journals, books, and calendars).

2. Through their encounters with print and their participation in several kinds of literacy events, children try to make sense of environmental print. Indeed, they elaborate concepts about the nature and function of these written marks.

3. Children try to interpret environmental print. They also try to produce written marks. Their attempts constitute the early steps of reading and writing. Thus, reading and writing activities go hand in hand, contributing to literacy development as comprehension and production both contribute to oral language acquisition. The use of the term *literacy* in the phrase *emergent literacy* indicates that the acquisition of reading and writing take place simultaneously.

4. The pioneer authors of the emergent literacy approach avoid the use of terms like *pretend reading* or *pre-reading, pretend writing* or *pre-writing*. Such terms, in fact, establish a frontier in the developmental process instead of a developmental continuum.

5. From a careful observation of spontaneous writing and reading activities as well as from data obtained through some elicitation techniques, it becomes possible to infer how children conceive the writing system and the social meaning of the activities related to it.

6. Emergent literacy is a child-centered concept that not only takes into account relevant experiences (like sharing reading books in family settings), but also takes into consideration that children are always trying to make sense of the information received in a developmental pathway that is characterized both by some milestones common to all and by individual stories.

Transformations of the Original Meaning

What is the use of the expression *emergent literacy* fifteen years after its first introduction into the literature? This expression competes with others such as *beginning literacy, early literacy,* or even *preschool literacy.* It is not unusual to see alternative terms used by the same authors (for instance Dorothy Strickland and Lesley Morrow). The term *emergent* remains restricted to English users. It is not used in Spanish nor in Italian or French, where expressions like "éveil au monde de l'écrit" ("awakening to the world of writing") convey similar ideas.

The emergent literacy approach affects preschool settings and shapes new educational practices. Instead of exercises to train basic skills as a prerequisite to reading, researchers frequently observe teachers and children engaged in real reading activities. Instead of exercises of copying letter forms, teachers encourage children to produce pieces of writing.

Independent research conducted in the linguistic and historical fields by such people as David Olson, Florian Coulmas, and Geoffrey Sampson contributed, during the closing decades of the twentieth century, to a reconsideration of writing systems. As long as alphabetical writing systems (AWS) are being conceived as visual marks for elementary units already done (i.e., the phonemes), the task of the child is reduced to the learning of a code of correspondences. But AWS are highly complex because they are the result of a long history, in which phonic considerations interfere with historical, pragmatic, and even aesthetic considerations.

However, the old pedagogical ideas are still so strong that the term *emergent literacy* has begun to be used as a new component of old practices. Expressions such as to *teach beginning literacy, evaluation of emergent literacy skills,* and even *emergent literacy teachers* are a commonplace in books, articles, and papers devoted to teachers, parents, and decision-makers. It is clear that emergent literacy cannot be taught, even if it can be improved or stimulated. The reduction of this concept to a set of trainable skills goes against the term's original meaning.

In the meantime, "phonological awareness" began to be considered the single strong predictor of school reading skills (reading, in that case, is evaluated in tasks of letter-sound correspondences in front of lists of words and pseudo-words). Some authors started to look for the components of emergent literacy—a set of skills—to allow similar assessment as phonological awareness.

When emergent literacy skills include phonological awareness it is clear that the new label is being applied to old ideas: emergent literacy originally indicated concepts built up by children through many encounters with print other than explicit teaching, whereas phonological awareness is clearly an acquisition that does not develop without explicit intervention, even if it is closely related to the acquisition of an AWS. For instance, when parents engage in shared reading, they offer the child the opportunity to learn about many relevant aspects of books but they are not explicitly teaching a particular literacy component.

This shaping of new ideas into old paradigms is present also in psychological research, such as the 1998 publication by Grover Whitehurst and Christopher Lonigan. It could seem, at first glance, entirely justified to inquire about the components of early literacy, and the weight of each one of them as predictors of school achievements in reading. However, the identification of these components and the assessment of their individual weight shows that literacy continues to be conceived mainly as reading behavior and that written language is still conceived as a coding of already given elementary units (the phonemes) into a graphic form (the letters of an alphabet). The persistent confusion between the teaching activities and learning processes (i.e., how children contribute to the task, how they transform the available information through their own assimilatory processes) is at the core of the weak results that try to discover the relevant correlations between early literacy and future school achievements.

Policy

For the time being, the best recommendation for any preschool program is to offer children many opportunities to engage in real reading and writing activities, with the grounded conviction that children—who are intelligent human beings—are eager to learn and will take advantage of a stimulating environment. The old view that prevented children from sharing literacy learning opportunities until they were ready to learn lessons is a discriminatory one, as not all parents all over the world are able to provide literacy experiences.

See also: EARLY CHILDHOOD EDUCATION; LITERACY AND READING; READING, *subentry on* BEGINNING READING.

BIBLIOGRAPHY

CHOMSKY, CAROL. 1971. "Write Now, Read Later." *Childhood Education* 47:296–299.

CLAY, MARY. 1966. "Emergent Reading Behaviour." Ph.D. diss., University of Auckland, New Zealand.

COULMAS, FLORIAN. 1989. *The Writing Systems of the World.* Oxford and Cambridge, Eng.: Blackwell.

FERREIRO, EMILIA, and TEBEROSKY, ANA. 1983. *Literacy Before Schooling.* Exeter, NH and London: Heinemann.

GOODMAN, YETA. 1986. "Children Coming to Know Literacy." In *Emergent Literacy: Writing and Reading,* ed. William Teale and Elizabeth Sulzby. Norwood, NJ: Ablex.

OLSON, DAVID. 1994. *The World on Paper.* Cambridge, Eng.: Cambridge University Press.

SAMPSON, GEOFFREY. 1985. *Writing Systems.* London: Hutchinson.

SNOW, CATHERINE, and NINIO, ANAT. 1986. "The Contracts of Literacy: What Children Learn from Learning to Read Books." In *Emergent Literacy: Writing and Reading,* ed. William Teale and Elizabeth Sulzby. Norwood, NJ: Ablex.

STRICKLAND, DOROTHY, and MORROW, LESLEY M., eds. 1989. *Emerging Literacy: Young Children Learn to Read and Write.* Newark, DE: International Reading Association.

STRICKLAND, DOROTHY, and MORROW, LESLEY M., eds. 2000. *Beginning Reading and Writing.* Newark, DE: International Reading Association and New York: Teachers College Press, Columbia University.

TEALE, WILLIAM, and SULZBY, ELIZABETH, eds. 1986. *Emergent Literacy: Writing and Reading.* Norwood, NJ: Ablex.

WITEHURST, GROVER, and LONIGAN, CHRISTOPHER. 1998. "Child Development and Emergent Literacy." *Child Development* 69(3):848–872.

EMILIA FERREIRO

INTERTEXTUALITY

A teacher asks students to find ways in which the stories "The Emperor's New Clothes" and "Chicken Little" are similar and ways they are different. A member of a book club compares last month's selection to the current month's. A book review includes some of the dialogue from the reviewed book. People leaving the movie theater after seeing *Lord of the Rings* comment that the book was better. The movie *Pocahontas* is criticized by historians for misrepresenting established historical events. In each of these examples, different texts are brought together, related to one another, or connected in some way. This juxtaposition of different texts is called *intertextuality*. Intertextuality occurs at many levels, in many forms, and serves a variety of functions; the foregoing examples reflect only a small subset of the possibilities.

Levels, Forms, and Functions of Intertextuality

Juxtapositions may occur at multiple levels including word or phrase, sentence or utterance, larger units of connected text such as a paragraph or stanza, and genre. Intertextuality can be created through the following means:

- duplication (a string of words occurring in two texts such as occurs in quotation) and stylistic means (repetition of a stress, sound, or rhyme pattern across two or more texts)

- naming and reference (as occurs in citations)

- proximal association (as occurs among chapters in an edited book which are presumed to have some relationship to each other)

- sequential association (an established sequence of related texts such as a reply to a letter or e-mail).

Intertextuality can be explicit or implied through a variety of literary devices (e.g., allusion, metonymy, synecdoche).

Intertextuality can be viewed as a function of social practices associated with the use of language. It is a social practice of scholars to refer to previous scholarly works through the use of quotations, citations, and bibliographies. The reading and use of book reviews, movie reviews, and similar texts can be viewed as social practices, which by definition are overt intertextual practices. Intertextuality can be created when an unexpected text occurs within a social practice. For example, if instead of receiving a report card at the end of a grading period, a student received a poem, part of the meaning of the poem would be from its placement in a particular social practice and its contrast with the genre of report card.

Locations of Intertextuality

A key question to ask about intertextuality is its location, because questions about location reveal different definitions and approaches to the analysis of intertextuality. Some scholars locate intertextuality in the text itself when explicit or implied reference is made to another text. The intertextual relationship exists whether or not it is detected by the reader and whether or not it was intended by the author of the text. From this perspective questions can be asked about how one text signals another text and what meaning is conveyed by the text through the intertextual reference.

A second location of intertextuality is in the person. As a person interacts with the target text (whether spoken, written, or electronic), the person brings to the interaction with the text previous texts and his or her experience with them. Some of these previous texts may be conversations, books, or other printed texts, narratives of personal experience, memories, and so forth. The person may use these previous texts to create meanings for the target text or to help with the process of comprehending the text. For example, previous experience in reading a mathematics text provides guidance and procedures for reading a new mathematics text. Because, for example, individuals have different background experiences and histories of encounters with conversational and written texts, the texts a particular person might bring to any interaction with a target text would vary. So too would their use of those texts. Other questions of interest pertain to understanding the cognitive processes involved in using texts from previous experiences.

Closely related to locating intertextuality in the person is locating intertextuality in the task. For example, an academic task might require a person to interact with multiple texts in order to understand some phenomenon, such as a historical event. In such a case, the task explicitly requires the use and juxtaposition of multiple texts. In some cases, multiple texts may even be provided as part of the presentation of the task. However, it may also be the case that the person addressing the task conceives of the task as involving multiple texts, whether or not it is an explicit part of the task. For example, a student given a literary text to explicate may conceive of the task as involving the juxtaposition of the target text, other texts written by the author, the teacher's lectures on the target text, and his or her previous efforts at explicating literary texts with the resultant teacher comments and grades. From this perspective, questions of interest concern the explicit and implicit intertextual demands made by the task and the interpretation of those demands. Interpretation reflects the person's representation of the task and its intertextual demands and are manifest in what and how texts are used to address the task. Questions can also be asked about the cognitive processes involved in the representation of the task and in its completion. There are interesting questions about the cognitive, affective, and social dimensions of the task, including their role in task interpretation and execution.

A fourth location of intertextuality is in the social practices of a community or social group. Over time, a social group establishes shared standards and expectations for what texts can and should be juxtaposed, and under what circumstances. That is, there are shared, abstract models for the use and juxtaposition of texts in particular types of situations. For example, in a court room, it is a shared social practice of lawyers and judges to interpret testimony and evidence in terms of previous court cases and a specific sets of legal documents (such as the U.S. Constitution). Within an academic discipline, there are specific intertextual practices and these vary from discipline to discipline. For example, in scholarly publications in the social sciences it is customary to cite previous work on the topic of interest. In writing a novel, however, authors do not cite previous novels that have addressed similar themes. In classrooms, teachers and students establish shared intertextual practices for engaging in academic work. For example, there are shared intertextual practices for completing worksheets (e.g., using the text book to answer the worksheet questions), for studying for tests, for writing an essay, and so on.

Although individuals enact intertextual practices, what they are enacting is an abstract model that has evolved over time. As such, the material environment that people encounter may be structured to facilitate certain intertextual practices and inhibit others. For example, many scholastic literature texts are organized to facilitate genre study and the comparison of texts within a particular genre. They do not foster comparison of texts across genre (e.g., poems and short stories). Textbooks often have end-of-chapter questions that refer readers to material in that chapter, but which do not ask readers to use information from previous chapters. From the perspective of intertextuality as located in social

practices of communities and groups, questions can be asked about the intertextual demands of the social practices that make up an institution such as schooling and how various intertextual practices came to be associated with particular social institutions.

A fifth location of intertextuality is in the social interaction of people in an event. As people interact with each other they propose intertextual links, acknowledge the proposals, recognize the intertextual links, and give the intertextual links meaning and social consequence. That is, intertextuality is socially constructed as people act and react to each other. In classroom conversations, a teacher may propose an intertextual link between a story the class is reading, a movie being shown at a local theater, and a mural in the surrounding community. But the proposed intertextuality does not become actualized until the students acknowledge that an intertextual link has been made, recognize the story, the movie, and the mural and the potential connections among them, and give meaning and consequence to those connections. As people interact with each other, the proposed intertextual link may be negotiated and transformed such that the construction of intertextuality is a joint accomplishment shared by all involved in the event. From this perspective, questions can be asked about the interpersonal processes involved in proposing, ratifying, and giving meaning and consequence to intertextuality.

The multiple locations of intertextuality reflect, in part, different disciplinary perspectives on intertextuality, as suggested by the kinds of questions proposed for each location. Cognitive perspectives tend to locate intertextuality either in the text, in the person, or in the task; social, anthropological, and related perspectives tend to locate intertextuality in social, cultural, and historical practices; perspectives associated with sociolinguistic ethnography and symbolic interactionism tend to locate intertextuality in the social interaction of people in an event. Regardless of perspective, intertextuality is inherent to every use of language whether written or spoken, verbal, or graphic. It is ubiquitous in education, in every classroom conversation, instructional task, curriculum guide, educational policy document, and debate. What may be less obvious about intertextuality is the impact it has on delimiting texts that may be juxtaposed as well as establishing participation roles, rights, and responsibilities for interacting with texts. This aspect of intertextuality can be discussed in terms of power relations.

Intertextuality and Power Relations

Two kinds of power relations associated with intertextuality can be distinguished for heuristic purposes. The first concerns the establishment of boundaries on the set of texts that may be intertextually related in any specific instance. Through historical practice, some authority, material circumstances, or simply the limitations of a person's experience, boundaries are placed on what texts may be candidates for juxtaposition. For example, consider the set of texts that may be considered for a high school course on American literature. It is unlikely that folk songs, rap music, personal journals of ordinary people, or comic books would be considered as possible candidates—much less be included in the course. By establishing particular boundaries some texts and the ideas, people, places, and ideologies they represent are centralized, others are marginalized. However, these boundaries can be crossed; indeed, the *Norton Anthology of African American Literature* includes folk songs, rap music, and a compact disc of oral performances, and the *Norton Anthology of Jewish American Literature* includes a comic-book-like entry.

The second kind of power relations related to intertextuality concerns intertextual participation rights—who gets to make what intertextual links, when, where, how, and to what social consequence. Intertextual rights are not necessarily distributed equally or equitably. Consider a classroom example. A low-achieving student might propose an intertextual link between a novel being read in a class and a rap song. The teacher might dismiss the proposed intertextual link simply because the low-achieving student proposed it. A high-achieving student might make a similar intertextual proposal that is accepted by the teacher and other students. Precisely because intertextuality is ubiquitous in academic and social practices, severely circumscribed and differentially distributed participation rights have important consequences for individuals, the institutions within which they may operate, and the ways in which they operate within those institutions.

The Educational Significance of Intertextuality

In many ways, teachers and researchers have been using the construct of intertextuality without naming it. Teachers often ask students to relate one text to another, and researchers are often interested in how various conversations and written texts have been juxtaposed. Thus, the explicit naming of intertextual processes and attention to them can be seen as an attempt to create systematic inquiry about intertextuality and to build an understanding of its nuances and consequences.

Recognition of the ubiquitous nature of intertextuality provides educational researchers with a set of heuristics for analysis of classroom conversations, reading processes, writing processes, instructional practices, and assessment practices. Similarly, attention to intertextuality can lead to redesign of curriculum in reading, language arts, literature studies, and social studies. Emphasis can be placed on ways to create understanding and meaning through intertextuality rather than the current emphasis on understanding texts as if they stood alone. There is preliminary evidence to suggest that such an emphasis increases academic achievement, although such increases are probably related to the ways in which texts are juxtaposed rather than simply juxtaposition. Attention to intertextuality also provides ways to enhance connections between academic texts and texts outside of the classroom, including community texts, workplace texts, and family texts.

See also: LITERACY, *subentries on* LEARNING FROM MULTIMEDIA SOURCES, MULTIMEDIA LITERACY; READING, *subentry on* LEARNING FROM TEXT.

BIBLIOGRAPHY

BAKHTIN, MIKHAIL. 1981. "Discourse in the Novel" (1935). In *The Dialogic Imagination,* ed. Michael Holquist and trans. Caryl Emerson and Michael Holquist. Austin: University of Texas Press.

BEACH, RICHARD, and ANSON, CHRIS. 1992. "Stance and Intertextuality in Written Discourse." *Linguistics and Education* 4:335–358.

BLOOME, DAVID, and EGAN-ROBERTSON, ANN. 1993. "The Social Construction of Intertextuality and Classroom Reading and Writing." *Reading Research Quarterly* 28:303–333.

CHAMETZKY, JULES; FELSTINER, JOHN; FLANZBAUM, HILENE; and HELLERSTEIN, KATHRYN. 2001. *Jewish American Literature: A Norton Anthology.* New York: Norton.

GATES, HENRY LOUIS, and MCKAY, NELLIE Y. 1997. *The Norton Anthology of African American Literature.* New York: Norton.

HARTMAN, DOULAS. 1992. "Intertextuality and Reading: The Text, the Author, and the Context." *Linguistics and Education* 4:295–312.

KAMBERELIS, GEORGE, and SCOTT, KARLA. 1992. "Other People's Voices: The Co-Articulation of Texts and Subjectivities." *Linguistics and Education* 4:359–404.

LEMKE, JAY. 1992. "Intertextuality and Educational Research." *Linguistics and Education* 4:257–268.

ROWE, DEBORAH. 1994. *Preschoolers as Authors: Literacy Learning in the Social World of the Classroom.* Cresskil, NJ: Hampton.

SHORT, KATHY. 1992. "Researching Intertextuality within Collaborative Classroom Learning Environments." *Linguistics and Education* 4:313–334.

DAVID M. BLOOME
SUSAN R. GOLDMAN

LEARNING FROM MULTIMEDIA SOURCES

The predominant means of instruction has traditionally been through verbal medium, either as spoken lecture or written text. As more instructional resources of many different media types become available to students through the Internet, there is a need for educators to understand when these sources may be used effectively for instruction, as well as a need for students to develop an additional set of literacy skills in order to learn from these sources. Although there is much optimism that multimedia sources will be a great tool for instruction, research in cognitive science has demonstrated that the use of these resources does not always lead to better learning. It is important to recognize the potential cognitive implications of multimedia presentations, including text, graphics, video, audio, and virtual reality simulations. Multimedia has been incorporated into instructional materials in a variety of ways: decoration, illustration, explanatory simulation, and "situating" simulation. The first three uses may be best thought of as adjuncts to a verbal lesson, while in the final use, the entire "lesson" is embedded and conveyed by situating the learner in a virtual context.

Uses

Often multimedia is used to decorate text, with the goal of making the text more interesting for the reader. A second use for multimedia, illustration or description, can be used to help a reader visualize a place or time or object. A third use of multimedia involves the explanation or explication of concepts. Especially in complex domains, understanding often requires that learners develop a dynamic mental model of phenomena or processes. Multimedia animations, narrations, and diagrams have all been used to support the understanding of complex subject matter by illustrating or highlighting important relations, thereby attempting to convey a correct mental model directly to the student.

Improved Learning

One reason why multimedia might be expected to lead to improved learning is consistent with a constructivist approach that posits that conditions that make knowledge acquisition more self-directed and active are beneficial for student understanding. The presentation of loosely connected texts and images in hypermedia environments allow learners to navigate information with more flexibility. At the same time, in order to build coherence, students must construct their own elaborations, inferences, and explanations. Thus, there has been reason for optimism surrounding the benefits of learning from hypermedia.

Another reason one might expect benefits from illustrated text and multimedia presentation in general is that it allows for information to be represented in multiple ways (i.e., both verbal and visual). A great deal of previous research within cognitive psychology, such as that of Allan Paivio in 1986, has suggested that the more codes one has for a given memory, the more likely one is to remember that information. Multiple media may also make the learning experience more vivid or distinctive. And, given the different preferences of different learners, multimedia may allow learners to choose the code best suited to their abilities.

A related reason why multimedia, and graphics in particular, may improve learning is that some particular domains may lend themselves to visual presentation, such as when information is inherently spatial. For instance, learning about different ecologies and climate zones may benefit greatly from the presentation of a map. Further, even when the understanding of the subject matter does not require a visual representation, images can still facilitate understanding if the image provides the basis for an abstract model of the content of the text. Figures, graphs, or flow charts that may allow the reader to think about abstract concepts and relations through images support the creation of more complete mental models and as a consequence may improve comprehension of text. Also, when subject matter is as complex and dynamic as streams of data from weather satellites or space stations, then visuals and animations may be especially important. Similarly, visual or audio representations (sonitizations) of complex data can give human thinkers the ability to consider many more dimensions, and the salient relationships between those dimensions, than they might otherwise.

Finally, it should not be overlooked that instructional materials with visual or audio adjuncts are simply more interesting to readers than plain text. Such motivational issues may contribute to advantages in learning with any multimedia presentation.

Criticisms

With all these potential benefits of images, it is perhaps surprising that since the 1960s, the empirical results on learning from illustrated text have been less than positive. In a 1970 review of studies using illustrated texts, Spencer Jay Samuels found little support for the superiority of illustrated text over plain text. In fact, in some cases illustration leads to poorer learning than simple text presentation. Follow-up investigations suggest that one reason for the lack of a consistent positive effect of images on learning is that any learning effect depends greatly on the kind of image that is used. In a 1987 review of Joel Levin and colleagues that discriminated between decorative illustrations, and conceptually-relevant images, decorative illustrations were found to lead to the smallest improvements and sometimes negative effects in learning. Decorative illustrations are often not relevant for the concepts that are described by the text, yet they are still interesting for the reader, and will attract the reader's attention. For this reason, interesting but irrelevant illustrations can be seen as part of a larger class termed *seductive details* as coined by Ruth Garner and colleagues, and others. Similarly, color, sound effects, and motion are preattentive cues that necessarily attract a reader's focus. If they are not used to emphasize conceptually important information, they too can seduce the reader.

Even when images are relevant for understanding the target concept, there is a further danger that images or animations can make learners overestimate their level of comprehension. People tend to feel that a short glimpse of an image is generally sufficient for understanding. This can lead to an illusion that they understand a graphic or image, even when they have not really engaged in deeper thought about the information. Further, students are notoriously bad at comprehending complex graphics, especially data-related charts or figures, and will interpret the data in support of their own ideas.

Another danger with images and especially animations, is that they can provide so much information so easily that although the reader is able to grasp a basic idea of "how" a dynamic system works, a good understanding of "why" the system works the way it does is lacking (i.e., they are unable to recreate the system or apply their knowledge to a new instance). This effect has in fact been demonstrated in several studies. The research of Mary Hegarty and colleagues, and other research, indicated that still pictures, or still sequences of pictures, in which the reader needs to infer movement for themselves, led to better understanding of dynamic systems than animations that actually show the motions. Similarly, animations that are reproductions of real-world actions are more effective if they are "doctored" to emphasize important features of the display. And, animations that are stoppable and restartable under the learner's control may lead to better learning than real-time simulations. However, images that provide readers with the basis of a mental model, and animations that show the dynamics of a model, may be especially important for people who lack knowledge and spatial ability. Finally, even conceptually relevant adjuncts run the risk of distracting the learner, and they need to be presented in a way that does not compete with the processing of the text. A number of studies, such as the work of Wolfgang Schnotz and Harriet Grzondziel, have shown that students learn better from diagrams and animated graphics when they were presented separately from text. Alternatively, learning from multimedia has been supported by structured computer learning environments, where different media and sources are presented to students, but students are given instruction both in how to use the environment, and are given a specific learning goal.

Other multimedia adjuncts have been studied, most notably narrations and sound effects. The bottom line from these investigations is that narrations only benefit learning when they are nonredundant with text. However, narrations may be especially helpful for poorer readers, especially when they accompany diagrams, and highlight the conceptually important features. Sound effects and music in general are distracting, and as adjuncts to text, they do not contribute to better conceptual learning. They do however help simulated environments seem more authentic, and may be helpful for situated learning and anchored instruction. Realistic sound effects may be especially important in skill learning environments. Similarly, in terms of conceptual learning, animations may help only when readers cannot generate mental models on their own, although realistic video may help when learning a procedural task and also in "situating" contexts.

The Simulation of Reality

The final use of multimedia considered here is where multimedia is used, not as an adjunct to verbal instruction, but more extensively as the entire means of presentation. In these lines of application, multimedia is used to simulate reality, through video and audio streams, to produce a sense of learning "in context." This may be especially important in skill-training environments, when learning in an actual cockpit or surgical operating room would be unsafe and costly. In more academic domains, simulations can give students the feel of an authentic experience, and both situated learning and anchored learning approaches have attempted to capitalize on this advantage of multimedia presentation. Another application of multimedia simulation is the creation of artificial agents that can act as tutors or peers. The presence of an interactive human-like entity may be an especially important coaching tool, and multimedia simulation may make such tutoring experiences more effective than feedback or prompts that appear in text messages. Simulations may also be used to support distance education and collaboration, again by providing a sense of real "co-presence" to the users.

Virtual reality is the ultimate multimedia tool, combining realistic video and audio streams (i.e., three-dimensional), and sometimes even tactile experience. Here, the potential exists to convey an understanding of new concepts in ways that surpass real experience, and many have heralded virtual reality as a powerful educational tool. Most researchers refer to the multisensory-based sense of "presence" that virtual reality affords the user as the characteristic that separates it from other training approaches. Where procedural knowledge and visuo-spatial skills are concerned there seems to be support for this optimism. However, results on more academic subject matter understanding have been less convincing.

Most studies that have been performed on people's uses of virtual reality have included only self-report data that reflect the user's interpretation of her or his experience in the virtual environment, while fewer investigations include more direct measures of learning. Among the few virtual reality studies with learning measures, Chris Dede and colleagues examined in 1999 students' understanding of electromagnetic field concepts from a virtual environment called Maxwell World. Students in the virtual reality condition were better able to define concepts and demonstrate them in three-dimensional terms.

At the same time, pilot studies, such as those of Andrew Johnson and colleagues in 1999, on using virtual reality to promote understanding of astronomical physics concepts have found that the virtual reality environment can also be prone to seductive distractions. For example, to learn that the earth's shape is round, younger elementary school-age children engaged in a virtual reality game, which included traversing a spherical asteroid to gather objects. The students failed to exhibit a substantial and robust improvement in their understanding, presumably because of the distracting and nonrelevant aspects of the game.

It would seem that virtual reality would be a prime candidate to demonstrate the positive effects of multimedia sources on learning. Yet, virtual reality experiences are not easily translated into learning experiences, and the results of studies on the educational uses of virtual reality underscore the same principles as have been discussed above. Virtual reality may add value to educational contexts when real training is not possible, and where it goes beyond "realistic" experiences in ways that emphasize conceptual understanding.

As an Effective Strategy

As the nature of instructional materials changes to include more images, sounds, animations and simulations, it is important to recognize the conditions under which multimedia can be an effective learning tool, and that new literacy skills are needed to learn from those materials. Instead of being presented with a single message, multimedia learners are presented with many information sources on a topic, and those sources can represent a number of media. The sheer number of resources available through the Internet is enormous. The availability of so much information means that students have the ability to direct their own learning, by performing searches and selecting documents, evaluating sources of information, and allocating attention to images and animations, without being confined by the linear structure of a single text or lecture. Although this flexibility in the learning environment has been seen as an opportunity for more active student learning, it is clear that in order to learn from multimedia and electronic sources, students will likely need additional skills in searching, document evaluation, strategic reading, strategic understanding of graphics, and integrating information across sources, including the integration across text and graphics. A specific set of skills may also be necessary for learning in more immersive multimedia environments.

A recurrent question focuses on how multimedia helps learning. Some have suggested that positive effects due to multimedia may be simply due to the motivating effect of its novelty. Unfortunately the literature of the early twenty-first century contains few controlled studies and few tests of when multimedia helps understanding. Further research is needed to identify what conditions enable the best learning from multimedia, and what new literacy skills students will need to support that learning.

See also: MEDIA AND LEARNING; LITERACY, *subentry on* MULTIMEDIA LITERACY; TECHNOLOGY IN EDUCATION.

BIBLIOGRAPHY

COGNITION AND TECHNOLOGY GROUP AT VANDERBILT. 2000. "Adventures in Anchored Instruction: Lessons from beyond the Ivory Tower." In *Advances in Instructional Psychology: Educational Design and Cognitive Science 5,* ed. Robert Glaser. Mahwah, NJ: Erlbaum.

DEDE, CHRIS. 1995. "The Evolution of Constructivist Learning Environments." *Educational Technology* 35:46–52.

DEDE, CHRIS; SALZMAN, MARILYN C.; LOFTIN, R. BOWEN; and SPRAGUE, DEBRA. 1999. "Multisensory Immersion as a Modeling Environment for Learning Complex Scientific Concepts." In *Computer Modeling and Simulation in Science Education,* ed. Nancy Roberts and Wally Feurzeig. New York: Springer-Verlag.

FARADAY, PETER, and SUTCLIFFE, ALASTAIR. 1997. *An Empirical Study of Attending to and Comprehending Multimedia Presentations.* New York: ACM Press.

GARNER, RUTH; GILLINGHAM, MARK; and WHITE, C. STEPHEN. 1989. "Effects of 'Seductive Details' on Macroprocessing and Microprocessing in Adults and Children." *Cognition and Instruction* 6:41–57.

GRAESSER, ART, et al. 2000. "Autotutor: A Simulation of a Human Tutor." *Journal of Cognitive Systems Research* 1:35–51.

HARP, SHANNON, and MAYER, RICHARD. 1998. "How Seductive Details Do Their Damage." *Journal of Educational Psychology* 90:414–434.

HAYS, TIMOTHY. 1996. "Spatial Ability and the Effects of Computer Animation on Short-Term and Long-Term Comprehension." *Journal of Educational Computing Research* 14:139–155.

HEGARTY, MARY, et al. 1999. "Multimedia Instruction: Lessons from Evaluation of a Theory-Based Design." *Journal of Educational Multimedia and Hypermedia* 8:119–50.

JOHNSON, ANDREW; MOHER, TOM; OHLSSON, STELLAN; and GILLINGHAM, MARK. 1999. "The Round Earth Project: Collaborative VR for Conceptual Learning." *IEEE Computer Graphics and Applications* 19:60–69.

LEVIN, JOEL; ANGLIN, GARY; and CHARNEY, RUSSEL. 1987. "On Empirically Validating the Functions of Pictures in Prose." In *The Psychology of Illustration,* ed. Dale M. Willows and Harvey A. Houghton. New York: Springer-Verlag.

NARAYANAN, N. HARI, and HEGARTY, MARY. 1998. "On Designing Comprehensible Interactive Hypermedia Manuals." *International Journal of Human–Computer Studies* 48(2):267–301.

PAIVIO, ALAN. 1986. *Mental Representations: A Dual Coding Approach.* New York: Oxford University Press.

REISER, BRIAN, et al. 2001. "BGuile: Strategic and Conceptual Scaffolds for Scientific Inquiry in Biology Classrooms." In *Cognition and Instruction: Twenty-Five Years of Progress,* ed. Sharon Carver and David Klahr. Mahwah, NJ: Erlbaum.

ROMANO, DANIELA M., and BRNA, PAUL. 2001. "Presence and Reflection in Training: Support for Learning to Improve Quality Decision-Making Skills under Time Limitations." *Cyberpsychology and Behavior* 4(2):265–277.

SAMUELS, SPENCER. 1970. "Effects of Pictures on Learning to Read, Comprehension, and Attitudes." *Review of Educational Research* 40:397–407.

SCHNOTZ, WOLFGANG., and GRZONDZIEL, HARRIET. 1999. "Individual and Co-Operative Learning with Interactive Animated Pictures." *European Journal of Psychology of Education* 14:245–265.

SHAH, PRITI; HEGARTY, MARY; and MAYER, RICHARD. 1999. "Graphs as Aids to Knowledge Construction: Signaling Techniques for Guiding the Process of Graph Comprehension." *Journal of Educational Psychology* 91:690–702.

SLOTTA, JAMES D., and LINN, MARCIA C. 2000. "The Knowledge Integration Environment: Helping Students Use the Internet Effectively." In *Innovations in Science and Mathematics Education: Advanced Designs for Technologies of Learning,* ed. Michael Jacobson and Robert Kozma. Mahwah, NJ: Erlbaum.

SPIRO, RAND, and JEHNG, JIHN-CHANG. 1990. "Cognitive Flexibility and Hypertext." In *Cognition, Education and Multimedia,* ed. Don Nix and Rand Spiro. Hillsdale, NJ: Erlbaum.

WEIDENMANN, BERND. 1989. "When Good Pictures Fail." In *Knowledge Acquisition from Text and Pictures,* Heinz Mandl and Joel Levin. North Holland, Amsterdam: Elsevier.

WRIGHT, PATRICIA; MILROY, ROBERT; and LICKORISH, ANN. 1999. "Static and Animated Graphics in Learning from Interactive Texts." *European Journal of Psychology of Education* 14:203–224.

JENNIFER WILEY
JOSHUA A. HEMMERICH

MULTIMEDIA LITERACY

The term *multimedia* is among several terms that have been associated with literacy to emphasize that literacy extends beyond reading and writing the alphabetic code, and should include a variety of audiovisual forms of representation. Associating multimedia with literacy also highlights a belief among many scholars and educators that conceptions of literacy and how it is developed should not focus exclusively on printed materials, but should include electronic media that have moved into the mainstream of communication, especially at the end of the twentieth century. Implicit in these views is that research and practice related to literacy must be transformed to accommodate new ways of accessing, processing, and using information.

Related Concepts

Kathleen T. Tyner argued in 1998 that in the information age the concept of literacy has been simultaneously broadened and splintered into many literacies in part because "the all purpose word literacy seems hopelessly anachronistic, tainted with the nostalgic ghost of a fleeting industrial age" (p. 62). Associating the term *multimedia* with literacy is consistent with that trend, although it might be thought of as encompassing a diverse set of related and sometimes ill-defined terms used in scholarly, and often popular, discourse. For example, related terms highlighting media and forms that go beyond the alphabetic code include *media literacy, visual literacy, technological literacies, metamedia literacies,* and *representational literacy.* Broader terms, such as the following, might also be included in this set because they typically acknowledge the role of diverse media and new technologies in broadening conceptions of literacy: *multiliteracies, information literacies, critical literacy,* and even the negatively stated term *cultural illiteracy.* Narrower terms such as *computer literacy* and neologisms such as *numeracy* also reflect expanding views of literacy, but such terms focus on specific skills and abilities.

Past and Present Conceptions

Broadening the scope of literacy, specifically in relation to diverse media, is not entirely a phenomenon of the late twentieth and early twenty-first centuries. Interest in how new media might affect conceptions of literacy can be traced to the widespread use of electronic audiovisual media such as television and film in the first half of the twentieth century. For example, Edgar Dale, well known among a earlier generation of educators and researchers for his work related to literacy, discussed the need for critical reading, listening, and observing in contending with the new literacies implied by audiovisual media of the 1940s.

Nonetheless, beginning in the latter decades of the twentieth century, the impetus for broadening the scope of literacy has been the increasing integration of digital technologies into the mainstream of everyday communication and the inherent capability of those technologies to blend diverse modes of representation. New modes of digital communication exist not only in parallel with conventional printed forms, but they have replaced or moved to the margins conventional forms of reading and writing. For example, the obsolescence of the typewriter, the ascendance of e-mail as the preferred alternative to diverse forms of correspondence on paper, the emergence of the Internet as a prominent cultural phenomenon, and the appearance of the electronic book represent a steady yet incomplete and unpredictable progression away from conventional printed forms. Likewise, students in the early twenty-first century routinely encounter digital information employing diverse audiovisual media presented in formats that are more interactive and dynamic than printed texts, although those encounters have been more likely to occur outside the school, as revealed in a national survey sponsored by *Education Week* in 2001.

Nonetheless, the opportunities for seeking out and creating such texts in schools have grown steadily. For example, the availability and use of the Internet, applications for creating digital documents and presentations, and similar digital activities has increased substantially since the mid-1990s. The parallel increase of electronic texts in academia, which includes electronic versions of dissertations and the gradual recognition of electronic journals as respected outlets for rigorous scholarship, suggests a continued expansion of multimedia forms into the mainstream of literate activity at all academic levels.

A further impetus to broadening the scope of literacy in relation to multimedia is the shift from viewing literacy primarily as a set of isolated, minimal, functional skills for reading and writing in schools: Literacy is a much larger sociocultural phenomenon that has implications for personal agency and for a nationalistic competitiveness and globalization. The imperatives for literacy, the definitions of its importance in world of the early twenty-first century, and the ideas about how it might best be developed have changed rapidly in both a technological and a sociocultural sense. Multimedia literacy, and the constellation of contemporary literacies that it encompasses, implies a broad conception of educational imperatives and an understanding that digital transformations of reading and writing go far beyond the development of technological competence.

Thus, multimedia means can be thought of as an orientation of perspectives and values about a variety of literate activities across the sociocultural spectrum. For example, in law and ethics it may mean a transformation of concepts such as plagiarism, intellectual property, and copyright. In government and politics it may mean a transformation of the possibilities for shaping or controlling public opinion through the dissemination of information. In economics it may mean a transformation of commerce and how people purchase goods and services and how they manage their personal finances. In mass communication it may mean the transformation of how news organizations gather and disseminate information and who has access to it. In popular culture it may mean a transformation of the pragmatics of writing and reading texts such as determining what is acceptable and unacceptable when using e-mail. In education it may mean a transformation in what is considered a text, how texts are written and used, and ultimately perhaps the goals of education and the roles of teachers and students. Such potential transformations and how they might be accommodated in educational endeavors define the broad imperatives for considering literacy in terms of multimedia.

Theory and Research

On a theoretical plane, it is challenging to define precisely the relation between multimedia and literacy. What exactly comprises literacy has always been debatable and has increasingly been so in light of sociocultural perspectives. But, defining precisely what is meant by the term *multimedia* is equally challenging. That challenge is reflected in what might be considered a grammatical redundancy or, at least, an ambiguousness. Media is technically a plural form of the word *medium,* making multimedia somewhat redundant in a literal sense. Yet, media in popular usage has become a collective noun that originated in the field of advertising to designate agencies of mass communication. Whereas considering multimedia in relation to literacy may include an understanding and critical analysis of mass media in the collective sense, it implies much more in light of the digital forms of representation. That is, digital forms of representation often blend what might intuitively seem to be individual media into combinations heretofore not possible or feasible. Doing so, however, begs the question of where the boundaries are between media. Put another way, what precisely is a medium? Is a medium elemental in terms of a perceptual mode? That is, might audio and visual presentations be different media? Or, is a medium defined in terms of its technological materiality? That is, the writing of a conventional essay with pen, pencil, typewriter, or word processor employs the use of distinctly different media with potentially different effects. Or might a medium be defined in terms of technological capabilities? That is, a picture or video on a television and computer screen may be identical in appearance, but they are not necessarily equal in their potential opportunities for viewer interaction, and might, thus, be considered different media. Or, does identifying an individual medium require considering all these differences in some ill-defined way? Addressing these and similar questions and issues may be important in translating how literacy might be seen in terms of multimedia into agenda for practice and for research. In other words, knowing what a medium is and what individual media, if any, comprise a means of communication seem fundamental to understanding literacy from the perspective of multimedia and how such literacy might be developed.

In 1979 Gavriel Salomon offered a well-developed and often-cited theory of media and learning relevant to these questions and issues, and it illustrates the type of theory that might be useful. It is useful in part because it transcends more superficial, popular definitions of media that are linked to longstanding forms of communication, and it more readily recognizes and accommodates rapid changes in the technologies of communication. In his scheme a medium can be defined, and thus analyzed and reflected upon, as a configuration of four elements: symbol systems, technologies, contents, and situations. Symbol systems and the technologies used to present them are intertwined and critical because they define the cognitive requirements for extracting information from a medium and consequently what skills become necessary for those who wish to use the medium successfully. In this view, a conventional musical score and a topographical map are different media because they require different cognitive skills for extracting information. Symbol systems and technologies also importantly set the limits of the degree to which a medium can assist those who do not have the requisite skills to extract useful information. For example, Salomon demonstrated that the technological capabilities of the film camera (now also the video camera), specifically the capability to zoom in for a close-up, could increase attention to relevant detail among learners who had difficulty doing so on their own. Contents and situations, the remaining components that define a medium, are more socially defined correlates than necessary qualities of individual media. For example, textbooks rarely have overt advertisements (con-

tents), although they could, and breaking news events are rarely viewed in a movie theater (situations), although they indeed used to be. Thus, among its other advantages, this theoretical perspective accommodates both cognitive and sociocultural dimensions of multimedia and literacy.

There are other relevant theoretical perspectives that might define multimedia and guide research. Research and practice in relation to multimedia literacy has frequently been ad hoc and atheoretical, however. Further, within mainstream literacy research there have been relatively few published studies guided by an awareness of new technologies and media. The body of research focusing on literacy is overwhelmingly aimed at the conventional use of printed materials. However, three studies illustrate the range of possibilities for research in this area and the type of approaches that may lead to important understandings about literacy in terms of multimedia, including learning from texts, integrating multimedia into instruction, and expanding students' sociocultural awareness of textual information. For example, in 1991 Mary Hegarty and colleagues used a cognitive perspective to demonstrate how students with low mechanical ability learned more from text describing a machine when its operation was animated on a computer screen than when it was shown as a series of static pictures in a conventional printed text. Ruth Garner and Mark G. Gillingham, using case studies, documented in 1996 how literate activity as well as the roles of teachers and students changed when e-mail and Internet access were introduced into classrooms. Jamie Myers and colleagues described in 1998 how involving students in creating multimedia hypertexts about literacy and historical figures such as Pocahontas led to a critical stance toward various sources of information.

Further Thoughts

For the early twenty-first century, considering literacy in terms of multimedia relates directly to important changes and trends in conceptions of literacy beginning in the late twentieth century. This perspective makes particularly poignant the shift from printed to digital texts and the implications of that shift for reconceptualizing literacy in light of new and diverse modes of communication. Yet, incorporating multimedia into conceptions of literacy remains imprecise and has yet to provide an unambiguous guide for theory, research, and practice.

See also: LITERACY, *subentry on* LEARNING FROM MULTIMEDIA SOURCES; MEDIA AND LEARNING; TECHNOLOGY IN EDUCATION.

BIBLIOGRAPHY

ADONI, H. 1995. "Literacy and Reading in a Multimedia Environment." *Journal of Communication* 45:152–174.

BERTELSMANN FOUNDATION, ed. 1994. *Media as Challenge: Education as Task.* Gutersloh, Germany: Bertelsmann Foundation.

THE COGNITION AND TECHNOLOGY GROUP AT VANDERBILT UNIVERSITY. 1994. "Multimedia Environments for Developing Literacy in At-Risk Students." In *Technology and Education Reform: The Reality Behind the Promise,* ed. Barbara Means. San Francisco: Jossey-Bass.

CUMMINS, JIM, and SAYERS, DENNIS. 1995. *Brave New Schools: Challenging Cultural Literacy.* New York: St. Martins.

DALE, EDGAR. 1946. *Audiovisual Methods in Teaching.* New York: Holt, Rinehart, and Winston.

FLOOD, JAMES, and LAPP, DIANE. 1995. "Broadening the Lens: Toward an Expanded Conceptualization of Literacy." In *Perspectives on Literacy Research and Practice: The 44th Yearbook of the National Reading Conference,* ed. Kathleen A. Hinchman, Donald J. Leu, and Charles K. Kinzer. Chicago: National Reading Conference.

GARNER, RUTH, and GILLINGHAM, MARK, G. 1996. *Conversations across Time, Space, and Culture: Internet Communication in Six Classroom.* Hillsdale, NJ: Erlbaum.

HAGOOD, MARGARET C. 2000. "New Times, New Millennium, New Literacies." *Reading Research and Instruction* 39:311–328.

HEGARTY, MARY; CARPENTER, PATRICIA.; and JUST, MARCEL A. 1991. "Diagrams in the Comprehension of Scientific Texts." In *Handbook of Reading Research,* Vol. 2, ed. Rebecca Barr, Michael L. Kamil, Peter Mosenthal, and P. David Pearson. New York: Longman.

KAMIL, MICHAEL L.; INTRATOR, SAM M.; and KIM, HELEN S. 2000. "The Effects of Other Technologies on Literacy and Literacy Learning." *Handbook of Reading Research,* Vol. 3, ed. Michael L. Kamil, Peter Mosenthal, P. David Pearson, and Rebecca Barr. Mahwah, NJ: Erlbaum.

LANKSHEAR, COLIN, and KNOBEL, MICHELLE. 1995. "Literacies, Texts, and Difference in the Electronic Age." *Critical Forum* 4(2):3–33.

LEMKE, JAY L. 1998. "Metamedia Literacy: Transforming Meanings and Media." In *Handbook of Literacy and Technology: Transformations in a Post-typographic World,* ed. David Reinking, Michael C. McKenna, Linda D. Labbo, and Ronald D. Kieffer. Mahwah, NJ: Erlbaum.

LEU, DONALD J. 2000. "Literacy and Technology: Deictic Consequences for Literacy Education in an Information Age." In *Handbook of Reading Research,* Vol. 3, ed. Michael L. Kamil, Peter Mosenthal, P. David Pearson, and Rebecca Barr. Mahwah, NJ: Erlbaum.

MYERS, JAMIE; HAMMETT, ROBERTA; and McKILLOP, ANN M. 1998. "Opportunities for Critical Literacy and Pedagogy in Student-authored Hypermedia." In *Handbook of Literacy and Technology: Transformations in a Post-Typographic World,* ed. David Reinking, Michael C. McKenna, Linda D. Labbo, and Ronald D. Kieffer. Mahwah, NJ: Erlbaum.

THE NEW LONDON GROUP. 1996. "A Pedagogy of Multiliteracies: Designing Social Futures." *Harvard Education Review* 66:60–92.

SALOMON, GAVRIEL. 1979. *Interaction of Media, Cognition, and Learning.* San Francisco: Jossey-Bass.

TYNER, KATHLEEN T. 1998. *Literacy in a Digital World: Teaching and Learning in the Age of Information.* Mahwah, NJ: Erlbaum.

INTERNET RESOURCE

INTERNATIONAL SOCIETY FOR TECHNOLOGY IN EDUCATION. 1998. "National Educational Technology Standards for Students: Essential Conditions to Make It Happen." <www.cnets.iste.org/condition.htm>.

DAVID REINKING

NARRATIVE COMPREHENSION AND PRODUCTION

Narratives convey causally and thematically related sequences of actual or fictional events. Narratives have a hierarchical schematic structure. At the highest level, they consist of a setting, a theme, a plot, and a resolution. The components of the setting are characters, a location, and a time. Thus, the typical opening sentence of a fairy-tale, "Once upon a time in a far-away kingdom, there was a princess who . . ." conveys the setting in a nutshell, as does the more colloquial "Last night I was at a restaurant when . . .". The theme can consist of a goal (the princess wanted to get married) or an event and a goal (a fire broke out at the restaurant and I was trying to call 911). The plot is a causally related sequence of events, usually describing the character's attempts to achieve his or her goal. The resolution describes the achievement of the character's goal. Of course, many literary narratives omit the resolution. An example is Samuel Beckett's play *Waiting for Godot* (1953), whose main characters, Vladimir and Estragon, are waiting for a third character, Godot, to arrive. But Godot never arrives, thus spawning decades of literary analysis about the meaning of the play. However, most stories exhibit the stereotypical structure described above.

Aristotle in *Poetics* identified the plot as the major organizing structure of narratives and admonished poets to describe events only when they are relevant to the plot, just as Homer had done centuries before them. They were to refrain from giving a blow-by-blow chronological account of an episode. This Aristotle considered to be the province of historians.

Cohesion and Coherence in Narratives

In order to make sense, narratives need to be cohesive and coherent. Two successive sentences are said to be cohesive when they share information, as indicated by linguistic markers, such as pronouns or connectives. Thus, the sentence pair in (1) is cohesive because the pronoun he in the second sentence refers back to the runner mentioned in the first sentence.

> (1) The runner jumped over the puddle. He did not want to get his feet wet.

On the other hand, the sentence pair in (2) is not cohesive; there is no word in the second sentence that directly refers back to the first.

> (2) The runner jumped over the puddle. It is unpleasant to get your feet wet.

Yet, sentence pair (2) does seem to make sense: The second sentence provides a motivation for the action in the first sentence. Thus, the two sentences can be connected by generating a bridging inference. A sentence pair like (2) is said to be locally coherent. Now consider sentence pair (3).

> (3) The runner jumped over the puddle. Airplanes seldom leave on time.

This pair is neither cohesive nor locally coherent (i.e., it is not easy to generate a bridging inference). Thus, the connection between successive sentences can be established through cohesion markers or through bridging inferences (or a combination of the two). Is this sufficient to produce a coherent text? Consider the following passage.

> The runner jumped over the puddle. There were some frogs in the puddle. Frogs are often used as characters in fairy tales. Fairy tales are narratives. This entry is about narratives.

Although this "text" maintains local coherence—each sentence can be connected with its predecessor—it lacks an overall point. Thus, an important characteristic of narratives is that they have an overarching point or theme. This is called global coherence.

Empirical Approaches to the Study of Narrative

Cognitive psychologists have been able to uncover a great deal about how people understand narratives by assessing, among other things, what people recall from a story, how quickly people read certain words or sentences, or how quickly they respond to probe words. For example, it is clear that people use their expectations about the stereotypical structure of stories when understanding a story. It is also clear that people make inferences about the motives behind characters' actions and about the causes of events when these are not explicitly stated in the text in order to establish both local and global coherence. Consider the two sentence pairs below.

> (5) The spy threw the report in the fire. The ashes floated up the chimney.

> (6) The spy threw the report in the fire. Then he called the airline.

In sentence pair (5) the bridging inference that the report burned is needed to establish local coherence between the two sentences, but in (6) no such inference is needed because of the cohesive link between *spy* and *he*. In experiments, participants respond more quickly to the probe word *burn* after sentence pair (5) than after sentence pair (6), suggesting that the inference about the report burning was activated during the reading of (5) but not during the reading of (6).

There is a wealth of evidence that comprehenders do more than simply generate bridging inferences to connect sentences. What they do is construct mental representations of the situations that are described in the text, situation models, rather than just mental representations of the text itself. Consider sentence pairs (7) and (8).

> (7) Mike started playing the piano. A moment later, his mother entered the room.

> (8) Mike stopped playing the piano. A moment later, his mother entered the room.

Participants in experiments responded more quickly to the probe word *playing* after sentences such as (7) than after sentences such as (8). The reason for this is that in (7) Mike is still playing the piano after his mother has entered, whereas in (8) he is not. Thus, in (7) playing the piano is still part of the situation, but in (8) it is not. If the subjects were merely constructing representations of the texts, no difference should have been found, given that the word *playing* appeared in both texts.

Narrative Production as a Window into Comprehension

Writing involves cognitive operations that are the result of thinking, such as collecting information, generating ideas, turning these ideas into written text, and reviewing the text for its meaningfulness. In narratives, the thoughts, perceptions, fantasies, and memories of the writer are incorporated in a coherent narrative structure, either in oral or written language.

Knowledge of the prototypical structure of a mode of discourse is important for its construction and comprehension. A narrative about a major disaster, such as the explosion of the *Challenger* shuttle, will be written and processed in a different manner than a newspaper article about it. Whereas a newspaper article will focus on the facts, a narrative would include other elements, such as a plot and a narrator or a character-based perspective leading the reader through the sequence of events. The comprehension strategies of a narrative or a newspaper article about the explosion will be different as well, with a stronger focus on stylistic aspects and smaller focus on criteria of truth when using literary comprehension strategies than when using expository text comprehension strategies.

Although the boundaries between narratives and other forms of discourse are not clear-cut, narratives share certain features, such as a narrative structure that enables the reader to seek meaning and generate meaning from the narrative, and a potential to have an emotional impact on the reader or listener.

Affective and Esthetic Aspects of Narrative Comprehension and Production

Most narratives possess a dramatic quality that is created from an imbalance between narrative components, for instance different characters with opposing goals or a sequence of events leading to a tragic outcome for one of the characters. The dramatic quality as well as the style of the narrative will draw the reader into a convincing fictional world of goals, emotions, and motivations. Narrative style will stir the reader's imagination. For example, foregrounding of narrative elements, such as references to the devil in Elizabeth Bowen's *The Demon Lover* (1959), will aid the reader in imagining the true nature of the relationship between the main characters.

An imbalance in the sequence of events can affect the emotional response of the reader, in particular suspense, curiosity, and surprise. According to the structural affect theory, suspense is evoked by postponing the narrative's outcome, thereby creating uncertainty for the reader on the issue of what is going to happen next in the narrative. Curiosity arises when the outcome of the narrative is presented before the preceding events, whereas surprise occurs as a result of an unexpected event in the narrative, such as the sudden appearance of the pawnbroker's half-sister when Raskolnikov kills the pawnbroker in Dostoyevsky's *Crime and Punishment* (1866).

The kinds of emotions that readers experience while reading or listening to a narrative can be the result of being drawn into the fictional world of the narrative and identifying with the characters. These emotions are called "fictional emotions." Reader emotions can also be the result of analyzing and appreciating the narrative structure and techniques, called "artifact emotions" by Eduard Tan. The overall enjoyment of reading the narrative is based on both types of emotions. Narrative techniques, in particular switches in the role of narrators, can be used to make the reader go from observation to identification in different parts of the narrative or throughout the narrative.

Comparisons of Narratives in Different Cultures

Apart from being entertaining, many narratives also reflect moral values as a commentary on a society, include the preservation of events central to a culture, or aim to create an identity of a group. A culture is a shared perspective regarding ways of life and symbolic systems maintained within a social group. Narratives can help to establish an identity in a multicultural context, such as postmodernist literature, or preserve or create a group's identity within one culture, such as feminist poetry or Navajo narratives. Group identity is especially important for minority groups within a multicultural society. These groups share common interests and customs that act as a basis for constructive memory to be passed on to future generations.

The preservation of cultural elements from a group and the manner in which they are delivered can be one focus of narratives in cultural groups. Many Native American narratives preserve and transfer cultural traditions and tribal discourse through oral techniques of pause, pitch, and tempo. Another focus of narratives in cultural groups is the reflection of moral and aesthetic values within those groups. This can be the result of exclusionary mechanisms from a dominant cultural group that urges minority cultures to develop their own means of literary production and aesthetic norms with their own unique features. The incorporation of blues lyrics in African-American poetry is unique to that group, as is the inclusion of the native or modified language into poems and narratives in Chicano, Caribbean, and African-American cultures.

Narrative production and reception in one culture will strengthen and preserve the aesthetic norms and traditions within that culture. For individuals from other cultures, reading or listening to these narratives may help to translate these specific cultural elements into their own experiences and provide a better understanding of cultures and cultural issues other than their own, such as the dual personality issue in Chinese-American and Japanese-American culture. The narrative structure and the elicitation of fictional and artifact emotions will help this process. As Eileen Oliver suggests, part of the reception process may be that readers and listeners become more aware of the dynamics of cultural exchange in which assimilation, retention, and transformation of new cultural features are in constant progress.

See also: LITERACY AND READING; READING, *subentries on* COMPREHENSION, READING FROM TEXT.

BIBLIOGRAPHY

BARTLETT, FREDERIC C. 1932. *Remembering: A Study in Experimental and Social Psychology.* New York: Macmillan.

BREWER, WILLIAM F., and LICHTENSTEIN, EDWARD H. 1981. "Event Schemas, Story Schemas, and Story Grammars." In *Attention and Performance,* Vol. 9, ed. John Long and Alan D. Baddeley. Hillsdale, NJ: Erlbaum.

BRUNER, JEROME. 1990. *Acts of Meaning.* Cambridge, MA: Harvard University Press.

CHAN, JEFFERY P.; CHIN, FRANK; INADA, LAWSON F.; and WONG, SHAWN H. 1982. "An Introduction to Chinese-American and Japanese-American Literatures." In *Three American Literatures. Essays in Chicano, Native American, and Asian-American Literature for Teachers of American Literature,* ed. Houston A. Baker Jr. New York: The Modern Language Association of America.

FOKKEMA, DOUWE W. 1984. *Literary History, Modernism, Postmodernism.* Amsterdam and Philadelphia: Benjamins.

GRAESSER, ARTHUR C.; SINGER, MURRAY; and TRABASSO, TOM. 1994. "Constructing Inferences during Narrative Text Comprehension." *Psychological Review* 101:371–395.

HALLIDAY, MICHAEL A. K., and HASAN, RUQAIVA. 1976. *Cohesion in English.* London: Longman.

KELLOGG, RONALD T. 1994. *The Psychology of Writing.* New York: Oxford University Press.

KINTSCH, WALTER, and VAN DIJK, TEUN A. 1978. "Toward a Model of Text Comprehension and Production." *Psychological Review* 85:363–394.

OLIVER, EILEEN I. 1994. *Crossing the Mainstream: Multicultural Perspectives in Teaching Literature.* Urbana, IL: National Council of Teachers of English.

PROPP, VLADIMIR. 1968. *Morphology of the Folktale.* Austin: University of Texas Press.

SHERZER, J., and WOODBURY, ANTHONY C., eds. 1987. *Native American Discourse: Poetics and Rhetoric.* Cambridge, Eng., and New York: Cambridge University Press.

STEIN, NANCY, and POLICASTRO, MARGARET. 1985. "The Concept of a Story." In *Learning and Comprehension of Text,* ed. Heinz Mandl, Nancy Stein, and Tom Trabasso. Hillsdale, NJ: Erlbaum.

TAN, EDUARD S-H. 1994. "Film-Induced Affect as a Witness Emotion." *Poetics* 23:7–32.

THORNDYKE, PERRY W. 1977. "Cognitive Structures in Comprehension and Memory of Narrative Discourse." *Cognitive Psychology* 9:77–110.

WILLIAMS, SHERLEY A. 1978. "The Blues Roots of Contemporary Afro-American Poetry." In *Afro-American Literature. The Reconstruction of Instruction,* ed. Dexter Fisher and Robert B. Stepto. New York: The Modern Language Association of America.

ZWAAN, ROLF A., and RADVANSKY, GABRIEL A. 1998. "Situation Models in Language Comprehension and Memory." *Psychological Bulletin* 123:162–185.

ROLF A. ZWAAN
KATINKA DIJKSTRA

VOCABULARY AND VOCABULARY LEARNING

How does one help students learn vocabulary? Solutions take two general directions: one focuses on learning word meanings from context through wide reading and the other on the need for direct instruction about word meanings.

What Is Known and How to Know It

The divergent recommendations of wide reading versus direct instruction derive from different assumptions about the extent of vocabulary knowledge, that is, how many words children typically know, and how readily new words are learned. For example, rapid word learning and large vocabularies would indicate a lesser role for instruction, while slower growth would indicate need for intervention.

Vocabulary size and growth. A key issue is that estimates of vocabulary size vary widely. For example, estimates of total vocabulary size for first graders have ranged from about 2,500 (Edward Dolch and Madorah E. Smith) to about 25,000 (Burleigh Shibles and Mary Katherine Smith), and for college students from 19,000 (Edwin Doran and Edwin Kirkpatrick) to 200,000 (George Hartmann).

Situations with such wide variations make it impossible to simply ask people how many words they know, so estimates must be based on testing people's word knowledge of a sample of words and extrapolating to a final figure. To construct such tests, decisions must be made about what is taken as evidence of knowledge of a word, what constitutes a single word (e.g., should individuals who know the word *walk* be credited with knowing the word *walking?*), and how a sample of words is chosen to represent the language. All these decisions open the door to wide discrepancies in vocabulary size estimations.

Work on what constitutes a word and on techniques for constructing a language sample have helped bring estimates into greater agreement. Consequently, estimates in the early twenty-first century place vocabulary size for five- to six-year-olds at between 2,500 and 5,000 words. But although the problems of older work on vocabulary size are understood, there are (as of 2001) no recent, large-scale studies that correct these problems.

Estimates of vocabulary size at different ages are also used to estimate rates of vocabulary growth. Specific estimates of vocabulary growth, not surprisingly, vary widely, from three (Martin Joos) to twenty new words per day (George Miller). A figure of seven words per day is probably the most commonly cited.

Whatever the reality, it is certain that there are wide individual differences in both vocabulary size and growth. Studies have found profound differences among learners from different ability or socioeconomic groups, from toddlers through high school. For example, Mary Katherine Smith reported that high-knowledge third graders had vocabularies about equal to lowest-performing twelfth graders. These differences, once established, appear difficult to ameliorate. This is because children whose backgrounds provide rich verbal environments not only learn more words initially, but they also acquire understanding about language that enables them to continue to learn words more readily.

Learning from context. Most word meanings are learned from context. This is true from the earliest stages of a child's language acquisition onward, but the type of context changes. Early learning takes place through oral context, while later vocabulary learning shifts to written context. Written context lacks many of the features of oral language that support learning new word meanings, features such as intonation, body language, and shared physical surroundings. Thus, written context is a less efficient vehicle for learning. Research shows that learning from written context occurs, but in small increments. Machteld Swanborn and Kees de Glopper estimate that of one hundred unfamiliar words met in reading, between three and eight will be learned.

Thus, students could substantially increase vocabulary if two conditions are met. First, students must read widely enough to encounter a substantial number of unfamiliar words. Second, students must have the skills to infer word-meaning information from the contexts they read. The problem is that many students in need of vocabulary development do not engage in wide reading, especially of the kinds of books that contain unfamiliar vocabulary, and these students are less able to derive meaningful information from context. So depending on wide reading as a source of vocabulary growth could leave some students behind.

Direct instruction. The most commonly cited problem with direct instruction to address students' vocabulary needs is that there are too many words to teach. This is certainly true if the goal is to teach all the words in a language. Consider, however, a mature vocabulary as comprising three tiers. The first tier consists of basic words—*mother, ball, go*—that rarely require instructional attention. The third tier contains words of low frequency that are typically limited to specific domains—*isotope, peninsula, refinery*. These words are appropriate for specific needs, such as introducing the word *peninsula* during a geography lesson. The second tier contains high frequency, general words, such as *compromise, extraordinary,* and *typical.* Because of the large role tier-two words play in a language user's repertoire, instruction directed toward these could be valuable in contributing to vocabulary growth.

What kind of instruction should be offered? The answer depends on the goal. Typically, educators want students to know words well enough to facilitate reading comprehension and to use the words in their own speech and writing. Facilitating comprehension seems a reasonable goal, given the well-established relationship between vocabulary knowledge and comprehension. Although virtually all studies that present vocabulary instruction result in students learning words, few have succeeded in improving comprehension. In analyzing this discrepancy, researchers, such as Steven Stahl and Marilyn Fairbanks, found that to influence comprehension instruction needs to: (1) present multiple exposures of words; (2) involve a breadth of information, beyond definitions; (3) engage active processing by getting students to think about and interact with words.

Effective instruction should accomplish the following:

- Begin with information about the word's meaning, but not necessarily a formal definition.
- Immediately prompt students to use the word.
- Keep bringing the words back in a variety of formal and informal ways.
- Get students to take their word learning beyond the classroom.
- Help students use context productively.

Status of Vocabulary Issues

Although there is general consensus on effective vocabulary instruction, little of this kind of instruction is found in classrooms. Attention to vocabulary in classrooms focuses on looking up definitions and perhaps writing sentences for new words. The typical dictionary definitions, however, do not promote students' learning of new word meanings. In fact, often students do not even understand the definitions of the words they look up. Thus it is important to implement what is known about effective instruction into classrooms.

Much about the way vocabulary is learned and stored in memory is still unknown. How much learning comes from oral contexts past initial stages of acquisition? How much do early learning experiences matter and is it possible for children who lag early to catch up? What characteristics of verbal environments are most useful for word learning? For example, what are the roles of the amount of talk in a child's environment, the kinds of words used, and interactions within the environment? How is word knowledge organized? Research makes it clear that a person's vocabulary knowledge does not exist as a stored list of words, but rather as networks of relationships. This leads to the question, how do these networks of word relationships affect how readily and how well words are learned?

To help students improve their vocabulary, it will be necessary to put into practice what is already known about vocabulary learning and evaluate and refine the results.

See also: INSTRUCTIONAL DESIGN, *subentry on* DIRECT INSTRUCTION; LITERACY AND READING; READING, *subentries on* COMPREHENSION, CONTENT AREAS; SPELLING, TEACHING OF.

BIBLIOGRAPHY

ANGLIN, JEREMY M. 1993. *Vocabulary Development: A Morphological Analysis.* Chicago: University of Chicago Press.

BEALS, DIANE E., and TABORS, PATTON O. 1995. "Arboretum, Bureaucratic, and Carbohydrates: Preschoolers' Exposure to Rare Vocabulary at Home." *First Language* 15:57–76.

BECK, ISABEL L., and MCKEOWN, MARGARET G. 1983. "Learning Words Well: A Program to Enhance Vocabulary and Comprehension." *The Reading Teacher* 36(7):622–625.

BECK, ISABEL L., and MCKEOWN, MARGARET G. 1991. "Conditions of Vocabulary Acquisition." In *Handbook of Reading Research,* Vol. 2, ed. Rebecca Barr, Michael L. Kamil, Peter Mosenthal, and P. David Pearson. New York: Longman.

BECK, ISABEL L.; MCKEOWN, MARGARET G.; and OMANSON, RICHARD C. 1987. "The Effects and Uses of Diverse Vocabulary Instructional Techniques." In *The Nature of Vocabulary Acquisition,* ed. Margaret G. McKeown and Mary E. Curtis. Hillsdale, NJ: Erlbaum.

BIEMILLER, ANDREW. 1999. *Language and Reading Success: From Reading Research to Practice,* Vol. 5. Cambridge, MA: Brookline Books.

DOLCH, EDWARD WILLIAM. 1936. "How Much Word Knowledge Do Children Bring to Grade 1?" *Elementary English Review* 13:177–183.

DORAN, EDWIN W. 1907. "A Study of Vocabularies." *Pedagogical Seminar* 14:177–183.

GOERSS, BETTY L.; BECK, ISABEL L.; and MCKEOWN, MARGARET G. 1999. "Increasing Remedial Students' Ability to Derive Word Meaning from Context." *Reading Psychology* 20(2):151–175.

GRAVES, MICHAEL F.; BRUNETTI, G. J.; and SLATER, WAYNE H. 1982. "The Reading Vocabularies of Primary-Grade Children of Varying Geographic and Social Backgrounds." In *New Inquiries in Reading Research and Instruction,* ed. Jerome A. Niles and Larry A. Harris. Rochester, NY: National Reading Conference.

HART, BETTY, and RISLEY, TODD. 1995. *Meaningful Differences.* Baltimore: Brookes.

HARTMANN, GEORGE W. 1946. "Further Evidence on the Unexpected Large Size of Recognition Vocabularies among College Students." *Journal of Educational Psychology* 37:436–439.

JOOS, MARTIN. 1964. "Language and the School Child." *Harvard Educational Review* 34:203–210.

KIRKPATRICK, EDWIN ASBURY. 1891. "The Number of Words in an Ordinary Vocabulary." *Science* 18:107–108.

LANDAUER, THOMAS, and DUMAIS, SUSAN. 1997. "A Solution to Plato's Problem: The Latent Semantic Analysis Theory of Acquisition, Induction, and Representation of Knowledge." *Psychological Review* 104:211–240.

MCKEOWN, MARGARET G. 1985. "The Acquisition of Word Meaning from Context by Children of High and Low Ability." *Reading Research Quarterly* 20:482–496.

MCKEOWN, MARGARET G. 1993. "Creating Effective Definitions for Young Word Learners." *Reading Research Quarterly* 28:16–31.

MEZNSKI, KAREN. 1983. "Issues Concerning the Acquisition of Knowledge: Effects of Vocabulary Training on Reading Comprehension." *Review of Educational Research* 53:253–279.

MILLER, GEORGE A. 1985. "Dictionaries of the Mind." *Proceedings of the 23rd Annual Meeting of the Association for Computational Linguists.* Chicago: Association for Computational Linguists.

NAGY, WILLIAM; HERMAN, PATRICIA; and ANDERSON, RICHARD. 1985. "Learning Words from Context." *Reading Research Quarterly* 20:233–253.

SHIBLES, BURLEIGH H. 1959. "How Many Words Does a First-Grade Child Know?" *Elementary English* 31:42–47.

SMITH, MADORAH ELIZABETH. 1926. "An Investigation of the Development of the Sentence and the Extent of Vocabulary in Your Children." *University of Iowa Studies in Child Welfare* 5:219–227.

SMITH, MARY KATHERINE. 1941. *Measurement of the Size of General English Vocabulary through the Elementary Grades and High School.* Provincetown, MA: The Journal Press.

STAHL, STEVEN A., and FAIRBANKS, MARILYN M. 1986. "The Effects of Vocabulary Instruction: A Model-Based Meta-Analysis." *Review of Educational Research* 56:7–110.

STERNBERG, ROBERT J. 1987. "Most Vocabulary Is Learned from Context." In *The Nature of Vocabulary Acquisition,* ed. Margaret G. McKeown and Mary E. Curtis. Hillsdale, NJ: Erlbaum.

SWANBORN, MACHTELD S. L., and DE GLOPPER, KEES. 1999. "Incidental Word Learning While Reading: A Meta-Analysis." *Review of Educational Research* 69(3):261–285.

WATTS, SUSAN. 1995. "Vocabulary Instruction during Reading Lessons in Six Classrooms." *Journal of Reading Behavior* 27(3):399–424.

MARGARET G. MCKEOWN
ISABEL L. BECK

WRITING AND COMPOSITION

Skills or process? Visible in the history of writing instruction is the same controversy found in the rest of the language arts. Historically, writing instruction focused on handwriting and on correctness of the product produced through emphasis on what are sometimes referred to as the mechanics of writing (i.e., sentence structure, spelling, correct punctuation, etc.) and on rules. Students were usually asked to write to assigned topics or for purposes such as essay exams. They were seldom asked to write for an audience other than the teacher and the quality of the writing was much more likely to be judged on the basis of the correctness of its content and mechanics than on style or creative expression of ideas.

Writing Process Instruction

Gradually research began to make visible the processes of writing. With the writing project movement in the mid- to late 1970s concern for teaching the writing process emerged as a strong force. In the early stages of that movement the process was often described in a linear fashion as a series of four steps: pre-writing, writing, editing, and revision. Over time those concerned with writing instruction came to recognize and acknowledge through instruction that real writing is a much more messy reflexive and recursive process. With this understanding came the push to encourage students to write on topics of their own choosing, write for their own purposes, and perhaps most significantly, write to real audiences. As with most swings of the educational pendulum, by the late 1980s writing instruction in some schools had reached an extreme point where students might write exclusively in the genre of their choice and where attention to mechanics was seldom taught and/or required, even in pieces for publication.

During the 1990s politicians and the public at large increasingly called for rigorous academic standards and writing instruction shifted once again. In the early twenty-first century, teachers of writing or composition typically try to balance their desire to have students engage in writing in which they are personally invested, with the challenges of attention to correctness issues and to writing in a range of genres. Often these demands are tied to distinguishing between private and public writing. When the intended reader is an audience other than the author, the needs and expectations of that reader must be addressed if the writer's work is to be positively received.

With these shifts in the view of the writing process came the realization that the idea that *writing is writing* is not valid. That is, each discipline, indeed each piece of writing, has its own demands in terms of genre, audience, purpose, situation, and even what is viewed as correctness. This realization, coupled with the belief that engaging in writing can influence cognitive development, led to the writing across the curriculum movement, resulting in pressure on all teachers, not just English or Language Arts teachers, to be teachers of writing. After all, which teacher is better prepared to help students develop the genre of lab report writing, the chemistry teacher or the English teacher? Accompanying this movement has been increased emphasis on tying reading and writing instruction together.

Technology As Tool

Within a decade of the emergence of the writing process movement, technology began to exert a significant influence on writing instruction. Early arguments centered around whether or not classrooms (especially elementary classrooms) should have a computer, and how or even if that computer should play a role in language arts instruction. Some argued for placing computers in one centralized lab, which students would visit as a whole class once or twice a week, rather than distributing computers across classrooms. Most of the educational software available by the mid-1980s provided little more than computerized versions of skill drills or workbook sheets, occasionally accompanied by programs to teach typing or rudimentary word processing. Even under these less than ideal circumstances, students and teachers recognized the potential of technology for contributing to the writing process. When one fourth grader was asked how the computer helped her to revise she stated succinctly, "you don't have to worry about the paper ripping." What she and others recognized was the power of technology to assist writers with the physical process of encoding their messages so that more time and effort could be given to the composing process.

While educators were arguing about if or how computer technology should affect classrooms, technology was continuing to evolve at a rapid pace and the accessibility of affordable computers outside the classroom soon rendered the argument moot. Children who came to school computer literate were supported by their parents in expecting (sometimes demanding) similar access at school. The impact on the school writing curriculum was profound, with computer literacy quickly becoming a major issue for both students and teachers.

As computers have become more affordable and pervasive in society at large they affect not just formal writing instruction in K–12 schools, but also instruction in other educational venues. Adult education and community college programs offer a variety of classes and programs aimed at developing computer literacy in a wide range of students and for a huge variety of uses. Colleges and university now typically expect their students to be computer literate, even in some cases providing or requiring a personal computer for each entering student.

Technology in Development of Writing and Composition Skills

These new writing technologies provide new choices and, in some cases, have led to a shifting emphasis in the development of writing abilities. Where there previously was an emphasis on traditional (paper-and ink-based) products and processes, there is now an emphasis toward an evolving set of products and processes enabled by electronic technologies. Handwriting is no longer an issue. To a large extent issues of mechanics (e.g., spelling, grammar) are taken care of by employing the computer as editor.

At the same time, shifting definitions of literacy have affected technology and software use in educational settings. Moving from the early days of computer drills and grammar checkers, to expressive freewriting or "invisible" writing on computer screens, to cognitive-based heuristic programs, to social functions of networked writing, technology use in writing instruction has mirrored the important theoretical and empirical approaches to teaching writing in traditional classrooms. This emphasizes a shift from viewing writing technology as a tool for delivering instruction to a technology that engages students as socially interactive participants. A new genre of writing with its own vocabulary and conventions has been born through such technology-related venues as e-mail, chat rooms,

listservs, and MOOs (Multiple User Dimensions/ Object Oriented, which arose out of online game-playing in text-based virtual reality environments). Writing in hypertext, with its ability to link writing through the click of a pointing device, is one example of this powerful new interactivity for writers and readers.

Traditional writing concerns such as understanding purpose and the importance of audience awareness have a renewed emphasis in technologically rich writing environments. Some teachers have successfully used technology to show students the importance of these traditional writing concerns in a writing environment with social relevance to students' lives. For example, discussions about audience naturally follow when writing is published on the Internet, whether to a known audience, as in personal e-mail, or a potentially unknown audience, as part of a website. Likewise, purposeful writing is given new importance when writers communicate with readers via electronic mail, electronic bulletin boards, synchronous discussion, or web sites—how readers interpret meaning in these contexts may shift, and students writing electronically need to carefully consider the crucial role of purpose in their writing.

Although issues of organization and style have always been important aspects of writing and composition (though sometimes underemphasized instructionally), technology provides a myriad of new options for writers to consider. Issues that previously were the concern of copy editors, publishers, and graphic artists have become the concern of authors. Developing writing skills in technologically rich environments may include elements of visual literacy skills, such as using graphics or integrated images within a text. Word processing and publishing software give developing writers the option, or in some cases the need, to learn about document design as it relates to writing. Composing in hypertext allows the writer to insert links from one part of a document to another, or if the document is made available online, writers can link to different texts and sites available over the network. Whether a document is composed on a word processor or marked-up for World Wide Web publication, writers are presented with previously unavailable choices of font styles, sizes, colors, and other symbols, including moving or still images and graphics. Writers can vary patterns of organization manipulating texts using electronic "cut and paste" tools, and writing in hypertext offers a nearly infinite number of organizational options controlled, in part, by the reader.

Taken together, these new choices and shifting emphases represent a changing literacy landscape. In this new context, writing instruction continues to evolve as the uses and processes of writing change.

See also: TECHNOLOGY IN EDUCATION; WRITING, TEACHING OF.

BIBLIOGRAPHY

BAZERMAN, CHARLES. 1988. *Shaping Written Knowledge: The Genre and Activity of the Experimental Article in Science.* Madison: University of Wisconsin Press.

FLOWER, LINDA, and HAYES, JOHN. 1981. "A Cognitive Process Theory of Writing." *College Composition and Communication* 32:365–387.

GRAVES, DONALD. 1980. "Research Update: A New Look at Writing Research." *Language Arts* 57:913–919.

GRAY, JAMES. 2000. *Teachers at the Center: A Memoir of the Early Years of the National Writing Project.* Berkeley, CA: National Writing Project.

HAIRSTON, MAXINE. 1982. "The Winds of Change: Thomas Kuhn and the Revolution in the Teaching of Writing." *College Composition and Communication* 33:76–88.

HAWISHER, GAIL E. 1994. "Blinding Insights: Classification Schemes and Software for Literacy Instruction." In *Literacy and Computers: The Complications of Teaching and Learning with Technology,* ed. Cynthia L. Selfe, and Susan Hilligoss. New York: The Modern Language Association of America.

HAWISHER, GAIL; LEBLANC, PAUL; MORAN, CHARLES; and SELFE CYNTHIA. 1996. *Computers and the Teaching of Writing in American Higher Education, 1979-1994: A History.* Norwood, NJ: Ablex.

MURRAY, JAMES. 1990. *A Short History of Writing Instruction: From Ancient Greece to Twentieth-Century America.* Davis, CA: Hermagoras.

NESSEL, DENISE; JONES, MARGARET; and DIXON, CAROL. 1987. *Thinking Through the Language Arts.* New York: Macmillan.

CAROL N. DIXON
CHRISTOPHER JOHNSTON

LITERACY AND CULTURE

Literate practices are learned within dynamic cultural systems that structure roles and scripts (alphabetic, pictographic), privilege modes of reasoning, and offer tools through which such practices may be carried out. In modern, often Westernized, societies, these tools include books, newspapers, magazines, film, digital technology, and television. Historically, the advent of new technologies—such as the printing press—made possible new explorations of literacy and opportunities for more people to become literate. With greater global immigration, more students for whom English is a second language are entering U.S. classrooms. In some cases both U.S.-born and immigrant populations are involved in literate practices that operate under different assumptions than those that characterize school-based literacies. The digital age in particular offers opportunities to many more people to self-publish, create and interpret multimedia texts, privilege non-linear approaches to reading, for example, in hypermedia texts, engage in visual as well as oral communication across borders, and access rich databases internationally. These and other advances are ushering in new kinds of literate practices that now challenge schools to learn to integrate them meaningfully and to provide equitable access across groups. This entry will focus on literate practices defined by ethnicity (including language use) and by academic discipline, considering their implications for classroom instruction and student learning.

Induction into literate practices involves socialization in the ability to decode scripts and to reason in patterned ways. People demonstrate their membership in literate communities through ways they use language—knowing the right lexicon, the structure of appropriate genres, as well as when, where, and how talk should proceed. In reading and writing, such cultural models may be influenced by ethnicity, nationality, disciplines, and professions. Reading literature, for example, requires one to infer motives, goals, and internal states of characters based not only on clues from the text, but also from one's reading of the social world. Reading primary historical texts requires readers to invoke disciplinary norms, questioning the point of view of the author, drawing on knowledge of historical contexts. Some challenges that students face in literacy instruction derive from differences between community-based cultural models and school-based literacies.

Cultural Conflicts in Classroom Practices

Schools are seen as the repository of "standard" English, which is assumed to be the proper medium of communication for advancement in the marketplace and the academy. Not only is the standard a historically moving target (syntactical and lexical forms considered proper, say, in eighteenth-century Great Britain or the United States are considered archaic and inappropriate in the twenty-first century); in addition, certain syntactic markers have different values. For example, "It is me" is not considered "improper" English (as opposed to the "standard" form "It is I"), whereas "It be me," a marker of African-American Vernacular English (AAVE) is seen as "incorrect." In the 1970s researchers documented how students of color, English Language Learners (ELL), and students living in low-income communities were marginalized through classroom practices, particularly in the area of literacy instruction.

Susan Phillips's work helped the field to understand how opportunities to participate in instruction were actualized in classrooms. She examined relationships of power that are constructed through norms for talk in classrooms. She documented the conflicts between norms for talk in the Navajo Nation and ways Anglo teachers expected Navajo students to participate. Using Anglo norms, teachers interpreted long stretches of silence by Navajo students as evidence that students were not learning.

In a similar vein other researchers, such as Courtney Cazden and colleagues, documented how oral language practices by low-income African-American primary level students were interpreted as deficits rather than resources. The function of sharing time is to scaffold young children from oral storytelling to the production of features of the kinds of academic writing that they will be expected to produce in later grades. Teachers viewed the African-American children's stories as ill formed and saw the students' language as a deficit. By contrast, Sarah Michaels analyzed the children's stories as fitting a different structure, which she termed topic-associative in contrast to the topic-centered stories of the Anglo children. James Gee extended Michaels's analysis to claim that the topic-associative story structure included complex literary elements. The consequences of teachers' abilities to recognize the literate features of children's oral language has important consequences for the ways they are or are not able to extend the funds of knowledge that stu-

dents bring to classrooms in order to help students learn school-based ways of reading and writing.

Other research has found more African-American students employing topic-centered stories than topic-associative. Tempii Champion identified an array of narrative genres used by African-American children. Champion's findings illustrate how children across different communities "take up various narrative styles, structures, and content [that] include formal instruction, informal instructional contexts, family contexts and others" (p. 72). If one moves away from the social address model that categorizes people into discrete cultural communities, one can understand the ways that children and adolescents, for example, traverse multiple cultural communities. In the process they adopt, adapt, and hybridize a variety of oral and textual genres that become part of their literate repertoires. They learn to engage such repertoires in different contexts, with different actors, for different purposes.

Language is central to literate practices. Research in bilingual education has explored how ELL use resources in the first language as they engage in reading and writing in the second language. When faced with a breakdown in comprehension while reading English texts, Spanish-speaking students, for example, would think in Spanish to repair comprehension. How a first language other than English may be drawn upon in support of school literacy often depends on how much formal schooling students had in the first language before entering U.S. schools.

Another area of study is literate practices of children and families outside school, shedding light on how schools can make connections with what students know and ways they learn that are not currently reflective in mainstream school literacy practices. The church in many low-income communities is a site for multilingual literate practices. For Spanish-speaking families, researchers documented literate practices associated with *doctrina*, catechism classes for children that involve reading and writing extended texts in both Spanish and English. Beverly Moss documents the oral as well as reading-writing practices in African-American Christian churches. For example, call and response is a dominant discourse pattern in black churches that requires the audience to attend closely to nuances of the delivered text and invites a high level of engagement by the audience. However, call and response is seldom invoked in classrooms serving African-American students (Carol Lee reports exceptions).

Schools value children's emergent literacy experiences outside school as preparation for learning to read, write, and speak. Reading books to young children at home is seen as an important predictor of future school success and white middle-class patterns of storybook reading are considered a norm that all families should emulate. However, Carol Schneffer Hammer reports both low-income and middle-class African-American mothers employing an interactive storybook reading style different from the white middle-class model. These mothers did not employ a question-asking routine but were still able to elicit appropriate language responses. Others have noted the value of oral storytelling as an emergent literacy practice, with an emphasis on its performative features; comparable mismatches with low-income Anglo students, particularly Appalachian students, have also been documented.

Many communities and individuals grapple with the question of which community-based language and literate practices to abandon in order to succeed in school. Ethnic and language cultural communities are not homogeneous in their response to this challenge. For immigrant populations, socioeconomic status and the number of generations removed from the country of origin are the most significant factors. Gail Weinstein-Shr documented two Hmong communities in Philadelphia with very different orientations toward cultural integration into U.S. "mainstream" values. Daniel McLaughlin has reported similar debates regarding reading and writing in Navajo versus English.

Community-based literate practices in low-income neighborhoods often involve reading functional and religious texts, and forms of writing such as letters, lists, and journals. Such reading and writing often involve both English and the community-based language. By contrast, the standards movement in literacy focuses on longer and discipline-based texts. Basil Bernstein characterizes language practices of working-class students as localized to the immediate context and not characterized by the more abstract and generalizable strategies that many associate with school-based literacies. The counter-voice to this position argues that literate practices are always context bound, socially co-constructed by the participants.

Culturally Responsive Pedagogy as Zones of Proximal Development

Lower literacy achievement rates for African-American, Latino, some Asian-American, and most low-income students have been attributed to three sources: cultural mismatches between instruction and the backgrounds of students; structural inequalities in the society manifested in the organization of and resources allocated to schools serving these populations; and ineffective instruction that is not based on enduring best practices. Culturally responsive pedagogy (CRP) is one response that addresses cultural mismatches directly and often addresses macro-level structures indirectly.

Studies of culture and cognition show that through repeated and patterned experience in the world, we develop schema through which we filter future experiences. New learning is strongest when we are able to make connections to prior knowledge. CRP explicitly fosters connections between students' cultural funds of knowledge and disciplinary knowledge to be learned.

This approach is particularly relevant to literacy because both language use and socially shared knowledge are central to acts of reading and writing. In addition, CRP often structures ways of talking that appropriate cultural norms for discourse from students' home communities. Examples below illustrate CRP focusing on generic reading and writing.

A classic example is the KEEP Project with Native Hawaiian children. Discussions of stories read were structured to resemble Talk Story, a community-based genre that involved multiparty overlapping talk. Students achieved significant gains in reading. Luis Moll coined the phrase "cultural funds of knowledge" in an ethnographic investigation of routine practices in a Mexican origin community in Tuscon, Arizona. Moll documented ways adults in the community engaged in practices involving carpentry, plumbing, and other skills, and the literate practices embedded in them. He then designed an after-school structure that allowed teachers to learn about these practices and forge relationships with community residents, resulting in teachers' incorporation of adult mentors in the classroom. Students learned to build projects around the cultural practices of the community, each requiring extensive reading, writing, and speaking.

Other work with ELL focuses on the competencies children and adolescents develop as language brokers, translating in high-stakes settings for their parents. Translating involves negotiating across different codes, understanding appropriate registers, anticipating audience, negotiating perspective, and often involves reading and writing in two languages.

The Fifth Dimension Project (FD) is a network of after-school computer clubs operating nationally and internationally. Through play, adults and children together work their way through a maze by developing competencies in commercial computer games and board games. The children are low income, many ELL for whom Spanish is the language used at home. Literate practices involve reading game instructions, writing to a mythical wizard who responds to questions, and communicating orally and in writing to others. Through this project children have structured access to multiple mediational means—invited use of English and Spanish/AAVE, and so forth, peer and adult mentors, the mytical wizard, and opportunities to move fluidly across roles. FD students have shown significant increases in reading achievement, despite the fact that didactic teaching of reading and writing are not the focus of the intervention.

Carol Lee has developed a design framework for CRP called Cultural Modeling (CM). CM has focused on response to literature and narrative composition. CM works on the assumption that students—in this case speakers of AAVE—already tacitly engage in modes of reasoning required to interpret literary tropes and genres. Instruction engages students in what Lee calls metacognitive instructional conversations where the focus is on how students know, for example, that rap lyrics are not intended to be interpreted literally, and what clues/strategies students use to reconstruct the intended meaning. In addition, in CM classrooms—with African-American students—classroom discourse reflects AAVE norms with overlapping multiparty talk, high use of gesture, and rhythmic prosody. In CM classrooms, high school students with low standardized achievement scores in reading display very complex literary reasoning with rich, canonical texts. A. F. Ball found secondary African-American students displayed in their writing a preference for a set of expository features that are rooted in what Geneva Smitherman has called the African-American Rhetorical Tradition. Smitherman found that the presence of these features correlated positively with higher evaluations on National Assessment of Educational Progress samples.

See also: INDIVIDUAL DIFFERENCES, *subentry on* ETHNICITY; LANGUAGE AND EDUCATION; LITERACY; RACE, ETHNICITY, AND CULTURE.

BIBLIOGRAPHY

BALL, A. F. 1992. "Cultural Preferences and the Expository Writing of African-American Adolescents." *Written Communication* 9(4):501–532.

BERNSTEIN, BASIL. 1970. *Primary Socialization, Language and Education.* London: Routledge and Kegan Paul.

BLOOME, DAVID, et al. 2001. "Spoken and Written Narrative Development: African American Preschoolers as Storytellers and Storymakers." In *Literacy in African American Communities,* ed. Joyce L. Harris, Alan G. Kamhi, and Karen E. Pollock. Mahwah, NJ: Erlbaum.

CAZDEN, COURTNEY; JOHN, VERA P.; and HYMES, DELL. 1972. *Functions of Language in the Classroom.* New York: Teachers College Press, Columbia University.

CHAMPION, TEMPII. 1998. "'Tell Me Somethin' Good': A Description of Narrative Structures among African-American Children." *Linguistics and Education* 9(3):251–286.

GEE, JAMES PAUL. 1989. "The Narrativization of Experience in the Oral Style." *Journal of Education* 171(1):75–96.

HAMMER, CAROL SCHNEFFNER. 2001. "'Come Sit Down and Let Mama Read': Book Reading Interactions between African-American Mothers and Their Infants." In *Literacy in African-American Communities,* ed. Joyce L. Harris, Alan G. Kamhi, and Karen E. Pollock. Mahwah, NJ: Erlbaum.

LEE, CAROL D. 1995. "A Culturally Based Cognitive Apprenticeship: Teaching African-American High School Students' Skills in Literary Interpretation." *Reading Research Quarterly* 30(4):608–631.

LEE, CAROL D. 1997. "Bridging Home and School Literacies: A Model of Culturally Responsive Teaching." In *A Handbook of Research on Teaching Literacy through the Communicative and Visual Arts,* ed. James Flood, Shirley Brice Heath, and Diane Lapp. New York: Macmillan.

LEE, CAROL D. 2000. "Signifying in the Zone of Proximal Development." In *Vygotskian Perspec-

tives on Literacy Research: Constructing Meaning through Collabative Inquiry, ed. Carol D. Lee and Peter Smagorinsky. New York: Cambridge University Press.

LEE, CAROL D. 2001. "Is October Brown Chinese: A Cultural Modeling Activity System for Underachieving Students." *American Educational Research Journal* 38(1):97–142.

MCLAUGHLIN, DANIEL. 1989. "The Sociolinguistics of Navajo Literacy." *Anthropology and Education Quarterly* 20(4):275–290.

MICHAELS, SARAH. 1981. "Sharing Time: Children's Narrative Styles and Differential Access to Literacy." *Language in Society* 10:423–442.

MOLL, LUIS. 1994. "Literacy Research in Community and Classrooms: A Sociocultural Approach." In *Theoretical Models and Processes of Reading,* 4th edition, ed. Robert B. Ruddell, Martha P. Ruddell, and Harry Singer. Newark, DE: International Reading Association.

MOSS, BEVERLY, ed. 1994. *Literacy across Communities.* Cresskill, NJ: Hampton.

PHILLIPS, SUSAN URMSTON. 1983. *The Invisible Culture: Communication in Classroom and Community on the Warm Springs Indian Reservation.* New York: Longman.

SMITHERMAN, GENEVA. 1977. *Talkin and Testifyin: The Language of Black America.* Boston: Houghton Mifflin.

WEINSTEIN-SHR, GARIL. 1994. "From Mountaintops to City Streets: Literacy in Philadelphia's Hmong Community." In *Literacy across Communities,* ed. Beverly Moss. Cresskill, NJ: Hampton.

CAROL D. LEE

LITERACY AND READING

The terms *literacy* and *reading,* though related, are neither synonymous nor unambiguous. Typically reading is subsumed by literacy, with the latter term referring to reading, writing, and other modes of symbolic communication that are valued differently for social, economic, and political reasons often imposed by a dominant culture. Simply broadening the definition, however, does not alleviate the ambiguity. For instance, the assumption that literacy exists in the singular has been criticized by Brian Street in 1995 and others for ignoring the socially situated aspects of one's multiple literacies (print, nonprint, computer, scientific, numeric) and their accompanying literate practices.

A preference for literacies, as opposed to literacy in the singular, also signals a critique of the autonomous model of reading that has dominated Western thinking up to the present. It is a model that views reading largely from a cognitive perspective—as a "natural" or neutral process, one supposedly devoid of ideological positioning and the power relations inherent in such positioning. Conceiving of literacies in the plural and as ideologically embedded does not require giving up on the cognitive aspects of reading. Rather, according to Street, the ideological model subsumes the autonomous model of reading in an attempt to understand how reading is encapsulated within broader sociocultural structures (schools, governments, families, media) and the power relations that sustain them. This focus on literacies and reading as social practices within various contexts is central to untangling the "realities" (the so-called knowns), unsupported assertions, and controversies that surround the practices.

Realities

Definitive paradigm shifts since the last quarter of the twentieth century have marked transitions from behaviorist to cognitivist to sociocultural models of the reading process. Although these changing conceptions have altered how researchers and practitioners think about the reading process generally (and instruction, specifically), overall the field has remained largely focused on two major topics: reading acquisition and comprehension. This is not to say that other topics have been neglected. For instance, sufficient evidence exists for linking reading directly and inextricably to writing, such as the work of Robert Tierney and Timothy Shanahan, and Ian Wilkinson and colleagues; and other evidence connects various instructional practices to students' reading engagement and motivation to learn content, such as that of John Guthrie and Allan Wigfield. In terms of sheer quantity of research findings, however, the focus remains on reading acquisition and comprehension.

Reading Acquisition Research

Reading acquisition is no longer seen as the sole responsibility of the school; nor is it viewed as a "lockstep" process that moves from oral language development (speaking and listening) to print literacy (reading and writing). Currently, learning to read is viewed as a developmental process, one that emerges gradually from the time a child is born. The role of the family is paramount in fostering a child's growth in language and in creating a literacy-rich environment. Parents, educators, researchers, and policymakers constantly look for ways to provide all children with access to the world of print, largely because knowing how to read and knowing what to do with information gained from reading is thought to be key to a child's future well-being.

The Report of the National Reading Panel in the year 2000, a major reference for U.S. education policymakers, is an evidence-based assessment of the experimental and quasi-experimental research literature on reading. The National Reading Panel (NRP) used strict selection criteria in analyzing a comprehensive body of research that focused primarily on early reading and reading in grades three to eight, with the research being limited to studies published in peer-reviewed journals written in the English language. One of the panel's goals was to report how instruction in phonemic awareness, phonics, and fluency impacts children's early reading development and achievement in school settings.

Phonemic awareness. Phonemic awareness and knowledge of the alphabetic principle (commonly known as letter recognition) are said to be the best school-entry predictors of a child's success in reading during the first two years of schooling in an alphabetic language, such as English. Phonemic awareness is not an innate skill; it can and must be taught. Children are said to be phonemically aware when they are able to manipulate phonemes (the smallest sound units of a word that impact meaning) in spoken words. The NRP found that children (regardless of socioeconomic class) who received between fifteen and eighteen hours of phonemic awareness instruction, prior to being taught how to read and/or before entering the first grade, benefited greatest from such instruction.

Phonics. Unlike phonemic awareness, which refers to the blending and pulling apart of the various sounds that make up spoken words in an alphabetic language, phonics refers to the sound-symbol correspondences in that language. Phonics is a tool for decoding words; it is not a reading program. Knowledge of phonics does not ensure that one will comprehend printed texts because reading is a far more complex process than simply sounding out words.

The NRP concluded that children (regardless of socioeconomic class) who receive systematic phonics instruction in kindergarten and first grade show greater improvement in word recognition skills than do children who receive no such instruction; however, phonics instruction after first grade does not significantly contribute to gains in children's word recognition abilities. The panel also concluded that the type of systematic phonics instruction (e.g., synthetic, analytic, analogy) children receive, either individually or in small or large group settings, does not significantly affect the contribution such instruction makes to reading achievement.

Fluency. According to the NRP, phonemic awareness and knowledge of phonics are tools for helping children achieve fluency in reading. Fluent readers can decode words rapidly and accurately with good comprehension. Caution needs to be exercised, however, in interpreting these findings. Possessing well-developed word recognition skills—a condition often associated with having knowledge of phonics—does not necessarily translate into fluent reading. As the NRP pointed out, fluency is thought to develop when individuals have sufficient opportunities for, and practice in, reading. Typically, such practice is associated with independent or recreational reading both in and out of school. At this point, however, only correlational data exist to support the hypothesized connection between increased reading practice and improved reading achievement.

The NRP examined research on guided repeated oral reading practice as well as on methods that attempt to increase the amount of time a child engages in independent and/or recreational reading. The panel concluded that explicit guidance during oral reading has consistent and positive effects on word recognition, fluency, and comprehension. However, researchers have yet to agree on the best approach for helping children achieve reading fluency. In sum, although many have applauded the efforts of the NRP for its concise compilation of relevant research pertaining to reading in schools, others have criticized the panel for failing to address the early learning that occurs before a child goes to school, and for failing to provide information about home support for literacy development. Still others have called attention to the fact that the studies the NRP selected for analysis did not address issues related to teaching children whose first language is other than English how to read.

Comprehension Research

Research on reading comprehension has been limited largely to print-based texts and various strategies for studying and learning from those texts. The NRP concluded that seven comprehension strategies (comprehension monitoring, cooperative learning, using graphic and semantic organizers, generating questions, answering questions, using story structure, and summarizing) are effective in helping students learn from text. Although the NRP reported trends supporting conventional wisdom that vocabulary instruction leads to improved comprehension, it offered no conclusive evidence on this point due to the limited number of studies that met its strict criteria for inclusion. Nor did the NRP draw conclusions about the most effective instructional methods for teaching vocabulary.

Caution needs to be taken in interpreting the NRP's findings. The report did not include research on second language reading and reading to learn in domain-specific areas. Nor did it include studies using qualitative research designs, the absence of which severely limits what can be known about the contexts in which instruction occurred. Moreover, six of the seven comprehension strategies that were considered effective were ones that teachers would use if they believe reading comprehension consists of students working individually to extract information from printed texts. This rather narrow view of comprehension instruction risks disenfranchising students who may learn better in more socially interactive settings or whose literacies span a broader range than those typically associated with school or assessed by traditional reading measures.

Beyond strategic knowledge, readers who possess and activate relevant prior knowledge, who demonstrate an awareness of text structure, and who apply appropriate metacognitive skills to comprehending texts are more proficient learners than those who either do not possess such skills or who lack appropriate background knowledge. That is to say, constructing meaning involves using information and experiences gained previously to interpret new information in light of the old. It also entails recognizing the various reasons that authors structure their texts as they do (e.g., to inform, to persuade, to elicit appreciation for certain literary devices). Finally, comprehension calls for monitoring the de-

mands of a particular reading task, knowing what background knowledge and strategies are relevant to the task, evaluating the inferences one makes while reading, and applying any of a number of fix-up strategies when understanding falters or breaks down completely.

Unsupported Assertions

Intuitively appealing literacy practices are often linked to improved reading achievement without adequate support in the research literature. Although a lack of empirical evidence for their use does not make such practices wrong, it does call into question the wisdom of making curricular or programmatic decisions on the basis of custom alone or anecdotal evidence at best. A good example of this phenomenon is the widespread acceptance of the idea that encouraging students to read more will translate into improved fluency and higher reading achievement. As the Report of the National Reading Panel has shown, most of the studies that met the panel's stringent criteria for qualifying as scientifically sound research failed to find a positive relation between encouraging students to read and improved reading fluency and achievement.

Another intuitively appealing practice—using technology to improve reading instruction—has only a meager research base to date. Its overall and long-term effectiveness is simply an unknown according to the NRP. Although the panel described several trends suggesting the usefulness of computer technology for reading instruction, too little evidence presently exists to make informed recommendations. Lacking evidence as to whether or not the knowledge students gain from online instruction is superior to that gained from more traditional instruction, reading educators are likely to remain ambivalent about making drastic changes in the way instruction is delivered.

Equally unclear is the degree to which integrated literacy instruction fosters outcomes such as authentic reading tasks, better applicability of learning, deeper and more coherent understanding of subject matter, and greater efficiency in teaching and learning. Thought to be one of education's most elusive constructs, integrated literacy instruction generally involves organizing the curriculum is ways that promote students' use of language and literacy processes to learn school subjects (e.g., science, social studies, math). An extensive review of the research literature on integrated literacy instruction led James Gavelek and colleagues to remark in the year 2000 on the exceedingly low ratio of data-driven articles to general papers on the topic. Although they remained optimistic about integrative approaches, these researchers questioned whether or not the push toward such integration was a bit premature, or possibly ill-founded.

Controversies

A controversy exists in the United States about how to teach reading effectively and efficiently to students whose home or first language is not English, the language of mainstream education. The U.S. Census Bureau of 2000, relying on data from the 1990 census, reported that 6.3 million children, ages 5 through 17, speak a language other than English in the home; of these children, 4.1 million speak Spanish. Since 1990 the Hispanic population has increased by 57.9 percent in the United States, a demographic factor that accounts no doubt for people of Hispanic, Latino, and/or Spanish origin receiving the most attention in terms of educational program development. Programs developed primarily to facilitate English language learners' entry into English-speaking schools vary in the degree to which they provide support in the students' home language. Depending on the English language learners' needs and the availability of funding, children may be submersed in classrooms where English is the medium of instruction. This means they will not be offered any first-language literacy support; nor will they receive the three to six years of transitional bilingual education that has been shown to be effective. Although sheltered English language programs are becoming more popular in the United States, they do not offer opportunities for children to become bilingual, biliterate, and bicultural. Two-way bilingual programs, with their emphasis on instruction in both the home language (in many cases in the United States, Spanish) and English, provide such opportunities.

Elizabeth Bernhardt reported in 2000 three possible ways of looking at the relationship between first and second language learning experiences. She noted a transfer relationship where the knowledge and skills of the dominant language transfer to the learning of the second language; an interference relationship where the dominant language impedes the learning of the second language; and a dominance effect where the behaviors of the first language control those of second language literacy. Bernhardt

pointed out that in the case of second language reading, it is unclear as to whether first language skills transfer or interfere with learning to read in a second language. Controversies surrounding the interference model show no sign of abating. In fact, literacy educators, such as Georgia Ernest García, who question the validity of such a model, often cite a well-known longitudinal study of Spanish-speaking children by J. David Ramírez and colleauges, which showed in 1991 that instruction that fosters bilingualism and biliteracy does not place youngsters at an academic disadvantage. In that study, children who were enrolled in a late-exit bilingual program scored higher on standardized tests of English language and reading proficiency than did their monolingual peers.

Another controversy surrounding reading instruction has its roots in what Harvey Graff has labeled in 1988 the "literacy myth." Part of the dominant world view of the Western world for over two centuries, the so-called literacy myth equates the ability to read with personal and individual worth, social order, and economic prosperity. Its tenets reach deep into the American psyche, and its implications for reading instruction regularly place teachers in the public eye. Evidence of the literacy myth's stranglehold on the teaching profession is the fact that educators in the United States often fall under attack by politicians, the media, and the general public for not serving students well enough to ensure that they join the U.S. workforce and compete favorably in the rigors of a world market place.

The problem deepens when the media and other information sources convince the general public that a literacy crisis exists. Word of such a crisis leads parents, teachers, administrators, and policymakers to search for a universally effective way to teach all children to read, and just as predictably, to a proliferation of commercially prepared reading programs. School districts adopt commercially prepared programs in an attempt to solve the perceived problem. For example, programs such as Success for All, Core Knowledge, Accelerated Reader, and Saxon Phonics exist side by side (and in company with many other such programs) in the current educational market. Many of these programs are intended to help teachers concentrate more of their attention on student learning and less on lesson preparation. The developers of these programs also claim they offer continuity and consistency of instruction. Individuals who are critical of commercially prepared reading programs point to their scripted nature and to the narrow focus of their academic content. Teachers, in particular, sense a loss of autonomy and professionalism when local or state mandates force them to rely on one particular kind of commercial reading program. They know that in the field of literacy instruction the concept of "one-size-fits-all" does not apply to the children they teach. Nor does this type of instruction take into account the multiple literacies children living in the twenty-first century already possess or need to develop.

See also: LITERACY, *subentries on* EMERGENT LITERACY, LEARNING FROM MULTIMEDIA SOURCES, MULTIMEDIA LITERACY, NARRATIVE COMPREHENSION AND PRODUCTION; LITERACY AND CULTURE; READING.

BIBLIOGRAPHY

ALEXANDER, PATRICIA A., and JETTON, TAMARA L. 2000. "Learning from Text: A Multidimensional and Developmental Perspective." In *Handbook of Reading Research,* Vol. 3, ed. Michael L. Kamil, Peter B. Mosenthal, P. David Pearson, and Rebecca Barr. Mahwah, NJ: Erlbaum.

BARTON, DAVID; HAMILTON, MARY; and IVANIC, ROZ, eds. 2000. *Situated Literacies.* New York: Routledge.

BERNHARDT, ELIZABETH. 2000. "Second-Language Reading as a Case Study of Reading Scholarship in the 20th Century." In *Handbook of Reading Research,* Vol. 3, ed. Michael L. Kamil, Peter B. Mosenthal, P. David Pearson, and Rebecca Barr. Mahwah, NJ: Erlbaum.

CORE KNOWLEDGE FOUNDATION. 2001. *Core Knowledge Sequence, K–8.* New York: Doubleday.

GAFFNEY, JANET S., and ANDERSON, RICHARD C. 2000. "Trends in Reading Research in the United States: Changing Intellectual Currents over Three Decades." In *Handbook of Reading Research,* Vol. 3, ed. Michael L. Kamil, Peter B. Mosenthal, P. David Pearson, and Rebecca Barr. Mahwah, NJ: Erlbaum.

GARCÍA, GEORGIA ERNEST. 2000. "Bilingual Children's Reading." In *Handbook of Reading Research,* Vol. 3, ed. Michael L. Kamil, Peter B. Mosenthal, P. David Pearson, and Rebecca Barr. Mahwah, NJ: Erlbaum.

GAVELEK, JAMES R.; RAPHAEL, TAFFY E.; BIONDO, SANDRA M.; and WANG, DANHUA. 2000. "Integrated Literacy Instruction." In *Handbook of Reading Research,* Vol. 3, ed. Michael L. Kamil, Peter B. Mosenthal, P. David Pearson, and Rebecca Barr. Mahwah, NJ: Erlbaum.

GEE, JAMES P. 1996. *Social Linguistics and Literacies: Ideology in Discourses,* 2nd edition. London: Taylor and Francis.

GRAFF, HARVEY J. 1988. "The Legacies of Literacy." In *Perspectives on Literacy,* ed. Eugene R. Kintgen, Barry M. Kroll, and Mike Rose. Carbondale: Southern Illinois University Press.

GUTHRIE, JOHN T., and WIGFIELD, ALLAN. 2000. "Engagement and Motivation in Reading." *Handbook of Reading Research,* Vol. 3, ed. Michael L. Kamil, Peter B. Mosenthal, P. David Pearson, and Rebecca Barr. Mahwah, NJ: Erlbaum.

INSTITUTE FOR ACADEMIC EXCELLENCE. 2000. *Getting Started with Accelerated Reading and Reading Renaissance.* Madison, WI: Institute for Academic Excellence.

RAMÍREZ, J. DAVID; YUEN, SANDRA D.; and RAMEY, DENA R. 1991. *Executive Summary: Final Report: Longitudinal Study of Structured English Immersion Strategy, Early-Exit and Late-Exit Transitional Bilingual Education Programs for Language Minority Children.* San Mateo, CA: Aguirre International.

Report of the National Reading Panel. 2000. Washington, DC: National Institute of Child Health and Human Development.

SIMMONS, LORNA. 2001. *Saxon Phonics K–2 Classroom Kit.* Norman, OK: Saxon.

SLAVIN, ROBERT E. 2001. *One Million Children: Success for All.* Thousand Oaks, CA: Corwin.

SNOW, CATHERINE E.; BURNS, M. SUSAN; and GRIFFIN, PEG, eds. 1998. *Preventing Reading Difficulties in Young Children.* Washington, DC: National Academy Press.

STREET, BRIAN V. 1995. *Social Literacies: Critical Approaches to Literacy in Development, Ethnography, and Education.* New York: Longman.

TIERNEY, ROBERT J., and SHANAHAN, TIMOTHY. 1991. "Research on the Reading-Writing Relationship: Interactions, Transactions, and Outcomes." In *Handbook of Reading Research,* Vol. 2, ed. P. David Pearson, Rebecca Barr, Michael L. Kamil, and Peter B. Mosenthal. New York: Longman.

WILKINSON, IAN; FREEBODY, PETER; and ELKINS, JOHN. 2000. "Reading Research in Australia and Aotearoa/New Zealand." In *Handbook of Reading Research,* Vol. 3, ed. Michael L. Kamil, Peter B. Mosenthal, P. David Pearson, and Rebecca Barr. Mahwah, NJ: Erlbaum.

INTERNET RESOURCE

U.S. CENSUS BUREAU. 2000. "Language Use." <www.census.gov/population/www/socdemo/lang_use.html>.

DONNA E. ALVERMANN
M. KRISTIINA MONTERO

LIVING AND LEARNING CENTER RESIDENCE HALLS

American higher education can mark the beginning of living and learning centers (LLCs) with the founding of the Harvard house program in 1926, made possible by a gift from William Harkin. The intent of this gift was for Harvard to develop a residential experience similar to those at Oxford and Cambridge universities. Yale University established a similar housing program in 1933, and a few years later Princeton University established what is commonly referred to as the quadrangle plan. All these plans focused on joining the classroom experience with the out-of-class experiences in the residence halls. The goal was to bring faculty and students into closer contact and to promote an environment that allowed students increased opportunities to discuss classroom subjects and other academic topics with peers in their residence halls.

Based on the English residential college model, the LLC environment is designed to foster a closer relationship between students' classroom experiences and their experiences outside the classroom. LLCs offer one of the best environments for partnerships between faculty and student affairs professionals to advance student learning.

Students usually gain residence in an LLC following an application and selection process. Academic courses for credit and enriched educational and cultural programs for student residents are part of the LLC experience. LLCs are usually compared with conventional residence halls, which commonly offer educational programs, organize recreational activities, and have some form of hall counsel or student government organization. The primary differences between conventional residence halls and LLCs are the programs and class experiences that are offered and the selection and application process used. Students who live in LLCs usually take one or more of their courses in the residence hall and/or take one or more courses with the other residents of their living unit. In addition, the administrative organization of LLCs differs from conventional residence halls in that faculty members have some administrative responsibilities in the LLC and some faculty often live in the LLC. Faculty normally do not have administrative responsibilities or live in conventional residence halls.

At the beginning of the twenty-first century, hundreds of universities have some version of the living and learning center. Some are based around a particular academic college such as the college of engineering, but most are interdisciplinary.

Organization and Administration

There are many versions of LLCs. They vary with regard to their history, academic programs, and degree of involvement with the faculty. The most successful of these programs place the students' living environment in the closest proximity to the location of faculty offices. Residence halls specifically designed as LLCs usually have classrooms, faculty offices, and one or more faculty apartments built into the residence hall. LLCs are most often organized to house both male and female students in the same building.

LLCs bring together the expertise of faculty and student affairs professionals to build a residence hall community focused on fostering students' personal and intellectual growth. Management of the LLC facilities, room assignments, crisis intervention, hall government, and the enforcement of institutional policies are usually responsibilities of the student affairs professionals. Classroom instruction, selection of LLC participants, and criteria for common courses or similar academic experiences are usually the responsibility of the LLC faculty. Educational programming, the selection of resident assistants, and issues concerning individual students or groups of students commonly are shared responsibilities.

Because of the way residence halls are built and funded, LLCs are usually the financial responsibility of the director of housing and residence life and the vice president for student affairs. Staffing in LLCs is similar to a conventional residence hall with undergraduate resident assistants (RAs) living on each floor and a student affairs professional living in the building. The faculty head of the residence hall might be called something like head of house, headmaster, or director. The closer the integration between the student affairs professional and the faculty of the LLC, the more likely the program will be successful.

Research Findings in Living and Learning Centers

Educational advantages supported by the LLC environment are derived through a combination of factors. Among these are increased opportunities for informal interaction with faculty, an enriched academic experience with a greater intellectual atmosphere, a greater sense of community among students, and support for a wider range of creative endeavors. The benefits of LLCs have been recognized by the National Institutes of Education, the Wingspread Group on Higher Education, and the National Association of State Universities and Land Grant Colleges. Reports by these institutions cite the LLC as a model that details how to integrate the academic experience of the classroom with student life outside the classroom. Research on colleges that have been successful in broadening the undergraduate experience point to the benefits of LLCs, giving as examples programs that integrate and involve students in the campus community.

Research on residence halls shows that students living in conventional residence halls have an advantage over students who are living at home with parents, at least in their first year of college. These advantages include greater psychosocial development, higher retention and graduation rates, greater satisfaction, greater educational aspiration, and similar positive outcomes associated with student learning. The question addressed by most of the research on LLCs concerns the extent to which living in an LLC may further enhance the college experience.

On most educational criteria, research shows that living in an LLC is more beneficial to students than living in a conventional residence hall. Students in LLCs, when controlling for past academic performance, perform better academically, perceive the intellectual atmosphere of their living environment to be more academic, have more faculty interaction, and report a better social climate. Some studies have

also shown that students living in LLCs have lower attrition rates and higher graduation rates.

Problems Associated with Creating and Sustaining Living and Learning Centers

Despite the benefits of LLCs, most attempts at creating and sustaining them fail. LLCs require a faculty commitment to spend more out-of-class time with students and to focus an increased amount of their creative energy on designing programs and activities with students. Unfortunately, the reward system for faculty, including tenure and promotion, does not always recognize the value of these contributions. Unless the academic department and the LLC are closely joined, faculty can be drawn between the departmental culture of scholarship and the LLC culture of student engagement. The most successful LLC programs are tied closely with an interdisciplinary department. This relationship allows for a wider range of faculty expertise and for the faculty reward system to more generously recognize the value of out-of-class commitments to student learning.

LLCs usually demand a greater financial commitment for educational programming and complicate the campus room assignments procedures because of the selection process used to admit LLC students. Both factors can be sources of concern for housing and residence-life professionals who must consider every student living in residence halls when allocating resources and meeting the demand for on-campus student housing. Even with these concerns, institutions that have invested in LLC residence halls find that the benefits to student learning, graduation, retention, and the value of an engaged and committed student body, outweigh the difficulties that must be overcome.

See also: ADJUSTMENT TO COLLEGE; COLLEGE AND ITS EFFECT ON STUDENTS; COLLEGE AND UNIVERSITY RESIDENCE HALLS; COLLEGE STUDENT RETENTION; RESIDENTIAL COLLEGES.

BIBLIOGRAPHY

BLIMLING, GREGORY S. 1993. "The Influence of College Residence Halls on Students." In *Higher Education: Handbook of Theory and Research*, Vol. 9, ed. J. Smart. New York: Agathon Press.

BLIMLING, GREGORY S. 1998. "The Benefits and Limitations of Residential Colleges: A Meta-Analysis of the Research." In *Residential Col-*

leges: *Reforming American Higher Education,* ed. F. K. Alexander and D. E. Robertson. Murray, KY: Oxford International Round Table and Murray State University.

COWLEY, WILLIAM H. 1934. "The History of Student Residential Housing." *School and Society* 40:705–712; 758–764.

DUKE, ALEX. 1996. *Importing Oxbridge: English Residential Colleges and American Universities.* New Haven and London: Yale University Press.

NATIONAL ASSOCIATION OF STATE UNIVERSITIES AND LAND-GRANT COLLEGES. 1997. *Returning to Our Roots: The Student Experience.* Washington, DC: National Association of State Universities and Land-Grant Colleges.

NATIONAL INSTITUTE OF EDUCATION STUDY GROUP ON THE CONDITIONS OF EXCELLENCE IN AMERICAN HIGHER EDUCATION. 1984. *Involvement in Learning: Realizing the Potential of American Higher Education.* Washington, DC: U.S. Department of Education.

PASCARELLA, ERNEST T.; TERENZINI, PATRICK T.; and BLIMLING, GREGORY S. 1994. "The Impact of Residential Life on Students." In *Realizing the Educational Potential of Residence Halls,* ed. Charles Schroeder, Phyllis Mable, and Associates. San Francisco: Jossey-Bass.

SMITH, TERRY B., and HODGE, LIBBY. 1991. *National Residential College Living-Learning Unit Directory.* Kirksville: Dean of the College, Northeast Missouri State University.

TERENZINI, PATRICK T.; PASCARELLA, ERNEST T.; and BLIMLING, GREGORY S. 1999. "Students' Out-of-Class Experiences and Their Influence on Learning and Cognitive Development: A Literary Review." *Journal of College Student Development* 40(5):610–623.

WINGSPREAD GROUP ON HIGHER EDUCATION. 1993. "An Open Letter to Those Concerned about the American Future." In *An American Imperative: Higher Expectations for Higher Education,* ed. Wingspread Group on Higher Education. Racine, WI: Johnson Foundation.

GREGORY S. BLIMLING

LOCAL GOVERNANCE

See: FINANCIAL SUPPORT OF SCHOOLS, *subentry on* CAPITAL OUTLAY IN LOCAL SCHOOL SYSTEMS; INTERGOVERNMENTAL RELATIONS IN EDUCATION; IMPACT AID, PUBLIC LAWS 815 AND 874; SCHOOL BOARD RELATIONS; SCHOOL BOARDS; SCHOOL REFORM.

LOOPING

Looping is a practice in which a teacher stays with the same class for more than one year; it is a multiyear placement for both the students and the teacher. For example, a teacher begins with a group of first-grade students and rather than sending those students on to a new teacher continues with them through second grade. Looping can occur for two or more consecutive years. In this example, the teacher could choose to remain with those students and move up to third grade. Looping can be used in conjunction with, or as a transition to, multiage programs but does not necessarily include students of a wider age range.

How Widespread Is Its Use?

The level of implementation varies widely. In some school districts looping options are offered at every grade level. In other instances, an individual teacher or pairs of educators initiate looping. Looping occurs most frequently in elementary schools and occasionally in middle schools. It is used in public and private school settings. Looping has gained popularity, but it is still considered innovative.

Rationale

The rising interest in looping has been in direct response to the diverse needs of students. Looping provides stability for the growing number of students with less stable home environments. Looping classes develop a family-like environment, providing teachers with the opportunity to build strong, meaningful relationships with students. Students also have the additional time to develop positive relationships with classmates.

More instructional time is another benefit of this teaching design. Teachers and students "hit the ground running" at the beginning of the school year instead of starting from scratch each year. Teachers begin instruction immediately, rather than spending time assessing student achievement or developing classroom procedures. Students pick up where they left off instructionally and socially and are able to get into the swing of school quickly. Instructional time is gained at the end of the school year as well. Instead of packing up and checking out, looping teachers are able to continue instruction through the end of the year and end the year on a high note. The additional four to six weeks of instructional time allows teachers to gain an understanding of students' academic and social strengths and to plan instruction accordingly.

Another benefit is that teachers are able to give students projects to complete over the summer, in between the looping years, which keep students involved in learning. The momentum of learning continues and more continuity is provided for the students. These extended learning opportunities help students to realize that learning can occur outside of the classroom.

Increased parental involvement is another advantage of looping. Parents are able to gain a better understanding of their child's educational development and needs. Looping provides a means by which stronger parent–teacher relationships may be built. This bridge between home and school can help create a more family-like atmosphere in the classroom and beyond.

Looping requires minimal additional funding and is easy to implement. Additional curriculum resources and staff development are useful in implementing a looping classroom; however, most teachers will have the necessary skills to move up a grade with their students. Looping does not require additional classroom space and teachers can loop without disrupting other organizational aspects of the school.

By working with two or more sequential grades and the related content, teachers develop an overall view of the scope and sequence of the curriculum and the school program. This in-depth understanding allows them to maximize instructional time and provide remediation or enrichment based on student needs.

Although most teachers and students have positive experiences with looping, it is not appropriate for all schools, teachers, or students. Difficulties can and do occur. Integrating new students into an established looped class can be a challenge. Class dynamics and peer relationships can also go awry; there are times when too much togetherness wears on the students. Occasionally a personality conflict

between a student and teacher may arise. These conflicts are most often resolved. However, if resolution seems unreachable, then the student is transferred to a different class. Another concern with looping is that students and teachers become emotionally attached and separations are difficult when the looping cycle ends.

Evidence Supporting Its Use

The Looping Handbook by Jim Grant, Bob Johnson, and Irv Richardson provides evidence supporting the use of looping. Beyond the benefits reported by teachers and parents, there is evidence that looping results in increased student attendance, decreased retention rates, a decline in discipline problems and suspensions, and increased staff attendance.

The Attleboro, Massachusetts, School District has provided looping assignments to its entire first-through eighth-grade students and all of its 400-some teachers. In addition there are cited examples of looping around the country, such as Ashby Lee Elementary School in Virginia, Liberty Center Elementary School in Ohio, Lac du Flambeau in rural Wisconsin, and schools in Chicago, Illinois. *The Looping Handbook* provides a list of several schools that are open to visitors. In addition, there exist numerous educational studies and articles on looping.

The Waldorf school system, with private schools located around the country, follows the tenets of its founder, Rudolf Steiner. One of these practiced beliefs is looping. A Waldorf teacher in the United States stays with a group of students from first through eighth grade.

It has been suggested that looping has occurred in thousands of schools across the United States. However, many of the looping classes have not been documented. For example, a teacher in California has looped with his students from second grade through sixth grade, but this case has not been studied or documented in educational research.

In a report from the National Middle School Association (NMSA), Paul S. George and John H. Lounsbury stated that looping is a major way of achieving long-lasting teacher–student relationships. According to the report, "increasing numbers of middle school educators believe that the education of young adolescents can be enhanced when teachers and students are members of classroom and small team groups characterized by long-lasting relationships" (p. 2).

The authors also reported that several middle schools around the country have implemented looping with success in an attempt to make a big school small. For many students the transition from a small elementary school environment with one teacher a year to a large middle school with several teachers a day can be overwhelming. Looping at the middle school level provides a nonthreatening environment for students. This allows the students to succeed academically and socially.

See also: ELEMENTARY EDUCATION, *subentry on* CURRENT TRENDS; STEINER, RUDOLF.

BIBLIOGRAPHY

GEORGE, PAUL S., and LOUNSBURY, JOHN H. 2000. *Making Big Schools Feel Small: Multiage Grouping, Looping, and Schools-within-a-School.* Westerville, OH: National Middle School Association.

GRANT, JIM; JOHNSON, BOB; and RICHARDSON, IRV. 1996. *The Looping Handbook: Teachers and Students Progressing Together.* Peterborough, NH: Crystal Springs Books.

GRANT, JIM; JOHNSON, BOB; and RICHARDSON, IRV. 1996. *Multiage Q & A: 101 Practical Answers to Your Most Pressing Questions,* 2nd edition. Peterborough, NH: Crystal Springs Books.

CHERYL A. FRANKLIN
MARY S. HOLM

LOWENFELD, VIKTOR
(1903–1960)

Viktor Lowenfeld, professor of art education at the Pennsylvania State University, helped to define and develop the field of art education in the United States. His life and career have been a continuing topic of study in the field.

Early Career and Influences

Lowenfeld was born in Linz, Austria, of Jewish parents. He taught art in the elementary schools in Vienna while attending the Vienna Academy of Fine Arts, which he found "very dry and academic." Lowenfeld then transferred to the Vienna Kunstgewerbeschule, which he likened to a "Vienna Bauhaus." He studied sculpture under Edward Steinberg, who required that his students blindfold themselves when working with clay. Lowenfeld visited the Institute for the Blind to validate or disprove Steinberg's approach. He also studied at the University in Vienna in art history and psychology, graduating in 1928. While still engaged in his studies, he became a member of the staff at the Institute for the Blind.

Sigmund Freud read an article about Lowenfeld's work with the blind and visited him at the institute. As a result, Lowenfeld became more seriously involved in research as a scientific venture. His ideas on the therapeutic uses of creative activity in the arts resulted in several books. The first was titled *Die Entstehung der Plastik* (The genesis of sculpturing, 1932), which was based on his doctoral dissertation. The second was titled *Plastiche Arbeiten Blinder* (Sculptures of the blind, 1934). A third, though initially written in German, became his first English publication, *The Nature of Creative Activity* (1939).

Lowenfeld's American Career

With the German invasion of Austria in 1938, Lowenfeld and his family fled to England, later settling in the United States, where he met Victor D'Amico, who was director of education at the Museum of Modern Art in New York City. D'Amico took credit for introducing Lowenfeld into the circles of American art education. During World War II Lowenfeld taught psychology at the Hampton Institute in Virginia. Having experienced racial prejudice at the hands of the Nazis, he was acutely aware of the racism experienced by his African-American students at Hampton. Though his field was psychology, Lowenfeld was directly responsible for establishing the art department at Hampton. A number of his Hampton students became prominent artists, including John Biggers, Elizabeth Catlett, and Samela Lewis. In 1945 Lowenfeld was invited to teach summer courses at Pennsylvania State College (now the Pennsylvania State University) and, in the following year, was invited to become chairman of art education, a position he held until his death in 1960. Several of his Hampton students followed him to Pennsylvania State College to continue their studies.

In 1947 *Creative and Mental Growth* was published and became the single most influential textbook in art education during the latter half of the twentieth century, having gone through seven editions. This text was widely adopted in courses for prospective elementary school teachers throughout the United States, a time when teacher education programs were undergoing rapid expansion in response to the shortage of teachers that followed World War II. This book describes the characteristics of child art at each stage of development and prescribes appropriate types of art media and activities for each age. Its strong psychological orientation provides a scientific basis for creative expression and the practices that cultivate it.

Lowenfeld's views of child art were grounded in constructs drawn from two sources. One was the psychoanalytic school of psychology in which evidence of aesthetic, social, physical, intellectual, and emotional growth is reflected in the art of children. The second was the concept of stages of growth in art, which originated in German and Austrian sources. The stages consisted of (1) scribble—uncontrolled, controlled, naming of scribble: two to four years; (2) preschematic: four to six years; (3) schematic: seven to nine years; (4) dawning realism/gang age: nine to eleven years; (5) pseudorealistic/age of reasoning: eleven to thirteen years; and (6) period of decision/crisis of adolescence: fourteen years and older.

Lowenfeld did not claim to originate these stages but adapted them from earlier sources. He also identified two expressive types of individuals that arise with the onset of adolescence. The first is the *haptic type,* which is primarily concerned with bodily sensations and subjective experiences in which individuals are emotionally involved. By contrast, the *visual type* usually approaches the world from the standpoint of appearances. Such students feel more like spectators than participants. Lowenfeld suggested that each creative type needed a different instructional approach.

He saw the free expression of children in artistic media as necessary for the healthy growth of the individual. Emotional or mental disturbance results when children are thwarted, either by a loss of self-confidence or by the imposition of adult concepts of so-called good art.

Concern for mental health had social consequences as well. In the second edition of *Creative and Mental Growth* (1952) he injected a personal note:

"Having experienced the devastating effect of rigid dogmatism and disrespect for individual differences, I know that force does not solve problems and that the basis for human relationships is usually created in the homes and kindergartens. I feel strongly that without the imposed discipline common in German family lives and schools the acceptance of totalitarianism would have been impossible." (p. ix)

Lowenfeld never regarded child art as an end in itself. He was critical of his former teacher Franz Cizek, who emphasized the aesthetic aspects of child art as the sole purpose for art education. This "is much against our philosophy, and I believe also against the needs of our time." The goal of education "is not the art itself, or the aesthetic product, or the aesthetic experience, but rather the child who grows up more creatively and sensitively and applies his experience in the arts to whatever life situations may be applicable" (Michael, p. xix).

Influence on Art Education

A number of students were drawn to Lowenfeld both through his text *Creative and Mental Growth,* and through extensive lectures and presentations given at state and national conferences throughout the late 1940s and 1950s. Many came to the Pennsylvania State University to study, and by 1960 its graduate program had become the largest one in art education in the United States. Lowenfeld wrote about the similarity of creativity in the arts with that of the sciences, suggesting that general creativeness might transfer from the arts. A number of doctoral dissertations were inspired by these views on the psychological importance of creativity cultivated in the arts for creative abilities in general.

Although revered by numerous students, Lowenfeld was not without his critics. D'Amico felt that Lowenfeld had over-psychologized art education and that too many future teachers were pursuing psychological research rather than deepening their powers of creative expression. In addition, with the onset of the curriculum reform movement that was spurred by Soviet space achievements, such as the launch of *Sputnik* in 1957, the importance of discipline-oriented forms of study began to challenge Lowenfeld's ideas about creativity as the central purpose of art education.

See also: ART EDUCATION, *subentry on* SCHOOL; BARKAN, MANUEL.

BIBLIOGRAPHY

D'AMICO, VICTOR. 1958. "Coming Events Cast Shadows: A Reappraisal of Art Education." *School Arts* 57(1):5–19.

HOLLINGSWORTH, C. 1988. "Viktor Lowenfeld and the Racial Landscape of Hampton Institute During His Tenure from 1939 to 1946." Ph.D. diss., the Pennsylvania State University.

LANIER, VINCENT. 1963. "Schizmogenesis in Contemporary Art Education." *Studies in Art Education* 5(1):10–19.

LOWENFELD, VIKTOR. 1939. *The Nature of Creative Activity.* New York: Harcourt Brace.

LOWENFELD, VIKTOR. 1947. *Creative and Mental Growth.* New York: Macmillan.

LOWENFELD, VIKTOR. 1952. *Creative and Mental Growth,* 2nd edition. New York: Macmillan.

MICHAEL, JOHN A., ed. 1982. *The Lowenfeld Lectures.* University Park, PA: Pennsylvania State University Press.

SAUNDERS, ROBERT. 2001. "Lowenfeld at Penn State: A Remembrance." In *Exploring the Legends: Guideposts to the Future,* ed. Sylvia K. Corwin. Reston, VA: National Art Education Association.

SMITH, P. 1983. "An Analysis of the Writings and Teachings of Viktor Lowenfeld in Art Education in America." Ph.D. diss., Arizona State University.

ARTHUR D. EFLAND

ISBN 0-02-865598-2